By Townsend Hoopes

THE LIMITS OF INTERVENTION
THE DEVIL AND JOHN FOSTER DULLES

THE DEVIL
AND JOHN FOSTER DULLES

THE DEVIL
AND
JOHN FOSTER DULLES

BY TOWNSEND HOOPES

AN ATLANTIC MONTHLY PRESS BOOK
LITTLE, BROWN AND COMPANY — BOSTON — TORONTO

FIRST EDITION

T 11/73

Library of Congress Cataloging in Publication Data

Hoopes, Townsend, 1922-
    The devil and John Foster Dulles.

    "An Atlantic Monthly Press book."
    Bibliography: p.
    1. Dulles, John Foster, 1888-1959. I. Title.
E835.D85H66   973.921'092'4 [B]   73-12690
ISBN 0-316-37235-8

ATLANTIC—LITTLE, BROWN BOOKS
ARE PUBLISHED BY
LITTLE, BROWN AND COMPANY
IN ASSOCIATION WITH
THE ATLANTIC MONTHLY PRESS

Published simultaneously in Canada
by Little, Brown & Company (Canada) Limited

PRINTED IN THE UNITED STATES OF AMERICA

TO ANN

For her patience and her love

Contents

Acknowledgments

I AM GRATEFUL to a number of people and institutions for their individual and collective assistance during the preparation of the manuscript; especially to the Trustees of the Woodrow Wilson International Center for Scholars for a two-year fellowship that greatly facilitated the research, and to the Director, Benjamin H. Read, for his warm interest in the work and his helpful comments on it. I am indebted to William Dunn of the Center for his unfailing administrative support; to librarians Mary Anglemyer and Marcella Jones for whistling up needed reference volumes, cheerfully and on short notice, from a wide variety of libraries in Washington; to Helen Clayton for typing the early drafts with discernment and patient skill; and to Frances Hunter and Mernie Weathers for a thousand undefinable kindnesses.

For access to the John Foster Dulles papers at Princeton University Library, and for permission to quote from the various articles, speeches, memoranda and letters contained therein, I am grateful to the Committee for the John Foster Dulles Papers. The identification and reproduction of particular papers, including interviews from the Dulles Oral History Project, were greatly assisted by Mrs. Wanda Randall, Assistant to the Curator of Manuscripts in the Rare Books Collection of the Princeton University Library, who together with her associates extended every courtesy and consideration.

The manuscript benefits greatly from interviews, attributable and otherwise, which a large number of former government officials, journalists, historians and other close observers of the Eisenhower years were willing to give me. Many of these persons are friends of mine or were professional associates in government during the Truman or Johnson administrations. All of them either worked directly with John

Foster Dulles or were otherwise involved in the foreign policy process of his era.

My friend and editor Robert Manning was a much valued source of professional counsel, as were his associates Michael Janeway, Upton Brady, and Natalie Greenberg. Melissa Clemence was a gentle fanatic in the matter of perfecting the voluminous, often imprecise, source notes.

To Mrs. Frank Carlin, who somewhat inadvertently provided that snug and sea-bound hut on the Connecticut shore for the final drafting, and to Cynthia Vincent who typed the final manuscript with pace and verve, I want to say a special thanks.

Preface

IN EARLY 1968, when the Tet offensive and Lyndon Johnson's withdrawal from further political combat tore away the final veil hiding
the misperception and failure of America's freedom-defending and nation-
building in South Vietnam, I faced, along with many others, the
dawning realization that an era in American foreign policy had ended.
It was an era of some twenty years' duration in which the American
people found a large measure of their *raison d'être*, as well as moral
comfort, in fusing their perception of the national interest with what
seemed an unarguable ideological imperative — the absolute need to confront and defeat, or at least oppose, every manifestation of Communism
at every point on the globe.

Standing in 1970 among the crumbled premises of that posture, it
seemed necessary to ask how and why America had come to press its quite
legitimate concern for freedom and world order to extremes that increasingly failed to meet the tests of interest or reason, proportion or morality.
The question led inevitably backward in time to an examination of the
roots and tendrils and spreading branches of the cold war. That dominating phenomenon, of course, had its origins in the period immediately
following World War II, in the fundamental clash between the demand
of the Western democracies for "self-determination" in Eastern Europe
and the counterdemand of the Russian tyranny for "Soviet security." It
was fed by the Russian threat to paralyze Western European recovery
through both direct subversion and the manipulation of large Communist
minorities within the West. The initial Western responses — Greek-
Turkish aid, the Marshall Plan, and NATO — were bold and strong, but
they were in the main guided by a conscious rhetorical restraint, a determined effort by the Truman administration to avoid setting in motion
the runaway locomotive of a global ideological crusade. That barrier was,
however, bent and then broken by the nation's intensely emotional reaction to the victory of the Communist faction in the Chinese civil war, by
the Russian-supported attack on South Korea, and by the Chinese Com-

munist entrance into that war. All were events that provoked severe American frustration, fear, anger, and sense of betrayal.

In the ensuing period of the Eisenhower presidency the cold war was pervasively institutionalized in the United States. Its chief manifestations were a strident moralism, a self-righteous and often apocalyptic rhetoric, a determined effort to ring the Soviet Union and China with anti-Communist military alliances, a dramatic proliferation of American overseas military bases, and a rising flow of American military equipment for foreign armies accompanied by American officers and men to provide training and advice. The posture of imperative, total confrontation thus came to full development during the Eisenhower period. By 1960, the United States government was not only positioned and determined to restrain the major Communist powers, but also determined — through an implicit extension of logic and the inertial momentum generated by a large and powerful military-foreign affairs bureaucracy — to control the pace and character of political change everywhere. From the vantage point of the early seventies, the compelling questions to be asked about these developments in our foreign policy were what caused them and whether or not they were inexorable — to what extent were they an unavoidable legacy of the Truman-Stalin period, to what extent a conditioned response to events and political pressures arising during the Eisenhower period itself, and in what measure a product of the philosophy, conviction, intellect, and style of particular American leaders?

The attempt to answer such questions led to a close look at the foreign policy of the Eisenhower years and so moved in a straight line to an appraisal of John Foster Dulles — what he thought, considered, understood, misunderstood, did, tried to do, or failed to carry out. While Eisenhower knew his own mind in foreign policy and demonstrated at several critical junctures a humane, practical wisdom and a firm restraint, Dulles was indisputably the conceptual fount, as well as the prime mover, of United States foreign policy during those years. His was the informing mind, indeed almost the sole keeper of the keys to the ramified web of understandings and relationships that constituted America's posture of categorical anti-Communism and limitless strategic concern. Because in his nearly six years as Secretary of State, Dulles came gradually not merely to dominate but to personify United States foreign policy, it is fair to say that it was in large measure *his* legacy that was bequeathed to Presidents Kennedy and Johnson. This book is about the nature of that legacy, the power of its impact, the length and density of the shadow it cast upon successor presidents, foreign policy practitioners, and the national psyche.

TOWNSEND HOOPES

May, 1973
McLean, Virginia

THE DEVIL
AND JOHN FOSTER DULLES

1

In the Beginning

HE STOOD on the steps of the State Department in the penetrating January cold, a solid tree trunk of a man, gnarled and weathered and durable. The sandy gray hair was tousled by the wind, crowning a rectangular brow and aquiline nose, a thin and drooping mouth, a strong jaw, the whole creating an effect of ultimate seriousness and at the same time of ultimate plainness, as if fashioned by Grant Wood. The flat blue eyes, at once assured and suspicious, peered intently from behind thin-rimmed glasses across the nest of microphones into or beyond the faces of the several hundred people — Foreign Service officers, officials, secretaries, clerks and curious bystanders — gathered below. His overcoat was open, hands thrust into the trouser pockets of a vested suit, well-tailored but conventional and worn without distinction. Thus John Foster Dulles on January 28, 1953, a week after he became Secretary of State in the first Republican administration to gain the White House in twenty years.

It was remarkable that he stood there at all. That he did, while ultimately attributable to Dwight D. Eisenhower's electoral triumph, owed much to his own missionary concern for the fate of the world, a tenacious ambition for high office, a capacity for shrewd maneuver between the warring factions of the GOP, and the conspicuous competence with which he had handled advisory assignments for successive Democratic Secretaries of State since 1945. He was sixty-five years old, and he had reason to doubt that he had been Eisenhower's first choice for the senior cabinet post. Four years earlier, his chief political sponsor, Thomas E. Dewey, had gone down to a second straight defeat in his quest for the White House, an event that eclipsed the tough prosecutor and New York governor as a national figure when he was only forty-six. In the aftermath, Dulles had seemed merely one more distinguished victim of Republican hopes dashed yet again, and at sixty-one too old for further consideration. Nor were his prospects visibly brightened a year later when, after serving four months as an appointed United States senator from New York, he lost a bitterly contested special election to Herbert H. Lehman.

At low ebb in his public fortunes, he had turned to his powerful friend Senator Arthur Vandenberg, of Michigan, for help in engineering a return to the State Department as the symbol of continuity in bipartisan policy beyond the water's edge. And because they badly needed Vandenberg's support against the mounting hostility of the "new isolationists" in the Republican right wing, President Truman and Secretary of State Acheson had taken him back, but without enthusiasm, as a political necessity. Yet they had asked him, in the late spring of 1950, to take the lead in negotiating a peace treaty with Japan, and his performance on that assignment had established him as a widely known and highly regarded public figure, architect of "the peace of reconciliation." A 1952 poll conducted by the *Saturday Review,* on the question "What Living American?" would make the most effective and distinguished President of the United States, showed Dulles in fourth place, behind Dwight Eisenhower, Robert Taft, and Estes Kefauver, but ahead of Earl Warren, Harold Stassen, and Eleanor Roosevelt.

Leaving the State Department in the late winter of 1952, he had abruptly discarded the mantle of bipartisanship to become a rough, hardhitting critic of the Truman-Acheson foreign policies, with many of which he had been intimately and sympathetically associated. Gaining the confidence of both leading Republican candidates, Taft and Eisenhower, he had accepted their joint call to author the foreign policy plank of the party platform. A few hours before the convention turned to formal selection of the nominee, he had declared publicly for Eisenhower. The rest was history.

Positive Loyalty

The ceremony on the steps had been hastily arranged — Dulles was flying that evening to Europe to inquire pointedly of six North Atlantic Treaty Organization members why the project for integrating their armed forces into the European Defense Community was not moving more rapidly toward ratification by their parliaments, having been initialed by their governments the previous May. But his worried aides were persuaded that some special effort must be made to take the curse off two characteristically blunt statements — statements that had further shaken a department already brought to near panic by Senator Joseph McCarthy's demonic search for Communists and security risks in government, particularly among those in any way related to the conduct of United States foreign policy in the period since the end of the Second World War. Their somewhat remarkable solution was a pep rally in the raw open air of a January afternoon.

The first offending statement was an internal memorandum, issued on January 21 after Dulles had developed it in longhand on a lined yellow pad as he flew from New York to Washington. It said in part: "We are front-line defenders of the vital interests of the United States which are being attacked by a political warfare which is as hostile in its purpose and as dangerous in its capabilities as any open war." Such a situation of peril, it added, required the Foreign Service to demonstrate not only competence and discipline, but "positive loyalty" to policies "that our President and Congress may prescribe." Less than that was "not tolerable at this time." [1] The second statement was contained among the concluding paragraphs of his maiden address as Secretary of State, delivered just the previous evening over nationwide television. Offering on the latter occasion "new policies" based on the principles of "openness, simplicity, and righteousness," he had also dealt with the issue of public doubt regarding the trustworthiness of the department he now headed: "Now I suppose some of you are wondering whether the State Department can really be trusted to take a strong lead against Russian communism. There have been some shocking revelations which showed that some Communists and sympathizers have found their way into high places and betrayed secrets, even that of the atomic bomb. I can assure you that all of the resources of Government, and that includes the FBI, are going to be employed to be sure that any such people are detected and cleaned out." [2]

In a less traumatized political climate, such words might have passed without arousing the special concern of a confident foreign affairs bureaucracy. In January 1953 they could only be received with foreboding by people already living in an atmosphere of anxiety, and who had rather desperately hoped the new chief would be, in combination with the Eisenhower White House, their stout and effective defender against bitterly partisan attack. But Dulles had other priorities. His principal concern was to reassure Republican leaders in the Congress that the new Secretary was alive to their own fears of Communism (whether in or out of government) and to their pronounced antipathy to policies of the previous management. He was moved also by personal suspicion that the State Department's senior operatives, who had worked under Democratic auspices for twenty years, were prepared to resist new initiatives and directions in foreign policy put forward by Republicans; he wanted to put them on notice that the penalties for sabotage would be high. Thus, when he arrived in Paris the following day, his first words to a private gathering of senior American diplomats amounted to a stiff paraphrase of the "positive loyalty" injunction. There must be no illusion, he said, that things remained as before in Washington. A new administration was in charge, and loyalty to that new administration was the highest imperative. The words themselves and the graceless manner of their delivery left a bad taste with his auditors, nearly all of whom were professional diplomats, pledged by oath and habituated by experience to faithful, nonpartisan service to their country. "He assumed our disloyalty," one of them said later.[3]

So the prospect that a special mass meeting could mitigate the effect of hard words was not bright, for Dulles had not arrived at his position inadvertently. There was, moreover, the factor of personality, including, as time would show, a marked inability to foresee the impact of phrases he had painstakingly shaped and polished. Tough, self-centered, suspicious, insensitive, he was not cut out to project warmth and reassurance to a large assemblage of worried employees (as an admirer, Elliott Bell, once noted, "Foster was not a man with a great deal of come-hither").[4] But his aides did not yet know this. Standing on the steps, he now contented himself with designating the assemblage before him as " 'shock troops' in the cold war that is being waged against us,"[5] then turned to the introduction of three new Republican appointments to the State Department: the Undersecretary, General Walter Bedell Smith; the Assistant Secretary for Public Affairs, Carl McCardle; and the Undersecretary for Administration, Donald Lourie. Except for Bedell Smith (who had been Eisenhower's exceptional chief of staff in World War II, later ambassador to Russia, and most recently Director of the Central Intelligence Agency), the appointments were not impressive. Of Lourie, a former president of the Quaker Oats Company, whose diffidence and ignorance of politics were soon to prove him conspicuously unsuited for government service, Dulles said: "A few years ago, he was an all-American quarterback. And I think that that is the kind of thinking and creative action we are going to see."[6] In the main, however, he talked about himself and his family's historic linkages with diplomacy and the State Department, thus signalling the proprietary attitude he would take toward the formulation and conduct of foreign policy over the next six years, and confirming the widely held supposition that to become the President's First Minister had indeed been a lifelong quest. His remarks were pervaded by a vibrant sense of personal and family pride which, as frequently happens, tended to an unconscious stretching of the facts. "I could tell you that it is a wonderful thrill to me to

John Foster Dulles
in christening gown (1889)

Grandfather John W. Foster
(a former Secretary of State)
and Grandmother Foster

feel that I can be here with you as your chief and Secretary of State. I don't suppose there is any family in the United States which has been for so long identified with the Foreign Service and the State Department as my own family." [7]

Forebears

Dulles's grandfather, John Watson Foster, had served as Secretary of State during the last eight months of President Benjamin Harrison's administration (1892–1893), and it was in the Victorian comfort of that family patriarch's house on Eighteenth Street in Washington that John Foster Dulles was born on February 25, 1888. If normal southern criteria are applied, it was a stern winter; snow fell frequently, and there was at least one blizzard. The baby's father, the Reverend Allen Macy Dulles, was in transition from the Trumbull Avenue Church in Detroit, Michigan, to a parsonage in the small northern village of Watertown, New York, and it was natural that his wife, Edith Foster, should want to be with her parents on the arrival of her first child. Not accidentally, it would seem, he was named for his grandfather, for that worldly, affluent man was to exercise a decisive influence on his education, ambition and career, providing motivation, encouragement and financial support at each of several critical junctures. Always known within the family as "Foster," he was the eldest of five children — himself, Margaret, Allen, Eleanor, and Nataline.

His father, as the young minister of the First Presbyterian Church in Watertown and later as a teacher of philosophy at Auburn Theological Seminary, also exercised a broad influence on the development of his older son. Sired by John Welsh Dulles, a missionary of more than ordinary zeal who sailed for 132 days in an open boat to carry God's word to the heathen in the Indian state of Madras and who was buried in Ceylon, the pastor of Watertown was less peripatetic, but perhaps more liberal than his father in matters of doctrine. A staunch advocate and defender of science, intellectual inquiry and individual freedom, he held, among other things, that true Christianity does not depend upon a literal acceptance of the virgin birth, and that divorced persons should be permitted remarriage within the church. At the turn of the century, these were far from majority positions in the presbytery. (Indeed, a quarter-century later, the Reverend Dulles urged his son Foster, now a lawyer, to assist the "modernists" in a showdown debate at the 1924 Presbyterian General Assembly against the "fundamentalists." The latter group, led by William Jennings Bryan, was seeking to excommunicate Dr. Harry Emerson Fosdick for having cast doubt on the virgin birth. After some shrewd parliamentary maneuvering, in which Foster Dulles played a role, the "modernists" won on the final vote.) [8] But the father's liberality extended no accommodation to slackness in the matter of religious training and observance in his home. Foster and the other children were expected to hear him preach three times on Sunday, to take notes on the sermon, and to join in prayer meeting each Wednesday evening. They were obliged to memorize songs from the hymnal and passages from the Bible, and to recite these standing before their father, while their mother, who had coached their preparation, sat quietly to one side.[9] His sister Margaret, who herself married a clergyman, remembered that "our Sundays were quite strict, but they were happy days." [10]

Grandfather Foster was the third son of Mathew Foster, a pioneer enterpriser who at seventeen had joined a wagon train going west from the Mohawk Valley in northern New York. Two years later, in 1819, he staked a claim to eighty acres of timberland near Vincennes, Indiana, built a log cabin with his own hands, and returned to New York on foot to bring his aged parents to live with him. Moving on to Petersburg, Indiana, he married Eleanor Johnson, grew affluent through the ownership of a gristmill, helped to build the Cumberland Presbyterian Church, and served as a probate judge although he had never gone to school. His son, John Watson Foster, born in 1836, attended Indiana University, entered upon the practice of law, and was shortly thereafter engulfed in the Civil War, ending as colonel of the Sixty-fifth Indiana Volunteers. For faithful services rendered, President Grant appointed him Minister to Mexico and he saw subsequent service as Minister to Russia (1880) and Minister to Spain (1882). Ten years later, when James G. Blaine resigned as Secretary of State to make a final run for the presidency, John W. Foster was on duty at the State Department. President Harrison named him to succeed Blaine, and he thus served in the cabinet during the final eight months of that administration. While this added up to more than an honorable career, it fell somewhat short of earning him a prominent place in history, a deficiency which seemed in part the product of circumstance, in part attributable to qualities in the man — a certain heaviness of mind and manner, a plodding, if steadfast, devotion to duty which lacked imagination. John W. Foster's influence on his grandson's career was nevertheless decisive for several reasons: he had achieved the secretaryship of state (a fact that established a tangible level of emulation); his moderate political liberalism (which stressed tolerance, gradual evolution, and individual freedom and which rested comfortably beside his affluence and worldly attainments) tended on the whole to reinforce the liberal theology of the boy's father, for both men believed strongly in "social utility" as the rightful measure of men and their actions; finally, his career had given his daughter, Edith, a rather glamorous upbringing in the diplomatic swim of foreign capitals, and this became a principal source of her own worldly ambition for both her sons.

Growing Up

Foster Dulles showed evidence of superior mental capacity at an early age. His mother, herself intelligent and energetic, recorded in her diary on his fifth birthday that "he has fine acquisitive powers, and such things as interest him he very promptly takes hold of and retains . . . mentally, he is really remarkable for his intellectual acuteness. His logical acumen betokens a career as a thinker . . . he reasons with a clearness far beyond his age." In the same entry, she noted with equal pride the boy's responsiveness to religious training: "He is reverential to a striking degree. . . . Whenever he sees . . . his father or mother in the attitude of prayer, he will instantly assume the same attitude and so remain until they rise." His occasionally "naughty spirit" was gradually "growing toward self-control." [11] Through the long and cold Watertown winters, Dulles applied himself to schoolwork and winter sports, and was graduated from the local high school at the early age of fifteen, not, it appears, because he was an especially zealous student, but rather because he possessed a naturally powerful and disciplined mind. His brother Allen and others were frequently to observe that, throughout his school and college days, Foster, while always earnest and diligent, earned high marks with considerably less than a total effort.

Each summer Grandfather Foster and his wife removed themselves from the tropical heat of Washington to the cool, dependable breezes of Henderson Harbor, a simple resort town on Lake Ontario some twenty-five miles south of Watertown, New York. And there in later years Edith and her children came for the long summer holiday, journeying over from Watertown by horse and buggy; for the most part, her husband seems to have stayed in Watertown, writing sermons and ministering to his flock. In a cluster of rustic cottages on the shore of the lovely lake, Foster Dulles thus spent the better part of every summer until he was well into his teens, learning to fish and sail, and listening to his grandfather talk about pioneering, war, diplomacy and the law. After retirement as Secretary of State, the family patriarch became legal adviser to the Imperial Government of China, helping in that capacity to negotiate the Treaty of Shimonoseki in 1895 following China's harsh defeat at the hands of the Japanese on the bloody ground of Korea, in what proved to be the first test of arms for modern Japan.

Age eight at Henderson Harbor,
with a large fish

At Shimonoseki not many mitigations were available to his corrupt, incompetent and doomed clients, and they were forced to surrender both Korea and Formosa to the Japanese. But the perspective of the Dulles children was widened and enriched by a steady stream of distinguished visitors to Henderson Harbor: Chinese gentlemen, European ambassadors, American politicians, journalists, and other men of marked or moderate consequence who came briefly to rest and rusticate and talk. Another frequent visitor was Robert Lansing, a young Watertown attorney and aspiring Democratic politician, who married Edith's sister, Eleanor, became "Uncle Bert," and later served as Woodrow Wilson's Secretary of State.[12]

Henderson Harbor was a benign, turn-of-the-century remove, a wholesome sheltered place where young lives could put down roots close to nature and there develop, under the firm but loving guidance of their elders, a moral purpose, a family pride, and a sense of the opportunities and obligations that lay ahead in life and the great world. But even summer vacation did not mean escape from religious instruction, nor any relaxation of strict moral tutelage. Mornings began with hymns and prayer, and there was a requirement to learn large segments of *A Pilgrim's Progress* by heart — a memory test which led the children to identify pieces of the Henderson landscape with symbolic elements of the book: a steep bluff became the Hill of Difficulty, a marsh the Slough of Despond.[13] Still, with these daily observances behind them, they were free to seek innocent adventure in the surrounding woods and waters, and from early on Foster showed a natural boldness tinged with careful calculation. Wishing to add a particular bird's egg to his extensive collection, he made a rather thorough survey of a high maple tree, noting those branches that would bear his weight. Then with practiced care he climbed to the top, collected the egg from the nest, put it in his mouth, and descended by the same route. Over another summer, he diligently practiced longer and longer swims until he could convince his father he was ready to try the two miles of open water across Henderson Bay. He then made it without strain, his father leading in a rowboat.[14]

In company with a kindly fishing guide, Foster and his brother Allen also spent a good deal of time sailing small boats on the wide and choppy reaches of Lake Ontario, making for islands ten or fifteen miles from home. In those early days of no auxiliary engines, Allen remembered that "if the wind went down, you jolly well rowed home." [15] Occasionally, to the anguish of their elders, they struck out for a site some forty miles away, called Duck Island, which Foster was to buy in 1941 and in whose Spartan solitude he was to find both physical and spiritual refreshment. Lazy afternoons were sometimes spent in wood

Age twelve,
with Margaret, Allen, Eleanor, and Nataline

carving and Foster, who was rarely without his pocketknife, later occupied himself with industrious whittling at international conferences, while he listened to the interminable translations of interminable diplomatic speeches.[16]

But, as Allen Dulles recalled, the "really serious business" at Henderson was fishing.[17] About eight-thirty, after morning prayers, they would set out in two small sailboats, one brother and one or more members of the older generation in each boat. "The girls would go out occasionally — my sister, Margaret, who was just between my brother Foster and myself. And later my sisters, Eleanor and Nataline. But not so often." [18] Uncle Bert Lansing was a frequent fisherman, as were more occasionally the Chinese gentlemen and other houseguests. Through steady practice Foster and Allen learned a number of fundamentals: how to sail, how to cook, how to choose their fishing ground, how to hook the smallmouthed bass in the upper lip just as it takes the bait. Foster, who learned extremely well, was soon able to hit the bass at just the right moment from a rocking boat in twenty feet of water. Their fishing guide, a local man named Will Stevens, taught the brothers "a ditty" which they applied with mental reservation: "When the wind is in the north, then the fisherman goeth not forth; when the wind is in the east, then the fishes bite the least; when the wind is in the south, it blows the bait in the fishes' mouth; when the wind is in the west, then the fishes bite the best." [19] The usual pattern was to fish until noon — using minnows, worms, frogs, and tiny water crabs for bait — and then to go ashore for lunch on any one of a hundred small islands. There they would scoop out a shallow depression in the earth, wall it with hard rocks, find a particularly flat one for their cooking platform, and gather twigs and fallen branches for the fire. The food consisted of fish ("broiled or fried with pork fat and corn meal"), potatoes, corn in season, and coffee. "Always the same," Allen remembered, "but always delicious." [20]

Many years later, Dulles received a letter from Jack Bristol of Tacoma, Washington, who had learned from the *Saturday Evening Post* that the Secretary of State was in the habit of baking trout by wrapping it in mud. Bristol proposed a variant which he said had been learned from a Blackfoot squaw: "Tuck a few mint sprigs inside the fish, then wrap in grass or leaves"; next seal the fish in an inch of "clay mud" and place on a bed of coals in an open fire. Bake for two hours, when the mud will be dry. "When the leaves are unwrapped, the skin of the trout comes away with the leaves. Remove the mint and serve your fish. You will note that no salt or pepper is used, and the odd thing is it does not seem to be needed." [21] Dulles wrote back, defending his own preference for wrapping the fish directly in mud (no mint or leaves), and then encasing it in newspapers to hold the mud in place. "After about two hours, I take the fish out, and the mud then comes off taking the skin with it and leaves the flesh clean and full of juice. Like you, I do not use salt or pepper." [22]

During and after lunch, the principal activity was talk — of the wind, the weather, the habits of fish, the affairs of the world — and the two boys formed an attentive audience for stories and comments by men who had made their place, exercised some measure of authority, and struggled with large problems of political and international diplomacy. From this amalgam of opposites — serious talk of Paris and Peking amid the lonely pines and rocky ledges on the shore of a northern lake — John Foster Dulles emerged as a rare blend of Spartan and sophisticate. On occasional visits to Washington he enjoyed the pomp and punctilio of receptions at his grandfather's house. Ambassadors, lesser diplomats, military attachés in their bright plumage came and went; and as his sister Margaret remembered it, she and her brother would "glue our faces to the windowpane to see those equipages roll up with their coachmen and their footmen, and then someone would get out all dressed in regalia . . ." [23] James Reston remarked many years later that, as Secretary of State, John Foster Dulles dearly loved the "diplomatic Chautauqua circuit." [24] Yet, loving power, status, ceremony and rich living, he was a man whose roots remained deep in the gnarled, unfashionable and puritan simplicities of his boyhood in northern New York.

2

Princeton, the Hague, and Paris

CONSIDERING Foster too young for entrance into college at the age of fifteen, his mother took him and his sister Eleanor off to Europe near the end of summer 1903, staying mainly in Lausanne where the children studied French.[1] Returning the following spring, he went to stay with his grandfather in Washington, where he spent several months with a tutor, preparing for his entrance into Princeton in the fall of 1904. Princeton, as Eleanor later wrote, was an "inevitable" choice; [2] not only his father but several uncles were graduates, and one of these, Joseph Dulles, the minister who had baptized him in Watertown, was librarian of the Princeton Theological Seminary.

Insecurity and Philosophy

Not much is known of Dulles's undergraduate days at Princeton, most of his classmates being unable to recall that he made any particular impact until near the end of senior year. Arthur Krock of the *New York Times,* who was a classmate until he dropped out for lack of money, recalled "a nodding acquaintance" and an awareness that Dulles's grandfather had been Secretary of State, but "I was in a couple of classrooms with him. And I have no recollection of him." [3] The reality seems to be that, during most of his time at Princeton, Dulles was an obscure member of the student body, serious, shy, poor, and markedly younger than those around him. A publicity handout prepared by Dulles's personal public relations adviser in 1944 (during his developing prominence as a lay church leader in the fight to establish the United Nations) contained the statement that it was Dulles's "own wish" not to accept membership in one of the social, class-conscious eating clubs; the handout attributed this stance to Dulles's sympathy for the position of the university's president, Woodrow Wilson, who held that on moral grounds the clubs ought to be abolished because they were breeding grounds of snobbery and an antidemocratic spirit. The statement may be true; one senses, however, a strong element of post facto rationalization: it avoids the compelling fact that, despite an honorable legacy, the young Foster Dulles, reared in the stern simplicities of a devout upstate family and village, unaccustomed to social drinking, with no spending money, and lacking fashionable clothes or an automobile, was hardly a prime candidate for a club system that laid heavy emphasis on "sophistication" and invited less than half of each class to join. Given his later drive for success and acceptance at the highest levels of the New York establishment, it seems likely that this particular memory was tinged with mortification. In any event, after he became an established and wealthy lawyer, he accepted an invitation to join the Cottage Club.

A number of colleagues and observers of Dulles's life over the years attribute the rigid, grave and graceless manner with which he moved through most of his relationships to the fact that circumstances had denied him a normal young manhood. His tender years, his puritanical background, his lack of money all made it very hard for him to make friends on an equal basis in either college or law school, and the painful chagrin of these circumstances must have been deepened by his own fierce awareness, indeed enlargement, of his heritage — not merely an upstate parsonage but the corridors of diplomatic power. Needing defenses to hide the gap between his sense of who he was and the apparent facts of the situation, he built up heavy layers of reserve against spontaneity, easy confidences and a light touch. He "kept greatly to himself," [4] gave intense concentration to intellectual and philosophical problems, and played chess. Such psychological pressures had the effect of forcing him to grow up unevenly and rather too fast; and although he demonstrated manly fortitude, there were consequences, chief among them a persisting social unease, combining shyness and suspicion. In the bosom of his family or with close and trusted associates, he could be warm, sentimental, occasionally jocular, exhibiting a hearty, even bubbly Victorian humor. In all other groups he was notable for a flat hardness and a striking insensitivity to people in the large.

If he was uncomfortably young and socially insecure at Princeton, he was also uneasily aware of deficiencies in his early education. During freshman year, he wrote a paper for English class that revealed a curious mixture of apology and defiance in the face of the undisguisable truth that the Watertown schools had not prepared him precisely in gram-

At Princeton (1907)

mar or widely in literature: "It is hard to write five hundred words on one's preperation [sic] in English when one has not spent five hundred minutes preparing it. . . . It is true that I have never taken an English course at school. Altho [sic] I have, at one time or another, entered classes, I have as often, voluntarily or otherwise, dropped out. As a result of this my knowledge of grammatical rules and parsing is slight. . . . My knowledge of English Literature is somewhat larger, but that is not saying much for it. Whatever of the masterpieces of literature that I have read, I have read not as a task. In this way they are much more enjoyable. . . . I have memorized — and forgotten — several short poems of Longfellow, Tennyson & Whittier, but am not so thoroughly acquainted with those books which are required for anterance [sic] into most Universities as those who have studied and dissected them with an eye, more directly, toward the examination. . . . As to compositions and essays I have written very few, as the present writing will testify. In fact I am surprised that I was ever allowed to enter the college, as far as English preparation is concerned." [5] The instructor started to correct the paper with blue-penciled interlineations, but gave up halfway through and wrote at the top: "Where did you study English? Rewrite." [6] Forty-eight years later, in 1952, when Dulles stood on the threshold of high public office, the same defiance, but none of the candor, was discernible in a short speech he gave to the assembled townspeople of Watertown: "My family could not afford to send me to private school, and I am glad that they could not. I learned here solidly the fundamentals of reading, writing, and arithmetic, plus American history." [7]

By senior year, however, Princeton had improved his prose style, and the developing force of a naturally bold, powerful and logical mind was evident in both debate and written argument. He was a serious and able student headed for a strong finish. Having enrolled at Princeton in the parental expectation that he would prepare for the ministry, he majored in philosophy, taking courses in logic and pragmatism under Professor John Hibben and one in ethics under Woodrow Wilson. In one essay, which analyzed the works of William James and John Dewey, Dulles doubted that pragmatism was in any way superior to other philosophies as an explanation of reality; he argued that it went too far in its tendency to "supplant all reason by feeling and desire." His conclusion was that "reason must be left the ultimate judge of truth." [8] His senior thesis (a modest nineteen pages of double-spaced typescript) addressed "The Theory of Judgment," and was good enough to earn him the Chancellor Green Mental Science Fellowship, providing a year of study at the Sorbonne under the preeminent French philosopher Henri Bergson. One passage is indicative of the Dullesian logic: "When

I cry 'fire' in a house, my total judgment is 'there is a fire here which is dangerous.' But I am pressed for time. I know that if I simply express a part of my judgment, the rest of it will be awakened by constant association and habit in the minds of my hearers . . ." [9] As Secretary of State, and pressed for time, he often found it convenient to avoid lengthy explanation of difficult situations by crying fire. At Princeton, he was elected to Phi Beta Kappa, stood second in the class of 1908, and was chosen to deliver the valedictory speech at graduation exercises.

The Question of a Career

All during his Princeton years, Dulles was pondering the question of a career. His father especially wished him to enter the ministry, thereby to carry on a long and strongly held family tradition. On the other hand, his mother, beneath a surface deference to her husband's wishes, seems to have encouraged wider and more worldly prospects both directly and through her father. In any event, the attraction of a career in law or politics or diplomacy, stimulated by the examples of Grandfather Foster and Uncle Bert Lansing, exerted an ever stronger pull upon Dulles's imagination and ambition, especially after the spring of 1907, when he went off to Europe as a minor participant in the Second Hague Peace Conference. Grandfather Foster, who was designated as a delegate for the Imperial Government of China, persuaded Princeton to part with his grandson before the end of junior year, making special arrangements for him to take the year-end exams the following autumn. As he later wrote in the second volume of his *Diplomatic Memoirs,* "I sailed from New York on May 31, 1907, accompanied by my wife and my grandson, John Foster Dulles, a student of Princeton University, aged nineteen, who, on our arrival at The Hague, was made a secretary of the Chinese delegation, and because of his knowledge of the French language was enabled to render useful service to the delegation." [10]

Like its predecessor of 1899, the Second Hague Conference of 1907 (both convened on the formal invitation of Czar Nicholas of Russia) was precluded from a discussion of arms limitation by opposition from the Great Powers. It turned accordingly to a series of important secondary questions, offering in the end thirteen separate treaties on subjects that ranged from the peaceful settlement of international disputes to rules for warning civilian populations of impending military attack. On the whole, this buffet table of diplomatic hors d'oeuvres was viewed with cynicism by the leaders of Europe, and seven years later the fateful spark was struck at Sarajevo. But the tragic inadequacy of European diplomacy in 1907 was at the moment less impressive for a young man from Princeton than the opportunity to see the operation of a major international conference at firsthand, rub elbows with men of high reputation, and himself play a modest but exhilarating part in the proceedings.

Dulles's task was to assist the Chinese delegation with French translations and a range of modest problems involving administration and diplomatic etiquette, and he appears to have abetted the solution of a silly but sticky problem created by a failure of the participating nations to agree on the order of precedence for courtesy calls. Protocol required that such calls be exchanged before the conference could begin, but no nation was willing to move first, the principle of sovereign primacy demanding obeisance from other nations before reciprocation. After an embarrassing impasse, during which it seemed that the conference might well be canceled, cool heads determined that honor could be satisfied if every delegation called on every other at the same time. This meant in practice the simultaneous delivery of calling cards all around. On behalf of the Chinese delegation, Dulles thus set out one fine afternoon in a hired carriage, attired in a Prince Albert coat and high silk hat, to deliver neat bundles of engraved cards.[11]

As for his contribution to French translations, there seems room for dispute. His grandfather's memoirs are the authority for his "knowledge" of French, and no doubt he spoke better French than Chinese. It is also possible that he was relatively more proficient in the language during his college years. But close associates of later years, at both his law firm, Sullivan and Cromwell, and the State Department, hold firmly to the view that he was competent only in English. A professor of international law at Columbia, who as a young law associate in the 1930s worked closely with him on a number of legal problems in Europe and Latin America, has said that Dulles could usually understand spoken French and Spanish, and was especially keen at picking out those foreign words that were crucial to the legal transaction at hand and thus in need of meticulous translation. But his ability to carry on a conversation in either language reminded the professor of a line from P. G. Wodehouse: " 'Oui,' the man said in fluent French." [12] At a private luncheon in Paris on May 5, 1952, given in Dulles's honor by the French Foreign Minister, Maurice Schumann, C. L. Sulzberger recorded the proceedings: "Schumann speaks excellent English but made the mistake of saying to Dulles that, of course, the latter spoke French. Dulles smugly agreed and from there on a crisscross of misunderstanding developed with conversations like: 'Do you think German rearmament is a good thing?' being answered with observations such as 'I am sorry she isn't here.' I was sitting next to André Maurois who was equally fascinated." [13]

A year after the Hague conference, on June 10, 1908, Dulles was graduated from Princeton, still apparently undecided about a career, but possessed of a six-hundred-dollar scholarship to the Sorbonne. If his sister Eleanor's account is taken at face value, "he meditated on his father's life" and reached a conclusion "which he did not often discuss but which I knew was a genuine feeling — that he could not follow adequately in his father's footsteps." [14] He wondered if he was "good enough." [15] In the light of a subsequent career that revealed little self-doubt, not to mention a central striving for place and power, one finds it easier to interpret this plea of unworthiness for the ministry as the means chosen, in part perhaps subconsciously, for letting down his father as gently as possible. On the one side stood the example of Grandfather Foster, holding out the prospect of money, fame, travel and the world; on the other stood devoted service to a Presbyterian flock in a small town at three thousand dollars a year. For a strong-willed young man in the dawning awareness of his exceptional powers, the choice seemed foreordained, and one senses his mother's acquiescence. Yet Dulles put off a formal decision, and the whole family (showing either a remarkable capacity to stretch a very small income or further assistance from Grandfather Foster) went off to Paris for the summer, taking a corner apartment in the Boulevard Raspail. There was a brief period of mountain climbing in Switzerland — the Dent du Midi at the head of Lake Geneva and the Diableret.[16] Then they packed for home again, placing Allen (age fifteen) in a French boarding school, L'Ecole Alsacienne, and leaving Foster (age twenty) to pursue his scholarship at the Sorbonne.

The ensuing school year found Foster, affecting a bowler hat and umbrella, busily tasting the fruits of French culture at the Sorbonne and the canapés at embassy parties. At one point he was caught up in a student riot incited by members of the "action française" (who were responding to slurs on the memory of Jeanne d'Arc by a certain Professor Thalamus), doused with a fire hose, and arrested by the French police. Many years later the French chargé in Washington, Charles Lucet, had the matter researched, and reported to Secretary of State Dulles that his arrest had been a mistake.[17] While concentrating his studies on philosophy, in accordance with the terms of his scholarship, Dulles revealingly elected to take some courses in international law, and there remains among his personal papers a book of notes which he wrote out, more or less in French, while attending lectures on international fishing rights.

Law and Marriage

At the end of a stimulating and maturing year, Dulles went home to Auburn, New York, where the family was now established, his father having assumed the chair in apologetics at Auburn Theological Seminary. Almost at once he broached to his parents the concept of a career that would combine the practice of law with dedicated lay service to the church. His father's disappointment was apparently overcome by the maturity and logic with which he presented the case, and both parents ended up thoroughly approving his decision to become "a Christian lawyer." That delicate hurdle surmounted, he made arrangements to enter the George Washington Law School and to live with his devoted, supportive grandfather in the four-story brick house on Eighteenth Street. Then, prefiguring a persistent peripatetic urge, he left the somnolent summer pleasures of Auburn and took himself off to Madrid, where he lived for six weeks in the house of a middle-class Spanish family that spoke no English, an experience that he later felt had given him a rudimentary ability to read and speak Spanish, and that thus proved helpful to his extensive legal work in Latin America.

At law school, Dulles plunged into his studies with the vigor and intensity that were to characterize all of his later life in law, religion, politics and diplomacy. His intellectual powers were fast maturing, and he was refining the uses to which a good memory can be put. On the night before an exam, he would memorize important case citations and their substantive judicial findings. Arriving at the examination room, he would quickly write down the essence of what he had memorized. Then attacking the examination questions, he would apply appropriate citations to the particular points of law he was expounding. This technique suggested a thoroughness and precision which his instructors found very impressive.[18] Whether inadvertently or by design, he completed the three-year course in two years, but was refused a degree on the technical grounds that a diploma from George Washington University required three years of resident study — a matter that was rectified only twenty-five years later, when he received his diploma, backdated to 1911.

Those two years in Washington, for all their intense application to the dry bones and living spirit of the law, appear to have been one of the few really gay social periods of Dulles's life. His grandparents' position gave entrée to houses of the politically and socially prominent, President Taft occupied the White House, and Dulles was frequently in attendance at parties with the President's two sons, Robert and Charles. Occasionally he squired Martha Bowers, who was later to marry Robert Taft, and he appears to have danced a good deal, returning home from a hard day of law classes to take a nap before rising late in the evening to put on his dancing shoes and go off to some embassy ball.[19]

Back home once more in Auburn in the early summer of 1911, he crammed sixteen hours a day for the New York State bar exams, but also found time to rediscover a local girl named Janet Avery, who had been keeping company with his brother Allen. At twenty-three, his formal education now completed, he was, although inexperienced with women, ready to consider love and marriage, and he found in Janet's attractive, shy reserve an appealing and manageable dependence to complement his own assertive character. By all accounts it was a genuine love match and, in what may have been his first application of brinkmanship, Dulles skipped the last several questions on the bar exam in Rochester in order to catch an afternoon train back to Auburn for a dinner date with Janet. His calculation, which proved correct, was that he had already written enough to pass.[20]

But success on the bar exam cut no ice with the leading Wall Street law firms with which he then sought to make a connection. Most of their partners, having been trained at Harvard or Columbia, found Dulles's superlative record at a little known and little reputed school in the southern village of Washington something less than an impressive credential; he lacked, moreover, any formal law degree. And some of his interviewers, showing no concern for consistency, disdained Princeton as both a parochial seminary and a country club. After six weeks of making the rounds, Dulles found himself without a single offer, facing an apparent stone wall. Despairing, he turned once more to his worldly grandfather, and the old lawyer-diplomat was able to draw upon an association that went back to Cincinnati and the years before the Civil War: as a young lawyer there, he had worked for Algernon Sullivan, who later moved to New York to form Sullivan and Cromwell. By 1911, Sullivan was dead, but Cromwell proved responsive to the frankly emotional plea of the former Secretary of State: "Isn't the memory of an old association enough to give this young man a chance?"[21] Dulles, exhibiting a mixture of shy gratitude and humiliation, was thus taken on as a law clerk at fifty dollars a month, this munificent sum reflecting the enlightened personnel policies of Sullivan and Cromwell in a day when it was the practice of many firms to apprentice young lawyers without any monetary compensation.

The connection was to prove of great mutual benefit. Sullivan and Cromwell was a firm already expanding the concept of the lawyer's relationship to the corporate client, in a sense anticipating the later development of management as a professional function. The firm's lawyers made it their business to be thoroughly conversant with the competitive position of each client company, with the growth prospects for the industry of which it was a part, and with broad political developments that might affect the economy as a whole. William Nelson Cromwell had also been a leader in the effort to persuade the United States to build the Panama Canal, and was counsel for both the Panama Canal Company and the Panama Railway Company. The firm served a number of foreign clients, including French, German, and British investors in Latin America. Aided by his rudimentary grounding in the Spanish language, Dulles was soon traveling to that region on legal business. On one trip to British Guiana, where his task was to persuade the authorities not to impose a tariff on United States flour entering the various British territories in the Caribbean, he contracted malaria and nearly died. The heavy quinine dosage that saved his life also damaged the optic nerve, leaving him with slightly impaired vision and a noticeable tic in his left eye.

At the end of one year, Sullivan and Cromwell raised his salary to one hundred dollars a month, and this persuaded him he could now afford to marry. What gave confidence to an otherwise still precarious financial condition was the promise of further support from Grandfather Foster who, having announced his intention to leave twenty thousand dollars to each grandchild, invited Dulles to begin drawing on the bequest as needed. He thought well of Janet Avery and warmly encouraged the marriage.[22] Thus buttressed, the young couple was married on June 26, 1912. After three days of waiting at her family's summer house on Owasco Lake to complete a prescribed course of treatment for Foster's malaria, they departed for a honeymoon in the Catskills. Though a happy match, it was hardly a marriage of equals. Janet gave wholehearted devotion, bordering on worship, to her strong and intellectually remarkable husband, and found comfort in his steady, protective domination. Their life together soon came to revolve almost entirely around him and his career, and was lived rather precisely as he prescribed it. With the financial cushion provided by Grandfather Foster's legacy, she began at once to accompany him on his far-flung business trips, a practice she was to continue even after the arrival of their three children, and all through his years as Secretary of State.

The First World War

Dulles had been practicing law for five years, developing as a respected associate at Sullivan and Cromwell, when he received a confidential assignment from his uncle Robert Lansing, who was now Secretary of State. It was early 1917, and America's entrance into the merciless stalemate that was bleeding Europe to death was an event that President Wilson and his cabinet now grimly anticipated; precautionary planning was in order. Wilson and Lansing needed assurances that the governments of Panama, Costa Rica, and Nicaragua would harmonize their policies toward Germany with that of the United States, that they would in fact synchronize a declaration of war. German agents were known to be operating in Central America, and Washington feared sabotage of the

A major in the Army, World War I

Panama Canal if, after the United States became an enemy of Germany, the agents continued to enjoy safe haven in adjacent neutral states. Dulles was picked for the job, it appears, both because of his family connection with Lansing and because Sullivan and Cromwell, as legal counsel for the Government of Panama, could send an American lawyer into the area under the guise of doing normal business. In the event, Dulles carried out his assignment with professional competence, and the cooperation of the Central American governments was assured.

Barred from combatant military service in 1918 because of his defective eyesight, he received a direct commission in the army and went to Washington to serve as a lawyer on the War Trade Board. Working to assure that American trade with the major neutrals — the Scandinavian countries and Holland — was conducted under agreements that denied the transshipment of American exports to Germany, he became a valued assistant to Vance McCormick, the board chairman (who was also chairman of the Democratic National Committee). A frenetic shipbuilding program was under way to augment the small American merchant marine, but concurrent efforts were going forward for the lease of immediately available shipping. When lease negotiations with Holland broke down, owing to strong counterpressures from Germany, Dulles helped to draft an executive order that resulted in the seizure of eighty-seven Dutch merchant ships then sitting in American ports. Though the seizure was accompanied by public dispute regarding its constitutionality, it brought an additional 350,000 tons of shipping capacity under direct American control. Dulles also served as liaison between the War Trade Board and the War and Navy Departments, and in that capacity gained a certain appreciation of the complexities and inefficiencies of industrial mobilization in wartime. By the end of the war, he had been promoted from captain to major and was highly regarded for exceptional competence and judgment, not only by Vance McCormick, but also by Bernard Baruch, who headed the War Industries Board.

Peacemaking in Paris

When President Wilson decided personally to lead the American delegation at Versailles, he selected both McCormick and Baruch for major supporting roles, together with a number of other prominent Americans including Herbert Hoover, Norman Davis, Russell Leffingwell, and Thomas Lamont. Baruch became United States Representative on the Reparations Commission, and promptly asked Dulles to serve as his legal counsel. So Dulles was once more in Paris, this time a seasoned younger lawyer of thirty, sharing the incandescent hopes of his former ethics professor at Princeton, and wrapped in the aura of brilliant promise that hovered round the heads of a whole group of young men — Walter Lippmann, Adolf Berle, William Bullitt, Joseph Grew, Stephen Bonsal, Gordon Auchincloss — whom Wilson had chosen to assist him in the arduous quest to make the world safe for democracy. On the British side was John Maynard Keynes, and in the French delegation a brilliant young planner, Jean Monnet, with whom Foster and Allen Dulles were to form a close and lasting friendship.

To the Hotel Crillon, which served as headquarters for the American delegation, journalists came to call each afternoon at six o'clock for the latest word on progress or regression as interpreted by Colonel Edward M. House. One of the reporters was Arthur Krock, by then working for the *Louisville Courier-Journal*. House's young assistants came and went during the course of the press interviews and, as Krock recalled, "one of these turned out to be this old classmate of mine, Foster Dulles. So . . . we had a few drinks together." [23] Krock found the Dulles of the Paris Peace Conference "impressive indeed," well known to President Wilson and "in his relaxed time . . . witty and merry and very, very companionable." [24] It was during this period that Lansing's relations with Wilson were severely strained; the Secretary of State was unable to ascertain just how the President proposed to conduct the peace negotiations, it being clear only that he neither had an organized plan nor wished the State Department to develop any systematic approach. Already retreating into the posture of secret, ad hoc dealings that was to confuse his associates and ensure the hostility of the United States Senate, Wilson was also moving to rely primarily on the advice of his unofficial counsellor, Colonel House.[25] Krock later surmised that, had Dulles been the nephew of House rather than the nephew of Lansing, "I rather think that Wilson would have . . . given . . . him the function and authority he gave to Colonel Stephen Bonsal" [26] — that is, the role of adviser to the President at major meetings with Lloyd George, Clemenceau, and Orlando.

As it was, Dulles served with distinction on reparations matters, striving in company with his chief, Baruch, to dilute the spirit of vengeance that so pervaded the exhausted victors, to establish acceptance of the truth that Germany's capacity to pay war damages was finite and that attempts to press claims beyond reasonable limits would sow the bitter seeds of a new war. This position brought them into sharp disagreement with the British and French demand that Germany must accept the obligation for "war costs," a formulation loose enough to cover not only war pensions for soldiers, but compensation for every citizen of any state in the allied coalition who might have mortgaged his house to buy war bonds. The formulation was open-ended, logically absurd, and politically dangerous. Yet neither the statesmen concerned nor their publics could rise above the deep, implacable grievances they held against Germany. At one point in the proceedings, Dulles engaged in debate with the Prime Minister of Australia, W. M. Hughes, a passionate advocate of the hard line. Because their treaty obligations had put them in the position of policemen sworn to uphold the law, Hughes argued, Britain and France had been *bound* to go to Belgium's rescue; they were thus entitled to recovery of total costs; moreover, all other nations, being in the position of private citizens on a city street, were *entitled* to participate in Belgium's defense and, having done so, they too should receive full compensation. Opposed to this open-ended view, the American delegation was working to establish the principle that Belgium alone (because her neutrality had been clearly violated) was entitled to full damages, while other nations should confine their claims to those arising from direct physical injury to civilians and from direct physical damage to property. Indeed, this was the principle on which Germany had been persuaded to sign the armistice agreement. The United States was asking no more than that the Allies live up to this agreement. But when it came to reparations, as Dulles later wrote in a private memorandum, "there was not one of them which recognized the binding force of this provision." [27]

Rising to rebut Hughes, Dulles argued that the prearmistice talks among the Allies had produced an agreement on reparations containing every necessary element of a contract: "We have not before us a blank page, . . . it is true; but one which is already filled with writing, and at the bottom are the signatures of Mr. Wilson, of Mr. Orlando, of Mr. Clemenceau and of Mr. Lloyd George. It is the agreed basis of peace with Germany." [28] Then attacking the Australian Prime Minister's logic, he asked: "Does the policeman receive his hire from the wrongdoer whom he arrests? No; in making the arrest the policeman has performed his duty — nobly, gallantly, at great sacrifice, if you will; but still his duty. And the reparation paid by the wrongdoer is made to the victim — not to the guardian of the law." [29] But all such self-denying advocacy came to naught, for, as Bernard Baruch sadly conceded, "in the reparations clauses, the conference was not writing a mere contract of dollars and cents; it was dealing with blood-raw passions still pulsing through people's veins." [30]

Dulles was, however, unready to accept that all was lost. His tenacity and sense of tactical maneuver led him to propose (on June 3, 1919), that, whatever the formula used for computing "war costs," at least a fixed upper limit should be established. And when this effort failed, he developed a rather more Jesuitical approach: a draft statement which, on the one hand, met the political necessity of certain governments for a declaration that "the German Government shall . . . make reparation for the entire cost of the war," but which, on the other hand, stipulated that "the ability of the German Government . . . to make reparation is limited." Governments at war with Germany could in their discretion "renounce" their right to payment beyond a specified level.[31] Unfortunately for all concerned, this informal, deliberately ambiguous effort was transformed by successive revisions, especially those attributed to Lloyd George, into a statement of such moral righteousness that it was later denounced by Hitler as the "infamous war guilt clause." As Article 231 of the final treaty, it read: "The Allied and Associated Governments affirm and Germany accepts the responsibility of Germany and her allies for causing all the loss and damage to which the Allied and Associated Governments and their nationals have been subjected as a consequence of the war imposed upon them by the aggression of Germany and her allies." The caveat recognizing Germany's finite capacity to pay appeared in a separate article.[32]

The Shock of Disillusion

Allen Dulles was also at the peace conference, having joined the Foreign Service in 1916, and finding himself on duty at the American legation in Berne at the time of the armistice. He was brought to Paris to work on problems of administrative support for the large American delegation, but was later assigned to the Czechoslovak Boundary Commission along with Charles Seymour, who later became president of Yale. His recollection was cheerfully detached: "We had commissions for Czechoslovakia, and for Poland, and for Rumania, and then we had one for Austria and Hungary. . . . I don't know that I deserve any great credit for the shape of . . . Czechoslovakia. It looks something like a banana lying across the map . . ."[33] He remembered more vividly the date of his arrival in Paris — December 16, 1918 — because it was the same day President Wilson set foot in France to be met by frenzied demonstrations of mass adulation. What shocked both brothers in the weeks that followed was the swift transformation in Paris from a climate of euphoria to one of cynicism and bare-faced greed. With a kind of horrified fascination, they and all the other earnest young men watched at close hand as Wilson's popularity and prestige were tested and steadily eroded in the hard process of bargaining out the claims of the sovereign victors. The American President had arrived in Paris as "Savior of the World," but as he opposed specific demands — the French incorporation of the Rhineland, the Italian claim to Fiume, the widespread demand for heavy reparations — the frustration of his erstwhile allies changed to bitter anger and resolve. When the collective vengeance was finally set down in the Treaty of Versailles, signed by the victors and presented to the Germans, Foster and Allen were both present. Allen recalled that "the German delegate couldn't stand up, he was so affected with emotion. Everybody attributed it to insolence. Poor fellow, he wasn't insolent that day . . . I was sitting there not more than thirty, forty feet from him. The fellow couldn't get up — under the weight of the Treaty." [34]

Depressed by events and impatient to return home to resume the practice of law, Dulles received on June 27, 1919, a personal letter from President Wilson asking him to remain in Paris for some additional period "to handle the very important and difficult matters with which you have become so familiar and which you have so materially assisted in handling." The President thought the request for further service was justified "by the confidence we have all learned to feel in your judgment and ability." [35] Dulles thus remained in Europe through the summer and fall of 1919 as United States Representative on the Reparations Commission, discharging responsibilities that brought him into direct contact with men far senior to him in age and rank, including the finance minister of France and the chief justice of England. Much work still remained with respect to Austria, Hungary, and Turkey, but late in the year the Senate Foreign Relations Committee adopted a resolution expressing the view that the United States should discontinue its participation in the reparations effort. It was a part of the broader congressional effort to undercut President Wilson's plan for American leadership in the League of Nations. Although not binding on the executive branch, it had the intended effect; the group that Dulles headed closed up shop and packed for home.

Dulles's ingrained impression was that, beyond injustice, the Versailles treaty was an exercise in self-destructive madness. Thus, while he shared with his uncle Robert Lansing very serious reservations regarding President Wilson's handling of the negotiations in Paris, and even more of the Senate in Washington, his view was not so much that Wilson had failed but that democratic Europe had proved unworthy. This perspective was later to make him slow to recognize the danger of Hitler and Mussolini and slower to sense the full dimension of their menace. But it was also to make him insistent on a "peace of reconciliation" with Japan in 1951 when those negotiations were placed largely in his hands. From the collapse of Wilson's towering hopes Dulles also drew the conclusion that policy makers must respect and accommodate to domestic political realities, however unpalatable they may be; that an eroded political base is not a platform on which significant diplomatic achievement can ever be built or sustained. To many critics of his years as Secretary of State, it seemed that he applied this last conclusion rather too uncritically.

3

Struggle and Success in Wall Street

DURING THE FINAL WEEKS in Paris, Dulles had been approached by Thomas Lamont, one of President Wilson's senior advisers and a partner of J. P. Morgan. Impressed by the young lawyer's ability, Lamont offered him an immediate partnership in a law firm beholden to the Morgans. Dulles carefully considered the proposal and then turned it down. Back at Sullivan and Cromwell, he informed his superiors of the offer and his decision and they, appreciating that he could have used the situation for direct trading purposes, substantially increased his salary and soon made him a member of the firm.[1]

A Swift Ascent

During the next two decades, in which he combined law with international finance and diplomacy, the inherent tendencies of a powerful mind and personality gave specific structure and content to ambitions whose seeds had been sown as boyhood dreams during the long, benign summers at Henderson Harbor. His forceful nature, moved to achieve mastery and exercise dominance, steadily expanded the area of its influence and control.

Plunged into a variety of client assignments, he soon made his mark with Royall Victor, the senior partner of Sullivan and Cromwell, who ran the firm in close collaboration with Alfred Jaretzki and Henry Hill Pierce. Initially, he assisted Victor on several large corporate reorganizations involving, among others, the American Oil Company and the Chicago and Indiana Coal Railway, and he helped with a proxy fight for

control of the Remington Typewriter Company. The vexatious problem
of reparations also continued to command his time and attention, and
he found himself affronted by the tendency of the Coolidge administration to press Britain and France for repayment of their debts to the
United States, while urging those same countries to show moderation in
the matter of their own immense claims upon Germany. As to German
debts, he continued to argue for establishing a fixed indemnity, and at a
level that would effectively cancel a large percentage of the Allied claims.
In 1923, he was retained by J. P. Morgan as special counsel to the Dawes
committee, a body set in motion by Secretary of State Charles Evans
Hughes to devise measures for simplifying the reparations tangle, which
had by that time brought payments to a virtual halt. The essence of the
Dawes Plan, put forward in 1924, was a series of proposed American
loans to Germany, so that the Germans could repay the British and
French, and they in turn could repay the Americans — a circular arrangement that suggested the irrational consequences of simple logic when
applied to international affairs. Dulles recognized the inadequacy of the
proposals, and especially regretted that the Dawes committee lacked
authority to set a fixed level of German reparations and a fixed date for
final payment.[2]

Meanwhile, dramatic events were transforming the internal situation
at Sullivan and Cromwell. Jaretzki died suddenly in 1925, and the following year Victor, a brilliant man in his early forties and apparently in
perfect health, suffered a fatal heart attack "on his sailing boat, down
off Oyster Bay." [3] At about the same time, Pierce, who had been ill since
1923, determined that his retirement could no longer be postponed. Thus
in the space of a few months, two deaths and a serious illness had wiped
out the top leadership of the firm, leaving a vacuum which, on careful
analysis, could be adequately filled only by reaching down to the ablest
of the younger men. Dulles was chosen for the responsible and prestigious
role of senior partner, to run the firm with assistance from Edward
Green, Eustace Seligman, and Wilbur Cummings. Only six years after
his return from Paris, fourteen years after graduation from law school,
and at the age of thirty-eight, he found himself catapulted to the top of
a large and famous law firm, a journey that in normal circumstances
would have taken thirty years.

The Mind and the Manner

The Wall Street ambience is not, of course, congenial to gentle be-
lievers in the brotherhood of man. Its transactions are marked by a
pervasive coldness; the dealing is hard, tough, impersonal and not infre-

quently ruthless; the stakes are high and the play is for keeps. Having been thrust into this arena to be tested for survival, Dulles proved in the event to be a shrewd and powerful gladiator, and, not surprisingly, took on along the way a number of characteristics essential not for survival alone but for conspicuous success. If his background indicated there would be at least an initial collision between the values of Watertown and the values of Wall Street, it seems to have been cushioned by the influences of Grandfather Foster, Princeton, law school and European travel. If Dulles understood that the hard calculations of advantage which dominate the American business ethic are of doubtful compatibility with the teachings of Christ, he found he could readily live with the discrepancy, meanwhile pursuing a pragmatic course for the benefit of his client, his firm and himself.

Thomas E. Dewey, who did not meet Dulles until 1937, later commented that "I think he spent some years as an atheist," [4] but the better explanation may be that the theological baggage he brought with him from Watertown was a good deal lighter than has been supposed. Even after his "rediscovery" of religion in 1937, his theology consisted almost solely of a generalized faith in a "universal moral law," which he failed to define, yet assumed every man could grasp and should obey; that, plus a belief that the church has a role to play in the political process, and a conviction in the supreme worth of the individual. The theologian John Coleman Bennett thought Dulles had evolved his own form of "secularized Calvinism"; [5] like his father's doctrine of "social utility," this was able to coexist quite comfortably with Wall Street. In the dozens of speeches he later made to church groups, in the many articles he wrote, and in his moralistic pronouncements as Secretary of State, there was rarely any reference to sin, no admission that ethical decisions are fraught with moral ambiguity, and no evidence of an understanding that the dimension of self-interest, self-preservation and self-righteousness is implicit in every exercise of power. But what he lacked in theology, he more than made up for in self-certitude; and as the years passed, and particularly following his categorical commitment to anti-Communism and his coming to power as Secretary of State, this quality seemed to transform itself into an awesome moral self-righteousness. The judgments continued to be those of Dulles, but he conveyed the sense of acting as the agent of a higher power, as if, someone said, he had "a pipeline to God." He left Jamison Parker, a young aide of his latter years at the State Department, with the strong impression that "to cross him was to cross the deity."

Confronting, in the 1920s, not only ambition but the need to compensate for his relative youth in dealings with older men, he developed early on — in part from observing international leaders at the Hague and

Paris conferences — a manner of grave reserve and an operational style that managed to combine an attitude of moral superiority with the hard, cold blankness of the professional poker player. Physically imposing, he conveyed in negotiations an impression of massive immovability, technical mastery, and — hovering just beneath the surface — an instinct for the jugular. He was a more than competent lawyer, but the law seemed essentially a vehicle for the growth and self-expression of a powerful personality. Several men who knew him in Wall Street believed that, had he not succeeded early at Sullivan and Cromwell, the momentum of his ability and ambition would have carried him readily into the higher reaches of banking or corporate management.

As senior partner he added to this formidable armory an air of veiled condescension and expected obeisance, an unspoken assumption that he was the natural center and ultimate arbiter of the discussion at hand. The duty to speak first thus fell upon others, and included the obligation to be succinct. Always controlled and never spontaneous in business dealings, he listened with a palpably physical intensity, fixing the speaker with a steady stare that often rattled him and never failed to put him on the defensive. Each speaker received in turn the same treatment; then Dulles would summarize, synthesize, recommend, and decide. To these tasks he brought a remarkable memory, a rare analytic capacity, and a masterful sense of timing. He brought also an extraordinary method of speaking — slow, almost tortured, with long pauses in midsentence while he blinked his eyes, opened and closed his mouth, and groped for the precise word or phrase. His friend Elliott Bell has said that Dulles, when speaking, vividly conveyed the impression that the mind in motion is an intense physical act; to many of his auditors he seemed in actual pain.[6] Finally would come forth a well-formulated, carefully phrased comment that seemed to reflect the consensus of the meeting, resolve the major issues, and lay out the logical next steps. Carefully dissected, the Dullesian formulations were usually found to be simple in conception, confined to the basic issues, more tactical than fundamental in their approach to action, and cast in almost banal language. Their chief virtues were clarity and apparent precision. But what gave them decisive weight with the men who heard them was the sense of almost passionate conviction with which they were propounded, an impression reinforced by the evident physical labor accompanying their gestation and birth. Honed to a fine edge, such techniques made Dulles an unusually effective advocate and persuader in small groups. In the caucus he was supreme; at the rostrum, speaking before large audiences, he was apt to seem merely wooden.

His partner, Eustace Seligman, wholly admired his ability to go quickly to the heart of a matter. "Many . . . lawyers, when they sit down to write a brief . . . start dictating without being quite sure where they're going to end up. . . . Foster Dulles always had just the opposite approach. He would outline very brief notes on the points which were essential." That was "his gift," not only in legal work, but also later at the State Department: "He always tried to analyze things down to the essence and then was able to, in his writings, and in his speeches, make them very clear. Sometimes some people thought that he went too far in eliminating important things in order to get down to essentials." [7] Some at Sullivan and Cromwell (and later many more in government and the press) felt that Dulles was a compulsive oversimplifier; a few believed this pronounced tendency reflected the inner need to establish, however dogmatically, a few basic reference points to guide his own thought. In the judgment of one law colleague, "Dulles was never guilty of complex or sophisticated legal formulations, and there were several better legal theoreticians at Sullivan and Cromwell." [8] In this view, the Dulles mind was fundamentally shrewd and practical, but quite narrow in range, seeking always an immediate and a tangible result. Combined with his instinct to dominate, it was a quality that made him an advocate with an ever-present tendency to overstate his case — a tendency not confined to the law, in the view of his critics, but readily extended to the realms of theology and foreign affairs. Reinhold Niebuhr was later to complain that "Mr. Dulles' moral universe makes everything quite clear, too clear. . . . Self-righteousness is the inevitable fruit of simple moral judgments." [9]

Through the 1930s, as Dulles grew in reputation and prestige, he also showed an increasing tendency to insulate himself from much of the immediate environment around him, to cultivate associations only on the highest financial, political, and social levels, and to act with condescension, abruptness or indifference to a range of lesser people and problems. It was a tendency that showed itself in a variety of situations, both important and trivial. While professing, for example, a serious interest in the selection of outstanding young men from the leading law schools to become associates in Sullivan and Cromwell, in fact he rarely found time to interview any candidate, and was oblivious of the identity of half the lawyers in the firm. At the office party before Christmas, it was standard practice for one of the older partners to stand at his elbow and whisper the name of each young associate as he approached deferentially to pay his respects. Admirers explained this abstract, impersonal style by saying that Dulles was always concentrating on some larger, more urgent matter; moreover, that his austere demeanor protected an innate shyness and concealed a genuine warmth. These observations were accurate as far as they went. He loved hard work, drove himself at a terrific pace, and was wholly absorbed by his professional problems, displaying

The senior partner of Sullivan and Cromwell,
in Berlin (1930)

the lawyer's tendency to "compartmentalize" by intense concentration on
one problem at a time. In the company of family and close friends, he
could be relaxed and considerate, and he showed a voracious appetite for
recreation and diversion after a long stint of hard work.

What this explanation left out, however, was the central fact that
Dulles was an intellectual loner — a man who relied not merely in the
last resort, but almost exclusively, in large matters and in small, on his
own counsel. His views on important matters were developed by an
apparently elaborate, structured, and wholly internalized process which
consisted of linking together relevant (to him) pieces of evidence, tangible
and otherwise. The resulting conclusion thus stood at the end of a long
chain of logic and, when finally arrived at, was not easily reversed. Especially was this the case since Dulles also possessed an almost unlimited
confidence in his own reasoning power, his own judgment, and his own
power of persuasion.

The British ambassador, Sir Oliver Franks, discovered this "solitary
method" when the two men discussed aspects of the developing Japanese
peace treaty in early 1951. Franks asked for certain amendments, but
found that Dulles, instead of addressing these points, insisted on leading
him through a logical labyrinth. He was "a very intelligent person work-

ing out all the angles of his brief and completely prepared to tell you where he was and why he was there, but unable to free himself from the process by which he, himself, had reached the position . . . so he had to tell you this enroute to the real discussion." There was, Franks added, a sense that Dulles was "always finding the evidence, weighing it — as it were, establishing a pleading — and there was a sense in which the person opposite him in the room was assumed by him to be doing the equal and opposite process, with the result that what you got was this confrontation of views and then an exploration to see whether accommodation was possible. But you did not have a conversation in the ordinary sense." [10] Because Dulles was thus locked into his own structured process, it was not possible, Franks found, to have "an open, freewheeling discussion . . . to see where the balance of truth, the balance of expediency, the issues of principle lay." [11] The only way to modify Dulles's position was to enter the labyrinth and to point out that one of the premises or considerations on which he had built his conclusion was not quite what Dulles had supposed it to be.

These were qualities of mind rather certain to produce a personality with a strong tendency to self-isolation — one that either actively rejected or itself proved repellent to a wide range of differing viewpoints.

Private Life

As he built his success in Wall Street, Dulles acquired along the way a town house on Ninety-first Street, a country house in Cold Spring Harbor, and a cruising yawl. The houses were well staffed — his son Avery remembered that a cook, a governess, and two Irish maids was about normal; and in 1928 "we got a Lincoln with a very large Irish chauffeur." [12] Each day during three seasons of the year, he rode the Third Avenue elevated from Ninety-first Street to Wall Street, the third car of the nine-thirty train being unofficially but zealously reserved by a class-conscious motorman for gentlemen wearing Chesterfield overcoats. In the summer he commuted to Long Island, often arriving early enough for a game of tennis, at which, according to David Bruce, he was reasonably proficient: "He wouldn't have been a tournament man, but he played well — and aggressively." [13] Then he would change into white flannels and blazer and take cocktails on the terrace with Janet before joining their three children, John, Lillias, and Avery, for a carefully planned, excellent and well-served dinner. Father, Avery recalled, was "definitely the master of the house." [14]

With his financial position assured, he also found increasing pleasure in those modestly sensuous indulgences that are the secret temptation of every self-denying Victorian. He developed a special fondness for French wines, caviar, brandy and cigars, and to a lesser extent for the diversions of European nightclubs. Arriving in Paris, where Sullivan and Cromwell had an office, he would put in a long, hard day's work, then give over the evening and much of the night to good food and wine, and to making the rounds of half a dozen cabarets, in company with Janet and a few close associates. Possessing a singular physical vitality, he could repeat the whole process the next day. David Bruce also recalled that the first time he met Dulles was at a wine auction in New York, organized to dispose of the private cellar of someone who had died: "Foster was not only the largest buyer, but certainly the most discriminating." [15] By the time he became Secretary of State, however, his doctors, concerned with his gout, had forbidden him both wine and cigars; for the former he seemed to find an acceptable substitute in Overholt rye, but nothing could assuage his longing for a good cigar. For years, he suffered a recurring nightmare in which he was turning a rich-smelling panatella under his nose and preparing to light it; then he would awake in a cold sweat, never certain whether or not he had actually followed through.[16]

Yet for all his obvious pleasure in the good life, Dulles never really metamorphosed into a stylish, artistically sensitive, socially cultivated New Yorker. He had absolutely no interest in music or art, and read detective stories in the evening for relaxation from the rigors of the law. Except for outer trappings, he remained a plain, rugged and rather gauche figure whose roots were deep in the simplicities of northern New York. "He was a man of Watertown rather than a man of New York," his sister Eleanor has said,[17] and his admiring State Department assistant, Roderic O'Connor, later called him "plain as a stick." [18] For one journalist, he brought to mind something "out of Kansas." [19] His expensive clothes, showing a partiality to subtle hues of green, came from Brooks Brothers and his ties from Charvet in Paris, but he tended to wear them with a somewhat rumpled lack of distinction. His manners were inelegant. At work or in conference, he played constantly with a pencil, tapping it against his yellow pad, rolling it on the table, twirling it in his hair or up his nose. He stirred his whiskey with a thick forefinger, and then sucked the finger. In later years, he wore no garters, in an effort to avoid pressure on the veins in his lower legs, and his socks were always falling down. As O'Connor recalled it, "He was constantly ducking down to pull them up," and when he sat down "his very long legs would dangle out completely bare. . . ." At gatherings of foreign ministers or in office meetings with visiting ambassadors, "this was a bit disconcerting." [20]

For recreation and reflection, he persistently returned to the scene of his youth, finding perhaps his truest pleasure in fishing the northern lakes, hiking the woods, or sailing his cruising yawl, *Menemsha*. Sailing, and particularly sailing in rough weather, may have been his greatest satisfaction. From boyhood this had taught him patience, self-reliance, physical endurance, and the hazard of unexpected storms, and he relished the challenge, as his son Avery said, of "battling with elements that he couldn't control," for this represented "an allegory of life itself." [21] An expert shiphandler and intrepid navigator, he preferred an all-male crew as this permitted "a more rugged life," [22] and he laid down Spartan rules for everyone aboard — a compulsory swim before breakfast (if the temperature was above fifty degrees), another before dinner no matter how cold the water, and only two meals a day. He rose early in the morning, enjoyed being soaked by the waves for eight or ten hours in an open cockpit, and frequently sailed all night. But when port was reached, the puritan yielded to the sybarite and with the zeal of a gourmet he would go ashore to select choice meats, vegetables, fruit, cheese and wine for the coming feast. He had a special fondness for cheese, and dinner would often be topped off with Belleville cheddar and brandy under a canopy of velvet black night and stars. As Avery said, all this showed his father's belief in a "combination of pleasure and pain." [23]

In 1941, he sold the *Menemsha* and bought Duck Island, an isolated landfall in the eastern part of Lake Ontario to which he had frequently sailed as a boy. There, in a rough but comfortable log cabin, built to his specifications by the local Indians, with no radio or telephone and wholly cut off from the outside world (except for an arrangement with the lighthouse keeper for the delivery of emergency radio messages), he retreated at frequent intervals to rest and review his problems. Alone with his wife, who did crossword puzzles and occasionally read aloud, he found refreshment in chopping wood, cooking, doing the dishes, walking on the beach, and whittling. Sitting on a rock in the pale northern sunshine, he seemed as naturally a part of the scene as the tough and gnarled old trees. His roots were in this northern lake and surrounding woodlands and in his upbringing there which had stressed simplicity, duty, determination, and no excuses.

Family Matters

In 1926, the year he became senior partner, Dulles used his new authority to bring his brother Allen into the firm. The younger Dulles, then thirty-three, was slowly going broke in the Foreign Service. While serving a tour in Washington he had managed to take his law degree at George Washington University by attending evening classes, a fact that rendered him a rather unlikely candidate for Sullivan and Cromwell, but Foster was now calling the shots. Allen had just received notice of his impending assignment to China: "I decided if I went to China, I would probably go bankrupt, as I had run out of money pretty much, and that I'd better get out of the Service. So I did." [24] He came into the law firm as an associate, and was elevated to the partnership in 1930. An intelligent and cultivated man, who in later years developed the deceptive manner and appearance of a rather jolly Victorian uncle, he worked hard at learning the lawyer's trade, and was soon earning his keep through a better-than-average ability to attract new clients. More gregarious than Foster and taking a more genuine pleasure in people, he enjoyed the business of nurturing prospective clients through companionship and entertainment. Initially there existed an unwritten house rule that, in working out the technicalities of a case, Allen was always to be supported by a "good lawyer," but over a period of years he made the transition successfully and contributed to the success of the firm. In the nature of things, he remained beholden to his powerful older brother.

In 1931 their father, the Reverend Dulles, died in his late seventies, and it fell to Foster, as the older son, to assume moral responsibility for the family and its problems. Allen was now well established; Margaret was happily married to the Reverend Deane Edwards in Rye, and Nataline comfortably settled in Utica as Mrs. James Seymour. His third sister, Eleanor, who was later to have a long career in the State Department, was teaching international relations at Johns Hopkins in Baltimore. Intellectual and bearing a strong resemblance to Foster, she possessed a career drive that many felt reflected an envy of her brothers and a wish that she had been born male. For some six years she had been "going with" a philologist named David Blondheim, who was an orthodox Jew. Insofar as they were aware of the relationship and its prospects, the Dulles family appeared to be relaxed, but the Blondheim family was violently opposed to any consummation. When the marriage nevertheless took place in 1932, family pressures on him mounted. Two years later, while Eleanor was pregnant, David Blondheim committed suicide by "putting his head in the oven." To muffle the scandal, Foster, who could be very overbearing in family as well as in business affairs, put a great deal of pressure on Eleanor to take back the Dulles name. This she soon did, giving it also to the boy she had been carrying at the time, and later to an adopted daughter.

Any number of people — foreign officials, comparative strangers, close friends — have remarked on the harmony, charm and mutual devotion they saw and sensed in Dulles's relationship with his wife, over a span of nearly forty years. Janet did not, with the passing years, emerge perceptibly from the shy dependence which had first attracted him, but remained a quiet, orderly, rather humorless person given to books and crossword puzzles and to arranging their domestic and social life exactly the way her husband wanted it. For his part, Foster continued to be attentive, solicitous and supportive.

Janet greatly preferred private to public life, and was reported to have been "miserable" at the 1952 Republican convention and "inwardly saddened" by his appointment as Secretary of State. The life of controversy and political strife in Washington made her tense and "fluttery," and ceaseless official travel to foreign countries meant for her hours and days of solitary waiting in hotel suites while he conducted endless diplomatic business. After several years of this, she seemed to many a rather forlorn and even embittered figure, barely suppressing an inner hostility to her general situation. The British journalist Henry Brandon, arriving at Claridge's for an interview one afternoon in 1956, found that Dulles was still at the Foreign Office dealing with the developing Suez crisis. Janet invited him in, apologizing for her husband's absence and the need for Brandon to wait. Then moving her hands in an involuntary gesture of helplessness, she said sadly: "Waiting is my life." [25] But it was a course she had long since, and irrevocably, chosen, and in the final years he seemed to need her more than she needed him. One day in 1957 on a trip to Bonn, Dulles returned to Ambassador David Bruce's residence at Bad Godesberg after a session with Adenauer. The American team was about to assemble for a postmortem review, when Dulles abruptly broke away, strode across the foyer and up the broad staircase to the second floor, where he knocked anxiously on Janet's door. She opened it immediately.

"Here I am, Foster," she said in a quiet voice.

"Oh, there you are," he replied, and kissed her. Thus reassured, he returned to his meeting. [26]

An evident truth about the Dulles marriage was that it was emotionally complete without the children. Indeed, they seemed intrusions upon an idyll, and all three were classic cases of parental neglect. No doubt the basic trouble was that Dulles had been totally absorbed in his own career from the beginning and that, as between him and the children, Janet always put him first. Beyond simple neglect, however, he displayed a heavy ineptitude that combined unbending reserve and sternness with more than a little derision. His idea of how to inspire them to achievement — in reading, tennis, sailing, chess — was to place great demands on them (often beyond the capacity of their years) and then, having done so, to bait them with pointed indications that, in his opinion, they really couldn't meet the demands and would accordingly never amount to much. By such techniques, they seem to have been not infrequently reduced to sobbing tantrums in the early years. "There was no coziness in that family," one friend has said, "no basic acceptance of the children as children." Caught between an imperious father and a passive mother, they were always on trial, on their guard, and emotionally on their own. One law associate sensed that at some point in the process Dulles, concluding that the children were not turning out well, acted to "cut his emotional losses" by putting further layers of insulation between himself and them.

The older son, John, who was perhaps his mother's favorite, succeeded at an early age in putting some respectable spiritual distance between himself and his father and in avoiding all thoughts of emulation. More lighthearted than the others, he was often "the life of the debutante parties" on Long Island and occasionally came home "wearing only a silk hat." As soon as practicable, he removed himself physically to an engineering career in Mexico. But if the first-born thus made good a relatively graceful escape, one that muted the resentment he felt, the other two seemed to be under psychological compulsion to strike back.

Lillias, the only daughter, who was graduated from Bennington and later from Union Theological Seminary, was an intelligent girl who inherited her father's large bone structure and lantern jaw. After a debutante season in which she suffered miserably from not being pretty, she married, as one friend of the family put it, "the first man who came along." He proved to be the son of a public relations man who had once worked for Dulles, and a young man with a penchant for promotional and self-promotional schemes that never quite panned out. Together he and Lillias developed a quietly spectacular capacity for running up bills, and, on at least one occasion, used for other purposes the checks that Dulles had sent them to pay for their children's schooling. Lillias stuck defiantly by her husband through every embarrassment, and Dulles anxiously bailed them out for many years, worried and waiting for the next shoe to drop.

The rebellion of Avery, the younger son, took the initial form of rather wild drinking at Harvard, but was followed by the more definitive decision in 1939 to renounce the Presbyterian faith for Catholicism. In the middle of the Second World War, when he was hospitalized for battle wounds, he decided to become a Jesuit priest. While there is no evidence to suggest that Dulles "disowned" him, the shock and embarrassment to both parents were considerable, notwithstanding the thinness of Dulles's own spirituality. Reconciliation when it did come seems to have been partial, and to have been based largely on the quality of Avery's performance as a priest. He was brilliant, gentle, and obviously well suited to the calling, and Dulles was disposed to honor excellence. Janet, however, continued to give the impression that the family "still loved him anyway," not for but in spite of his achievements; and although she professed to be proud of his books, she made no pretense of understanding them. In the end, however, as one friend said, "Avery was considered the great success of the family."

4

Response to World Crisis

As THE WORLD CAREENED through the 1930s on its reckless run toward the Second World War, Dulles, though deeply disturbed by the advance of destructive forces, viewed the impending crisis as grimly inevitable and placed almost all of the blame on the democratic powers. Moreover, he assigned this blame with arguments at once so trenchant and so vehement that, as also happened later when he was Secretary of State, he lost his sense of proportion and ended by misjudging and underestimating the menace that Hitler's Germany and Imperial Japan presented to America and to democratic hopes throughout the world.

He believed there were inherent defects in the existing international system of nation-states, indeed in human nature itself, and that these had been aggravated by the gross inequities of the Versailles treaty, producing severe rigidities that made war more than likely. The victors in the war of 1914 were guilty of a "grave misconception of the nature of peace," [1] for they had chosen to identify it with a rigid status quo and had sought to use the League of Nations as the instrumentality for repressing legitimate demands of the defeated nations, whose conditions of life had in consequence become intolerable. "Aggression," he wrote in 1935, had become "the capital international crime" for those who equated the status quo with "security" and "peace." [2] Speaking at Princeton in March 1936, he viewed the gathering war clouds in Europe as another chapter in the historic struggle "between the dynamic and the static — the urge to acquire and the desire to retain." [3] Change, as Henri Bergson had taught him, was the "ultimate fact to which we must accommodate ourselves," [4] yet the leading nations of the world were refusing to acknowledge this truth, refusing to accommodate the rising energies of Germany, Italy and Japan. Change would inevitably come, he argued, but the probability now was that it would be violent and destructive rather than peaceful and manageable.

On balance, it was better to accept change and avoid war, "even though one could not understand or approve the forces compelling it"; [5] although distasteful, Hitler and the National Socialist movement in Germany represented change which it was better to accept. As Dewey said in retrospect, Dulles thought "Hitler was a passing phenomenon . . . reflecting a basic economic problem. . . . His thesis was that the fat and happy should gracefully yield to avoid war." [6] John J. McCloy, who was later United States High Commissioner in Occupied Germany, said with reference to the prewar period that "I was always puzzled to see just where Foster Dulles stood . . . with the Nazi business and what his feeling was about the oncoming menace from Germany. I rather gathered the impression that he was not particularly concerned about it." McCloy thought Dulles was "a peacefully disposed man" with "a great deal of faith in . . . the arbitrament of disputes other than by means of violence," and that this posture somewhat disposed him "to rationalize this Hitler movement." [7] Dulles indeed opposed the rising resistance to Hitler's demands on the grounds that Britain, France and the United States had all committed "blunders so colossal that they must be paid for." [8] President Roosevelt's increasing efforts to alert public opinion to the rising dangers seemed to him a deplorable cultivation of "mass emotion on a substantial scale," which threatened to create the dangerous ideology of the "nation-hero" versus the "nation-villain." [9] He was especially anguished at the impending heavy cost of American rearmament.

Sullivan and Cromwell had close ties with Germany, where the firm handled bond issues and related matters for several provincial governments and private corporations. It maintained an office in Berlin, and the business from German clients was lucrative. Sometime in 1935, after the vicious Nazi persecution of German Jews was no longer deniable, Dulles found himself suddenly confronted by a quiet but determined partners' revolt. At a special meeting, called for the purpose, they informed him flatly that the moral implications of continuing to do business with German firms had become intolerable and that, unless connections were severed, they would resign en bloc and organize a new law firm. As Allen Dulles later told the story to Robert Amory, Foster Dulles was at first bewildered, then adamant, protesting among other things the loss of substantial profits; finally, however, he capitulated "in tears." [10]

Political Philosophy

Dulles's comprehensive reflections on the nature of man, society, and the international system were set down in a book, *War, Peace and Change*, which, though published in 1939, was "the result of much thinking and study since the Paris Peace Conference of 1919." [11] It seems to represent his matured reflections on the tragedy of Versailles, and was probably completed before 1938, for it is wholly devoid of the moral preachments with which his later writings and speeches were so heavily laden. The book is indeed notable for its qualities of abstract thought and moral detachment, being the inquiry of a philosophically pragmatic mind into the question of man's strong propensity for conflict and war; at the same time, it is a lawyer's brief for the Wilsonian view that solution of the problem of world peace lies basically in the establishment of international institutions that run on abstract principles of justice.

The history of the human race, Dulles argued in his book, is largely a history of "the effort to reconcile selfishness with gregariousness." [12] Unfortunately, the social cohesion of one group depends on the existence of external enemies, for "upon this foundation is built that form of patriotism which personifies the nation as a living being endowed with heroic qualities, who lives bravely and dangerously in a world of inferior, and even villainous, other-nation personalities." [13] The crisis of 1939 was, he found, traceable directly to the Paris Peace Conference of 1919. The tragic failure of Versailles was rooted in the insistent, purblind selfishness of the victors. Like most satisfied persons, "they conceived of peace as the avoidance of all change, the creation of a situation such that they would be left in tranquillity to enjoy their existing status." [14] How had they erred? By placing all emphasis on the enforcement provisions of the League Covenant (namely, Articles 10 and 16), which were designed to prevent aggression, and by choosing to ignore Article 19, which was the inspiration of Woodrow Wilson's genius. Article 19 permitted "reconsideration" of treaties whose relevance had become questionable, as well as "consideration" of international conditions "whose continuance might endanger the peace of the world." [15] Dulles conceded that the language of Article 19 was "cautious and halting" and that it provided no mechanisms or procedures for actually bringing about treaty revision; he insisted nevertheless that "here resided the germ of 'peaceful change,' without which violent change becomes inevitable." [16]

To what sort of proposals did such analysis lead? To the creation of "international mechanisms" (which he nowhere defined) that could manage change, accommodating to a reasonable and legitimate extent the thrust of dynamic forces, while providing unspecified safeguards against general violence. Specifically, his international system of guidance and arbitration would (1) "detect at their inception" those forces in the world that were operating for international change; _ (2) "appraise intelligently" the potential of such dynamic forces for growth and "intensification"; (3) assess the likelihood that such forces would find "adequate outlet" within the framework of "internal opportunities" (both those in existence and those that might be created); and (4) "recommend *promptly* such alteration of the international status as may seem necessary to prevent the growth of powerful forces emotionally committed to exaggerated and drastic change." [17] In sum, the "practical" road to peace required "procedures" designed to "check the tendency to identify one's personified state with deity," and to "check the tendency to identify the other-nation personality with evil." [18]

War, Peace and Change is striking for its relentless insistence on logic, for the abstract and legalistic quality of its arguments, and for the high-minded impracticality of its proposals. Still it stands, whatever its inadequacies, as an earnest effort by a serious person to find a nonviolent solution to the gravest problem of twentieth-century man. In the light of Dulles's later posture as Secretary of State, however, it is most striking for its tone of moral detachment, a determined avoidance of value judgments on the issues of right and wrong. Dulles was arguing in this work that men everywhere — by the mere fact that they are men — contribute to the causes of war and the dangerous imperfections of the international system; to guard against war, men must somehow transcend the innate tendency to equate their particular ingroup with the deity and all outgroups with the devil; to assist them in so fundamental an undertaking, they must develop "mechanisms" able to manage peaceful change. However, by the time he became Secretary of State, some fourteen years later, his view had shifted significantly. The primary causes of international strife were no longer in the system of nation-states, per se, but only in certain of its malignant members; the dangers of war sprang not from inadequacies in human nature distributed rather impartially across the human race, but from evil intent peculiar to certain nations and philosophies; and while peaceful change was, of course, necessary for the avoidance of war, that requirement now translated into mandatory reform of the evil-doers, rather than concessions by defenders of the good and the true.

It is no doubt correct to say that Dulles as Secretary of State maintained a basic belief in the inevitability of change and in the surpassing desirability of avoiding major war. But it is instructive to note that, as he descended from philosophy to assume the roles of public servant and politician, he rather conspicuously lost his objectivity. In part this loss was the result of compelling circumstance, yet the rising stridency of his moralistic assertions was a major contributing factor. What is most ironic is that Dulles the preacher-politician, in sharpest contrast to Dulles the lawyer-philosopher, saw no apparent reason to check the tendency to equate the personified nation-state with God and the other-state personality with the devil.

"Rediscovery" of Religion

If Dulles had in fact, as Dewey thought, fallen into atheism during his early and middle years in Wall Street, the year 1937 seems to have marked a revival of his faith — at least his faith in the relevance of the Christian ethic to the problem of international peace and order. The "rebirth" or "rediscovery" seems to have come from the striking contrast he perceived in the tone and effectiveness of two conferences he attended that year, the first a gathering of intellectuals in Paris organized under the auspices of the League of Nations, the second a meeting of church notables in Oxford. Both groups had been brought together to ponder the precarious prospects for world peace.

According to the account of his son Avery, Dulles was painfully disappointed by the inability of any speaker at the Paris meeting to transcend his own narrowly national perspective or to put forward any imaginative proposals. But when he moved across the Channel to Oxford the following week, he was immediately impressed by the refreshing readiness of the church leaders to give weight to the claims of mankind as a whole. A 1944 publicity handout, issued by the Federal Council of Churches, is authority for the statement that he found the Paris meeting "absolutely futile," [19] whereas at Oxford "he was struck by the spirit of unity and fellowship with which it [the conference] tackled problems in contrast to the suspicious atmosphere of diplomatic conferences"; he realized that "peace must have a spiritual basis . . . diplomacy had failed. His search for a successful method led to the conviction that the qualities taught by the great religions were needed for the practical solution of world problems." [20]

As these 1937 conferences marked the beginning of Dulles's association with the Federal Council of Churches, which led in 1940 to his appointment as chairman of its Commission on a Just and Durable Peace, some thought that the more than casual effort to demonstrate a revival of his faith reflected an attempt to give himself a more appropriate "image" for church work. One leading journalist thought his symbolic donning of the church uniform was "shrewd," [21] but, as the executive secretary of the commission recalled it, Dulles was chosen not only for his experience and competence in world affairs, but also because of "his real orientation to the Christian approach. . . . It sounds a little overly pious maybe, but I think he really had a sense of Christian vocation about this." [22] Moreover, the church leaders who worked with him for the next five years did not perceive any ulterior motive, although they recognized that motivation exists on many levels and that "Mr. Dulles — as all big men — was complex." [23]

Dulles's reasons for moving deeply into church work at this time may indeed have been complex. The showdown with his partners over the moral meaning of Hitler had somewhat shaken him; relationships with his children had proved a disappointment; as he approached fifty and the world seemed to slide toward catastrophe, the relevance of devoting almost all of his time to the problems of a large law firm began to seem questionable. Facing "a growing boredom with the routine of success," [24] and a genuine concern for the fate of mankind, he sought new channels for large and restless energies, and church work offered both intellectual challenge and a public forum for the expression of his opinions on a range of burning international issues, moral and political. At the same time, there is no reason to doubt that a genuine "rediscovery" of religion (as an important component of peace and order) may have been a major factor in his decision; in any event, he stressed the point on several occasions. Addressing the Princeton Theological Seminary on May 16, 1945, he asserted that the church's influence in shaping the postwar peace would be decisive, and added: "That judgment is very different from that with which I started a career of international activity. For many years it never occurred to me that the Christian Gospel had any practical bearing on the solution of international problems. So I came to my present views only after 30 years of experience with futility." [25]

Beginning in 1938, his traveling, writing, and speechmaking on behalf of the Federal Council of Churches developed into a formidable commitment of time and energy. He kept four or five dozen speaking engagements a year, talking to church and business groups, YMCA organizations, luncheon clubs and colleges; he also found time to write a growing number of articles for publications ranging from *Foreign Affairs* to *Presbyterian Life*. Writing or speaking, his major themes were basically political — the obsolescence of national sovereignty, the need for long-range national objectives, and the vital importance of the undefined "spiritual element." Before Pearl Harbor, he also made plain his view that America should stand aloof from the impending cataclysm in Europe. Thus, addressing the Detroit YMCA on October 28, 1939, two months after the onset of the "phony war" phase in Western Europe, he saw "neither in the underlying causes of the war, nor its long range objectives, any reason for the United States becoming a participant in the war. Were we now to act, it would be to reaffirm an international order which by its very nature is self-destructive and a breeder of violent revolt." [26] And as Charles A. Lindbergh began to emerge as an outspoken champion of isolationism, and of a modus vivendi with Hitler, Dulles wrote to him in cautious but sympathetic terms: "I am very glad you spoke as you did. I do not agree with everything that you said, but I do agree with the result, and I feel that there is grave danger that, under the influence of emotion, we will decide upon a national policy which is quite the reverse of what we had more or less agreed upon when we were thinking clearly." [27] His speech the same year to the Foreign Policy Association seemed to combine vehement refusal of an American war effort with near despair. "The tragedy is that we seem to have learned nothing. I hear the same talk about 'sanctity of treaties,' 'law and order,' 'resisting aggression,' and 'enforcing morality.' Such phrases have always been the stock in trade of those who have vested interests which they want to preserve against those in revolt against a rigid system." [28]

In the spring of 1940, he wrote to a friend that "so far as Europe is concerned, I do not think there is anything we can do, or that anyone can do, that will prevent the present war from impoverishing the nations of Europe . . ." [29] To another audience he said, "I dislike isolation, but I prefer it to identification with a senseless repetition of the cyclical struggle between the dynamic and static forces of the world. . . . The fundamental fact is that the national system of wholly independent sovereign states is completing its cycle of usefulness." [30]

A year *before* Pearl Harbor, in a speech to the New York YMCA, he noted the British unreadiness to define Britain's postwar aims, and feared that Churchill and Roosevelt sought "little more than to recreate the very conditions which have bred the present war." [31] Believing such conditions could be changed only within a flexible international "federation," he argued three months *after* Pearl Harbor for a modification of national sovereignty, so that the world's political evolution could be resumed "through the genius of the federal system." [32] Repeatedly and with rising fervor he preached his opposition to the war by ignoring its reality and by taking refuge in the Christian prescriptions for perfect universal harmony. World peace depended, he said, on mankind's acceptance of "basic thoughts which Christ himself expressed — humility, repentance, avoidance of personal hatreds and hypocrisies, recognition of the spiritual supremacy of God rather than of the state." [33]

His persisting emotional detachment from the life-and-death struggle against Hitler was apparent on a trip in 1942 to an England still under siege, with Londoners still receiving flaming nightly visits from the Luftwaffe. Dulles seemed genuinely surprised to find a general lack of interest in postwar planning, and was chagrined that leading churchmen, immersed in war work on the home front, showed no particular interest in even talking to him. As a result, he had to turn to the American ambassador, John G. Winant, for help in arranging some appointments with British politicians and other public figures. He met Clement Atlee and Ernest Bevin, who failed to impress him, but he was delighted by Barbara Ward and reassured to find that Professor E. H. Carr was "a great believer in the necessity of federation in Europe." [34] Anthony Eden, then Foreign Secretary, agreed to invite him to lunch. Dulles wrote in his report of the trip that Eden was polite, but not very forthcoming and "mostly listened to me" on the necessity for postwar planning and American-British coordination on European policy after the war, failing which "the whole situation might easily get out of hand with turmoil and confusion in Europe for many years." [35] Eden's later recollection of that first encounter was of a vaguely pleasant interlude, but Sir Alexander Cadogan (later Britain's permanent representative to the United Nations Security Council), who was also present, made the following entry in his diary: "Monday, 13 July [1942]: Lunched with A. in his flat. J. F. Dulles there. . . . J.F.D. the wooliest type of useless pontificating American. . . . Heaven help us!" [36]

Introduction to Politics

Nineteen thirty-seven also marked the beginning of Dulles's long association with Thomas E. Dewey, who was to be the Republican presidential nominee in 1944 and again in 1948 — and almost in 1940 as well. They had met in the course of Dulles's search for a replacement for his senior partner in litigation, a colleague who was being forced into retirement by bad health. Dewey, only thirty-five, was the young and rising rackets investigator in New York City. After several lunches and dinners, an impressed Dulles invited Dewey to become a partner of Sullivan and Cromwell, and an impecunious Dewey readily accepted. At that point, however, politics intervened to prevent consummation. Dewey was being pressed hard to run for district attorney by the reform forces who were concerned that the Fusion candidate, Irving Ben Cooper, lacked the standing or experience to win election against the Democratic-controlled Tammany Hall. As Dewey explained it: "I didn't want to run for District Attorney of New York County any more than

I wanted a great big hole in the head. No Republican candidate had won in New York County since 1911 . . . it was an absolutely hopeless race, and the Democrats had nominated a perfectly respectable fellow." Unfortunately, the "general impression was about to get around that I was a skunk because I wouldn't run for an office I didn't want. . . . In the final analysis it got so bad that I had to sit down with Foster, and we talked about it. He agreed that I had to do it, and therefore I was excused from my commitment. I did run. And to my great surprise I was elected. I was then launched in politics." [37]

The Dewey-Dulles relationship grew steadily closer after 1938 when Dewey, having made a splendid but losing fight for the governorship of New York, found to his "horror and astonishment" that he was the leading GOP candidate for President, according to Gallup polls. In 1940, the year of the presidential election, he was thirty-eight years old and had never held an office higher than district attorney. But after watching the polls sustain his high standing for a number of months, he and his advisers concluded that the situation, "while impossible to believe," nevertheless warranted serious attention; "we decided to do the best we could with it." [38] From that point onward, in company with Roger Straus and George Medalie, Dulles was a close adviser to the new Republican hopeful, drafting foreign policy speeches and helping with strategy sessions that lasted well into the small hours of many nights. Dewey entered a number of primaries and appeared to have an edge over the conservative-isolationist Senator Robert Taft, but both were eclipsed at the convention by the political phenomenon of Wendell Willkie, "the barefoot boy from Wall Street." Dewey found Dulles in those years "thoughtful, decisive, bright — occasionally a little brittle — a very hard worker, efficient with the use of his time, but generous with his time." [39] The journalist Richard Rovere has expressed the retrospective view that in this relationship Dulles may well have been the true sponsor, who, holding the ambition to become Secretary of State, substantially created and nurtured the Dewey candidacy.[40] On the available evidence, this appears to assume a greater political competence, though not perhaps a greater ambition, than Dulles possessed in 1940.

The Church in World Affairs

As the far-flung, intensive, bloody, and precarious drama of the war unfolded, Dulles labored to make the Commission on a Just and Durable Peace an effective voice in the developing debate about war aims and how to organize the postwar world. The commission was thus increasingly a political instrument, but remarkably it escaped all serious

charges of partisanship, even though Dulles continued to serve concurrently as a political adviser to Dewey. The political nature of the
commission's work, carried on within the framework and under the
auspices of a church organization, did, however, have the effect of producing a gradual fusion of the religious and political elements in Dulles's thinking. In 1937 he had warned that "too often spiritual and
secular motives become unconsciously mixed, and it requires unusual
practical experience to detect the pitfalls which the worldly constantly
prepare to secure for themselves the appearance of church benedic-
tion." [41] By 1942, however, in the dark and uncertain months following
Pearl Harbor, he was emphasizing the urgent need for Americans to
obtain a "righteous faith . . . a faith so profound that we, too, will feel
that we have a mission to spread it throughout the world." [42] This, he
felt, was a practical necessity, for the present "cynical and disillusioned"
state of American opinion was conducive to neither military victory nor
subsequent peace. Without spiritual strength, "new faiths will rise to
attack us, and in the long run we will succumb." [43]

Dulles proved an excellent commission chairman, working flexibly
toward consensus with those, like Reinhold Niebuhr and John Coleman Bennett, whose emphasis differed from his own. He was generous
with his time, he listened carefully. Bennett thought him "not dominating in an objectionable sense. He always did his homework, he always
had drafts, he always knew the line he wanted to take." [44] He showed
a special gift for reconciling positions through skillful editing and he
"didn't polarize things as much in regard to the war as he did later with
regard to communism." [45] With all his flexibility, however, there was
general agreement with the assessment of another member, Henry Van
Dusen, that the commission was "really a one man show . . . a rubber
stamp for John Foster Dulles' ideas." When he departed, "the keystone
dropped out of the structure." [46]

Dulles's overriding aim was to create a successor organization to the
defunct League of Nations. On September 18, 1941, shortly after the
Roosevelt-Churchill meeting at sea off Argentia, the commission published a critique of the Atlantic Charter, finding it noble in purpose,
but "tentative and incomplete," largely because it contained no commitment to a new world organization, nor sought consciously to avoid
a repetition of the Versailles failure. Dulles was prepared to accept as
a "reality" a concentration of postwar power in "the Anglo-American
architects of a new military victory," but he argued that this could
become a "beneficent reality" only if Anglo-American power was willing
"not to perpetuate itself, but to create, support and eventually give way
to international institutions drawing their vitality from the whole
family of nations." [47] This was clearly an expression of the purest Wil-

sonian idealism — and, in the context of the engulfing storm of war in
1941, more than a little naïve.

In October 1942, the commission published a pamphlet of essays entitled "A Righteous Faith for a Just and Durable Peace," and this led
in March 1943 to the "Statement of Political Principles," which was
reissued and widely circulated in May 1943 as "The Six Pillars of Peace."
Acknowledged by other commission members as primarily Dulles's work,
the "Pillars" document reflected his new conviction (in notable contrast
with the thesis of *War, Peace and Change*) that moral law is ultimately
controlling in world affairs, that international political affairs must accordingly be organized in conformity with moral law, and that the
United States had been assigned a special role in the establishment and
maintenance of world peace. Accompanied by a longer supporting paper,
the "Six Pillars" was a careful distillation of the elements which Dulles
considered essential to the establishment of lasting world order. While
idealistic, most of them seemed within the bounds of feasibility; while
succinct, they were general enough to avoid serious controversy over
details. They called for: (1) a political framework to ensure the continuing collaboration of "the fighting United Nations"; (2) international
agreement on those economic and financial acts of nations that have
"widespread repercussion"; (3) the means to adapt treaty structures to
changing world conditions; (4) the goal of autonomy for all subject
peoples; (5) adequate procedures for controlling military establishments;
and (6) the universal right to religious and intellectual liberty.[48]

Securing an appointment with President Roosevelt on March 26, 1943,
Dulles * explained that the document's main purpose was to develop
wide public support for a new international organization of which the
United States would be a leading member. To cement the fighting United
Nations in the postwar period, Dulles said, required "the willingness of
the American people this time to go the way of organized international
collaboration." [49] Roosevelt asked him to leave a copy of the document.
The Federal Council of Churches, in company with like-minded groups
throughout the country, then waged an intensive public campaign for
the United Nations organization — an effort that was crowned with success when both houses of Congress passed supporting resolutions. President Roosevelt, who had resisted Churchill's wish to include a new organization in the Atlantic Charter, was now persuaded that a new effort
might be feasible. He sent Cordell Hull to Moscow in October of the
same year on a mission that led to the Dumbarton Oaks conference of
August 1944, where the wartime Big Four † sat down to write a detailed
charter for a United Nations organization.

* Accompanied by the Presiding Bishop of the Protestant Episcopal Church, the Reverend H. St. George Tucker, and by Dr. Roswell P. Barnes.
† United States, USSR, Britain and China.

There followed an incident which demonstrated the duality of Dulles's rising role as church leader and political operator, and which was to make him a leading symbol of bipartisan foreign policy. Hull, long an advocate of the doctrine that partisanship should stop at the water's edge, began in the spring of 1944 a series of consultations with congressional leaders of both parties, with the aim of keeping the proposed new international organization from becoming an issue in the upcoming presidential election. There was natural anxiety in the Roosevelt administration that, if controversy developed, the concept of a United Nations organization might suffer the fate of the League, dooming Roosevelt to the kind of humiliation that Wilson had suffered. Hull had received encouraging assurances from Republicans in Congress, but these came to nothing on August 16 when the GOP presidential nominee, Thomas E. Dewey, delivered a public attack on the Dumbarton Oaks proposals, claiming they would "subject the nations of the world, great and small, permanently to the coercive power of the four nations holding this conference." [50] The White House issued an immediate denial, and Hull called a press conference that was widely attended by reporters who thought they had caught the scent of a major campaign issue. Asked if he would welcome a talk with Dewey to clarify their alleged differences, Hull replied in the affirmative. Before Roosevelt, who was not pleased with Hull's reply, could evade the consequences, Dewey had wired Hull accepting the offer and designating Dulles as his spokesman. There is little doubt that Dulles had inspired and written the complaining Dewey statement (as Senator Vandenberg, then emerging as the powerful and responsible Republican advocate of bipartisan foreign policy, had noted in the margin of a letter of June 20 from Dulles: "Dulles speaks for Dewey in respect to foreign relations — and will probably be his Secretary of State").[51]

In what came to be regarded as a landmark of bipartisan collaboration, Dulles went to Washington on August 23 for talks with Hull, after first conferring with Vandenberg and other Republican leaders on the Foreign Relations Committee. Hull wrote in his memoirs that he had "seldom worked harder" [52] in his preparation for the meeting, being convinced that a failure to agree might seriously jeopardize American participation in the new world organization. In the event, Hull was rather quickly able to dispel Dewey's alleged concern relating to the danger of Big Power coercion — primarily by letting Dulles read the confidential working texts of the charter, then under consideration at Dumbarton Oaks; both men also agreed that a United Nations organization would fail of Senate ratification without strong and positive Republican backing. But difficulty arose in attempting to frame an agreement in writing, for, according to Dulles, Hull wished to extend bipartisan restraint during the electoral campaign to all matters relating to a future peace, including, for example, possible negotiations with Russia over the future of Poland. Dulles insisted on confining the agreement to the world organization. The joint communiqué was thus confined to the usual hopeful imprecisions — essentially that the new organization should be kept out of the partisan arena and that both groups would continue to confer on developments. Dewey said in 1965 that the private agreement had, in fact, been confined to a mutual promise not to discuss "the very thorny issue of whether there should be a United Nations army"; but that in the last week of the campaign, "Roosevelt broke his commitment and said in a very deft way that the town hall didn't have any power unless it had a policeman, thereby satisfying a great many people who felt that there should be a United Nations army, about which I had a good many reservations. I have been proved right, and he won the election." [53]

To some observers, the whole Dewey-Dulles intervention looked like a political ploy designed to demonstrate, for the benefit of ethnic minorities within the American body politic, that candidate Dewey felt a special concern for the rights of small nations like Poland and Czechoslovakia. This view fails to give due weight to Dulles's genuine concern for the rights of small nations, but there is no doubt that Dulles's later sensitivity to "ethnic politics," as reflected in his vague but emotional "liberation" rhetoric, was acquired in the arena of New York politics, and primarily from Dewey.

The event provided publicity, good and bad, for Dulles. As he was suffering from a severe attack of thromboid phlebitis * and could not walk without crutches, Governor Dewey had dispatched him to Washington in a chauffeur-driven New York State car. The columnist Drew Pearson promptly attacked him for wasting scarce and rationed gasoline in wartime. Dulles was indeed in severe pain, and got himself to bed each evening by crawling up the stairs of the Georgetown house where he was staying with friends. A few days later he went to the hospital for an operation that involved crushing the nerves in his foot behind the ankle; recovery was complete.[54] On the positive side, the talks established him as a principal Republican spokesman on foreign policy. Roosevelt remained skeptical of the whole enterprise and even withheld Dulles's appointment as a delegate to the 1945 United Nations Conference in San Francisco until pressure was brought to bear by both Vandenberg and Baruch.

Idealism and Eastern Europe

In early 1945, America was approaching the climax of her momentous war effort, relentlessly grinding down the Axis powers with unanswerable

---

* An inflammation of the veins complicated by the presence of a blood clot.

industrial strength, technology, organization and human bravery. Military victory was assured both in Europe and the Pacific, although the remaining price to be paid in time and lives would be very high. Whether or not the American people possessed the sustained will and political wisdom to consolidate the victory, and whether or not the allied coalition could hold together in the postwar period, were the problematical questions. Dulles evidenced at this time little anxiety about either "International Communism" or the policies of the Soviet Union; he was more concerned that America would slip back into isolation, and especially worried that the Roosevelt administration would shrink from a determined effort to play a positive role in Eastern Europe. In January 1945, six months before the end of fighting in Europe, he criticized "the American nation" for not yet having adjusted itself to "the working conditions of collaboration," particularly in eastern and southeastern Europe.[55] He recognized, he said, that the assertion of an active United States role in settling boundary questions and other peace terms in Poland, Hungary, and Greece would bring domestic criticism from affected ethnic groups in America, and indeed from all American Catholics, if the ultimate settlement seemed to them unjust. He could thus understand Roosevelt's preference for "lofty pronouncements . . . upon which all can agree." [56] But such prudence and expediency simply would not do. America, he insisted, must not again shrink from grappling with unpleasant, intractable problems by retreating into isolation, nor even by acknowledging spheres of influence as between the major powers. America had chosen such passive courses in 1919 with disastrous results. To redeem the vast sacrifices of the Second World War and establish world peace on a firm and lasting basis, America must in the coming period plunge totally and irrevocably into the world, asserting an American interest and an American role in the achievement of just solutions to all problems that threaten peace. America must roll up its sleeves and "collaborate, . . . working in the muck and mire," and showing the necessary strength of purpose to deflect or absorb "the criticism which will be heaped upon it when it comes back with some of the mire adhering to its hands and feet." [57]

The speech is a curiosity. It may be read as the sincere assertion of a universal American interest, reflecting a Wilsonian conception that reduces to a syllogism: (1) peace is indivisible; (2) America has an interest in peace; (3) therefore America, in its quest for peace, can accept no geographical limits on its interest. On the other hand, the speech may be read as a cynical effort to push Roosevelt into assuming direct responsibility for settlements in Eastern Europe which were bound to be determined by the requirements of Russian power, and thus to create a situation which was bound to stir up an anti-Roosevelt hornet's nest among the ethnic groups, when the realities of Russian power produced a harsh solution. That is, of course, what happened. The "cold war" between Russia and the West began in Eastern Europe, over the sharply drawn issue of whether the small nations there were to be truly "democratic and independent" or under the undeniably brutal hegemony of the Soviet Union. The heavy sacrifices of the war and the declared American war aims (including those embodied in the Atlantic Charter and the principles of the United Nations organization) had created a public opinion fervently insistent on self-determination everywhere, through free elections, leading to democratic governments in the Western sense of the term. Roosevelt, fully mindful of this, was trying to obtain Russian agreement to an American domestic imperative, or, failing that, then at least to a formula that would blur the power realities in Eastern Europe and possibly inhibit Russian seizure of total control. Stalin proved willing to accept a "democratic" formula, but not in fact to modify his paranoid insistence on establishing an iron security belt that involved crushing governments and peoples across the whole of Eastern Europe. When the gross disparity between formula and consequence became evident, the Republicans courted the ethnic vote by charging the Democrats with treasonous sellout. And indeed it was Dulles who inserted in the 1952 GOP platform a scathing denunciation of the Yalta Agreements and a demand for their wholesale renunciation.

Such considerations make tempting the cynical interpretation of Dulles's January speech. Yet most of the evidence runs in the opposite direction. In early 1945, Dulles was still a remarkably abstract and rather isolated observer of the world scene, sustained by Wilsonian principle and idealism, but lacking serious practical experience in diplomacy since 1919 (experience of the kind that is acquired only through the sustained discharge of official responsibility). He was also, along with most Americans, still a stranger to the operational theory and practice of Soviet Communism, particularly as applied by Stalin. In another speech just a month later (to the Economic Club of Detroit in February) he stressed the need for friendly relations with the Soviets, acknowledging the Western belief that "atheist-materialists" could not be trusted, but adding that the Soviets "on their side, have little reason to trust us." [58] And when he first heard about the Yalta Agreements, he hastened to tell the Foreign Policy Association of New York (in March) that these surely opened a new era of diplomatic promise: they meant, he said, not only the end of American aloofness, but also the beginning of Soviet willingness to accept "joint action on matters that it had the physical power to settle for itself." [59] Evidently, he assumed the Soviets would live up to the Yalta undertakings. In company with most of his countrymen, he did not anticipate that Stalin would impose total Russian control over Eastern Europe while blandly describing the process as democratic.

With malice toward none, with charity for Russian policy, and with rather little feel for the political realities in Eastern Europe, Dulles looked forward in early 1945 to a struggle for peace that would be hard and demanding, but basically hopeful — provided only the United States government would "adopt and publicly proclaim long-range goals which reflect our high ideals," [60] and thereafter enter the international arena prepared to fight for them. As Dewey later remarked, "I would say that [before and during the war period] Foster was a man who knew the techniques of diplomacy and had a very high-minded approach to it. I wouldn't say that he was naive, but he was certainly idealistic." [61]

5

Discovering the Russians

As THE POSTWAR PERIOD BEGAN, Dulles was an established national
leader in foreign affairs, providing advice and counsel not only
to church and party, but also to the Truman administration as a senior
symbol of bipartisan unity beyond the water's edge. As Republican adviser to successive Democratic Secretaries of State at a series of protracted
meetings of the Council of Foreign Ministers, he was deepening his education in the hard school of undisguised power struggle for control of
Germany and Western Europe, a struggle against physical and spiritual
prostration aggravated by large Communist minorities whose determined
tactics of disruption were reinforced by the overhanging threat of Russian military power. Stalin gave every evidence of acting on the belief
that the dislocation now apparent in Europe created unexpectedly broad
opportunities for widening the Soviet security belt and moving toward
realization of Lenin's prophecies. Confrontation with Molotov, Andrei
Vishinsky and other cold-faced Soviet negotiators brought Dulles rather
quickly to a far graver assessment of the world situation than he had
previously held.

The London meeting of the Council of Foreign Ministers in the early
fall of 1945 appears to have been the turning point. There, while admiring the professionalism of Molotov's performance, he reached the conclusion that further accommodation to Soviet demands would be disastrous,
that the United States, Britain and France must take a stand against
further sacrifice of Western interests in Europe. Following preliminary
consideration of the proposed Italian, Greek, and Finnish peace treaties,
Molotov suddenly demanded that the French and Chinese Foreign Ministers withdraw from the discussions on the grounds that their nations

were not parties to the "surrender terms." Behind this simple procedural demand was a basic Soviet drive to split the non-Communist allies, sustained by Molotov's argument that, as satisfactory political settlements and world peace depended on agreement between the Soviet Union and the United States, American diplomacy had little practical choice. The issue thus confronting the Secretary of State, James Byrnes, was whether or not the United States was prepared to accommodate further an increasingly arbitrary and opportunistic Soviet policy for the sake of continued surface agreement. Byrnes, a former senator and Supreme Court justice with a reputation and seasoned Irish faculty for constructive compromise, was in some doubt as to how to handle the hard proposition put by Molotov. A basic consideration was how American opinion would react to a diplomatic showdown, for this was only three months after the armistice in Europe and a mere six weeks after the Japanese surrender. The image of Russia established by official American propaganda, abetted by wartime censorship, was of a valiant fighting ally, with a different social-political system, to be sure, but with a basic need and desire to cooperate in the building of a better postwar world. Roosevelt, had he lived, might have taken steps more quickly and directly to correct the distortions in this view, but Roosevelt had died in April and a staunch but inexperienced Truman was struggling to avoid inundation by the massive problems of the American presidency at this juncture in history. According to Dulles's account, he met alone with Byrnes in the latter's room at Claridge's Hotel on Sunday morning, September 30: "We explored together the problem, and the Secretary asked whether I did not feel that there was some basis upon which we could effect a compromise. I told him that I saw none." [1] The following day, in an act which signaled the end of Western efforts to sustain wartime collaboration with the USSR, Byrnes rejected the Soviet demand. Thus began the fateful confrontation of diametrically opposed beliefs concerning the nature of international relations and the nature of man.

Know Your Enemy

Returning home from the London conference, Dulles said in a radio report of October 6, 1945, that the meeting with the Russians "has not *created* difficulties. It has merely *revealed* difficulties of long standing which war has obscured. It is healthier that we now know the facts." [2] The facts, however, were far from fully known. Like many other leading Americans, Dulles remained unclear as to the precise nature and extent of Soviet ambitions, and confused by the complexity and rationale of Stalin's tactics. He wondered why the Russian nation, in a state of near collapse, did not welcome and encourage Western help, but maintained a hard, mistrustful posture toward its wartime allies. For enlightenment he turned to a quick study of Communist theory, in particular to one book — Stalin's *Problems of Leninism* — and therein discovered the Kremlin's intensely paranoid view of the outer world. "We must remember," Stalin wrote (quoting Lenin), "that we are surrounded by people, classes and governments who openly express their intense hatred for us." [3] Bourgeois states send "spies, assassins and wreckers into our country and are waiting for a favorable opportunity to attack it by armed force . . . ." [4] We must remember that we are at all times but a hair's breadth from every manner of invasion." [5] In a situation of such peril, he argued, safety for the Soviet Union could lie only in a constant outward push to eliminate the threat, to the end that "a Socialist encirclement exists instead of a capitalist encirclement." [6] Peaceful coexistence of the two systems over a long time was "unthinkable"; one or the other must triumph in the end, which made "a series of frightful collisions" inevitable.[7]

Dulles memorized this work as thoroughly as he had the Bible and the Federalist Papers, kept a heavily underlined and well-thumbed copy on his desk and another at his bedside, and quoted it frequently. In 1950, noting that 18 million copies of the book had been printed up to 1947, he wrote: "This work of Stalin's has become to the Communist Party what Hitler's *Mein Kampf* was to the Nazi Party. It spells out the creed and purposes of Soviet Communism and its plans and methods for achieving world domination. The world neglected Hitler's book until it was too late for anything but regret. We should not make the same mistake. . . ." [8] Several close observers of his period as Secretary of State regarded his infrequent reliance on State Department experts in Soviet affairs as a reflection of his self-confidence that, through his own study of Communist ideology, he had cracked the Kremlin's operational code.

The first product of this intensive effort at self-education was a long memorandum he presented on May 8, 1946, to the Commission on a Just and Durable Peace; a covering letter expressed his view that "our Commission has been derelict in not facing up to the Russian problem." [9] A month later the memorandum appeared as two articles in *Life* magazine (June 3 and June 10). Divided into analysis and prescription, they reflected, first and foremost, Dulles's desire to prevent war. "The most urgent task of American statesmanship is to find the policies which will avert a serious clash with the Soviet Union." The danger of such a clash arose, he thought, not out of a deliberate Soviet desire for war, but from the view of its leaders that security depended on eradicating all non-Communist political systems and establishing the "proletariat dictatorship" everywhere. To the Soviet leadership, "democracy" was a word that applied only to the "proletariat dictatorship"; all other forms of government were "fascist" and "unfriendly." Stalin and the Politburo, while maintaining an absolute hold on the Soviet Union itself (the "inner zone"), had now established a *cordon sanitaire* from the Gulf of Finland through Eastern Europe to the Kurile Islands north of Japan (the "middle zone"). But even this did not satisfy their obsessive search for security. As evidenced by their current efforts to subvert Greece, Iran, Turkey, and Kurdistan, they sought compulsively to extend their control throughout the rest of the world (the "outer zone"). In the farthest reaches of the outer zone, Soviet policy was already stimulating independence movements among 750 million people who still lived under colonial rule.[10]

Soviet policy was carried out in "a rigid, mechanistic and uncompromising way," and in considerable part by men in Moscow who were ignorant of foreign conditions and foreign peoples: "To them it is like playing a game of chess . . . . Soviet diplomats and private agents abroad are the pieces who move as directed by the master mind." [11] On the whole, however, the policy was succeeding: "It is natural, it is simple, it is positive," and expansion is relatively easy into areas which are "largely a vacuum, as far as faith and order are concerned." Such conditions have led Soviet leaders to "feel confident of peacefully achieving their *Pax Sovietica*." But Dulles thought that the Kremlin's hope for an essentially nonviolent takeover seriously "underestimates the Western world's repugnance to human suffering and its attachment to personal liberties," and that this fact increased the dangers of miscalculation and war.[12]

Turning to prescription, he laid down the principle which, above all others, was to guide his later approach to the problem of deterring war: make clear to the Soviet leaders that their efforts to expand would be resisted, for history shows that most wars arise, not out of deliberate intention, but from "miscalculation." Deterrence would require maintenance of reasonable military strength because "they believe in force," but it would be a serious mistake to "place our reliance wholly on our military and economic power and to use it to coerce Soviet leaders." Such a program "would probably fail," for they "are tough, they are not afraid of fighting, and they cannot be arbitrarily pushed around." Moreover, an attempt to crush the Bolsheviks, even if it did not precipitate war, would "prove nothing"; it would "not end the challenge to a society of personal freedom"; on the contrary, it would "intensify that challenge, for the Soviet experiment would then seem to have succumbed not to our merit, but to our might. New disciples of that faith would spring up everywhere." Beyond a moderate defense effort to ensure against miscalculation, the real solution lay elsewhere: "What we need at this critical juncture is an affirmative demonstration that our society of freedom still has the qualities needed for survival. We must show that our free land is not spiritual lowland, easily submerged, but highland that, most of all, provides the spiritual, intellectual and economic conditions which all men want." Moreover, "the most significant demonstration that can be made is at the religious level," for the ultimate justification for individual freedom is that "men are created as the children of God, in His image. The human personality is thus sacred and the State must not trample upon it." [13]

On the whole, Dulles's analysis of the Soviet system, its motivation, its operational doctrine of expansion without war, was solid and impressive. Furthermore, the prescriptive elements showed a balance and restraint, both substantive and verbal, that were rarely to be seen again in Dullesian formulations regarding deterrence and the right path to a lasting peace. In both its call for a proportioned and controlled American military effort and its insistence that the "real" solution lay in reestablishing a vigorous and effective free society at home, the Dulles statement closely resembled the deeply informed "X" article which appeared in *Foreign Affairs* some nine months later, and was subsequently identified as the work of George F. Kennan, the leading Foreign Service expert on Soviet affairs. The Dulles analysis also showed the marked development since 1940 of his belief in the role to be played by Christian faith and ethics in world affairs. His 1939 book had located the sources of war in a selfish human nature and a rigid international system in which rich, static nations refused accommodation to the dynamic poor; the *Life* articles of 1946 showed that he had moved from a sort of economic determinism to a sort of spiritual determinism; the principal source of war was now to be found in a confrontation of universalist faiths: Christianity versus Communism, spirituality versus atheism. He defined the cold war explicitly as a moral rather than as a political or economic conflict.

Reaction to the articles showed the variety of a nation whose leaders and opinion makers had not yet crystallized their attitudes toward Russia, the cold war, or America's role in the postwar world. Henry Luce wrote that "the Editor of *Life* is deeply proud of having been associated with them. . . . They had the unusual quality of concluding an argument. Oh, I don't mean that there are no Max Lerners left — but I do mean that for a great many people, directly and indirectly, your articles ended all doubts as to the inescapable reality of the Russian-Communist problem." [14]

A leading pacifist, A. J. Muste, wrote deploring what he perceived as Dulles's failure "to realize the fear we inspire in them [the Soviets]" with "our tremendous military establishment and on top of that the atomic bomb." [15] On the other hand, Senator Vandenberg, while offering congratulations on the "magnificent Russian poem," took some exception to the statement that a policy of coercion based primarily on military force would probably fail: "I seem to miss a sturdy call to 'hold the line' beyond which both we and Russia must understand that surrender for us is impossible." [16] Alfred Kohlberg, who later emerged as kingpin of the single-minded, well-financed American backers of Chiang Kai-shek known as the China Lobby, thought the articles "unrealistically hopeful" of restraining Russian aggression.[17] Dulles's reference to America's "far-flung bases which threaten others" brought a retort from Stuart Symington, the Assistant Secretary of War for Air, that the statement "worried us here in the War Department a great deal." He enclosed a memorandum from General "Toohy" Spaatz which called Dulles's remark "a misconception of United States' objectives in the Pacific Basin," and went on to a spirited defense of the overseas base structure noting that, except for the Philippines, Korea, and Japan, all bases were located on U.S. territory.[18] It seems likely that the criticisms from Senator Vandenberg and the air force tended to move Dulles a notch or two toward a tougher anti-Communist stance and a gingerly reticence about intervention in professional military matters.

There was also some hate mail, the most spectacular being a thirty-four-page collection of scurrilous allegations and comments drawing on material from *Who's Who, Moody's Manual,* the *Fuehrer Lexicon* and Drew Pearson, all packaged under the *Life* cover from the issue in which the first Dulles article had appeared. It was mailed to several thousand people in New York City and was thought to be the work of the American Communist party.[19]

Showdown over Germany

Dulles's speeches continued in an almost garrulous flow, always bearing religious titles — "Spiritual Bases of Peace," "Christian Responsibility," "A Diplomat and His Faith" — but invariably dealing with specific and current issues of foreign policy. His emphasis was Germany and Europe, and he felt passionately that the system of national sovereignties in that cramped and arson-prone quarter of the globe could no longer be tolerated. Influenced by his good friend Jean Monnet, he advocated European political and economic integration, warning repeatedly against rebuilding "the rickety fire hazard of the past." [20] Within the "European deathtrap," Germany was the "worst fire hazard": this time "Germany's industrial potential should be fully integrated into the peacetime economy of Germany's neighbors so it can work for the greater prosperity of all, but never again be a separate German thing which Germans might use in a war of revenge." [21] In late 1944 he had written a private memorandum which proposed, as to Germany, a solution at least as severe as the Morganthau Plan for pastoralization. To prevent resurgence of German militarism and Hitler's "heinous philosophy," he proposed that "German life" be incorporated into the surrounding countries, "leaving only a small nucleus in Prussia": the Rhineland should go to France, southern Germany to Austria, and eastern Germany to Poland.[22] Although never made public, the memorandum is interesting for the sharp contrast it presents not only to Dulles's previous excoriation of the Versailles treaty and his tolerance of the Hitlerian dynamic in the 1930s, but also to his later conciliatory approach to peace with Japan. In the crucial year of the war, with millions of fighting men locked in struggle on the Continent, Dulles seemed to reflect the predominant American emotion toward Hitler Germany: break it into pieces and never let it join together again.

The initial Allied policy toward defeated Hitler Germany was similarly harsh, although it never extended to formal dismemberment, but by September 1946 the United States and Britain had concluded that the calculated suppression of German living standards (to be certain they did not rise above those of Germany's prostrate neighbors) had become a self-defeating policy for the whole of Western Europe; the result was economic stalemate everywhere, grimly revealing the full depth and breadth of the devastation and dislocation wrought by the war. In the absence of economic revival, or even of serious near-term hopes for it, despair was spreading, and despair was a breeding ground for anarchy and political extremism, the milieu in which Communist parties and agents thrived. At Stuttgart, Secretary of State Byrnes declared that Germany must not be turned into an economic poorhouse, and Western policy quickly shifted to the promotion of German economic revival, primarily under local management; four months later, in December, plans were announced to merge the American and British zones of occupation. These actions, taken to arrest the steady sinking of Western Europe, set in motion the East-West showdown over Germany in 1948, for Soviet policy both desired a deepening of stagnation in the West and feared economic revival in Germany.

Byrnes having resigned in late 1946, Dulles was with Secretary of State Marshall at the Moscow meeting of Foreign Ministers in March of 1947, where the Russians seemed initially to be pursuing a course of determined delay. In a letter to Senator Vandenberg, with whom he corresponded frequently, Dulles noted that "the third week has now wended its weary way," with the Soviets "unwilling to get to grips with the real problems, apparently feeling that the process of exhaustion has not yet gone far enough." [23] However, as Marshall and British Foreign Secretary Ernest Bevin underlined their determination to move ahead with merger of the American and British zones, Molotov unexpectedly proposed not only German reindustrialization but also the establishment of a strong central German government. It was a dramatic and rather desperate shift of stance, designed to counter the move to create "Bizonia" and stimulated by fear that industrialization would now proceed in the Western zones, beyond Russian control and directed against Russia. The shift also reflected acute Russian industrial backwardness, for the new proposal included a demand for further German reparations — $10 billion in finished goods! Under the Potsdam Agreement, whole German factories had been removed to Russia, but miles of machinery rusting on railroad sidings between Berlin and Moscow stood as mute testimony to the inability of Russian engineers and managers to convert them to productive power. Desperate for goods, the Kremlin was apparently willing to gamble that it could control a central German government through a sizable Communist party participation, and through penetration of the German labor movement. That there existed some grounds for Russian optimism on this latter point was reflected in another comment by Dulles to Vandenberg which noted that "results of the labor union elections in Berlin this week were very disappointing." [24] The West rejected the Russian proposal, but Dulles was deeply impressed by the revealing light it cast upon Russian economic and technological weakness. "Soviet economic needs are so acute and vast," [25] he declared over CBS radio on April 29, 1947, that they were ready to run major political risks on the central issue of Germany. This strengthened his belief that war was not inevitable.

Secretary Marshall was more concerned with the fact of debilitating stalemate in the West — "the patient is sinking while the doctors deliberate." With major assistance from his Undersecretary, Dean Acheson, and his Undersecretary for Economic Affairs, Will Clayton, he soon set in motion measures which a few months later took shape as the Marshall Plan for European economic recovery. On May 8, Acheson delivered a speech at Cleveland, Mississippi, which pointed to Europe's need for $16 million in economic aid and urged the reconstruction of the "two great workshops — Germany and Japan — upon which the ultimate recovery of the two continents so largely depends." Marshall's famous speech at Harvard followed on June 5, urging, among other things, the attainment of a self-sustaining German economy at the earliest practicable date. "Bizonia" had become a fact on May 29, and shortly thereafter the French added their zone to the merger. The stage was being set for showdown.

Seven months later, in February 1948, the Russians seized Czechoslovakia, adding it to the group of totally controlled Soviet satellites in Eastern Europe. On March 17, the West European countries signed the Brussels Defense Pact. The Soviets retaliated three days later by walking out of the Allied Control Council in Berlin and blocking military (but not civilian) traffic to Berlin. The West responded with a "little airlift." Meanwhile, the United States, Britain and France plus the Benelux countries * developed plans to bring the three western zones of Germany into coordination with the Marshall Plan, which had just been enacted into law. Final proposals were announced at London in early June and included the introduction of currency reform in the Western sectors of Berlin. That proved to be the final straw for the Soviets, who then applied a full and total blockade of the ground corridors to Berlin. Truman and Marshall, refusing both retreat and the aggressive advice of the Berlin commander, General Lucius Clay, to force entrance into Berlin with armed convoys, decided to rely on a continuous and massive airlift to sustain the beleaguered city.

The 1948 Election

As the 1948 election approached, President Truman was faced with serious defection on both flanks — the South, in anger at his civil rights program, broke away to form the right-wing Dixiecrat party; and former Vice-president Henry Wallace, in protest against the foreign policy of confrontation with Russia, gathered an odd assortment of populists and pacifists to raise a challenge from the left fringe. Dewey was renominated by the Republicans and, given the Democratic disarray, his victory in the fall seemed virtually assured. Herbert Bayard Swope wrote to Dulles shortly after the Republican convention, saying: "Dewey's nomination is attributable to you in substantial measure. Your steadying of his course on foreign policy had a definite influence on the outcome. I hope you go on to more successes." [26]

With all the political signposts pointing toward a Republican administration, Dulles now began to be widely courted as the heir-presumptive Secretary of State. Taking advantage of his presence in Europe in early summer, Queen Juliana of the Netherlands invited him for a morning visit followed by luncheon with the Dutch Prime Minister. A lady journalist in Paris, Genevieve Tabouis, wrote a note saying "how welcomed is in France the certitude of your coming to direction of Foreign Affairs in a few months' time," [27] to which Dulles prophetically replied, "There is in human affairs no 'certitude' as you should know." [28] In the autumn, James Reston of the *New York Times* sketched a flattering portrait in *Life* magazine, calling Dulles thoughtful, idealistic, well-read, and "something of a whiz" in small gatherings. "He has a sense of

* Belgium, the Netherlands and Luxembourg.

history, and he is good at the vanishing art of simple speech and definition. . . . He stubbornly persists in the old-fashioned habit of thinking
before he opens his mouth." [29] Reston's only major caveat was the fear
in some quarters that Dulles "might be tempted to use the power of
office to launch something of a crusade." [30]

His unusual position as agent-symbol of bipartisanship, foreign policy
adviser, and probable successor to Secretary Marshall encouraged inti-
macies at the State Department as events ran toward the presidential
election and what nearly everyone assumed would be a change at the
White House. Led by the great wartime Army Chief of Staff and his
distinguished deputy, Robert Lovett, that department enjoyed in 1948
an unusual degree of independence, reflecting Marshall's great prestige
and Truman's first-term uncertainties in foreign affairs. In mid-July,
shortly after Truman had gained the Democratic nomination, dramatically branded the "Do-nothing Eightieth Congress," and called it back
into special session, Lovett took Dulles out of a larger meeting at the
State Department to his own room and there "privately expressed his
chagrin at the Democratic Platform on foreign policy, saying that he
and M[arshall] were bitterly disappointed; that they had worked with
the President to get a decent platform which would not claim all credit
for the results of bipartisan cooperation." Truman had seemed to support them, Lovett added, but "in the end the political advisers had
written it their way." Dulles replied to Lovett that "if the President
went on through the campaign in that way, it would be disastrous for
the country." [31]

In mid-September, Dulles emplaned for Paris with Marshall to attend
the United Nations General Assembly, leaving Lovett in charge at the
State Department. Reporting regularly to Vandenberg, Dulles described
his efforts to avoid a handling of the Berlin situation that would, by
precipitating a showdown with the Soviets, risk polarizing public opinion in the United States. He opposed going to the Security Council
with an "action" resolution, he wrote, for he feared this would produce
a Soviet veto, which in turn would stimulate the two extremes of
American public opinion: the isolationists, "who would claim that this
spectacular veto demonstrated once and for all the futility of the United
Nations"; and the " 'preventive' war" advocates, who would claim that
"the . . . resolution created a moral, if not legal, obligation, on the
United States to use force." He hoped for "discussion" in the Security
Council by "fresh minds" representing those countries "not actual parties
to the dispute," as a means of promoting compromise and gaining
additional time.[32] His political purpose was to avoid presenting Dewey,
as President-elect, with a full-blown crisis in January, but his approach
also reflected a sensitivity to the dangers of major explosion in the

Berlin situation and, equally, an innate caution with respect to the actual use of military force.

With the presidential campaign now under way, Dulles flew back to New York on October 1 for three days of political consultation with Dewey, following which he returned to Paris, keeping in touch with

Listening to American election returns from Paris (November 1948) with Secretary of State George C. Marshall, Counsellor Benjamin V. Cohen, and Ambassador Warren Austin

the Republican campaign entourage through State Department cable channels under a special arrangement worked out with Marshall: messages from Dulles were delivered to his brother Allen and young McGeorge Bundy in Dewey's New York office. At about this same time, Truman, at the urging of White House aides, developed a plan to send Chief Justice Fred M. Vinson to Moscow for direct talks with Stalin in a broad but exceedingly vague effort to "ease cold war tensions." Whatever may have been in the President's mind, his White House aides viewed the trip as the kind of dramatic gesture toward peace that Truman desperately needed to hold the support of the Democratic Left which, they feared, was slipping away to Henry Wallace. With time

arranged over the national networks for a major presidential announcement of the Vinson mission, Truman finally informed the State Department by telephoning Marshall in Paris. The Secretary of State expressed
his flat and unalterable opposition to the scheme, whereupon the
President, with some public embarrassment, dropped it. Dulles, who
strongly supported Marshall, cabled Dewey that the trip to Moscow
would have greatly complicated the effort to maintain a firm and united
Western policy on Germany and Berlin: "From the standpoint of
bi-partisan cooperation you may want to suggest necessity of unity
behind Marshall. You are seeking through me to present united front
in face of foreign perils but you cannot at the same time cooperate
with irreconcilable policies one developed by Secretary of State at Paris
the other developed under political influence at Washington." [33]

Also in the final month before the election, Marshall opened a very
private exchange with Dulles on the delicate matter of "transition"; the
fact that the initiative on such a matter came from the State Department
without knowledge of the President says a good deal about relationships in the first Truman administration, and about assumptions
regarding the impending election results. On October 25, Marshall
suggested in a note to Dulles that, if Dewey were elected, Truman might
at once appoint Dewey's choice for Secretary of State, on the ground
that the "emergency character" of the world situation justified "unusual
measures." Marshall was personally quite ready to go: "The present
Secretary would welcome his own resignation," which he thought could
be explained by a genuine need to undergo a kidney operation. But if
this seemed too drastic a step, then perhaps Lovett could succeed Marshall, opening the way for the "prospective Under Secretary" to be
brought in immediately.[34] Dulles shared Marshall's purpose, but rejected
the proposal, giving Marshall along the way a short lecture on constitutional law: "I am doubtful. The President, not the Secretary of State,
has, under the Constitution, the ultimate responsibility for the conduct
of foreign affairs. President Truman has virtually abdicated in this
respect. Nevertheless, every effort should be made to avoid extra-Con-
stitutional devices if, without them, our national safety can be
secured." [35] He then cabled Dewey that "the President-elect should, if
at all possible, avoid taking over general responsibility for foreign policy
until the new Administration actually takes office." [36]

Dulles had planned to be in the United States to vote in the election
and share in the celebration of the first Republican triumph in sixteen
years, but Dewey decided at the eleventh hour that a special trip would
look too partisan in the midst of a delicate international situation to
which the GOP had pledged full bipartisan support. Expressing personal
disappointment "not to be with you," Dulles cabled his agreement with

the decision, saying "my presence [in Paris] tends somewhat to allay nervousness" arising from "uncertainty as to what will be the situation between now and January." He added that, among the foreign delegates to the General Assembly, there was "nothing but praise" for the "statesmanlike quality" of the Dewey campaign.[37]

The blow fell on November 3, a stunning shock and surprise. CBS correspondent David Schoenbrun had arranged to interview Dulles in Paris on the morning after what nearly everyone assumed would be an electoral triumph for Dewey and the Republicans. The Philippine Foreign Minister, Carlos Romulo, had arranged a dinner in Dulles's honor for the next evening. When Dulles went to bed, the returns were still inconclusive, but Schoenbrun telephoned him at four in the morning with the bad news, saying, however, that he would still like to proceed with the interview if this were acceptable. Pondering in the dark at the other end of the telephone, no doubt deeply distressed at the news of Dewey's defeat, which had the most painful implications for his own hopes and ambitions, Dulles managed a wry and sardonic piece of humor. Yes, he told Schoenbrun, he would be agreeable to doing the interview, and "you could introduce me as the former future Secretary of State."[38] A few hours later he cabled Dewey: "Am deeply disappointed. Your campaign had dignity and elevation and was in the best American tradition. I am rather frightened by the influences which prevented it from succeeding."[39]

Marshall left Paris in mid-November, after persuading President Truman to appoint Dulles as acting chairman of the United States delegation. It was a generous move, helping to restore Dulles's suddenly deflated prestige even as it expressed Truman's continuing commitment to bipartisan foreign policy. But it could hardly conceal the bleakness of his personal situation. Approaching his sixty-first birthday, Dulles's chances of becoming Secretary of State seemed gone forever.

6

Pleasures and Perils of Partisanship

O N JULY 6, 1949, Dulles and his wife were vacationing alone in their Lake Ontario retreat when the lighthouse keeper from the other end of the island came to their cabin with a radio message that Governor Dewey wanted to talk to Dulles on the telephone. There being no telephone on Duck Island, it was necessary to go to the mainland, but a stiff north wind was whipping waves across the reefs and ledges along the south shore; for the moment he was stormbound.[1] When he reached Dewey the next day from a phone in the town of Picton, Ontario, he learned that the governor wanted to appoint him to the Senate seat rather suddenly vacated by Robert F. Wagner. As Dewey recalled the fragmentary conversation:

Dewey: Wagner has resigned.
Dulles: I heard that on the radio.
Dewey: I want to appoint you to the Senate in his place.
Dulles: Oh, I couldn't run for the Senate. [Accepting] means I would be agreeing to run in the fall.
Dewey: I don't care whether you run or not. I think you may decide to, but I will never urge it. I think that this would be a very fine experience. It will stand you in good stead in the future. I think that it would be good for the party and good for everything.[2]

Dewey had the impression that Dulles was "a little scandalized by the whole idea, frankly. I don't think he'd ever considered it. . . . [But] I wanted to appoint him. I thought he was a great American. . . . I thought he would make a great contribution even if he were only there six weeks." [3] So on the understanding that he wouldn't be expected to run for election in the fall (a special off-year election required by New York State law), Dulles accepted. Moving swiftly, he was sworn in as a member of the Senate on July 8 and on the same day resigned from Sullivan and Cromwell, his law career now technically at an end.

NATO Ratification

Within a few days, he had made his maiden speech on the Senate floor (which may have scandalized those traditionalists who hold to the view that junior members should be seen but not heard for at least the first year), and was thereafter deep in the debate over ratification of the North Atlantic Treaty. His credentials as a spokesman in support of the treaty were impressive, for the original discussion of the idea had taken place fifteen months before in a meeting of Marshall, Lovett, Vandenberg, and Dulles. At the time, he had favored a relationship less formal than the NATO arrangement that had now emerged, feeling that a unilateral statement of American intentions coupled with practical military cooperation would suffice. Apparently he was concerned that a formal, semipermanent American commitment to help defend a specified group of governments in Western Europe would risk attenuation of their impulse to economic and political integration, which he judged to be the categorical imperative. Nevertheless, he believed wholeheartedly in the principle of regional defense and had been instrumental, in 1945, in embedding that principle in the United Nations Charter. On May 9, 1949, Dean Acheson, by then the Secretary of State, had expressed elaborate thanks for Dulles's "brilliant exposition of the case for the Treaty" at the United Nations in the spring. It "has helped very much in contributing to public understanding of some of the more complex issues involved." [4]

Whatever his private reservations, Dulles in the Senate debate gave unstinting support to the Truman administration, in the face of stiff opposition from isolationist senators, including the towering Republican conservative Robert Taft. Citing Article 51 of the UN Charter as the authority for those nations "which had common values" to "organize their own collective defense," he argued that regional security arrangements were necessary to "lift from the UN a burden and anxiety which it was never designed to carry." Thus, "far from being a step backward, NATO is a step forward"; and with a prophecy which later events placed him in a position to fulfill, he asserted that the building of adequate security for the free nations must "advance progressively through a series of organizations for collective self-defense." [5]

The central problem for NATO ratification in the Senate proved not to be in the treaty itself — that is, in the commitment to participate in the defense of Europe — but rather in the presumed cost of its implementation. The Truman administration planned to seek authority and appropriations for a military assistance program on the order of $1.5 billion as soon as the treaty was safely laid to rest, a fact widely known but officially denied. The senior Republican senators, all residual isolationists faced with the massive fact of American intervention across the world, were now ready to enter a plea of nolo contendere on the issue of "Gibraltarism," but they continued to insist that a policy of international defense must not cost money. When Taft, who was seeking to establish the connection between treaty and military assistance program, asked Dulles if ratification of the one did not in fact carry a legal or moral obligation to proceed with the other, Dulles tried to stand on the too narrow ground of legal fact by saying no. The answer proved politically inadequate, and also drew him into a further technical quibble that, even if "military assistance" should be approved, it would not necessarily mean "arms" for the Europeans. However, with the treaty ratification in some doubt, he joined with Vandenberg in an appeal to Acheson for major revisions in the military assistance plan. A more palatable substitute bill was introduced, and this ensured approval of both measures. On the large issues of the debate, Dulles performed with distinction.

China and Asian Communism

From the beginning, Dulles's views on China and the Chinese seem to have been composed about equally of sentiment and illusion, which may have reflected the influence of his missionary relatives and his grandfather's job with the Imperial Dynasty. Speaking to a church audience in Cleveland in 1945, he explained that America's "special friendship and admiration for the Chinese people" resulted from the "splendid qualities of the Chinese people becoming known to us through the activities of Christian missionaries"; [6] and, redolent of Chinese gentlemen at Henderson Harbor, he went on to assure them that John Hay's policy of "open door," Charles Evans Hughes's policy of "territorial integrity" and Henry Stimson's policy of "non-recognition of the fruits of aggression" had all been entirely honest, high-minded efforts aimed at protecting Chinese interests and showing America's friendship. On his first trip to the Far East, in 1938, he had left Janet in Hong Kong to fly in a primitive craft through turbulence and fog to a meeting with Chiang Kai-shek in Hankow, and had come away with admiration for the Generalissimo's patriotism and courage in the face of profoundly discouraging conditions inside China. The issue of Communism in China was not prominent at the time; indeed, the Mao faction was cooperating with Chiang against the Japanese invader. But the fact that Chiang and his wife were Christians was very important to Dulles, and created for him a genuine bond. A senior American diplomat, George Allen, who was a dinner guest in Dulles's home some years later, recalled the Secretary of State's sharp and emotional retort to certain disparaging remarks Allen had dropped concerning the quality of democratic leadership being provided by Chiang in Formosa and Syngman Rhee in South Korea. Dulles leaned forward in his chair and his eyes were blinking: "Well, I'll tell you this. No matter what you say about them, these two gentlemen are modern-day equivalents of the founders of the Church. They are Christian gentlemen who have suffered for their faith. They have been steadfast and have upheld the faith . . ." [7]

By the fall of 1949, Chiang's position on the mainland had totally collapsed and his corrupt and diminished followers were en route to Formosa with the Chinese gold supply. Dulles rose in the Senate on September 21 to warn that "our Pacific front" was now "wide open to encirclement from the east. Stalin himself wrote some 25 years ago that the west was most vulnerable to attack through the east, and the Soviet government has been supporting Communist revolutionaries in China ever since. I saw that support with my own eyes in Hankow in 1938, and it is somewhat surprising that our government seems to have been totally unprepared to meet the danger. Today the situation is critical." [8] By the winter of 1950, he had become deeply concerned about the danger of Chinese Communist military expansion into the Pacific, convinced that it was a strategic imperative, no matter what the cost, to keep them bottled up on the mainland. In the course of a serious after-dinner conversation in New York with several prominent guests, including Ernest Gross, the U.S. ambassador to the United Nations, he stressed this point with great vehemence. Formosa, he told the group, was only a hundred miles from the mainland and the nearest Philippine island only a hundred miles from Formosa. If you once let the Communist regime push out beyond the mainland, then they were going to move and keep on moving. The Truman-Acheson decision to draw a perimeter defense line excluding Formosa and South Korea was thus a serious misconception of strategic reality. His listeners, for the most part, considered this a "startling thesis" which, among other things, grossly exaggerated the Chinese military capacity.[9] The origins of this rather new Dulles view are not entirely clear, but it is likely that it derived chiefly from his own rather literal application of Marxist-Leninist thought to the new situation in

China. It seems likely also that he was to some extent influenced by his fellow senator, William Knowland of California, who was already a charter member of the China Lobby. Knowland had sponsored an amendment to the military assistance program, creating a special fund of $125 million for Nationalist China. Dulles had supported the amendment.[10]

The Run against Lehman

At the time of his Senate appointment, Dulles announced publicly he would not stand for election in the fall, but once he got accustomed to the political "hurly-burly," he found himself enjoying the experience. Time passed quickly and, although Dewey later insisted that he exerted no pressure ("I kept my word . . . I didn't influence him by so much as a hair"),[11] few other Republicans proved willing to make a run against Herbert H. Lehman, a former governor of New York and a capable campaigner. Dulles's assistant, Roderic O'Connor, believed, however, that "Dewey really pushed him into it" by simply postponing the selection of any other candidate. "I kept telling Dulles that I thought, if he didn't push Dewey into getting a candidate, he was going to get sucked into it." But Dulles apparently did not act on this advice, and "he had a lot of conferences with Dewey that I didn't attend." [12] In the event, four months after his interim appointment, Dulles ended up as the GOP nominee.

The "Dewey forces" of 1948 came into the campaign en masse. Herbert Brownell and Elliott Bell directed basic strategy, Gabriel Hauge headed up research, James Hagerty handled the press, and Tom Stephens supervised the advance men. Partially, it would appear, to compensate for his own disappointingly bland and losing effort of 1948, Dewey spurred his cohorts to ensure that Dulles waged an aggressive "fighting" campaign. Dulles proved amenable. After a slow and rather stiff beginning, he was soon in the swing of speechmaking for fourteen hours a day, traveling by chartered bus and concentrating mainly on the "upstate" areas outside of New York City. As Dewey recalled it, "Foster campaigned as though he were running for alderman. He did a glorious job. . . . He learned the trick — any hotel he went into, he left through the kitchen and shook hands with every waitress. He was patient. He put up with a lot of nonsense, which he never would have done before." [13]

On the issues, he generally avoided foreign affairs and concentrated his fire on the iniquities of Truman's Fair Deal "welfare state." He did, however, accuse Lehman of accepting Communist support, adding that, in the event of his own defeat, the greatest rejoicing would be "not . . . in New York or Washington but in Moscow." [14] Lehman, in turn, accused Dulles of both anti-Semitism and anti-Catholicism. The former

Campaign for the Senate (1949)

charge was based on a distortion (but, in the context of even a reasonably decent political campaign, not a blatant one) of a speech Dulles made at Geneseo on October 5. Referring to the welfarists and their fellow-travelers in the city, he told his conservative upstate audience: "If you could see the kind of people in New York City making up this bloc that is voting for my opponent, if you could see them with your own eyes, I know you would be out, every last man and woman of you, on election day." [15] The *New York Post* castigated him for having the gall to suggest that "upstate Republicans have nobler features than their fellow men," and Lehman called the speech "a diabolical and deliberate insult to the people of New York City." [16]

The anti-Catholic charge had a less tangible basis, consisting largely of the rumor that Dulles was alienated from his younger son, Avery, because he had chosen to become a Jesuit priest, and that he had in consequence "disowned" him. As Roderic O'Connor later pointed out, the latter charge was "rather silly" on its face, as "young men entering the priesthood are not accompanied by a burden of worldly goods." But the general rumor was widespread and, in political terms, far more damaging than the charge of anti-Semitism. Dulles could not hope, in any event, to make serious inroads on the Jewish vote in New York City, but the middle-class Catholic vote there was disenchanted with Lehman and had a documented tendency to support Republicans when Lehman was running. Getting that Catholic vote was Dulles's best hope of holding down Lehman's plurality in the city, and thus of winning with a wide margin of upstate Republican support. "So," as O'Connor put it, "this rumor hit us right, you might say, in the bread basket." [17]

For the aggressive "Dewey forces" the obvious solution to this serious problem was to bring Dulles together with his son for an amicable meeting that could be photographed and widely distributed. As the

Listening to election returns in the Senate race,
with Mrs. Dulles (November 1949)

"Catholic" on Dulles's personal staff, O'Connor was dispatched to see Father Robert I. Gannon, who was a former president of Fordham and "well known as a strong Republican in the Jesuit Order." [18] Avery Dulles was at the time in a seminary near Woodstock, New Jersey, and permitted to leave only one weekend every six months. With Father Gannon's help, however, his weekend leave was advanced, he met cordially with his father at their townhouse on Ninety-first Street, and a smiling photograph was taken. Hagerty had carefully planned to release the picture only to New York City papers, in an effort to avoid alienating the genuine anti-Catholic attitudes upstate. But the "Lehman forces" made certain that it was printed all over the state, which essentially neutralized the ploy. Avery later described the incident as "one of those sort of unpleasant things one had to go through" for the sake of "general historical truth" and the "reputation of the family." [19] It was perfectly clear on the facts that Dulles was neither anti-Semitic nor anti-Catholic; nor indeed was he pro-Hitler, as certain disgruntled leftists sought to show. It was equally clear that Lehman was neither a Communist nor influenced by Communist support. Perhaps to a greater than normal extent both candidates were victimized by their own campaign organizations.

Even by New York standards, it was an exceptionally harsh and unsavory campaign. In the end Lehman won, as expected, but by a margin of fewer than 200,000 votes, which some Republicans regarded as a "remarkable achievement" for Dulles. Janet was visibly unhappy about the whole affair and lastingly embittered by the false and nasty charges against her husband. On the whole, however, and after he gained his stride in the campaign, Dulles appeared to enjoy the rough and tumble, for he was essentially a hard-boiled advocate who did not shrink from a fight. And one thing more was certain: the campaign marked the beginning of the end of both his reputation and his inner capacity for nonpartisanship. During the previous years as adviser to Byrnes, Marshall and Acheson, "he might as well have been a career Foreign Service officer," as a senior diplomat, Robert Murphy, remembered.[20] But the run for the Senate changed things a good deal. Except for the notable interlude of the Japanese treaty negotiations, Dulles was thereafter an avowed Republican partisan. The Dewey staff had shown him how to shorten his sentences, simplify his phrases, and pitch his arguments more to the "average person." As such techniques served mainly to reinforce innate and already manifest elements of his mind and operating style, he absorbed them quickly, but many believed in retrospect that they did not serve him well as Secretary of State.

A Reflective Interlude

In the quiet winter of 1949–1950, following his defeat in the Senate race, Dulles wrote his second book, *War or Peace*. It is an interesting work on several levels, being a rather lively reportorial account of his experiences at international conferences since 1945, a statement of his then current position on specific foreign policy issues, and a reflection of his progressive tendency to fuse morality with politics in the power struggle against the Kremlin. Apparently dictated and polished in the space of only a month or so, its brisk, choppy, journalistic style and tendency to polemic suggest the influence of the recent political campaign and distinguish it sharply from *War, Peace and Change*, which was a rather more detached and philosophical inquiry. Comparison with the 1946 *Life* articles shows also that four years had measureably toughened his anti-Communism, deepened his pessimism, and enlarged his self-righteousness.

For Dulles, the nature of the struggle had now become pervasively moral: "Soviet Communism starts with an atheistic, Godless premise. Everything else flows from that premise" [21] — especially the totally expedient behavior of Communists. The Kremlin's offensive was succeeding because Communism had a "universal appeal," because it had "perfected a superb organization to conduct indirect aggression" — and because "it had no counteroffensive to fear." [22] Here was the first appearance in Dulles's thought of the "liberation" virus. The proposals were indirect, yet in notable contrast to his 1946 dictum that an attempt to crush alien systems would "prove nothing."

The Truman-Acheson policies of containment were, he argued, sensible enough; they had temporarily rescued Western Europe, Greece, Turkey and Iran. But they had failed to save Eastern Europe or China. Moreover, a great disadvantage of regional security pacts like NATO was that they drew lines on a map and thus permitted the inference that "we would not fight an aggressor who kept on the farther side of the line." [23] The NATO boundaries offered "immunity to aggression in the Pacific, Asia and the Near East"; even worse, they implied a readiness to "divide the world with Communism." To draw precise lines might "leave us in the position of consolidating about one-fifth of the population of the world and acquiescing in the consolidation of the other four-fifths by hostile, despotic forces." [24] The Soviet despotism suffered from major weaknesses, but these would prove "fatal" only under pressure. "If there is no pressure, purges can occur, organizational wounds can be healed at leisure, and the despotism can go on." [25] This

Dullesian thesis was, at least on the level of rhetoric, a clearing of the ground for a clarion call to ideological crusade, to a "manifest universalism" in which democracy must everywhere prevail, to the preparation of a diplomatic posture which, by transforming every difference with the Soviet Union into a moral issue, would make every compromise settlement seem immoral, and thus politically unacceptable.

Precisely because of the dangers involved in thus unleashing the latent self-righteousness in American public opinion, Truman and Acheson had rather carefully suppressed the natural urge to declare holy war on Communism — with the notable exception of Truman's speech of March 17, 1947, which placed a request to Congress for a program of arms and economic assistance for Greece and Turkey in the context of a broad fight against "International Communism." No one can doubt their temptation. To expose the difficulties of containment was easy enough, but to devise a formula for counteroffensive was either to openly court a large-scale war or else to cruelly dash the hopes that would be raised behind the Iron Curtain. The Democratic administration had chosen instead to concentrate on matters more nearly within its control — i.e., a series of major measures to strengthen the non-Communist areas, particularly Western Europe. By 1950, such restraint seemed to run against the messianic strain in Dulles, for in *War or Peace* he plunged without hesitation into the bog.

If counterpressure beyond containment was needed to open up the "fatal" weaknesses in the diabolical Stalinist system, what kind of pressure did he advocate? He acknowledged candidly that armed revolt was not feasible: "The people have no arms, and violent revolt would be . . . worse than futile, for it would precipitate massacre." [26] He stood firmly against "preventive war" or any direct U.S. military coercion, and was indeed concerned by the danger of overmilitarization in America: "Top policy decisions have been influenced too much by the military," resulting in the concentration of attention on a "hot" war that might never come. "It is time to think less of fission bombs and more of establishing justice and ending terrorism in the world." [27] But how? By what program and set of operational measures? His attempts at definition were all very vague, never moving beyond an anguished protest of the grisly brainwashing in Eastern Europe and of related Stalinist inhumanities. "We can picture these haggard persons; for example, Cardinal Mindszenty and Robert A. Vogeler in Hungary. . . . We see what can happen to minds and spirits when individuals are cut off from all normal contacts, terrorized and exposed to the insistent repetition of falsehood." There was accordingly "a duty to prevent whole peoples from being broken in mind and spirit . . . free peoples must try to frustrate this gruesome process." [28]

There is no reason whatsoever to doubt the passionate sincerity of this call to "moral offensive," but it was intellectually thin and politically mischievous. For there was here, and there remained in his later formulations of "liberation," a marked and dangerous gap between analysis and prescription, between the necessary action implied by the cruel nature of the problem and the actual constraints to action imposed by overpowering circumstance. While the book thus contained a number of interesting and perceptive observations, it seemed, taken as a whole, to complete the fusion in Dulles of a rather simplistic anti-Communism and a simplistic moral ethic. The result was a triumph for ideology, but not for wise diplomacy, yet the pith and clarity of his exposition undoubtedly gave sharper focus to the views of a large segment of American public opinion.

Rescue from Oblivion

A few weeks after Dulles's defeat in the special Senate race, Lucius Battle, who was personal assistant to Secretary of State Acheson, received an evening telephone call. The caller was a Philadelphia journalist named Carl McCardle who had come to know and respect Acheson since the days of the Bretton Woods conference when Acheson had given him material help with the esoterics of international finance, thereby enabling him to win a Pulitzer Prize. It now appeared he had also been courting John Foster Dulles. The talk lasted for more than an hour. The burden of McCardle's story was that Dulles hoped that his partisan thrusts, made in the heat of the Senate campaign, would not disqualify him for further work in foreign affairs under the Truman administration; in short, at the age of sixty-one, Dulles wanted rescue from the threat of political oblivion.[29]

Battle reported the conversation to the Secretary's staff meeting the following morning, adding that he himself judged the idea worthy of serious consideration. The collapse of the Chiang Kai-shek regime and its retreat to Formosa in October were raising gale winds of partisan anger and protest in the Congress; nor were these calmed by cumulative evidence that Truman and Acheson intended to wash their hands of the Chinese civil war — no further political involvement with Chiang, nor any use of U.S. armed forces to defend Formosa. (It was also their hope to extend recognition to the Chinese Communist regime in due course, but the Mao group proved so harsh in word and deed, jailing the American consul general in Mukden and subjecting other American officials to related humiliations, that a full-scale withdrawal of the United States diplomatic representation was carried out by the end of 1949.) The ugly demagoguery of Senator Joseph McCarthy (which would combine with explosive effect the "Communists-in-government" issue with the "fall of China" issue) was gathering in the wings. Moreover, the Soviets had detonated their first atomic weapon in September, forcing Washington to reappraise the extent to which it could in future rely on the nuclear deterrent, and pushing it toward a decision on the question of H-bomb production. It seemed to Battle that the need to restore a larger measure of bipartisanship in foreign policy was urgent and self-evident.[30]

Undersecretary James Webb, who was presiding over the staff meeting that day (Acheson being out of town), acknowledged the need for bipartisanship, but nonetheless found the Dulles initiative a remarkable piece of gall. He instructed Battle not to pursue it, not even to raise it with Acheson, as he thought President Truman would be most irate. Battle obeyed his instructions. In late December, however, when Battle was with Acheson at a NATO meeting in Paris, a cable arrived from Webb urging that Dulles be taken on as a special adviser. The Undersecretary had been turned around by Senator Vandenberg, who had expressed, informally, an urgent need to restore "unpartisan unity" following "the fall of China," and who believed Dulles the best qualified Republican for a high advisory position in the State Department. Acheson's first reaction was strongly negative, but Battle persuaded him to weigh the advantages and disadvantages with care, and, after reconsidering, Acheson cabled Webb that he would agree if the President found the arrangement acceptable.[31] Webb then approached the White House, but, encountering opposition in the President's staff, chose not to press the proposal.

Accordingly, the matter did not come to a head for another three months when, at the end of March 1950, Dulles went to Washington to press his own case with the senator from Michigan. Vandenberg's conversion to internationalism had been quite probably the decisive factor in congressional support for the Greek-Turkish Aid Program, the Marshall Plan, and the North Atlantic Treaty (almost certainly, there would have been no Marshall Plan without his wholehearted cooperation and support). Now he was dying of cancer, a fact that may have added an intangible increment to the already great weight of his influence at the White House. According to Dulles's confidential memorandum of record (which he dictated following his talk with the senator in the latter's apartment at the Wardman Park, March 30), Vandenberg told him he was "much disturbed . . . by the collapse of bipartisanship."[32] Moreover, while Vandenberg had no objection to the recent appointment of another defeated Republican senator, John Sherman Cooper of Kentucky, as a consultant to the State Department, "he did not think . . . that bipartisanship would have much reality so long as the Democrats chose to ignore my position in this field . . . the needs of bipartisan cooperation . . . could only be met by dealing with me." [33] Vandenberg said the "one embarrassment" which had kept him from pressing the matter formally was the question of whether or not Dulles would be running for the Senate again. Dulles replied "that I was reluctant to run; that I had no desire to be for six years in the Senate." If he could "play a responsible part" in averting the serious danger of war which he perceived, then that, he told Vandenberg, would constitute "a greater call of duty" than running for office again. Vandenberg replied that this statement "cleared away the last vestige of doubt" and that he would accordingly write an appropriate letter to Acheson for delivery the following morning.[34]

Later the same day, Dulles called on Dean Rusk, then Deputy Undersecretary of State, who told him that "top people" at the State Department were anxious to bring him back, but that there was an obstacle at the White House. They talked about the recent political campaign and Dulles, revealing an open bitterness about his run against Lehman, told Rusk he felt "a grave blow had been struck to bipartisanship when the Democratic high command during the Senatorial campaign had tried to smear me and to destroy public confidence in my qualifications for international work, and to belittle my contribution to bipartisan foreign policy." How he conducted himself from this point forward "would depend on the attitude of the Administration. If they really wanted bipartisanship, they could have it so far as I was concerned. If they did not want it, that would be their choice, not mine." Although he had given Vandenberg a rather categorical indication of his disinclination to run again for the Senate, he now dangled the positive possibility before Rusk, using it as a bargaining chip to bring the State Department to a decision. He would have to decide "whether or not to make the Senate race within the next two or three weeks"; indeed he was breakfasting the next morning with Dewey's chief party factotum "to discuss the state political situation." [35]

As the conversation with Rusk was ending, Acheson sent word that he would welcome a short chat, and Dulles thus moved on to see the Secretary of State. He told Acheson that he and Rusk had enjoyed a "very full and frank" talk, which Rusk "was authorized [sic] to report to him." [36] In the course of pressing Acheson on the need to restore bipartisanship, he complained again of having been smeared in the Senate race "as [a] fascist, nazi and bigot by the Democratic political organization, when none of the Administration had publicly or privately said a word of protest." [37] There was apparently no direct discussion of Dulles's possible return to the State Department, but Acheson closed the meeting cordially by saying he looked forward to reading Dulles's new book when he went abroad in May. However, after receiving the Vandenberg letter the following day, he telephoned Truman in Key West on April 4 and recommended an affirmative decision.[38]

It was now the President's turn to react with negative feeling. In his peppery way, Truman was angry at Dulles's sharp campaign attacks on the Fair Deal domestic policies, and he was not in a forgiving mood. Acheson chose not to press the matter, confident that his chief would develop a more reflective view after a few days, and indeed this happened. Weighing the administration's need for bipartisan support, Truman concluded it would be cavalier to risk the loss of Vandenberg's momentous assistance in the Senate; and Dulles, whatever his shortcomings, was an able man. However, in view of the hard positions Dulles had taken in the campaign, Truman was unwilling to make him a part of the administration with the title of ambassador at large: he was prepared to make him a "consultant," provided Senator Lehman agreed to the appointment. Acheson promptly undertook to clear the appointment with Lehman, who was glad to have the assurance that Dulles would not run again for the Senate. Dulles, although unhappy about the measured denigration of his new title, promptly accepted, and was sworn in on April 26.[39]

Two days later, he had a long conversation with the President in which he expressed his pleasure and gratitude for this further opportunity to work for bipartisanship. Aware of Truman's cool reaction to his return, he added that his ability to serve effectively depended, of course, on the President's confidence in him, as well as on the development by the administration of policies which he could, as a Republican, loyally endorse. He had no wish, he said, to run again for elective office; indeed his acceptance of the Senate appointment had reflected the consideration that, with Dewey's second defeat and Vandenberg's illness, it behooved him as a Republican internationalist to gain some personal stature, so that he would not be wholly reliant on the influence of distinguished sponsors. Bipartisanship, Dulles told Truman, was the key to regaining the confidence of the American people in the fight against Communism. Truman was sympathetic, saying that he understood Dulles's position in the recent campaign, and that he fully shared Dulles's views on the importance of a bipartisan approach to foreign policy. Moreover, he had read and liked Dulles's "very good book," which had been published just a month before.[40]

Dulles was thus back in harness. His return owed something to his own initiative, more to Vandenberg's sponsorship, and most to the acute need of the administration for the kind of bipartisanship that would, by rallying the Republican moderates, help to neutralize the rabid right wing. Three personal negatives (Webb, Acheson, and Truman) had been, on reflection, converted into an official affirmative.

7

Japanese Peace —
Korean War

I n the spring of 1950, events were moving American opinion toward the view that a rather prompt peace treaty with Japan was an intrinsically desirable step — and a political imperative if Japan were to be brought to America's side in the cold war. The cost of military occupation was a rising popular concern, the *New York Times* having declared editorially as early as August 1949 that "no agreement and no moral law requires us to perpetuate a situation which costs us hundreds of millions of dollars yearly," and Senator Taft having soon thereafter expressed his own fiscal alarm. As early as 1948, General Douglas MacArthur, the Supreme Allied Commander in Tokyo, recommended a prompt and generous peace treaty, arguing that Japan's "spiritual revolution," which he had largely engineered, had prepared that once-warrior nation for a new era of peace and democracy.[1] In MacArthur's view, Japan should be neutral, "the Switzerland of the Pacific," but not stripped of industrial capacity, except for the right and ability to manufacture armaments and aircraft. There should be a well-trained national police to deal with internal disorder, but no regular military forces, Japan's best defense against external threat being, in his judgment, the moral authority of the United Nations. By 1949, however, the deepening cold war had moved him away from this somewhat idealistic position; now, he argued, Japan should be allowed, following a peace treaty, to "assure herself of security in the Communist-threatened Western Pacific by entering into a pact providing her with military defenses."[2]

While State Department thinking had by no means coalesced, it was in 1948–1949 generally doubtful about the efficacy of a "hasty" treaty. The democratic reforms imposed by the Allied Occupation had been dramatic and pervasive — e.g., the effective removal from influence of 180,000 professional army officers, 30,000 imperial police officers, 10,000 imperial teachers, and most of the high bureaucracy. But the purging of those who were responsible for the prewar policies of military conquest had also removed most of the nation's trained leadership, and in the State Department view, not enough time had yet passed for the Japanese people to bring forth a new group of able leaders and functionaries who wholeheartedly embraced the reforms. State thus feared that an early termination of controls would reveal a vacuum of leadership that only the old ruling cliques could fill. Moreover, Japan was still enfeebled economically; to set it loose in a fiercely competitive world might well bring on economic collapse, which would in turn brand the whole occupation effort a failure and, worst of all, open the doors to Communist infiltration.[3] By early 1950, however, the State Department had swung around to the conclusion that, however cogent its reservations might be, the occupation was a wasting asset, and an early treaty a political necessity. As Dean Acheson later wrote: "Force can overcome force, but a free society cannot long steel itself to dominate another people by sheer force." [4] In addition to fiscal and political unease in the United States, the Japanese themselves were becoming restive. And the European and Asian peoples who had suffered death and destruction at Japanese hands were beginning to press for reparations, for punitive restrictions on postwar Japanese trade and industry, and for strong assurances against a revival of Japanese militarism. At the same time, the rising tempo of the cold war strengthened the argument for bringing the Japanese power potential into alignment with the free nations.

As a general consultant to the State Department, Dulles was without specific assignment, but at Acheson's suggestion he was soon conferring on Asian policy questions with ranking Republican members of the Senate Foreign Relations Committee. Although Vandenberg continued to urge "maximum cooperation" on a "unified foreign policy" in every part of the world, it was evident that his fellow Republicans were not in fact willing to accept and support the Truman-Acheson policies in Asia. These policies, centering on the decision to let the dust settle in the Chinese civil war, seemed to them dubious and imbued with high risk, making failure a probability; and Democratic failure spelled Republican political advantage in the next presidential election, which lay only two years ahead. Japan seemed the only area in the Far East where they were willing to offer genuine bipartisan support. A few days after these consultations, Dulles asked for a briefing on the department's plans for a Japanese peace treaty. After listening closely for an hour, he turned to Walton Butterworth, the Assistant Secretary for Far Eastern Affairs, and said to him: "You'll never get anything done unless you select someone in whom you have confidence, give him a job to do, and then hold him to results." [5] The logic of the situation soon led to a decision that Dulles should work on the treaty.

Obstacles

Yet if an early treaty was now broadly regarded as necessary, the problems of conception, methodology, and procedure remained largely unresolved. How to satisfy the victims of Japan, while avoiding a punitive and self-defeating settlement? How to prevent the Russians from creating an endless conference deadlock that would frustrate the signing of any treaty? How to determine which "China" should participate in the proceedings, now that Mao had captured the mainland and driven Chiang Kai-shek to Formosa? There remained, moreover, a serious split inside the United States government. As Acheson described it: "In planning content and method, four groups had to be reckoned with: the Communists, the Pentagon, our allies, and the former enemy. Of these, the Communists gave the least trouble. Their opposition to any tenable ideas was predictable and irreconcilable. It could only be ignored. The most stubborn and protracted opposition to a peace treaty came from the Pentagon." [6] Setting themselves against both General MacArthur and the State Department, the Defense Secretary, Louis Johnson, and the Joint Chiefs of Staff argued that it would be feckless to exchange the "secure" status of military occupation for the manifold uncertainties of a multilateral peace conference. For the Pentagon, military strength was the overriding consideration, and its leaders wanted to retain unrestricted use of Japanese territory for American bases.

The British had begun pressing for a treaty in early 1949, both as a matter of British interest and on behalf of the Commonwealth countries. Acheson's talks with the British Foreign Secretary, Ernest Bevin, in September of that year, revealed a common desire to draw Japan into the free world camp. But they also uncovered the British feeling that more attention must be paid to the Commonwealth anxieties concerning the revival of Japanese militarism and economic competition, and to strong Commonwealth demands for reparations.

There also existed a good deal of international opposition to the idea of a treaty without the participation of Russia or Communist China. Such a "separate peace" was incompatible with India's hopes for moderating the ideological struggle and strengthening the neutral bloc, and a number of neutral countries supported India. Australia was also opposed, fearing that a settlement dominated by the United States would lead rapidly to Japanese rearmament. American opinion appeared to be plastic and as yet unformed, a Gallup poll of November 1949 showing only 20.5 percent in favor of any long-term United States–Japanese relationship that involved American political or military obligations.

The Dulles Approach

On May 18, 1950, a presidential announcement formally assigned Dulles to work on the treaty, adding that responsibility for the project rested with the Secretary of State; the latter point was designed both to underline Dulles's consultant status and to signal foot-draggers at the Pentagon to fall in line. Working without staff, except for John Allison, the able director of the Bureau of Northeast Asian Affairs, who was detailed as his special assistant, Dulles quietly examined all of the miscellaneous drafts, analyses, and memoranda that had served as raw material for three years of inconclusive debate within the U.S. Government. These included a National Security Council paper (approved by President Truman in November 1948) which had aimed at beginning to treat Japan less like a defeated enemy and more like a potential member of the family of free nations: MacArthur was authorized to create a 150,000 man national police force; the Japanese were granted wider discretion in determining the pace and method of assimilating the occupation reforms; new efforts were aimed at strengthening the economy. This approach reflected the work of the policy planning staff at the State Department and of its director, George Kennan.[7]

Dulles then prepared an initial memorandum. Because it drew substantially on the 1948 NSC paper and because these elements were embodied in the treaty as eventually negotiated and ratified, the Asian scholar Frederick S. Dunn was led to write that it was perhaps not accurate to refer to Dulles as "the architect of the Japanese peace treaty," but "rather as the [statesman] who successfully negotiated and carried out, albeit with various improvisations and innovations, a previous blueprint."[8] Intellectual vanity appeared, however, to create an obstacle to Dulles's acknowledgment of this essential truth, and he sought to create a different impression at a press conference on July 11, 1951, two months before the treaty was signed at San Francisco. A reporter asked, "Did you start with a clean sheet of paper, or did you have a good deal of work already prepared and the outline given over to you?" Dulles answered, "There were, I suppose, a good many drafts of a Japanese peace treaty which had been the product of various stages of thinking over the preceding five years. I will have to admit I never read any of them."[9]

In any event, his initial memorandum had the great virtue of brevity and it reflected two deeply held personal convictions: (1) that any attempt to impose vengeful terms on a defeated enemy was a self-destructive approach; and (2) that the intensity of the cold war now made it imperative to align Japanese interests and assets with the coalition of free nations.[10] On the first point, he was insisting that the world must finally learn and apply the tragic lesson of Versailles — that magnanimity and generosity were essential ingredients of any sane solution, on both moral and practical grounds. (At about this time, his friend Elliott Bell taxed him with the statement that surely it was impossible to forgive the Japanese for an outrage like the Bataan Death March; to which Dulles replied, "Jesus teaches us that nothing is unforgivable.") [11] On the second point, he was reflecting the growing view that the former Asian enemy must now become an ally.

The memorandum also contained three procedural recommendations. One called for a preliminary conference of all interested nations to consider proposals put forward by the United States. A second defined a method for handling the difficult "two Chinas" problem — i.e., both the Nationalist and Communist regimes would be invited to send delegates to the conference; on issues where they agreed, only one vote would be cast for "China"; where they disagreed, each would be given a vote. The third aimed at encouraging Japanese immigration into the United States as a means of stimulating a Japanese feeling that they were racially preferred by America in comparison to the Chinese, Koreans and other Asians; by this means Dulles hoped to induce a Japanese desire to join the free world club.[12] Acheson disapproved all three procedures. Taking account of both the Russian capacity for procedural obstruction and the heavy pressure for reparations and restrictions certain to be applied by the victims of Japan, he considered the idea of a general conference to be unworkable. The proposal for dealing with the China question, while legalistically adroit, looked equally unworkable in the cold light of practical diplomacy. The suggestion that the United States should pander to Japanese racial prejudices seemed to Acheson a shallow and divisive approach to Asian problems. In putting forward these rather curious measures, Dulles — for neither the first nor the last time — apparently became rather too absorbed in the tactics of the problem.

Heading into Storm

On June 14, Dulles embarked with Allison on a reconnaissance trip to Japan to begin his firsthand education into the details of the problem. Traveling by way of South Korea, so that he could assure his friend Syngman Rhee that a treaty with Japan would not be developed at the expense of that small country, he ran head on into the Korean war. Arriving in Seoul just a week before the fighting broke out, he toured what Allison later described as the "meager" defenses at the 38th parallel near the town of Uijongbu, with South Korean and American military officers. The Russians later distributed a photograph of the occasion, charging that Dulles had been sent to start the war that began on June 25.

Dulles had been something of a sponsor of South Korean independence, having argued the case for it in the 1948 UN General Assembly. Strong American and other Western support had made this a reality, but a corollary effort to obtain Seoul's membership in the United Nations had been blocked by Soviet insistence on equal treatment for North Korea, which the Western majority refused. Dulles admired Rhee as a tough-minded Christian and anti-Communist, and it was rather clear from views he had expressed both on the Senate floor and in his book *War or Peace* that he did not agree with the Truman-Acheson decision to let the dust settle in Asia. To him the struggle against Communism had become unavoidably universal, without room for accommodation in any sector.

All during 1949 while his regime fell apart, Chiang Kai-shek had worked at trying to build an anti-Communist alliance in the Pacific comparable to NATO. He found support in South Korea, Australia, and the Philippines, but the United States held firmly to the view that the time was not ripe for an Asian alliance despite "serious dangers." [13] Acheson supported Nehru's view that internal conflicts in several Asian countries should be resolved first. Even when President Quirino of the Philippines pleaded in Washington for American endorsement of an all-Asian "organizing conference" to be held in the spring of 1950, Truman and Acheson promised only to "watch sympathetically." At its meeting in September 1949, the new NATO Council had strongly rebuffed the idea of a Pacific pact, with the British Foreign Secretary, Ernest Bevin, expressing the view that it was useless to try to "save" the Chiang regime on Formosa. The NATO action accurately reflected the considered judgment of the Truman administration: the recovery and protection of Western Europe was the vital first priority; and given the major commitments to Greek-Turkish aid, the Marshall Plan, and NATO defense, the American political system could neither undertake nor sustain a comparable effort in Asia.

On December 23, 1949, the State Department had sent to all Far Eastern posts a circular telegram advising that Formosa was expected to fall to the Chinese Communists and that it was United States policy not to interfere. On January 2, Senators Taft and Knowland demanded that the United States Navy be ordered to defend Formosa against invasion; on January 3, the circular telegram was leaked from Tokyo, which raised the first suspicions of MacArthur's collusion with the Republicans, and which forced Truman to be more explicit than he would have preferred. The President did not flinch. At a press conference on January 5, he read a prepared statement saying that the United States would *not* give "military . . . aid or advice" to Chiang and would *not* "pursue a course which will lead to involvement in the civil conflict in China." [14] On January 12, Acheson, in a carefully considered policy speech, defined the United States defense line in Asia to exclude both Korea and Formosa — a position fully endorsed by the Joint Chiefs of Staff. He added that, if military attack should occur on areas outside that line, "initial reliance must be on the people attacked to resist it and then upon the commitments of the entire civilized world under the Charter of the United Nations." [15]

By mid-January 1950, then, it was plain that United States policy intended no defense of either Formosa or South Korea, but it was equally plain that angry and anxious resistance to this position was rising in the Congress, particularly among Senate Republicans. McCarthy's attack on the State Department began the same month. In South Korea Syngman Rhee was increasingly unpopular, but the basic issue was his harsh and dictatorial method of governing in the south; there was not much illusion, even among liberal South Koreans, that a negotiated unification with North Korea was a wise or desirable course. On March 31, Rhee issued a decree postponing prescribed parliamentary elections from May until November. Acheson quickly and severely warned him that South Korea would lose all United States aid unless the elections were held on schedule. Compliance followed, and proved a near catastrophe for Rhee, whose supporters won only 45 out of 210 seats. About 60 percent of the seats were won by "independents" who, although detesting Rhee, were strongly anti-Communist. It is plausible that North Korea may have read these election results as indicating that it could count on substantial support in the south, if it should try to resolve the unification problem by force. In any event, its military preparations were well advanced. On May 10, the South Korean defense minister cited North Korean troop movements and warned of imminent danger of invasion.[16]

Dulles was, of course, generally aware of these developments, and tried to take account of them in an address to the South Korean parliament on June 19. The people of South Korea, he said, were "today . . . in the front line of freedom, under conditions that are both dangerous and exciting." The danger was "Soviet communism . . . north of the 38th Parallel," which "seeks, by terrorism, fraudulent propaganda, infiltration, and incitement to civil unrest, to enfeeble and discredit your new Republic." [17] Then, moving to provide assurances of American moral support, and at least to imply some promise of unspecified help in time of trouble, he said: "The United Nations considers you as, spiritually, one of them. . . . The American people welcome you as an equal partner in the great company of those who make up this free world, a world which commands vast moral and material power, and whose resolution is unswerving. . . . Therefore, I say to you: You are not alone. You will never be alone, so long as you continue to play worthily your part in the great design of human freedom." [18] John Allison thought at the time that, through these remarks, Dulles had "rather tried to make up for what he thought Dean Acheson had omitted in his January speech . . ." [19]

Dulles and Allison flew on to Tokyo the following day, where Dulles went immediately into a private ninety-minute conference with General MacArthur. Emerging in a cheerful mood, he told a press conference he "predicted 'positive action' by the United States to preserve peace in the Far East." [20] Pressed as to the meaning of "positive action," he retreated into generalities, saying merely that he was confident his talks with MacArthur and others would lead to a positive result. He insisted later that this reference was confined to the Japanese peace treaty. But he added a comment which was broader, and also at cross-purposes with the Truman-Acheson position: American foreign policies are, he said, "constantly under review, taking account of changing situations. This generality applies to Formosa also." [21]

Over the next four days, he talked to a wide range of Japanese, beginning with Prime Minister Yoshida and the opposition leader, Mr. Miki. He met with members of the Diet, industrialists, labor union leaders, journalists, and intellectuals; also with various American businessmen and churchmen living in Japan, and with foreign diplomats, including especially the British and French ambassadors in Tokyo. His aim was to gain a wide sense of what kind of treaty was considered desirable and acceptable. One vital purpose was to bring the Japanese themselves into the discussions from the beginning, which to the world's sorrow had not been done with the Germans at Versailles. In the main, Dulles found the Japanese leaders remarkably vague about methods and arrangements for safeguarding their nation's security in the aftermath of a peace treaty, some choosing to place their faith solely in the United Nations, arguing rather desperately that Japan's constitutional renunciation of war would ensure her safety. Prime Minister Yoshida indicated that, while he had developed no clear defense concept of his own, neither was he ready to commit himself on the question of United States base rights in a post-treaty period.

War Comes to Korea

When the Korean War started on Sunday, June 25, Dulles and his wife were sightseeing in Kyoto; Allison was in Tokyo lunching with his old friend, the Norwegian Minister. Returning to the Imperial Hotel at three in the afternoon, Allison found the foreign editor of *Newsweek,* Harry Kern, drinking tea in the lobby with a former Japanese ambassador to the United States. Kern asked him if he had heard about the war in Korea. Allison, who was "dumbfounded," immediately telephoned MacArthur's headquarters and there learned that Dulles had been notified and was returning to Tokyo. Ambassador William Sebald, MacArthur's political adviser, who had been making a speech in Yokohama, was also on his way back. A meeting in the Supreme Commander's office was set for six o'clock.[22]

At the meeting, Dulles and Allison learned that Washington had already requested a UN Security Council meeting for the next morning. They also learned, to their surprise, that MacArthur's assessment of the fighting was bland and nonchalant. Striding about his palatial office in an open-necked khaki shirt, he called the attack a reconnaissance in force, and easily handled by the South Koreans alone. Syngman Rhee had asked for some fighter planes and MacArthur would send them, but recognizing they would contribute only to morale since the South Koreans were incompetent airmen. There were no American combat troops in Korea and, in MacArthur's view, no need to send them. The situation was not serious: "If only Washington will not hobble me, I can handle it with one arm tied behind my back." [23]

Although they had no independent sources of intelligence information, both Dulles and Allison reacted uneasily to such imperial complaisance; both instinctively felt the situation to be more serious. As soon as they left MacArthur, they conferred in Dulles's embassy apartment. Dulles had "vividly in mind" the moral implications of his "you are not alone" speech to the Korean National Assembly; both men wondered if this attack was the first fruit of the Soviet-Chinese mutual defense treaty of February 1950, and if the assault on Korea was a prelude to the building of a direct threat against Japan. After twenty minutes of discussion they sent a joint cable to Acheson and Rusk through Sebald: "It is possible that the South Koreans may themselves contain and repulse the attack and, if so, this is the best way. If, however, it appears that they cannot do so, then we believe that United States force should be used." To remain passive "would start a disastrous chain of events leading most probably to world war." [24]

En route to lunch at the British embassy the following day, the two men stopped by MacArthur's office for the latest word. The general now acknowledged that the fighting was somewhat more severe, but still thought it within the capacity of the South Koreans to handle. Ambassador John Muccio in Seoul had asked for help, including air cover, in evacuating American women and children, and MacArthur was going to accommodate him, although he thought Muccio's action somewhat premature.[25] That afternoon Dulles had a final meeting with Prime Minister Yoshida and later with a group of Japanese labor leaders. He and Mrs. Dulles then dined quietly with General and Mrs. MacArthur, and afterwards attended a movie in MacArthur's quarters. There was little or no talk of Korea.[26]

Meanwhile, Allison had gone to a black-tie dinner at the home of one of the embassy officers, and there got ominous word from the Australian ambassador, a cantankerous personality named W. R. Hodgson who was brimful of anti-Americanism. Hodgson described with some relish a telephone conversation he had just completed with the Australian member of the UN commission in Seoul: "Well, I've just had the last conversation anyone will have with Korea. . . . The Korean army is retreating all along the front and . . . the American military advisory group is getting ready to pull out."[27] On hearing this report, the NBC Tokyo correspondent, George Folster, left the party, returning an hour later to confirm Hodgson's information. Allison, by now alarmed, went to the American embassy, where he telephoned Ambassador Muccio in Seoul. It was a quarter to eleven Monday night, June 26. The boom of artillery fire and the hectic rattle of small arms were plainly audible over the telephone. Muccio told him flatly that South Korean resistance was "disintegrating."[28] Allison then telephoned Dulles, who had returned unenlightened from MacArthur's dinner. They quickly concluded that MacArthur's subservient staff, under strict orders not to disturb him after office hours, had decided to hold the bad news until the following day. Thinking this was folly, Dulles immediately called the general and gave him the Hodgson-Allison-Muccio report. The general assured him he would "get something started." The following morning Allison again called Muccio, who now told him the Rhee government was evacuating Seoul and retreating ninety miles south to the city of Taejon, below the Han River.[29]

Their own business finished, Dulles and Allison were scheduled to take a Pan American flight back to Washington at noon that same day (Tuesday, June 27). The general and Sebald arrived at the airport to see them off, "a vastly different MacArthur from the jaunty, confident General" of Sunday evening. In a mood of deep pessimism, he now told them the position in Korea was down the drain: "All Korea is lost," and the only remaining action was to "get our people safely out of the country."

With South Korean officers at the 38th Parallel
(June 18, 1950)

With General Douglas MacArthur in Tokyo
(January 25, 1951)

To Allison, he seemed a "completely despondent man." [30] While they waited in the VIP lounge, one of the general's aides arrived with a message that the Secretary of the Army desired a telecon discussion with him at one o'clock. But as the Pan Am flight showed no signs of leaving on time, MacArthur brushed off the aide, saying he was engaged with Mr. Dulles and that his chief of staff should take the conference call, if he did not return by one o'clock. Allison and Sebald, by now deeply distressed at this casual treatment of both Korea and Washington, concocted on the spot (with Dulles's nodded approval) a ruse to get MacArthur back to Tokyo. In a few minutes, the loudspeaker in the sealed VIP waiting room announced the readiness of the Pan Am flight, and asked "Ambassador Dulles" and his party to board the aircraft. This they did, with final handshakes and good-byes at plane-side. When the aircraft door was closed, MacArthur climbed into his limousine and returned to Tokyo. As soon as he was gone, Dulles and his party returned to the waiting room.[31] The one o'clock telecon with Army Secretary Frank Pace informed MacArthur of Truman's decision to authorize the use of American air and naval power in Korea, to interpose the Seventh Fleet between Formosa and the Chinese mainland, to increase military assistance to the French in Indochina, and to order MacArthur to make a personal inspection of conditions in Korea and report his findings to the President.[32]

Dulles was in a dark and troubled mood as he flew back across the Pacific, his gloom only marginally lifted by the comforts of the cheerful bar in the belly of the Pan American Clipper. And the patience of all concerned was sorely tried when the aircraft lost an engine going out of Wake Island, and had to return there for extensive repairs, involving an overnight stay. "Dulles was frantic," [33] but the next morning brought a radio report of Truman's decisions, and despair vanished. With perhaps understandable hyperbole, Allison wrote that Dulles "completely forgot that he was a Republican," regarding Truman at that moment as "the greatest President in history." With an hour remaining before departure, "a happy and buoyant John Foster Dulles went swimming." [34]

Allegations of Conspiracy

From a selection of public materials, several observers, notably the journalist I. F. Stone, later developed a theory of right-wing conspiracy involving MacArthur and Dulles, according to which Republicans linked to the China Lobby in Washington concocted the Korean War out of fear that a "normalization" of events in Asia, which Truman and Acheson sought, would have proved fatal to Rhee and Chiang Kai-shek.[35]

Central to the theory is the assumption that on June 25 South Korea attacked North Korea, rather than the other way around, or at least that the south maneuvered to provoke an attack from the north. But Khrushchev, if his account can be accepted, has demolished the vital point by stating unequivocally that the war was planned by the North Korean premier, Kim Il Sung, and blessed by both Stalin and Mao (although there seems to have been minimal consultation with the Chinese). There was, Khrushchev remembered, some worry about American intervention "but we were inclined to think that if the war were fought swiftly — and Kim Il-sung was sure that it could be won swiftly — then intervention by the USA could be avoided." [36]

The essence of the charge against Dulles was that, as an agent of the Senate war hawks, he went to South Korea to assure Rhee that, if Rhee could succeed in provoking North Korean attack, the United States would be forced to intervene, thereby opening the way for the "rollback" of Communism in North Korea, and eventually in all of Asia. Dulles's speech to the South Korean parliament, his prediction of "positive action" at the Tokyo press conference, and his rather too clever inclusion of Formosa in the reference to policies under "constant review" are all circumstantial points against him in the light of what happened on June 25. It is also true that he opposed letting Formosa go by default. Yet the case is compellingly weak.

In the first place, as an eastern seaboard internationalist, an adviser to Dewey, a colleague and protégé of Vandenberg, and the leading symbol of bipartisan cooperation, he was at the time still distrusted and generally opposed by members of the China Lobby, most of whom were recent and rather mindless converts from "Gibraltarism." Moreover, while he was no pacifist, most of his thinking and writing since Versailles had concentrated steadfastly on the problem of how to prevent war. "War is intolerable," he wrote in the *Presbyterian Tribune* of October 1947; "Christians must reject, and see to it that their nations reject, the Soviet thesis of the inevitability of violent conflict, and they must not imitate Soviet leadership by placing reliance on violent means." And on June 4, 1950, just two weeks before he went to Korea, he warned an audience at Vanderbilt University against the small group of domestic military zealots and amateur strategists who thirsted for a showdown: "A few people talk as though it would be smart to fight a so-called preventive war. . . . That would be a folly which I am sure the American people would never tolerate." [37] Beyond this central point the charge implied that Dulles possessed special intelligence information relating to North Korean battle plans and timing (not to mention special political intuition as to how Truman and Acheson would react to attack). As a consultant assigned to a particular problem (Japan) and outside the mainstream of daily departmental operations, it would have been very unusual bureaucratic practice if he had been made privy to intelligence reports and operational telegrams concerning a different problem (Korea).

When the charges surfaced some ten months after the outbreak of the war, Dulles was plainly stupefied at the thought that any rational, reasonably informed person could so misconstrue his character and conduct. Receiving on March 15, 1951, from A. J. Muste, spokesman for the pacifist Fellowship of Reconciliation, a lengthy recitation of the allegations, he dictated in some heat an even longer point-by-point rebuttal. It began: "I have your letter of March 15. It seems incredible that you should regard as 'plausible' the tissue of lies and insinuations which are woven together in your letter. It is more than a little discouraging that a lifetime of devotion to peace should seem to count for nothing in the face of insinuations of vile and treasonable conduct." As to the charge that he had returned to the State Department at the behest of the China Lobby, he asked: "What is there in my life, record or position which makes it seem 'plausible' that I should accept such a servile role?" As to the allegation that he had special access to intelligence reports: "Your suggestion is utterly grotesque in its misunderstanding of the functioning of government agencies." [38] Having thus vented his spleen on an alternately plaintive and scalding rough draft, he put it aside and wrote out a shorter, more deliberate and rather forebearing reply which ended:

Possibly the words of Paul will carry some weight with you: "Finally brethren, whatsoever things are true, whatsoever things are honest, whatsoever things are just, whatsoever things are pure, whatsoever things are lovely, whatsoever things are of good report; if there be any virtue, and if there be any praise, think on these things." [39]

The charge against MacArthur is that he deliberately "played dumb" during the winter and spring, discounting threatening intelligence reports and advising Rhee to do the same, in the expectation that an attack by North Korea would produce an American reaction that would throw the United States irrevocably on the side of the Asian anti-Communists. There are more serious ambiguities in the case of MacArthur, but this is not the place to attempt their analysis and resolution. It ought to be said, however, that his remarkable passivity *beyond* the onset of the fighting, his statement to Dulles and Allison on June 27 that the situation in Korea was irretrievably lost, and his reluctance to treat the problem as his own all serve to dilute the theory that he concocted the war in order to involve American forces and reverse United States policy in Asia. What such immediate reactions do plausibly suggest is MacArthur's preoccupation with affairs in Japan. That he was more than a little intoxicated by his remarkable transformation of Japanese society there is no doubt. As Arthur Schlesinger and Richard Rovere wrote, "Contemplating his handiwork, MacArthur found the miracle of the occupation a source of constant wonder," and he was "often in a philosophical mood, pulling on his corncob pipe, letting his mind roam freely along the spacious reaches of history." [40] He was also on record as agreeing with the Joint Chiefs of Staff that the American defense line in Asia excluded Korea. Moreover, whatever its strategic value, it lay outside his area of responsibility, and if he received ominous intelligence reports from South Korea, he also received consistent assessments from American military advisers there that the ROK's * were "the best doggoned shootin' army outside the United States." For all of these reasons, MacArthur did not appear to be sharply focused on the problem of Korea in the spring of 1950. It was outside the official defense perimeter; it seemed defensible by South Koreans; it was someone else's responsibility. He seemed more concerned with the Olympian matter of a Japanese peace treaty, which he sought as the final jewel in his crown.

On June 29, however, after being ordered by President Truman to address the problem as his own, he apparently changed his mind. Following a hazardous flight from Tokyo in an unarmed transport, harried by fog and a North Korean Yak fighter, he landed at Suwon and immediately set off with Syngman Rhee on an eight-hour inspection of the ragged battle lines. Reporting to Washington early on Friday, June 30, he gave his military opinion that only the introduction of American ground forces offered a chance of saving South Korea, and he recommended that this action be promptly taken. On hearing this report, President Truman, without further consultation with the National Security Council, at once ordered the Secretary of the Army to send in the troops. [41]

Truman regarded his decision as fundamentally political, a point that MacArthur missed or later chose to misunderstand. What seemed to Truman to imperil world security in late June 1950 was not the possible loss of Korea as a geographical entity — the agreed U.S. defense perimeter made clear that its loss could be accepted in military terms. Peril was perceived, rather, in the broader strategic implications of the attack, which administration policy and Acheson's January 12 speech had surely failed to appreciate. "Communism has passed beyond the use of subversion to conquer independent nations and will now use armed invasion and war," [42] Truman declared. In the administration's revised judgment, that psychological-political fact could have untold consequences for the

* Republic of Korea soldiers.

defense of free nations everywhere, unless they could demonstrate that the aggression would be resisted. It was necessary "to provide a rallying point around which the spirits and energies of the free world can be mobilized to meet the world-wide threat which the Soviet Union now poses." [43] But this was not, as MacArthur later construed it, an invitation to go for total victory in Asia.

Negotiating the Treaty

The onset of Korean hostilities, which created an urgent American need for Japanese logistical support, evaporated remaining reservations at the Pentagon concerning an early peace treaty. Another important factor was MacArthur's continued support for it. By August 7, Dulles had set down his own modified concept in a seven-point paper of admirable brevity, together with a separate memorandum of instructions addressed to himself for the President's signature. To these were added a list of "governing principles" spelling out the security requirements of the Defense Department. The whole package was approved by the Secretaries of State and Defense on September 7 and by the President on September 8. Dulles now had his mandate.

The seven-point paper was circulated confidentially to the Far Eastern commission, that advisory body in Tokyo which had been carefully designed to give Allied participants in the occupation a "position of pompous futility" in relation to the plans and decisions of the United States Supreme Commander.[44] The paper left no doubt that the United States intended to conclude a treaty without the Soviet Union, if the Kremlin refused to accept the American approach. On September 9, Dulles told a press conference that the treaty would be developed not through a general conference of the interested nations, but through a series of bilateral discussions conducted by the United States representative.

Having again been appointed a delegate to the UN General Assembly in the fall of 1950, Dulles decided to use that forum for initial diplomatic explorations on the treaty, a course made feasible by the presence in New York of numerous Foreign Ministers who were urgently caught up by the fateful drama unfolding in Korea. But his proposal for a short treaty bereft of both reparations and controls on Japanese rearmament did not warm the cockles of many hearts. Allison remembered that the first reaction of Australia's Foreign Minister, Sir Percy Spender, was "apoplexy," [45] and the Philippine response was bitter. But whereas the Australians, and especially Spender, later found Dulles's arguments persuasive and worked hard to achieve both the peace treaty and its corollary security agreements, the Filipinos remained sullen to the end. As had been expected, India objected to a treaty without the Russians, while all parties without exception opposed the absence of restrictions on Japanese rearmament and the waiver of reparations. The British, who postponed any written reply, complained that the American document was lacking in sufficient detail.

Preliminary soundings at the UN included talks with the Russian representative, Yakob Malik, who, though he refused to be seen conferring with Americans in the broad light of day at Lake Success, was agreeable to meeting privately in the evening. Three discussions took place at Dulles's house on East Ninety-first Street. The following day might find Malik denouncing Dulles as a "fascist beast," but over whiskey and soda in the quiet of the small library, the talk was civilized, if lacking in agreement.[46] Dulles's purpose was to keep the Russians fully informed of American intentions and of the developing attitude of other governments toward the peace treaty. The official Russian response, when it came on November 20, took the form of a detailed *aide-mémoire*. It was an attempt to derail the entire American negotiating effort by insisting that a Japanese treaty must be based on the unanimous agreement of the Big Four.* All in all, Dulles had his work cut out for him.

Toward the first of the new year, 1951, he and Allison once again left Washington, this time on a longer trip to conduct detailed negotiations with the Philippines, Australia, New Zealand, Britain and France. In a letter of January 10, Truman elevated Dulles from consultant to ambassador at large, and set forth supplementary instructions beyond the basic State-Defense directive of September 8, 1950: he was to proceed without awaiting a favorable resolution of the Korean conflict; he was to understand that the United States was willing to conclude mutual security arrangements with Japan, the Philippines, Australia, New Zealand "and perhaps Indonesia"; the "principal purpose" of settlement was to "secure the adherence of the Japanese nation to the free nations of the world, and to assure that it will play its full part in resisting the further expansion of communist imperialism." The letter also said: "Your discussions will in no way involve any final commitments by the United States Government, and you will avoid giving any contrary impression." [47] Dulles's subsequent effort was to prove an exercise in "imposed morality" (as *Time* magazine put it on August 13, 1951), for not one other country in the world wanted the kind of peace with Japan that the United States government had entrusted him to negotiate.

Thus in the Philippines, with evidence of Japanese devastations and cruelties still visible everywhere, his arguments for a magnanimous settle-

* United States, USSR, Britain, France.

ment fell on stony soil. Allison recalled a luncheon at Malacanan Palace "as the worst two hours [of] my life," [48] listening to Foreign Minister Romulo and several Filipino senators recount the trials of the war, the bitter losses, the massive human suffering inflicted by the Japanese invaders. President Quirino had personally lost his wife and daughter. Adamantly these leaders demanded $8 billion in reparations and detailed guarantees of future Philippine security. Dulles met their claims with sympathy, but implacable logic, doggedly insisting that everyone concerned must recognize the hard realities created by the cold war, realities which made it imperative to enlist Japan on the side of the free nations. The *principle* of reparations, he said, was valid, but the amount demanded must be reasonable, must not drive Japan to feelings of frustration and revenge that would lead only to another round in the vicious cycle of war. Ultimately Quirino yielded, with profound reluctance and misgiving, because he had no choice, but also because Dulles's patient persistence had made an impact. He told the American: "I have no reason to do anything but hate the Japanese. But, I've listened to you and what you've said, and after all we must remember that God put us both in the same ocean and we've got to get along with each other in the future." [49]

In Canberra, where he was invited to an initial joint session with the leaders of both Australia and New Zealand, Dulles found far greater fear of Japan than of Russia, and thus an overriding concern with measures to prevent the revival of Japanese militarism; they also wanted monetary compensation for the suffering of war prisoners. According to Allison, Dulles was invited to sit at the cabinet table, where he expounded his conception of the treaty in a "very eloquent and forceful" manner and generally dominated the proceedings. "There wasn't too much give and take there. I don't know whether you'd call it negotiation or not." [50] Flying then across the world to Paris, he learned that the French wanted $2 billion in reparations, an agreement protecting French commercial interests in Indochina against the dumping of Japanese goods, and participation in the treaty-signing ceremonies by Vietnam, Laos and Cambodia. Only the third point was accepted. Ambassador David Bruce noted Dulles's "single-handed, masterly performance." [51] By late February 1951, Dulles had completed his consultations and prepared and circulated to the interested nations a refined draft of the peace treaty. Once more, it was admirably succinct, comprising thirteen pages.

In early April, the British came forth with their own treaty draft. While it was longer than the Dulles version, the differences were accounted for primarily by a more detailed treatment of claims to property and damages. The United States accepted most of London's amendments with good grace, and invited a British working party to come to Washington to synthesize the two documents. But Dulles quietly rejected the British proposal that Formosa be returned to "China," as well as the related British effort to obtain Peking's participation as a signatory. On this stubborn issue — which Chinese regime should be recognized by Japan — there was no hope of agreement. Although London's early move to recognize Peking had produced no useful result (even diplomatic relations were delayed until June 1954), it was stuck with the position. Washington, on the other hand, had tried to maintain a pragmatic ambivalence while waiting for the dust to settle, but Chinese Communist entry into the Korean War and the subsequent UN action to brand Peking as an aggressor had inevitably hardened American opinion — and shifted U.S. policy. By mid-1951, the pressures of circumstance and the formidable pro-Chiang minority in the Senate had pushed Truman and Acheson into a posture of strong support for the Chinese Nationalist regime on Formosa.

In June, Dulles went to London to consider this touchy matter with the British Foreign Secretary, Herbert Morrison, and they appeared to reach a compromise understanding. As Dulles recorded it in a private memorandum, neither Chinese regime would be invited to sign the peace treaty with Japan, but Japan's "future attitude toward China" would be left to "the exercise of the sovereign and independent status contemplated by the Treaty." [52] It was understood by Morrison that Japan could not legally exercise a choice until the treaty was ratified by the several signatories. Dulles, however, took the view that the timing of legitimate Japanese action "would depend upon the degree of freedom which might, in fact, be restored to Japan after the signature of the Treaty, but before the coming into force, particularly if the latter was considerably deferred." [53]

Security Arrangements

In addition to the peace treaty, Dulles's instructions empowered him to negotiate a broad regional security pact, but his encounters in the Pacific began to make clear that more flexible arrangements were called for. Australia and New Zealand strongly desired a security arrangement that would bring the United States to their side against a rearmed Japan, but they refused to enter a pact that included Japan. The British made it known that, if the Philippines were included, they would want the arrangement extended to cover Malaya and Hong Kong as well. But inclusion of these British protectorates would give rise to similar expec-

Signing the Japanese Peace Treaty (September 1951) with Senator
Alexander Wiley, Prime Minister Yoshida,
and Secretary of State Dean Acheson

tations by the Dutch in Indonesia and the French in Indochina. United States military authorities began to be appalled by the mushroom growth of potential commitments, and Truman and Acheson were equally opposed.

In addition, Dulles believed the moral tone of the security arrangements would be sounder if there were no participation by European colonial powers. Exclusion of France and the Netherlands presented no problem, but Britain was visibly irritated when Australia and New Zealand were approached on this basis and proved willing to conclude a security agreement without Mother England — an act which revealed a new readiness in the Commonwealth countries to assert their independence of London on matters of interest which they perceived as vital. In the end, the solution was to devise three interlocking pacts: (1) a bilateral United States–Japan security agreement providing for the continued presence of American forces in Japan at the invitation of the Japanese government; (2) a bilateral United States–Philippine security agreement incorporating previous base agreements and placing obligations on a mutual basis; and (3) a tripartite agreement involving the United States, Australia, and New Zealand (the ANZUS Pact) assuring the latter two countries of American support in the event of external aggression.

Triumph at San Francisco

The conference to sign the peace treaty was convened at San Francisco on September 4, 1951, the document for consideration being the final Anglo-American draft. Circulated to interested governments on August 13, it was accompanied by an invitation from "The United States Government to a Conference for Conclusion and Signature of a Treaty of Peace with Japan." The basic condition of the invitation was stark in its clarity: *the sole purpose of the conference was to sign the Anglo-American draft in the form presented;* there were to be no amendments and no discussion of substance. To hold firm to such a position against a tide of unhappiness and resentment demanded tough rules of procedure, and these were found in the "closed rule" provisions governing debate in the United States House of Representatives; under this procedure, there is a fixed time for debate and no amendments are permitted. As Acheson later wrote, "Never was so good a peace treaty so little loved by so many of its participants," [54] but the issues at stake "required a determination mounting at times to ruthlessness in dealing with the opposition." [55] In his address to delegates, Dulles called his effort "an eleven month peace conference," but in fact the chosen method of bilateral negotiations had been devised precisely to avoid the unmanageable pitfalls of a large assemblage in dealing with the sensitive problems of reparations, security and Chinese representation.

Even more fundamentally, the method had been designed as a barrier to Russian obstruction. After remaining sullenly on the sidelines for a year, the Soviets in late August suddenly announced their intention to attend the conference, declaring that Foreign Minister Andrei Gromyko would lead a delegation to "present the proposals of the Soviet Government." This unexpected challenge raised fears of a Russian "wrecking crew," and stirred anxiety in Washington. *Newsweek* reported that "a sense of high fate hung over San Francisco this week like the fog on the city's hills," for what the United States had envisaged as a relatively simple endorsement ceremony was being "transformed into one of the momentous showdowns between East and West." [56]

The Americans and their closest allies were, however, well prepared, and determined, to parry and defeat Soviet obstruction; and Acheson, as the presiding chairman of the conference, carried through the prearranged plan with great skill, firmness, and circumspection. Quickly gaining a majority vote for the ironbound rules of procedure, he was, thus armed, able to turn back every angry Russian sally led by Gromyko and his Polish colleagues. As the Turkish ambassador told him, the Russians never fully appreciated the devastating consequences of the rules of procedure, and Acheson himself later wrote: "Once they were adopted, the parliamentary battle was over." [57] In his closing remarks to the conference, the Secretary of State hailed the treaty as "a true act of reconciliation," made possible "because all of us, in the words of Benjamin Franklin, 'doubted something of our infallibility.' " To the Japanese he said, "A great broad highway to a position of equality, of honor, of friendship in the world lies open to you." [58]

The development and negotiation of the splendid "treaty of reconciliation" represented a signal personal triumph for Dulles, an accomplishment that for the first time gave him a truly independent status and prestige apart from his erstwhile sponsors, Dewey and Vandenberg. Operating with a mandate that permitted him the exercise of broad discretion, reinforced by firm and unstinting support from both the President and the Secretary of State, and unencumbered by the burdens of managing a large staff, he handled the assignment with energy, realism, imagination, and distinction. While the problem was large and ramified by countless subtleties, it was nevertheless comprehensible as a single problem, and that fact made it ideally suited to his talents. In the perspective of history, the conclusion of this magnanimous peace settlement may well be judged his finest hour, the single most tangible and durable achievement of his long career. In a meeting with the

President on October 3, Truman offered warm congratulations and then asked if Dulles would be willing to serve as the first postwar ambassador to Japan. Thanking the President for the offer, Dulles declined on the spot, explaining his belief that he "could be more useful . . . at the powerhouse than at the end of the transmission line." [59]

Ratification and the Yoshida Letter

With bipartisan support vital to treaty ratification, Dulles was the natural choice to guide the matter through the Senate debate and, on October 22, he informed Acheson of the conditions he attached to handling this further assignment: one was assurance that the President firmly intended to seek prompt Senate action; the other was assurance that Truman would "assume my loyalty in this matter" despite the inevitable partisan pressures and sniping in an election year.[60] Acheson discussed these conditions with Truman, who accepted them the same day.

With the Korean War dragging on against both Red Chinese and North Korean forces, the ratification process in the Congress turned vitally on the question of Japan's attitude toward mainland China and the Chiang regime on Formosa. Owing to the irreconcilable British and American positions on the Mao government, Prime Minister Yoshida was under conflicting diplomatic pressures, and as a consequence was led into a series of ambiguous pronouncements concerning Japan's future course. Returning from the San Francisco conference in the same airplane, Herbert Morrison and Dulles talked further about this question. As Dulles recorded it, Morrison expressed once more the hope that "nothing would be done to crystallize" the Japanese position until the treaty actually came into force through ratification, but Dulles once again warned that "we could not suppress indefinitely the natural desire" of a government which was "strongly anti-Communist" and which needed "at least such recognition of the Nationalist Government as would assure their good will in various U.N. organizations." [61] The Dulles position was soon reinforced by a stiff letter from fifty-six United States senators to President Truman, taking note of Yoshida's ambiguities and warning that ratification would be jeopardized if the Senate remained in doubt as to Japanese intentions.

Acting swiftly after the signing ceremonies in San Francisco, the Supreme Commander of Allied Powers (SCAP), who was now General Matthew Ridgway, authorized Japan on September 13 to deal directly with those foreign governments whose diplomatic representatives were accredited to SCAP. Although this list included the Nationalist Chinese mission in Tokyo, the Japanese government carefully refrained from making any immediate moves toward Formosa. Nevertheless, in November, Acheson sought the concurrence of Anthony Eden (who had by then succeeded Morrison as Foreign Secretary) in a course that would sanction Japan-Formosa preliminary talks looking toward an agreement that would conform to the realities, but Eden felt he should adhere strictly to the Foreign Office position against any form of recognition before the treaty came into force. The British Parliament had ratified the treaty in late October, but the United States Senate was not scheduled to act before February 1952.

With no "give" in the British position, but with favorable Senate action dependent on a clear statement of Tokyo's intentions, Dulles traveled to Japan in early December, accompanied by Senators John Sparkman and H. Alexander Smith, the ranking Democratic and Republican members of the Far Eastern subcommittee of the Foreign Relations Committee. Rather bluntly they told Yoshida that the Senate "would doubtless want to have clarification of Japan's attitude, in view of the large number of practical post-treaty problems between the United States and Japan that would involve Congressional action." [62] They pointed out that, if the treaty were ratified, the United States would assume "a certain responsibility for Japan's security and that inasmuch as the threat to that security came primarily from Communist China, already convicted by the United Nations of military aggression in Korea, the Senate would doubtless want to know whether or not Japan contemplated giving moral, political or economic support to the aggressor regime against which the United States would be expected to defend Japan." [63] From this formidable demarche came the famous Yoshida letter, which was received in Washington on January 7, 1952. Almost certainly drafted by Dulles himself and handed to Yoshida for signature, it said in part: "My government is prepared as soon as legally possible to conclude with the National Government of China, if that government so desires, a Treaty which will reestablish normal relations between the two Governments." [64] It stated further that such a treaty would "be applicable to all territories which are now, or which may hereafter be, under the control of the National Government of the Republic of China." [65] It noted that, the United Nations having condemned the Peking regime as an aggressor, Japan "is now concurring and expects to continue to concur" in measures against that regime which were recommended by the United Nations.[66]

After its receipt in Washington, the letter was shown to the British ambassador, Sir Oliver Franks, and its substance conveyed to Eden. Winston Churchill and Eden were apparently willing to ride with the situation if the matter were left to a public announcement by the Japanese sometime *after* the treaty came fully into force, but this of course failed to meet the condition required for success in the Senate debate and, on the morning of January 16, 1952, at the outset of the Senate debate, the Yoshida letter was released simultaneously in Washington and Tokyo. It produced angry protests and questions from Labour spokesmen in the British Parliament who embarrassed Eden by alleging his complicity with the Americans in rescinding the Dulles-Morrison agreement. Morrison asserted in the House of Commons that Dulles's pressure on Yoshida before ratification violated the spirit of their agreement. Dulles, defending himself with a lawyer's shrewdness, asserted that Japan's sovereign status had, as a practical matter, come into being with the termination of the occupation controls on September 13, 1951. Acheson defended Dulles at a press conference, saying he did not think Mr. Dulles violated the so-called Dulles-Morrison agreement in any way, and he had "supported Mr. Dulles throughout in what he had said to Mr. Yoshida." [67] He later wrote that Dulles's argument was "not unanswerable, but respectable." On the other hand, he regarded the manner of the letter's release — without specific private warning to Eden — as "an inexcusable bungle." [68] While Acheson did not quite say so, his implication was that Dulles was responsible for the "bungle."

It was surely a political fact in Washington that early release of the Yoshida letter was an unavoidable price to be paid for Senate ratification of the treaty. That being the case, or in any event Dulles's judgment of the case, he showed no moral qualms about putting pragmatism above the obligations of a less-than-ironclad understanding with Morrison. This cutting of corners with the British was, however, the beginning of Eden's distrust. But as John Allison remarked, when Dulles "felt he had to do something," he showed "all the marks of a Jesuit." [69]

8

"Victory" and
the American Temperament

As previously noted, Dulles had stood solidly with Truman and Acheson at the outset of the Korean War, even recommending United States intervention from Tokyo while MacArthur blandly discounted the danger. At the Washington airport on his return, he asserted that the attack involved "open defiance" of the United Nations and was for that reason "a serious affair . . . no use pretending any different." [1] Lucius Battle, entering his office on June 30, 1950, to escort him to a meeting with Acheson, found him on the telephone to Senator Taft, vigorously supporting Truman's intervention. Later, as they walked down the corridor, Dulles told Battle he was "filled with admiration" for the administration's response; it had made the United Nations "a living thing." [2]

Six months later, when the Chinese had come into the war and there was hell to pay, he began to change his position. Sometime in late November, when the United States faced the stark possibility of military evacuation, several reporters called Battle to tell him that Dulles was now disowning his earlier support, telling the press privately he had never been a party to the decision to intervene (which was literally true), and had counseled against the use of ground troops (which was demonstrably false). An indignant young Achesonian loyalist, Battle joined a solitary Dulles at a corner table in the executive dining room, and pointedly recalled each of the many Dulles statements in support of the administration's Korean action. A glacial Dulles glared at him, but attempted no other response; when Battle's compendium ran out they continued glaring at each other for several additional minutes. [3]

This Dullesian shift of position seemed to combine a genuine new fear of Chinese Communist expansion with a case of political cold feet. At a moment of apparently impending national humiliation on a far-off peninsula, he both judged the Truman-Acheson policies inadequate, and sensed the need not to get too far out of step with developing Republican prejudices and partisan opportunities. On November 30 (four days after MacArthur's "Home by Christmas" offensive was crushed by 200,000 Chinese), he sent to Senators Taft and Eugene D. Milliken a bitingly pessimistic memorandum, passing a copy to an irritated Acheson: "We may have been sucked into a major military disaster," he wrote, because the dangers of Soviet-Chinese cooperation were underestimated. The Soviets and the Chinese were carrying out a "comprehensive program . . . designed as a present phase to eliminate all Western influence on the Asiatic mainland, and probably also in relation to the islands of Japan, Formosa, the Philippines, and Indonesia." Indeed the Chinese Communist revolution, Ho Chi Minh's struggle to expel the French from Indochina, Huk banditry in the Philippines, the Communist uprising in Malaya, and the attack on South Korea were "all part of a single pattern of violence planned and plotted for twenty-five years and finally brought to a consummation of fighting and disorder" across the whole vast arc of Asia.[4]

Although he had given impetus to liberation and rollback with his call for a "moral offensive" in the 1946 *Life* articles, the November 30 memorandum appeared to be his first explicit urging of counteroffensive at the level of subversion and paramilitary operations. Here he argued that "there should be a review of our attitude towards Formosa. Our sea and air power and the presence of the Chinese Nationalists, should make it possible to salvage Formosa, and perhaps to use it as a base for covert and perhaps open Chinese activities against the China mainland. . . . Consideration should be given to . . . stimulating guerilla and insurrectional activities . . ." In Europe, because there now seemed to him not enough time to build an effective European army, he urged "stepping up subversive activities within areas of Soviet control." In any event, "we can not safely go on playing a purely defensive role, as this enables the potential enemy to organize themselves [*sic*] at one place or another with a pre-arranged time table which we have no will or capacity to disarrange."[5]

Taken as a whole, the memorandum reflected an inflated estimate of Chinese and Russian power in Asia and of Chinese-Russian policy coordination, and it gave rather too little weight to the thrust of dynamic local forces determined to change the status quo in the name of anticolonialism, self-determination, or a better economic deal. But in late 1950, all violent change in Asia seemed to be instigated and propelled by an ominous Communist momentum, and Dulles was hardly

alone in his disproportionate reaction. It was a misperception involving official Washington, the press, and the general public. Nor was Dulles
unique in his instinct to move from a precarious defensive to a determined counteroffensive, from containment to liberation and rollback.
This too was something of a national phenomenon, an idea that sprang
up in many places, more or less simultaneously, as an instinctive American response to the malevolent purposes and brutal methods of the
Communist system. It reflected American commitment to individual
liberty, American will-to-win, American resistance to half-measures,
American frustration at the psychological strain, the danger, the complexity, and the persisting inconclusiveness of a challenge that had to be
met, yet could not be eliminated.

This national impulse was about to be magnified and personified
by General MacArthur's dramatic defiance of Washington's restraints,
and by his insistence (before and after his dismissal) on the stirring
theme "there is no substitute for victory." From this episode would be
generated powerful new political forces that would run headlong
through the 1950s, mutations of the old isolationism and the new unilateralism, which Dulles, as Secretary of State, could not avoid. In part,
he would espouse them; in greater part he would seek to accommodate
or to harness and ride them.

Containment versus Counteroffensive

From 1947 onward, the Truman administration was steadfastly committed to meeting the challenge of Soviet Communism through selective containment, a strategy that required (in the words of George Kennan, the trenchant Foreign Service officer who was its foremost exposi-
tor) "the adroit and vigilant application of counter-force at a series of
constantly shifting geographical and political points, corresponding to
the shifts and manoeuvres of Soviet policy." [6] Although this formulation was not wholly free of ambiguity, the strategy's clear aim was not
to "win" at any point, but to contain, and by containing to shake Soviet
Communism's confidence in the "historical inevitability" of its triumph,
to discourage the appetite for Soviet risk-taking that could lead to war,
and thus gradually to force a change of attitude and policy on the
leaders in the Kremlin. Soviet challenges at particular points along the
extensive East-West perimeter were to be treated as situations requiring
local response, not as invitations to central war. Broad, all-out response
would be confined to direct attack on the United States or on NATO
Europe.

Yet defensive reaction was not the essence of the strategy. Because its authors believed that the Communist threat, in its profoundest aspects, reflected the crisis of individual man — man's personal disarrangement in the modern world, where politics and economics moved steadily toward ever larger concentrations of mass — they also believed that solutions to the Communist problem lay primarily in restoring confidence in free men, in Western political ideals, in the feasibility of societies unified and harmonious. As Kennan wrote, the "real victories" in the struggle against Soviet tyranny must be registered "within ourselves in our own Western world." [7] In the main, and taking account of the widespread devastation and demoralization existing at the end of World War II, the containment strategy had succeeded brilliantly. By early 1950, it had blocked a Soviet thrust into Iran, greatly weakened the internal Communist threats to Italy and France, ended (with an inadvertent assist from Tito, whose defection closed the Yugoslav-Greek frontier) the guerilla war in Greece, protected Turkey, generated the economic revival of Western Europe through the Marshall Plan, established NATO, moved ahead on the economic and moral recovery of West Germany, and withstood the blockade of Berlin.

But a potential difficulty was that the strategy required endurance, steadiness, patience, and resistance to the temptation of "all-out" response, qualities that tended to run against the American temperament in war. Moreover, it showed itself, both as formulated by Kennan and as orchestrated by Truman and Acheson, to be a doctrine oriented primarily toward Europe and lacking the same confident clarity when applied to the less familiar terrain and conditions of Asia. As the profound dislocations in China produced the traumatic collapse of Chiang's armies and brought to power a regime that many thought was a direct agent of the Kremlin, the cold war seemed to spread relentlessly despite effective containment in Europe. Troubled, impatient Americans began to view it as a negative, overly defensive policy, a treadmill going nowhere, yet at the same time absorbing vast amounts of national attention, energy and resources. On a more scholarly level, there was a spreading sense that, while containment was a correct response insofar as it went, it was by itself inadequate, requiring some more positive supplement. Even the reflective and experienced Walter Lippmann feared that the logic of containment was leading to a wider and wider dispersion of limited American resources, a development he thought would so dilute American power as to deprive it of decisive effect at any single point in the global struggle.

Truman's Brush with Rollback

In early 1950, there appeared on the Washington scene a small book which gave focus and a certain measure of intellectual respectability to what had previously been, in the main, an inchoate collection of doubts and anxieties. Written by James R. Burnham, a professor of political science at Georgetown University, *The Coming Defeat of Communism* expounded the thesis that, in its mortal struggle against the "Communist octopus," the West must now "turn to the offensive" for "if we do not smash the communist power, we shall cease to exist as a nation and a people." [8] From a competent analysis of weaknesses in the "overextended Soviet empire," Burnham moved to the prescription of detailed measures for exploiting these, thus bringing down what he perceived as a house of cards. The book struck profoundly sympathetic chords in important segments of the State Department, the Central Intelligence Agency, and among military planners at the Pentagon. And when the attack on South Korea came a few months later, dramatically reinforcing the arguments of those who already saw inadequacy in a purely defensive American response, there proved to be decisive sentiment in the upper reaches of the national security bureaucracy for putting the liberation-rollback doctrine to its first practical test.

Immediately after the aggression (and well before MacArthur's "end-around" landings at Inchon in September which permitted the United Nations forces to break out of the grimly held Pusan perimeter), a debate developed inside the Truman administration over the question of whether or not to carry military operations beyond the 38th parallel. The Far Eastern division of the State Department, led by Dean Rusk and John Allison, argued that a crossing of that line by allied forces should not be excluded as a matter of policy if military developments should make it a feasible course.[9] Their central point of reference was a UN General Assembly resolution of 1948, establishing a unified and independent Korea as the basic objective. The resolution was not a precisely apt base point in the circumstances, for its supporters had never contemplated the unification of Korea by force. But the North Korean attack had created a fluid situation, and the Pentagon gave strong support to the Rusk-Allison approach, with the important proviso that the United States must concurrently mobilize sufficient resources all over the world to guard against the danger of Soviet countermoves elsewhere — i.e., in Europe. If, however, such a major precaution were taken, American military leaders were confident that rollback in Korea could proceed without serious risk of Soviet intervention there or elsewhere.[10] The danger of Chinese Communist intervention seems to have been, at that stage, rather heavily discounted. Against these bold tendencies, the State Department policy planning staff (now headed by Paul Nitze) argued that the United Nations commander should announce his intention to restore the *status quo ante,* and should not pursue enemy forces beyond the 38th parallel. After the spectacular success of the Inchon landings, debate moved from the theoretical to the operational realm, and resulted in a qualified victory for advocates of the bolder course.

Carefully drawn instructions for MacArthur, authorizing the cautious exploitation of military opportunities north of the 38th parallel, were approved by President Truman on September 27, and then converted into a British-sponsored resolution approved by the UN General Assembly on October 7. Recalling the essential objective of "a unified, independent, and democratic Korea," it recommended that "all appropriate steps be taken to ensure conditions of stability throughout Korea." [11] While embodying the germinal idea of rollback, the language was sufficiently ambiguous to win support from those countries who were nervous about the implications, and who were not prepared to press Korean unification against serious Chinese or Russian military opposition. Thus the Truman administration, emboldened by a dramatic upturn in military fortunes on the Korean battlefield and willing to conclude "the chances were . . . good" [12] that the Red Chinese would not come in, led a docile but wary United Nations coalition into the first effort to recapture territory seized by the Communists during and after World War II. For Truman and Acheson, this appeared to represent a calculated risk, a tentative probe that could be arrested and retracted if serious Chinese or Russian interference should materialize. It also reflected a tempting, intuitively arrived at middle course between the rising demands of congressional and military war hawks for an all-out offensive, and the requirements of maintaining a broad coalition effort in both Asia and Europe.

It proved in the event to be a decision of catastrophic consequence for nearly everyone concerned, bringing in its wake not only a sanguinary, demoralizing war of attrition against the Chinese, but, worse still, an American misconception of Chinese motivations and thus a poisoning of United States–Chinese relations for the next twenty years. The decision went awry, in some large part, because it discounted the powerful idiosyncracies of General Douglas MacArthur and his readiness to defy Washington's restraints, to challenge the President to an almost open struggle for the control of American foreign policy, with peace or general war hanging in the balance. But it also went awry because there was a failure to gauge the strength of popular enthusiasm for a policy of counteroffensive, and thus a failure to anticipate the tide of emotional and political support that flowed outward to the general for his defiance of the President. When the President belatedly asserted his constitutional position by dismissing the general, the action deeply divided public opinion, inflamed right-wing Republicans to a reckless and punishing castigation of the President and his Secretary of State, increased the scope and intensity of the savage McCarthyite witch hunts for "security risks," and thus paralyzed foreign policy for the balance of Truman's term.

These events and their political meaning were not lost upon John Foster Dulles, as he worked at negotiating the Japanese peace treaty.

No Substitute for Victory

As of late November 1950, after the Chinese had come openly into the war and crushed MacArthur's "Home by Christmas" offensive, the real case against the general was not that he had provoked the Chinese. That charge was to some extent true, but provocation was inherent in his directive, and it is doubtful that the use of South Korean troops (instead of American) in the vanguard would have altered the Chinese reaction. The real case against him was that, even after his own warning (in early November) that the Chinese armies in Korea and Manchuria far outnumbered and thus "threatened the destruction" of his own forces, he made no preparations against the contingency of a major Chinese counterattack. Not only did he continue the advance, but spread his vastly inferior forces along a three-hundred-mile front, at the same time parrying or defying every cautionary instruction from his worried superiors in Washington. Why he acted as he did even the long Senate inquest following his dismissal failed to make clear beyond doubt, but it seems close to the truth that he was betting everything on his "superior grasp" of oriental psychology to overawe the Chinese and thus deter their further intervention. He had more than once expressed the belief that "it is the pattern of the Oriental psychology to respect and follow aggressive, resolute, and dynamic leadership." [13] There accordingly existed good grounds for sacking MacArthur for military incompetence at the end of 1950.

After General Ridgway, as field commander, had stabilized the bitter retreat in mid-January 1951, on a line below Seoul, the case against MacArthur became his refusal to accept the fact that, short of major war with China, which both the United States government and the United Nations emphatically opposed, forcible unification of Korea was no longer a viable policy. Fighting back to the 38th parallel and there restoring the *status quo ante* seemed to represent the feasible outer limits for a nervous UN coalition that wanted no further involvement in the Chinese civil war. But such a compromise proved wholly alien to the absolutist tenor of MacArthur's thinking. He had expected victory in Korea; deprived of it by the Chinese intervention, he never seemed to grasp the fact that his superiors no longer shared his expectation. He recognized the opposition of Truman and the United Nations, but passed it off as the folly of politicians who do not understand the real world. By January he was openly appealing to the American people over the heads of the President and the Secretary of State, in a determined effort to win public support for his own policy of uncompromising counteroffensive.

The point is that, in the winter and spring of 1951, there was a good deal of emotional and political support in America for MacArthur and his policy. Three acts of defiance finally led to his dismissal on April 11, of which the last, though not the most egregious, involved a letter to Congressman Joseph Martin, the Republican minority leader. Written on March 20, it surfaced on April 5. Martin, a rather mindless political hack and a formerly staunch isolationist, now advocated the use of Nationalist Chinese forces in Korea, and had asked for Mac-Arthur's comment. The general replied that Martin's view was in conflict with "neither logic" nor the American tradition "of meeting force with maximum counterforce as we have never failed to do in the past." He added with exquisite gratuitousness "that here in Asia is where the Communist conspirators have elected to make their play for global conquest, and that we have joined the issue thus raised on the battlefield; that here we fight Europe's war with arms, while the diplomats there still fight it with words. . . . As you point out, we must win. There is no substitute for victory." [14]

Six days later, President Truman, exercising his authority as commander in chief, relieved MacArthur of his several commands. But popular opinion tended to blur the President's undoubted constitutional right to act, and preferred to focus on the more controversial issue of which strategy — Truman's or MacArthur's — was in the national interest. On that question, MacArthur's convictions concerning the American way of war seemed to be more firmly attached to the public viscera. In the wake of dismissal, thousands of hate telegrams descended upon the White House: IMPEACH THE LITTLE WARD POLITICIAN STUPIDITY FROM KANSAS CITY; RUN THE UNITED NATIONS BACK TO SWITZERLAND; IMPEACH THE JUDAS IN THE WHITE HOUSE WHO SOLD US DOWN THE RIVER TO LEFT-WINGERS, et cetera.[15] In their first instinctive reaction, probably a majority of the American people were for the general and against the President, for the President was working against the grain of American history.

The New Unilateralism

Pulling back from this brief but deadly experiment with rollback, the Truman administration locked solidly onto the familiar strategy of containment, which meant reaffirming the necessity for collective effort, particularly in the NATO coalition; it meant a readiness to use limited war, where unavoidable, as an instrument of policy, but to take care that this involved Kennan's "adroit" rather than MacArthur's "maximum" counterforce; it meant finally a set of priorities that started with Europe.

But now the MacArthur genie was out of the bottle, challenging the Truman-Acheson doctrine at all its points. MacArthur disdained allies and argued for going it alone if allies proved unwilling to follow a bold American lead; he insisted on responding to challenge with maximum counterforce, and considered limited war a prescription for appeasement. Finally, he refused to regard the Soviet Union as the primary source of the trouble: the enemy was "Communism" — a detached, floating ideological virus — a view which not only undercut the rationale of a Europe-first policy, but suggested a series of wholly open-ended American crusades in countries large and small, whether or not their situations presented any conceivable security threat to the United States: "There can be no compromise with atheistic communism — no halfway in the preservation of freedom and religion. It must be all or nothing." [16] MacArthur was probably not, as a matter of careful study and conviction, an Asia-firster; it was more a case of his believing that war, having started, must be carried on to the end — and it had started in Asia. But the political message he preached was clarity itself: the only unpardonable sin is self-restraint.

Such a bold and dashing philosophy propounded by a national folk hero proved to be meat and drink for residual isolationists of the Republican right wing. Isolationism, in the sense of Gibraltarism, had lost all respectability in the course of America's global struggle and triumph in World War II, yet isolationist politicians continued to feed on the anti-Europeanism of the ethnic groups, who remained important voting blocs in both local and national politics. Given the postwar circumstances, some form of American participation in foreign affairs seemed unavoidable. But what kind? Residual isolationists found MacArthur's doctrine appealing because it seemed to permit some redeeming action, while avoiding involvement with Europe. Asia and the Pacific Ocean were areas where, if action was necessary, America could at least act alone, unencumbered, uncontaminated by entangling alliances hatched in the devious, self-serving societies of the old continent. MacArthur's formulations thus provided American isolationism with a "new crystallization," at a time when its intellectual lease on life was precarious in the extreme. As Schlesinger and Rovere described the impact in 1952: "Unilateralism . . . has become the new isolationism. Go it alone; meet force with maximum counterforce; there is no substitute for victory; do not worry about consequences: these are the tenets of the new faith. It is a more vivid, more adventurous, more dangerous faith than the placid, small-town isolationism. . . . It provides scope for men of global vision or of messianic bent. Moreover, it seems to provide a clear-cut and viable alternative to the [Truman] philosophy. . . . It promises action and a victorious conclusion, against the slow death of the cold war." [17]

Dulles was not in the old sense an isolationist, yet he was to become, through the alchemy of politics, a dramatic exponent of the new unilateralism in Asia, and under circumstances in which his major domestic political support would come from the old (now the new) isolationists.

9

The Partisan's Return

As the japanese peace treaty moved toward Senate ratification in the winter of 1952, Dulles was eager for release from the State Department and its obligation of bipartisanship. Increasingly critical of the Truman-Acheson doctrine of containment, he was also aware that both the doctrine and its executors were steadily sinking in public esteem. A vast sum of public grievances, real and imagined, accumulated over twenty consecutive years of power, was now threatening to submerge the Democrats, and central to the trouble was the endless Korean War. Because its conduct ran so hard against the grain of war-making in the simpler American past, it was producing strains, anxieties, and problems of credibility that became fertile breeding grounds for the new unilateralism and a vicious demagoguery. Nineteen fifty-two looked like a Republican year at last, and the indefatigable Dulles, moved by an unflagging ambition, did not intend to be left on the sidelines.

Yet why he chose over the next six months a course of blatant partisanship has remained a substantial mystery to many, for there is no doubt that it damaged him; his campaign speeches and statements generated intense anxiety at home and abroad, and led to feelings of personal distrust and hostility which, as Secretary of State, he never was able to overcome. As one of the master builders of bipartisanship, he bewildered moderate internationalists of both parties and foreign statesmen of various persuasions by political charges that clearly repudiated his own previous positions. The answer to the riddle would seem to lie in a complex personal mix of elements, including conviction, ambition, a tendency to focus on immediate tactical requirements, and a power of advocacy that frequently transcended good judgment. Moreover, having reached this posture by a wholly internal intellectual process, he was more or less insensitive to side effects or wider implications including, one must assume in this case, the unmistakable appearance of his own hypocrisy. In any event, as the year unfolded, he steadily emerged as an advocate of uncompromising anti-Communist crusade, seeking to build upon the national mood of anxiety a sense of moral urgency and missionary zeal. In a speech on February 16, he asserted that Communism was vulnerable because the Soviet empire was vastly overextended: "A dozen people in the Kremlin are attempting to exert absolute dictatorial control over increasing numbers of mankind. . . . All of this is evidence not of strength but of desperation." The United States should accordingly move to exploit this weakness: "It is nothing new for America to lead a psychological and political offensive for freedom and against despotism. Indeed that was the basic conception of our founders. . . . If we get back into that mood, then we would not tremble at the menace of Soviet despotism. It would be the despots who would do the trembling." [1]

As he left the State Department, there was also the matter of which horse to ride in the upcoming presidential election. If the Democrats were exhausted and in disarray (and their future complicated by Truman's March statement that he would not run again), the Republicans were philosophically sundered between the old and the new, between the residual isolationists and the liberal internationalists, between the faction of Taft and the faction of Eisenhower. Dulles had known Taft since his law school days in Washington, and the relationship, while never close, had always been cordial; Eisenhower was only a passing acquaintance. Dulles had asked for the latter's support in the Senate race of 1949, but the general had declined, pleading that his position as president of Columbia University and his continuing military status * precluded active political participation.[2] The two men had met infrequently thereafter, and not at all since Eisenhower's departure in early 1951 to establish the NATO command in Paris.

Taft's views on foreign policy were well known, and Dulles found them, on the whole, too narrowly isolationist and conservative for his taste. Taft was moreover a stubborn, rigid man whose convictions went deep and seemed unlikely to change. Eisenhower's views, though less well known to Dulles or the world at large, seemed to reflect a basically generous and pragmatic internationalism. There was, in addition, the compelling probability that Eisenhower, unlike Taft, could be elected. After discussing the matter with Dewey and Lucius Clay, the retired commander of Berlin who was now an investment banker and a key Eisenhower backer, Dulles decided to support Eisenhower, but to hold off a public

* A five-star General of the Army for life.

announcement until he could meet with the general in Paris. This was arranged for early May. In preparation for the meeting, he developed an extended essay on United States foreign policy which set forth his developing doctrines of deterrence and liberation. This was sent ahead via Clay and was the focus of the talks in Paris.[3] Three weeks after Dulles's return from his visit with Eisenhower, the essay was published in *Life* magazine under the title "A Policy of Boldness."

A Policy of Boldness

One finds in the *Life* article the matured fusion of Dulles the policy thinker, Dulles the moralist, and Dulles the politician; all the strands are there and all are now closely interwoven. The document represents a proposed shift in American strategic posture advanced by a known expert and careful thinker on foreign policy, but a shift also suffused with righteousness and the word of God, inviting a moral crusade, and shrewdly calculated for partisan advantage in the forthcoming presidential election. It is an expression of conviction, yet also a skillful brief reflecting the lawyer's dictum that he is under no obligation to point out the weaknesses in his own case. As one scholarly observer later noted, Dulles frequently showed a tendency to adopt the "preacher's style" as a means of excluding factors which he found it awkward or distasteful to deal with on their merits.[4] But that this was the conscious employment of a device, that he had carefully calibrated the boundaries between statesman, moralist and politician, is doubtful. Especially as the years passed, the once separable elements ran together. And yet he showed an evident ability to move back and forth between them: as a pragmatic, worldly statesman, he could attack his opponents as hopeless idealists; as a preacher-politician, he could attack them as immoral appeasers. On these counts, and because Dulles privately acknowledged to his personal assistant in 1956 that he really never developed any new ideas after coming in as Secretary of State, the *Life* article is worth examination.[5]

In mid-1952, he found American policies to be dangerously inadequate, despite the Truman Doctrine, the Marshall Plan, NATO, and the response to aggression in Korea; indeed, all major policies since World War II were, he thought, reactive, negative, emergency measures, alarming in both their budgetary implications and their tendency to militarize American society: "Such gigantic expenditures unbalance our budget and require taxes so heavy that they discourage incentive." Worse still, "this concentration on military matters . . . transfers from the civilian to the military decisions which profoundly affect our domestic life and our foreign relations." [6] Yet, despite horrendous domestic consequences, none of the policies was designed to terminate the peril. "We are not working, sacrificing and spending in order to be able to live *without* this peril — but to be able to live *with* it, presumably forever. . . . Ours are treadmill policies which, at best, might keep us in the same place until we drop exhausted." [7] The strategy of linear containment pursued by Truman and Acheson could only mean "strength nowhere and bankruptcy everywhere." [8] The way out of this self-made trap lay in the devising of a new military strategy, one that would meet not only the military problem, but also the attendant problems of cost and overmilitarization. His dominant aim here was to *settle* the military factor, so that "we may no longer be so overridingly preoccupied with purely military necessity." [9] How to do this? His formulation in 1952 was, almost verbatim, the one with which he ushered in the doctrine of massive retaliation in January 1954. "There is one solution and only one: that is for the free world to develop the will and organize the means to retaliate instantly against open aggression by Red armies, so that, if it occurred anywhere, we could and would strike back where it hurts, by means of our choosing." [10] He was confident this doctrine would not only put a stop to overt aggression, but would also impose conclusive restraints on internal subversive movements.

With the military problem thus in hand, the free world could move to the political offensive. There existed "a moral or natural law" determining right and wrong to which men must, in the long run, conform or meet with disaster; and America was the chosen agent of God's vengeance: "This law has been trampled by the Soviet rulers, and for that violation they can and should be made to pay." America must make known that "it wants and expects liberation to occur," for that would electrify the mood of captive peoples and "put heavy new burdens on the jailers." [11] He then sketched a series of implementing measures: "task forces" to develop "a freedom program" for each of the captive nations (which he did not define beyond finding ways to stimulate escape from behind the Iron Curtain and to refocus the Voice of America and Radio Free Europe on a more direct advocacy of liberation). He insisted this was not a call for "a series of bloody uprisings and reprisals," that "separation from Moscow" could be peacefully achieved.[12]

As to the proposed new emphasis on deterrence, Dulles, as student and practitioner of foreign affairs, presumably understood that nuclear retaliation was already a vital component of the containment strategy — indeed the principal NATO deterrent, the ultimate backdrop to American diplomacy. The Strategic Air Command was a force in being and its primary mission was to deliver the nuclear counteroffensive. Accordingly, he was not really calling upon the free world to "organize the means" for retaliation, but rather to "develop the will" to use it "instantly." Taken at face value, this was a proposal to transform the awesome nuclear capability from an instrument of last resort to one of first resort. Whether or not this was a policy consonant with power realities in 1952, three years after the USSR had exploded its own nuclear weapon, was a question he did not elect to explore.

As to "liberation," his contention that such a process could be peaceful was buttressed by the single example of Tito. But Yugoslavia was an atypical case involving both a physical boundary on the West and a loyal indigenous army and secret police apparatus capable of resisting Russian penetration. Moreover, Tito's was the triumph of *national communism*, which was not the victory for individual freedom that Dulles preached. Emmet John Hughes, then foreign affairs editor of *Life*, who worked closely with him to edit the long memorandum into suitable shape for the magazine, experienced special difficulty in bringing him to a tangible definition of the liberation doctrine. "What are you proposing that U.S. policy should *do?*" Hughes kept asking. But Dulles, leaning against the mantlepiece in his library on Ninety-first Street, remained entirely vague concerning the operational implications.[13] There was no doubt that his proposals lacked content, but he was perhaps also loath to acknowledge that the liberation rhetoric was, in some large part, an exercise in domestic ethnic politics.

The Eisenhower Reaction

Eisenhower was rather taken with the doctrine of deterrence, although he thought Dulles's formulation too simple and unqualified. But he liked its essence because he shared Dulles's concern that, in defending itself against Communism, America might well spend itself into bankruptcy. On April 15, the NATO commander wrote Dulles a letter thanking him for the paper and saying he was "as deeply impressed as ever with the directness and simplicity of your approach to such complex problems." [14] Then with typical Eisenhower diplomatic finesse, he expressed his reservations not to Dulles, but to Lucius Clay. The threat of overwhelming retaliation, he wrote Clay, was no doubt the efficacious posture in those places, like Berlin, where an American vital interest existed and was formally recognized. But what about minor aggressions or internal subversions in remote places? "What should we do if Soviet *political* aggression . . . successively chips away exposed portions of the free world? So far as our resulting economic situation is concerned, such an eventuality would be just as bad for us as if the area had been captured by force. To my mind, this is a case when the theory of 'retaliation' falls down." [15] Eisenhower was thus, with certain reservations, sympathetic to deterrence. He expressed no opinion whatsoever on the doctrine of liberation, but silence concealed misgivings to which he would later give voice. In all probability he did not, at the time, recognize the domestic ethnic politics embedded in the arguments.

The two men met cordially on May 3 and again on May 5 at the Supreme Headquarters of the Allied Powers in Europe (SHAPE) at Fontainebleau. Over a long luncheon with Clay and General Alfred Gruenther, they found themselves in agreement on the main lines of global strategy, including steady opposition to Soviet Communism, the principle of collective defense, and the promotion of European unity through various organizational devices including the European Defense Community.[16] Dulles promised full political support, but thought it best to withhold a public announcement until he could confer with Senator Taft. After the meetings, however, he seems to have felt some distress at what he regarded as Eisenhower's naïveté, not merely about domestic politics, but especially about the Communist threat and the world power balance. According to Joseph C. Harsch of the *Christian Science Monitor,* who saw him at the Ritz Hotel immediately after the second meeting, Dulles paced the floor of his room in agitation, complaining that Eisenhower somehow failed to see that the world was in acute crisis; incredibly, he told Harsch, the general thought "the British are right," that, with patience and firmness, things would work out.[17]

Back in the United States, Dulles was soon summoned by Taft, who asked support for his candidacy, or at least neutrality. He told Taft he had decided to support Eisenhower, but wished to act in the best interest of the whole party. By prearrangement with Eisenhower's advisers, he then steered the conversation toward the possibility of cooperation on foreign affairs, as a means of preventing fratricide between the two dominant factions of the GOP. Rather surprisingly, Taft agreed with this view, and suggested that Dulles might prepare the foreign policy section of the party platform on behalf of both himself and Eisenhower. Dulles's "recent speeches," Taft said, had led him to believe there existed "a large area of possible agreement." [18]

With Eisenhower's approval, Dulles thus undertook the tricky task of devising a foreign policy plank satisfactory to both the isolationist and internationalist wings of the party, an effort at grafting which many thought could not bring forth good fruit. Taft had voted against NATO, argued for no commitments in Europe, flirted with the MacArthur thesis of unilateral action in Asia, and thought of American military force solely in terms of air power. Eisenhower was the living embodiment of global interdependence, free trade, collective security and Europe-first.

Taft Republicans were vocally unhappy with the selection of Dulles, and Eisenhower enthusiasts like the *New York Herald Tribune* called attention to unbridgeable differences. Dulles, however, seemed undaunted by either the intellectual or the moral nature of the challenge; from being the symbol of bipartisanship, he was prepared to become, as a witty journalist put it, "the leading prophet and agent of bi-factionalism." [19]

The Preacher-Politician

Dulles was also prepared to accept a basic rationale of the Taft forces that was personally distasteful to Eisenhower and of little help to him in appealing to the independent voters on whose support his electoral chances turned. As the rationale ran, Dewey had been twice defeated by embracing bipartisanship in foreign affairs, by forgoing the electoral benefits to be gained from sharp attack upon those Democratic wartime agreements that had led to cruel Soviet domination of those East European entities — Latvia, Lithuania, Estonia, Poland, Czechoslovakia, Hungary and Rumania — many of whose former citizens were now voting Americans. The basic strategy was thus to detonate bipartisanship and make foreign affairs a major issue in the campaign. The emotion-laden prose of the platform accordingly promised to "repudiate all commitments contained in secret understandings such as Yalta which aid Communist enslavements." And it promised that "we shall again make liberty into a beacon light of hope that will penetrate the dark places. It will mark the end of the negative, futile and immoral policy of 'containment' which abandons countless human beings to a despotism and godless terrorism which in turn enables the rulers to forge the captives into a weapon for our destruction." It added that "the policies we espouse will revive the contagious, liberating influences which are inherent in freedom." It sounded like pure Dulles.

Whether Dulles was a full party to the cold political calculation that lay behind the hot-eyed prose, or merely a double agent and arbiter, the result was a foreign policy platform that made little sense except on the assumption of a Taft nomination. Eisenhower was persuaded to accept it only with difficulty and as a repugnant necessity of the new, to him, game of politics. In the campaign he did not regard himself bound by it, and his principal speech writer on foreign affairs never bothered to read it.[20] Not unnaturally, however, its content dismayed several Eisenhower advisers and strained their confidence in Dulles. The standard argument used in his defense was that, of course, heavy concessions in the platform language were necessary to assure active con-

THE PARTISAN'S RETURN   131

servative support for the ticket, following Eisenhower's nomination; and there was the corollary point that a platform writer is "by definition a dealer in grotesqueries" who should thus be allowed a certain moral discount.[21]

These arguments would perhaps be more convincing in this case if Dulles had subsequently shown himself more restrained on the political stump. But his speeches during the campaign were filled with inflammatory right-wing oratory, which sounded strange indeed coming from the mouth of one who was widely regarded as a moderate, wise and mellow internationalist: "We are marked down for destruction by those who today control one-third of the world. . . . Our policies are inadequate."[22] "Why should we assume that what Soviet Communism can *do* in China, we cannot *undo*. . . . For our own safety we need and must have a positive China policy."[23] One is left with several possible conclusions: either he was passionately convinced of what he was saying; or he was convinced that this line of attack was essential to electoral success for the Republican party, even with Eisenhower as the party standard-bearer; or he felt an overriding personal need to ingratiate the congressional conservatives, so that he would have their support for the cabinet post and so that as Secretary of State he could expect sympathetic treatment from them, having in mind the grievous personal assaults and official paralysis that Acheson suffered as a consequence of their opposition. Given the fusion of the dominant elements in his character, it is probable that all three conclusions are partially true.

In August there was a television colloquy with Averell Harriman, who was assumed to be the Democrats' first choice for Secretary of State. Walter Cronkite was the moderator:

Dulles: The first thing I would do would be to shift from a purely defensive policy to a psychological offensive, a liberation policy, which will try to give hope and a resistance mood inside the Soviet empire . . .

Harriman: Those are very fine words, but I don't understand the meaning of them. . . . We have the initiative in many parts of the world [but] it's very dangerous to talk about liberation because liberation in the minds of Europeans means war, and I can assure you that the word "liberation" terrifies the people who are under Communism that we are going to be the aggressor. . . . When the time comes, when we are strong enough, then I believe there will be a beginning of the weakening behind the Iron Curtain. But nothing can be more cruel than to try to get people behind the Iron Curtain — I have been there and I know what it is — to try to revolt and have a new tragedy and a massacre . . .

Cronkite (to Dulles): Your Party doesn't support such a move?

Dulles: No, we don't support a move which would start a massacre. I wrote quite a little piece in *Life* magazine.

Harriman: I read it twice, but I couldn't understand what you meant.

Dulles: You should have read it a third time.

Harriman: I did. I still don't understand it.

Cronkite: Mr. Harriman, being impartial, we don't know whether Mr. Dulles can't write or you can't read.[24]

Whatever the reasons, Dulles gave in the final weeks of the campaign an ultrapartisan performance, with rather predictable results. To the Democratic nominee, Adlai Stevenson, his line on "liberation" was a "cynical and transparent attempt, drenched in crocodile tears, to play upon the anxieties of foreign nationality groups in this country." [25] Senator Paul Douglas accused him, accurately, of sharing responsibility for many of the policies he now chose to call futile and sterile. To Europeans, he became a "fire-breathing warmonger who would obliterate Europe with hydrogen bombs in order to free Poland and so gain votes in Hamtramck." [26] The British press feared that he would, in office, support offensive bombing operations against the Chinese mainland. And Anthony Eden, drawing heavily on a long and close friendship, went so far as to "express the hope" privately to Eisenhower that Dulles would not receive appointment as Secretary of State.[27]

Stung by this barrage of personal criticism, Dulles insisted with considerable heat that his liberation doctrine was not intended to foment violent revolution, and he answered Senator Douglas's charge by angrily accusing the Democrats of wrecking bipartisanship! [28] A more artful defense employed was that the platform and his vocal support for it did not necessarily express his own convictions, that he was simply an advocate making a case for his client — in this case the Republican party. The following January, during his confirmation hearing before the Senate Foreign Relations Committee, he elaborated this theme with perfect composure: "Under our constitutional system we have a general election every four years. . . . One side presents his case and the other side presents the other case, as two lawyers do when they go into court. At that stage the two parties are . . . not judicial. In my opinion they should not be. They are in a controversial position. My job as a lawyer is to present the case for my client. Your job is to present the case for your client. It is not my job to present your case, and it is not your job to present mine." The language used, he thought, "took on the tones of a normal presidential campaign." [29] A case could be made for a limited application of the agent theory to politics. What made the theory disquieting in Dulles's case was his claim, in other guises, to be not only a man of integrity who expressed and stood upon his own convictions, but a man of God who tirelessly warned of "confusion in men's minds and a corrosion in their souls" and who urged upon his countrymen a spiritual renaissance. It is quite possible that he never noticed the discrepancy. What mattered in the fall of 1952 was electoral success for Eisenhower and enough support from Taft to assure his appointment as Secretary of State. He was the quintessential tactician at work.

On November 3, he summed up in a final speech: "Foreign policies, if they are good, should give happiness, not dread: they should give solvency, not bankruptcy; they should give life, not death. . . . Now we have war again and no end to killing is in sight. Our defense expenditures and tax rates are being fixed by the Soviet Union . . . and it surely fixes them high. So we have crippling taxes and expenditures which constantly shrink the dollar's value. . . . Therefore, if you want more of the same, more war, more taxes, more depreciation of your dollars, and more peril, you know where to get them. If you want change, you must look to General Eisenhower." [30]

10

The New Dispensation

MANY OBSERVERS of American affairs in the fall of 1952 felt that a
Republican presidential victory was almost a prerequisite to the
continued workability of the American political system, for Lord Acton's
dictum, they argued, applies equally in reverse: lack of power corrupts
and total lack of power corrupts absolutely. No Republican had sat in
the White House for twenty years, and, deprived of that sobering
perspective, conducive to responsible behavior and a large view, the
party had fallen into the hands of its senior representatives in the
Congress who were, on the whole, backward-looking, penny-pinching
men — quintessential nay-sayers who turned instinctively away from any
form of American involvement in the turbulent world of the mid-
twentieth century. With Eisenhower's nomination, the objective need
for a Republican victory could be accepted with greater confidence, for
he seemed to promise a responsible transition. The Democrats had led
the nation since 1932, up from the Great Depression and through a
bloody and noble triumph for mankind over the blackest tyranny of
modern times. Their postwar readiness to cope with global dislocation
and to confront the dangerous ambitions of the Soviet Union showed
courage and imagination on a grand scale. But now they were tired and
running out of seasoned leaders. They needed respite from the burdens
of office almost as badly as the Republicans needed to assume these. A
Democratic victory in 1952 might drain the party's remaining reserves
of energy and public goodwill for long years to come; a Republican
defeat would almost certainly throw the GOP into mindless subservience
to its most irrational and regressive elements.

General Eisenhower's victory, when it came, was accordingly a source of relief and encouragement to millions of thoughtful citizens — Republicans, Democrats, and independents alike. The impressive margin of victory * reflected the nation's confidence in the man, far more than in the party, and in his most visible characteristics — strength and moderation in equal measure. Although time and retreat from the vexations of office, aggravated by heart attack, ileitis, and cerebral stroke, would dim it, the dominant first impression of the President-elect, as a close observer recalled, was one of strength and commanding presence: "The timbre of his voice, . . . the vigor of his gestures, the authority of his movements . . . that loose, rolling, yet somehow assertive stride . . . the blue eyes of a force and intensity singularly deep, almost disturbing, above all commanding"; his "easy air of personal authority seemed, of all hopeful facts of 1952, the most promising for the future." [1]

Dulles and Eisenhower

Dulles had been conspicuously absent from the Eisenhower entourage during the campaign, and his assistance and advice had been rather conspicuously unsought on any of the candidate's foreign policy pronouncements.[2] These facts suggested that, at least during the summer and fall, Eisenhower was less than anxious to have Dulles's counsel and less than certain that he wanted to appoint him Secretary of State. Dulles campaigned vigorously, but alone, and was at least once admonished by Eisenhower for what the candidate regarded as his rather too unqualified exposition of the "liberation" doctrine. Nor was he among the first cabinet appointees. There was an awkward three weeks after the election before Eisenhower named him to the State Department, and he thus missed the meeting with Truman on November 18 at which the problems of transition were discussed, the President-elect being accompanied on that occasion by Henry Cabot Lodge and Joseph Dodge.

There are conflicting versions of how the appointment came about. According to Herbert Brownell and Lucius Clay, who comprised the core of a small committee to advise on cabinet selections, Eisenhower never considered anyone but Dulles. However, according to a view attributed to C. D. Jackson (vice-president of Time, Inc., who became the President's assistant for "psychological operations"), Eisenhower informed his close advisers a few days after the election that he wanted John J. McCloy as his Secretary of State. McCloy had served as Assistant Secretary of War and High Commissioner for Germany, and was a close friend and professional colleague of the President-elect. According to this version,

* He carried 39 of 48 states and won 442 electoral votes, as against 9 states and 89 electoral votes for Adlai Stevenson.

Clay and others told him that such an appointment would cause an uproar in the Taft wing of the GOP; among the few serious candidates, Clay is reported to have said, only Dulles would sit well with Taft. After some argument, Eisenhower reluctantly accepted this judgment, but then went on to formulate a scheme whereunder McCloy would come in as Undersecretary with the understanding that, after one year, he would move up to head the department and Dulles would move into the White House as a special adviser. As Eisenhower knew, Dulles had frequently expressed the wish that he could play a major role in "planning" foreign policy without having to assume the administrative burdens of running the State Department. Dulles's age (he would be sixty-five in February 1953) was said to have been a factor in Eisenhower's thinking. Eisenhower then invited Dulles to enter the cabinet on the basis of these conditions and understandings. Dulles appeared to accept, and asked who should talk to McCloy. Eisenhower indicated he would be glad to have Dulles do it.[3]

The foregoing must be judged hearsay evidence, in part because Jackson died in 1964 without leaving a written account. What appears to be solid fact is that Dulles did telephone McCloy for an appointment, and the two men met in New York. Dulles did not immediately present the Eisenhower proposal, but asked McCloy how he would rate certain other men for the position of Undersecretary; he ran down a short list of names headed by Lewis W. Douglas. The talk continued for several minutes, with McCloy responding forthrightly, but being somewhat mystified about the point and purpose of the queries. At last, Dulles asked McCloy if *he* would accept that position for a short time, to be followed by promotion to Secretary. When McCloy asked where this would leave Dulles, the reply was that he, Dulles, would move over to the White House as a personal adviser to the President. Further probing gave McCloy the clear impression that Dulles expected to remain the chief policy adviser on foreign affairs, while McCloy ran the State Department "from the administrative point of view." McCloy declined this kind of arrangement, feeling that the Secretary of State must also be the chief adviser to the President on foreign affairs. So the matter ended there. McCloy never spoke to Eisenhower about it, feeling that any further initiative lay properly with the President. But General Walter Bedell Smith, who became Undersecretary of State, later told McCloy that Dulles's presentation of the proposal had not been consistent with Eisenhower's intentions.[4]

Explanation of this apparent conflict may lie in a proposal put forward at the same time by the Commission on Government Organization, a group appointed by the President-elect and comprising his brother, Milton, Arthur Fleming, and Nelson Rockefeller. The proposal was to create a supracabinet post to coordinate the nearly forty agencies engaged in some aspect of foreign affairs and, according to Milton Eisenhower, this was discussed with both the President-elect and Dulles.[5] Superficially, it had a certain appeal — nine months before, on the eve of his visit to Eisenhower in Paris, Dulles had told his law partners, Arthur Dean and Eustace Seligman, that "I don't think I really want to be Secretary of State. . . . The job I would like to have would be head of the planning group — to plan foreign policy." [6] On closer examination, however, he doubted that sufficient power and prestige would reside in some new position unsupported by tradition; and he possessed an unspoken desire to succeed his grandfather and uncle as the Secretary of State. After careful consideration, according to Milton Eisenhower, both Dulles and the President-elect opposed the proposal for a supracabinet post in 1953;[7] it is thus possible that the approach to McCloy was made in the context of their examining it, but before they decided it was not feasible. On the other hand, Emmet Hughes thought the circumstantial evidence of Eisenhower's indifference to Dulles during the campaign and his restless unease in Dulles's presence during the first weeks and months of their relationship were "overpowering." [8]

Having made a quick and secretive inspection trip to the Korean battle-field in early December (in fulfillment of his campaign promise that "I shall go to Korea"), Eisenhower was joined at Wake Island on his return by the men he had appointed to State, Defense, and Treasury — Dulles, Charles Wilson of General Motors, and George Humphrey of the Hannah Company — and by Admiral Arthur Radford, then Commander in Chief, Pacific (CINCPAC), who would soon become Chairman of the Joint Chiefs of Staff. For three days they sailed in the battle cruiser USS *Helena,* en route to Hawaii, a voyage billed by the press secretary as the setting for an urgent "mid-Pacific conference" arranged "to decide how best to combat Soviet-dominated Communism throughout the world." In fact, the meeting's purpose was to afford Eisenhower an opportunity to gauge the minds and temperaments of men he did not know, but had selected for key roles in his administration, and for them similarly to gauge him and each other. The deliberations produced only one tangible piece of work — a brief statement on the Korean War, pressing the other side to acceptance of an honorable settlement; otherwise the talk was wide-ranging, informal and inconclusive, running from global strategy to the removal of war-induced price controls.[9]

According to Emmet Hughes, who was among those present, both he and C. D. Jackson noted an uncharacteristic diffidence and uncertainty in Dulles, which was deepened by painful evidence that Eisenhower found him boring, whether he was "expanding at philosophic length upon his estimate of the Communist challenge, or responding at legalistic length to a specific question . . ." Whenever Dulles spoke, Eisenhower's "all-too-expressive face" and gestures betrayed an impatient lack of interest. He nodded briskly "to nudge a slow voice faster onward toward some obvious conclusion," tapped a pencil on his knee in restless rhythm, and finally gazed at the ceiling "signaling the end of all mental contact." To Eisenhower's eagerness for tangible fare, Hughes thought, "the lawyer offered a surfeit of abstractions and generalizations." And from this encounter, both he and Jackson judged that the two men could not work together, and would shortly come to a parting of the ways. Some years later, he acknowledged this as a memorably erroneous conclusion.[10]

Although Eisenhower later denied it, there does, however, seem to be little doubt of an initial strain in the relationship. Dulles's special assistant, Roderic O'Connor, sensed that, during the first several months in office, his chief was somewhat nervous about his relations with the White House, and others noted the sharp difference, in tone and style, between Dulles and Undersecretary Bedell Smith in their frequent telephone conversations with the President. Staff members gathered in the Secretary's office would hear: "Yes, Mr. President, I understand." Those meeting with the Undersecretary were more apt to get: "God damn it, Ike, I don't think . . ." But after a while, as O'Connor watched, "everything seemed to go more naturally," and thereafter Dulles had the President "in his palm." [11]

Throughout his period as Secretary of State, Dulles never forgot that his relationship to the President was the absolute first priority: the vital lifeline. He nourished it with extreme care, giving Eisenhower advance notice of upcoming problems in need of decision, laying out his own analysis, and listening carefully to the President's comments. As the relationship developed, the two men would normally talk on the telephone three or four times a day, and when Dulles was out of the country he sent the President each evening a summary cable of his actions and reflections; these cables came to be regarded around the White House as literary gems. He suffered initially from Eisenhower's insistence on encapsulated analyses of complicated situations and their further reduction to one proposed course of action, but he gradually adjusted to this requirement. His basic conception was that he was the President's lawyer for foreign affairs and that, as in other lawyer-client relationships, his job was to provide advice and counsel. He was in no doubt that it was the client who possessed the ultimate authority and power, but as the relationship matured he left nobody else in doubt that the President would very probably accept his recommendation. In his view there could be only one adviser on foreign policy, and he was extremely sensitive to the slightest threat of intrusion from any quarter, defending his turf with an aggressive, guileful, absolute single-mindedness that brooked no opposition. Eisenhower had come into office with an announced determination to strengthen the National Security Council and himself to

The Eisenhower Cabinet (1953). Left to right: Lodge (Ambassador to UN), McKay (Interior), Humphrey (Treasury), Nixon (Vice President), Brownell (Justice), Weeks (Commerce), Mrs. Hobby (Health, Education and Welfare), Adams (The Assistant to the President), Dodge (Budget Bureau), Fleming (Emergency Planning), Durkin (Labor), Summerfield (Post Office), Dulles (State), President Eisenhower, Wilson (Defense), Benson (Agriculture), Stassen (Foreign Aid); standing, Rabb (Cabinet Secretary) and Cutler (National Security Council)

"orchestrate" the State, Defense, CIA and Treasury contributions to a fully coordinated foreign policy. His progressive reliance on Dulles, however, soon compromised this approach, for the intimacy of the relationship made the Secretary of State unchallengeable inside the administration — because he spoke for the President, he could encroach on the jurisdictional territory of others, but they could neither effectively resist nor retaliate. This later made for friction with Harold Stassen and Nelson Rockefeller, whose attempt to conduct aspects of foreign policy independent of Dulles led to showdowns and their resignations. Aware of his determined predominance, various other men around the President (including Sherman Adams, C. D. Jackson, William H. Jackson, Robert Cutler, and Gordon Gray) never chose to challenge him. Dulles's aggressiveness here reflected not only personal force and a passion to control events, but also the lesson learned at Versailles, where he had witnessed the steady erosion of his uncle Robert Lansing's position by the encroachments of President Wilson's personal assistant, Colonel House.

Sherman Adams, the President's principal staff man in the White House, found Dulles an altogether "tough-fibered individual . . . an aristocrat in his own domain," [12] who insisted on maintaining a strictly personal and private line to Eisenhower; he was "a rather secretive person" who "shrank away from [White House] staff intervention, or even [from] giving the staff knowledge of the particular problem." [13] The President had somewhat unguardedly invited cabinet members "simply to walk in" on him if they had pressing problems to discuss, but only Dulles's sangfroid consistently surmounted the procedural obstacles erected by Sherman Adams to guide and protect his chief's schedule. Dulles would walk into Eisenhower's anteroom, bypassing Adams, and ask the lady secretary if the President was engaged; "if the answer was no, he just opened the door and walked in." [14] Adams complained mildly that Dulles's "lengthy discussions . . . rather ate into the schedule," [15] but the Secretary of State's meticulous preparation, down to and including a recommended course of action to meet the problem at hand, moved Eisenhower to a steady growth of confidence and respect. If, however, the President progressively welcomed unscheduled visits from his precise Secretary of State, it was otherwise with his imprecise Secretary of Defense. "Engine Charlie" Wilson, who had recently guided the fortunes of General Motors, "discombobulated" Eisenhower with rambling, exploratory discourses on defense problems which "the President thought he ought to have taken a stand on himself," [16] and Adams was encouraged to close him off.

Adams had no doubt that it was Dulles who initiated and gave primary shape to United States foreign policy during the greater part of the Eisenhower era, but he perceived that the President frequently "smoothed the sharp edges of Mr. Dulles' incisiveness" by bringing to bear "the human side of the equation" — by which he meant the need for a more empathetic understanding of the opposition, whether in Congress or the Kremlin. In Adams's view, Dulles consistently advanced a hard line and Eisenhower consistently softened it.[17]

Dulles and the State Department

Having concluded that it was infeasible to define himself as a kind of "Super Secretary of Foreign Policy" with policy authority but no administrative burdens, Dulles thus formally accepted the full range of responsibilities that devolve upon a major department head in Washington; in fact, however, he instinctively concentrated almost wholly on policy-making. As Dewey put it: "Foster was not an executive . . . he didn't have the instinct of an executive. Very few lawyers do." [18] And a loyal aide remarked, "Administrative matters failed completely to interest Mr. Dulles. I may say that he failed completely to comprehend them either." [19] Had he been willing, in earlier years, or even in 1953, to turn his powerful and orderly mind to the problem, he could undoubtedly have made himself a passably adequate manager. But at sixty-five and shaped by the habits of a lifetime, he was determined to concentrate his energies on what he regarded as the transcendent issues facing a world in turmoil. The implicit corollary was to avoid, insofar as possible, what seemed to him the petty annoyances of time-consuming administrative detail. His ceaseless traveling was in part a means of escaping the burdens of management and the tedium of congressional testimony. Aloft over the oceans, he could "compartmentalize" and concentrate on the immediate policy problem.

To observers, his subsequent conduct of office seemed like the performance of a one-man band, and the cliché was widely repeated that he "carried the State Department in his hat." A loyal inner circle of subordinates fiercely disputed this, insisting that he conferred with all relevant sectors of the department on important matters, and citing in evidence his twice-weekly staff meetings. The truth is he conferred selectively, very selectively, albeit with refreshing unconcern for rank and formal channels of command, but the consultations were of a rather special sort. His own ideas being largely self-developed, he needed facts, and relished debate with those he considered informed and tough enough to defend their position, but the purpose of the process was to produce, at most, minor refinements of his own handiwork. Each morning he would arrive at his office with a sheaf of handwritten notes, set out on the sheets of a lined yellow pad, to be typed and distributed; almost invariably the information or comment he sought was with reference to an idea, a formulation, a decision that he himself had already roughed out. As Dewey said, "His disposition was to do his own thinking, talk or confer if he had to, but to go ahead and act." [20]

He had a strong sense of relevance and priorities, and a rather disconcerting habit of turning off his attention if the report or comment of a subordinate was not fully meshed with these. As Charles E. Bohlen, who was Counsellor of the department before his departure to be ambassador to Moscow, put it, "you would almost hear the click as he turned off the mental hearing aid." [21] And, according to O'Connor, "you'd wonder if he'd just turned off the engine. . . . And mind you, he was totally polite, patient, and so forth. But . . . you would lose him . . . you might just as well not [have] been in the same room with him. . . . He became unaware . . . that you were there." [22] O'Connor likened Dulles's power of concentration to a flashlight: "He would turn it on and point it down on something, and you couldn't shake him. . . . He would always put it [down] on what he thought was [a] priority. If you didn't think so, it was just too bad. . . . In that degree, he appeared to be exceedingly rude to people which he wasn't at all." [23]

Many officers in the department found him forbidding and unapproachable. Nor were these qualities apparent only in dealings with underlings; he could be equally abrupt and discourteous with very high people. A part of the problem, though by no means the largest part, was his suspicion that most of the State Department's senior career officers, having served Democratic administrations for twenty years, were partisan in their loyalties and therefore not fully to be trusted. As chairman of the Carnegie Endowment for International Peace in 1946, he had accepted, and been stung by, a favorable State Department recommendation of Alger Hiss — an incident which not unnaturally inclined him to caution in matters involving reliance on the professional Foreign Service. But basically the problem for the officers in the department was the man and his style, and they could hardly avoid the contrast between the new Secretary and his immediate predecessor, who had led them through four difficult, creative and tumultuous years. Both Dulles and Acheson were men of exceptional intellectual power and purpose, occasional arrogance, and tough inner fiber; there the similarity ended. Acheson projected the long lines and aristocratic bearing of a thoroughbred horse, a self-assured grace, an acerbic elegance of mind, and a charm whose chief attraction was perhaps its penetrating candor. Dulles projected the heavy opaqueness of a large bear — massive in physique, in energy, in capacity for work, in self-certitude. Where Acheson was swift-flowing and direct, Dulles was ponderous and Jesuitical; where Acheson was perceived as a cultivated eighteenth-century rationalist ready to apply an irreverent wit to matters public and private, Dulles came across as an austere nineteenth-century moralist, a one-dimensional man who could not bring himself to relieve, for any reason, the self-conscious gravity of his every public utterance.

Dulles's inner circle defended him with the same arguments that had been used by admiring law partners — that the Dulles mind was always in motion on some more consequential problem, that he was very busy, that he intensely disliked the distraction of administrative or personal details. To demonstrate his humanity, they pointed out that he did not drive his subordinates by ordering them to work, but by setting an extremely stiff pace in his own work. And it was true that he did not explicitly condemn poor staff papers — he simply ignored them. He could ignore them without anguish, for he was in no real sense concerned with the performance and well-being of the corporate body of the State Department. The Secretary was one thing; the department another. But it was the Secretary who formulated, recommended, and carried out, relegating the corporate competence of the career service to a narrow advisory role, precluding it from significant initiatives, and rarely giving it his full confidence. He wrote all his own speeches and his briefing notes for the President, as well as many memoranda for the National Security Council, cables to ambassadors, and statements for the press. One curious consequence of this intensely proprietary attitude toward U.S. foreign policy was that his press conferences were notable for their heavy attendance by officers of the State Department, junior and senior alike, who had concluded that it was not otherwise possible for them to be adequately informed of the Secretary's thinking about problems and areas for which they were responsible.

In brief, by acting out of the imperatives of his character and personality, Dulles made himself, for all practical purposes, the sole intellectual wellspring of conception and action in foreign policy during his period in office. No feature of his performance did more to wither the creative impulses of the Foreign Service, weaken its sense of purpose and self-esteem, and sap its morale. He thus came to the department rather like the High Commissioner of an occupying power: determined to impose his will, to extract from local resources whatever was necessary to accomplish his mission, but to do so without making himself dependent on the local elite. Being an ambassador under Dulles, one senior diplomat remarked, "created a Kafka-like situation. You had a telephone up to the Castle, but nobody answered it." [24]

But if his colleagues and subordinates were thus made aware of his conspicuous intellectual vanity, his disposition to see himself as chess master of the free world daily engaged in a mortal contest against a monolithic adversary whose every move was carefully designed to outwit

Dulles, they were equally impressed by the energy and skill he brought to the undertaking. Also admirable in their eyes was an ability to take hard decisions without anguish, and let go afterwards. He was "a rough weather sailor," O'Connor thought, with "a lot of confidence, that sooner or later, he was going to get the boat into port . . ." [25] And after a harrowing eleven-hour day, he could go home, "sit out on the terrace with his wife and have a cocktail and dinner, and . . . wipe it out of his mind." [26] Beneath the thick outer crust, they found a man of kind consideration and, occasionally, of hearty old-fashioned good humor, and they were amused and protective when intense preoccupation with his problems made him something of an absent-minded professor in social situations. Over a drink with friends he would unconsciously eat an entire bowl of nuts on the coffee table, and Janet's personal secretary, Eleanor Thomas, regularly pinned notes to the clothes in his closet, reminding him that "the dark gray suit is necessary for Tuesday's meeting with Eden." She was also responsible for keeping him supplied with the detective stories he read for relaxation before going to sleep. One evening, some thirty minutes after he had come home from the office, changed into pajamas, and climbed into bed with a paperback mystery, an agitated Miss Thomas knocked on his door: "Mr. Secretary, the King of Thailand is downstairs for his meeting with you." [27]

The endless round of official white-tie dinners quickly palled on him, in part because the rigid rules of protocol seemed always to place him beside elderly cabinet wives, the limits of whose charm and intellect were quickly reached. One of his more or less constant companions was Jessie Wilson, wife of the Secretary of Defense and a lady of somewhat lumpish mind and body, whose napkin was constantly slipping to the floor (after several months, this awkward situation was finally remedied when Attorney General Brownell anchored it with a large safety pin).[28] In any event, Dulles soon asked his special assistant to see what could be done to enliven these leaden affairs, and a few weeks later O'Connor presented him with proposals worked up by the protocol division. The centerpiece was a guest list of rather glittering notables headed by Marlene Dietrich. Dulles scanned the list and cocked a quizzical eyebrow: "Rod," he said, "perhaps the department has gone too far." [29]

On one occasion, however, he had the good fortune to be seated beside the attractive Mrs. Thomas Gates, wife of the then Undersecretary of the Navy. But he was preoccupied, and began pulling the wax off the table candles and chewing it. The young Mrs. Gates, who had never met him and was somewhat apprehensive at such proximity to the formidable Secretary of State, found the courage to admonish him. "Now, Mr. Dulles, I scold my children for doing that; it's bad manners, and it messes up the tablecloth." The formidable Secretary gave her the look of a child caught with his hand in the cookie jar: "I know; it's awful, it's a terrible habit, but I just love to chew candle grease. I've done it all my life." Then they both laughed and got on swimmingly. A day or two later, Mrs. Gates bought two boxes of beeswax candles and shipped them to Duck Island where Dulles was spending the weekend. She received a note of thanks which read: "Dear Mrs. Gates: The candles arrived. They look good, they light good, and they chew good." [30]

The Inner Staff

With the appointment not only of Bedell Smith as Undersecretary, but also of Douglas MacArthur II as Counsellor, and Robert Murphy as Deputy Undersecretary for Political Affairs, Eisenhower gave at least the appearance of having arranged to surround Dulles with men whose loyalty to himself had been tested over a number of years. The apparent effort to recruit John J. McCloy as Undersecretary would fall into the same pattern. The appointment of Bedell Smith was interesting because it appeared to have come from Dulles's initiative,[31] and was not of particular interest to Smith. He was already the Director of the Central Intelligence Agency, and moving to the second place at State looked like being a slight demotion. When Eisenhower first asked him if he would like to play a part in the new administration, he had replied that "what I would like to do is get a fifth star and retire." [32] But there were to be no more fifth stars (they required special legislation), and Dulles was pressing to obtain his services.

Bedell Smith was a first-class staff officer, a tough and competent executive, and he had also been ambassador to Russia, all superb qualifications for the major administrative job at the State Department. But Dulles had still another reason for wanting him. Allen Dulles, who had become something of a spy master during World War II, operating out of Geneva for the OSS, was now Deputy Director of CIA. Moreover, as a condition of taking that job, he had exacted a promise from Bedell Smith that, in the event Smith departed CIA, he would recommend Allen as his successor. Smith, however, had developed reservations about Allen's administrative capacity and was worried at the prospect of leaving CIA in his hands. Therefore, after he decided that loyalty to Eisenhower required his own move to the State Department, he went to the President, told him of his promise to Allen and of his later reservations, and argued that in any event it would be impolitic to have the brother of the Secretary of State running the CIA. He then recommended another deputy, Lyman Kirkpatrick. His approach had apparently been anticipated. The President told him he had already discussed the matter with Foster

Dulles, who saw no problem at all, and, this being the case, he planned to appoint Allen Dulles as Director of CIA.[33]

Bedell Smith went to the State Department on the assumption that, as Undersecretary, he would serve as Dulles's chief of staff, sitting astride all the channels of command and communication, and serving as the screen for all people and papers reaching the Secretary. But Dulles refused any formal screen, decided what issues he wanted to handle personally, and passed the balance on to the regional Assistant Secretaries, using the Undersecretary primarily for the execution of matters that had been decided. As a result of this sharp difference in operational technique, there was initial tension between the two men.

Robert Murphy was an experienced professional diplomat who had gone through the war as Eisenhower's political adviser. Douglas MacArthur II, also a career diplomat and a nephew of the famous general, had played a similar role during Eisenhower's period at NATO. Dulles never placed more than limited confidence in Murphy as a policy thinker, but valued him as a seasoned and thoroughly reliable diplomatic operator. MacArthur, who served as principal planner and coordinator for major conferences and overseas trips, won the Secretary's increasing respect for his ability and sound judgment. MacArthur's wife, called Warvie, was the daughter of Truman's Vice-president, Alben Barkley of Kentucky. One evening after eight o'clock, with Dulles and MacArthur due to leave Washington within a few hours on a long overseas trip, MacArthur was still working feverishly on the "briefing books." He had just left Dulles's office to return to his own when an irate Mrs. MacArthur telephoned to give someone a piece of her mind about the intolerable working hours demanded by the State Department. By coincidence Dulles and his secretary picked up the phone simultaneously and Warvie, unaware she was speaking to the Secretary of State, proceeded to deliver an earful of remarkable barracks language, for which she was widely reputed. Dulles listened impassively, then hung up and called MacArthur on another phone: "Boy, I insist that you leave your office right away. Your homefront is crumbling." [34]

In addition, the inner staff came to include Livingstone Merchant, a capable if rather bland career officer who was chosen to be Assistant Secretary for European Affairs, and Walter Robertson, a courtly banker from Richmond who had served in China during World War II. In his bid for conservative support in the Congress, Dulles had asked for suggestions from Congressman Walter Judd of Minnesota, a former missionary in China and a staunch supporter of Chiang. Judd had recommended Robertson, who believed in the absolute rectitude of Chiang's cause and the absolute evil of Chinese Communism. When confronted a few years later by a CIA estimate of growing steel production in China, Robertson indignantly told the briefing officer that he must be wrong: "No regime as malevolent as the Chinese Communists could ever produce 5 million tons of steel." [35] O'Connor sensed that, while Dulles had great respect for Robertson, occasionally "Walter annoyed him terribly." [36]

Robert Bowie, whom Dulles recruited from the Harvard law faculty to be director of policy planning, played the role of chief devil's advocate (one aide called him "the paid hair shirt"). He served up a variety of "think pieces" to challenge the conventional wisdom and debated issues face to face with Dulles, displaying a sinewy mind that showed no particular deference to the position of Secretary of State. As Dulles relished a real argument when he respected his opponent, Bowie became an important catalyst on a range of major issues. The Dulles-Bowie arguments tended always to move around a central point: whether or not to be a little more forthcoming, a little more magnanimous, a little more accommodating — with Moscow, Peking, Cairo, London or Paris — than the immediate power realities required. By his own account, Dulles always took the hardest line.[37] Bowie's imagination and relative liberality, which he did not disguise, made him an increasing target for dark innuendo from absolutist cold warriors in the Pentagon (later, he and Admiral Radford each referred to the other as a "devilishly clever" man). He made a major personal contribution until his return to Harvard in 1957, but owing to Dulles's style, with its emphasis on one-man operations and short-term tactics, the planning staff as a whole, which had been the creative center of the Acheson State Department, fell progressively into disuse.

Dulles's closest and most valued colleague may have been Herman Phleger, the legal adviser of the department and a noted San Francisco lawyer. Both men were tough, pragmatic operators, quick to absorb a briefing and ready for adversary proceedings on short notice; and because Dulles fully trusted him, Phleger exerted an influence on matters well beyond the scope of his official position.

While he rejected a formal chain of command and refused any well-defined delegation of authority to his Undersecretary, Dulles also fought shy of organizing any coherent alternative system for managing the State Department. Jealous of his own time, he shunned meetings and was only with great difficulty persuaded to make himself regularly available to the regional Assistant Secretaries, each of whom carried wide and often urgent responsibilities in vast areas of the globe. This default on administration, the product of personality and lifelong habits, inevitably meant that the many and intricate parts of the sprawling department were left more or less to manage themselves as best they could. At the end of the first Eisenhower term, when the air was thick with criticism of Dulles's constant traveling and loose administrative grip, Dewey made a special effort to persuade him that he must "stay home more" and "take command of the State Department." [38] When Dulles replied that he had to attend major meetings abroad, Dewey told him: "Yes, but you've also got to survive and keep your own standing and influence. You will not be as useful to the President and the country if you lose them." Dulles did not disagree; "he was just puzzled over how he could accomplish it." [39]

Congressional and Public Relations

Dulles entered office with a strong sense of the need to develop and maintain a dialogue with Congress and the country that would provide the necessary public support for foreign policy. He judged rightly that, whatever the merits of the case, Acheson had lost his public base shortly after the collapse of Chiang Kai-shek in 1949, and that thereafter it had become somewhat academic to debate the wisdom of his policies; whether good or bad, they were unsupported by Congress and public opinion. Congressional demagogues charged Acheson and the State Department with iniquities ranging from "softness on Communism" to treason. His loyalty was frequently impugned and his resignation regularly demanded. Only Truman's total support kept him in office, and even that could not prevent the steady erosion of his effectiveness. Dulles was determined, above all else, to avoid a similar fate.

In an effort to ingratiate himself with the GOP panjandrums in Congress, he had gone rather a long way in the 1952 campaign to espouse their major frustrations and prejudices (not only those held by Senator Taft, but even those of men like Styles Bridges, William Jenner and Joseph McCarthy, who were wildly irrational in their opposition to the whole movement of events that had transformed America's relationship to the world since 1941). Dulles's shift of stance in the campaign had damaged his reputation for prudence and good judgment in internationalist circles; whether or not it had bought him effective protection from right-wing attack was a question yet to be answered. But having before him what Hans Morganthau called the "terrifying spectacle" of what had happened to Acheson, he judged the necessity of continuing to accommodate those who could hurt him most.

To cultivate the press and public opinion, he developed an elaborate set of arrangements — from press conferences open to all and cocktail parties open to a good many, to intimate dinners confined to a few key members of the Washington press corps — each type of meeting being notable, however, for the fact that it placed Dulles himself at the epicenter. He was his own press officer for all but the most mundane announcements, reporting to the American people from the State Department, from airport microphones in Paris or Bangkok, from luncheon rostrums and television studios in a garrulous outpouring of speeches, statements, and warnings. He seemed driven by a compulsion to dominate the moving public dialogue, as Churchill noted perceptively: "Mr. Dulles makes a speech every day, holds a press conference every other day, and preaches on Sundays. All this tends to rob his utterances of real significance." [40]

He considered the speeches, usually thirty minutes in length, his most important form of public communication, and they were always highly personal efforts written largely or entirely by himself. From the outset he resisted all proposals that he take on a speech writer, feeling that no one else could accurately reflect his own perspective on a particular issue, or his view of how it was woven into the fabric of wider situations. Moreover, he regarded each speech as an intellectual challenge, an important discipline forcing him to think through a problem and present it in simple, orderly language. As a result, he would spend three or four hours in the preparation of a draft acceptable for comment by others, and another twelve to fifteen hours on further editing, refining and redrafting. He could dictate a thirty-page draft in forty minutes, using three secretaries in rotation. By the time he had finished, the first ten pages would be ready to read (typed in triple-space), and he would turn immediately to marking them up and returning them page by page for revision. Working this way, he might go to a third or fourth draft in the space of three hours. When the result was judged acceptable, it would be circulated for comment — usually to Bedell Smith, Bowie, MacArthur, Merchant and Phleger within the department; to Robert Cutler at the National Security Council; to Wilson (but more often to Admiral Radford) at Defense; to Allen Dulles at CIA. Occasionally, an early draft would also go to the President, but Eisenhower's exposure to a Dulles speech usually occurred at a somewhat later stage.

Where planning was possible, the first draft was blocked out three weeks in advance of the speaking date, and Dulles would work through successive revisions of the text over weekends, a task which in his post-athletic years he considered a genuine recreation. As William Macomber (who succeeded O'Connor as special assistant) said, "It was what he liked to do best." Staff comments were duly considered, but he was more receptive to suggested shifts in emphasis than to specific changes of language. The average speech would go through ten or twelve drafts before Dulles sat down with the inner staff around his conference table to go over the final version page by page.

Technically, he did not speak well — his voice was flat, his delivery unanimated, his words occasionally slurred (he called himself the "Sek-katary of State"). But he spoke to very large audiences — 10 million people on national television — and his strong, simple sermons were heard and absorbed, even if sometimes subliminally. Listeners on the eastern seaboard were inclined to find his concepts overly simple and heavily draped in synthetic moralizing, but such judgments did not render them immune to the message. In other regions of the country, where piety and patriotism mingled more comfortably, he was far more favorably received.

In what seemed his one acknowledgment of need for specialized public relations advice, Dulles hired the Philadelphia newspaperman Carl McCardle. He valued his loyalty, but also believed him to possess an uncanny, wholly intuitive ability to predict public reaction to pieces of Dullesian copy destined for release. The basis for this belief was never revealed and was certainly not self-evident, for McCardle was painfully inarticulate in conversation, but Dulles apparently thought he was acquiring a journalistic divining rod. With characteristic indifference to administrative consequences, he appointed McCardle Assistant Secretary for Public Affairs, a position which involved responsibility for managing one of the largest and most sophisticated subempires in the State Department. Unfortunately, McCardle's managerial incompetence was at least as great as Dulles's own, and to complicate matters he had a drinking problem. Joseph C. Harsch of the *Christian Science Monitor* said, "It was too bad. I always thought Carl made an awful mistake in taking that job." [41] James Reston agreed, with equal gentleness, that "the McCardle thing was kind of a sad story . . . Foster was not as well served as he might have been." [42] Richard Rovere thought there "could scarcely have been a worse choice from the point of view of the press," and that reporters frequently had to do McCardle's work for him at conferences.[43] The consensus seemed to be that it was not an outstanding appointment.

Even at his instinctive specialty, McCardle drove Dulles crazy with an almost total inability to articulate his views. Asked to comment on a proposed speech, he might send it back with an inscription in red pencil: "This is no good." Called in to provide some more specific rationale for such a flat assertion, he would mumble incoherently. Dulles would then proceed to a merciless cross-examination in an effort to get to the bottom of the judgment. McCardle would stand in the middle of the room, inarticulate, miserable, perspiring, giving nonsensical answers, but refusing to budge from his basic position that the paper was "no good." Finally, in exasperation, Dulles would give in, throw the paper in the wastebasket, and turn away to pick up the telephone.[44] In view of his own rather marked inability to anticipate the public impact of several of his most carefully polished and cherished phrases, there was little doubt that Dulles needed assistance. On the doleful record of repeated mistakes, however, it is not clear that McCardle provided a great deal.

In his direct dealings with the press, Dulles was respected for his forensic skill, but was not much liked or trusted. Reston admired his knowledge and his precision: "He knew his brief. . . . And he'd put a subject and a predicate and an object together and then he stopped. He wasn't like his boss over in the White House. He spoke in sentences . . ." [45] But Reston also suspected "a wide streak of hypocrisy" reflected in the constant contradiction between the "very moralistic man" and the "very shrewd political and diplomatic operator." [46] Henry Brandon of the *London Times* thought no reporter was ever sure that Dulles was telling him the truth: "He told you 'something,' but he used the press." [47] David Schoenbrun of CBS felt that talking to Dulles was a chess game: "Acheson would either tell you or not tell you, but Dulles played games." He was brilliant, but clever and opportunistic with "a little bit of . . . Elmer Gantry in him." [48] Dulles was far more available to the press than Acheson had been and, in small groups and protected by the rule of nonattribution, he could be startlingly frank. He rather hoped the press liked him. On the whole, however, he encountered wary intellectual respect, but progressive emotional antipathy — after the first year, the press corps even refused to stand up when he entered the room for his press conferences. Yet whatever their reservations, Dulles was the absolutely indispensable source for reporters who covered foreign affairs during the Eisenhower years. He was the principal, indeed the sole, initiator of policy and the single keeper of all the ramifications, subtle interrelationships, and crucial details of America's far-flung dealings with the external world.

The Naked Foreign Service

O'Connor thought Dulles was "remarkably relaxed" about delegating authority when the task "wasn't on his list of priorities." [49] Personnel administration was one of those tasks, and there is no doubt that his determined inattention to it greatly facilitated the continuing savage assault on the career service by Senator Joseph McCarthy — and his henchmen in the Senate, the Hearst and McCormick press, and the China Lobby. Moreover, through his reluctance to antagonize the Republican right wing, he permitted the assault to be conducted not only from outside, but from inside the citadel itself by dedicated and implacable agents of the purge.

That McCarthy was in 1953 a formidable political power to be reck-oned with, no one could doubt, even though his influence was based almost solely on the national mood of anti-Communist hysteria. In whole or in part, he had engineered the defeat of two senior Democratic senators, Millard Tydings of Maryland and Scott Lucas of Illinois, in 1950, charging them with an attempt to "whitewash" his own investiga-tion of the State Department and the U.S. China policy. Exploiting the public outcry at General MacArthur's dismissal in 1951, he had put into the *Congressional Record* a 60,000 word attack on General Marshall (who was then Secretary of Defense), castigating Marshall's "affinity for Chinese Reds" and arguing that the crux of the "great debate" over military strategy in Asia was "whether we approve the judgment of General MacArthur or whether we intend to follow the appeasement policies as enunciated . . . by General Marshall." [50] The Republican leadership, while perhaps deploring McCarthy's rough-and-tumble meth-ods, was impressed by the public resonance that his thrusts produced. Their vote-getting power seemed exceptional. Thus, when even candi-date Eisenhower declined to defend his old friend and mentor against McCarthy, it was clear that the "Communist conspiracy" issue had be-come central to the GOP campaign. Richard Nixon promised in early September to make it "the theme of every speech from now until elec-tion." [51] In the fall of 1952, the GOP thus rather fully and officially embraced "McCarthyism," if not quite the senator himself. It was a decision which made for moral ambivalence in the aftermath.

Even granting that Dulles was more the victim than the creator of this highly charged atmosphere, his administrative carelessness regard-ing the fate of State Department people who then came under his juris-diction was rather remarkable. It was reflected in two early appoint-ments. As previously noted, Donald Lourie, the president of the Quaker Oats Company, was appointed Undersecretary of State for Administra-tion, a position raised in authority and prestige at Dulles's specific urging, so that he himself might be wholly freed of cloying detail. As the chief operating officer of a large corporation, Lourie appeared to be a man of broad competence and judgment, and Dulles accepted him at face value. He turned out to be a quiet disaster. Innocent of politics, noncombative, compliant, awed by Dulles's intellect and personality, Lourie was totally bewildered by the vicious political whirlwinds kicked up in the bitter struggle between those angry Republican forces who demanded a "clean out" of the State Department and those who fought to preserve the integrity of a scarred career service. Like a number of others on the scene in those nightmare months, Lourie seemed hyp-notized by the awesome unfolding of Senator McCarthy's ruthless ingenuity, each day revealing some previously unimagined depth of malignant intent. Transfixed, he never got his bearings. But he had in any event impaled himself and the department in the very first days by hiring as his deputy for personnel security a henchman from the enemy camp. Like Lourie's own appointment, the hiring of Scott McLeod was an act combining innocence with inadvertence. Lourie lived in Chicago and knew absolutely no one in Washington. One evening he dined with a Chicago business acquaintance who happened to be a former member of the FBI; the man suggested that Scott McLeod might be helpful. When Lourie arrived in Washington, he got in touch with McLeod, liked his looks, and hired him on the spot.[52]

Scott McLeod was a former FBI agent and former reporter for the powerful right-wing *Union-Leader* in Manchester, New Hampshire, published by William Loeb. He had worked in the campaigns of Senator Styles Bridges, a close McCarthy collaborator, and was in fact administrative assistant to Bridges at the time Lourie hired him. As might have been expected, he was violently anti-Communist; he was also simplistic, anti-intellectual, shrewd, conspiratorial, quick-tempered, vindictive, and a hopeless administrator.[53] As another Dulles assistant, John Hanes, said of him, "Scotty lived in an essentially simple world" and was "accident prone whenever he opened his mouth." [54] This was the man chosen to install a personnel security system that would, by identifying and dealing with real cases of measurable disloyalty and breaches of security, thereafter permit the new Secretary of State to defend the vast majority of loyal and competent departmental officers and employees against malicious and unfounded charges.

In a true sense, however, these appointments were only aggravations of a basic condition, for no one in the new administration appeared to have foreseen the swiftness or severity of McCarthy's attack on the State Department. The prevailing belief was that Eisenhower's election had more or less automatically cut away any legitimate grounds for suspicion that "Communist sympathizers" would henceforward be tolerated in the making of foreign policy, and that Congress would leave the matter in the President's hands. But this view was too reasonable; it grossly underestimated the sheer primitive ferocity of the GOP right wing and its bitter distrust of Eisenhower's internationalism. Almost as soon as Dulles reached office, heavy political seas driven by hurricane winds were upon him, and the instinctive reaction of the "rough weather sailor" was to assure his own survival whatever the cost. Faced with the need to decide several prominent security cases — including those of John Carter Vincent and John Paton Davies — Dulles read through the voluminous dossiers and reached the firm conclusion that, contrary to McLeod's urging, no finding of disloyalty or breach of security could be substantiated. To reinstate them, however, meant defying very powerful Republican forces

"I Hear There's Something Wrong With Your Morale"

From *Herblock's Here and Now*
SIMON & SCHUSTER, 1955

who had repeatedly charged them with a conspiracy to destroy Chiang Kai-shek and bring the Communists to power in China. In reality, these men were on trial for their objective judgment that Chiang was a corrupt, nonviable force and that Mao represented the future in China. But their accusers were not interested in reason; they demanded blood sacrifices. Dulles met the problem with tactical ingenuity and cold calculation.

Finding that Vincent was neither disloyal nor a security risk, he dismissed him from the Foreign Service on the grounds that his "reporting of the facts, evaluation of the facts, and policy advice during the period under review show a failure to meet the standard which is demanded of a Foreign Service officer of his experience and responsibility at this critical time." [55] His ruling thus turned on the conclusion that Vincent's professional judgment fell below a certain standard which was "demanded" but which he, Dulles, nowhere defined. John Paton Davies had undergone nine separate security investigations before a panel could be formed that was ready to pronounce him a security risk. In reviewing that case, Dulles again altered the finding, but dismissed him for "disregard of proper forbearance and caution in making known his dissents outside privileged boundaries." [56] In less lofty language, John Hanes said that the Secretary had cleared these men on loyalty and security grounds, but fired them for "bad judgment and stupidity." [57]

George Kennan, whose name was synonymous with the containment policy, had inadvertently nettled Dulles by making a speech in Scranton (on January 15, 1953) that denigrated the wisdom of a policy of "liberation." The speech was reported in the press on the same day that Dulles went to the Senate committee for his confirmation hearing. He was not pleased, but the incident served merely to underscore a deep-seated philosophical and personal antipathy between the two men. In July 1950, just after the outbreak of the Korean War, Kennan had urged in closed meetings of the top State Department staff that the United States should (1) make clear its intention to stop military operations at the 38th parallel and (2) interpose no obstacles to Chinese Communist membership in the United Nations, if there was a "majority feeling in the UN that they ought to be there." [58] At the same time he expressed his view that the United States should not sponsor such a move and should not itself grant diplomatic recognition to Peking. In the meetings, Dulles opposed him on the UN membership question, arguing that public opinion would not support greater military expenditures unless Communist China were clearly categorized as an enemy. Kennan said he could understand the force of Dulles's point, but "shuddered" at its implication, for it assumed that "we could not adopt an adequate defense position without working our people up into an emotional state," and that future American policy in Asia would accordingly have to be based on "an emotional anti-

Communism." A week later, he learned Dulles had told at least one newspaperman that he now regarded Kennan as "a dangerous man." [59]

Kennan had been ambassador to Russia during most of 1952, but in December the Soviet authorities chose to take offense at certain unflattering statements he had made concerning the confined life of a foreign diplomat in Moscow. They declared him persona non grata, and he was accordingly back in Washington as the new administration took office. As a career minister, he would be automatically retired from the diplomatic service unless he received a new assignment within three months. It soon became apparent that Dulles intended to let time run its course, which would mean closing out several decades of Kennan's distinguished service without even the courtesy of an acknowledgment. Sherman Adams and Emmet Hughes at the White House, having gotten wind of this calculated insult, arranged such comfort as was possible by having Eisenhower send a warm and appreciative letter to the condemned and departing diplomat. [60]

By offering up these sacrifices to Republican idols in the Senate, Dulles sought to satisfy what he judged to be the cold political imperatives of the situation, and thus to secure his own personal position against attack. He was without question in circumstantial difficulties, and could hardly proceed as though the 1952 election had not taken place. Moreover, Eisenhower's curious but determined adherence to a theory of the separation of powers (between executive and legislative branches) that might have sprung full-blown from the pages of a high school textbook further inhibited active resistance. The President would not interfere with the inherent congressional power to investigate, even if this meant — as it surely did in the McCarthy case — a refusal to defend against encroachment upon the presidential power to conduct foreign policy. Eisenhower's attitude thus reinforced Dulles's own deep-seated instinct for prudence, yet could hardly excuse his conspicuous failure to provide any protection to hundreds of State Department employees whose reputations and careers were savaged by the witch-hunt.

The purpose of Executive Order 10450 (signed by Eisenhower on April 27, 1953) was to provide adequate safeguards for the government against violations of "loyalty and security"; it was also a device to protect the new administration against further McCarthy attacks by demonstrating that it was itself dealing responsibly with the problem. But the aim of the Republican right-wing was far more ambitious. Based on frustrations and suspicions of twenty years, it was to root out all the "middle-aged New Dealers" who, having come into government with Franklin Roosevelt via NRA or WPA or during the war years, had gravitated to the State Department where they were now protected by the career systems of the Foreign Service and the civil service. Nor was this a view confined to

Republicans in the Congress. Within the new administration the natural political instinct to throw the rascals out was widely felt, though in varying degrees of intensity; and for many reasons, the impulse focused principally on removing the "architects of disaster" in the State Department. As John Hanes reasoned it, "We felt that there was an overwhelming predominance of, let us say, Democratic as opposed to Republican thinking in the Department," [61] and that it was both legitimate and necessary to change this. Merely to change the President and a few top people around him would be to cheat the electorate.

Dulles's expectations from a new security system were probably not far-reaching. He wanted chiefly to tranquilize the opposition in Congress, as a means of protecting his own position so that he could get on with the main business of making foreign policy. Confident that he could carry on the substantive work with a handful of loyal colleagues, he did not overly concern himself with questions of competence and morale as they applied throughout the ranks and reaches of the department. And that being the case, he was essentially indifferent to the danger that an all-embracing security system might breed conformity and mediocrity and dry up the creative wellsprings of the career service. It was a curiously insensitive posture for one who professed to be a staunch defender of human liberty. But, judging that McLeod's FBI background provided adequate professional credentials for a delicate task, and regarding his link to Senator Bridges as a political plus, Dulles chose to conclude that personnel matters were well in hand, permitting him to concentrate on the substance of policy.

McLeod, however, shared the wider aims of Senators McCarthy, Bridges and Jenner, and was soon applying "loyalty and security" procedures to a large number of people whose records indicated neither disloyalty nor breach of security. He and his hastily assembled staff of some 350 inexperienced but zealous investigators quickly identified several hundred Foreign Service officers as drunkards, homosexuals, incompetents, or "incompatibles" (a flexible category that included those whose past, present or prospective policy judgments were displeasing to the Republican right-wing and to McLeod). Asked, at one of his many speaking appearances before Republican audiences, to define a "security risk," McLeod replied with a laugh that "not *all* New Dealers are necessarily security risks." [62] But the "loyalty and security" framework of the executive order was in fact technically too narrow to accommodate McLeod's political purpose, and he acknowledged the problem. Speaking to the American Legion at Topeka in the summer of 1953, he said it was "extremely difficult" owing to civil service and Foreign Service regulations, and the Veterans Preference Act, "to replace an individual whose viewpoint does not coincide with that of the Republican Party." [63] He did not, however, say it was impossible. The result was that a very large number of what John Hanes termed "simple personnel actions" were incorrectly "rammed into that pattern." [64]

In an atmosphere of hysterical anti-Communism, largely created and sustained by McCarthy and his rooters, but neither checked nor effectively challenged by the White House, it was an easy matter to force resignations using the threat of dismissal on loyalty or security grounds. The evidence did not need to be conclusive; the implied threat of a leak to the McCarthy committee, carrying with it the certainty of public branding as a homosexual, "com-symp," "dupe," or worse, was usually sufficient. For the man thus branded, there was no protection. His public career was finished; even his ability to secure private employment was in grave doubt. Dulles was sporadically concerned by McLeod's excess of zeal, and "really used to get boiled off at him sometimes," [65] which led McLeod, who wanted to go much further, to Irish despondency and complaints that the Secretary didn't understand him. But owing to Dulles's helpless impatience with "administrative work" and his unwavering instinct to avoid antagonizing the right wing, no remedial action was taken. The quiet reign of terror, conducted as a collaboration between McLeod and McCarthy's committee, burned its deadly way through the State Department for nearly two years, immolating along the way the careers of several hundred officers and employees.

The Bohlen Appointment

On at least one occasion, however, McLeod almost went too far. Charles E. Bohlen, a distinguished Foreign Service officer, Roosevelt's translator at Yalta, and an admired friend of the new President, was personally chosen by Eisenhower to succeed George Kennan as ambassador to Russia. McLeod, charged with running a security check, reluctantly reported to Dulles that there were no grounds for withholding a clearance under Executive Order 10450, but he went on to argue that Bohlen ought to be dismissed for "other reasons" relating to his judgments of Soviet policy and his role at Yalta.[66] Meanwhile, Dulles was conferring nervously with Bohlen, who candidly anticipated difficulties in the Senate and told the Secretary: "I was afraid I was not going to be able to give a version of events [at Yalta] that would be exactly in harmony with the Republican platform." [67] Dulles expressed the hope that Bohlen could finesse the substantive controversy by stating he had acted merely as an interpreter, but Bohlen demurred. Dulles then asked him "very definitely" if there was anything in his record that might prove an embarrassment. Bohlen gave him "the requisite assurances," to which he

With President Eisenhower and Ambassador-designate to Moscow,
Charles E. Bohlen (April 2, 1953)

replied: "I'm glad to hear this. I couldn't stand another Alger Hiss." [68]
At his confirmation hearing, Bohlen forthrightly defended the Yalta
Agreements, placing the blame for evil consequences on blatant Soviet
violations, and denying the existence of "secret understandings . . .
which aid Communist enslavements," as charged in the Republican
campaign platform. His testimony caused "a certain amount of consternation in the Republican Party," [69] and deepened the moral dilemma for
Dulles, who had written the party platform.

Not content with his advice to Dulles, McLeod went directly to the
White House staff to argue that Bohlen's appointment would be a "public
relations risk" owing to his role at Yalta. Met there by Sherman Adams,
who showed surprise and anger at "his unmitigated gall," McLeod moved
undaunted to tell his former mentor, Senator Bridges, that Bohlen's
record contained "derogatory information." [70] Shortly thereafter (March
20), Senator Pat McCarran of Nevada, a McCarthy supporter, rose on the
Senate floor to charge that McLeod had been "unable to clear" Bohlen
"on the basis of information received from the FBI"; moreover, that
McLeod had been "summarily overridden" by Dulles. When the Secretary
of State denied this, McCarthy accused him of lying. [71] The nomination

was suddenly in doubt. As Bohlen was the President's personal choice for a major diplomatic post, Dulles was now confronted with a problem that could not be evaded. Recognizing what had to be done, and applying himself with characteristic energy, he studied the Bohlen file in detail, then invited two leading senators, Taft and Sparkman, to share this information at a meeting in his office. For six hours, Dulles led them painstakingly through the voluminous material, and the next day they both publicly supported his statement to the Foreign Relations Committee that Bohlen's record was fully compatible with the proposed appointment. Confronted by such heavy artillery, "McCarthy never dared open his yap." [72] At the same time, Senator Taft, who disliked expending his political capital in intraparty fights, sent word to the White House that he wanted "no more Bohlens." [73]

For his performance on this occasion, McLeod (whose desk was adorned by a photograph of Senator McCarthy inscribed "To a great American") was nearly fired by Dulles. The Secretary was apparently ready to act on the morning after McCarran's charge, but was dissuaded by Bedell Smith, who felt the President did not want an open break with the right wing.[74] The picture of the testy, short-fused Undersecretary restraining the cold, calculating Secretary from an angry and impulsive act is not easy to imagine.

Until the nomination was absolutely secured, however, Dulles displayed acute nervousness and did not exclude the possibility of recommending to Eisenhower that Bohlen's name be withdrawn. En route in an automobile to a second hearing of the Foreign Relations Committee, Bohlen recalled that Dulles "asked me not to be photographed with him." [75] And after the nomination, he worried over Bohlen's plan to fly to Moscow a week or two ahead of his family, telling Bohlen with cold unsubtlety that such a circumstance could open him to veiled charges of homosexuality, no matter how baseless such charges might be.[76] Such was the measure of hysteria and malevolence in the Washington air in the spring of 1953. The relationship between the two men was never confident or trusting, but Bohlen left Washington in April with the strong impression that Dulles was a man who lived in mortal terror that events would conspire to turn the McCarthy attack on him, that "so strong were his preoccupations with his job and staying in it, that this affected his attitudes and actions" in nearly every realm. Dulles was a man with "one obsession: to remain Secretary of State." [77]

11

Policy Beginnings

(PART ONE)

A s DULLES ENTERED OFFICE in January 1953, his major thoughts and plans about policy seemed to be carried on the rushing streams of heady campaign rhetoric, not least of all his own. The essence of the struggle he now entered as a major commander was, as he judged it, neither political nor economic, but moral — a clash of universalist faiths that was by its nature only marginally, if at all, susceptible to negotiation or compromise. In his maiden address of January 27 (which three of the four Washington newspapers criticized, the conservative *Evening Star* calling it a piece of gross "oversimplification"), he defined the framework in which he would be operating. "We have enemies who are plotting our destruction. . . . Any American who isn't awake to that fact is like a soldier who's asleep at his post." [1] Communists "completely dominate" a vast area from "Kamchatka near Alaska, [to] the northern islands of Japan, and right on to Germany in the center of Europe." In that area, "800 million people . . . are being forged into a vast weapon of fighting power backed by industrial production and modern weapons that include atomic bombs." [2]

He inveighed against Communism in stark terms because he believed the threat was real, but also because he believed that, unless the warning were blood-curdling in its effect, the American people would "let down their guard"; worse still, that powerful Republican Neanderthals would attack him for being "soft on Communism." But while it was inherently difficult to separate the elements of conviction, manipulation, and self-protection in his posture, it seems clear that conviction formed the bedrock. Marxism-Leninism was, he believed, a well-articulated creed embraced by the whole of the Communist hierarchy, both in the Kremlin and outside Russia, and there was little place in his thought for the view that a shift of individual leaders would make any significant difference. Stalinism was a normative manifestation, and the free world must accordingly be girded for ceaseless battle until the vicious system was finally subdued. His basic approach was to develop a policy of unrelenting counterpressure designed not merely to prevent further Communist advance, but to keep the adversary off balance, deprive it of the outside resources presumed necessary to its industrial growth, deny it moral acceptability in the eyes of respectable nations, and thereby arrange its decline and ultimate collapse.

This could be described as a policy of "containment plus," differing from the basic Truman-Acheson strategy chiefly in its urge to be more activist, not merely "for" the free nations but "against" the Communist adversary. The rhetorical decibel count was also a good deal higher, which reflected in some large part Dulles's judgment that public support would quickly go slack unless it were continually pulled taut by emotional reminders of imminent danger. (In *War, Peace and Change,* he had written that "unfortunately" the social cohesion of one group depends upon the existence of external enemies, and he had later deplored Roosevelt's efforts to arouse the American people to the Hitler threat as "mass emotion on a substantial scale." By 1953, however, he appeared to be thoroughly convinced that this was a necessary technique of statecraft.) There was no detailed blueprint for the new approach — Dulles was inherently a tactical operator — but as 1953 unfolded, American foreign policy was tranlated into four main lines of action: (1) to prevent any reduction in East-West tensions, (2) to unify Western Europe, (3) to erect anti-Communist defenses in the Middle East, and (4) to achieve an armistice in Korea while avoiding a general Asian settlement.

The European Defense Community

The scheme for an integrated European army had begun as the Pleven Plan in mid-1951, named for the French defense minister who put it forward as a hasty rejoinder to the Anglo-American demand for immediate West German rearmament. That basic decision by Washington and London had been a strategic response to the Chinese Communist entrance into the Korean War (and to inconclusive evidence that the Russians were creating an East German army). At what seemed a deadly peril point in the cold war (the Communist adversary having demonstrated a readiness to use open force), President Truman had called upon General Eisenhower, who was resting quietly in the groves of academe, to return to Europe, take command of NATO, by his presence restore

Greeting Chancellor Adenauer at Washington Airport,
with Vice President Nixon (April 7, 1953)

a shaky European morale, and begin the rebuilding of respectable military power on the Continent. Western Europeans seemed prepared to undertake a serious defense effort, but the demand for German rearmament had shocked them, even as they were forced to concede, in logic, that an effective European defense was unlikely without a German contribution. Fear of a German military revival was deeply felt and not confined to France. At a 1951 meeting at Claridge's Hotel in London, Konrad Adenauer, the staunch democratic leader of still-occupied West Germany, told Paul-Henri Spaak of Belgium and Joseph Bech of Luxembourg: "It is grotesque that I am being forced to create a German national army again . . . . We must not resign ourselves, we must not capitulate to nationalism. We must use every possibility to unify Europe." [3] Thus the Pleven Plan (which became the European Defense Community) was a desperate counterproposal to buy time for debate and modification of the Anglo-American demand.

By the time Dulles came into office, the six governments in question (France, Germany, Italy and Benelux) had initialed an EDC treaty, but none of their parliaments had yet ratified it, and popular opposition seemed to be gathering. Influenced by his good friend Jean Monnet,

Dulles had long believed that the "world's worst fire hazard" must not be rebuilt on the old foundation of "rickety national structures," and he thus made EDC the heart of his European policy. It was to be another vital building block — to be placed beside the Coal and Steel Community, the Council of Ministers and the Consultative Assembly — in what must become the sturdy edifice of the supranational European system. Noting in his maiden speech that "the plan now seems to be somewhat stalled," [4] he promptly flew to Paris to push it forward.

Aside from the gracelessness of his encounters with senior American diplomats, that first European trip was notable for the sheer intensity of willpower he applied to the discouraging prospects for EDC. Gathering all the mission chiefs or their deputies at a meeting in the American embassy in Paris, and after rather curtly paraphrasing his expectation of "positive loyalty," he stressed the absolute necessity for full ratification of EDC within six months. Then he listened with mounting distaste to a lucid but somber assessment of the German paliamentary situation by Samuel Reber, the American deputy in Bonn, and to the even more depressing estimate of the French situation from Ambassador James Dunn. One participant remembered that Dulles glared intently at Reber as though he were blaming the messenger for bearing bad news.[5] Julius Holmes, the American Minister in London, advised that, while the British supported EDC in principle, the extent of their support was problematical and they would flatly refuse to join. At the end of the meeting, Dulles told the assembled diplomats that EDC was so urgent a necessity, so fundamental a goal of United States policy, that they were not to tolerate any discussion of alternatives within their embassies, nor to admit in their dealings with European officials and the press that alternatives even existed.[6] This instruction reflected the effort of a powerful idealist to harness power to a specific ideal and thereby bring it to life in the real world. It was a noble effort, yet in the end self-defeating: by binding so ramified a question in an unnatural diplomatic straitjacket for the next eighteen months, Dulles left the whole Western Alliance adrift and without a coherent fallback position when the final collapse came. It was then left to Anthony Eden, in a remarkable diplomatic tour de force, to pick up the pieces and put together a workable alternative.

French ratification was crucial for EDC, but the French were a troubled people, deeply divided by an inability to define a postwar role that was at once satisfying to the national ego and financially sustainable; they were, moreover, gnawed by a sense of weakness and a continuing fear of Germany. Abroad, their government was attempting to maintain an essentially unchanged hold over colonial territories at a time when colonial peoples everywhere were ready to fight for their independence, and when the exertions required for a French policy of suppression served primarily to underline the economic backwardness and political weakness of metropolitan France. But while France was thus beset by contradiction and self-doubt, West Germany across the Rhine was building a healthy and bustling new society on the ghastly ruins of the old. Stripped of both the honors and burdens of their former empire, the West Germans were developing their economy, expanding their exports, and emerging as the major creditor nation of Europe. The French people, in a state of emotional agitation over what seemed the profound unfairness of life, balked at EDC because it both threatened the disappearance of the French army (which was a national symbol dear to the hearts of even the most unmilitary Frenchmen) and forced them into intimate military collaboration with a feared and hated neighbor. The uncertainty of British military support for the enterprise further fed French anxiety, for it opened the appalling prospect that, if Britain defaulted, they would once again be left alone on the Continent with an uncaged German tiger.

A month before Dulles arrived in Paris, Premier René Mayer, who had newly come to office with the open support of anti-integrationist followers of General de Gaulle, had asked for "clarifications" of EDC that were in fact so far-reaching as to require renegotiation of the treaty. The amendments were aimed at retaining for France a large measure of control over the French army, particularly the right to withdraw French forces from EDC for emergency use within the French Union (i.e., Indochina and North Africa). But they also sought a tighter promise from Britain to maintain substantial military forces on the Continent, and the permanent separation of the Saar territory from Germany and its transference to "European" status (which amounted to French economic control). Although these were stiff demands, the five other treaty powers addressed them seriously, and by mid-June had conceded all that was in their authority. All five powers granted Paris the right to withdraw French troops under certain emergency conditions. And the Germans, although affronted by French insistence on the Saar question, were willing to pay a high price to end the Allied occupation and restore West German sovereignty, which were linked features of the EDC proposals. Moreover, Adenauer, who strongly supported EDC, pressed the Bundestag to a favorable vote on ratification (on March 19) after a bitter debate. Of the conditions asked by France, only the matter of a stronger British commitment remained unresolved by mid-1953. Yet French reluctance was unaffected.

Dulles and Eden

But now in early February Dulles flew from Paris to London for talks with a British government still far from ready to merge its institutions with those on the Continent, and indeed in active resistance to the construction of a supranational Europe.

Beyond a lack of political foresight that was later to prove painful (when Britain, having scorned the Treaty of Rome in 1955, was later refused entrance to the Common Market by De Gaulle's curt veto), the negative British position in 1953 appeared to reflect something more than traditional Foreign Office ambivalence toward Europe. A significant factor was Prime Minister Churchill's passionate hope to reestablish the special Anglo-American intimacy that had been at the heart of all planning and action in the wartime Western Alliance. With his old comrade-in-arms now established at the center of American power, the hope must have seemed tantalizingly real. But the world had moved swiftly onward since 1945, creating a wider discrepancy of power between the United States and Britain than had existed (or than had seemed to exist) during the war years. And while the gap had been partially camouflaged during the Truman-Acheson period by Washington's dedication to genuinely collective efforts, it was soon to be exposed by Dulles's rather different approach; for Dulles was, as a consequence both of Versailles and of his international law practice, oriented to the Continent, to the problems of France and Germany, rather than to Britain. He had played no official role in the Second World War. More to the point, as one historian wrote, he "never went through the experience of that peculiarly close wartime partnership with the British," [7] which was so formative an experience for Eisenhower (as for Marshall, Harriman, Lovett, Forrestal, McCloy, et al.).

What Dulles saw when he came to office was that Europe's urgent need was integration and that Britain opposed this; that British power was in serious decline, while America's superiority was indisputable; that this established a power relationship in which Washington needed to pay no special attention to London's views or sensitivities in formulating policies for the future. The judgment was accurate enough as to the facts. It was Dulles's readiness to proceed from blunt analysis to blunt action, unsoftened by ties of sentiment, that dashed whatever element of reality remained in Churchill's dream of reestablishing the "inner club." The tragedy for the British was that, holding out hope where there was none, they put themselves in a rather false position.

When Dulles arrived in London on February 3, however, a discussion of EDC had to be deferred, for it was first necessary to deal with the running Anglo-American differences over China. Eisenhower had delivered his first State of the Union Message the previous day and, even as Dulles put down at the London airport, Eden was trying to soothe a House of Commons angered by the passage that "unleashed" Chiang Kai-shek by changing the orders of the Seventh Fleet. Since the outbreak of the Korean War, its mission had been to interpose itself in the Formosa Strait as an obstacle to hostilities initiated by either side. Now Eisenhower had asserted there was no "logic or sense" in having the United States any longer assume "defensive responsibilities on behalf of the Chinese Communists . . . a nation fighting us in Korea." [8] Like other informed and experienced men, Eden was less worried that this pronouncement would lead to serious Nationalist Chinese operations against the mainland than that it would, as he told the Commons, "have unfortunate political repercussions without compensating military advantages." [9] It was, as he saw it, a mischievous device, deliberately employed to please the China Lobby by seeming to reopen the Chinese civil war. And he probably judged that Dulles was the mastermind behind the ploy. After his arrival, however, Dulles was able to persuade Eden to make a further statement, assuring the Commons that "grave events" would not necessarily follow from the President's new orders to the fleet and that, in any event, Her Majesty's Government would be fully consulted. He may have told Eden that one purpose of the ploy was to increase the pressure on mainland China for an early settlement in Korea.

Eden gratified his guest by agreeing that EDC was indispensable and that London fully supported it short of direct British participation. This latter was a helpful, even handsome reassurance in the circumstances, for the British Foreign Office had been quite affronted by the passage in Dulles's maiden speech that threatened to give "a little rethinking" to basic American relations with Europe "if . . . France, Germany, and England should go their separate ways." [10] The implication here was that both Marshall Plan aid and the U.S. commitment to NATO had been based on the condition that Europe, including Britain, must quickly achieve institutional unity. The implication having no basis in fact, the British took it unkindly as a dishonest form of pressure.[11] In this first meeting, Dulles tried to put his best foot forward in an earnest effort to lay to rest the widely expressed British displeasure at his appointment. But despite his efforts, and Eden's reciprocal gestures of goodwill, there was tension in the relationship from the outset. Dulles was obviously vexed to find not only that his campaign hyperbole had created mistrust, but

With Eden at the White House (June 1954)

that his first official policy speech had apparently deepened it. Try as they might, Dulles and Eden were probably doomed to mutual misunderstanding and dislike, for they were utterly different kinds of men.

In appearance and style, Eden was the quintessential upper-class Englishman, with a calculatedly languid manner to match the elegance of his tailoring and the perfection of his cravat. He was handsome. He was brilliant. He had studied Oriental languages at Oxford, with emphasis on Persian; he had also studied Arabic and the Koran. Like many seasoned diplomats, his judgments tended to be rather intuitive, based on long experience, and he was in any case not very receptive to lengthy and didactic dissertation. Dulles was surely a contrasting study in his green-hued suits, indifferent neckwear, and garterless socks. He hunched slightly forward when he talked and showed a tendency to slur his words (he called Eden "Ant-ny"), and was chronically afflicted with bad breath. More intellectual, more legalistic, more insistently logical, less experienced than Eden, he was given to droning, slow-motion monologues, which carried him and his listeners (always with painful care and precision, occasionally with impressive sweep) down the winding path of his thought. In this first meeting, according to his special assistant, "it was quite obvious that [Dulles] was carefully weighing every word and putting it down on the table exactly next to the last word." [12] But Eden, whose own speech was "all flowing rose petals," [13] was temperamentally incapable of following Dulles's every labored step through the logical forest. He half listened and, at the end, often turned the conversation in ways that seemed to depreciate or wholly ignore many of the subtler points in the Secretary of State's dissertation.

At this first set of meetings, the talk turned to the Middle East and more particularly to Egypt, where Britain was beginning the painful negotiation of its withdrawal from the major military base at Suez. Eden referred passingly to the treaty of 1936, an instrument running for twenty years and which constituted Britain's legal right to maintain military forces in Egypt. The pre-Nasser Egyptian government had unilaterally abrogated the treaty in October 1951, amid riots and bloodshed, but had been unable to achieve any practical result in the face of British military power based at Suez. Dulles asked to see a copy of the document. The British side of the table seemed much taken by surprise at this request, and there ensued an embarrassing half-hour's search by Eden's private secretary before the document was finally produced. Dulles, in his formidable lawyer's manner, locked onto it, quickly devoured it line by line, and then turned to a blunt cross-examination of the Foreign Secretary, discovering that Eden was imprecisely informed on a number of details. From this he drew the sharp and rather too hasty conclusion that Eden ran a slipshod operation and did not personally do his homework. It was the beginning of his growing contempt for Eden's ability.[14] On the other side, Eden thought Dulles's mania for legal detail was irrelevant in the context of a general discussion, and resented his overbearing manner. The incident, which foreshadowed more consequential friction between the two men over Indochina and Suez, was also rich in ironies, not the least of them being that Eden had personally negotiated the treaty in question and was widely regarded as the "official in politics" with the rather narrow talents of a technician. Dulles, on the other hand, was considered by admirers as a seminal thinker with the wide-ranging perspectives of a statesman, unconfined by detailed staff papers. At the 1948 UN General Assembly meeting in Paris, for example, he had enlivened an interview with Henry Brandon of the *London Times* by tossing a large stack of staff-written "position papers" high into the air and exclaiming "words, words, words," as they fluttered to the floor beside his desk.[15]

Opposition to Détente

The pervasive intensity of the Stalinist threat was, in early 1953, the dominating fact in every capital of the world. From the perspective of official Washington, moreover, it seemed that the malignant qualities of the Soviet system were heavily institutionalized and would not be much affected by the passing of one chieftain. Thus, when Stalin died rather suddenly on March 4, U.S. diplomats and intelligence experts expected the new Soviet regime to move cautiously and with a careful concern not to repudiate the recent past. But in his oration at Stalin's funeral, the new premier, Georgi Malenkov, stressed "peaceful coexistence and competition," and soon thereafter declared the categorical need for the world (not merely the Communist system) to avoid global war; he also hinted at a major shift in Soviet economic allocations away from heavy war-supporting industries and toward measures aimed at raising the levels of public consumption. Eisenhower found these statements to be "startling departures from the ways of his predecessor." [16]

Stalin's death, the ensuing evidence of both flexibility and weakness in the new Soviet government, and the question of how the United States should respond uncovered in fact a significant difference of instinct and feeling between the President and his Secretary of State. It became clear that Eisenhower stood instinctively on the side of hope, seeing the new situation as an opportunity for renewed appeal to the common aspirations of mankind, while Dulles stood sternly on the side of moral rectitude, seeing enhanced opportunity for a policy of pressure. Eisenhower found in the Malenkov speeches a signal that a forthcoming American response might just possibly reduce suspicions and lead to a climate in which rational negotiation was possible. Dulles read them as evidence of weakness and uncertainty in the Kremlin, indicating that it was time to apply the thumbscrews. On March 20, he told a press conference, "I can say we have evaluated these speeches, but we do not receive any great comfort." [17] And he said later to the President, "What they are doing is because of outside pressures, and I don't know anything better we can do than to keep up those pressures right now." [18] On March 24, while acknowledging "a certain softening" in Soviet language and behavior, he argued, in remarks before the White House Conference for the Advertising Council, that the key to understanding such gestures was to be found in *Problems of Leninism*. He then proceeded to read from the chapter on "tactical retreats," and ended by declaring the Soviets were now engaged in a "peace offensive" because they feared "the forces of disintegration at work within the Soviet empire." [19] He was girded for, indeed seemed temperamentally to require, uncompromising struggle against a Communism whose goal was total conquest of the world in the most literal and physical sense. Stalin was capable of making such a goal seem real, as his successors were not. In an important sense, Stalin did Dulles a philosophical and practical disservice by dying, but Dulles retaliated by continuing to act as though the death had not occurred.

By late March, however, Eisenhower was seriously considering some public acknowledgment of this major political event and some reflections on what it could mean for the world. As he told his favorite speech writer, Emmet Hughes, he and everyone else were tired of "just plain indictments of the Soviet regime"; indeed it would be "asinine" for him to get up before the world and deliver another one. The main question, he thought, was what the United States was prepared to offer by way of a positive approach, in a new situation, to the overriding problem of peace.[20] He went on, with Hughes's encouragement, to develop the idea of making an appeal to the new Soviet leadership. He would assert America's belief that security could not be found in the amassing of armaments, for an arms race would lead "at worst, to atomic warfare. At best, to robbing every people and nation on earth of the fruits of their own toil . . ." [21] He would express an earnest American desire for cooperation and détente, and he would regard even a few "clear and specific acts" of reciprocation as "impressive signs" that the new men in the Kremlin shared this desire.[22] Dulles had serious objections to such an approach, but sensing the President's strong attraction to it and being at an early stage in their relationship, he confined himself to oblique expression of his doubts. Such an approach, he told Eisenhower, would show that the United States was taking the baited hook of a new Communist "peace offensive," a hook concealed not only in the Malenkov speeches, but in Chou En-lai's initiative of March 30 for a Korean prisoner exchange. His suspicion extended even to Russia's agreement to join with the West in supporting Dag Hammarskjöld as the new Secretary-General of the United Nations! [23] Indeed, evidence of American-Soviet agreement on any issue troubled him, for he judged it could only be a ruse designed to cause the free world to "let down its guard."

Eisenhower, however, was now determined to make the speech, and Hughes was preparing it for delivery in mid-April. Dulles accordingly addressed his objections to Hughes. In a written notation on the semifinal draft, he commented that the "reference to ending of wars in Asia" caused him concern because it might seem to *"commit us to end the Chinese civil war* and again to 'neutralize' Formosa," [24] a comment which made plain to the dedicated, world-weary Bedell Smith that "Dulles is still dreaming his fancy about reactivating the civil war in China." [25] What the Secretary wanted in the speech was a posture that would give the United States a free hand to run a liberation-rollback policy against mainland China, but would at the same time refuse U.S. agreement to a Korean armistice unless the Kremlin explicitly promised to end the anti-French rebellion in Indochina. Neither Hughes nor Paul Nitze (who as outgoing director of policy planning made a major contribution to the tone and content of the final speech) was sure that Dulles was fully conscious of this highly selective approach to peacemaking in Asia, but they decided to "forget" his proposals (while not disputing the broadly held, erroneous view that Communism was a tightly efficient monolith which, for example, gave the Kremlin decisive control over events in Indochina). Beyond the Asian question, Dulles thought the speech should also demand of the Soviets a list of "deeds" as a test of their desire to improve relations: not only an Austrian peace treaty and the release of German prisoners of war still held in Russia (which were acceptable to Eisenhower), but also a manifest move toward genuine political self-determination for the captive nations of Eastern Europe. As Dulles surely understood that this last point went to the roots of the emotional Soviet concern for its own security, it is safe to say that his move to include it was another effort to foreclose any possibility of serious negotiation with the post-Stalin government.

The speech, when finally delivered on April 16 to the American Society of Newspaper Editors, was eloquent, noble, and somewhat naïve: "The cost of one modern heavy bomber is this: a modern brick school in more than thirty cities. . . . We pay for a single fighter plane with a half million bushels of wheat. . . . This is not a way of life at all, in any true sense. Under the cloud of threatening war, it is humanity hanging from a cross of iron." [26] "We seek, throughout Asia as throughout the world, a peace that is true and total." The "first great step" must be "conclusion of an honorable armistice in Korea"; then the United States government would declare "total war, not upon any human enemy, but upon the brute forces of poverty and need," and would "ask its people to join with all nations in devoting a substantial percentage of the savings achieved by disarmament to a fund for world aid and reconstruction." [27]

The *New York Times* called the speech a "magnificent and deeply moving" peace initiative. Richard Rovere of the *New Yorker* found it "an immense triumph" for the President, one which "reëstablished American leadership in the world." [28] And reflecting the fluid new order in Moscow, both *Pravda* and *Izvestia* printed the full text. For his own part, however, Dulles moved swiftly to fit the speech within the frame of a strategy of pressure. "When President Eisenhower first took office," he told the same audience of newspaper editors just two days later, "a plea for peace such as he made this week might have been interpreted as a sign of weakness or a mere gesture of sentimentality. . . . It was first necessary to demonstrate . . . [the] will and capacity to develop foreign policies so firm, so fair, so just that the Soviet leaders might find it expedient to live with these policies rather than to live against them." [29] This amounted to a wildly unreal claim that the Eisenhower-Dulles policies had transformed the international situation — in the space of two months! Of graver consequence than the crass effort at credit-taking was the subtle distortion of Eisenhower's generous humanitarian impulse. The clear signal from Dulles was that only a policy of pressure had made the President's speech possible, and that a policy of pressure would therefore continue. Guardedly disturbed by what he felt to be Eisenhower's naïveté, he was in any event temperamentally incapable of pursuing the intended implications of the President's speech. Eisenhower, of necessity, turned to other pressing problems. The President's brave little speech was thus a paper boat launched against the tide. The currents of opposition, on both sides of the Iron Curtain, were too strong and too dependent for their political or bureaucratic survival on a posture of continued hostility.

Opposition to a Summit Conference

Anxious to be certain that Europe also got his message, Dulles was back in Paris in late April warning the NATO Council that Malenkov's moves were purely tactical, that the West must not drop its guard, indeed that the new situation underlined the urgent need for ratification of EDC. He left Paris feeling he had convinced the allies that they must resist the deadly perils of Malenkov's "phony peace campaign," [30] and so reported to Eisenhower. In fact, the Europeans were rather unconvinced. Carefully pondering the evolution in the Kremlin, they discerned new possibilities for East-West accommodation which it seemed to them unwise to foreclose without exploration. The feeling spread, particularly in France, that EDC and German rearmament were now less urgent, and on May 11 Prime Minister Churchill proposed a parley at the summit with an informal, flexible agenda and an avoidance of specific prerequisites. It would be unwise, Churchill argued, "to assume that nothing can be settled . . . unless or until everything is settled." [31]

Eisenhower, who now became confused by the evidence (contrary to Dulles's report) of disarray in the Western Alliance on the fundamental issues of Russia and EDC, asked the Secretary to arrange a quiet meeting with the French and British heads of state. Churchill was anxious to see the President, and the new French premier, Joseph Laniel (another of those minor parliamentary figures thrown up by the revolving door system of the weak and troubled Fourth Republic), was equally willing. A meeting in Bermuda was set for early June. Dulles, however, was unhappy at Eisenhower's insistence that the three Western heads of state should meet to unify and coordinate their approach, for he felt that differences within the alliance would be magnified by the publicity attending a meeting at the top, and that dramatic failure might well strengthen isolationism in America. And he was particularly irritated by Churchill's initiative, for it seemed to him to imply Britain's "incipient tendency" to mediate the conflict between the free world and Communism.[32]

But the Western Big Three meeting did not come off in June. Churchill had suffered a stroke in April, the full seriousness of which had been withheld, and Eden was still recuperating from an operation for gallstones that would keep him out of action until late in the year. Rather than cancel the meeting, however, the decision was made to transform it into a conference of Foreign Ministers. Hence the "Little Bermuda," convened in Washington on July 10, with Dulles playing host to Georges Bidault of France and the Marquess of Salisbury, who was acting head of the British Foreign Office in Eden's absence. The main topic was Churchill's idea for a four-power summit, a proposition ably argued by Salisbury. The Russians, Salisbury said, were not in fact dealing from weakness; they could march to the English Channel in two months and their nuclear weaponry was growing. Malenkov's general softening of the Soviet line should therefore not be rejected out of hand, but carefully and thoroughly probed at the earliest opportunity.[33] Bidault reinforced the British position by making quite clear that the French Assembly could not be persuaded to ratify EDC until there had been a serious effort to negotiate the German question with the new Soviet regime; at the same time, however, he opposed a wide-open meeting featuring, in Churchill's phrase, "a fluid or flexible agenda." [34] From the Anglo-French differences, Dulles was able to fashion a compromise agreement: the West would ask the Russians for a four-power conference of Foreign Ministers in early autumn, with an agenda limited to Germany and Austria. Salisbury, who did not fully share his own Prime Minister's optimism about a summit, accepted the compromise in good grace, but indicated publicly as he left Washington that a summit conference remained a distinct possibility.

A major factor in Dulles's willingness to countenance any meeting at all with the Russians was a recent plea from Adenauer, whose regime, still an instrument of the Allied High Commission, was facing its first electoral test on September 6. The German leader, with whom the American Secretary of State was to develop bonds of special trust and warmth, urged that a four-power conference on the German question be held soon, as a means of dramatizing Russia's categorical opposition to free elections in the truncated German nation. Adenauer stood absolutely for free elections, while his Social Democratic opponent, accepting the reality of a Soviet veto over such a process, proposed that unification be achieved through negotiations between East and West Germany. Adenauer's electoral tactic was to show that both his German opponent and the Russian devils held the same position — namely, opposition to free elections.[35] The Russians, however, declining to play this game, balked on both the scope and timing of the Western proposal for a conference. They wanted a wider agenda, to include arms levels and foreign base agreements, and they seemed in no hurry. Thus, as the autumn approached without agreement to a meeting, Dulles apparently concluded that some other form of dramatic help for Adenauer would have to be found. And at a press conference on September 3, after declaring that Russia's enforced partition of Germany was not merely "a scandal," but "a menace to the peace," he took the unusual step of directly endorsing Adenauer's candidacy, asserting that any other result would be disastrous for Germany and the cause of freedom.[36] The State Department staff was dumbfounded. Whether this was a calculated diplomatic indiscretion (in the manner of the Yoshida letter), or, as Robert Bowie thought, another instance when Dulles was momentarily carried away by the strength of his conviction and the power of his advocacy, Adenauer's coalition won a smashing victory at the polls, thereby assuring a continuity to Western policy that Washington, London and Paris considered vital.

Two Ghosts of Yalta

The Republican party platform for 1952 contained the promise to "repudiate all commitments contained in secret understandings such as those of Yalta which aid Communist enslavements." While this was a wish deeply embedded in the demonology of the GOP perspective on world affairs, still it was surprising that Dulles should have initiated implementing action by dictating a paragraph for the President's first State of the Union Message in early February — for despite the fixation of the right wing, there were no "secret understandings . . . of Yalta." What had produced enslavement in Eastern Europe was not secret American acquiescence, but clear Russian violation of a Yalta agreement that called for democratic and independent states in that area. Dulles's proposed language nonetheless used the word "repudiate" in keeping with the GOP platform. Fortunately for the administration, Emmet Hughes, who was editing the speech, struck that verb in favor of more ambiguous language, and as finally delivered the passage read: "I shall ask Congress at a later date to join in an appropriate resolution making clear that this Government recognizes no kind of commitment contained in secret understandings of the past . . . which permit [this kind of] enslavement." [37]

But ambiguity is a limited virtue, and the Republican senators and congressmen who heard the speech found in it confirmation of their belief that secret understandings did in fact exist. And they wished to proceed to a vote on a resolution of righteous repudiation. At this point embarrassment set in. As there existed no secrets to repudiate, the administration hardly wished to sponsor or endorse a resolution that the Democrats would tear factually to shreds. What was therefore needed, the White House now decided, was a resolution in which the Democrats could join, but they, of course, were not prepared to condemn Roosevelt and Truman, even obliquely, and especially not for a crime never committed. A watered-down version, merely deploring Communist enslavement of Eastern Europe, was at length painfully sold to Senator Lyndon Johnson and the other Democratic leaders by Thruston Morton, the hard-working Assistant Secretary of State for Congressional Affairs. At the last moment, however, Dulles nearly upset the applecart a second time by persuading Eisenhower to sign a message to Congress which again asked for the *repudiation* of "past agreements committing us to such enslavement." Another eleventh hour intervention by Emmet Hughes was needed to save the day.[38] Knowing Dulles's precision as a legal technician, it is difficult to believe he was merely careless with language on two separate but related occasions. Yet to assume that his actions were knowing and deliberate is unavoidably to condemn his judgment, for his course, before it was deflected, led straight to acute political embarrassment for the President.

The final point of absurdity was reached when the congressional Republicans, discovering the administration intended no rebuke to its Democratic predecessors, angrily refused their support. The result was that no resolution of any kind issued from either the Senate or the House.

A sturdier ghost of Yalta was the Bricker amendment to the Constitution, which sought drastic limitations on the presidential treaty-making power and the assertion of broad congressional control over foreign affairs. Sponsored by the conservative senator from Ohio who had been Dewey's running mate in 1944, it reflected not only concern over excessive executive power, but fear that the United Nations could legislate international covenants (in areas like human rights) that would be binding on the United States. In the 1952 campaign, Dulles had warned publicly of "great dangers" inherent in presidential authority, and had added that modification of the treaty-making power was "desirable under modern conditions." [39] Now of course the shoe was on the other foot.

The most notable features of the struggle, which lasted into early 1954, were the President's determination to avoid a head-on collision with Republican leaders in the Congress, and his exasperation at their refusal to support him. Bricker needed two-thirds of the Senate to win, but it was not clear that he could be defeated. Broad support came from the South and Middle West, and from organizations that included the Daughters of the American Revolution and the Vigilant Women for the Bricker Amendment. "If we can't get thirty-three senators to vote with us," Eisenhower asked impatiently, "what kind of a *team* is this?" [40] Seeking a compromise, he talked at length with Bricker, but found no satisfaction. By the middle of July, Dulles said rather sharply at a cabinet meeting: "We just have to make up our minds and stop being fuzzy about this." The President replied tartly that he had not been fuzzy: "There was nothing fuzzy in what I told Bricker. I said we'd go just so far and no further." To which Dulles responded with equal tartness, "I know, sir, but you haven't told anybody else." [41] So finally the President went on record declaring himself "unalterably opposed" to an amendment which, if passed, "would be notice to our friends as well as our enemies that our country intends to withdraw from its leadership in world affairs." [42] Despite his great popularity, his intervention had almost no effect. When the vote was finally taken in early 1954, the Bricker amendment failed of passage by only one vote! Sixty senators voted for it (including thirty-two Republicans and twenty-eight Democrats) and only thirty-one voted against it.

12

Policy Beginnings

(PART TWO)

Liberation Is Tested

On June 16, 1953, rioting broke out in East Berlin and quickly spread to Halle, Jena, Leipzig and other cities in the Soviet-occupied zone of Germany. From the perspective of twenty years, it now seems doubtful that vague, even though strident, Republican promises to assist captive peoples on the day of liberation were ever more than a minor motivating factor in producing those acts of supreme courage and supreme folly by angry, desperate East German workers. The evidence is that they began as spontaneous protests against "higher work norms" imposed by the East German authorities, quite possibly against the advice and wishes of the Malenkov regime. The Soviets had themselves just announced several minor concessions to workers, apparently to sweeten public opinion on the eve of the arrival of a new Soviet High Commissioner for East Germany.[1] Moreover, since Stalin's death there had been a perceptible relaxation of Soviet policy in the belt of satellite states, attributable to the Malenkov speeches and no doubt to uncertainty on the part of the resident Russian proconsuls as to the plans and intentions of the new ruling group in the Kremlin. Dulles always feared that any evidence of American-Soviet agreement to relax tensions would deepen the discouragement of the captive peoples. But Ambassador Bohlen in Moscow believed it would have precisely the opposite effect: as he reasoned it, the Soviets could not publicly come to terms with the West and at the same time justify retention of harsh police controls that were ostensibly aimed at protecting "Socialism" from "imperial wreckers, spies and assassins"; he thus thought a relaxation of tensions would stimulate internal dissension. It does not seem implausible to argue that the East German rioters drew as much subconscious encouragement from the hope (which proved false) that a new and apparently more tolerant regime in Russia might take their side against an old and intolerable regime in East Germany, as they drew from campaign rhetoric in distant America.

But whatever the causation, the uprising put the Dulles doctrine of liberation to immediate and critical test in the halls of Congress and the chancellories of Western Europe. While brave and angry rioters piled Communist banners on blazing bonfires along the Unter den Linden, broke into Communist jails to free wretched political prisoners, and fought Russian tanks with fists and stones, Washington remained inert. Beyond campaign rhetoric, there was neither strategy nor plan. In twenty-four hours the workers had been ground under and a deathly silence descended. It was all over. While Europe watched and waited with tense anxiety, Washington officially concluded (what all serious observers had known) that no meaningful action was possible without unacceptable risk of general war. After moral protest, Dulles offered $15 million worth of free food, which Molotov contemptuously spurned, calling it a deliberate provocation. Soup kitchens were briefly established in West Berlin for those East Berliners who would come over, but the Russians quickly closed down the traffic. The episode added nothing to Dulles's reputation for probity at home or abroad, yet American inaction was in fact the occasion of considerable relief in Western Europe; it encouraged the feeling that, however bombastic his rhetoric, neither Dulles nor President Eisenhower was disposed to rash action in an actual crisis. Moreover, by putting an end to whatever hopes of American support existed in Eastern Europe, the tragedy gave inadvertent support to the case for a more peaceful evolution. The unfolding of the ill-fated Hungarian rebellion three years later was not much influenced by the prospect of Western support; tragedy there resulted from serious Hungarian miscalculation as to the limits of Russian tolerance.

But the East German riots also threw Dulles onto the defensive with his domestic critics and produced another of those reactions that seemed to combine conviction with heavy layers of political self-protection. He now argued that the Soviet empire was seething with restlessness and turmoil, and that steady Western pressure upon an uncertain, mutually distrustful leadership group could break the Kremlin's control or force it to a series of formal accommodations with the West. He took the July announcement of Lavrenti Beria's summary execution as a sign that "freedom is again in the air. A new convulsion is underway. The old system may remain and may continue to threaten, but inherent weakness is disclosed." [2] He told a cabinet meeting that "this is the kind of time when we ought to be *doubling* our bets, not reducing them — as all the Western parliaments want to do. This is the time to *crowd* the enemy — and maybe *finish* him, once and for all." [3] Moreover, both Dulles and his immediate subordinates displayed a tendency to portray these convulsions behind the Iron Curtain as at least the indirect result of their own handiwork. Emmet Hughes recorded a telephone conversation in which Roderic O'Connor told him: "Well, this is the time for us to *talk it up* — remind people how our policy has been getting results right on down the line. *Anyone* can see, with this business of Beria, that we're accomplishing everything we *said* we could with a *dynamic* policy." [4] Stalin's death, the riots in East Germany, the fall of Beria, and the uneasy new Kremlin leadership were indeed evidence of grave weakness in the Soviet system, but they were also evidence of change, gestation, and the possibility of new direction in policy. Ambassador Bohlen, who arrived in Moscow in April, believed in retrospect that the situation in the spring of 1953 had presented a rare opportunity. There were rumors that the new Russian leaders were considering "the possibility of giving up East Germany," [5] a piece of information which he felt tended to be confirmed several years later when Khrushchev charged both Malenkov and Beria with plotting such a policy. Had the West accepted Churchill's appeal for prompt parley with the Kremlin, Bohlen thought, "this would have been a very fruitful period," and might have "led to a radical solution in our favor on the German question." [6] He readily acknowledged, however, that such hopeful prospects were less clear at the time. What *was* clear at the time was Dulles's firm opposition to any form of détente.

Cross-Currents in the Middle East

When Dulles flew off to the Middle East on May 9, accompanied by Harold Stassen, the director of mutual security, he seemed to have three purposes in mind: (1) to promote the idea of a Middle East security pact as a barrier to Soviet Communist penetration; (2) to restore a greater measure of balance and evenhandedness in American policy toward Israel and the Arabs; and (3) to acquaint himself at firsthand with the leaders of the area.

Attempts to establish indigenous support for a Middle East command desired by London and Washington had foundered badly in the last two years of the Truman administration. A British effort, in April 1951, to embody joint defense arrangements and British retention of the military base at Suez in a revision of the 1936 treaty had been rejected by an Egyptian government that was pledged to get Britain out of both Egypt and the Sudan. In September of that year, a British-American working group had developed another plan. This centered on a Supreme Allied Commander with headquarters in Cairo; he would be British, but high Egyptian officers would participate, the base at Suez would be turned over to Egypt, and all British forces not allocated to the Supreme Commander would be withdrawn. By such means it was hoped to transform the character of remaining British forces from occupiers to defenders. Although the plan was quickly endorsed by several non-Arab nations, including Turkey, it had wholly failed to measure the rising force of Arab nationalism and the Arab inability to perceive any serious Russian threat to the Middle East. When it was presented to Egypt on October 13, Prime Minister Nahas Pasha rejected it without reading it, and two days later moved to abrogate both the 1936 treaty and the Anglo-Sudan condominium. As Dean Acheson later remarked, "If ever there was a political stillbirth, this was it." [7]

The British, refusing to accept these proclaimed abrogations, stood fast on the power of their large resident armed force, but guerilla fighting soon broke out in the Suez Canal Zone. And on the following January 26 (1952), mobs incited and led by agents of the government sacked and burned downtown Cairo, killing several dozen Europeans including nine Englishmen who were forced by fire out of the exclusive Turf Club and then slaughtered in the street — this episode came to be known as Black Saturday. Churchill and Eden, who had been returned to power just two months before, warned King Farouk that British forces would move out from their Suez base to reoccupy Cairo and Alexandria if Egypt refused to protect British lives and property. Farouk promptly capitulated. Six months later a group of young Egyptian army officers deposed the jaded monarchy, changed the political order in Egypt without bloodshed, and demanded serious negotiations for British withdrawal. Getting rid of the British was, initially, the most profound commitment of the Nasser revolution.

But ending the British occupation proved to be a difficult and bitter task, for the concern in London focused not only on the tangible problem of how to guarantee passage through the Suez Canal for the oil supplies on which British industry increasingly depended. It extended, particularly among Tory politicians, to the psychological question of British power and prestige, creating dense emotional barriers to acceptance of an orderly reduction and transformation of the British role in the Middle East — and indeed throughout the world. The ensuing Anglo-Egyptian negotiations were hot-tempered, and were played out against a backdrop of intense anti-British feeling in Egypt. Sabotage, thievery, terrorist attacks on British soldiers steadily increased, converting a supposed free-world operating base into a besieged redoubt and making it abundantly clear that, without Egyptian goodwill, the base could only be a heavy liability in time of war.

Fundamentally, the West wanted to trade British military evacuation for Egyptian membership in a defense pact that would secure the British right of return to the Suez base in a crisis affecting Western strategic interests. Nasser, on the other hand, was firmly opposed to any Arab pact with the West, although he seemed ready to countenance Western defense arrangements with non-Arab states of the "northern tier" — e.g., Turkey, Iran, and Pakistan. He understood that any "outside aggression" must necessarily come from a Communist source, for the West was already present in the Middle East, indeed engaged in the protection of its lines of communication and its oil investments. In the Arab countries of the "southern tier," however, he wanted an Arab pact without Western participation. In time, as he told Nuri as Said of Iraq, the Arab people might come to understand the need for new defense agreements with Western powers, but first there had to be a period of complete Arab independence.[8]

Churchill and Eden sought to strengthen their hand by bringing the United States directly into the negotiations, but Nasser stubbornly resisted this, and both Eisenhower and Dulles refused to join the talks without Egyptian consent. Their refusal reflected an instinctive American reluctance to associate U.S. policy with a colonial power in confrontation with a nation aspiring to gain its independence from that power. But a major consideration was also to maintain at least the appearance of primary British responsibility for Western interests in the area. Yet refusing a larger American role created a certain dilemma, for Dulles believed the Middle East was vulnerable to Communist penetration, and that American counterforce was an essential ingredient of its prevention. In 1953, however, he was still feeling his way through the intricate and treacherous minefield of the Middle East situation.

Arriving in Cairo, where he first met with the nominal leader of the junta, General Naguib, he presented him with a plated .38-caliber pistol from President Eisenhower (a gift which, though not an inappropriate offering from one soldier-statesman to another, evoked a wide range of different yet uniformly negative symbolism in Cairo, Tel Aviv and London). At the same time, he took a rather tough pro-British line, telling the Egyptian leader that Washington desired a settlement satisfactory to both sides, but one that would retain the elaborate military installations at Suez in effective readiness, "available for immediate use on behalf of the free world in the event of future hostilities." [9] Over dinner at the American embassy amid "the usual gold-plated and elegant trappings," [10] Dulles found, however, that the junta leaders — Naguib, Nasser, Sabry, Sadat, Amer, et al. — were nearly impervious to warnings of Soviet

Communist menace to the Middle East. They had no illusions that Russia was friendly, but a threat seemed to them remote, far lower on their scale of fears than British imperialism and Israel; as Roderic O'Connor remarked later, "It was a little hard to get them convinced that they really had to take some steps." [11] On the record, Egyptian skepticism about the Communist menace seemed understandable. During the 1920s and 1930s, Russian diplomatic relations with the Arab world were almost nonexistent, and the Kremlin treated such bumbling and beleaguered local Communist cells as were formed with almost total indifference; and these made no inroads into Moslem society. Even when diplomatic relations were established after World War II, the Kremlin seemed remarkably blind to the advantages of identifying with the emergent anti-colonial forces. And during the current negotiations for British withdrawal, the Soviet press was still depicting Nasser as a "Fascist lackey of the West," castigating his every reluctant concession to the British as a step that would ensure the permanence of British control.[12] The Cairo junta therefore regarded Russian policy as an annoyance, but, with Greece and Turkey in NATO and the American Sixth Fleet in the Mediterranean, the idea of a military threat from the north seemed far away.

Dulles appeared to accept the thrust of Egypt's position during this first trip, although it complicated his felt need to widen the anti-Communist barrier to Soviet expansion southward. In a broadcast on June 1, shortly after his return, he said that while "the northern tier of nations shows awareness of the danger," the Arab countries to the south were far more concerned with their disputes with Israel, Britain, and France.[13] This set of facts led him to the conclusion that a regional security system was not an immediate prospect, for any such system would have to "grow from within out of a sense of common destiny and common danger." [14] And in a private memorandum, he showed an accurate perception of the realities and the limits that these factors imposed on his preferred policy line. Noting that "almost the entire area is caught in a fanatical revolutionary spirit" that was causing local countries to "magnify their immediate problems and depreciate the Soviet threat," he concluded that "we must accept the fact that the political situation is such that Arab states will not, at this time, openly join defense arrangements with a combination of Western powers." [15] The memorandum added bleakly that the British and French positions in the area had probably deteriorated beyond the point of repair, and that the "Israeli factor" plus the Arab tendency to link the United States with the colonial policies of European states were "millstones around our neck." [16] From this analysis, he drew the wise conclusion that it was necessary to "avoid becoming fascinated with concepts that have no reality." [17] Yet a year later, when he was fresh from exhilarating efforts to bring the Southeast Asian Treaty Organization into being and to rebuff the Chinese Communists at Quemoy, he sent a new ambassador to Iraq with special instructions to see what could be done to promote Iraqi adherence to a northern tier pact.[18]

Israel

Also high on Dulles's list of Middle East objectives was a desire to restore a greater measure of evenhandedness to American policy toward Israel and the Arabs. The Truman administration, he thought, had "gone overboard in favor of Israel," [19] through a combination of Zionist pressure and personal preference, and he was resolved to restore the balance, encouraged by the fact that Eisenhower's victory had not depended in any important sense on the American Jewish vote. The Israeli leader, David Ben-Gurion, thus received him in Tel Aviv with a mixture of hope and apprehension, but apparently paid lip service to the new thesis, for Dulles was able to say in his televised report of June 1 that "the leaders in Israel themselves agreed with us that United States policies should be impartial so as to win not only the respect and regard of the Israeli but also of the Arab peoples." [20]

In truth, however, the Israeli leaders were not at all receptive to the idea that their influence in Washington should be diluted, as they were soon to make plain in word and deed. And as time passed, the Dulles shift seemed more apparent than real. As Abba Eban, then Israeli ambassador to Washington, later reflected on this phenomenon, the Eisenhower administration in 1953 was characterized by "a certain reluctance to confess that American policy anywhere was a continuation of what it was before. . . . Everything had either to be different, or one had to pretend that it was different." [21] From Dulles came "certain moralistic and virtuous assertions that American foreign policy would not be influenced by internal considerations, that the Arab interest would be upgraded, that Israel would be looked after, but downgraded. . . . Nothing very much came of it in terms of fact . . . but there was substantial misjudgment and a deep psychological error in the talk of change. It gave the Israeli public the impression that American friendship for Israel had been a fleeting and accidental circumstance of history, linked organically with the Truman administration." [22] The resulting uncertainty produced a sense of isolation in Israel which led in turn to a posture of militant self-reliance, finding expression in "a very active policy of retaliation on the frontiers." [23]

But if Dulles's earnest efforts, in 1953 and later — to allay Arab resentment against the United States without at the same time abandoning Israel — fell short of his hopes, the central difficulty lay in the impossibility of the task. From the day of Israel's creation, the Middle East was riven beyond foreseeable repair; and the United States, having sponsored and supported Israel, yet having undeniable economic interests in the Arab countries, could not subsequently find a policy that met with the acceptance of both parties. The Arab-Israeli struggle proved too bitterly irrational for evenhanded compromise.

Ending the Korean War

An immediate goal for Eisenhower and Dulles was ending the Korean War. It had run on for two and a half years when the new administration entered office and its high cost in human life, money, and societal disruption had contributed in a major way to Eisenhower's victory. But now the problem was his, and it needed prompt solution, for its debilitating inconclusiveness continued to fuel the wild demagoguery of McCarthyism.

Eisenhower was firmly decided against any attempt to "win" the Korean struggle, but his military experience told him that an honorable compromise depended on convincing his adversaries that the United States under his leadership was prepared to intensify the fighting unless a satisfactory settlement were promptly reached. By a combination of words and deeds — the "unleashing" order to the Seventh Fleet, disclosure of plans to enlarge the South Korean army, the dispatch of more American airpower to Korea, the placement of nuclear missiles on Okinawa — he and Dulles set out to persuade the other side that this was indeed the U.S. posture. On the continuing leg of his Middle East–South Asian trip, Dulles visited India on May 22 and is said to have quietly passed the word through Nehru to Chou En-lai that, failing an early settlement, the United States would bomb the Manchurian sanctuaries north of the Yalu River.

By late March, the ice jam at the negotiating table in Panmunjom had begun to show signs of breaking up, a development perhaps attributable as much to Stalin's death as to the combination of threats from Washington. On March 28, the Communist side accepted a long-standing UN proposal for the exchange of all sick and wounded prisoners, and two days later Chou En-lai advanced a formula to accommodate Western insistence on the principle of nonforcible repatriation: those prisoners refusing to go home could be handed over to a neutral state. Negotiations moved forward until by late May the United Nations was ready to state its "final offer" for a settlement.

But the idea of any compromise was hemlock to Syngman Rhee, the Princeton-educated, Christian septuagenarian who still ruled South Korea. He informed Eisenhower that he could accept an armistice only if he had an ironclad American promise to resume the war, should the unifi-

With Nehru and Stassen in India (May 1953)

cation of Korea not be achieved by political conference within ninety days. Eisenhower's reply argued that "we would not be justified in prolonging the war with all the misery that it involves" if the other side proved willing to sign an agreement reflecting "clear abandonment of the fruits of aggression." [24] He thought the proposed truce met that test. To mollify Rhee, he promised a bilateral security pact, further economic aid, and every effort to achieve Korean unification by peaceful means. But the seventy-eight-year-old Rhee refused these entreaties. When the opposing negotiators at Panmunjom nonetheless signed a June 8 agreement on the prisoner repatriation issue, his bitterness led him to a dramatic act of sabotage. On the night of June 18, he released nearly 27,000 North Korean prisoners who had refused repatriation, and they were soon scattered all over South Korea. A dumbfounded Dulles dispatched Assistant Secretary Robertson to try to restore the bizarre, yet delicate and dangerous, situation. Robertson spent nearly two weeks in patient and sympathetic listening, while the tough old South Korean poured out his anger and frustration. Then, after Rhee had talked himself out, Robertson made it plain that the United States was going to negotiate a truce. It would give full support to South Korea's desire for unification, at a subsequent political conference. Meanwhile, Eisenhower wanted Rhee's promise to keep South Korean forces under UN command and to avoid any act of obstruction. With persistence and southern charm, Robertson persuaded Rhee to trust Eisenhower and Dulles and accept the U.S. position. The Chinese Communists, while they denounced Rhee's sabotage, declined to use the incident as a basis for breaking off negotiations. They too wanted an agreement.

Rhee's stand was, however, supported by a number of Republican leaders in the Congress whose uncomplicated purpose had now become the overthrow of the Peking regime and the restoration of Chiang Kai-shek, and who saw in a Korean compromise a measurable victory for Mao and a serious danger that UN membership for Communist China would shortly follow. Senator Knowland thought that acquiescence in a divided Korea would mean a truce without honor, and that "inevitably we will lose the balance of Asia." Senator Taft found the prospective settlement "extremely unsatisfactory," because it would leave the Chinese free to attack elsewhere.[25] But Eisenhower was firmly resolved on a Korean truce, and the American people seemed to recognize the larger wisdom of his course. The armistice was finally signed on July 26. It was promptly followed by a declaration that reflected the new, but as yet unannounced, Eisenhower-Dulles doctrine of deterrence. Issued in the name of the sixteen nations who had fought for the United Nations, but sounding like Dulles, it warned that the consequence of any renewed aggression on the Korean peninsula "would be so grave that in all probability it would not be possible to confine hostilities to Korea."

The Big Bermuda

After the middle months of *Sturm und Drang* in East Germany and Korea, Dulles's attention in late 1953 shifted back to the issues of EDC and a parley with the Russians. In order to advance the prospects of EDC in France, give support to Adenauer's election in West Germany, and avoid undue strain on the Anglo-American tie, he had compromised his opposition to Soviet talks at any level, but he continued to resist the idea of a summit conference. October found him in London, explaining to the Prime Minister that President Eisenhower, beset by the widely diverse duties devolving upon him under the American Constitution, could not afford to be away from Washington for an extended period; moreover, EDC must be ratified first. Churchill, who was irritated by this line, said he might meet alone with Malenkov, to which Dulles replied that such a move would give the American people the unfortunate impression that Britain was shifting from ally to intermediary. In spite of this somewhat disagreeable exchange, he departed London with the impression that neither Eden nor Salisbury, who had been present, were enthusiastic supporters of a summit conference.[26]

The Western heads of state finally met in Bermuda in early December, with Winston Churchill, a "visibly enfeebled figure, housing a visibly unenfeebled spirit," [27] in the role of host. Eden was physically recovered and on hand. The French team was composed of Premier Laniel and Foreign Minister Georges Bidault, but Laniel spent much of the conference in bed with a cold (real or diplomatic), leaving the burden of presenting the French case to the brilliant and courageous, but erratic, former hero of the underground and former professor of philosophy. The talks covered four or five subjects, of which the most consequential was EDC. Here Bidault, in the presence of Laniel and several other ministers in the precarious new French coalition, set forth at great length the French conditions and misgivings. It was a brief that depressed his allies by its profound negation. Not only, he told Eisenhower and Churchill, must West Germany permanently accept the Saar territory as an autonomous political state under French economic control, but American and British ground forces must remain in Europe at substantially their present strength for twenty years. When Eisenhower and Churchill promptly protested that such a guarantee of their forces was not possible, Bidault replied that without it the EDC treaty stood no chance of approval by the French Assembly. A point that struck Bidault's listeners was his repeated reference to the "humiliating sacrifice" involved for France in integrating her forces with those of a long-standing enemy, a "sacrifice" that the EDC protocols demanded only of France, among the Western Big Three.[28]

Churchill's response noted, with characteristic candor, that the underlying theme of Bidault's whole presentation was French fear that Germany would dominate EDC. He did not share Bidault's pessimism, he said, for under the EDC protocol Germany would have neither a complete military force nor the industrial means of its support. Still, he was convinced there must be a German contribution to the defense of Western Europe; only that could give adequate strength and geographic depth to the NATO military position. He was astonished, he said, that Bidault should speak in such negative, defeatist terms, for surely EDC was an alternative preferable to a national German army. EDC must therefore be accepted; if it were not, he would urge national German rearmament as a measure indispensable to the safety of the West. Eisenhower supported Churchill, adding that "EDC would function effectively as a part of NATO." But it proved impossible to modify Bidault's position, and the French refusal to confront the inexorable alternative cast a pall over the proceedings.[29]

Discussion aside, the only action taken at Bermuda was a note to the

USSR agreeing to January talks in Berlin. The Western leaders were prepared to hold such a conference, at the Foreign Minister level and provided the agenda was confined to Germany and Austria. Eisenhower explained to his colleagues that the United States would also insist on the exclusion of Communist China from both the conference table and the United Nations until the Mao regime met a number of moral and political-military conditions. These were: withdrawal of Chinese forces from Korea, cessation of support for the anti-French rebellion in Indochina, abandonment of the military threat to Formosa, and adoption of "decent deportment" in contacts with the West.[30] These unrealistic demands, reflecting the administration's strong disinclination to challenge the rampant prejudices and presumed power of the Republican right wing, reflected no less Dulles's own determination to pursue a policy of pressure in Asia, unembarrassed by any serious prospect of a general Asian settlement. The President's brave speech of April 16 seemed far away. Recognizing the categorical nature of the American position on this issue, Britain and France did not press their differences.

This first postwar meeting of the Western heads of state does not rank as either very notable or consequential. For one thing, its news value was immediately eclipsed by Eisenhower's dramatic "Atoms for Peace" proposal to the United Nations, which he flew directly from Bermuda to deliver before the General Assembly on December 8. For another, it was further overshadowed, two weeks later, by Dulles's public warning that the United States could not avoid an "agonizing reappraisal" of its basic commitments in Europe if EDC were not soon ratified. Clearly exasperated by the French performance at Bermuda and now gathering his full stride at the end of an arduous yet exhilarating first year in office, he moved on the mistaken assumption that he could frighten the French into enlightened behavior. According to CBS news sources in Paris, the Dulles move was a "calculated political risk" which recognized and accepted the dangers of an emotional French reaction.[31] It was also a performance that rather perfectly reflected Dulles's particular blend of qualities — a persistent sense of tactical urgency, a strong impulse to act, a stubborn will placed in the service of a genuine idealism, too much logic, too little intuition, and an almost total absence of empathy. His threat exploded like a bomb at the NATO Council where he delivered it, and quickly raised a mushroom cloud of infuriated protest from Frenchmen in every walk of life. Senator Michel Debré, who was later to be Premier in De Gaulle's government, set the tone with his charge of "intolerable interference in internal French affairs." [32] Bidault, who acknowledged that Dulles had grounds for anger at the skittish unreliability of the French Assembly, said privately: "But what a thing to say to me, when I was doing everything conceivable" to obtain ratification.[33]

On the other hand, the aging vice-premier, Paul Reynaud, thought Dulles "spoke the truth" and was "perfectly justified." [34]

It is unlikely that any tactic, any form or combination of threat or inducement, could then or later have brought the French Assembly to approval of EDC. The trauma of defeat in 1940 had produced a national malaise too deep and too complicated to permit a rational response. If anything, the prospect for ratification was to grow worse in 1954, when France faced the bitterness of defeat and humiliation in Indochina. But when EDC was finally defeated eight months later, and there ensued no basic American reappraisal, agonizing or otherwise, Dulles merely added to his reputation for making hollow threats.

Despite its seeming inconsequence, however, the Bermuda meeting recorded a tentative new Western consensus that an old era had ended and a new one begun. In its quiet assessment that "the danger of aggression now seems less imminent," the conference communiqué seemed to confirm the world's arrival at a new stage in the cold war. The immediate postwar fear had been that Western Europe would succumb to local Communist penetration supported by the threat of Russian invasion; that fear had been surmounted by the Truman Doctrine, the Marshall Plan and NATO. In 1950 the attack on South Korea raised the new fear that "International Communism" would now use open force at many confrontation points; this fear had been relieved by valiant collective response in Korea, the dispatch of U.S. forces to Europe, and the swift arming of NATO. Stalin's death and the armistice in Korea now seemed to usher in a declining sense of apocalypse. And although Dulles deplored and feared the implications of even partial relaxation, there was widening evidence at the end of 1953 that the world was beginning to breathe normally again for the first time in many years.

13

Massive Retaliation and the New Look

THE "NEW LOOK" POSTURE took its name from a 1953 reexamination of military policy by a newly appointed group of military chiefs of staff. It was later applied not only to this analysis, but to the substance of a modified grand strategy which emphasized the threat of nuclear punishment against centers of Communist power and deemphasized localized efforts to block or contain Communism's expansionist tendencies. It was the product of two compelling impulses of the new administration: to save money, and to regain control of an American policy that was perceived to have become largely a reflexive reaction to Communist initiative. In Greece and Turkey, in Berlin, in Korea, the Communists had precipitated crisis, forcing a hasty, costly, disruptive American response. The new men were determined to put an end to such humiliation and discomfort. As he entered office, Eisenhower seemed overridingly concerned with the danger that he might inadvertently spend the country into bankruptcy; at the same time, he shared Admiral Radford's instinct that the major part of American military forces abroad should be drawn back from their far-flung outposts into a strong home-based reserve, and that the United States should henceforward guard against violent change across the world by placing more reliance on threatened American action and less on the physical presence of American forces. As both men were aware, such military redeployments were necessary concomitants of serious budget reduction.

Dulles, who fully shared both the budgetary and strategic impulses, had been a persuasive force in the development of Eisenhower's outlook. In his *Life* article of May 1952 * (which was in substance the memoran-

* "A Policy of Boldness."

dum he had sent to Eisenhower a few months before), he complained that, in response to the Communist "strategy of encirclement and strangulation," the Truman administration had "adopted a series of emergency measures which are fantastically costly not only in money but in their warping of our American way of life." Present "negative policies . . . will never end the peril nor bring relief from the exertions which devour our economic, political and moral vitals." [1] The only escape from a fatal treadmill was to develop "community punishing power," the means "to hit with shattering effectiveness the sources of power and lines of communication of the Sovietized world." [2]

Yet there was here something of a paradox, for despite the deliberate *schrecklichkeit,* Dulles was, on the record, philosophically opposed to war and also something of an antimilitarist, convinced that a steady growth of military expenditures must inexorably produce a disturbing increase of military influence in the life of the nation. In 1950, when the defense budget stood at a level of $13.5 billion,* he feared "we have gone militaristic." And in his book *War or Peace,* he had warned against the tendencies of military leaders both to enlarge their own establishments and to encroach upon foreign policy. "Military advice is professional advice" and "naturally and properly, they advise *full* insurance," but "it is not their business to measure the resources of diplomacy." [3] It is "always tempting to accede to military requests because they take a tangible, concrete form. You can see guns, battleships, airplanes, bases. . . . On the other side are intangibles, things not seen. In reality, these are vitally important." [4] The arms race is "very exciting," but precisely for that reason there is danger that the military men who must follow it closely will "lose their sense of proportion." [5] He noted admiringly that Soviet political leaders were never "overawed by military advice," nor were their tactics dominated by military considerations.[6]

These expressions of undoubted conviction help to throw needed light on Dulles's real attitudes toward nuclear deterrence. What he evidently sought was a military posture sufficiently powerful to support an effective warning to those who dared pursue a course of violent change in the world, yet sufficiently moderate in cost and size to avoid the adverse economic and political implications he feared. It would be incorrect to suggest that he was unwilling to use force, particularly against an opponent of secondary strength like Communist China. At the same time, the evidence suggests that because he abhorred war and had concluded from his study of Marxism-Leninism that the leaders in the Kremlin would not risk destruction of their home base for the sake of peripheral expansion, he regarded the nuclear strike force more as

* Compared to $78 billion in 1970.

a political instrument to brandish than as a military force to use. That his listeners, particularly in the free nations he sought to protect, could not fully share this perspective, but were bound to examine the appalling implications for them should deterrence fail, seems in the main not to have occurred to him.

A Bigger Bang for a Buck

The driving force in the "New Look" planning was a determination to reduce military spending. Coming into office, Eisenhower inherited a military budget of about $42 billion,* as well as a paper (NSC-141) prepared by Acheson, Lovett, and Harriman which proposed an additional $7 billion to $9 billion in defense expenditures, mainly for an improved air defense against the growing Soviet capacity to attack the United States with bombers carrying nuclear weapons. With the Secretary of the Treasury leading the way, but reinforced by considerable pressure from Senator Taft, the figure for the new fiscal year (beginning July 1, 1953) was pared down to $36 billion, a reduction accomplished primarily by *deferring* certain long-range financing for air force procurement, and by lowering the somewhat abstract force goal for that service from 143 to 120 wings. Critics like Senator Stuart Symington charged that the new administration was effecting a dangerous "stretch-out" in the buildup of air power, but the economy mood in the Congress not only sustained the President, but resulted in further defense budget reductions — down to $34.5 billion.

On April 30, the President also announced a "radical" change in the approach to defense planning. It involved rejection of the idea that "we must build up to a maximum attainable strength for some specific date" on the assumption that the Soviets intended to go to war at the theoretical peak point in their own military development.[7] "Defense is not a matter of maximum strength for a single date," he said, but rather a matter for the "long haul," meaning that military programs should be stabilized at a level which the economy could sustain for many years without serious strain.[8] The presumed antithesis of the "long haul" idea was the concept of the "crisis year," a term that had appeared in studies made during the Truman period (especially in NSC-68, a comprehensive reassessment of the American security position prepared by the State and Defense Departments in late 1949 following the first Soviet nuclear explosion). NSC-68 had argued that by 1954 the Soviets would probably achieve the capability of launching a devastating nuclear

* In "new obligational authority"; the actual spending level was slightly higher.

attack on the United States, a fact that would neutralize the existing American nuclear advantage. Thus, 1954 would be the year in which the Soviets *might* take advantage of their great superiority in conventional forces; it would be a "crisis year" unless America and the West moved, before that date, to redress the balance in conventional forces. However, the sponsors of NSC-68 had proposed not a vast and precipitous military mobilization, but rather a moderate and balanced strengthening of forces that could be sustained indefinitely after the "crisis year." As General Omar Bradley, Chairman of the Joint Chiefs of Staff, wrote in 1949: "Our way toward security lies not in any sudden burst of activity, but in the steady, unwavering, purposeful application of energy over a long period of years. . . . We are in for a long pull." [9] While the sudden onset of the Korean War severely upset this deliberate approach, producing a swift and somewhat open-ended mobilization, still the Eisenhower "long haul" was not so radical a shift from the "long pull" as the administration supposed it to be.

Also in late April 1953, Senator Taft and other powerful Republicans in Congress urged the immediate appointment of a new set of military chiefs, a recommendation reflecting their conviction that the holdovers in the Pentagon were deeply imbued with the Truman-Acheson policies and thus bound to resist new departures in military policy. General Bradley had publicly scorned Taft's "Gibraltar theory of defense," and his colleagues on the Joint Chiefs of Staff seemed to the Republicans wholly oriented toward a Europe-first policy. As a result of these strong representations, Eisenhower was persuaded to appoint new chiefs in early May, and to put them to work on defining future policy about four months before they would assume full responsibility as chiefs of their respective services. Defense Secretary Wilson obtained Taft's approval of all the names over whiskey and soda in the latter's apartment in the Wardman Park. [10] Thus Admiral Radford (as chairman) and General Ridgway, Admiral Robert Carney, and General Nathan Twining (as chiefs of army, navy and air force) became the new Joint Chiefs of Staff. The Radford appointment in particular went a long way toward satisfying GOP complaints of an excessively Europe-first orientation, for the dashing, articulate naval commander (whose maxim as a carrier admiral in the war against Japan had been "kill the bastards scientifically") advocated a "strong" and "positive" policy toward China, and was known to favor primary reliance on air and sea power. The President promptly put the new group to work on the next year's military budget (to take effect on July 1, 1954), instructing them to make their study without benefit of staff and enjoining them to strike a proper balance between an ideal military posture and the danger of economic bankruptcy. It was quite untraditional to ask military men to consider factors outside their area of professional concern, but Eisenhower stressed his desire for personal views based on broad and varied experience. He did not want an exhaustive military staff study. Moreover, he wanted no "split papers," only unanimous decisions.[11]

Concurrently, the President launched a reexamination of basic political-military strategy, a study that came to be known as "Operation Solarium" (for the White House sunroom where he met on May 8 with Bedell Smith, Allen Dulles, C. D. Jackson, and Robert Cutler, to define the problem). This involved the creation of separate task forces to examine three possible approaches: (1) whether to continue the "containment" strategy essentially as pursued by the Truman administration; (2) whether to "draw a line" between the Soviet orbit and the free nations, and warn the Kremlin that it ran severe risks if it dared to move across the line; or (3) whether to adopt a serious "liberation" strategy based on a vigorous program of psychological, political, economic and paramilitary measures. By October (and having the benefit of several important intervening events — i.e., the Korean armistice, the unsuccessful East German uprising, and the Soviet detonation of a hydrogen bomb), the senior planners essentially confirmed the validity of "containment" with the understanding that American air-nuclear deterrent power might play a somewhat larger role in containing proxy insurgencies in the unstable Third World. The alternative of "liberation" was firmly rejected.[12] Robert Bowie represented Dulles and the State Department on the senior staff group that reached these conclusions.

As the new military chiefs analyzed the related problems of military force composition and cost, they found themselves working in an atmosphere of rising expectations for budgetary savings. The Secretary of the Treasury, George Humphrey, who wanted both a balanced budget and a tax cut in February 1955, had established a savings target of $12 billion and was expecting to obtain at least half of this from cuts in defense spending. Eisenhower also wanted a balanced budget, but was unwilling to cut deeply into defense in order to achieve it. Nevertheless, he judged that the end of the Korean War should produce significant savings in manpower and hence in money. This consequential process came to a kind of climax on October 13 at a meeting of the National Security Council, at which Secretary Wilson and Admiral Radford presented their conclusions. Their estimated requirement for the new fiscal year was $35 billion in "new obligational authority," or $500 million *more* than the sum finally appropriated for the then current year. To this conclusion Humphrey reacted with "surprise and dismay," as he had anticipated a figure of about $30 billion; the President was also disappointed.[13] Meeting this decidedly cool reaction, Radford then undertook to argue that the desired economies might well be feasible if the basis for military planning were more sharply defined — that is, if, instead of having to develop forces for a wide range of contingencies (all-out nuclear war, conventional general war, limited nuclear war, and limited conventional war), the Joint Chiefs of Staff were allowed to make plans on the assumption that nuclear weapons would be used whenever it was technologically advantageous to do so. No decision was taken at the October 13 meeting, but these remarks of Radford's were soon to become the heart of the "New Look" doctrine and the official rationale for manpower reductions in the army and navy.[14]

On October 30, the President approved a new paper (NSC-162/2) which approved the *planning assumption* that nuclear weapons would be used in limited war situations. While such situations were not defined, the implication was that they included potential conflicts in which the United States would previously have used moderate-to-large-scale conventional forces — e.g., Korea. The President retained in his own hands sole authority to order the use of nuclear weapons, but the new planning guidance had the effect of stimulating the development of "tactical" nuclear weapons and of operational doctrine for their use in a wide variety of contingent situations; it also had the effect of virtually foreclosing the army and navy from establishing requirements for manpower and equipment on the assumption that the United States would have to fight a sustained and large-scale conventional war. Impassioned and cogent, but unavailing, protests came from General Ridgway, the Army Chief of Staff, and from Robert Anderson, the Secretary of the Navy. They argued that, faced with an impending neutralization of American nuclear forces (owing to the growth of Soviet nuclear power), it was dangerous to base the security of American interests so heavily on the narrow doctrine of nuclear retaliation. The official rejoinder by the Deputy Secretary of Defense, Roger Keyes, was a dubious, technologically inspired assertion that the nation must "have the courage to discard the outmoded procedures and weapons which no longer serve more than tradition." [15] And the Secretary of the Treasury applied the budgetary clincher: "There would be no defense," he declared, but only "disaster in a military program that scorned the resources and problems of our economy — erecting majestic defenses and battlements for the protection of a country that was bankrupt." [16]

The "New Look" was thus, in its essence, a military posture based not upon a rigorous analysis of enemy capabilities (present or potential) nor even of enemy intentions; it grew out of domestic considerations of economy and political-psychological preference. It consisted, first and foremost, of a presidential decision to *plan* for the use of nuclear weapons in situations short of all-out war (though it involved no absolute increase in American nuclear striking power). Its philosophy was to accept greater destructiveness in war in return for a lower cost in the preparation for war.

The "Massive Retaliation" Speech

Dulles played only a small role in the detailed debate leading to the new posture, particularly with respect to its military logic and the question of whether or not it would seriously weaken the American capability to fight limited, "brush-fire" wars. In part, his limited participation simply reflected his nonmilitary background and his preoccupation with foreign affairs, but it also reflected his concentration on the "deterrent" as distinguished from the "war fighting" aspects of the doctrine — that is to say, on the political as distinct from the military problem.

It was characteristic of his approach that he did not often find it necessary to think about military matters beyond the problem of devising and issuing political warnings. All through his tenure as Secretary of State, he displayed a broadly uncritical acceptance of Pentagon representations as to what American armed forces could or could not do — a tendency that dismayed his senior staff assistants, like Robert Bowie, who felt that Radford seriously misled him with assurances that tactical nuclear weapons were only "moderate" in their destructiveness and that American conventional forces were "adequate" for a range of contingent situations in which the use of even small nuclear weapons would be appallingly inappropriate. In part, Dulles's aloofness from military detail reflected a simple lack of interest; in part, it seemed a piece of calculated political prudence. As Dulles reasoned it, according to Bowie, the President was a military expert whereas he was not; thus, an effort on his part to debate military issues with Eisenhower could only reveal Eisenhower's greater understanding; this in turn would tend to diminish Eisenhower's respect for Dulles's judgment — a diminution which might extend beyond military affairs into the domain of foreign policy. For the same reason — a concern to maintain preeminence in his own domain — Dulles generally declined to cross swords with Radford and the Pentagon on technical military issues.[17]

Nevertheless it fell to Dulles, by inadvertence or design, to make the first, most inclusive and most dramatic announcement of the new military strategy — on January 12, 1954, in a speech to the Council on Foreign Relations. Previously, Dulles told his audience, he had spoken of "various parts of our foreign policy"; on this occasion he would present the "over-all view of those policies which relate to security." [18] What followed was a terse, choppy lawyer's brief, faithful to fact in its description of the considerations set out in NSC-162/2, but giving that document a more dramatic interpretation than its framers had intended. It was also a strikingly personal interpretation, for the threat of nuclear retaliation was couched, almost verbatim, in the vivid language of his 1952 article in *Life*

There was some good in past policies, the Secretary said, but "we need to recall that what we did was in the main emergency action, imposed on us by our enemies. . . . Emergency measures are costly, they are superficial and they imply that the enemy has the initiative." The new aim, he said, must be to make collective security more effective and less costly "by placing more reliance on deterrent power, and less dependence on local defensive power." Local defense must be reinforced by "the further deterrent of massive retaliatory power." He then briefly traced the transition from the old to the new posture: "So long as our basic policy concepts were unclear, our military leaders could not be selective in building our military power. If an enemy could pick his time and place and method of warfare — and if our policy was to remain the traditional one of meeting aggression by direct and local opposition — then we needed to be ready to fight in the arctic and in the tropics; in Asia, the Near East and in Europe; by sea, by land and by air; with old weapons and with new weapons." But all this had now been changed by reason of the President's having taken "some basic policy decisions." The "basic decision was to depend primarily upon a great capacity to retaliate, instantly, by means and at places of our choosing," for that "permits of a selection of military means instead of a multiplication of means." [19]

It seems doubtful that Dulles was fully aware of the difficulties he faced in making a persuasive case for the new doctrine; more likely, its virtues were to him self-evident, but if he did recognize vulnerable points he trusted to his own powers of advocacy to shore them up or make them disappear. In any event, his text revealed itself as an advocate's pleading, more declaration than analysis, and carefully avoiding logical weaknesses and awkward questions. It concentrated, for example, entirely on what the United States could do to the enemy, and ignored both what the enemy might do in return and what this would mean to people and nations located near the point of nuclear conflict. Thus it failed to mention that the Soviets also possessed nuclear weapons and the means of their delivery, or that their capability was steadily growing. Nor did it try to anticipate the question of whether or not it was reasonable for the world to assume that the United States would "instantly" apply maximum destructive power to any breach of the peace wherever it might occur, knowing the Soviets could respond in kind against European or American cities. The failure in this respect was probably another example of

Dulles's chronic trouble in dealing with multiple audiences. The speech was written as a stern warning to the Kremlin; unfortunately, the rest of the world was listening in.

The speech also revealed the strong unilateral, quasi-isolationist strain in the outlook of the new administration. In declaring that American military action would be "by means and at places of our choosing," Dulles served notice that whatever the complexities of treaty obligations and alliance politics, the United States reserved the right to act alone and would no longer tolerate a situation wherein the Soviets, by creating a provocation through a satellite, could commit America to inconclusive collective action. Showing through the argument for greater reliance on "massive retaliatory power" was a yearning to disengage from complexity, while at the same time continuing to exercise a dominant influence. And beyond this discernible unilateralism, at least one passage seemed to reflect Dulles's personal zeal for a sort of "pacifist reform" of the international system (which had its roots, certainly not in NSC-162/2, but in Woodrow Wilson and in Dulles's first book, *War, Peace and Change*). It implied accepting for the United States the role of world policeman, but to give this conception a logical framework, he found it necessary to define the world as if it were a homogeneous community. Thus, he argued that maintenance of a central deterrent power "is accepted practice so far as local communities are concerned. We keep locks on our doors; but we do not have an armed guard in every home. We rely principally upon a community security system so well equipped to punish any who break in and steal that, in fact, would-be aggressors are generally deterred." That, he argued, was the "modern" way to get "maximum protection at a bearable cost.[20] It was neither a happy nor an apt analogy.

Reaction

The Dulles theory of deterrence (as previously propounded) had possessed one overriding aim: to make United States intentions "crystal clear," so that a "potential aggressor" would not "miscalculate" the certainty and the strength of the American response. Perhaps the deepest irony of the January 12 speech was that its net effect was to compound the ambiguities for friend and foe alike. No doubt, in addressing the Soviets, a measure of ambiguity had its uses, but the speech failed to define any single area, interest or objective which the United States would definitely defend, with nuclear weapons or otherwise; at the same time it broadly implied that the new policy extended the prospect of instant nuclear retaliation well beyond the agreed NATO commitment to the farthest fringe areas of Asia. Public reaction was thus not surprisingly an uproar of confusion, consternation and disbelief. While the speech did contain a few caveats ("Local defense will always be important"), the press and public read it either as the serious intent of the U.S. government to transform every border incident into a nuclear showdown, or else as a glaringly transparent bluff that would (by proving wholly inapplicable to the task of guiding revolutionary change in the fringe areas) serve to weaken the credibility of American policy everywhere. The tactical advocate had loosed a verbal rocket at the Kremlin, but the side effects spread psychological devastation in a hundred other capitals. All the logical weaknesses of the doctrine, all the awkward questions, which his presentation had consciously or unconsciously pushed under the rug, were now embarrassingly thrown up to the administration in a thousand protests. A hasty and endless attempt was made to answer them, which led Walter Lippmann to the comment that "official explanations of the new look have become so voluminous that it is almost a career in itself to keep up with them." [21] Dulles's law partner, Eustace Seligman, later put his finger on the psychological flaw in the doctrine with a disarming and innocent candor: Dulles "felt that the ideal way of preventing another war would be for us to have such a powerful aviation force with nuclear weapons that no other country would dare to start a war. . . . Of course, it subsequently proved that the weakness was that nobody took the threat seriously. And in so far as they did take it seriously, our allies got very worried that we might start a nuclear war without their approval — so we were caught between those who were afraid we'd do it, and those who didn't believe we would." [22]

Thrown once more on the defensive, Dulles published (on March 16 in *Foreign Affairs*) a heavily qualified version of his thesis. This acknowledged that "massive atomic and thermonuclear retaliation is not the kind of power which could most usefully be evoked under all circumstances"; [23] it also denied that, in the event of "a Communist attack somewhere in Asia, atom or hydrogen bombs will necessarily be dropped on the great industrial centers of China or Russia." [24] Nevertheless, reflecting the basic policy decision (NSC-162/2), it insisted that should the free world attempt to "match the potential [of the] Communist forces, man for man and tank for tank . . . it could bankrupt itself and not achieve security over a sustained period." [25] A "better strategy for its defense" must be devised by the free world, based upon "its own special assets" of air and naval power and atomic weapons; "imaginative use" must be made of these for deterrent purposes, with the aim of building "a system in which local defensive strength is reinforced by more mobile deterrent power." [26] This far more careful formulation of the "New Look" suggested that it was much closer to the original intent of the Eisenhower decision. There are times when style makes all the difference. Stentorian warnings appeared to be a compulsive element of the Dulles theory of deterrence. Eisenhower, on the other hand, tended to view the nuclear force as a quietly unassailable backdrop whose relation to policy should be rather more subtly communicated. He had ordered the phrase "retaliatory striking power" deleted from the GOP platform in 1952, and presumably he felt at least as great a distaste for "massive retaliatory power," which was Dulles's current phrase. It is interesting to imagine how the doctrine might have emerged if he himself had chosen to announce and explain it. The difference probably would have been notable. Yet he presumably approved the Dulles presentation.

After all the explanations and qualifying amendments were in, Lippmann commented that, while the words of the Dulles speech "convey the impression that something momentous and novel has been decided," the sum of the subsequent comments by the military chiefs and by Dulles himself nevertheless "make it plain that there has been no radical change in our strategy policy." [27] This was broadly speaking an accurate statement, but it was not quite precise to imply that nothing had changed. The "New Look" did involve a deliberate shift toward greater emphasis on nuclear warning, and this did have a marked effect on the administration's attitude and approach to possible conflict and "crisis management." Moreover, it greatly influenced military planning and the composition of U.S. armed forces (stimulating development of small nuclear weapons and their supporting operational doctrines, and discouraging consideration of non-nuclear weapons, forces and techniques). The effect was to make the United States progressively dependent on a nuclear capability it could not safely or rationally use, and at the same time to deny it a confident capability for engaging in limited conventional war. From the perspective of 1973, it is plausible to argue that the absence of a strong conventional capability was an important factor in keeping the Eisenhower administration from a military intervention in Vietnam, both in 1954 and toward the end of the decade. In any event, the "New Look" represented changes from the Truman-Acheson period.

14

"United Action" in Indochina

NONE OF DULLES'S ACTIONS was to bring forth a darker harvest than his refusal to allow United States policy to support or even countenance a diplomatic settlement of the French colonial war in Indochina in the period from 1954 to 1956. That the opportunity for genuine settlement was there seems now beyond reasonable dispute. The new Soviet government, still moving to reduce its arms burden and shift its resources toward greater emphasis on consumer goods, evidenced a serious desire to avoid a new confrontation. The Peking regime was on its best behavior, anxious to end its isolation and restore its prestige in the world community by playing the role of peacemaker. Both Russia and China imposed concessions on the Vietminh which the military situation did not require and which Ho Chi Minh, left to his own devices, would probably have successfully resisted. The British worked firmly and responsibly for a compromise solution. The French, after the fall of the Laniel government, were at last prepared to accept reality. Only the United States refused the uses of genuine diplomacy. Although he demonstrated tactical flexibility beneath a strident rhetoric, Dulles steadfastly refused to acknowledge the existence of any reasonable or legitimate claims on the Communist side. When these were nonetheless reflected in the Geneva Agreements, he refused all entreaty from Eden, Molotov and Chou En-lai that he be bound by them; this would, he said, risk "prejudicing basic principles to which the United States must adhere if it is to be true to itself." [1]

His posture owed a good deal to his fear of the Republican right wing. Acheson had paid dearly for his considered conclusion in 1949: "The unfortunate but inescapable fact is that the ominous result of the civil war in China was beyond the control of the government of the United States. Nothing that this country did or could have done within the reasonable limits of its capabilities could have changed that result." [2] Senators Knowland, Bridges, Jenner, and Wherry and other members of the China Lobby scathingly denounced the State Department's China White Paper as "a 1,054-page whitewash of a wishful, do-nothing policy which has succeeded only in placing Asia in danger of Soviet conquest." [3] Nor was this the worst. In an atmosphere supercharged by the Russian coup in Czechoslovakia, the first Russian atomic test, and the convictions of Alger Hiss and Dr. Klaus Fuchs, the archdemagogue McCarthy raised the cry of treason. "How can we account for our present situation unless we believe that men high in this government are concerting to deliver us to disaster? This must be the product of a great conspiracy on a scale so immense as to dwarf any previous venture in the history of man." [4] In 1954, McCarthy's personal power was waning, but the Republican Asia-firsters remained a reckless and destructive cabal.

But if Dulles demonstrated a strong disinclination to challenge these forces in the Congress, acting with a prudence that seemed to verge at times on moral cowardice, it must be appreciated that he shared many of their views: their militant anti-Communism, their impatient unilateralist tendencies, and their belief that America possessed the power — and the moral right to use it — to make the world safe for a moral America. He had argued that the geographical boundaries of NATO were too restrictive to meet the global Communist problem. He endorsed rollback and liberation in Asia. At the "Little Bermuda" in 1953, he had told Bidault that the further French measures of July 3 to "perfect" Indochinese independence were deeply gratifying because they removed the colonial stigma from the struggle. And speaking before the American Federation of Labor, three months later, he claimed that this action "transformed" the struggle, making it far easier for Americans to support victory for the anti-Communist forces with a clear conscience.[5] Dulles's contemporary Victor Bator has called his negative contributions to Geneva and its somber aftermath a genuine tragedy "caused not by his weakness, but by his innate moral and spiritual strength, which made his anti-Communist fervor a blinding dogma and deprived him of flexibility when wisdom demanded it." [6] Thus, lacking the foresight and the capacity for objectivity which are the marks of genuine statesmanship, Dulles fastened the United States to a policy which (as Molotov said with prophetic truth on April 29, 1954) seriously erred in its tendency to "attribute to Communism every movement of the oppressed peoples toward freedom and national independence," and had "no prospects whatever, for it is in conflict with the entire course of the historical development in Asia." [7]

French and American Perspectives

After seven years of cruel and frustrating struggle, the French forces had steadily lost ground to the insurgency led by the Communist-trained Ho Chi Minh; the war had become a running sore, draining away French blood and treasure and bitterly dividing metropolitan France. But although the national will to carry on the battle was in fact ebbing fast, the French government, pressed by a willful bureaucracy whose strength lay in its continuity, still dreamed elaborate dreams. In early 1954, the new scheme for victory was the Navarre Plan, a forerunner of "Vietnamization," which called for raising another 100,000 Vietnamese forces and for sending out from the metropole another 50,000 volunteer French legionnaires. If everything went well, total forces on the French side would be increased from 400,000 to 550,000. But it would take time, and there was general agreement that it could *never* succeed unless the French provided the Vietnamese with sufficient incentive to make their own larger, more effective fighting effort. The only adequate incentive was genuine political independence.

Here lay the rub: not only all the French political parties who wanted to fight on, but also most of those who favored a negotiated settlement, were passionately wedded to the view that Indochina must remain within the French Union, that there must be impediments upon the sovereignty of the Associated States of Indochina, or else there was no warrant for further struggle. If the Emperor Bao Dai were so ungrateful for the fruits of French culture as to demand total independence, so the reasoning ran, why then should Frenchmen fight for Bao Dai? The French constitution imposed a particular legal status on the Associated States, and the existing chaos of parties in the French parliament precluded amendment. But beyond legalities lay more fundamental political and strategic obstacles, related to France's self-image as a Great Power. Genuine independence for Indochina would trigger similar demands in the French colonies of Tunisia, Morocco, and Algeria; for this reason, it was a development to be avoided at all costs. Caught in the toils of an identity crisis, proud in spirit, poor in resources, divided in purpose, unwilling to fight and unable to settle, France drifted.

The United States showed itself to be, on the whole, unsympathetic to the French dilemma. For Dulles and his colleagues in Washington, Indochina was less a deplorable colonial problem than a crucial link in the chain of global resistance to International Communism. Still judging the Mao regime to be basically the agent of a unified, compulsively expansionist movement controlled by the Kremlin, they thought a breaching of the chain in Southeast Asia would set off a whole series of Communist insurrections throughout Asia. Dulles, who seemed most concerned by the threat of direct Chinese military invasion on the Korean model, had warned in September 1953 that "the Chinese Communist regime should realize that such a second aggression [sic] could not occur without grave consequences which might not be confined to Indochina." [8] But while American politics was thus transfixed by the menace of Chinese Communism in Asia, there was no broad-based public readiness to underwrite a deeper American commitment or involvement, the strident minority in the Senate to the contrary notwithstanding. Less than a year away from the pain and frustration of the Korean War, the American people were not yet ready to countenance more American bleeding and dying. The evident gap between the sense of threat and the willingness to meet it thus tended to be filled by a judgment that the French must go on fighting in Indochina. Continued French resistance on the rim of China for the sake of "freedom" everywhere became something of an American political imperative. The United States would supply the arms.

The Berlin Conference

The French policy of drift came to an end in late January 1954, at the Foreign Ministers conference in Berlin, the first such meeting to be held with the Soviets in five years. Although its agenda was ostensibly confined to the problems of Germany and Austria, Molotov soon proposed a five-power conference — to include the Chinese Communists — hinting that in such a forum the questions of both Korea and Indochina could be discussed. Dulles's reply was hardly calculated to advance the proposition: "Who is this Chou En-lai whose addition to our circle would make possible all that so long seemed impossible? He is the leader of a regime which gained de facto power on the China mainland through bloody war, which has liquidated millions of Chinese . . . which so diverts the economic resources of its impoverished people to military efforts that they starve by millions; which became an open aggressor in Korea and was so adjudged by the United Nations; which promotes open aggression in Indochina by training and equipping the aggressors and supplying them with vast amounts of war munitions. Such is the man Mr. Molotov urges would enable the world to solve all its problems and to gain lasting peace and mounting prosperity." [9]

Bidault, to whom the proposal seemed more directly addressed, replied that France did indeed desire negotiations, but first needed "pledges of goodwill" [10] that China would cease its material support of the Vietminh. This seemed to close the matter for a while. As the conference wore on, however, the French military situation in Indochina steadily worsened, and soon reached such a point of deterioration that Premier Laniel concluded that his government could not survive unless Bidault brought home from Berlin a firm agreement to negotiate the Indochina war.

Dulles now recognized that France could not avoid negotiations, and that the United States could not frontally oppose such an effort. A stiff-necked American reaction would split the Western alliance, confirming in Paris the widely held belief that the United States was insisting on unlimited French sacrifice for the sake of Washington's strategy of global anti-Communism, and raising the level of exasperation in London. He thus accepted the inevitable, but went to elaborate lengths to protect his domestic flanks. In agreeing to a Geneva conference on Korea and Indochina that would include Communist China, he insisted on inserting into the communiqué the understanding that "neither the invitation to, nor the holding of, the above-mentioned conference shall be deemed to imply diplomatic recognition in any case where it has not already been accorded." [11] And he drew a sharp, not altogether real, distinction between sitting down with Peking on broad matters "dealing generally with the peace of the world" and on narrow, practical matters. "It is . . . one thing," he told his American television audience on February 24, "to recognize evil as a fact. It is another thing to take evil to one's breast and call it good." [12]

Despite these legal caveats and moral disclaimers, the GOP right wing was not appeased. At meetings of the Foreign Relations Committee on February 23 and 24, Senator Knowland warned Dulles against any "slips" that might lead to diplomatic recognition of Red China, and said bluntly the administration would be held accountable. In public speeches, he and other members of the China Lobby then moved to vent their fury at any proposal that seemed to presage a negotiated settlement of the Indochina war, for this would be, in their view, an intolerable Far Eastern Munich.[13] Dulles defended himself fundamentally on the ground that Indochina was France's war, and that the United States could not obstruct a French desire to negotiate unless it were willing to sacrifice both EDC and basic relations with France. He laid particular emphasis on his refusal to attend a conference with Red China without a written agreement that no American recognition would be involved, and even sought to gratify his obsessive critics with an emotional account of his struggle with the devil at Berlin: until Molotov's final capitulation on this point, he said, the clever Bolshevik had "sought by every artifice and device, directly and through our allies, to tempt us to meet with Communist China. . . . We refused and our . . . allies stood with us." [14] Moreover, he assured the nation, the Chinese regime "will not come to Geneva to be honored by us, but rather to account before the bar of world opinion." [15] Political theatrics aside, these statements reflected deep-seated conviction. Dulles looked forward to the Geneva negotiations with pronounced distaste, and feared a French sellout of a vital free-world salient.

The Ely Visit

In mid-March, the French military situation in Indochina began to fall apart. Parachute battalions sent to form a strong fortress base at Dien Bien Phu, in a deliberate effort to lure an elusive enemy into a set battle and there destroy him with superior firepower, suddenly found themselves beleaguered. Vietminh raids destroyed more than a dozen troop-transport aircraft on the ground, cutting off the bastion's chief means of resupply. Within two days of the first attacks, General Navarre, who had conceived and ordered the operation, apparently concluded that Dien Bien Phu would fall, in the absence of some dramatic relief operation.[16] General Ely, the French chief of staff, fresh from an inspection trip to Saigon, now arrived in Washington on a diplomatic mission of gravest import: to inform the United States that France had decided it could not win a military victory in Indochina, and to ask for help in securing a settlement. While he was, of course, anxious for any immediate American assistance that might lift the siege of Dien Bien Phu, his main purpose was to convey the strong impression that time was running out for France, that the crisis was not remote but immediate, and that a settlement short of military victory was not avoidable.[17]

Washington encountered difficulty both in receiving and accepting the message. On March 22, Eisenhower met with Ely, accompanied by Admiral Radford, and heard his pessimistic assessment. But the President's soldierly concern focused primarily on the immediate military problem — the fate of the besieged fortress — and at the conclusion of the meeting he instructed Radford to do everything possible to meet French requests for help in lifting the siege. Eisenhower's preoccupation with Dien Bien Phu prevented Ely from laying emphasis on the far more fundamental strategic point. The next day, however, Ely was able to tell Dulles with clarity and force that France was now determined upon a settlement, and that all military operations would henceforward be restricted in time and scale to what was judged necessary to bring that about.[18] Dulles seems to have received this information with conspicuous coldness. Not even bothering to express an opinion on the French decision, nor to ask any questions about the military situation, he instead declaimed to Ely on the necessity of preventing Communist domination of Southeast Asia and the need for a regional defense pact.[19] With magisterial arrogance he then issued his own statement, which said: "We have no reason to abandon the so-called Navarre Plan. . . . There have been no military reversals. . . . I do not expect that there is going to be a Communist victory in Indo-china." [20] The statement also denigrated the forthcoming negotiations at Geneva by insisting that peace would come only through the achievement of military supremacy.

Meanwhile Radford, a very hard-liner who believed a showdown with Communist China was sooner or later inevitable, had taken his instructions from Eisenhower very literally. On March 25, he gave Ely his opinion that tactical air strikes on the surrounding enemy positions could relieve the garrison at Dien Bien Phu, and he thought it feasible to use B-29's based in the Philippines, covered by carrier planes from the Seventh Fleet. As he recalled it in 1965, "We could have helped the French with air strikes. Whether these alone would have been successful in breaking the siege of Dien Bien Phu is debatable. If we had used atomic weapons, we probably would have been successful." [21] But he added, "I never felt that it was basically a question of atomic weapons at all. That could have been decided one way or the other at the time of a specific military operation." But if conventional bombing had been tried and had failed, "then the question would have come up." [22]

Ely departed for Paris on March 26 with the impression that "everything was in the bag" regarding American air support for the beleaguered fortress, but Radford later insisted that the French general must have failed to grasp two central points: one, that Radford had no authority to commit the United States government; and two, that France could not realistically expect to obtain American air support without "internationalizing" the war. As he recalled it, "Ely wanted us to come in, strike Dien Bien Phu, and break the siege . . . then withdraw and leave the fighting to them." But "you can't just get one foot wet and then pull out again. . . . We would have to have a voice in the war — in the command — in the planning from then on. And the question was whether we should run it or not. I was in favor of running it." [23] Despite these polite disclaimers, the episode showed the disturbing readiness of a forceful, cocksure Chairman of the Joint Chiefs of Staff to push the administration into a military fait accompli of unknown dimensions, on the strength of a vague presidential instruction and without serious consideration and reflection by other responsible elements of the government. Immediately following Ely's departure, the upper echelons of the State and Defense Departments were locked in anxious debate on the Radford proposal: support was expressed for further aid to the French, and the possible need for American military force was not excluded; but serious doubts were cast upon the wisdom of any attempt to bomb Dien Bien

Phu, and troubled questions were raised as to whether or not the nation, through Radford, had given a commitment.

"United Action"

Details to one side, the Eisenhower administration was plainly sobered, even shocked, by the import of the Ely visit, for it brought home to them, really for the first time, how fragile was the French position in Asia and how imminent the prospect of its collapse. The first instinctive reaction was that France must not be allowed to quit. Dulles, noting with concern the general passivity of public and congressional opinion, quickly set about to arm himself and the President with a mandate for bold action in the event their worst fears should be realized. He had misgivings about the proposal to use American bombers at Dien Bien Phu, considering it "a poor way for the U.S. to get involved," [24] but his doubts were not rooted in an aversion to a tough policy involving war or the serious risk of war. He felt, rather, that the Radford proposal was too narrow in scope, that it imposed no conditions on French colonialism, that it failed to address the broad question of how to organize a long-term anti-Communist defense position in Southeast Asia. His own view was that the problem could be met by an organized warning, involving a tailored application of the deterrence doctrine he had expounded to such clamorous effect in his already famous "massive retaliation" speech of January 12. Such a warning implied the readiness to fight, and the political objective was not compromise settlement; it was Communist defeat. As he reported to the President at this time, he had reminded Ely that "if the United States sent its flag and its own military establishment — land, sea or air — into the Indo-China war . . . we would want to have a success." [25] The absolutist tenor of his thinking was similarly revealed at a press conference two weeks later:

Q: What would you regard as a reasonably satisfactory settlement of the Indochina situation?
Dulles: The removal by the Chinese Communists of their apparent desire to extend the political system of Communism to Southeast Asia.
Q: That means a complete withdrawal of the Communists from Indochina?
Dulles: That is what I would regard as a satisfactory solution.
Q: Is there any compromise that might be offered if that is not entirely satisfactory to the Communists?
Dulles: I had not thought of any.[26]

On March 29, he delivered a major policy address before the Overseas Press Club of America, to alert the American people to the prospect of dramatic and possibly grave choices. Putting the most favorable face on equivocal French measures to provide political freedom for the Associated States, he blamed Ho Chi Minh for "attempting to prevent the orderly development of independence." Then he turned to developing the theme of Indochina as a vital economic and strategic asset of the free world. It is important, he argued, not alone because it provides vital raw materials, but because it sits "astride the most direct and best developed sea and air routes between the Pacific and South Asia." If it should fall to Communist control, not only the Philippines, Australia, and New Zealand, but the entire Western Pacific area would be "strategically endangered." Indeed the imposition of such control "under the conditions of today" would be a "grave threat to the whole free community." Having set the stage, he then declared the operational policy: "The United States feels that that possibility [of Communist control] should not be passively accepted, but should be met by united action." [27]

The timing of the speech — only three days after Ely's departure — seems to reflect an urgent compulsion to reassert personal control over American policy, which had drifted toward Radford and the French. An official request from Paris for the American bombing effort was expected momentarily, and it was not certain how Eisenhower would respond. There were, in addition to Radford, several highly placed supporters for it in the executive branch, including Vice-president Richard Nixon and Chairman Lewis Straus of the Atomic Energy Commission. The Dulles counterformulation was certainly artful. The operational statement of policy, which seemed so resolute, proved on close examination to be a model of Sullivan and Cromwell ambiguity. It did *not* say that the grave threat must be actively resisted; it left open the possibility that ultimately it might have to be accepted. And what was "united action"? The ambiguity was surely deliberate, and for a very good reason — no clear line of action had been decided even within the executive branch, and no consultations had been undertaken with either Congress or allies. The fine print, although scrutinized in foreign chancelleries, was for the most part lost upon the journalists. What they heard and reported was in essence that holy struggle against Communism was necessary in Southeast Asia, because vital American interests were at stake, and because attempted settlement would compromise American principles. The *New York Times* said editorially: "Dulles was as plain as words would allow in insisting that the United States look upon this struggle as vital to its interests and . . . not stand passively by." [28]

Not until five days later was there a move to consult with Congress. On Saturday morning, April 3, Dulles called a secret meeting at the State

Department at which Radford explained his proposal for air strikes at Dien Bien Phu to eight senior members of the legislature (Senators Knowland, Milliken, Lyndon Johnson, Richard Russell, and Clements; Congressmen Joseph Martin, John McCormack, and J. P. Priest). Radford admitted that his proposal risked war with China, and acknowledged that it did not have the support of the other chiefs of staff. Under questioning, it became clear that, if the bombing failed to achieve its objective, the fact that U.S. prestige would have been committed might well require the sending of American ground forces (this was the central point of General Ridgway's strong dissent as Army Chief of Staff). The congressional reaction was mixed, but a majority was troubled by the unilateral nature of the proposed action and equally by the prospect of having to commit ground forces. The senior Democrats, Senators Russell and Lyndon Johnson, implicitly stated the Democratic condition for support in variants of the question: "Where do the British stand?" No one could answer that question.[29]

The following evening, Sunday, April 4, Dulles and Radford met alone with the President, from which discussion emerged Eisenhower's decision that the United States would not act in Indochina except with congressional support. And such support, it was calculated, would be contingent upon three conditions: (1) the United States must act as part of a coalition including the free nations of Southeast Asia, the Philippines and "the British Commonwealth"; (2) the French must "accelerate their independence program" for the Associated States, so that no American military action could be interpreted as support for French colonialism; and (3) the French must agree not to withdraw their forces if American forces were put in.[30] This was, as it turned out, an extremely important meeting, in which Eisenhower effectively sidetracked the Radford proposal for an immediate bombing effort, and reasserted presidential command in a fluid situation that could easily get out of control. Radford was a clever, fast-moving operator whose supporters on Asian issues included Vice-president Nixon, General Curtis Lemay of the Strategic Air Command, and most of the China Lobby senators. Over the years, Eisenhower treated Radford's judgments with skepticism and, on the issue of intervention in Indochina, he thought General Ridgway's dissents were cogent and compelling. The three conditions which Eisenhower imposed before he would seriously entertain intervention were not, at the time, considered impossible to meet, but to meet them would take time and wide consultation. In retrospect, they reflect the solid common sense of a President with a feeling in his bones that military adventures ought not to be undertaken without allies, and that decisions involving war and peace must have explicit congressional participation and support.

So the meeting neutralized Radford. Did it also neutralize Dulles? The

Secretary of State was not enthusiastic about an air strike at Dien Bien Phu, and one recent historian has suggested that the April 3 meeting was a deliberate stratagem by Dulles to defuse the Radford proposal by demonstrating the opposition of congressional leaders, thus avoiding a bruising struggle with Radford supporters inside the executive branch.[31] On this theory, Eisenhower's absence from the meeting was significant, for it implied that he was not prepared to argue for the Radford proposal. The theory tends to be sustained by Dulles's prompt and negative response when Laniel and Bidault, having conferred with General Ely, conveyed a formal French request for air strikes on April 5. He replied that the United States could not act without congressional approval or in advance of allied consultations. On balance, it seems clear that Dulles wanted and needed the new presidential ground rules as a means of restoring his own control of policy, and he had probably prepared the first draft. On the other hand, in light of his own hyperthyroid performance over the next month and his strong tendency to unilateral action, it also seems clear that presidential insistence on both British and congressional support were restraints on Dulles that constituted a helpful "management control" for Eisenhower.

The three ground rules now formed the boundaries of Dulles's operational guidance, and no one could charge him with giving them a passive treatment or a strict construction: during the next month he was galvanized to build a base of domestic and allied support for a wide range of apparently broad, though carefully unspecified, actions. Richard Rovere of the *New Yorker* wrote in early April that the Secretary of State was conducting "one of the boldest campaigns of political suasion ever undertaken by an American statesman."[32] Congressmen, political leaders of all colorations, newspapermen and television personalities were being "rounded up in droves and escorted to lectures and briefings on what the State Department regards as the American stake in Indo-China."[33] Were that area to be "lost," the color charts showed that "Communist influence" would radiate dramatically in a semicircle outward from Indochina to Thailand, Burma, Malaya and far down across the South China Sea to Indonesia; the briefing officers listed strategic raw materials that would accrue to Russia and China and thereafter be denied to the free nations; if America should fail to save the day, the prospect was faltering resistance to Communism in the whole Asian arc from India to Japan. On the basis of both his public and off-the-record remarks to the press, Dulles was represented as believing that "we should not flinch at doing anything that is needed to prevent a Communist victory"; indeed if American moral and material support should prove unable to hold the French in line, "then we ought to commit our own forces to the conflict."[34]

The Europeans Balk

As Dulles moved forward to win support for "united action," he seemed surprised at the nervous irritation and suspicion he had aroused in London and Paris by his presumption to speak for Europe, even tacitly to bind Europe to American concepts and plans, without consultation. He operated, instinctively, on the assumption that America's clear power superiority gave it an unquestioned right to lead in a peremptory manner, but to London and Paris in 1954, this was still an intolerable assumption. And reinforcing European resentment over his address of March 29 was a powerful emotional resistance to the apocalyptic implications of his "massive retaliation" speech.

There was also the ambiguity of "united action," and, while subsequent messages clarified this somewhat, the clarifications did not please the Europeans. In a letter to Churchill of April 4 (almost certainly drafted by Dulles), the President said a primary purpose of "united action" was to prevent a French capitulation and keep France in the war whatever the cost: "I can understand the very natural desire of the French to seek an end to this war which has been bleeding them for eight years," but "there is no negotiated solution . . . which in its essence would not be either a face-saving device to cover a French surrender or a face-saving device to cover a Communist retirement. The first alternative is too serious . . . to be acceptable." [35] The situation, Eisenhower wrote, called for a new grouping of nations which share "a vital concern" in checking Communist expansion in Asia: "The important thing is that the coalition must be strong and it must be willing to . . . fight if necessary." [36] A message of similar import was sent to the French. Though Dulles later emphasized the *deterrent* aspect of the proposal, the April 4 letter to Churchill in fact made plain the American intention to build a coalition prepared in the last analysis to fight beside the French in an ongoing war, and strongly to oppose any serious search for a settlement at the forthcoming Geneva conference. Some thought that, at this stage, Dulles hoped his coalition plan would scuttle the conference. To Dulles, and presumably to Eisenhower, any conceivable settlement was anathema.

The French and British were quick to see that the American proposal, particularly if promptly implemented, would absolutely close the door to settlement. The French reply accordingly suggested further study, explaining that the sudden creation of an anti-Communist united front would only harden the attitude of the Vietminh and the Red Chinese, thereby creating new difficulties for negotiation that French public opinion would not understand. The British response was equally tepid. Churchill, while not opposed in principle to a joint public warning to Red China, thought that to make it now would further diminish the already slight chances for successful negotiation at Geneva. And while he did not object to some new regional grouping in Southeast Asia, he felt this must be a careful diplomatic undertaking, involving months of preparation, not something to be thrown together in time for a conference at Geneva that was scheduled to begin just three weeks thence (on April 26).[37]

Meanwhile, Dulles was orchestrating a range of actions and statements designed to demonstrate Washington's resolve. The State Department began a vigorous round of diplomatic consultations, in an effort to line up members of the new coalition; the effort included talks with the Chinese Nationalists. Two aircraft carriers from the Seventh Fleet steamed into the South China Sea. Eisenhower held a press conference on April 7 at which he described the strategic situation in Southeast Asia as "a row of falling dominoes." Before the House Foreign Affairs Committee, Dulles called attention to the passage of his March 29 speech which asserted that the free world would be threatened by Communist conquest of Indochina, "by whatever means" it might occur. This phrase was quite deliberate, he said; it meant that United States concern "should not be mitigated by the fact that the means [of conquest] are perhaps technically evasive." [38] Rumors of impending United States intervention flew around Washington.

Having thus rather thoroughly confused his allies, Dulles flew to Europe on April 10 to continue his aggressive quest for their support. Talks with the British lasted for two days, with Dulles trying to convince Eden that the prompt formation of an ad hoc coalition would not undermine the Geneva negotiations, but would on the contrary strengthen the Western bargaining position. Eden's rejoinder was that a joint warning to China would be useless, if Dulles hoped thereby to frighten the Chinese into halting arms aid to the Vietminh. Dulles now said that, contrary to Eisenhower's April 4 letter, he no longer believed in the efficacy of a joint warning for that purpose. What he really sought was a regional security alliance that would deter China from *direct* intervention with her own forces; if this were accomplished, he said, then American and British military intervention in Indochina would be unnecessary.[39] This tactical shift, designed to sweeten the spoon for Eden, unfortunately overlooked the fact that the Vietminh could in all probability defeat the French without the help of Chinese troops; it thus left unclear just who would fight to save Indochina while the new coalition held off the Red Chinese. The charitable view is that this was simply another example of Dulles, the advocate, being carried away by the tactical necessities. To obtain congressional support for American action, it was imperative to bring the British on board; how and under what pretexts one got them there was a secondary consideration. Once they were committed, many things would be possible, not excluding unilateral American military action under the cover of a nominal coalition.

Eden was willing to move toward a regional security organization, but thought he made plain that, as the British saw it, this would take time and careful diplomatic preparation. He did agree that first priority should be given to coordinating allied preparations for the Geneva negotiations and that this effort might include some preparation for a regional grouping. The Dulles-Eden communiqué of April 13 thus said: "We are ready to take part, with the other countries principally concerned, in an examination of the possibility of establishing a collective defense . . . to assure the peace, security, and freedom of Southeast Asia and the Western Pacific." [40] That Eden had in mind no serious effort to form a coalition *before* the Geneva conference seems borne out by his statement to the Commons on the following day that the "desirability" of a collective defense arrangement would be greatly influenced by what happened at Geneva.

Dulles went on to Paris for a full day of talks with the French on April 14, where Bidault insisted that France's first consideration must be to gain an honorable peace at Geneva. He thought no steps should be taken that would risk a hardening of the Chinese attitude, for Red China's willingness to accept a compromise was of the essence for France. But Dulles now revived the joint warning proposal he had presumably discarded in London. A joint warning, he argued, could compel Russia to press both Red China and the Vietminh to accept a compromise. Why? Because the Soviets were just as worried as the Western powers over the risks attendant on "internationalizing" the war.[41] Bidault was not impressed, and the Paris communiqué, while granting the desirability of a regional defense pact, carefully subordinated it to the more urgent reality: "No effort should be spared to make the Geneva Conference a success"; moreover, the evolution of a defense arrangement "would be profoundly conditioned by the outcome of the conference." [42]

By any normal standard of judgment, this diplomatic mission had failed to achieve the purposes Dulles sought, yet within three days of his return to Washington he dispatched invitations to the ambassadors of nine countries (Britain, France, Australia, New Zealand, Thailand, and the three Associated States) to convene on April 20 in Washington for the purpose of establishing a staff-level group for preparatory work on a collective defense pact for Southeast Asia. Dulles acted, in short, as though he had clear British and French support for "united action." It is difficult to escape the conclusion that this move was an attempt to bull-

doze his allies, a blunt effort to build, upon the tenuous base of generalized public agreement, a fait accompli which they, overawed by American
power and determination, would not dare to defy openly. He may have
justified this action to himself by reference to the moral and strategic
imperatives of his cause; a more mundane truth was that, having committed his prestige in the speech of March 29, he could ill afford the
political consequences of a conspicuous allied refusal to support his policy
line.

The ploy failed. Eden reacted with swift and uncharacteristic sharp-
ness, cabling his ambassador not to attend the meeting, and adding:
"Americans may think the time past when they need consider the
feelings or difficulties of their allies. It is the conviction that this tendency becomes more pronounced every week that is creating mounting
difficulties for anyone in this country who wants to maintain close Anglo-
American relations." [43] Dulles received this news on Easter morning,
April 18, in the form of a telephone call from the British ambassador,
Sir Roger Makins. His sister Eleanor was standing alone with him in
the front hall of his house on Thirty-second Street in Washington: "He
was visibly disturbed," she reported, and he said to her, "Eden has
reversed himself and gone back on our agreement." [44] While it is very
doubtful that there was a meeting of minds in London, there is no reason to doubt the genuineness of Dulles's agitation, for the domestic
consequences were swift and sharp, and they unquestionably fed his
developing antipathy for Eden. One powerful senator castigated him
for having demanded broad action "before finding out in advance
whether he had the support of the Congress, the French and the British." [45] Another Republican legislator told him at a hearing that "you're
either a liar or Eden is a double-crosser." [46]

A Feverish Weekend

But Dulles was tough, determined, and resourceful. Back in Paris on
April 21 for a NATO Council meeting, he again conferred with Eden
and Bidault on the Indochina problem. On April 23, a highly agitated
Bidault showed him a message just received from General Navarre,
warning that the fall of Dien Bien Phu was imminent and that its loss
would permit the Vietminh to move rapidly into the Red River Delta.
Bidault again asked Dulles to save the situation by air bombardment
which, to be effective, would have to be delivered within seventy-two
hours; the only alternative for France, he said, was an effort to achieve
an immediate cease-fire. Dulles promised to report this urgently to the
President, and also to discuss it with Admiral Radford, who was arriving

in Paris the following day, but he told Bidault that a "B-29 intervention as proposed seemed to [be] out of the question under existing circumstances." [47] He added in a cable to Eisenhower that "Bidault gives the impression of a man close to the breaking point . . . it has been painful to watch him. . . . He is obviously exhausted and is confused and rambling in his talk." [48] Eden found Bidault's desperate request "all too reminiscent of the French demand for our last R.A.F. squadrons in 1940," [49] but Radford, when he joined the discussions on April 24, showed himself unready to forgo the bombing option: "There must be some military effort to assist the French without delay," he argued; otherwise the fortress would fall and "the whole military situation . . . would get out of control within a few days." [50] Dulles, however, concluded that the situation at Dien Bien Phu was too far gone to be saved by a bombing raid,[51] and Eisenhower cabled his agreement that "there would be no intervention without allies." [52] He meant the British. Dulles, who was becoming depressed by the irresoluteness of the French government and its strong tendency to view the fall of the fortress as a matter of strategic consequence, cabled the President: "There is, of course, no military or logical reason why loss of Dien Bien Phu should lead to collapse of French will, in relation both to Indochina and EDC.[53] Eisenhower in reply expressed his "full understanding of the feeling of frustration that must consume you. . . . There is little I can say now to help you . . . but I am so confident of the unity of conviction you and I hold on these and related matters, that I do not even feel the need of assuring you again of my complete support . . ." [54]

Dulles remained fiercely determined to obtain the necessary minimum of allied cooperation on which to build his case for "united action" — not to rescue Dien Bien Phu, but, as he saw it, to save Indochina and Southeast Asia. How he expected to do this, even assuming full British and French cooperation, remained a carefully veiled mystery, but when the three Foreign Ministers met again in the early afternoon of Saturday, April 24, he produced the rough draft of a rather peculiar paper. Addressed to Bidault, it stated that, while American support for Dien Bien Phu was now impossible, the United States was nevertheless prepared to move "armed forces" into Indochina, if France and the other allies so desired, for the purpose of protecting Southeast Asia as a whole.[55] The letter was passed to Eden, who read it glancingly, and then handed it on to Bidault. Dulles offered to send the letter formally if Bidault would find that helpful. After hesitating for several minutes, Bidault said he was prepared to receive the letter formally.[56] Suddenly events stood at a new watershed; if this striking new development were real, it meant the war would be internationalized. Eden concluded he must return at once to London to consult his cabinet colleagues. As he

put it to the Foreign Office in a cable sent just prior to his departure,
"It is now quite clear that we shall have to take a decision of first-class
importance, namely whether to tell the Americans that we are prepared
to go along with their plan or not." [57] Arriving in London, however,
he received a message from the British embassy in Paris saying that,
upon further reflection, Bidault was far from enthusiastic about the
American proposal and would probably advise Laniel against its acceptance.

Eden conferred with Churchill in the late evening of the twenty-
fourth, and reported his belief that Dulles and Eisenhower were now
prepared to ask congressional approval for broad but vague American
military actions, provided only that Britain pledged adherence and a
very nominal participation. Both men agreed that the action contemplated by the Americans would not solve France's problems, and might
well lead to major war; moreover, they thought they were being asked
to assist in misleading the Congress.[58] The circumstances indeed suggest
that the letter (which apparently was never formally sent) was a ploy
by Dulles to force the British to take a clear-cut stand on the issue of
intervention, without really committing the United States to particular
action; if it produced even a symbolic British willingness to associate
with "united action," then that might provide a sufficient color of alliance to persuade Eisenhower to seek congressional support for strong
American action; if it produced a negative response, then Britain and
not the United States would bear the onus of having refused the frantic
French plea for help. In terms at least of forcing the British hand, it
worked. The British cabinet met the next morning (Sunday, April 25)
and approved the position put forward by Churchill and Eden. The
essence of this was: "We are not prepared to give any undertaking now,
in advance of the Geneva Conference, concerning United Kingdom
military action in Indo-China." [59]

The matter, however, did not end there. The French cabinet, meeting
on Saturday evening, declined to accept the Dulles letter offering general U.S. intervention; it chose instead to draft another plea for an air
strike at Dien Bien Phu. This was the perhaps predictable course of a
panic-stricken government facing within hours the fall of a symbolic
fortress — an event certain to produce gripping anguish throughout
France, and to be followed by explosive resentment against the government that had exposed heroic soldiers to such humiliation and defeat.
According to the memoirs of Premier Laniel, the new French request
was discussed with Dulles that same evening, a few hours before his
departure for Geneva, where the negotiations were to begin on Monday.
Choosing to exploit the French panic, Dulles now told Laniel and
Bidault that, if *they* could bring the British even nominally into a

coalition "proclaiming their common will to check the expansion of communism in Southeast Asia," [60] and if France agreed to United States assumption of strategic command in Indochina, then President Eisenhower would seek congressional approval for intervention, and air strikes might well be carried out against the besiegers of Dien Bien Phu within the seventy-two-hour deadline defined by General Navarre. The desperate French apparently accepted this new proposition. [61] Dulles then flew off to Geneva.

There remained to be played out at least two more acts in the feverish weekend drama. A copy of the new French plea for an air strike was cabled to the French embassy in Washington and carried that same Saturday evening (Washington time being five hours behind Paris time) by Ambassador Henri Bonnet to Acting Secretary of State Bedell Smith. After speaking immediately with Eisenhower, Smith informed Bonnet (that same evening) that a response to the French plea could be made only within the context of a declared allied intention to establish a regional security organization, but that with such a declaration, supported by authorized signatures, a positive U.S. response was likely. Smith emphasized that British adherence was the keystone. If London were willing, then an agreement among ambassadors in Washington could be signed in two days (by Monday, April 26). Moreover, he told Bonnet, a resolution authorizing the President to use air and naval forces in Indochina had already been prepared; it might be approved by Congress as early as April 28. [62] Acting swiftly on the basis of this strong encouragement, which directly reinforced the line Dulles had taken at his last talk with Laniel, the French sent their ambassador in London, René Massigli, to the Foreign Office the following day (Sunday, April 25), where he met with Eden on the latter's return from the special cabinet session. Massigli detailed the talk between Smith and Bonnet and urged the British to accede. Eden was notably dismayed and irritated to learn that, on so pressing a matter, the United States had not only allowed and encouraged the French to be a direct channel to the British government, but was in effect using the French as an instrument of pressure. [63]

The British cabinet met again at 4:00 P.M. and reaffirmed its position. Eden then flew to Geneva, stopping briefly at Orly Airport to inform Bidault of the decision. Still the French persisted, apparently strong in their belief that if Britain would merely give nominal consent, American military action to save Dien Bien Phu would follow. On Tuesday, April 27, Massigli once more pressed the matter upon Churchill, who told him bluntly that the British government had made its decision. [64] Later that day, the Prime Minister rose in Commons to reassure the House that Britain had not entered upon "any new political or military

commitments" with the United States or France; and that, while the
French trial by fire at Dien Bien Phu was unfortunate, it should not
"prejudice the sense of world proportion" that ought to guide and
inspire the Geneva conference.

Even after this rebuff, Bedell Smith rather amazingly sought to find
a formula for action that was not dependent on the British. Without
consulting Dulles, he conceived a joint action under the ANZUS treaty,
and sounded out the Australian and New Zealand ambassadors on the
evening of Monday, April 26, reporting to Eisenhower that they were
"ready to listen" to any proposals the United States might put forward
with regard to "collective action for entering the Indochina war." [65]
Smith's purpose appeared to be prompt military action to save Dien
Bien Phu, rather than the more deliberate gathering of a nucleus for
a regional alliance. By April 29, however, the Australian and New Zealand governments (upon reflection and no doubt after consultation with
London) indicated that they were not prepared to pursue this line.[66]
It is also doubtful that Eisenhower could have been persuaded. It was
an inherently frail proposition and, in his memoirs, he recalled that he
would have been "most unhappy" to urge a collective action "without
sturdy Britain as a participant." [67]

This curious episode was vastly revealing of Dulles's mental attitude
toward allies, and of his operational style. Convinced of the imperative
need to halt further Communist advance in Southeast Asia and confident that solution lay in skillfully orchestrating threats of condign
punishment from afar, he moved to develop the elements of such a
solution with titanic energy, iron determination, and a tactical guile
that did not hesitate to mislead and manipulate his allies. He would
have been far happier to conduct a unilateral United States effort (as
he was later to do with the Formosa Resolution and the Eisenhower
Doctrine), but here both the President and the Congress had decreed
the necessity of allied support. His aim was accordingly to fashion a
nominal coalition, one that could provide at least the semblance of an
alliance as a cover for American power and initiative. What he sought
from both allies and Congress were broad precommitments, proxies
given in advance, that would leave the management of the affair to
himself and the President.

The British refusal to be stampeded by French and American pressures showed wisdom, moral courage, and a sense of proportion. Churchill and Eden simply did not share Washington's alarmist assessments of
the Chinese Communist threat to Southeast Asia; they recognized the
considerable political and military independence of Ho Chi Minh; they
were under no illusion that France could be persuaded to continue the
war for an indefinite period. For them a compromise settlement was

the unavoidable diplomatic requirement and, being relatively free of the impassioned anti-Communism that hypnotized American policy makers, they were confident that practical settlements of mutual benefit could be negotiated. Beyond these differences with Washington on substantive issues of policy, their resistance to signing on to a vague and open-ended plan for military coordination, in advance of negotiations, reflected their growing lack of confidence and trust in Dulles. At some point during this period, Churchill remarked privately that Dulles "is the only case of a bull I know who carries his china closet with him." [68] It was not a good omen for the Western Alliance.

15

The Geneva Negotiations — 1954

T HE UNITED STATES thus entered the Geneva conference on April 26 in a mood of apprehension and moral disapproval. The British arrived with a determination to be realistic, and with a confidence that both Russia and China desired a compromise. The French, who were determined to negotiate an end to the war, came to Geneva with a quite inflated view of what kind of settlement was possible.

It is customary to rotate the chairmanship of international conferences, but Dulles refused to countenance Chou En-lai or the North Korean, Nam Il, in the chair, and this obstruction led to an agreement between Eden and Molotov whereunder they would assume the duties of chairman on alternate days (excepting only that Prince Wan Waithayakon of Thailand would preside at the first session of the Korean phase of the talks).[1] Dulles accepted this arrangement, which had the dual advantage of subordinating the Chinese role and of providing the United States with a measure of detachment from responsibility. To underline the impression of detachment, he remained in Geneva for only one week, and while there conducted himself with the pinched distaste of a puritan in a house of ill repute, "quite brusquely" refusing to shake hands with Chou En-lai and instructing the American delegation to ignore at all times the presence and existence of the Chinese delegation. He also reopened the argument with Eden for immediate British-American action to create a Southeast Asian defense pact in time to influence the current negotiations. At dinner with Eden, Lord Reading, and Bedell Smith (who would remain as the U.S. representative after he departed), Dulles subjected the British to what Eden called a "prolonged, and at moments somewhat heated, onslaught upon our

Working in his limousine
at the Geneva Conference on Indochina (April 1954)

attitude," which included the blunt charge that Eden had repudiated their presumed understanding of April 13.[2]

Eden, who made plain that he would not "endorse a bad policy for the sake of unity,"[3] nevertheless sought to ease the tension. On April 30 he offered joint British-American military staff talks aimed at examining "the political and military problems in creating a collective defence for South-East Asia; namely: (a) nature and purpose; (b) membership; (c) commitments."[4] This was a relatively minor shift in the British position, conceding that exploratory talks on defense arrangements (but not the conclusion of a defense pact) could be undertaken before the results of the Geneva conference were known. It was a gesture of goodwill made in the hope of promoting the restoration of Anglo-American harmony, and hardly subject to misunderstanding. Unfortunately, Dulles promptly inspired statements by Eisenhower which sought to present the British offer as a belated acceptance of the original "united action" proposal. Anticipating the imminent formation of a new defense pact, Eisenhower thus said on May 5, "There is a general sense of urgency. The fact that such an organization is in process of formation could have an important bearing upon what happens at Geneva . . ."[5] The British, newly affronted, replied through the Foreign Office that "we refuse to go beyond military staff talks."[6]

This did not, however, put an end to the Secretary of State's vehement tenacity and persistence. As the celebrated *Life* article of January 1956 later made clear, he regarded the Indochina crisis as a major testing ground for his theory of deterrent warnings based on a readiness to threaten massive retaliation; and his call for "united action," followed ten days later by the dispatch of American aircraft carriers to the South China Sea, he considered "a modern version of the classic show of force, designed both to deter any Red Chinese attack . . . and to provide weapons for instant retaliation . . ."[7] Rebuffed in his effort to stretch the implications of the military staff talks beyond British intent, he again sought in early May to find a collective approach independent of British participation. The search led back to the ANZUS treaty and an attempt to obtain Australian and New Zealand support for an arrangement that would also include Thailand, the Philippines and Pakistan. Very preliminary talks were allowed to generate disproportionate publicity on the American side, even though the governments in both Canberra and Wellington showed themselves unready to strain their Commonwealth ties or risk an intervention that might put them "in the wrong with world public opinion, particularly in Asia."[8] Dulles and Eisenhower (who was persuaded at one point to state publicly that British participation might not be "indispensable") applied persuasion over a three-week period, but there was never a serious likelihood of

At the Geneva Conference on Indochina, with French Foreign Minister
Georges Bidault, Jean Chauvel, Lord Reading, and Walter Bedell Smith
(April 1954)

success, and the ploy died on May 20 when the New Zealand minister
of external affairs declared that a satisfactory alliance in Southeast Asia
was not "conceivable" without Britain.[9]

To a great many people it was not at all clear what Dulles was trying
to do, and in early May he went through a stiff session with the Senate
Foreign Relations Committee, whose members wanted to know if the
United States had *any* policy at Geneva. It seemed a fair question. Dulles
was undoubtedly frustrated by major aspects of the situation. He detested
the *fact* of the negotiations, but his allies were unwilling to cooperate
with his efforts to exchange the conference for a coalition war. At the
same time it was not clear that he really advocated war. At one level,
"united action" seemed essentially a means of asserting American control
over French and British actions in Asia; at another, it seemed a means of
demonstrating the efficacy of deterrent warning without resort to war; at
still another, it seemed the framework for full-scale American military
intervention with nominal support from allies. It is quite possible that
Dulles, whose true métier was short-term tactics, was himself unclear as to
how he would proceed if allied "united action" should become a reality.
His chief planning assistant, Robert Bowie, is authority for the view that

the Dulles approach was "to keep it vague, avoid the use of ground troops under any conditions, and be sure the United States did not simply supplant France." [10] Moreover, certain domestic factors were in opposition to his own abstract anti-Communist imperative, including a public opinion decidedly lukewarm about the prospect of American intervention, and the President's coveted budget ceiling which would be blown sky-high by war. Finally, he and Eisenhower were not at all times on the same wavelength. Thus, as the Geneva conference opened, the President delivered a speech in which he declared that the United States could not be the gladiator of the free world, but must work in Geneva for a "modus vivendi." [11] Dulles was reported to be dismayed by these remarks.[12]

It is possible that Eisenhower was seeking here to offset the effects in Asia of the Chinese-Indian agreement to the "five principles of peaceful coexistence" which were proclaimed at this time in Peking: (1) mutual respect for each other's territorial integrity and sovereignty; (2) mutual nonaggression; (3) mutual noninterference in each other's internal affairs; (4) equality and mutual benefit; (5) peaceful coexistence. Although apparently compiled with the aid of a dictionary of synonyms, they were soon to become the basis of the neutralist platform throughout the Third World.

The Fall of Dien Bien Phu

The Korean phase of the conference started first, and was hopelessly deadlocked from the opening day. Syngman Rhee's government naturally wanted unification by means of Korean elections supervised by the UN, but North Korea, supported by Molotov, argued that the UN had disqualified itself from playing a disinterested supervisory role by reason of its "illegal" intervention in Korean affairs in 1950. The Western participants vigorously rejected this contention, as well as Nam Il's proposal for an electoral commission that would give North Korea both equal representation and a veto in the development of an electoral law. At the heart of the difficulty was the fact that North Korea contained only a third of the Korean population, and thus could not win more than a minority position in a unified government under the most favorable circumstances. The final plenary session, held on June 15, ended with an exchange of unfriendly statements. The Thai representative insisted the UN was entirely competent to take collective action not only to repel aggression, but to restore peace. Nam Il replied that both the rejection of his government's proposals and the breaking off of negotiations were without justification.[13]

On May 7, one day before the Indochina phase of the conference was to open, the exhausted defenders of Dien Bien Phu were overwhelmed in a final human-wave assault, plunging France into anguish and pessimism. Yet as the talks began, Bidault's negotiating position took no account of the debacle. He called for an immediate and guaranteed cease-fire in Vietnam, with all the political problems to be settled later during a transitional period. He wanted to hold the Associated States at least nominally within the French Union, as a means of assuring protection for French commercial, economic and cultural privileges. He opposed partition. Pham Van Dong, who headed the Vietminh delegation, said that the French proposals proceeded from an "outworn imperialist colonial conception," and asked for a settlement that dealt concurrently with both military and political problems. He also demanded recognition of the "resistance governments" under Vietminh control in Laos and Cambodia. Eden and Bedell Smith supported Bidault, while Molotov and Chou lined up behind Dong.[14] A French spokesman who held a press conference to discuss this initial deadlock gave the unfortunate, though not entirely incorrect, impression that Bidault had rejected the Vietminh position more or less out of hand. An uproar rocked the French parliament, causing renewed and bitter debate on the war. It ended on May 13 in a vote of confidence, which the government survived by only two votes, making it clear that the Laniel-Bidault policy hung by a slender thread.[15]

Following the fall of Dien Bien Phu, the Washington air was filled with intense recriminations against Dulles and American policy on the one hand, and against Eden and British policy on the other. Senator Knowland called Britain an "undependable ally."[16] Harsh words were used against Eden in the State Department — among them that he was slipping, and lacking in moral stature — and some of the epithets were attributed directly to Dulles.[17] Walter Lippmann diagnosed the Western alliance as "shaken," but warned against the "most dangerous fantasy" of the Asia-firsters who believed "it would be feasible for the United States alone to take over the war in Indo-China and to win it."[18] For the Democrats, Senators Herbert Lehman and Theodore Green denounced the administration's Indochina policy as a "diplomatic disaster" and "insulting toward our allies and friends." And Senator Lyndon Johnson, declining ad hominem comment (but prophetically implying that the war in Indochina was America's own fight), declared that "American foreign policy has never in all its history suffered such a stunning reversal. . . . We have been caught bluffing by our enemies."[19]

Dulles Shifts Gears

On May 7, the day of final collapse at Dien Bien Phu, Dulles delivered a major speech in which he conceded that "present conditions . . . do not provide a suitable basis for the United States now to participate with its armed forces," although the administration would be "gravely concerned" by a settlement that opened a "road to a Communist take-over." [20] On May 11 he caused further pain to Paris by seeming in a press conference remark to write off the whole French effort: "Even if Indochina were lost," he said, "the balance of Southeast Asia *could* be defended." [21] In light of the subsequent shift of U.S. policy, this proved to be a revealing remark, signaling the conclusion that he and Eisenhower had basically given up on the efficacy of the French effort, yet remained determined to organize a wider Asian defense as a means of limiting the damage. To Paris, of course, the statement looked suspiciously like the beginning of an American retreat from serious support for the French negotiating effort, and it thus forced the Laniel government to reexamine its basic premises. Acting with a swiftness born of desperation, the cabinet on May 12 instructed Ambassador Bonnet to ask Washington what it would be prepared to do if an honorable cease-fire should prove impossible to obtain, or if the French military position in the Red River Delta should rapidly fall apart.[22]

The French demarche of May 13 thus posed anew for Washington the fundamental questions: What was the true nature and extent of United States interest in the Indochina struggle? What were the compelling domestic and international factors to be considered? What was the President prepared to do? The administration's response was, in terms of substance, a measurable retreat from the bold and rampant activism of March and April. But the substantive response, conveyed privately, was accompanied by a number of public gestures that were designed to demonstrate forward movement and tough American resolve, thereby to disarm domestic critics of immobilism and to bolster the sagging French negotiating position at Geneva. The public gestures were dramatized for the press: a swift but full-dress review by State, Defense and CIA, followed by formal discussion in the National Security Council, and ending with an undisclosed decision by the President. The May 14 edition of the *New York Herald Tribune* carried a story which said, "The U.S. and France will shortly begin discussion of the exact conditions under which the United States would consider military intervention in the French Indochina war." It added that agreement had been reached on a joint conference, to be held probably in Paris. Other newspapers later spoke of impending "Franco-American military discussions."

Under cover of these pyrotechnics, however, Ambassador Douglas Dillon delivered to the Quai d'Orsay on May 15 a memorandum bearing conditions so formidable that they could be judged only as having been carefully calculated to impede, if not indeed to preclude, American military involvement. For the weak and faltering coalition behind Laniel, they were manifestly impossible to meet. President Eisenhower, the memorandum revealed, could ask Congress to use American military forces (air and naval units, but no ground forces) in Indochina if seven conditions were met. These included the indefinite retention of French forces "during the period of united action"; "unqualified freedom" for the Associated States to withdraw from the French Union; United Nations willingness to send an observation commission to Southeast Asia; and agreement on American-French command arrangements and on training the Vietnamese armed forces. They also stipulated that the French request for assistance must be formal, must be approved by the French Assembly as well as the cabinet, and must be addressed to Britain and several Asian nations in addition to the United States (all of whom must agree to meet the request, except Britain, whose "acquiescence" would suffice).[23] From the American point of view, such conditions were perhaps not unreasonable, but they seemed hardly designed by an impulsive government eager to commit its military forces. Some observers have suggested that administration officials did not fully appreciate the difficulties for Laniel and Bidault, and thus put forward their memorandum in the serious expectation that all seven conditions could be met. This seems a highly dubious view. Even if the Laniel government had been willing to act, the French Assembly would most certainly have balked, which would have led to the immediate defeat of Laniel and the emergence of a new government far more disposed to make "peace at any price." Taken together, the seven conditions were a set of interlocking booby traps for the French, and, if by some miracle they had been able to render them harmless and acceptable, it is likely that a now thoroughly disenchanted Eisenhower would have developed further obstacles. Describing the May 15 memorandum in his memoirs, the President wrote that these were "preconditions under which I *might* ask Congress for authority to use armed forces." [24] (The italics were his own.) Robert Bowie, who was close to Dulles, called the conditions "makeweights." [25]

From that point forward, the French could hardly have been under any illusion regarding the likelihood of American military intervention, yet negotiations ensued in Paris over the next several weeks between Dillon and Laniel. Gradually it began to be clear that the French aim was not to *obtain* U.S. military support, but rather to use the aura of its possibility to strengthen French bargaining for a settlement at Geneva. Laniel emphasized his view that EDC would have no chance of ratification if the government were to pledge indefinite retention of the French troops in Indochina. The French people, he said, desired to save their army, not enmesh it in larger Asian adventures under foreign command; for that reason, the Assembly would never approve a formal governmental request to "internationalize" the war.

As to the right of the Associated States to withdraw from the French Union, Laniel predicted the French people would never grant it. Why? Because the people of Indochina had never asked for it; moreover, he anticipated that even the Vietminh would wish to join.[26] He also asked Dillon for a response to two questions: (1) could the United States guarantee the borders and the independence of Laos and Cambodia in the event the French withdrew from these countries? and (2) could the United States provide "written assurance" of prompt air intervention to meet a Chinese Communist air attack on French forces? Dulles (replying through Dillon) gave Laniel a flat negative answer to the first question "in view of the military and legal impracticalities." As to Chinese air attack, Dulles thought it so unlikely as to rule out the need for a written commitment, but he told Laniel that a collective regional defense arrangement would provide protection against such a contingency.[27] When the French, later in the month, pressed again for a U.S. promise to retaliate against a Chinese air attack without reference to the seven conditions, Dulles was reported to feel that unilateral U.S. action would be entirely proper in such a case of "overt aggression." The President, however, came down fiercely and categorically on the other side. The United States, he insisted to his NSC assistant Robert Cutler, "would not intervene in China on any basis except united action." Indeed, he "would not be responsible for going into China alone unless a joint Congressional resolution ordered him to do so. . . . Unilateral action by the United States in cases of this kind would destroy us" by creating the expectation that we would also be prepared "to intervene alone in other parts of the world."[28] Despite this stern presidential caveat, however, Dulles issued on June 11 what can only be interpreted as a warning of unilateral American action against China, in a statement that seemed to move the United States defense line to the Chinese border of Indochina. Referring to the possibility of Chinese attack, he said, "If such overt military aggression occurred, that would be a deliberate threat to the United States itself"; and while Washington would, of course, consult with its allies and avail itself of the United Nations, "we could not escape ultimate responsibility for decisions closely touching our own security and self-defense."[29]

Although the exchanges in Paris led Dillon on May 29 to the rather remarkable conclusion that agreement "in principle" had now been reached on the "political side," [30] in fact the seven American conditions and the French responses to them served mainly to underscore the gulf between the perspectives of Washington and Paris. But while these desultory exchanges remained secret, the public received the contrary impression that the United States might soon intervene, not only with air and naval forces, but with three ground divisions. The British having been neither consulted nor informed, Eden was left to read of these developments in fragmentary and misleading newspaper reports, until an aide of Bidault's showed him a copy of the secret American memorandum. He was understandably annoyed that Washington had "resurrected" the issue of intervention, for he felt this could only complicate and jeopardize his efforts to reach an acceptable settlement.[31] British irritation and anger over American policy had indeed been mounting since the Dulles attempt to stretch the intent of the military staff talks; now his effort to pull Australia and New Zealand into a separate defense pact, and the fact of the French-American talks, were adding fuel to a smoldering fire. For his own part, Churchill had shown patient forbearance, confining himself, in answering angry questions from the floor of the Commons, to brief and factual answers that fell short of criticizing Washington — e.g., "Britain had nothing to do with United States–France negotiations." [32] On May 20, however (the day after Eisenhower's remark that Britain was perhaps not an "indispensable" party to an Asian defense pact), the Prime Minister associated himself with the remarks of a Labour MP that the words and actions of American and French officials were contrary to the spirit of the Western Alliance.[33]

Fall of the Laniel Government

Following the press leak on May 13, which, by suggesting Bidault's categorical rejection of the Vietminh proposals, nearly brought down the Laniel government, Eden had taken the lead in obtaining general agreement to secret sessions, on the assumption that serious negotiations were possible only if they could be reasonably insulated from the daily pressure of public opinion. From that point the conference had gradually gained its stride, with Eden pursuing the goal of a negotiated end to the war with a skill, tenacity and objectivity that produced both admiration and irritation in the French and American delegations. Eden and Molotov having come to a good working relationship, there was some progress during the last ten days of May. On the twenty-first, Molotov put forward a five-point proposal for settlement: (1) cease-fire, (2) regroupment of troops into zones, (3) measures to prevent troop reinforcement after a cease-fire, (4) methods for controlling such arrangements, and (5) an international guarantee of a settlement. And while this proposal omitted any mention of disarming the "volunteers" in Laos and Cambodia, Bidault accepted it as a basis for discussion.[34] By May 29, the conference had agreed to establish a military committee of experts to study and report on the technical problems of cease-fire and regroupment; moreover, Pham Van Dong had agreed to de facto partition of Vietnam as an initial step, and both Molotov and Chou had agreed that there could be some transitional period between a military armistice and a political settlement.

The Vietminh continued, however, to make steady military progress in the Red River Delta and that fact, combined with Bidault's continued refusal to negotiate directly with Dong, or even to explore his offer of temporary partition, led to Communist stalling that became evident in early June.[35] Molotov and Chou now reversed their positions on political issues, demanding that they must be considered concurrently with a cease-fire, and the Vietminh showed a stiff resistance to Eden's statement that progress was impossible unless they were willing to withdraw their "volunteers" from Laos and Cambodia. The conference was suddenly stalemated. Eden, sensing that a critical point had been reached, indicated on June 10 that he was willing to act as intermediary for only one or two more weeks: "Gentlemen, if the positions remain as they are today, I think it is our clear-cut duty to say so to the world and to admit that we have failed." [36] Eisenhower and Dulles, who now concluded that the Communist side was "only spinning things out to suit their own military purposes," cabled Bedell Smith that, if the French insisted on continuing the negotiations "in spite of their obvious futility," he should return home, thereby reducing the level of American representation, and advise Eden to do the same.[37] This combination of events made it evident that the end was near for the government in Paris.

The Laniel cabinet fell on June 12, produced a suspension of formal negotiations at Geneva until July 14, and ushered in Pierre Mendès-France as the sixteenth premier of the Fourth Republic with a promise to achieve an honorable settlement within thirty days or resign. The new premier was a tough realist of the non-Communist Left who had declared a few months before he took office that "continuation of the Indochina war, with the human and material sacrifices it entails, does much less to bar the road to communism in Asia than to open it in France." [38]

Washington seemed to view the new situation with a mixture of apprehension and relief. On the one hand, there was distrust of the new premier's readiness to negotiate directly with the Vietminh and a feeling that the self-imposed thirty-day deadline could only benefit the Communists (there seemed a failure to appreciate the Mendès-France calculation that the deadline was a useful means of neutralizing an otherwise un-manageable Assembly during the specified period). On the other hand, the conference deadlock offered the hope that Britain might now be willing to participate in a collective security arrangement for all of Southeast Asia. On June 15, Dulles told a press conference he had never expected the negotiations to be "productive of anything good"; indeed, "it looked now as though the Geneva conference would be terminated, recessed, or reduced to a lower level of negotiation." [39] But he looked forward, he said, to talks with the British that would be held in Washington on June 25.

Before Eden left Geneva, however, there was evidence that a combination of events — Laniel's fall, Eden's decision to quit, the announcement of Anglo-American talks, the clear failure of the Korean phase, and Dulles's unilateral warning to China — had produced a certain shock effect on Russia and China, and led them to concessions which revived the conference. On June 17, Molotov called on Eden to express his willingness to accept a Communist minority (Poland and Czechoslovakia) on a five-nation supervisory commission, provided the other three members were "nonaligned" states (India, Pakistan, Indonesia). Pham Van Dong agreed to withdraw Vietminh "volunteers" from Laos and Cambodia, and Chou told Eden that China would be willing to recognize the royal governments in those two states.[40] These were concessions significant enough to indicate that the Communist side did not want the conference to fail.

Anglo-American Talks

Churchill and Eden came to Washington on June 25 for talks which had been originally set for a date in advance of the Geneva conference. They now seemed imperative to check the widening estrangement in Anglo-American relations, and to devise some definite plan for helping the French to make the best of a situation that was bad and growing worse. Mendès-France was pledged to a quick settlement (by July 20). The problem was how to ensure that his efforts did not end in a wholesale sellout. As the discussions opened, the London Times said editorially: "It is generally agreed by those who believe that the future of the free world depends on the intimacy of the relationship between its two leaders that the talks have not begun a minute too soon." [41]

Unfortunately for the "atmospherics," Eden made a speech in the House of Commons on the eve of the Washington talks which inadvertently exposed the American horror of "contact" with China and of any arrangement that would give the appearance of approving "the fruits of

Anglo-American talks on Indochina (Washington, June 1954); with Prime Minister Churchill, President Eisenhower, and Foreign Secretary Eden

Communist aggression." In the course of a cautious review ("I think there is a chance — I do not put it higher than that — there is a chance that, with continued patience, these long and difficult negotiations will produce an acceptable result"),[42] he expressed the hope that a settlement could be underpinned by an international guarantee — "a reciprocal arrangement in which both sides take part. . . ." [43] Or, as he later put it, "a reciprocal defense arrangement in which each member gives guarantees." [44] The speech caused immediate uproar in Congress, by no means confined to Republicans and their supporters, and the American press denounced Eden's proposals as a sellout of the free world. The idea of mutual guarantees was viewed as scandalous: it would lead to de facto recognition of Red China, and was based on the outrageous assumption that Communists could be trusted to keep their word. Several congressmen promptly introduced an amendment to the Mutual Security Act that would withhold aid funds from any country that agreed to guarantee Communist conquests in Asia.

The talks themselves (which Churchill described as a discussion of "family matters") went a fair distance toward composing Anglo-American differences. The British agreed to move promptly ahead with plans for a regional defense pact whether or not a settlement was reached at Geneva, while Eisenhower and Dulles accepted partition as an unavoidable ingredient of any Indochina solution. The two governments drew up a position paper defining an armistice agreement they would be prepared to "respect." It included partition at 17°30′ north latitude; the "peaceful and humane transfer" of people desiring to move from one zone to the other; the integrity and independence of Laos, Cambodia, and "retained" Vietnam; effective international supervision of a settlement; and the "possibility" of the ultimate reunification of Vietnam.[45] There was no mention of international guarantees, but the paper as a whole was encouraging to Mendès-France, particularly the point reflecting Washington's acceptance of partition. If he could arrange a settlement within its framework, it appeared he had a right to expect the support of his alliance partners.

Determined Evasion

In talks with Mendès-France at Bern on June 23, Chou En-lai reaffirmed his view that military and political aspects of a settlement could be separated, and that a military armistice should have priority. They also agreed that the joint military teams working on the technical problems of cease-fire and regroupment must complete their work and report back to the Foreign Ministers within three weeks.[46] This meant the full conference would resume on July 14. Mendès-France now asked Eisenhower to send Dulles back to Geneva as head of the U.S. delegation, so that the West could present a strong and united front in his effort to achieve a settlement that conformed to the Anglo-American paper. But Dulles was suspicious that both France and Britain considered the paper a "maximum hope," rather than an absolute minimum requirement for which they would be willing to bargain hard, and he thus advised Dillon in early July that the United States "would not want to be associated in any way" with a settlement that fell below the Anglo-American paper.[47] Politically, he was unwilling to act against the grain of American opinion, defy his Republican critics in the Senate and, as he saw it, risk his continued effectiveness in office. Personally, he wanted no part in what, it seemed to him, could not avoid being an immoral compromise bordering on capitulation.

Mendès-France insisted that the Anglo-American paper *was* the French negotiating position, that he did not intend to deviate from it, but that France absolutely needed high-level American support at Geneva if this position was to prevail. Dulles continued to resist. On July 11 he issued a statement through his congressional liaison man which seemed designed to foreclose the situation: "We have no way of knowing whether a settlement can be reached and, if one is reached, whether or not it will be acceptable." Nevertheless, it should be understood that "the United States will not become party to any agreement which smacks of appeasement." Nor will it "acknowledge the legitimacy" of Communist control over "any segment of Southeast Asia." [48] The same day Ambassador Dillon flew from Paris to Geneva with a presidential letter for Mendès-France explaining the administration's "reasons for preferring to avoid full diplomatic participation in a conference the results of which we could not approve." [49] The French premier was disturbed, particularly by the implication that he would not, or could not, obtain a settlement conforming to the Anglo-American guidance paper. He pressed Dillon, refusing to accept the President's conclusion, stressing again that a satisfactory settlement depended on the physical presence of a senior American representative.[50] Eisenhower then relented, agreeing to send Dulles — though not to Geneva but to Paris — for a private meeting with Mendès-France and Eden.

In the Paris meeting on July 13, Dulles continued to play the artful dodger, arguing initially that U.S. representation of middle rank would help to keep the Communists ignorant of American intentions. But Mendès-France did not regard ignorance as bliss, and he once again pressed Dulles with the thesis that a high-level American delegate at Geneva might mean the difference between an honorable settlement and none at all. Dulles, who was becoming impressed with the premier's toughness, was also pleasantly surprised to learn (from examination of a map) that the Frenchman was actually demanding a partition line farther north than the line recommended in the Anglo-American guidance paper.[51] Mendès-France was also agreeably surprised to find in Dulles a greater suppleness than was discernible in his public utterances. With regard to the level of representation, however, Dulles said he did not wish to be placed in the position of having to say no in public — which was an implied suggestion that Mendès-France should withdraw his request. The premier replied bluntly that Dulles could not so easily escape his dilemma: The United States, he said, was already represented at Geneva at the ambassadorial level; if it did not raise that level of representation when Eden, Molotov, and Chou returned, that would in itself represent a visible decision with public consequences.[52] From this exchange came Eisenhower's agreement to send Bedell Smith back to the conference, but with the American position still carefully hedged about by legal thickets.

Dulles had told Mendès-France the United States would have to dissociate itself from any agreement departing from the guidance memorandum; at the same time it would not guarantee even a settlement that fully conformed to that paper. Why not? Because American opinion would never tolerate a guarantee for "the subjection of millions of Vietnamese to Communist rule." [53] What then *would* the United States do if the settlement met this standard? It would "respect" the settlement, in the words of the guidance paper. What did this mean? To Britain and France, it implied positive obligations, but Dulles would not give a clear answer. His revised instructions to Bedell Smith made clear that the United States delegate was to play a passive role at the conference. If an agreement should be reached that "conforms substantially" to the Anglo-American guidance paper, Smith was authorized to issue a unilateral statement of general support, but this must not involve any U.S. guarantee of the terms; moreover, it must not involve the United States as a "cosignatory with the Communists in any Declaration." [54] It is surely one of the ironies of diplomacy that, despite this American posture of determined passivity and evasion, the Chinese Communists interpreted Bedell Smith's return as evidence of an American decision to wreck the conference, prevent a settlement, and thus pave the way for pursuing the war with American military forces.[55]

Also during their meeting on July 13, Mendès-France told Dulles that the French Assembly would probably not ratify the EDC in its present form. Although the British Foreign Office had reached the same conclusion a month earlier, Dulles seems to have reacted with surprise and anger.[56] He agreed, however, that the communiqué should make no mention of EDC.

Geneva Settlement

The conference was formally reconvened on July 14 and, after six days of inconclusive sparring, the heads of five delegations met on the afternoon of July 20 at the French villa: Eden, Molotov, Chou En-lai, Mendès-France, and Pham Van Dong (Bedell Smith and Tran Van Do of South Vietnam were both absent). The issue of a five-power supervisory commission was quickly settled. On the fundamental questions of cease-fire and partition, Molotov proposed a compromise at the 17th parallel, which Eden and Mendès-France immediately accepted, although it was thirty minutes south of the line specified in the Anglo-American guidance paper.[57] On the matter of all-Vietnam elections, Pham Van Dong insisted that these be held within six months. Eden and Mendès-France had privately agreed to accept eighteen months. When Molotov surprisingly proposed a delay of two years, they promptly accepted.[58]

Then a serious hitch in the proceedings arose when Cambodia notified the conference that it would not sign the agreements because they limited Cambodia's right to join an alliance or even to import arms. American activity seemed to lie behind this protest. On July 10, Dulles had encouraged the Cambodian ambassador in Washington to believe his country could become a member of a new collective security pact and thus to resist pressures for neutralization and demilitarization.[59] Bedell Smith had later told the Cambodian delegate in Geneva that, while his country probably could *not* join the impending regional pact (SEATO), it should be free to import arms and employ French instructors. In view, however, of the acute Chinese sensitivity to foreign military bases in Southeast Asia, Smith recommended that Cambodia state its intention not to establish these.[60] However, the Cambodian delegate, Sam Sary, who was invited to attend the evening session of the conference, refused to recede from either demand. Debate went on for several hours, and the thirty-day deadline for Mendès-France passed at midnight with the conference still in deadlock. At 2:00 A.M. the Cambodian blandly announced that he had seventeen additional demands! Molotov then moved quietly to accept the proposition that Cambodia be permitted to seek outside arms if its security was threatened; at French insistence, the same provision was accorded to Laos. That broke the logjam.[61]

The Final Declaration of July 21, 1954, was a thirteen-point paper which (1) took note of the separate military armistice agreements in Vietnam, Laos and Cambodia; (2) took note of the agreement to prohibit the introduction of foreign troops and "all kinds of arms and munitions" into Vietnam; (3) took note of a similar prohibition on foreign military bases in Vietnam, and of the Cambodian and Laotian declarations to avoid establishing such bases and joining outside military alliances; (4) recognized that the demarcation line in Vietnam was provisional only, and that a political settlement would be achieved by general elections in July 1956; (5) warned against reprisals; (6) took note of the French readiness to withdraw its military forces at the request of Cambodia, Laos, and Vietnam; (7) promised French respect for the sovereignty, unity and territorial integrity of these three states; and (8) provided for the possibility of consultation among the conference participants if that should be necessary to ensure respect for the agreements.[62]

Dulles was willing to "take note" of twelve of the thirteen paragraphs, taking major exception only to the last on the grounds that "this seems to imply a multilateral engagement with Communists which would be inconsistent with our basic approach." [63] He also insisted on indicating the U.S. preference for elections that were supervised by the United Nations instead of by the five-power supervisory commission as set out in the Final Declaration. Noting that the "ink is hardly dry" on a Churchill-Eisenhower declaration of June 29 endorsing UN supervision in the case of all "nations now divided against their will," he cabled Bedell Smith that "our apparent acquiescence" in the Geneva proposal on this point would be "rather humiliating." [64]

Until the final day of the conference, both Molotov and Chou insisted there could be no settlement which did not have formal United States approval — i.e., for which America assumed positive responsibility. But Eisenhower and Dulles steadfastly refused, with rather strange and certainly tragic consequences. Russia and China had both given Eden to believe they were prepared to participate in a multilateral guarantee of the settlement. However, the American refusal to be bound caused Russia and China also to back away from an endorsement of the agreements, and this led to a chain reaction of abdication involving all of the potential signatories. As a result, none of the nine conference participants signed the Final Declaration. A number of unilateral statements were made whereby particular participants associated or disassociated themselves with particular elements of the agreements. The result was a document with participants, *but no contracting parties and thus no collective obligations.*

In the U.S. unilateral declaration, Bedell Smith announced that his government was willing to "take note" of the several agreements and all save paragraph thirteen of the Final Declaration. Further, he said, "(i) it will refrain from the threat or the use of force to disturb them" and "(ii) it would view any renewal of the aggression in violation of the aforesaid agreements with grave concern and as seriously threatening international peace and security." [65] The striking fact to be taken hold of here is that, while Dulles maneuvered with determination to avoid any U.S. responsibility for the results of the Geneva conference, his actions not only drove away all other potential guarantors, but his own declaration amounted, in diplomatic parlance, to a unilateral U.S. guarantee of South Vietnam, Laos and Cambodia. Thereafter the United States guarantee stood in splendid isolation. It may be argued inferentially that Dulles expected the forthcoming SEATO pact to multilateralize the American obligation; that expectation failed, however, to materialize. SEATO was never a usable instrument for collective response, and in 1961 President Kennedy cited not SEATO but the Dulles-Smith warning against "any renewal of . . . aggression" as the basis of the United States commitment to South Vietnam.[66]

16

Vietnam — Aftermath and Prologue

T HE GENEVA AGREEMENTS met in nearly every particular the seven points of the Anglo-American guidance paper and, everything considered, constituted a respectable result for the West. The dominant reaction in France was relief, but it was a relief tempered by the reality of loss, both actual and potential, the collapse of French prestige in Asia, and the menacing new pressures against French colonialism gathering on the North African horizon. Mendès-France spoke with eloquent candor to the Assembly, which gave him a large vote of confidence for his skillful execution of a tragic task: "I do not have any illusions and I do not want anyone to have any illusions about the contents of the agreements. The texts are sometimes cruel because they consecrate facts which are cruel." [1] In Britain, the sense of relief at having averted an American-Soviet confrontation and the danger of nuclear war carried with it a broad and bipartisan appreciation for what Churchill called Eden's "patient, persevering skill." [2]

Malenkov declared that Geneva was a great success and one which convincingly demonstrated the constructive impulses and peaceful intention of the USSR. [3] Chinese statements emphasized the role of the conference in bringing Peking back onto the world stage: "For the first time as one of the Big Powers, the People's Republic of China joined the other major powers in negotiating on vital international problems and made a contribution of its own that won acclaim of wide sections of public opinion. . . . Its international prestige has been greatly enhanced." [4]

If relief was the dominant emotion in Europe, the prevailing public reaction in the United States was probably anticlimax. The perfervid official effort of March and April to demonstrate that American vital interests were at stake and to brace public opinion for military intervention had given way in May and June to melodramatic hand-wringing, which the general public intuitively took to mean they would not be asked to fight after all. Moreover, the protracted nature of the negotiations drew attention away to other issues, producing a measure of indifference when the compromise agreement was finally announced. Eisenhower encouraged the public inclination to believe that the result, while not ideal, was not a major cause for future worry. He expressed his pleasure that the bloodshed had been stopped, and told his press conference (July 21) that he was "not going to criticize" what has been done; while "the agreement contains features which we do not like . . . a great deal depends on how they work in practice."[5] Privately, however, the administration felt a deep concern that Communist control might soon extend throughout Indochina, and the concern was accompanied by a powerful determination to prevent it by every practicable means.

The Confusions of SEATO

The roots of what came later to be known as Dullesian pactomania first appeared in his book *War or Peace* published in early 1950. In discussing therein the existing Rio and NATO regional pacts, he expressed a clear preference for a pre-NATO idea put forward by Hamilton Fish Armstrong involving "a General Protocol under Article 51 of the [UN] Charter, open to all member nations."[6] Its central feature was an absence of regional boundaries or other territorial limits. Adoption of the Armstrong proposal, Dulles argued, "would have avoided one great disadvantage of our regional security pacts" — namely, the inference "that we would not fight an aggressor who kept on the farther side of the line." He was opposed to "offering immunity to aggression in the Pacific, Asia, and the Near and Middle East and impliedly offering to divide the world with Communism."[7] Dulles, "the possessed insurance salesman," wanted total coverage, and preferred a single, comprehensive policy. However, as he inherited not only the NATO and Rio pacts, but also the U.S.-Japanese, U.S.-Philippine, and ANZUS security pacts (which he himself had largely negotiated) it was probably inevitable that his practical line of advance should lie in the formation of additional regional and subregional arrangements.

Pursuant to the June agreement with Britain, arrangements were made for representatives of eight nations * to meet at Manila on September 6 to establish a Southeast Asian Treaty Organization. Dulles's view of what the new organization should be and do was abundantly clear: it should be primarily an instrument for military warning or military resistance, and it should be directed against every manifestation of Communist expansion in the area. Also, having refused to countenance U.S. adherence to the Geneva Agreements, because that would have appeared as acquiescence in Communist territorial gain, he necessarily regarded SEATO as an instrument of guarantee for South Vietnam, Cambodia and Laos. He wanted, in short, a military pact with teeth in it, "a new initiative in Southeast Asia" which could "stabilize the present chaotic situation . . . [and] prevent further losses to communism." [8]

Fortunately, or unfortunately, the British conception was quite a different one, a fact that the June talks in Washington had failed to illuminate, although it was certainly implicit in Eden's conduct at Geneva. The British Foreign Secretary was always clear in his own mind that specific guarantees for an Indochina settlement were something quite distinct from a broader regional security arrangement. He had advanced his ideas of mutual guarantee at Geneva, and Dulles had rebuffed him. But a regional arrangement, in his view, should be designed to deal with inherent instability between and among weak and developing Asian states, to localize such conflicts as might erupt, and to encourage a sense of political and economic cooperation in the region. A basic point in Eden's thinking was that the regional arrangement must be broad enough to permit the active participation or cooperation of neutral states, including India, Burma, and Ceylon. Its orientation should accordingly not be anti-Communist.[9]

When the basic differences surfaced at Manila, and proved resistant to genuine reconciliation, they led to awkward compromises which produced a weak and hybrid treaty. The British conceptions were not, however, the only inhibiting factors for Dulles. He started out bravely enough, declaring in his opening speech to the delegates that SEATO's purpose was to warn aggressors that "an attack upon the treaty area would occasion a reaction so united, so strong, and so well placed that the aggressor would lose more than it could hope to gain." [10] (This was a statement which made plain the modest role he had in mind for his listeners for, with the possible exception of the British delegate, they represented countries possessing no semblance of mobile striking power, countries that were indeed notable for their political insignificance or military weakness, or both.) But the Joint Chiefs of Staff, faced with force reductions pursuant to the "New Look" program, were not at all enthusiastic

* United States, Britain, France, Australia, New Zealand, Pakistan, Thailand, Philippines.

about earmarking specific forces for SEATO.[11] And soundings in the Senate showed an unreadiness for the kind of precommitment on the NATO pattern that would, in effect, permit the President to use armed force in an emergency without further consultation with Congress. Nor were the other SEATO participants willing to allow themselves to be automatically committed by an event, or by the action or reaction of any other treaty member. Yet precommitments were the very essence of the Dulles approach. The primary lesson he drew from Indochina was that the free world would continue to incur defeats unless collective defense arrangements were firmly agreed *in advance*. What he sought at Manila was: (1) a precommitment from Congress and (2) a precommitment from allies — or, as his brother explained it to a CIA colleague, a "justification in international law" that would avoid "tying our hands" in a future crisis.[12]

In the SEATO exercise, however, he was doomed to disappointment. Reflecting the general reticence, the operative heart of the treaty (Article IV) as finally agreed committed each member, in the event of armed attack on another member, to do no more than "meet the common danger in accordance with its constitutional processes." The approach to the difficult problem of subversion, infiltration and guerilla warfare was similar: members agreed merely to "consult immediately" if any part of the treaty territory was "affected or threatened by any fact or situation which might endanger the peace of the area . . ."

There were other frustrations. Dulles fought to include the Associated States as members of the new treaty organization, but was vigorously opposed by Jean Chauvel of France, who argued that such a move would violate certainly the spirit, and probably the letter, of the Geneva Agreements, and would, moreover, add no strength to SEATO.[13] France, like Britain, was committed to a political solution in Indochina, to be brought about by general elections in 1956. Dulles insisted, however, that SEATO "throw a mantle of protection" [14] over these three small states, and this was finally done by a protocol to the treaty which brought them within the framework of Article IV. The narrowness of Asian representation was also a weakness (both India and Indonesia were excluded, for example, as a result of Britain's objection to Nationalist China, and India's enmity was ensured by the inclusion of Pakistan). The treaty thus tended to aggravate national rivalries in the region, and for this reason proved unworkable as a conduit for economic development funds which was one of its intended purposes (under Article III).

Dulles further weakened the treaty's capacity to deal with the inherent instabilities of the region by insisting, in another treaty protocol, that the American commitment must be confined to situations involving "Communist" aggression. As written, Article IV clearly applied to armed attack of every character, including Communist, but Dulles insisted not only upon making this point explicit, but upon excluding all other forms of aggression, with respect to the American commitment (the United States would be prepared to "consult" in the event of non-Communist contingencies). Once again, it is difficult to apportion the proper shares of honest conviction, political accommodation, and Jesuitical tactics in these strange and curious moves. His stress on the Communist threat (SEATO is necessary to "prevent communism from rushing on into the Pacific area, where it would seriously threaten the defense of the United States") [15] seemed straightforward, if exaggerated. But his move to exclude non-Communist threats from the U.S. commitment seemed clever to the point of inanity: some thought it arose from the desire to forestall a potential Pakistani claim on United States support in a border dispute with India (a claim that was quite effectively blocked by the "constitutional process" clause of Article IV). But if this evidence is true (and it is plausible), then the move was another subtlety out of Sullivan and Cromwell revealing Dulles's innate inability ever to transcend a preoccupation with the immediate interest of his "client," no matter how great the resulting distortions for the broader enterprise at hand.

Driven by his powerful will, and his highly abstract anti-Communism, he thus achieved a framework of alliance at Manila, but it was one that fell far short of his aims. He failed to obtain a firm advance commitment to the use of American force from either Congress or his new treaty partners, and he thus failed to gain an instrument that could be wielded dramatically in future crises. SEATO was never invoked, and three years after Dulles died C. L. Sulzberger of the *New York Times* called it "the alliance that really never was." [16] A congressional committee later called it "not a going concern but a sham." [17]

The French Reject EDC

The noted French journalist Raymond Aron later wrote that nothing since the Dreyfus affair had so riven France as the fight over the European Defense Community.[18] Initiated hastily by nervous French leaders as a means of deflecting the Anglo-American demand for immediate German rearmament in September 1951, it had come to be embraced by integrationists both as a basic building block in the new European structure and as an ingenious means of holding West Germany on a firm tether. This view was endorsed without qualification by Konrad Adenauer, whose suspicion of his fellow Germans ran deep, and it was widely accepted throughout West Germany. To the French followers of General de

Gaulle, however, who were powerfully moved to undo the humiliations of 1940 by restoring French prestige and grandeur, EDC was anathema. They demanded a free and unfettered national state, and recoiled from the "humiliation" and "sacrifice" that would attend a merger of the sacred French army with the military forces of the German "enemy." These passions were, if anything, heightened by the hard pressures which Dulles and others continued to apply, while France lay traumatized by the agony in Indochina and by the onset of an even greater crisis in Algeria.

Returning from the final negotiations at Geneva and turning to the problem of presenting the EDC treaty to the Assembly, Mendès-France concluded, after political soundings, that any chance for ratification depended on very drastic amendments — amendments that in fact would vitiate the basic principles of supranationality and equal treatment for West Germany. He thus carried to Brussels for a meeting with other EDC signatories (on August 19) proposals to suspend the supranational provisions for eight years, to limit military integration thereafter to troops stationed in particular forward areas (principally West Germany), and to permit every signatory the right to withdraw from EDC if Britain or the United States should withdraw from the Continent, or if Germany were unified.[19] Although they accurately reflected political realities in the French Assembly, these proposals were met with open hostility at Brussels, where they seemed to the other signatories the crowning exasperation in the long series of French maneuvers for concessions that would give France a special and privileged place in the proposed structure. The U.S. special representative, David Bruce (who was relying on contacts of long standing in the Quai d'Orsay, all of whom were strongly biased in favor of EDC), was still convinced that majority support for an unamended treaty existed in the Assembly. Harsh words were exchanged, and some chose to believe Mendès-France was acting in bad faith — even that he had made a deal with Molotov to kill EDC in exchange for Soviet concessions on Indochina. The French premier, who felt France was being dragged through the mud at Brussels, grew obdurate and refused to heed the angry entreaties of his allies, including a cable from Dulles and a proposed "interpretation" by Paul-Henri Spaak, for modification of his position.[20]

The conference adjourned on August 22 without agreement and in an atmosphere of recrimination. Moreover, when Mendès-France returned to Paris, it was to find that Robert Schuman and other leading integrationists were now publicly declaring his proposals unacceptable. Thus caught between the upper and nether millstones, the premier, who was neither an opponent nor an ardent advocate of EDC, thereupon decided to submit the *unamended* treaty, but neither to advocate its ratification nor to make success an issue of confidence. In short, he chose not to risk the fall of his government on the EDC vote. Realizing defeat was almost certain, the integrationists now desperately prepared a motion to adjourn Assembly debate and instruct the premier to continue negotiations with the other signatories. But the EDC opponents countered with a motion to "pass on to other business," and this motion, according to parliamentary rule, took priority over the motion to adjourn. On August 30 the Assembly voted to pass on to other business (319 votes for, 264 against, and 43 absentions), thus killing EDC on a purely procedural question.

The Crisis of September

The final defeat of EDC, at the hands of the nation which had given birth to the idea, had a shattering impact — dramatically arresting the European momentum toward structural integration and producing an immediate crisis in the NATO Alliance. Dulles, who had nailed the EDC banner to the American mast from his first days in office, and who eight months before had solemnly warned that an "agonizing reappraisal" of American commitments to Europe must inevitably follow a failure to bring the European army into being, now called the situation "a crisis of almost terrifying proportions." [21] For him, the vote in the French Assembly was also a personal defeat, and, coming on the heels of his ambivalent performance during the Indochina negotiations, it raised a new chorus of outcries from domestic critics who charged that not only his Asian but also his European policies had now self-evidently failed.

For Dulles the crisis was "terrifying" because he believed that, unless West Germany were quickly tied to Western Europe through legal and structural bonds, political developments in that country would soon make such a move most difficult and perhaps impossible. It must be done, he thought, while Germany was still dependent and militarily weak, and while Adenauer was still in control.[22] Adenauer fully shared this view, fearing (or professing to fear) that, left to their own devices, the West German people would gravitate inevitably toward unification on Communist terms. Because Adenauer, too, had pinned his reputation on the success of EDC, he was, in the wake of the French vote, a lonely and much criticized figure in Bonn, and Dulles feared he was politically vulnerable as well. On this consequential point of West German tendencies, Eden and the British were somewhat more relaxed and even cynical, for they judged that both Adenauer and the great majority of West Germans were bitterly anti-Communist, and they concluded from this that the risks of a "deal" with East Germany or the Soviet Union were very slight. Their judgment here was sounder than Dulles's. British policy nevertheless strongly supported West German membership in NATO and a reasonable military contribution within that alliance, preferring such an arrangement to EDC because it both finessed the awkward question of supranationality and provided a framework in which Britain could maintain strong links with the United States without seeming to neglect Europe.

Dulles's heavy pressures on the French, including his public commitment to an "agonizing reappraisal" in the event of EDC's defeat, plainly paralyzed Washington's capacity for diplomatic initiative in the new situation, and it thus fell to London to take the lead in picking up the scattered pieces and resolving the crisis. At this critical turning point in European affairs, and newly arrived from what most of Europe regarded as his admirable diplomatic performance in Geneva, Eden unhesitatingly took up the new challenge, and within a month had put together the elements of a solution that has stood the test of time. To his credit, Dulles recognized the necessities of the situation and held himself in the background for the most part, constructively supporting Eden's lead. But Eden's performance was decisive, and it may have been his finest hour.

Eden left London on September 11 for visits to Brussels, Bonn, Rome and Paris, both "to test the atmosphere after the patient, EDC, had finally died," [23] and to lay out suggestions for a solution that would bring the West Germans into formal parity with Britain, France, and the United States within NATO, while at the same time placing some conditions and constraints on German rearmament. The key element of his proposal was an extension and conversion of the Brussels Treaty of 1948 — an idea which he later said occurred to him in his bath. That treaty bound Britain, France, and the Benelux countries to assist each other in the event of attack, and was directed primarily against Germany. Eden now proposed to add West Germany and Italy to the membership, and to provide authority under the treaty for regulating the armament *on the continent* of its members; this would, of course, include supervision of the German contribution (set at twelve ground divisions and a tactical air force). With acceptable and nondiscriminatory controls thus imposed on Western German rearmament by the component alliance (called Western European Union), the way would be cleared for the full restoration of sovereignty in Bonn and for that government's admission to NATO.

While Eden was thus engaged in a reconnaissance of diplomatic possibilities on the Continent, mindful of the dual need to move carefully, yet to find a solution that could be built promptly upon existing foundations, Dulles once more cut sharply across his bow by making a sudden flying visit to Adenauer on September 16. While Eden was affronted, the trip showed again Dulles's determination to do whatever he deemed necessary, regardless of how much crockery might be broken along the way, and here he apparently felt that the scale and intensity of Adenauer's anger against Mendès-France might gravely affect the prospects of a Franco-German rapprochement, which was a vital ingredient of any solution. Eden, who had been in Bonn only a few days before, had not perceived any serious dangers in Adenauer's natural bitterness about EDC, but the chancellor may not have fully confided in the British Foreign Secretary. In any event, from an angry communiqué in which the word "France" was not even mentioned, and from fragmentary reports from the American embassy in Bonn, Dulles gained the distinct impression that Adenauer now wanted a purely German-American-British solution to the problem of German rearmament and ties to the West, implying the total exclusion of France.[24] Although many years later NATO defenses were similarly split between a northern and a southern sector when De Gaulle terminated French association with the NATO command structure and ordered NATO units out of France, in 1954 this possibility was a nightmare that Dulles was determined to avoid at all costs. He thus flew to Bonn, where he was able to reassure the tough old chancellor that America stood, as always, firmly by his side, and that wisdom bade them both to take the long view. He also encouraged detailed discussions of how West German entry into NATO could be brought about, and when he returned to Washington (after a brief and awkward talk with Eden in London), he was convinced he had conducted a successful rescue operation. Whether or not Adenauer actually needed rescue from the particular pitfalls perceived by Dulles remains something of a question, but there is little doubt that this gesture of sympathy and support earned him Adenauer's undying gratitude and friendship. As one historian has put it, "On the plane of personal relations, the friendship between Adenauer and Dulles really dates from the visit which Dulles paid at that moment to the lonely Chancellor." [25]

After a month of intense diplomatic exchanges, a nine-power conference * was convened at London on September 28, 1954, at the level of Foreign Ministers. Its purposes were to make arrangements (1) for restoring West German sovereignty after nearly a decade of occupation, (2) for bringing Italy and West Germany into the expanded Brussels Treaty, and (3) for admitting West Germany to NATO. On the second

* Britain, France, Germany, Italy, Belgium, Holland, Luxembourg, United States and Canada.

day, Dulles rose to make what began as a tendentious speech, deploring the loss of EDC, playing hard to get, and seeming to skirt the edges of "agonizing reappraisal." Recalling Eisenhower's pledge to maintain in Europe a "fair share of forces needed for joint defense of the North Atlantic area," [26] he reminded his listeners that this pledge applied only if EDC were ratified. He could not now reaffirm that commitment, he said, because of "a great wave of disillusionment which has swept over the United States — a feeling that after all the situation in Europe is pretty hopeless." [27] Then he paused, and his words took a more positive turn: "I cannot say at this moment that a renewal of that commitment is possible. . . . But if, out of the elements of the situation within which we are dealing, if using the Brussels Treaty as a nucleus, it is possible to find in this pattern a continuing hope of unity . . . then I would certainly be disposed to recommend to the President that he should renew" the pledge.[28]

Eden followed, thanking Dulles for a statement of "very rare quality and much valued frankness." [29] He then went on to make a strong new pledge of British military support for Europe. Britain, he declared, would maintain in Europe its present four ground divisions plus a tactical air force, or such other forces as the NATO commander "regards as having equivalent fighting capacity." [30] And they would not be withdrawn against the wishes of a majority of the Brussels Treaty members, except in the event of "an acute overseas emergency." [31] Both Eden and Dulles had hoped that these strong force commitments, designed to reassure France, would elicit some comparable contribution to unity from Mendès-France. The Benelux countries renounced their right to manufacture nuclear, chemical and bacteriological weapons. And Germany moved to reassure France by promising to forgo the manufacture of bombers, guided missiles and naval vessels. The French premier, however, yielded nothing, but stirred new controversy by clinging stubbornly to his plan for European armaments of wholly standardized design and manufacture — a plan which would have vastly complicated the strengthening of NATO while indefinitely delaying a West German force contribution. This dilatory tactic, which was aimed at maintaining support for his government within the French Assembly, seemed particularly graceless to Eden, who thereupon permitted himself a rare and splendid outburst of temper, creating "a violent scene which left Mendès-France shattered." [32]

At the final session on October 3, Dulles said: "A large part of what was sought to be achieved by EDC has been salvaged. And there is now a tremendous asset not present in EDC — the generous committal of the United Kingdom to the defense of the Continent. . . . All of us, I know, want to pay tribute to the resourcefulness in paving the way for this of

Mr. Anthony Eden, the British Foreign Secretary, who served as our chairman." [33] Eden replied in a personal message the following day: "I cannot tell you how much I have valued your unwavering support during this critical week. I believe like you that we have made an historic step forward. Without you it would have been quite impossible. Warmest regards. Anthony." [34]

The conference was a passing moment when Dulles and Eden moved in nearly complete harmony. But it was a moment of high consequence, a fateful hinge on which swung the future of Western Europe and NATO. With America's help, Europe turned a hard corner. Nothing more was heard of "agonizing reappraisal."

American Compulsions in Indochina

Not only the American drive for the SEATO pact and the post-EDC crisis in Europe, but also the post-Geneva crisis in Indochina and the first offshore island confrontation in the Formosa Strait made the late summer and autumn of 1954 a period of frenetic diplomatic activity and major consequence. We shall deal presently with the brink at Quemoy. Suffice it to say that Dulles flew repeatedly to Europe during this period, spending hour after hour in the air, as well as countless days at conferences in London, Paris and Bonn.

Although the United States had refused formal association with the Geneva Agreements, it was soon evident that Dulles had no intention of allowing the postarmistice evolution in Indochina to proceed uncontrolled by Washington. The situation was anomalous. Under the Geneva Agreements, France was pledged to implement the armistice and to guide the all-Vietnam elections in 1956, which were in turn to assure the unity and sovereignty of Vietnam. To assure the power to discharge these heavy tasks, Paris was also pledged to retain the French Expeditionary Corps until its removal should be requested by the Associated States, and General Ely had been named French High Commissioner in Vietnam to assure the coordination of military, political and economic problems. It was thus widely assumed that France would remain in Vietnam for an extended transitional period; indeed, some French leaders were hopeful that French economic investment and cultural ties could be maintained, even in North Vietnam.[35] With this in mind, Mendès-France had sent an able emissary, Jean Sainteny, to Hanoi in August to find ways to preserve French business interests in Tonkin, and Paris began to look upon the whole Vietnam problem as a not unhopeful experiment in East-West coexistence.[36]

But against these formal commitments and hopes of commercial advantage stood several intractable facts. One was the intense and widespread Vietnamese antagonism to continued French influence of any kind, a feeling personified by Premier Ngo Dinh Diem, an ardent nationalist and rigid Francophobe, determined to expel every trace of the French presence at the earliest possible moment. (The Sainteny mission to Hanoi naturally strengthened the anti-French sentiment in Saigon, for it seemed to indicate Paris's intention to play a "double game".) A second intractable fact was Dulles's utter determination to prevent the further spread of Communist influence or control. Although the detailed circumstances of Diem's appointment are still obscure, there is little doubt that he was more or less the "American candidate" whom the French were persuaded to accept with reluctance and misgiving. A Catholic intellectual, well known to the group of non-Communist Vietnamese expatriates who gathered for many years in Paris, planning and hoping for independence, he was in early 1954 living obscurely in a religious retreat in the United States, but had been introduced by Cardinal Spellman to a handful of American moderates and liberals, including Senator Mike Mansfield and Justice William O. Douglas.

On a fine April evening in 1954, Robert Amory, a deputy director of the CIA, was leaving a cocktail party at the home of NBC commentator Martin Agronsky when Justice Douglas drew him aside and told him that Ngo Dinh Diem was the man who should be chosen to lead South Vietnam. Amory, who had never heard of Diem, reported the matter to Allen Dulles's staff meeting the following morning, and Frank Wisner, who headed the covert side of the agency, was instructed to follow up.[37] On July 7, Diem was appointed premier of South Vietnam by Emperor Bao Dai. Dulles strongly supported him, finding reassurance in both his Christianity and his tenacious anti-Communism; at the same time Dulles refused any dealings with Ho Chi Minh, which effectively stifled the hope in some quarters that Ho might be moved by inducements toward an independent position, toward becoming an Asian Tito.[38] United States policy in the post-Geneva period thus quickly moved into a "backseat driver's" role vis-à-vis France, with Dulles first requesting, and then progressively demanding, drastic shifts in French policy that refused to recognize the legitimacy of any French interests. What Washington required of Paris was (1) full independence for South Vietnam, (2) strong support for a regime that took the harshest anti-French and anticolonial line, (3) progressive relinquishment of French political, economic and cultural influences (and indeed acceptance of their inadvertent displacement by a variety of American programs), yet at the same time (4) maintenance of a large French military presence.[39] The French being heavily dependent on American arms, supplies and money for the maintenance of their position in Indochina, the U.S. leverage was very great. But its application by Dulles and Eisenhower had the effect of driving France out of Indochina for all intents and purposes within ten months, leaving an economic and military vacuum that the United States then felt compelled to fill.

To say that, in applying these pressures, Dulles foresaw and planned the consequences would probably be going too far. As always, he was a nearsighted tactician. He believed that, if French policy would bend to what he regarded as the anticolonial, anti-Communist necessities, France could continue to play a useful transitional role in nation-building, and he understood that the French Expeditionary Corps was the only guarantor of reasonable safety and stability in South Vietnam for some time to come. But there was an imperious and righteous determination in his posture. French policy must bend to the necessities as perceived in Washington, or else. Dulles hated colonialism and deplored and distrusted what he took to be the venal readiness of Paris to establish commercial relations with the Vietminh. He felt deeply that France had morally fouled the nest, and that a fresh start was required if "retained" Vietnam and the two smaller states were to survive as an anti-Communist bulwark. France must accordingly renounce and expunge her colonial sins. Both before and after Geneva, he thus imposed what proved to be impossible demands on the French political system.

The Fight for Control

Washington was the site, in late September (1954), for the first in a series of monthly trilateral (France, Britain, United States) meetings on Vietnam, a development which gave rise to the short-lived impression of "partnership." In the first meeting, the French argued hotly against an American proposal to channel American aid directly to the Associated States, but they ended by accepting an ambiguous compromise.[40] At the same time they agreed to maintain their expeditionary corps on the slender assurance that the United States would "consider the question of financial assistance." [41] Within a few weeks, however, Dulles had taken clear-cut unilateral action on the direct allocation of aid, apparently because he was galled by the Sainteny mission to Hanoi and by reports of strict French support for the specified elections in 1956 looking to "an eventual peaceful North-South rapprochement." [42] These actions and attitudes he interpreted as equivocal support for Diem.

On October 23, 1954, President Eisenhower signed a letter to Diem, which, after expressing his "grave concern regarding the future of a country temporarily divided by an artificial military grouping," declared that he was instructing the American ambassador in Saigon "to examine with you in your capacity as Chief of Government, how an intelligent program of American aid given directly to your Government can serve to assist Viet-Nam in its present hour of trial, provided that your Government is prepared to give assurances as to the standards of performance it would be able to maintain in the event such aid were supplied." [43] The French found this initiative a direct violation of the September agreement to "coordinate" French and American aid programs, and Ambassador Bonnet told Dulles that the action was a virtually unconditional gift to Diem requiring of him nothing in return; Paris wanted to stipulate "that he should first succeed in forming a strong and stable government." [44] These French statements were largely accurate, but Dulles blandly told Mendès-France that the Eisenhower letter was "in furtherance of the understandings reached at Washington" and he added that "many French officials have not concealed their belief that Diem has failed . . ." [45]

The breach with France was soon widened by a report issued by Senator Mike Mansfield after a fact-finding trip to South Vietnam. He supported the principle of direct aid to his old acquaintance Diem, who represented "genuine nationalism," was prepared "to deal effectively with corruption," and had demonstrated concern for "the welfare of the Vietnamese people." [46] If Diem were to fall, Mansfield argued, the United States should "consider an immediate suspension of all aid to Vietnam and the French Union Forces there," preliminary to a "complete reappraisal" of American policy — i.e., preparation for American withdrawal.[47] Dulles and Mendès-France had agreed in September that both countries would support a successor government if Diem for any reason lost power, but the Mansfield report effectively (and conveniently) undercut the administration's promise. For now, although Mendès-France might hold Dulles to their understanding, neither of them could bind Mansfield, who probably had enough influence in the Senate to bring about a suspension of aid if Diem were displaced. This is one of the facts of the American political system that consistently maddens foreign statesmen.

Meanwhile, the Joint Chiefs of Staff had added their own impetus to the compulsive American movement toward expelling the French and assuming unilateral U.S. responsibility. General John W. O'Daniel (who headed the U.S. military assistance mission to Indochina) asked for very substantial increases in his personnel before the ceiling imposed by the Geneva Agreements took effect on August 11. The JCS insisted that four preconditions must be met before the United States assumed any further military responsibility, one being the "phased, orderly withdrawal of French forces" and another the establishment of "a reasonably strong, stable civil government in control." [48] Dulles, however, felt it would be "militarily disastrous" to demand the withdrawal of French forces before a new Vietnamese army was trained and ready, and he characterized the JCS demand for prior political stability as another example of "the familiar hen-and-egg argument." He regarded it as necessary to build political and military strength simultaneously.[49] Dulles's more cautious approach carried the day in the National Security Council, but the resulting decision to "work through the French only insofar as necessary"[50] reflected the tacit consensus that the French presence was at best a transitional reality. Dulles also contended that the Vietnamese army should be scaled down from 230,000 and oriented primarily to internal security, but once more the military leaders demurred: the Vietnamese forces, they argued, must possess at least the capacity "to deter Viet Minh aggression by a limited defense of the Geneva Armistice demarcation line";[51] anything less would combine "limited beneficial effect" with the likelihood of military failure, and under such conditions they were opposed to assuming any responsibility.[52] Having thus made known their distaste for a small Vietnamese force with a limited mission and for collaboration with the French, they grudgingly consented, if "political considerations are overriding," to undertake the training of Vietnamese, but again, provided there were "safeguards against French interference."[53] In a word, the Joint Chiefs of Staff, "from a military point of view," wanted to do it their way or not at all. They held a strong belief in the superiority of American military methods, and they recoiled from collaboration with a French army whose failures were writ large in the history of World War II and equally in the eight years of inconclusive struggle in Vietnam.

The Collins Mission

Moving to bypass this stickiness in the Pentagon, Dulles and Eisenhower worked through the Operations Coordinating Board (the executive arm of the National Security Council), on October 22. On that day the board directed Ambassador Donald Heath and General O'Daniel in Saigon to implement a "crash program" of aid to Diem, including limited military training by American instructors.[54] At the same time, Eisenhower dispatched a special envoy to Saigon to get the program moving. He was a former Army Chief of Staff, General J. Lawton Collins, one of Eisenhower's favorite commanders in Europe, and a man chosen especially for his capacity to deal with General Ely. By November 17, Collins had recommended that the Vietnamese army be reduced to 77,000 men. By December 13, he and Ely had signed a minute of understanding, agreeing that the Vietnamese army should become autonomous in July 1955 (only six months ahead), that the United States would assume military training responsibilities in January (one month ahead), and that French trainers should be phased out. They also agreed that U.S. support for the French Expeditionary Corps should be about $100 million through 1955, with no financial commitment beyond that time.[55]

Paris was upset and dismayed by this paper. They thought it unrealistic to anticipate an effective autonomous Vietnamese army in six months' time, and the support figure for the expeditionary corps amounted to only a third of the French request. But even more basically, Mendès-France was nettled by the proposed withdrawal of French instructors.[56] Why should France be denied influence over the future Vietnamese army, he asked, while being asked to maintain the expeditionary corps and support other heavy burdens in Vietnam? The honest answer, never given, lay in the combined convictions and pressures of Diem, Dulles, and the Joint Chiefs of Staff, against which there was only limited recourse. Both Mendès-France and Ely argued with cogency that, if the French instructors were eliminated, the United States would have assumed primary responsibility for Vietnam.[57] Dulles and Collins disagreed, but their counterclaims were baseless. The American decision being implacable, however, the only prudent French action was to withdraw the expeditionary corps, and this they proceeded to do, running it down from 150,000 to 35,000 men by the end of 1955, and to 5,000 by the spring of 1956.[58] The public explanation was monetary stringency, but Paris was responding fundamentally to a political and psychological rebuff, and to strong sentiment in France for shifting the troops to North Africa.

The December meeting between Dulles and Mendès-France, which took place in Paris and was also attended by Eden, came close to being a confrontation. The French were disturbed by America's strong moves toward a unilateral approach, but perhaps even more by the single-minded American support for Diem, who galled Paris with his open Francophobia and his total lack of response to French advice on any subject. What became clear in this meeting was the fundamentally different French and American purposes at work. Mendès-France wanted someone in Saigon who could *unify* South Vietnam under conditions that permitted the retention of at least residual French influence. Dulles wanted primarily a strong anti-Communist position in the south and was drawn to Diem's ascetic, intransigent anti-Communism. That he was also a rigid Catholic in a predominantly Buddhist country, insensitive and dictatorial in relation to the majority religious and civic groups who opposed him, and temperamentally incapable of applying the political skills of compromise and conciliation, mattered less. Dulles,

Televised Cabinet meeting (October 23, 1954)

along with most other Americans, was magnificently ignorant of Vietnamese history and culture; at the same time he was transfixed by the abstractions of "national independence" and "anti-Communism."

Mendès-France made clear his view that the time had come for a change, and he proposed that the Emperor Bao Dai (who resided on the French Riviera) should either name a viceroy with full authority to unify the warring political factions in Saigon or should himself return to form a government. Dulles agreed that Diem was not ideal, but that "the problem must not be approached in [a] spirit of defeatism," and indeed he thought the situation contained a number of favorable factors, including popular opposition to Communism.[59] The "only serious problem we have not yet solved is that of indigenous leadership," but all concerned should recognize this could not be solved "ideally" because Vietnam lacked a self-governing tradition.[60] The two men finally agreed to support Diem a while longer, while studying alternatives; Ely and Collins were instructed to determine how much more delay could be tolerated. But Dulles then added a comment which revealed how very little flexibility existed in the American position. He thought that a considerable investment in Vietnam was justified "even if only to buy time to build up strength elsewhere in [the] area." [61] but that congressional willingness to continue that investment without Diem was very doubtful: "Mansfield believes in Diem." [62] Below myriad surface complexities, the underlying equation was thus rather simple: believing that a sustained and substantial investment of resources was essential to prevent the "further expansion of Communism" in Vietnam, Dulles was not prepared to press Diem for reforms or overturn him, for that might lead to a congressional cutoff of the entire Vietnam program. As Ambassador Heath summed it up: "The fear that a fiscal commitment of over $300 million plus our national prestige would be lost in a gamble on the retention of Free Vietnam is a legitimate one, but the withholding of our support at this juncture would almost inevitably have a far worse effect." [63] While the French case was weakened by the unpersuasiveness of Mendès-France's proposed alternative (the Emperor Bao Dai was a corrupt, debauched, and ineffective tool of the French without significant public backing in Vietnam), the point was that Diem now appeared to have gained a hammerlock on American policy.

Thus, by no later than December 1954, the United States had become the prisoner of its own transcendent fears of a Communist takeover, a state of mind which rendered U.S. policy doggedly, even fanatically, resistant to any course that would permit free play to the political forces at work in Vietnam. Allowed to evolve and mature, such forces (even though some were abhorrent to American political preferences) would surely have produced a government far more expressive of genuine national self-determination than the artificial counterweights the United States insisted on sustaining in Saigon over the next twenty years, in pursuit of a phantom "anti-Communist" solution. For this national self-imprisonment in an abstraction, which may have destroyed Vietnamese society and which has dragged both the Vietnamese and American peoples through oceans of blood and frightful bogs of learning, Dulles must bear a large measure of responsibility. His conviction, his willpower, his political maneuvering, his strident and simplistic rhetoric over a period of years made a deep imprint on the national psyche and thereby a major contribution to a national state of mind so persistent that three presidents after Eisenhower were convinced there could be no "letting go" in Vietnam.

Diem Wins a Showdown

In March 1955, the several pirate sects — Cao Dai, Hoa Hao, and Binh Xuyen — who possessed private armies the French had armed and used against the Vietminh, and who controlled much of the police, gambling and prostitution in South Vietnam, joined in a united front

In Saigon with Premier Ngo Dinh Diem
and American diplomat, Randolph Kidder (1955)

against Diem and demanded that he form a government of "national union." Diem called this move an ultimatum and on March 28 sent a paratrooper company to attack and capture a central police headquarters controlled by the Binh Xuyen. The following day the Binh Xuyen attacked Diem's palace with mortar shells, and Diem prepared a general offensive. On April 7, General Collins cabled Washington his considered agreement with Ely that Diem must be removed if civil war was to be avoided and South Vietnam preserved for the free world. Dulles's reaction was still that Diem's removal would damage American prestige in Asia by giving the appearance of abandoning a national leader who was under pressure from "colonial interests." Moreover, the pro-Diem sentiment in Congress, if affronted, could hurt the mutual security bill which was then under debate.[64]

When Paris insisted that Diem be at least subordinated to a "conseil superieur" comprising a balance of Vietnamese interests and opinion, including intellectuals, the sects, and other leading politicians, Dulles rejected this plan and argued that Diem should be given full support in his plan to strike back at the Binh Xuyen. At the same time, he sent a list of questions to the Quai d'Orsay designed to elicit the details of French plans for a proposed change of government. Paris replied that the questions ought to be answered jointly, but proposed that Collins and Ely draw up a list of candidates for major cabinet positions. Dulles then agreed to consider a change of government if Collins would personally come home for consultation.[65]

General Collins flew to Washington for a meeting with Dulles on April 27, and succeeded in persuading the Secretary to "consider" shifting support from Diem either to Dr. Quat or Tran Van Do.[66] A message to this effect was sent to the American embassy in Saigon, but Dulles wanted to keep knowledge of this tentative shift from the French until he had their full response to his questions.[67] Before any action could be taken, however, the uneasy truce in Saigon exploded. Diem had issued a decree charging the police commissioner, Lai Van Sang, with "very grave official misconduct," and discharging him. On April 28, the Binh Xuyen replied by putting heavy mortar fire on the presidential palace. Diem in turn ordered the Vietnamese army to open a general offensive which first drove the Binh Xuyen gangsters back into Cholon and then beyond into the Rung Sat swamps, an action in which hundreds were killed. Bao Dai, from his far-off seat on the French Riviera, ordered Diem to Cannes and placed a Binh Xuyen sympathizer, General Vy, in charge of the army. He also dispatched another Diem dissident, General Hinh, a former chief of staff, from Cannes to Saigon with special instructions. Diem ignored the summons, refused to allow Vy to command the army, and refused to allow Hinh into the country.[68] Although General Ely thought Diem "quite mad," he could not persuade American and British representatives on the spot to support his attempt to reimpose a cease-fire, and the American chargé d'affaires felt Ely himself was approaching hysteria.[69]

Amid Washington's favorable emotional response to the news of Diem's military triumph and defiance of Bao Dai, Dulles promptly countermanded his equivocal cable of April 28 and fell back to a position of full support for Diem. The premier's tough resolve, momentarily impressive, had created an opportunity for a wavering Dulles to return to a philosophically comfortable stance.[70]

At the next monthly trilateral meeting, held in Paris on May 10, the Franco-American split became explicit. As the reporting cable to the State Department, reflecting Dulles's remarks, stated: "Diem is [the] only means US sees to save South Vietnam and counteract [the] revolutionary movement underway in Vietnam."[71] He thought the newly proclaimed "revolutionary congress" which had repudiated Bao Dai and called for an elected national assembly to draft a new constitution was "not yet dominated or influenced by Communists to any appreciable degree" and that "Diem could sit on top of revolution."[72] On the other hand, the new French premier, Edgar Faure, saying it was "time to speak frankly," declared Diem "a bad choice, impossible solution. . . . Without him some solution might be possible, but with him there is none." [73] More explicitly than Mendès-France, Faure seemed prepared to challenge Dulles to acknowledge that France was still the essential political-military factor in Vietnam, or else to assume full and explicit American responsibility. He told Dulles that, since the French position in Vietnam was still dominant, he could have "claimed" that the United States should accommodate itself to French policy, but "I have rejected this." Still, he admitted, the answer to the problem was neither clear nor easy. Recognizing the "difficult position" in which French civilians and interests might be placed, he put a question to Dulles and then quickly provided his own answer: "What would you say if we were to retire entirely from Indochina and call back the FEC * as soon as possible?" To such a situation "I might be able to orient myself . . . if you say so," [74] for such a solution would have the advantage of ending the intolerable "colonial" reproach to France and of being responsive to Diem's demand for liquidation of the French position. What would Dulles say to this? Dulles answered cagily that "US interest in Vietnam is simply to withhold [the] area from communists." [75] And he added that "Vietnam is not worth [a] quarrel with France"; indeed, the United States would itself withdraw totally if that would solve the problem. This wary sparring reflected Dulles's reluctance to see a precipitate French military withdrawal and at the same time an unreadiness to accept explicit United States responsibility for the resulting vacuum. He wanted the French to stay militarily, but at the same time to accept and support Diem. And he warned Faure, as he had warned Mendès-France, that U.S. financial support could not be expected for any solution that did not include Diem.[76] Harold Macmillan, who had succeeded Eden as British Foreign Secretary in April (when Eden became Prime Minister) advised his French and American colleagues that the decision they were weighing was far too grave to be taken that evening. His advice was accepted.[77]

When the meeting reconvened the next day, Dulles had in hand further thoughts from the Joint Chiefs of Staff and from General Collins. The JCS had now swung around and strongly opposed a precipitate withdrawal of the French Expeditionary Corps, feeling it would produce "an increasingly unstable and precarious situation" leading to eventual collapse and Communist takeover.[78] Dulles used this JCS assessment in urging Faure to support Diem at least until a new national assembly could be elected. Against his own better judgment and against the grain

* French Expeditionary Corps.

of French opinion, Faure accepted Dulles's plea, on condition that these internal elections be held as rapidly as possible, that Bao Dai be retained as chief of state, and that certain abrasive officials (both American and French) be removed from Vietnam. Dulles agreed, but then added that, in the new situation, the United States and France should each proceed with its own policy.[79] Nine months of uneasy and superficial "partnership" were at an end. A year later (June 2, 1956) General Ely's mission was terminated, and the remaining elements of the expeditionary corps were progressively withdrawn.

Although both France and Britain pressed Diem to open up consultations with the Vietminh in July 1955 (as called for in the Geneva Agreements), looking toward the organization of all-Vietnam elections in 1956, Diem refused to do so. Washington's advice to Diem was, in effect, that he not openly refuse the elections, but that he demand conditions which excluded the possibility that he would lose them. Diem's key demand was free elections by secret ballot under strict conditions, a formula which had proved consistently unacceptable to Communists in Korea and Germany. As Dulles said: "While we should certainly take no positive step to speed up present process of decay of Geneva Accords, neither should we make the slightest effort to infuse life into them." [80] As the election date approached, Diem remained adamantly opposed, insisting that, as South Vietnam had not signed the accords, he was not bound by them. In December 1955, he went so far as to tell Paris that continued diplomatic relations depended on French renunciation of the Geneva Accords, including, of course, the requirement for North-South elections. The United States backed Diem. France was now impotent to influence Diem's policy, and neither Britain nor the Soviet Union pressed the matter. When Ho Chi Minh, feeling betrayed, reopened the civil war two years later, the United States, alone among the Western powers or indeed the SEATO powers, felt committed to uphold the regime in Saigon.

17

Ambiguity at Quemoy

In *War or Peace* Dulles had written that "if the Communist government of China in fact proves its ability to govern China without serious domestic resistance, then it, too, should be admitted to the United Nations." [1] But as American public opinion, steeped in sentimental notions of the Chinese people and Chinese-American relations, showed a deep sense of grievance at the Communist victory, and as Senator McCarthy developed his explosive charge that "loss" of the mainland had been engineered by a conspiracy of traitors in the State Department, Dulles changed his view. As on other issues, the conversion appeared to be a combination of conviction and political prudence. His continuing study of Leninist thought brought him progressively to the view that the Mao regime was a Russian instrument.* And when Chinese Communist troops poured across the Yalu River in October 1950 to prevent MacArthur's unification of Korea, turning America's sense of betrayal to cold fury, Dulles strongly endorsed the UN castigation of Peking as an aggressor, and with lawyerlike prudence used the occasion to explain and justify (in a footnote to later editions of his book) a reversal of position on China's admission to the United Nations.

It was a politic move. On the eve of the Korean War, the Gallup poll showed 40 percent of the American people opposed to recognition of the Communist regime; after the Chinese military intervention, that figure rose to 78 percent, and congressional expressions on the subject

* Although he never went as far as Dean Rusk, who said in a speech in New York City on May 18, 1951: "We do not recognize the authorities in Peiping [Peking] for what they pretend to be. The Peiping regime may be a colonial Russian government — a slavic Manchukuo on a larger scale. It is not the Government of China."

thereafter achieved new levels of vehemence. Dulles thus shared and reflected a pervasive public mood. By the time he came to office, he advocated a policy of pressure and isolation toward the mainland regime, and a policy of support for Chiang Kai-shek which, however, fell short of support for an attempt to recover the mainland by military force. In this latter respect, he was at odds with the rabid activists of the China Lobby, but he was naturally prone to conceal specific differences. His ambivalence was to contribute an acute lack of clarity and proportion to United States policy in the two offshore island confrontations of 1954–55 and 1958.

Chiang Seeks a Defense Treaty

Forced to flee the mainland, and insecure in his island redoubt (which the Japanese had called Formosa and the Chinese called Taiwan), Chiang was extremely anxious to obtain a formal American commitment at least to the defense of Taiwan, and he chafed at the tentative American attitude and the diplomatic limbo in which this left him. Governor Thomas E. Dewey, on a visit to Taiwan in the late summer of 1951, accidentally triggered the smoldering resentment of both the Generalissimo and his beautiful, tough and talented wife by mentioning the peace treaty with Japan. Not only, said the hot-eyed Madame Chiang, was the United States concluding major treaties of peace and defense with China's nemesis, while conspicuously failing to develop comparable arrangements with its faithful ally; it was even excluding the Nationalist Government as a signatory. As Ambassador Karl Rankin reported it, Dewey suddenly found himself in "one of the most violent political discussions he had ever had" with two of "the most furious people he had met in the Orient." [2]

With the end of the Korean War and the conclusion of the U.S. security treaty with South Korea in August 1953, Chiang began a sustained effort to obtain comparable treatment. In October, with Ambassador Rankin's encouragement, his government developed a draft that was handed to the State Department by the Nationalist ambassador, Wellington Koo, in December. Dulles, however, seemed to have other priorities. Five months later, in May 1954, Chiang raised the question with Defense Secretary Wilson, who was visiting Taipei, saying that the lack of progress was being widely interpreted as indicating the United States still desired to hold the door open to recognition of Red China. [3] Soon thereafter a prominent Taipei newspaper, reporting on a visit by General James Van Fleet, stated that tentative agreement had been reached on a bilateral defense pact; according to the story, this would provide U.S. protection not only for Taiwan but also the offshore islands, leaving the Nationalists free to attack Red China.[4] Although the story had no basis in fact, the Mao regime apparently took it with utmost seriousness, charging in the *People's Daily* of July 8 that the "warlike group" in the United States was attempting to "perpetuate its criminal occupation of Taiwan" by means of a treaty. Angered and concerned by this development, that regime began a campaign, combining propaganda and military action, aimed at asserting its claims to sovereignty in the area and at frustrating consummation of a U.S. defense pact with Taiwan. Amid declarations that "any treaties concluded between the U.S. Government and the traitorous Chiang Kai-shek group entrenched on Taiwan would be illegal and without any validity," [5] and that "the most important task before our people is the liberation of Taiwan in order to smash thoroughly the American imperialists' plot to invade and overthrow our country," [6] Red Chinese air and naval units clashed with Nationalist forces at several points along the coast and in the straits during late July and early August. On July 23, Red Chinese fighter planes shot down a British commercial airliner near Hainan Island, mistaking it for a Nationalist aircraft. The United States denounced "this further act of barbarity" and, at Admiral Radford's urging, two American aircraft carriers were ordered to the area to conduct an armed search for survivors. Their search continued for an abnormally long period and on July 26, just as the Peking radio began to broadcast an apology to the British, American jets shot down two propellor-driven Red Chinese fighter planes only thirteen miles off Chinese territory.

Chiang and the Nationalists were also contributing their full share to the tension and provocation. In his 1954 New Year's message, the Generalissimo had pledged attack on the mainland "in the not distant future," and on Easter Sunday had called for a "holy war"; both declarations were followed by aggressive Nationalist military activities along the China coast.[7] Then in August, Syngman Rhee, speaking from the rostrum of the United States House of Representatives (and abusing the hospitality of his American hosts), called on the United States to join him and Chiang in a full-scale invasion of the Chinese mainland. Two weeks later, "as if in reply" (as Eisenhower put it), Chou En-lai called for the "liberation of Formosa." [8] Then, almost predictably, on a bright and clear September 3, 1954, Chinese Communist shore batteries near the port of Amoy fired across the two-mile harbor separating the mainland from the Nationalist-held island of Quemoy. It was the beginning of a crisis that would last for eight months and gravely strain United States relations with its allies, as well as the nerves of humanity everywhere.

Eisenhower Restrains the Hawks

When the shelling started, Eisenhower was vacationing in Colorado and Dulles was en route to Manila to develop the SEATO treaty. Ambassador Rankin in Taipei informed the State Department that "I do not take the present fracas around Kinmen [Quemoy] very seriously from a purely military standpoint." [9] Washington, however, found the sudden eruption unsettling, and from the Senate hawks, frustrated by the actionless denouement in Indochina, came loud demands for a belligerent response. The Pentagon promptly approved retaliatory strikes by Chiang's air force against gun emplacements and transport shipping in the immediate vicinity of Quemoy, and there was a strong impulse in the Joint Chiefs of Staff for wider action. On September 6, the JCS voted 3 to 1 (Admiral Radford, Admiral Carney, and General Twining versus General Ridgway) for a more ambitious battle plan. They recommended to the President (1) that he authorize Chiang to bomb inland China and (2) if this produced an all-out Communist assault on Quemoy, that he order U.S. aircraft to join the battle.[10] This thinly disguised effort to provoke war with China accorded with Admiral Radford's long and deeply held view that a showdown with the Mao regime was inevitable and should be precipitated before that regime could consolidate its hold on the mainland. According to one source, Dulles who was still in Manila, cabled his concurrence with the JCS majority.[11] At the other end of the spectrum, Senators Lehman, Wayne Morse and John F. Kennedy urged the administration to give up any notion that the offshore islands were worth an American defense effort. In London, Foreign Secretary Eden proposed that the islands be neutralized by diplomatic agreement, and Hugh Gaitskell, leader of the Labour opposition, called for Chiang's retirement.

Although at considerable physical remove in his Colorado fishing camp, Eisenhower was in full communication with Washington, and he seemed swiftly to grasp the imperative need for an American policy of proportion and restraint. Reinforced by Bedell Smith, who was acting for Dulles at the State Department and who adamantly opposed the reckless course proposed by the JCS majority, the President concluded that the only sensible way to quench the inflammable situation was to offer Chiang the mutual defense pact he sought, but only in exchange for an absolute promise to forgo all further military actions against the mainland except with express United States concurrence. He promptly instructed Dulles to stop at Taipei en route home from Manila, to warn Chiang in strongest terms against provocative action, and to present the conditions for a defense pact. This Dulles did on September 9.[12] Meanwhile, Ambassador Rankin, on his own initiative, was warning the Nationalist foreign ministry against carrying attacks "further than could be justified," and this produced temporary restraint, even though the chief of the Nationalist air force claimed to be receiving contrary advice from members of the American military mission.[13]

Eisenhower had not yet acted on the JCS recommendation of September 6. He now ordered a special meeting of the National Security Council for September 12 at Lowry Air Force Base near Denver. At the meeting, Admiral Radford argued with articulate force for the majority JCS position, acknowledging that the offshore islands were not related militarily to the defense of Taiwan, but insisting that their loss would probably bring on a collapse of Nationalist morale, and that a high state of morale on Taiwan was of supreme importance to the cause of freedom in Asia.[14] This line of reasoning, although rejected by Eisenhower as a basis for overt military action against inland China, was nevertheless to become the accepted rationale for U.S. policy throughout the crisis, and was used to underpin the subsequent mutual defense treaty and the Formosa Resolution. It had little basis in fact — it was indeed the official line out of Taipei — and why the chairman of the Joint Chiefs of Staff should be advancing it as the heart of his argument was indeed a curiosity (General Ridgway, the lone JCS dissenter, had argued that the military chiefs ought not to take upon themselves the nonmilitary task of judging the psychological value of the islands).

Defense Secretary Wilson, who seemed opposed to precipitous action, but did feel that Chinese shellings required some United States response, generally failed to grasp the implications of the Radford proposal.[15] Bedell Smith, who attended the meeting with Dulles, placed himself in vehement opposition to Radford, arguing that it would very probably lead to war against China. Vice-president Nixon was also opposed, but primarily on the grounds that domestic political support was lacking for the scale of risks involved.[16] Dulles, who had previously stood with the JCS majority, was now moving uneasily back toward realignment with the President's determined restraint. After a full discussion, Eisenhower firmly rejected the Radford proposal, telling the group that such a response had very broad implications: "We're not talking now about a limited, brush-fire war. We're talking about going to the threshold of World War III." [17] Radford no doubt understood and accepted this implication. One official, deeply relieved that Eisenhower had firmly and sensibly pulled his advisers back from a perilous leap in the dark, said "the President personally saved the situation." [18]

As the situation quickly showed, Peking's purpose was primarily political — to create a nerve-racking stir in the straits area, thereby to demonstrate that it would not passively accept an American attempt to reinforce the de facto "two Chinas" situation by concluding a defense treaty with a territory which Peking regarded as a province of the mainland. The Chinese Communists did not possess the military capability to undertake a serious amphibious operation against Taiwan, and the presence of the Seventh Fleet made it virtually certain they would not try. The September bombardment was not a prelude to attempted assault on Taiwan; indeed, given the absence of massed landing craft and adequate airfields, as well as the sporadic character of the artillery fire, it is doubtful that there was an intention even to invade or blockade Quemoy. Ambassador Rankin reported in late September that the Nationalists were "exaggerating the military danger" as a means of gaining maximum American support.[19]

The Offshore Island Problem

A month earlier, on August 17, Eisenhower had been asked at a press conference what would happen if the Red Chinese tried to invade Taiwan. He had replied with relaxed matter-of-factness that any such attempt "would have to run over the Seventh Fleet." [20] But this did not meet the problem of the offshore islands, and the acute question from September onward was not whether or not to defend Taiwan; it was what to do about Quemoy, the Matsus and the Tachens. They occupied a different juridical status. Taiwan and the nearby Pescadores had been detached from China by the Japanese conquest of 1895, but restored to the "Republic of China" by the Cairo Declaration of 1943. The offshore islands had always been geographically and legally a part of the mainland. Since 1949, however, they had been occupied by Nationalist forces, who had bloodily repelled at least one major invasion attempt against Quemoy (October 1949) and who in 1954 numbered about 75,000 troops deployed in fortified positions: on Quemoy (50,000); on the rocky, treeless Matsu chain to the north (9,000); and on the Tachen Islands, 200 miles farther to the north (15,000).

American policy toward the offshore islands had been consistently ambiguous. On June 27, 1950, when President Truman's two-way order interposed the Seventh Fleet between Taiwan and the mainland, no mention was made of any other islands held by the Nationalists. As a matter of practice, the Seventh Fleet never made any attempt to interfere with Nationalist raids from the offshore islands, but on the other hand the military aid program for Taiwan (which began in February 1951) carried a secret understanding that American equipment was not to be sent to the offshore redoubts.[21] The United States, perhaps from inadvertance, perhaps from Acheson's awareness that to declare the islands explicitly outside the U.S. defense perimeter would precipitate a further eruption of the China Lobby, thus chose to regard Nationalist forces in the islands as neither under U.S. protection, nor subject to the same restrictions as the forces on Taiwan. There the matter rested, without evidence of further high-level attention within the American government, until March 1952, when Dulles, who was just completing his assignment on the Japanese peace treaty and about to begin the political campaign for Eisenhower, proposed to a group of State Department officials that the Nationalists ought to be encouraged to strengthen their position in the offshore islands.[22] Coming from a man who still had to be reckoned as a serious contender for Secretary of State in an election year that favored the Republicans, the proposal was taken seriously. By early 1953, responsibilities of the U.S. military advisory group on Taiwan were extended to the training and equipping of 75,000 Nationalist troops on Quemoy, the Matsus and the Tachens; and six months later, the Joint Chiefs of Staff advised Chiang that there was no objection to the rotation of American-equipped regular troops to the islands. The U.S. military advisory group even proposed a specific buildup in the Tachens.[23] Thus, the support of American military officials for a more aggressive Nationalist posture toward the mainland had grown considerably by mid-1953, with encouragement from Dulles. It was consonant with his policy of pressure against the Mao regime, and it was at the same time sufficient evidence of an incipient rollback posture to be useful in deflecting right-wing pressures against himself and the administration. It fell short, however, of a promise to support liberation, or even to defend the offshore islands. Thus when Chiang requested formal integration of the offshore islands with defense plans for Taiwan, in July 1953, Ambassador Rankin told him that action on such a request might take some time.[24]

The Crisis Deepens

The Communist artillery fire across Amoy harbor had now produced a deepening crisis. Peking, calling stridently for the "liberation" of Taiwan, continued to shell Quemoy; on November 1, Red Chinese planes bombed the Tachen Islands. Chiang, who resented but accepted the

Eisenhower demand that he strictly avoid the provocation of bombing inland China, expanded the scope of his air force activity within that constraint, hitting coastal ports, shipping around Quemoy, and a number of Communist-held islands. Senator Knowland, who had been told privately that this "releashing" was a precondition of a defense pact, chafed unhappily at the President's action until November 15, when he not only broke his silence, but passionately called on the Congress to ask the Joint Chiefs of Staff and other Defense officials to come before it to express their opinions on the heretical proposition of "peaceful coexistence" with Communist China. He wanted to know, he said, if the "clear and present danger" in the Asian situation warranted such "a basic change in the direction of our policy." [25] The unmistakable purpose of the Senate Majority Leader was to force a public exposure of differences between the Joint Chiefs of Staff and the President, but Congress did not take up the challenge.

Later in the month, on November 23, in response to an announcement that Peking had sentenced thirteen Americans (eleven of them airmen in uniform shot down during the Korean War) * to prison terms ranging from four years to life for espionage, Knowland urged a naval blockade of China. Eisenhower, who had privately warned the senator against such a rash countermeasure, rejected the blockade idea when it became public. "The hard way," he told Knowland, "is to have the courage to be patient." [26] During the same month an American reconnaissance B-29 was shot down by Russian MIG's over the sea north of Japan. The air force, which felt the facts were ironclad, was angered and dismayed when Eisenhower contented himself with a mild protest.

Thus, as 1954 drew to a close, perhaps the most striking fact on the Washington scene was President Eisenhower's visible effort to pull away from the bellicose advice that surrounded him and to reestablish a tone of reason and a sense of proportion in the conduct of U.S. foreign policy. On his own initiative and impelled largely by his own instincts, he seemed determined to dampen the inflammatory anti-Communist rhetoric that had run like a contagion through the first two years of his administration, raising temperatures on the political fever charts and engendering a mood of quick-tempered readiness for combat against the glaring frustrations of the world situation. Fundamental to the President's outlook was the assessment that there *now* existed a strategic nuclear stalemate, that Moscow was operating on that premise, and that for the sake of mankind the United States must do likewise. Knowland and Radford still spoke of nuclear stalemate as a *future* con-

---

* The other two were John Downey and Richard Fecteau of the CIA. Dulles refused to admit they were CIA agents. They were not released until March 1973 when President Nixon acknowledged their espionage role.

dition, indeed one that set finite time limits on an American policy of pressure and "decisive action" against its enemies. Dulles was more subtle, but the implicit premise of his January 12 speech was that Washington could threaten instant retaliation because the United States was not itself vulnerable to a blow in return. Already a dubious premise when Dulles spoke, it was recognized by Eisenhower a few months later as dangerously unreal. On October 19, he delivered a moving informal talk to State Department employees in which he pictured the world after nuclear war as one "very greatly in ashes and relics of destruction." [27] And his earnest searching, at a December 2 press conference, for a way out of the dilemma created by growing nuclear abundance on both sides, moved one leading journalist to observe that "considering the hysteria over Communism of the past two years, it is a tribute to Mr. Eisenhower that he has somehow thrown off those who would drive him into a dead end from which war would be the only escape. This is also a reflection of his innate caution, of his feeling against extremes, of his ability to gauge the temper of the mass of Americans and the masses elsewhere in the world on both sides of the Iron Curtain." [28]

The Sullivan and Cromwell Treaty

One reflection of Eisenhower's restraint in September had been a proposal by Dulles that the offshore island question be taken to the UN Security Council with the aim of obtaining "an injunction to maintain the status quo and institute a cease fire in the Formosa Strait." [29] Dulles assumed that Communist China would object and that this might well produce a Soviet veto, but he felt that such a development would help to focus blame for the crisis on the Communist side and thus to solidify opinion in the non-Communist countries. He assumed also that Chinese Communist military ambitions extended far beyond the capture of Taiwan, and that failure to stop them now would confront the free world with "disaster in the Far East," [30] but he was aware that an explicit U.S. commitment to defend Quemoy would leave the United States without allies. To legitimize the status quo seemed the answer. The British, Canadians, Australians, and others agreed.

However, before the Communist side could protest, an emphatic objection came from Chiang, who both rejected the idea of cease-fire and expressed his fear that any United Nations inquiry would scrutinize his shaky legal claims to mainland China and thus to the offshore islands (which were unanimously regarded as an integral part of the mainland). Nor was this necessarily the worst; the same line of examination could erode Chiang's claims to Taiwan. Dulles wrote to him on October 14, seeking to assure him that his understandable reluctance would be overshadowed by a vituperative Communist reaction and that this could be turned to Chiang's account; he added that the United States would always defend Chiang's right to rule Taiwan.[31] But the Generalissimo was unwilling to take any risks. The resulting impasse had the effect of strengthening momentum for a bilateral United States–Nationalist China security treaty, which was signed in Washington on December 2 by Dulles and the Nationalist Foreign Minister, George Yeh.

In form the document resembled the SEATO pact, declaring that in the event of armed attack on one party, the other party would act to meet "the common danger" in accordance with its "constitutional processes"; in geographical extent, it was similarly vague and indeterminate. Almost certainly, Eisenhower's strong preference was for a treaty absolutely restricting the U.S. defense commitment to Taiwan and the adjacent Pescadores, but there was, on the other side, the insistent argument that Nationalist morale on Taiwan would crumble if Quemoy fell, and the congressional eruption that had to be expected if another piece of territory, no matter how insignificant, were "lost" to "International Communism." Both Dulles and Radford were, in varying degrees, purveyors of these interwoven lines, Radford as a more open spokesman for the "positive China policy" group in Congress, Dulles concerned more with avoiding that group's hostility and with nurturing the remaining symbols of liberation and rollback.

Dulles met this dilemma by seeking to placate both viewpoints through deliberate ambiguity. Reflecting Eisenhower's strong desire to limit the U.S. commitment, the central emphasis of the treaty language was on the defense of Taiwan and the Pescadores. But reflecting the countervailing pressures, it also extended the commitment to "such other territories as may be determined by mutual agreement." Without committing the United States to such a course, the treaty thus carefully preserved the option to defend the offshore islands. It was a classic example of Dulles's legalistic approach and his Jesuitical preoccupation with the immediate tactical situation — i.e., with avoiding affront to the right wing, and with serving his chief while also serving his own convictions and preferences. It was a Sullivan and Cromwell treaty. Eisenhower's acceptance of it forfeited a major opportunity to force Chiang's retreat from a provocative forward position and thus to stabilize the situation in the Formosa Strait. There is little doubt that the President possessed the leverage to make either total withdrawal or very substantial reduction of Nationalist forces the price of any security treaty; his popular standing in the country could have ridden out the ensuing storm kicked up by the China Lobby and other critics. Four months after the treaty was signed, he tried in effect to do just this — proposing to Dulles a drastic reduction in Chiang's offshore garrisons, so that military defeat there, should it occur, could be accepted as the mere overrunning of minor outposts, without political consequence. But by that time it was too late.

Publication of the treaty on December 2 gave rise to severe Democratic criticism that the United States had needlessly tied itself to a hopeless regime and under conditions that encouraged Chiang to provoke a war in the Formosa Strait. And interpretations out of Taipei did nothing to invalidate such charges. The Nationalist Foreign Minister soon asserted (not incorrectly) that the treaty contained no undertaking *not* to attack the mainland, and Chiang added that indeed the treaty, by placing Taiwan under United States protection, put his regime in a stronger position to make such attacks. The Nationalists having thus demonstrated their intention to exploit the treaty for purposes which Eisenhower clearly did not share, it is reasonable to assume that the President was the prime mover in the supplementary exchange of letters on December 10, between Dulles and Yeh, which effectively "released" Chiang and cast a quite different light on at least Eisenhower's view of what the treaty was intended to achieve. The treaty supplement stipulated that the "use of force" from any area controlled by the Nationalists "will be a matter of joint agreement," excepting only a situation of dire emergency involving "the inherent right of self-defense." [32] Nationalist military action of any kind, from any place, was thus made subject to an American veto. Eisenhower appeared to have won his basic point, but soon lost it by agreeing that, while the treaty was public, the restraining supplement should be secret. Probably Dulles argued that secrecy was a necessary concession to morale on Taiwan, but it is plausible that he was more concerned to avert a right-wing backlash in the Congress. Such refusal of forthrightness was to make for further trouble.

The Formosa Resolution

As 1955 opened, it was apparent that the mere fact of the security treaty was not going to deter Chinese Communist probes, and would not therefore produce the administration's aim of a stabilized situation in the Formosa Strait. Peking seemed determined to test the ambiguities of the public agreement. Thus, on January 10, a hundred Chinese Communist aircraft raided the Tachen Islands, some two hundred miles north of Taiwan and of no significance to its defense. And on January 18, 4,000 Communist Chinese troops assaulted the island of Ichiang, on the flank of the Tachens, overwhelming 1,000 Nationalist guerilla troops in a fight that, according to Eisenhower, "lasted just two hours." [33] This action rendered the Tachens untenable without American air and naval support, for the Communist artillery, now established on Ichiang, could prevent resupply of the 15,000-man garrison and an equal number of civilians. When the Nationalist defense minister then asked Ambassador Rankin to declare that the Tachens would be protected by the Seventh Fleet, Washington was faced with another crisis. In the ensuing debate in the National Security Council, Radford argued that the United States should fight for the Tachens and bomb the mainland.[34] According to one source, Dulles's first impulse was to offer the Nationalists a flat guarantee to defend Quemoy and Matsu, in exchange for their evacuation of the Tachens,[35] but his later position involved a public promise of U.S. assistance in holding Quemoy and Matsu only "as long as the Chinese Communists profess their intention to attack Formosa." [36] Eisenhower still seemed to favor a commitment to Taiwan alone, but was now ensnared by the ambiguities of the treaty and the pressures created by the new Communist probes to test where it was bluff and where it was hard resolve.

The need was thus perceived to reinforce the treaty by some further grant of authority to the President, some new instrument that would show Peking it could no longer proceed with its rather clever surgical probes and thrusts in the confidence that the risks would remain low. The resulting Formosa Resolution was a classic Dullesian contrivance, embodying at once his tendency to sophisticated legalisms, his faith in the efficacy of dramatic public warnings, his belief in the fundamental need to precommit the Congress to the support of wide discretionary action by the President, and his preference for acting without allies. The Formosa Resolution was a refined version of "united action" in Indochina and a forerunner of the Eisenhower Doctrine for the Middle East. It amounted to the matured and seasoned Dullesian formula for effective deterrence. While the resolution was being debated by the Congress, Dulles explained it to his press conference on January 24. Most wars, he reminded them, including the Korean War, started because the aggressor miscalculated, and it was therefore basic to the prevention of war that the potential aggressor be left in no doubt of America's resolute will to throw its military weight upon the scales. Having advanced this dictum, however, he turned at once to the advantages of ambiguity in the instant case. "Well, are you going to nail your flag to this little bit of rock . . . which in fact could be pretty easily pulverized by artillery fire from the Mainland, and make that into a Dien Bien Phu? You certainly wouldn't want to do that. Nor would you want to give a notice to the Communists that they can come in and pick it up without a fight." [37] Here again was the tactical mind at work. Basic to his *theory* of deterrence was the certainty of retaliation, but in every application of theory from the "massive retaliation" speech onward, both the horrendous consequences of actual retaliation and the political forces arrayed against such a course forced him to manipulate ambiguity.

What the resolution asked of Congress was that it concur in the exercise of inherent presidential powers — in this case, to use force if, in Eisenhower's sole judgment, an attack on the offshore islands was a part of, or a definite preliminary to, an attack against Taiwan and the Pescadores. Without firmly committing the United States, it sought to prevent any assault on Quemoy and Matsu by strongly hinting that the American President might construe such an attack as a prelude to an attack on Taiwan. The rationale employed to gain congressional support indicated that Eisenhower had in effect succumbed to the rationale of Radford and Dulles, which was in fact the extremely pessimistic and self-serving assessment invented in Taipei. Why was it vital to prevent the loss of the offshore islands, when everyone agreed they were not remotely related to the military defense of Taiwan? Because Nationalist "morale" depended on holding them. What were the ingredients of this "morale," and why was it deemed of such importance? Eisenhower's correspondence with Churchill in early February 1955 gave the answer: Chiang and his followers "are held together by a conviction that some day they will go back to the mainland." Quemoy and the Matsus were thus "stepping stones" whose surrender "would destroy the reason for the existence of the Nationalist forces on Formosa." [38] Churchill made the wholly sensible reply that, while he fully understood the importance of defending Taiwan, he saw no reason why the West should hold a bridgehead for a Nationalist invasion of the mainland at the risk of World War III. He was confident that the Seventh Fleet could "drown" any invading force that sought to cross 120 miles of open water. He thought the United States should offer to Chiang the protection of its shield, but not the use of its sword.[39] Lewis W. Douglas, a former U.S. ambassador to London, also wrote to Eisenhower at this time, arguing that Quemoy and Matsu clearly belonged to mainland China and that United States policy should be based on law.[40]

The House of Representatives promptly endorsed the Formosa Resolution, 410 to 3, but the debate in the Senate was tougher. Senator Hubert Humphrey proposed an amendment limiting congressional consent to a defense of Taiwan and the Pescadores; this was defeated in the Foreign Relations Committee. During the floor debate, Senator Lehman introduced a similar amendment — to draw a defense line in the straits *outside* Quemoy and Matsu and confine the use of American

forces to the defense of Taiwan and the Pescadores. This was defeated
74 to 13. Senator Walter George, the Democratic chairman of the
Foreign Relations Committee, who endorsed the resolution and indeed
managed the floor debate for the administration, declared that abandoning Quemoy and Matsu would cause a "disintegration . . . swift,
quick, speedy, and final" of the whole Nationalist position,[41] which
led the Senate to believe that a vote for the resolution was very probably a vote for American participation in the defense of Quemoy and
Matsu. Eisenhower signed the resolution on January 29, 1955. Only on
February 7 did the White House release the supplementary Dulles-Yeh
exchange of December 10.

The Confrontation Hardens

While the Dulles-Yeh exchange provided some insurance against
Nationalist actions that might commit the United States to the use
of military force, the thrust of the Formosa Resolution moved in the
opposite direction — toward a greater American readiness to defend
Quemoy-Matsu. The Seventh Fleet evacuated 30,000 persons from the
Tachen Islands to Taiwan during the first week of February, and the
Chinese Nationalists moved 4,000 troops from Nanki Island to reinforce Matsu. An uneasy calm descended over the straits area, but there
was no resolution of the conflict, and the development of Communist
airfields and artillery concentrations continued along the China coast.

Before flying off to Bangkok in mid-February to attend the first formal
meeting of SEATO, Dulles combined warnings with concessions, big
sticks with small carrots, all couched in tenuous legalisms. In a speech
to the Foreign Policy Association on February 16, he declared that
Peking's mere celebration of its victory in the Tachen Islands demonstrated that it linked these coastal positions to Taiwan, and that such
linkage would permit the President to invoke the Formosa Resolution
and go to the defense of Quemoy and Matsu. On the other hand, he
suggested that a cease-fire in the straits could be based on a Communist
renunciation of force, without a renunciation of Peking's political
claims.[42] In Bangkok on February 21, he gave the SEATO Council his
considered view that Communist China was and had always been the
central source and coordinator of aggressive expansion in Asia. He saw
no distinction between Mao's essentially unlimited ideological aims
and his far more limited territorial goals. Peking, he said, "did not
turn the guerilla war of Indochina into full-scale war until the Korean
armistice gave safety to her northern flank." And it "did not stir up
military action in the Formosa area until the Indochina armistice had

given security to her southern flank." [43] Accordingly, South Korea, Nationalist China and SEATO (backed by the United States) constituted the indispensable elements of a restraining barrier in Asia.

Eden, who was also in Bangkok, did not, of course, share the American view that China was the monolithic fount of all revolutionary trouble in Asia, and he felt in particular that the risks being run by U.S. policy in the Formosa Strait were wildly disproportionate to the objective. The British wanted Washington to insist on a Nationalist withdrawal from Quemoy and Matsu, in exchange for a Chinese Communist renunciation of the use of force against Taiwan. But Dulles told him that the United States had no intention of bringing pressure to bear on Chiang for a withdrawal of his offshore island garrisons so long as Chiang "deemed their possession vital to the spirit and morale" of Taiwan. Attainment of a cease-fire might create some room for maneuver, he added, but unless it were reached soon, the United States could not much longer insist that Chiang maintain a passive posture of "watchful readiness" while the unimpeded Communist buildup proceeded opposite Quemoy.[44] Eden remained unpersuaded. Continuing on to Manila for a meeting of American mission chiefs and thence to Taipei, Dulles kept up a drumbeat of public statements underlining American resolve, while keeping the Communists guessing — e.g., "It cannot be assumed that the defense would be static and confined to Taiwan itself or that the aggressor would enjoy immunity." [45] He was indeed so garrulous and cute on this particular trip that Richard Rovere of the *New Yorker* was moved to comment that, although the Chinese Communists probably didn't believe their own charge that America was a paper tiger, they might reasonably conclude that it was a talking tiger.[46]

In Taipei, Dulles received the full Nationalist barrage of "dire consequences" that would flow from loss of the forward islands, whether by defeat or default. He received them, moreover, without the benefit of Ambassador Rankin's tempering presence and judgment. Rankin, whom Dulles inexplicably declined to take with him on his visit to Foreign Minister Yeh, noted afterward that the briefing had made an "evident impression" on the Secretary of State. As Dulles departed, the ambassador cabled the State Department that, with respect to the forward islands, Yeh "may have exaggerated their importance"; in Rankin's judgment, their loss would be "very serious but not necessarily disastrous." [47]

Dulles thus returned to Washington with what one press report described as a sense of foreboding, induced primarily by arguments of the Chiang regime. "The situation out there in the Formosa Strait," he told Eisenhower on March 10, "is far more serious than I thought." [48] And reflecting Yeh, he added, "The Chinese Communists are determined to capture Formosa. Surrendering Quemoy and Matsu won't end that determination." [49] It is surprising that the latter point should have been a revelation to Dulles in the spring of 1955, for Peking's claim to Taiwan had been clear, constant, and categorical. On the other hand, Peking obviously lacked the means to seize Taiwan by military force. There was accordingly no objective reason why the problem of holding Taiwan should be defined to require the military defense of the forward islands. But Dulles was now too engaged as political advocate and tactician to see the matter with detachment. He accepted Taipei's argument of linkage. Therefore, as he saw it, the only way out of the deepening dilemma was to apply more pressure — to force the Chinese Communists to back down by threatening the use of nuclear weapons. "If we defend Quemoy and Matsu," he further told Eisenhower, "we'll have to use atomic weapons. They alone will be effective against the mainland airfields." [50] He added gravely that "before this problem is solved, I believe there is at least an even chance that the United States will have to go to war." [51]

Eisenhower, despite his misgivings, appeared to accept his Secretary of State's assessment; in any event, he confined his reply to the passive, morally confident, and rather inane observation that "if this proved to be true it would certainly be recognized that the war would not be of our seeking." [52] The orchestration of American nuclear threats during the next several weeks showed more clearly than in earlier crises that Dulles was in full command of day-to-day operations, with the President reserving himself for the judicial role of weighing and deciding only transcendent issues. This was a division of labor inherent in Eisenhower's conception of the presidency, but by the spring of 1955 it was becoming an ingrained pattern of operation, as the cumulative pressures of the office bore down upon the man and as the man responded by trying (through frequent recreation and the army staff system) to escape or deflect them. Delegating broad powers of initiative to Dulles and others, Eisenhower seemed, as one observer noted, to have "organized his office staff and his Cabinet into a kind of conspiracy to perpetuate his own unawareness," of details.[53]

The new rhetorical effort about Quemoy now served a dual purpose: to frighten the Chinese Communists into accepting a cease-fire and to persuade American and world opinion that nuclear weapons represented no special menace to noncombatants. Dulles, who possessed a vast technical ignorance of nuclear weapons effects, based his comments on information received from Admiral Radford which, while reassuring, was factually untrue. The Secretary of State now spoke of "new and powerful weapons of precision which can utterly destroy military targets without endangering unrelated civilian centers. . . . I imagine that if the United States became engaged in a major military activity anywhere in the

In Taipei, with Chiang Kai-shek and Madame Chiang (1955)

world that those weapons would come into use." [54] Vice-president Nixon took up the theme, saying "tactical atomic explosives are now conventional and will be used against the targets of any aggressive force." [55] This spate of statements concerned Robert Bowie, who, distrusting Radford, was moved to ask the CIA for an independent estimate of civilian casualties in the heavily populated mainland area opposite Quemoy, if tactical nuclear weapons were used against airfields and artillery concentrations. The answer was on the order of 12 to 14 million people! Bowie showed the CIA report to Dulles, and believed the Secretary was sobered by the figures, although he betrayed no visible emotion.[56] In light, however, of Dulles's similar approach to the second Quemoy crisis in 1958, the effect of the new knowledge seems to have been inconclusive.

At one point in the process, Eisenhower was asked to comment on Dulles's talk about "new weapons." The President told his press conference that "I see no reason why they [nuclear weapons] shouldn't be used just exactly as you would use a bullet" or anything else, provided the application was against "strictly military targets and for strictly military purposes." He added, "The great question about these things comes . . . where you cannot be sure that you are operating merely against military targets." [57] Despite these careful caveats and disclaimers, the fact that he, Dwight Eisenhower (as distinguished from subordinates), had lent himself to such a casual attitude about the use of nuclear weapons produced an audible shock both at home and abroad, and he thereafter backed away. Radio Peking declared that Eisenhower was trying to sow the false impression that atomic weapons could be used tactically "without massacring civilians." [58] At his next press conference, on March 23, the President firmly evaded all questions related to tactical nuclear weapons, saying only that their use was impossible to determine in advance.

As the tension mounted, there were press reports of serious official differences over policy in the Formosa Strait, and one observer reflected the feeling of informed Washington circles that Eisenhower was perhaps the "one member of the administration who is determined not to go to war over the offshore islands if he can find any possible way of avoiding it"; [59] that "he stands almost alone . . . as an advocate of restraint in language and commitments." [60] The basic split lay between "a White House faction" favoring a minimum commitment and "a Pentagon–Capitol Hill faction" favoring a maximum commitment. "By and large it is recognized that the President wants out and the Joint Chiefs of Staff and Senator Knowland want in." [61] Dulles was also widely regarded as taking a more militant attitude toward Peking than his chief, as well as a more solicitous attitude toward Taipei; and some observers, noting the marked contrast between the Secretary's "dour Calvinist forecasts of doom and retribution" and the President's statements of "restraint and circumspection," professed to see a rift. Responding to a press conference query on March 15, Dulles replied with curious tentativeness that he "wouldn't think there is any basis" for reports of differences between himself and the White House. The fact is that there were wide differences of purpose between the President and the military chiefs, and also critical differences of emphasis between the President and the Secretary of State, but that Eisenhower, despite an outward passivity, seemed confident of his ability (on this issue as on others) to manage and manipulate these to produce a result that satisfied his own judgment and his own conscience.

At a briefing session on March 30 for legislative leaders of both parties, for example, Dulles explained that the Chinese Communists were "dizzy with success" and acting with "obvious arrogance," owing to their military victories — against MacArthur in Korea, against the French at Dien Bien Phu (sic), and most recently at Ichiang Island. House Speaker Sam Rayburn said that he drew from this presentation the inference that, if Quemoy and Matsu were attacked, the United States would intervene. Before Dulles could respond, Eisenhower quickly stepped in to say this was not necessarily the case, and led the Speaker once more through the somewhat unreal catechism of the Formosa Resolution.[62]

The President versus the Hawks

By late March, relative quiet reigned in the straits area, but the issues remained at impasse and time did not seem to be working for the United States. The glaring disproportion between risks and objectives in American policy continued to erode both domestic and international support. A typical newspaper editorial said on March 27 that "all of our allies, except Generalissimo Chiang Kai-shek, regard this as the wrong war, at the wrong time, and at the wrong place." Adlai Stevenson asked by what distortion of reason the honor and prestige of the United States had come to be "staked on some little islands within the shadow of the China coast." [63] Canada asserted that, like Britain, it would not join in any fight to defend them. And Carlos P. Romulo of the Philippines, a firm and tested friend of the United States, wrote in the *New York Times Magazine* of April 10 that Asians were baffled by the American obsession with Communism, repelled by the American tendency to perceive every serious political issue as a military threat, and frightened by the reflexive American response — which was to hold the threat of nuclear warfare to the world's head.

Such developments did not much affect senior operators at the Pentagon, who viewed the continuing Chinese Communist buildup opposite Quemoy as both disquieting and illegitimate. They wanted action. On March 26, newspaper reports later attributed to Admiral Carney, the Chief of Naval Operations, the view that Communist attack against the Matsus by mid-April, and against Quemoy by the end of May, was a virtual certainty; moreover, that the military advisers had urged the President to take *preemptive action* to destroy Red China's industrial base and thus to terminate its expansionist tendencies.[64] One newsmagazine report went so far as to suggest that "the President's military advisers have now set him a military deadline — April 15 — to do what, in their judgment, must be done." [65]

Eisenhower's prompt response reflected his innate privateness, his remarkable and largely benign detachment from much that went on inside his administration, yet at the same time his determined control of essentials, especially those bearing on the issues of war and peace. The same day as the Carney disclosure, he wrote himself a note, remarking that "hostilities are not so imminent as is indicated by the forebodings of a number of my associates," and added that "I have so often been through these periods of strain that I have become accustomed to the fact that most of the calamities that we anticipate really never occur." [66] He then "leaked" a statement to the newspapers through his press secretary which firmly rejected the military view: "The best political and military intelligence reaching the White House is that the Chinese Reds have not yet undertaken the kind of military and aviation build-up that would make an attack likely in the near future." [67] Thus did he turn back another effort by militant advisers who advocated a course of action that ignored all calculations of risk, and who, moreover, sought to force his hand by provocative public statements. His reaction was not wholly benign: Admiral Carney was denied reappointment as CNO after his two-year term expired.

Ten days later Eisenhower was moved to take a rare initiative in the realm of his Secretary of State. On April 5, he sent Dulles a memorandum urging that an effort now be organized to alter the character of Nationalist defenses in the offshore islands, so that an attack upon them would not produce "dire political consequences." In his new view, the status of the islands should be changed to "outpost positions," so that neither Chiang nor the United States need be committed to their "full-out defense." [68] This was a belated but unambiguous effort to extricate the United States from the worst risks and hazards of a position which, inherently dangerous, had now been rendered politically absurd as well by the ingenuities of Dulles the lawyer and the deficiencies of Dulles the statesman. Had Eisenhower insisted on such force reductions as a condition of the security treaty in December, the United States and its allies would have been better served. But now the United States was committed by both the treaty and the Formosa Resolution, Chiang's position was harder, and the Chinese Communist buildup continued.

By April 1955, it was more difficult to apply effective pressure on Taiwan, but, even so, Eisenhower proved unwilling to reinforce his sound instinct by sternly imposing his will; apparently he felt it would be improper to go beyond the point of bringing to Chiang's attention the many political and military advantages he himself perceived in a shift of stance. Success or failure for a new attempt to find an exit from the crisis thus hung on the ability to *persuade* Chiang to give way, and by the richest irony Admiral Radford and Assistant Secretary Robertson were chosen for the task. These fervid supporters of Nationalist China journeyed to Taiwan on April 20, under instruction to seek a solution "that will neither commit the United States to go to war in defense of the offshore islands nor will constitute an implied repudiation of the Generalissimo." [69] To induce the desired force reductions in the forward islands, Eisenhower was willing to station marines and an air force wing on Taiwan to reinforce its defense, but Chiang proved totally stubborn about redistributing any of his forces. As there were no reports of intemperate exchanges during the visit, it is safe to assume that Radford and Robertson did not press the President's case with excessive zeal. Perhaps they told Chiang that, if he found the proposal impossible, his reasons would be understood in Washington.

The Catalyst of Bandung

Although the President's gentle effort to turn Chiang around proved inconclusive, it did put Dulles on clear notice that Eisenhower did *not* favor U.S. participation in the defense of Quemoy and Matsu, and that in a crunch he would probably go to considerable lengths to avoid it. With characteristic resilience, the Secretary turned energetically to possible diplomatic solutions that had been either previously overlooked or unavailable. The much-heralded conference of Asian-African nations (representing nearly 1.5 billion people, or more than half the world's population) was about to convene at Bandung, Indonesia, and there seemed at least a chance that their growing anxiety of war off the China coast could be transformed into effective pressure against Communist China to renounce the use of force in pursuing its claim to Taiwan. On April 18, Eisenhower issued a statement calling attention to the "grave implications" of the Chinese Communist buildup opposite Taiwan, and expressing the President's hope that the Bandung Conference would seek agreement to a general renunciation of force with respect to the realization of national claims and objectives. The appeal soon had a positive effect. Although Krishna Menon of India found Chou En-lai still adamantly opposed to a cease-fire on the grounds that Taiwan was entirely an internal Chinese affair,[70] the Bandung Conference developed considerable support for a more ambitious proposal put forward by the Prime Minister of Ceylon, Sir John Kotelawala. This called not only for an immediate cease-fire in the straits, but for a five-year international trusteeship for Taiwan, and then a plebiscite.[71] Drawing on the analogy of Ceylon's recent achievement of independence from India, the proposal aimed at self-determination for the Taiwanese — a solution that was of course anathema to both Chiang and Mao (who shared the conviction that Taiwan was an integral part of China).

These pressures did force Chou En-lai to make a considered response. And adopting an attitude with his fellow delegates that was at once quiet, humble and forceful, Chou managed in the course of two statements on April 23 to place China at the center of the Asian-African yearning for a "relaxation of tensions" without either ensnaring himself in the risks of a multilateral negotiation about Taiwan, or agreeing to a cease-fire.

By all accounts it was a masterful performance. Speaking at a closed session in the afternoon, he said, "[We] do not want to have war with the United States. We are willing to settle international disputes by peaceful means." He thought the "constructive action" of other delegations would be "most beneficial . . . to the postponement and prevention of a world war." [72] But he rejected a cease-fire on the now familiar grounds that "there is no war between China and the United States, so the question of a so-called cease-fire does not arise." [73] That evening he made a public statement which said: "The Chinese people are friendly to the American people. The Chinese people do not want to have a war with the United States of America. The Chinese government is willing to sit down and enter into negotiations with the United States government to discuss the question of relaxing tension in the Far East, and especially the question of relaxing tension in the Taiwan area." [74]

Herbert Hoover, Jr., who had succeeded Bedell Smith and who was Acting Secretary during a brief absence by Dulles, at first rejected the offer, but a more considered and positive American response followed on April 26; with this evidence of mutual desire to back away from the tense confrontation, the crisis, although unresolved, was effectively over. Chou En-lai had fended off a formal cease-fire, offered peace negotiations, and raised Peking's international standing among neutralist nations and even among the NATO combine of Western Europe. In fact, he had accomplished more than that: by opening a peace offensive with broad appeal, he had both disguised Peking's military inability to force a showdown with the United States over Quemoy and Matsu, and deflated the American charge that Peking intended to assert its claims only by force.

The United States, in Eisenhower's words, had threaded its way "with watchfulness and determination, through narrow and dangerous waters between appeasement and global war." [75] He generously attributed this skillful course to his "Administration," but the credit belonged very largely to him alone. Radford had wanted to bomb the mainland and fight for the Tachens, Knowland to blockade the coast, and Dulles to use nuclear weapons if Peking attacked Quemoy. Eisenhower, in his relative detachment and deceptive passivity, saw the issues in a larger frame, maintained a superb sense of proportion, and managed (although at times precariously) to retain control of the United States government, including those powerful factors within it who did not share, but sought to foil, the President's peaceful purposes.

18

To the Summit

A s 1955 OPENED, segments of official and unofficial Washington began
to acknowledge a gathering awareness that conditions outside the
United States had changed markedly in the space of only a few months,
and that developments driving the change promised or threatened, in
their reinforcing interaction, to produce a radically transformed world
situation. The major developments were these: a rapid growth of Soviet
nuclear strength (weapons and deliverability), a more skilled and flexible
Soviet diplomacy, and a new determination in the underdeveloped world
not only to eliminate every remaining vestige of colonial tutelage, but
to forge a collective independence apart from the cold war conflict that
obsessed the Communist and anti-Communist blocs. Such developments
challenged the fundamental assumptions of United States foreign policy.

Resistance to a Changed World

Russian achievements in research and development, especially their
extensive hydrogen bomb tests in September 1954, were producing a
new power relationship. An Assistant Secretary of Defense might proclaim with factual accuracy that the United States was "militarily
stronger by far than its challenger," but the wider truth was that the
world had entered what Hanson Baldwin called "the age of atomic
plenty." [1] With stockpiles of deliverable weapons steadily mounting on
both sides, a situation was being created in which numerical superiority
provided little or no usable political advantage. If it had ever been
plausible to believe the United States could eject a major adversary

from a position considered by him to be of central importance, it was plausible no longer, for now the United States was also vulnerable to atomic attack and destruction.

The emerging strategic fact was nuclear stalemate which, translated, meant that a policy of nuclear threat against Russia or any lesser power under Russia's protection was either a policy of bluff or a policy of suicide. Ardent advocates of nuclear showdown with "International Communism" continued to assert that stalemate was a *future* condition, but wiser heads — notably Churchill and Eisenhower — accepted the truth that it had already arrived. Churchill indeed was already turning to "the universality of potential destruction" as a source of "hope and even confidence," owing to the stability that he perceived could be built into "the balance of terror." [2] And Eisenhower, heavily influenced by the American hydrogen bomb experiments at Bikini (which had torn a mile-wide hole in the coral atoll and showered radioactive fallout a hundred miles from ground zero) as well as by Russian developments, had said several times near the end of 1954 that "since the advent of nuclear weapons, it seems clear that there is no longer any alternative to peace." [3]

The United States and its allies were also operating against a more flexible and resourceful Soviet diplomacy, whose confidence was buoyed both by Khrushchev's perception of nuclear stalemate and by growing Soviet economic strength. A major asset of Western policy in the first years of the cold war had been the predictability of the Stalin regime and its gift for regularly setting off every alarm bell in the Western world. Stalin had assured passage of the Marshall Plan by rejecting an invitation to participate which the plan's sponsors had felt required to extend, yet which, if accepted, would almost surely have killed the plan in Congress. Similar doctrinaire rigidity and harsh threats had secured the Truman Doctrine and NATO, as well as cast away the allegiance of Tito, who controlled the second most powerful army in Europe. Stalin's support for the attack on South Korea had led not only to collective resistance on that peninsula, but to serious rearmament in Europe (including Germany, whose military renaissance was the single development most hated and feared by Russia). The uncivilized behavior of Russian representatives at the United Nations and in other international forums had served constantly to remind the West of Communist arrogance and brutality. But the tyrant's death had changed a good deal of this, at least on the surface. The new Soviet posture of "competitive coexistence" required some American reassessment and response, if only because its appeal to former colonialized nations threatened to spread neutralism and thus undermine both the ideological and geopolitical foundations of the existing American strategy.

But candid reassessment and forthright acceptance of new truths presented special difficulties for the Eisenhower administration, for the Congress, the press, indeed for the whole American establishment. And for none did such an exercise run harder against the grain than for John Foster Dulles. He had prepared himself intellectually and psychologically to meet and master the Stalinist challenge which he had assumed would be the dominant manifestation of "International Communism" for many years to come. A basic tenet of his belief was that Soviet Russia, behind its iron facade, was ultimately weak because it was morally rotten; a Western policy of political, military, moral pressure was accordingly the way to strain that basic weakness, to force major revisions in Soviet policies and attitudes, perhaps even to produce a total breakdown of the Communist system. To acknowledge that this morally evil system could now offset American strategic power was to admit that an American policy of pressure could not be sustained. Another basic tenet for Dulles (and many others) was that American economic and technical superiority rested in large part on the *moral* superiority of the free enterprise system. Only men operating in political freedom could achieve spectacular industrial progress. And as political freedom and economic progress were interdependent partners, it followed that emerging nations, given a choice, could not fail to choose allegiance with the West. To acknowledge that the Soviet system was now an emergent industrial power, capable of generating economic surplus and of employing this in ways that appealed to vast numbers of the world's people in Africa and Asia, was to yield up the moral foundations of his policy. Moreover, the basic Dullesian approach was to apply America's superior assets not as a means of opening, ventilating, and dealing with the Communist system, but rather as a means of surrounding it, isolating it, and denying it normal commercial and diplomatic intercourse. But the new developments indicated that the Soviets, employing the age-old factors of power and affluence, might now break out of Coventry and achieve respectable status in many parts of the world. Such a development would rob the West of what Dulles regarded as its indisputable and indispensable moral edge.

Perhaps understandably, the implications of these far-reaching changes were, collectively, more than Dulles and other senior administration leaders could admit to. Their reaction, in the main, was to discount Soviet nuclear power, to treat the new Soviet diplomacy as a desperate shift in tactics dictated by failure to achieve expansionist aims by military means, and to deplore actual and incipient neutralism. Dulles's speech notes for the NATO Council meeting of December 15, 1955, contained the phrase "Stalinism lives, though Stalin dead." [4]

Grudgingly toward the Summit

American reluctance to reappraise the basic strategic situation was not, by and large, shared by others. Western Europe and a broad range of countries in the Middle East and Asia recognized the outlines of consequential change, and were moved above all to find some modus vivendi in what seemed to them the mortal struggle between two un-comprehending giants. At the end of 1954, Mendès-France told the United Nations that France was ready to meet with the Russians at the highest level: "We shall not let the idea gain credence that the Western community rejects peace or brushes aside opportunities of effecting a *rapprochement* and conciliation." [5] He then called for a summit meeting in the early spring of 1955, which would have left French ratification of the Western European Union agreements (and thus West Germany's entrance into NATO and German rearmament) conditional upon the outcome. For these conditions Churchill sternly admonished him, insist-ing that full ratification of the WEU agreements must precede any high level East-West conference, but the British remained the driving force behind a summit. For Sir Winston it was only elementary prudence for the West to learn at firsthand what sort of men were now in charge in the Kremlin, and to let those new men gauge the quality and temper of Western leadership. And now in the spring of 1955, he had a second reason. On April 6, he was laying aside the burdens of office for the last time, and, given the mood of the British people, he and his chosen successor, Anthony Eden, felt it was very important to obtain four-power agreement to a summit meeting before the Tory party had to face the general elections in May. As it turned out, Eisenhower's readiness to help Eden (and thus avoid what Dulles thought would be the disad-vantages of having to work with a Labour government in which Aneurin Bevan might be Foreign Secretary) was a key factor in Washington's ultimate willingness to go to the summit.

Dulles continued, however, to view the idea with skepticism and distaste, complaining to Adenauer on a trip to Bonn that he was unhappy about the summit plan; [6] it would be much better to wait until greater strength had been gathered through West Germany's consolidation in NATO and the raising of twelve German divisions. He acknowledged that a meeting might be necessary as an exercise in alliance politics, but believed that nothing of benefit could be gained, for, in his judgment, no totalitarian society could afford to agree to a genuine easing of tensions — the regime's survival required a constant focusing of popular discontent on external enemies. Moreover, any

With Mrs. Dulles at the United Nations (1955)

In Madrid with Generalissimo Franco and U. S. Ambassador
John Davis Lodge (1955)

At the signing of the Austrian Peace Treaty with Foreign Ministers
Pinay, Molotov, Figl, and Macmillan on the balcony of the Belvedere
Palace in Vienna (May 1955)

meaningful accord with the Russians would have to involve Western acceptance of the status quo in Germany, and here Dulles shared Adenauer's foreboding that, unless Germany were unified on democratic terms before Adenauer passed from the scene, the West Germans would be lured into the trap of negotiating with the East Germans for unity on Soviet terms. The British heavily discounted this possibility, and were accordingly lukewarm about unification. Their own goal was a West Germany under reasonable control, and they felt this had been substantially realized in the WEU agreements. And France, far from being disheartened by the continued division of Germany in two parts, would have been pleased to see it divided into ten or twenty. Thus, beneath the facade of Western agreement, only Adenauer and Dulles cared very deeply about German unification, and their concern seemed to rest at bottom on a distrust of the West Germans — i.e., on a fear that they preferred the abstraction of "unity," even under painful conditions, to a secure place in a prosperous Western Europe. It was a notably bad judgment, and it had the effect of holding Western policy to the free-elections formula for unification (and of insisting that the German question be settled in advance of all European security and disarmament arrangements) long after it was crystal clear that the Soviets, who held a veto on unification, were unalterably opposed.

Yet it was a bad judgment rooted in a noble human impulse; for Dulles's opposition to the German status quo was linked to "liberation," to America's moral duty to work for the end of "enslavement" in Eastern Europe. At the NATO meeting in May 1955, he spoke so emphatically of his continued hopes for the advent of freedom behind the Iron Curtain that Paul-Henri Spaak privately took issue with him, arguing that insistence on a public posture of rollback cruelly implied assistance which the NATO alliance could not realistically give; moreover, Spaak pointed out, the diplomatic position of the West was exceedingly weak on this matter because it had already extended diplomatic recognition to all of the Eastern European regimes. Dulles replied that the goal of freedom everywhere was an objective for which the United States stood as a matter of sheer principle, and which it could never abandon. Spaak later said, "We never spoke of this very much afterwards. Dulles wanted to maintain the principle. We must remember that he was that type of man. I greatly admired him." [7]

With the pressures for a summit meeting in 1955 becoming irresistible, Dulles appeared gradually to yield to a conception put forward by the new British Foreign Secretary, Harold Macmillan — namely, that a heads of government meeting should be regarded not as the *end* of a process, but as a *beginning* — that it should open up a whole series of conferences at various levels and on various subjects extending probably over

Arriving on the island of Brioni to visit Tito (May 1955)

With Tito and his wife at Brioni (May 1955)

"Yes, We'll Be There, Rain And Shine"

From *Herblock's Here and Now*
SIMON & SCHUSTER, 1955

a period of years. At their first encounter in Paris on May 7, Macmillan found Dulles "more gracious than I had expected" and "rather dreamy — as if he were thinking about something else." [8] When they met again on May 9, the French had become strong proponents of the Macmillan idea, and Eisenhower had moved almost to full acceptance. A meeting at the summit was now a virtual certainty. At the outset of their talk, however, Dulles asked rather confidentially if Macmillan thought it would be suitable if the United States sent its Vice-president. Macmillan assumed Dulles was joking, and promptly launched into a music hall story about "poor Mrs. Jones" who had two sons: one was lost on the Titanic, the other became Vice-president of the United States; neither was ever heard of again. As the punch line was delivered, Dulles gave Macmillan the "look of Queen Victoria saying 'We are not amused' "; then, recovering, he broke the tension with an excessively hearty laugh. It was evident that he had meant his proposal to be taken seriously.[9] On May 10, the three Western powers sent identical notes to Russia proposing a series of three meetings: (1) a meeting of Foreign Ministers, to formulate the agenda and methods of procedure; (2) a meeting of the heads of government; and then (3) a second meeting of Foreign Ministers, to pursue in greater detail whatever promising avenues of consideration might have been opened at the summit. A quick succession of moves on the Russian side (including approval of the Austrian treaty, an invitation to Adenauer to visit Russia, an offer of formal peace with Japan, and Khrushchev's trip to Yugoslavia to make his bibulous amends to Tito) reinforced the sense of certainty that a summit meeting would be held.

Of the several Soviet contributions to an "easing of tensions," by far the most important was their willingness to break the long deadlock on the Austrian State Treaty, which had been an explicit American test of Russian good intentions for several years. And the public celebrations in Vienna, which marked the end of the oppressive Russian occupation, were perhaps one of the most moving experiences in Dulles's life. After the treaty signing, the Big Four Foreign Ministers emerged on the lofty central balcony of the magnificent Belvedere Palace to greet a jubilant Austrian throng in the gardens below. According to two seasoned reporters, as the crowd "cheered with a joy approaching delirium," a gradual change came over Dulles's face. "His expression altered from polite pleasure to immense happiness and delight." [10] He and Molotov (whom Macmillan thought looked "rather like a head gardener in his Sunday clothes") [11] began to "exchange handshakes, and soon embraces, in response to the crowd's cries for a display of East-West harmony — the same emotional plea that was propelling Dulles toward the summit. The Ministers then withdrew into the palace, but were called back.

Dulles raised both his hands and waved a handkerchief in one of them. Molotov, in turn, clasped his hands above his head in the fashion of a winning prize fighter. Macmillan and [French Foreign Minister] Pinay were slightly less demonstrative. . . . Vienna's doughty Foreign Minister Leopold Figl, with tears on his cheeks, hugged Dulles with one arm," and Molotov with the other.[12] The following day, May 15, Dulles told a press conference that "an area of Europe is, in a very literal sense, liberated by the withdrawal of Red Army troops . . ." and he found in this new development "something contagious."[13]

The tenth anniversary celebration of the United Nations, held at San Francisco in late June, was also marked by a measurable amity in East-West relations and, however fleeting or ceremonial this may have been, it served to stimulate Eisenhower's congenital optimism about Russia, the world, and life in general. The British foreign secretary, wanting to extend informal good wishes to his old commander and comrade-in-arms from the North African campaign of 1942, telephoned the President at his hotel:

Eisenhower: "How are you getting on with Foster?"

Macmillan: "I'm getting on fine."

Eisenhower: "Foster's a bit sticky at first, but he has a heart of gold when you know him. You have got to get to know Foster. He's all right when you get to know him."[14]

For some time the President had followed Dulles's lead in speaking of a summit as though its only constructive purpose was to serve as an object lesson for deluded optimists, but he returned from San Francisco in a far more hopeful state of mind. He was now persuaded that the Kremlin had excellent reasons of its own for wanting a détente, and that Russian statements on the need for arms reduction could be taken essentially at face value. Moreover, he would go to Geneva not to test Russian sincerity — which had been Dulles's theme for three years — but rather to establish Macmillan's pattern for a whole series of subsequent meetings aimed at bringing about a stable and orderly and peaceful coexistence.[15] Where Dulles had consistently deprecated Russian strength (causing Khrushchev to remark that "we are not going to Geneva with broken legs"), Eisenhower now made clear at a press conference on July 6 that nothing was further from his mind than the thought that the Russians would be negotiating from weakness.[16] By going out of his way to reassure Khrushchev that he was not contemptuous of Soviet power, he seemed to be acting on the wise insight that it was Russia's new strength and confidence that gave a hopeful prospect to the Geneva meeting. If there were a chance for settlement of important questions, including arms control, Eisenhower reasoned that it was based on the fact that the Russians had at least partially succeeded in their efforts to catch up with the West in nuclear weapons development and long-range delivery vehicles. In light of the long-standing American posture that meaningful settlements could be reached only when the West was negotiating from a position of evident superiority — i.e., from "situations of strength" — this presidential judgment was a fine piece of irony.

This instinct to be positive and forthcoming showed once more the underlying differences in temperament and outlook between the two men, and the President's calm insistence on his own ultimate judgment, for Dulles's briefing memoranda during the preparatory stage were filled with somber warnings and advice that ran in the opposite direction: "Undoubtedly, one of the major Soviet desires [at the summit] is to relieve itself of the economic burden of the present arms race." Another was to achieve the "appearance that the West concedes the Soviet rulers a moral and social equality which will help . . . maintain their satellite rule by disheartening potential resistance." Moreover, East-West fraternization in Geneva would encourage neutralism in other countries by "spreading the impression that only 'power' rivalries, and not basic principles,* create present tensions." [17] He estimated that a summit conference would probably lead to "considerable" Soviet gains of this kind. But now accepting the summit as a foregone conclusion, the lawyer sought means to limit the damage to his client. The President, he wrote, should seek to minimize the impact by "avoiding social meetings where he will be photographed with Bulganin, Khrushchev, etc., and by maintaining an austere countenance on occasions where photographing together is inevitable." [18]

On July 15, Premier Nikolai Bulganin told a press conference the Soviets were going to Geneva "to discuss frankly with the other great powers the most important international problems, to find a common language and by joint efforts to achieve a relaxation of international tension and the strengthening of confidence in the relations between states . . ." [19] Eisenhower's rejoinder was equally promising. The purpose of his trip, he said, was "to change the spirit that has characterized the intergovernmental relationships of the world during the past ten years." [20]

The Meeting at Geneva

The Summit Conference, convened at Geneva, July 18 to 23, 1955, was a far larger, more formal gathering than the intimate affair without agenda that Churchill had envisioned two years before. There *was* an

---

* In the handwritten first draft, the phrase "moral issues" was used in place of "basic principles."

agenda and it was rigidly confined and ordered: (1) German unification and European security, (2) disarmament, and (3) the development of East-West contacts. To the British Foreign Secretary, Harold Macmillan, a relatively new boy at international conferences, the physical arrangements were equally forbidding: "The protagonists were sitting at tables drawn up in a rectangle; the space between them was about the size of a small boxing ring. But this arena was itself surrounded by rows of benches and seats which . . . seemed to be occupied by a crowd of interested onlookers. The walls were decorated with vast, somewhat confused, frescoes depicting the End of the World, or the Battle of the Titans, or the Rape of the Sabines, or a mixture of all three. I could conceive of no arrangement less likely to lead to intimate or useful negotiations." [21]

Yet, despite the antiseptic formalities, it proved possible for the leaders of East and West to explore each other's minds with some candor, an achievement that owed much to the Russians' encouraging and dramatic departure from the infuriating incantations that had filled all Russian diplomatic discourse while Stalin ruled. At Geneva in 1955, the Soviet representatives were speaking not for the ear of that one strict auditor in the Kremlin, but actually to persuade their Western counterparts across the table. They displayed an unhurried self-confidence, making it possible to base exchanges on the accepted Western techniques of logic and debate, and their self-confidence extended to matters of personal security, where they presented an odd contrast with the Americans. Eisenhower's arrival was guarded by a covey of fighter planes, hovering helicopters, and squads of Secret Service men dogtrotting beside his limousine. Khrushchev and Bulganin landed without escort and proceeded to their villas in the rear of an open car.

Except perhaps for the somewhat staid French premier, Edgar Faure, the attending heads of government were all rather richly dramatic personalities. The Russians were, of course, represented by a tandem. Marshal Bulganin was Soviet premier, yet all were aware that Khrushchev was Boss. As one seasoned observer perceived it, "the relationship between the two men was approximately the same as that between a competent and self-assured prizefight manager and a heavyweight who is good but not so surpassingly good that the manager would have to retire if he lost him." [22] In surprising contrast to the "squat, tough, loud, indelicate, and altogether self-possessed" party boss, Bulganin was "well turned out, in an almost aristocratic style," and looked like "a successful Kentucky horse-breeder." [23]

Anthony Eden, Britain's most distinguished diplomat, arrived in Geneva for his first major performance as Prime Minister with the plaudits of the European press trailing behind him like triumphant streamers. All expressed the view that his seasoned experience in high conferences would make him the most effective spokesman on the free world side. Also, he had recently taken a new wife, the attractive and much younger Clarissa Churchill (Sir Winston's niece), and it appeared to some that he worked hard at maintaining an image of glamour as much for her as for the press and general public. Daily sunbaths gave his handsome features a blooming healthy tan, and he watched with obvious approval as his young wife entered the conference room each day "with quite a bit of posh and spit" escorted by two young aides from the Foreign Office.[24] Yet a combination of factors deprived Eden of a starring role. One was the rigidly prescribed order of the speeches — i.e., United Kingdom, USSR, United States, and France — for this meant that Eden's remarks were subject to immediate rebuttal by the Russians, who in turn could be answered by the Americans. As Dulles's assistant put it, "So that the Russians were knocking them down, and we were knocking the Russians down, you see."[25] Given the techniques of press coverage, this sequencing favored the United States and handicapped the British and French, in terms of scoring points in the East-West conflict. In addition, the Russians chose to lionize the Americans during the coffee breaks, leaving both Eden and Faure to form a nucleus of the "second best" club, or to sip alone in a state of relative pique.

But in the main, Eden and all others were overshadowed by Eisenhower's personality and performance. By a near-unanimous judgment he was the leading figure of the conference, and not merely because he spoke as commander of the great citadel of world capitalism. In every encounter he projected an earnest and pacific intent, a serious yearning for conciliation, a readiness to grant the other side a rectitude no less than his own. All this produced a sense of trust. When in the course of his unannounced "open skies" speech on the fourth day, he turned directly to the Soviet delegation and said, "The United States will never take part in an aggressive war," Bulganin immediately replied, "We believe that statement."[26] *Le Monde* of Paris, a notably anti-American journal, was moved the following week to say that "Eisenhower, whose personality has long been misunderstood, has emerged as the kind of leader that humanity needs today." Richard Rovere added in the *New Yorker:* "The man has an absolutely unique ability to convince people that he has no talent for duplicity."[27] Dulles worked at restraining public enthusiasm. At a press conference he was asked if reports were true that "the President's personal impact on the Russians has been considerable." He replied that the reports were accurate, but that "like everything else, it is not to be overemphasized."[28]

The Secretary of State had persuaded his chief to avoid what he conceived to be the acute domestic political pitfalls of social intercourse with the Soviets, but the British saw informal entertaining as a superior means of gauging the new Kremlin leaders and of assessing their major hopes and fears. On the first evening of the conference, the Russians dined at Eden's villa, a purely Anglo-Russian affair which, according to Macmillan, Eden conducted "with great brilliance, exerting all his charm, both during and after dinner." [29] As he further reported, "(a) They were very relaxed, after the removal of the tyrant, Stalin. (They said, with glee, that since 1953 they worked a normal day instead of all night!) (b) They do not want another Stalin — a bloody and uncertain tyrant. (c) Khrushchev is the boss, but *not* another Stalin . . . (d) They are unable to accept the unification of Germany in NATO . . . because their public would be horrified. After all, the Germans treated them terribly and they hate them. (e) They do not fear war; they do not really believe that the Americans are going to attack them. (f) They are anxious about China . . . they (like us) wish that Quemoy and Matsu could sink beneath the sea. (g) They may fear . . . that China will be a danger to them on their eastern flank . . . (h) They do not want the conference to fail." [30]

Indeed, on a range of matters great and small, inside and outside the conference hall, Macmillan, who did not on this occasion seem overburdened with responsibility, proved easily the spriteliest and most trenchant reporter. Thus, on the opening day, "we all lunched with the President — a disgusting meal, of large meat slices, hacked out . . . and served . . . with marmalade and jam. The French were appalled." [31] Four days later, however, he waxed lyrical over lunch with Premier Faure. "The French luncheon was certainly superb. There was a relaxed and happy atmosphere. . . . The French had not forgotten their experience and put on a long series of exquisite courses, with wines of equal distinction. It was the demonstration of the refinement of the Old World against the barbarism of the New, whether in the East or in the West." [32] On July 22, the day Eisenhower sprang his unannounced "open skies" proposal, all three Western delegations met at Eden's villa for breakfast: "Dulles came and ate boiled eggs one after the other . . . we tried to get him to talk. . . . But he ate and talked so slowly that we got little out of him which we did not know before." [33]

In the Palais des Nations, the conference settled down to the agenda, with Eden leading off for the West. On German reunification, he proposed the basic Western plan for free all-German elections, creating a government which would then decide between neutrality, or alignment with either NATO or the Warsaw Pact. The West had insisted on linking the German question to the issue of European security, on the magnanimous assumption that, after Germany was unified by free elections and had chosen alliance with the West, it would be helpful to offer assurances to Russia against potentially aggressive German behavior. Here Eden laid out three possibilities: (1) a mutual security pact involving the Big Four, plus Germany; (2) limitations on German forces and armaments, or (3) a demilitarized buffer zone between a unified Germany and the Soviet Union. But these proposals had about them an air of logical unreality. The Russians, who understood that their hold on East Germany could not survive free elections and that such a loss would spread dissension throughout Eastern Europe, were conspicuously not interested. In their view, broad arrangements for European security had to precede German unification. It was first necessary, they argued, for the major powers to agree on the "peaceful settlement of disputes," which, once accomplished, would lead to a dismantlement of Western European Union, NATO and the Warsaw Pact. This meant the withdrawal of all "foreign troops remaining on the territories of the European states," an unsubtle demand that the United States get out of Europe.[34] Within such a framework, Bulganin argued, the question of German unity could be considered.

On disarmament, the West stressed inspection, although Eisenhower's "open skies" proposal (calling for a full exchange of maps and blueprints identifying the location, size and character of military installations on both sides, and for a mutual grant of freedom to conduct photoreconnaissance over the territory of the other side) was an attempt to surmount the inherent Russian objection to on-site inspection. Once more the Russians showed little interest. But underlying the political objections, there was in this case a technical question of whether or not such a scheme, even if carried out in good faith, could provide adequate assurance against hidden stockpiles of significant size. The fact of nuclear abundance on both sides had created formidable practical difficulties to policing any agreed limitation, but there was no expert capacity to deal with these at the summit. Macmillan thus found Eisenhower's statement "a very moving, though not very coherent address."[35] The Russian disarmament proposals were more tangible, calling for an absolute prohibition on the manufacture and use of atomic weapons and a ceiling of 1.5 million men each in the armed forces of Russia, China, and the United States, 650,000 each for Britain and France, and lesser numbers for other nations. They were too tangible for the West, for their acceptance would have meant giving up the consolidation of an armed West Germany within NATO; moreover, they carried no assurance that the promised Soviet reductions would be subject to satisfactory Western inspection.

On the final agenda item (the development of East-West contacts), each side confined itself to general statements; the West desired entry of more printed materials into the Soviet bloc; the Russians were chiefly interested in a relaxation of Western controls on trade. There were also informal skirmishes, but no real debate, on several other issues, including the recognition of Communist China, and the status of Taiwan and the off-shore islands. Eisenhower, responding to congressional representations, privately took up with Bulganin the sensitive question of national self-determination in Eastern Europe. On all of these issues there was mutual rebuff.

The Spirit of Geneva

Out of the general politeness of those few days at the summit, there arose a public euphoria, promptly labeled "the Spirit of Geneva," but it could not long withstand the withering analysis of politicians and journalists who, expecting more, now pointed to the total absence of agreement on any of the agenda items. James Reston wrote: "The Russians are waiting it out . . . counting on our impatience and on Europe's weariness and divisions." [36] Roscoe Drummond found behind Russia's new cordiality "a massive hostility to any settlement . . . except on complete acceptance of Soviet terms." [37] Dulles continued his steady effort to deflate expectations. At a press conference as he was leaving Geneva, the following exchange occurred:

Reporter: The President today remarked that nobody doubts the sincerity of the Russians in their peace efforts. What are the reasons for the "era of good feelings" we are writing about?
Dulles: Well, I think it is a little premature to talk about the "era of good feelings." [laughter] [38]

Yet these points, while well taken, seemed to miss a larger truth: that the Geneva meeting had been a tentative probing exercise for both sides, without serious expectation of quick or far-reaching settlement. All parties found themselves in tacit agreement that a serious attempt to unify Germany was premature — for the one side, because it wished first to complete the integration of West Germany into NATO and to raise twelve German divisions; for the other, because it could not at this time hope to unify Germany on its own terms, and failing that, preferred a division. Thus neither side had more than an abstract interest in immediate German unification, although only the Soviets were blunt enough to say so. The conference was also notable for Eisenhower's emergence as a man of peace, transcending the bellicose image of his administration that had prevailed throughout the world for two and a half years; conversely, it was notable for making clear the harsh and negative Soviet position on Germany, which served to clear the air in Europe and to leave public opinion, especially in West Germany, rather satisfied with the status quo.

But far and away the most important result was the mutual understanding and the real, if tacit, agreement that resort to nuclear war by either side would be suicidal. Again, it was Macmillan who summed it up better than anyone else: "I felt some encouragement, largely because of the strong impression left in my mind that all the great nations who were in the nuclear game now accepted that modern war, that is nuclear war, was quite impossible and could only lead to mutual destruction. . . . [The Russians] do not want war. So long as nuclear weapons exist, they know it to be impossible." [39] And Khrushchev, returning from the conference via Pankow, publicly assured the East Germans that "neither side wants war," which may have been the first time Soviet leaders had ever suggested to their own constituents that the capitalist world was not compulsively bent upon aggression.[40] The Khrushchev statement seemed equally to reflect a greater Soviet reliance on reason at the expense of blind doctrine, and a confidence that Party control inside the Russian security belt was not entirely dependent on the promotion of external threats and tensions. Four months later, the Russian leader seemed even more convinced that nuclear stalemate was the central strategic fact. Completing a flamboyant visit to India, he said the Geneva meeting had "led to recognition by the Great Powers of the senselessness of war, which in view of the development of atomic and hydrogen weapons, can only bring misfortune to mankind. This fundamental admission — to rule out war as a method of settling international disputes — met with the wholehearted approval of the peoples and led to considerable relaxation of tension." [41]

Dulles Sums Up

In a long cable to all mission chiefs on August 15, 1955, the Secretary of State sought to make a comprehensive assessment of where United States foreign policy stood a month after the summit. He remained convinced that the Soviets had sought the meeting in order to gain a strategic respite: with an industrial base less than a third the size of America's and a faltering agriculture, they were overextended, and no match for the United States in an arms race that featured high cost and advanced technology. Realizing this, they had moved to meet the Western demands for "deeds" — e.g., concessions on the Austrian treaty. Thereafter, the summit was convened. Dulles candidly acknowledged that this meeting had given rise to new complications, which he did not minimize:

"Geneva has certainly created problems for the free nations. For eight years they have been held together largely by a cement compounded of fear and a sense of moral superiority. Now the fear is diminished and the moral demarcation is somewhat blurred. There is some bewilderment . . . as to how to adjust to the new situation." [42] But no consequence of Geneva "justifies the free world relaxing its vigilance or substantially altering its programs for collective security. . . . We must assume that the Soviet leaders consider their recent change of policy to be an application of the classic Communist maneuver known as 'zig-zag' — i.e., resort to the tactics of retreat . . . 'to buy off a powerful enemy and gain a respite' (Stalin). We must not be caught by any such maneuver." [43] It was possible, he thought, that what the Soviets had designed as a maneuver might "assume the force of an irreversible trend"; such a development was worth encouraging, provided "our side" avoids setting up its own "irreversible trend toward accommodation." [44] He ended on a strong moral note, which also reiterated his insistence on the principle of liberation and rollback: "The United States does not acquiesce in the present power position of the Soviet Union in Europe. . . . There are gross international injustices which need to be corrected. Human freedoms need to be restored in the vast areas where they are now denied. Soviet military threats and subversive efforts still create an intolerable sense of insecurity." [45]

19

A Gathering Immobility

The fall of 1955 and the ensuing winter seemed to work a deepening confusion in the administration's perception of the outside world. Certain far-reaching changes in the world situation had occurred or were in the making; on the strength of these, an ebullient new Soviet leadership was denigrating Stalin and rewriting Lenin, asserting that war was not "a fatalistic inevitability," and contending that Communism could triumph over capitalism without war. The cold war seemed to have reached a new stage in which the primary struggle was shifting from the military to the nonmilitary arenas. But while certain men — notably Nelson Rockefeller, Harold Stassen, and Richard Nixon — fought for a dramatic response to what they perceived as a wholly new challenge, the senior men in the administration tended to deprecate this analysis and to persist in a stubborn defense of existing policies, even as public criticism mounted and Moscow's drive for "competitive coexistence" gathered momentum in the Third World. The President's heart attack on September 24, 1955, was a further factor working against change and for the status quo, although there is no evidence that his presence in full health during that period would have made much difference.

The President's Heart Attack

Indeed, Eisenhower's attitude and actions in recent months had suggested to many observers that he was gradually receding from the presidency, ill at ease in the White House, bored with routine. While wise and vigilant in foreign affairs, it was evident after nearly three years that he possessed no considered view of American life, of what the country should be or might become. On a wide range of domestic issues he seemed indeed to possess a formidable indifference, which led him inevitably to find many day-to-day problems of government both tedious and fatiguing, and which led in turn to an impression that the U.S. government was almost leaderless, except in moments of crisis involving life-and-death issues. One observer found his lack of knowledge about current issues at times "so formidable that at times one wonders if it is not actually a revulsion." [1] Notwithstanding his immense personal triumph at Geneva, he had left Washington in mid-August for an extended vacation in Colorado amid mounting speculation that he would not run for reelection in 1956. As he departed the capital, he told a press conference that his decision would be easy if only the future were revealed to him, but "I do not have that gift of prophecy." For six weeks he lounged at Byers Peak Ranch, fishing, golfing, playing bridge at stag gatherings with nongovernmental colleagues whose professional concerns were far removed from his own, putting in hardly more than an hour a day of presidential office work. He received during this period a telegram from the Republican National Committee which read, "Looking forward to supporting you again in 1956. We like Ike better than ever"; to which Eisenhower replied that he was certain the party was not lacking in "high-quality personnel and leadership." He added, "Humans are frail — and they are mortal. [Never] pin your flag so tightly to one mast that if a ship sinks you cannot rip it off and nail it to another. It is sometimes good to remember that." [2] On September 23, which was to be the last day of his vacation, he played twenty-seven holes of golf and developed heartburn from a luncheon of hamburger and onions. At two-thirty the next morning, he suffered a moderate coronary thrombosis at his mother-in-law's house in Denver.

In the ensuing period of shock and uncertainty that enveloped official Washington, the country, and indeed much of the world, Dulles played a wise and steadying role, counseling the young Vice-president against precipitate initiatives and throwing his influence against a proposal to develop a legal-legislative basis for delegating presidential authority. Still vivid in his mind was the case of Mrs. Woodrow Wilson, who had shielded the stricken President and who later caused the dismissal of Dulles's uncle Robert Lansing when he attempted, as Secretary of State, to transform the cabinet into a decision-making committee. There was also in Dulles's mind, and those of other close Eisenhower adherents, a determination to retain control in trusted hands and to avoid delivering political power to an ambitious Richard Nixon, who was also the favorite of the Republican old guard. At Dulles's urging and under his guidance, James Hagerty, the White House press secretary, and Sherman

The Helicopter Era

From *Herblock's Special For Today*
SIMON & SCHUSTER, 1958

Adams were quickly dispatched to Denver, and an effort soon organized to give the appearance that the President and his administration were functioning normally. Eisenhower's encouraging recovery and the coming and going of cabinet officers lent a verisimilitude to the operation, and both the press and the public seemed to recognize the constitutional delicacy and chose not to probe a number of evident anomalies — e.g., although not permitted to read newspapers for a month, and otherwise shielded by his doctors from contact with problems that might prove emotionally disturbing, the President was nevertheless reported to be working actively on his State of the Union Message.

Fortunately his recovery was steady and visible to the public, which greatly eased the tension and uncertainty in Washington. And the cabinet members displayed a selflessness and unity that reflected, among other things, Eisenhower's singular gift for commanding the loyalty and affection of his associates. Vice-president Nixon presided over regular meetings of the cabinet, but with the now explicit understanding that the presidency was operative in Denver, and that measures that could not be decided routinely would be sent to the temporary White House through Sherman Adams. The quiet power play to neutralize Nixon was not lost upon the sensitive Washington press corps, Rovere reporting in the *New Yorker* on October 8 that Sherman Adams "as the President's appointed caretaker" was "doing everything he can to cut Mr. Nixon down to size." [3] In terms of policy, the U.S. government marked time for at least two months, but the vital constitutional appearances were preserved, and public opinion remained calm. Reflecting on this surrealistic situation, Rovere concluded that "the power to communicate is in fact the most important of the presidential powers," and that the press secretary, James Hagerty, who spoke in the President's name and who conveyed to the world each day the only authoritative view of the presidency in operation, was accordingly for a crucial period the largest figure in the administration. [4]

In late October, Eisenhower addressed a message to the cabinet: "The doctors are relenting slightly their rigid rules as to my conduct here in the hospital and have allowed me to try to thank, however inadequately, each one of you for the competent and completely selfless manner in which you have carried on the governmental business during these last few weeks. Sometimes I think I take too much for granted the loyalty and devotion of each of you." [5] By November 11, Eisenhower was back in Washington, able to walk down the ramp of the airplane without assistance. On November 14 he went to his Gettysburg farm for further convalescence. On January 13, 1956, he polled his closest colleagues on the question of running again, and they unanimously urged him to do so. (Dulles told him he should go on using his "God-given ability" for reconciling differences among men and nations.) On February 25, having evidently decided he was not ready for retirement, he told a press conference that his decision would be "positive; that is, affirmative," and four days later he spelled this out for a national television audience: while he had "not the slightest doubt that I can now perform" the presidential duties, his acceptance was necessarily conditioned upon a public understanding that his doctors insisted on "a regime of ordered work activity, interspersed with regular amounts of exercise, recreation and rest." [6] This pledge of further service was heartwarming to Republicans whose political salvation continued to depend decisively on Eisenhower's popularity (George Bender, a congressman from Ohio, declared, "I have faith in God and Dwight Eisenhower"). It seemed equally welcome to the great mass of Americans, who, whatever flaws they detected in the man, were deeply reassured by his saneness and practicality in foreign affairs, by his readiness to restrain Dulles and override the Joint Chiefs of Staff on the transcendent questions of war or peace. The conditions he attached to his future service, however, betokened no discernible change in his life style or habits of governing, and left the rather clear impression that the country should not look to an Eisenhower second term for exceptional intellectual energy, vision, or innovation.

Defending the Status Quo

With Eisenhower still in the hospital, Dulles faced the prospect of attending the post-summit meeting of Foreign Ministers in Geneva in solitary charge of American foreign policy. Although his outward appearance showed no change, Dulles was disquieted by the prospect of taking decisions visibly alone, without the assurance of Eisenhower's political support at his side, and without the benefit of Eisenhower's intuitive and sensitive judgment. Maxwell Rabb, the cabinet secretary, thought Dulles seemed "very upset, and not just because of his emotional feelings," and Sherman Adams found to his own surprise that "Foster seems lost without the Boss." [7] Perhaps sensing the problem, Eisenhower wrote a polite but firm note to Nixon a week before the new Geneva conference, reminding him (and through him the cabinet) that Dulles was going to Europe with "my complete confidence" and that there must be no attempt to circumscribe his position: "He must be the one who both at the conference table and before the world speaks for me with authority for our country." [8]

The Foreign Ministers meeting, held from October 27 to November

16, revealed all of the basic disagreements that had surfaced at the summit, but revealed them in an atmosphere of greater asperity. The West was still stuck with its unsalable demand for free all-German elections. The West also continued to insist that a German settlement was the priority question, to be settled ahead of disarmament and East-West security arrangements. For their part, the Soviets wanted not only an inviolable status for the East German regime, but also disarmament — by which they meant an end to NATO and a withdrawal of both British and American forces from the Continent.

One consequence of total deadlock was that Dulles was not burdened by the need to take any far-reaching decisions during the critical period of Eisenhower's convalescence; another was the tendency in Europe (and to a lesser extent in the United States) to blame Dulles for the "sterile, rigid" linkage between security arangements and German unification, for most Europeans were deeply interested in the former, while the latter left them quite cold. This criticism was mitigated somewhat by the harsh unreasonableness of the Soviet demands, for NATO was now universally recognized as the cornerstone of West European security. A third probable consequence of the Foreign Ministers meeting was that the specific focus of the issues under debate tended to obscure for Dulles the wider manifestations of change in the world power balance and of the new flexibility in Soviet diplomacy toward the Third World.

While Democratic critics, like Adlai Stevenson, charged that the nation was drifting into new peril because "our Government is unprepared for this new Communist offensive, which has been in the making since Korea and the death of Stalin," [9] Dulles continued to insist that the change in Soviet tactics proved the correctness of past Western policies and demonstrated the need for holding steady on the course of collective security backed by deterrent retaliatory power. Moreover, while others stressed the need to meet the new Soviet tactics with larger infusions of economic and technical assistance, Dulles continued to focus on the political-military aspects of global confrontation. He thus tended to see the Soviet economic aid drive not as a serious new challenge to be countered in kind, but rather as evidence that Soviet expansion by military means had been blocked; in short, as an indirect source of satisfaction. This was a position that placed him in comfortable alignment with most of the military professionals, and with the economic conservatives whose steadfast opposition to new foreign aid programs reflected a concern that these would unbalance the budget.

Nothing perhaps better revealed Dulles's inner judgment as to the crucial elements of his policy than the interview he gave to *Life* magazine in January 1956. This was not an extemporaneous exercise, but a planned

"Don't Be Afraid --- I Can Always Pull You Back"

From *Herblock's Special For Today*
SIMON & SCHUSTER, 1958

response to mounting expressions of doubt that the major premises of American foreign policy were any longer valid, and to charges that the administration was failing to take adequate account of the new situation. In the interview, Dulles attempted a categorical defense of a tough and vociferous confrontation policy — although he never used the particular word "brinkmanship" which the interview created. Insisting that a hard unyielding posture remained the only way to avert war while avoiding surrender to Communism, he claimed that his resolute action on three occasions had saved the free world from the agonies of further aggression and bloodshed: (1) to break the 1953 Korean stalemate, he had informed Nehru that the United States "would lift self-imposed restrictions on its actions and hold back no effort or weapon to win"; (2) in April 1954, aircraft carriers had been sent to the South China Sea in "a modern version of the classical show of force designed both to deter any Red Chinese attack against Indochina, and to provide weapons for instant retaliation . . ."; and (3) American resolution had faced down the Red Chinese at Quemoy, and he had "never doubted" that "Eisenhower would have regarded an attack on Quemoy and the Matsus as an attack on Formosa." [10]

The administration's response to these crises, he implied, demonstrated a considered pattern of theory and action: "You have to take chances for peace, just as you must take chances in war. Some say we were brought to the verge of war. Of course we were brought to the verge of war. The ability to get to the verge without getting into war is the necessary art. If you cannot master it, you inevitably get into war. If you try to run away from it, if you are scared to go to the brink, you are lost. . . . We walked to the brink and we looked it in the face. We took strong action." [11]

A dramatic storm of protest and outrage broke over Dulles's head following publication of this piece, reflecting a wide range of official and public dismay, at home and abroad. Many were appalled by a "public relations" ineptitude that cast grave doubt upon the nation's professions of peaceful intent, and tarnished the attractive image that Eisenhower had conveyed at the summit just seven months before. Others found it a dishonest performance based on specious claims — there was no solid evidence that a threat to use tactical nuclear weapons had broken the Korean deadlock, and Nehru denied any role in the proceeding; and the dispatch of aircraft carriers, while it may have made doubly unlikely an improbable Chinese invasion of Indochina, had no visible deterrent effect on the Vietminh, the real French nemesis. Only the outcome at Quemoy gave some color of plausibility to the claim of success for a policy of confrontation in the Dulles manner. Moreover, to his further detriment, he had embroidered the interview with a series of lesser claims that were demonstrably untrue. Thus, he tried to take credit for the failure of his "agonizing reappraisal" ploy by saying that France signed the WEU agreements primarily because it had "Dulles' warning in mind." [12] As to Indochina, he asserted, "It was also clear to the Communists that the French and the British, if they were pushed too far, would accept Dulles' suggestion for united action." [13] He even inflated his own role in the 1953 talks with the President-elect aboard the *Helena:* "Dulles led most of [the] discussions" because he had "probably devoted more thought to the subject of war and peace than any other man alive." [14]

The volume and intensity of the criticism that met the article were extraordinary by any standard. Several members of Congress demanded that the Secretary of State resign. The British Foreign Office flatly disavowed statements referring to them, and London newspapers called Dulles "an edgy gambler" whose "terrible doctrine will shock the United States." It was necessary for Eisenhower to come to his rescue, acknowledging some "unfortunate expressions" in the article, but insisting that Dulles was "the best Secretary of State I have ever known." [15] Even the publisher Henry Luce (who was, if anything, more of an uncompromising Roundhead than Dulles) felt obliged to attempt mitigation of the hurricane that whirled around the head of his favorite *Life* contributor and fellow Presbyterian. Said Luce, in a special statement in the January 30 issue: some aspects of the piece may have been unfortunately inflammatory, but "taken in the context of the whole article, there is nothing in Secretary Dulles' words which is contrary to common sense." [16]

The conscious or unconscious liberties taken by *Life* editors (and the inevitable loss of nuance involved) in the process of transforming a taped conversation into hard prose no doubt exacerbated the basic trouble. But even when full allowances were made, the interview could not escape assessment as a remarkably feckless, tactless, unnecessary piece of work by a Secretary of State. James Reston thought Dulles had "added something new to the art of diplomatic blundering . . . the planned mistake." The Secretary of State, he said, "doesn't stumble into booby traps: he digs them to size, studies them carefully, and then jumps . . ." [17] The interview seemed to reflect the man's strange quintessential inwardness, in its revelation of both his insensitivity to public mood and his tendency to let vanity outrun proportion and truth. New, however, was a greater gap between his view of what was central and essential and the view of his critics than had appeared before. Certain changes in the world situation seemed to them of marked or even decisive consequence. Apparently Dulles was not impressed.

Rationalizing Contradictions

In his State of the Union Message of January 5, 1956, President Eisenhower noted that at the Geneva summit, "all were in agreement that a nuclear war would be an intolerable disaster which must not be permitted to occur." [18] But what this meant, he warned, was that "Communist tactics against the free nations have shifted in emphasis from reliance on violence to reliance on division." [19] Did such a Communist shift have implications for United States military policies or for American programs of economic and technical assistance? Apparently not very many.

On the military side, despite the President's acceptance of nuclear stalemate, there was no move to alter, nor even to reexamine, a policy whose underlying doctrine and deployments were increasingly dependent on nuclear weapons. The proposed military budget * continued to place major emphasis on "air-atomic power," and proposed to allocate the lion's share of new money to the air force,† including several billions for procurement of the new B-52 bomber. Outlays for conventional weapons and for stockpiling would be decreased. On January 28, the Air Force Chief of Staff, General Nathan Twining, while granting the possibility of "peripheral action" of a non-nuclear character for "a few more years," asserted that developments were "rapidly approaching the day when any conflict would be waged with atomic weapons." [20] The Air Force Secretary, Donald Quarles, insisted that even the condition of "mutual deterrence" would not inhibit the United States from the use of nuclear weapons. No aggressor, he said, "should ever again expect us to employ our air power and weapons as we did in Korea" — i.e., with mere "iron bombs" and a conscious restraint. In future, the United States would use "modern quality weapons as are needed for the job in hand." [21]

This determined normalization of nuclear weapons seemed a remarkable exercise in unreason, in the face of the comparable power developing in Russia; for the question hung in the air: was the United States really prepared to respond "instantly" and "at places of our choosing," not only to attack upon the United States and NATO Europe, but also to inspired crises throughout the vast arc of Asia and Africa where poor peoples and weak governments were unavoidably immersed in the revolutionary gestation of the postcolonial period? In geographical terms, the U.S. commitment seemed almost total. But Soviet military doctrine

* For fiscal year 1957 (beginning July 1, 1956).
† $16.5 billion of a total military request of $35.5 billion.

sharply rejected the notion that anyone could use "tactical" nuclear weapons in a critical area without triggering the holocaust. "It is already impossible to fight and avoid retaliatory blows," warned Marshal Zhukov. "If you want to deliver atomic blows to your adversary, be prepared to receive the same and perhaps even stronger blows from him." [22] The unreason in Washington was real, but so was the dilemma confronting the administration planners. The official rationale began with the deeply felt necessity for a balanced budget and ended with the assumption that America's stronger scientific and economic base, given the inexorable march of technology, could maintain a meaningful margin of deterrent superiority for an indefinite period. The administration (from Eisenhower, Humphrey and Dulles on down) had in short decided to continue a military posture tailored to their own political and economic preferences, rather than to a detailed assessment of the type and location of aggressions or encroachments most likely to occur in the outside world. The threat of nuclear retaliation was a sensible stance for ensuring against attack on areas unmistakably "vital" to the United States — i.e., North America and the NATO area — but the attempt to extend nuclear deterrence as a means of guarding the entire East-West perimeter was bound to frighten allies and raise awkward questions of credibility.

The discrepancy between domestic preference and international reality was underlined on July 7, 1956, when a document labeled the "Radford Memorandum" was leaked to the *New York Times* (possibly by a disgruntled army staff). Although it had not received presidential approval, the document caused severe disquiet in Europe, for it seemed to many an authentic Pentagon plan to achieve a progressive application of "New Look" principles over the coming three years: it proposed a worldwide American force reduction of 800,000 men, including the scaling-down of troops in Europe to token level; and it strongly reaffirmed the commitment to "instant" retaliation. Adenauer, who faced serious internal opposition to the raising of twelve German divisions (and who needed constant psychological reassurance), now complained to Dulles that the American military presence in Europe was a factor no longer to be counted on, a situation he found shocking only a year after ratification of the WEU accords had produced a strong American promise to maintain "a fair share" of the NATO forces indefinitely. Dulles, who shared the felt need for a balanced budget, and generally accepted Radford's facile assurances that even a reduced force structure would provide a capacity for limited and non-nuclear response, in this case threw his influence against the Pentagon. The President was persuaded, and there were no American troop reductions in Europe.

On the matter of foreign aid, the economic conservatives in the administration — principally Humphrey at Treasury, Herbert Hoover, Jr., at

State, Rowland Hughes at Budget, and John Hollister who ran foreign aid * — doubted both the Soviet ability to fulfill their economic promises to underdeveloped countries and the capacity of such countries to absorb aid at more than very modest rates. On the other side, Rockefeller and Stassen urged increases in the size and flexibility of foreign aid, bold departures in trade, and a general bringing to bear of the full range of American ingenuity and imagination on an area of activity where the United States no longer enjoyed the advantage of a monopoly position. In the internal debates of the fall and winter, however, it was the economic conservatives who prevailed. Joseph Dodge, former Director of the Budget and now an economic adviser, warned in the cabinet that the United States should not get into a contest of bidding against Soviet shills. "What is a shill?" asked the President. Dodge explained that a shill is a decoy employed by an auctioneer to make offers to get the bidding up.[23]

Meanwhile, the Soviets were reducing their armed forces by an estimated 650,000 men (as well as relinquishing the naval base at Port Arthur to China and the naval base at Porkkala to Finland), and Bulganin and Khrushchev were journeying through India, Burma, and Afghanistan, carrying the new message. In a speech before the Indian parliament, Bulganin said, "We are ready to share with you our economic and scientific and technical experience." [24] And in a colorful elaboration of this theme at Bhakra on November 22, 1955, Khrushchev attacked the Western allegation that the Russian offers were deceptive and without content. He said:

To those who write this, we say: Perhaps you would like to compete with us in establishing friendship with the Indians? Let us compete. [applause] Why have we come here? We come with an open heart [applause], and with honest intentions. [applause] We say to you: You want to build factories. We are glad of it. Perhaps you have not sufficient experience? Then apply to us and we shall help you. [applause] You want to build electric power stations? If you have not the necessary know-how, if you need technical assistance, apply to us and we shall help. [applause] You want to send your students, your engineers to our country for training? Please do so. [applause] [25]

Was this mere bombast? No doubt there were discrepancies between promise and performance, but three months later the Indians announced an agreement whereunder the Soviets would build a $91 million steel plant with an annual capacity of one million tons. By March, the Soviets had agreed to provide a large number of tractors immediately, and to follow up with $10 million in farm equipment and the loan of several

* A quartet dubbed "the 4-H Club" by the Washington press.

expert technicians in oil exploration. Pending construction of the steel mill, they also agreed to sell India one millions tons of rolled steel, taking raw materials and manufactured goods in return.

"We need not get panicky," said Dulles in late 1955, "because Soviet Communism displays itself in this new garb," for Asian leaders will not be "easily duped by false promises." [26] Yet a principal element of the new situation was the Third World's broad receptivity to the new Soviet approach. At the Bandung conference, twenty-nine former colonial nations with an aggregate population of 650 million (roughly one-quarter of the world's people) signed a declaration that "colonialism in all its manifestations is an evil which should speedily be brought to an end." [27] Although Russia and Communist China also represented an incipient threat of colonialism (which the underdeveloped world would gradually recognize and, on the whole, effectively resist), "colonialism" in 1955 summed up for these countries their protracted and complicated "development-exploitation" relationship with the West. To Russian and Chinese offers they were more receptive.

The Fear of Nonalignment

The aims of the Third World movement were national independence, racial equality, and nonalignment in the East-West power struggle. Dulles could endorse the first two without reservation; the third made him uneasy. Regarding global resistance to Communism as the rock on which the safety and future of free men rested, he looked with grave concern on the development of large groups of "uncommitted" countries that showed little sympathy for Western efforts to hold back the barbarian tide, indeed that seemed intent upon normalizing relations with the major Communist powers. His distress on this point was probably more strategic than ideological, for the principal instruments of an American policy of pressure — namely, military bases and alliance relationships — were ultimately dependent on at least the tacit allegiance of the governments and peoples who owned the real estate in places of strategic interest to the West. Calculations of world stability and Western influence would be undermined by "uncommitted" governments in such places.

But Dulles deplored even benign forms of normal international intercourse — like Soviet political visits, economic aid, and cultural exchanges — believing they could lead rapidly to the seduction of innocent young countries and to the insidious growth of Soviet influence and control. On this latter point, he reflected a curious and telling dichotomy in American belief. On the one hand, Communism was evil incarnate, the antithesis of everything free and decent in human affairs; on the other hand, Communism had an irresistible appeal for all downtrodden and exploited races, who would not see the danger until they were caught in the totalitarian vise. The predictions and promises of Karl Marx and the Russian example of a backward state brought to industrial might through stern collectivist disciplines supported this appeal. Distance and unfamiliarity lent a certain enchantment to the Soviet image in Asia and Africa. What American policy makers of this period failed to see was that familiarity would expose Russian feet of clay, and would strengthen the Third World's demand for independence and its resistance to political encroachment from any quarter. In the mid-1950s, however, Dulles was not alone in believing that neutrality could only be a transitional state of existence on the way to Communist control.

The emergence of a pronounced Third World drive for independence and nonalignment thus met with uneasiness and distaste in Washington; there was inherent sympathy for the aspirations of colonial peoples, but there was disquiet at the prospect of widespread neutralism. As the leader of global resistance to the Kremlin, as the central power in regional military pacts, as the fount of economic and military aid to anti-Communists, as the primary source of moral and diplomatic pressure aimed at restraining and altering Soviet and Chinese Communist behavior, the administration looked on neutralism as a serious threat to a world order of free nations.

Yet it was evidently not a unanimous view. Once again, the President showed himself a free-floating exponent of candid personal opinion, above and apart from the policy process that was carried on in his name and presumably under his guidance. Reflecting his own groping search for an assessment that squared with the new facts, he undertook at a press conference (June 6, 1956) to defend neutralism, particularly as it applied to military alliances. If a nation stood aloof from such alliances, he said, this did not necessarily mean neutrality "as between right and wrong"; on the contrary, it might reflect understandable practicality and prudence, for if a nation openly announced its "military association" with a Great Power, "things could happen to it." [28] This earnest, but clumsy, thinking-out-loud, because it appeared to repudiate the principle of collective security, caused some agitation among America's allies. Two days later, however, Eisenhower was rushed to the hospital with an attack of ileitis, and on June 9, Dulles, once more in solitary charge of foreign policy, delivered a speech at Iowa State College which strove to reestablish the conventional wisdom. Emphasizing America's fundamental attachment to the principle of collective security, and excluding all possibility of a sound alternative, he argued that America's far-flung security arrangements, embracing forty-two countries, "abolish, as between the parties, the principle of neutrality, which pretends that a nation can best gain safety for itself by being indifferent to the fate of others. This has increasingly become an obsolete conception, and, except under very exceptional circumstances, it is an immoral and shortsighted conception." [29] With that *coup de main*, Dulles set the record straight. Washington would not enter into serious competition for the allegiance of neutral nations; indeed, it would react sharply to any indication that a neutral country was seeking to play off the United States against the Soviet Union or China, in any particular or general bargaining for advantage.

By mid-1956, American foreign policy, despite its strident rhetoric, gave evidence of having been placed on the defensive. Its perception of reality seemed blurred; through a failure to recognize, accept, and act upon far-reaching changes in the outer world, it was beginning to yield initiative and advantage to the other side.

20

The Middle East—
Prelude to Crisis

THE SUEZ CRISIS of 1956, which destroyed Eden, also did irreparable damage to Dulles's reputation both at home and abroad. The Middle East situation in the 1954–1956 period was, as it has historically been, a seething snake-basket of local conflicts, Great Power rivalries, and ideological struggles, all somehow connected by political hatreds of a pervasiveness and intensity unmatched anywhere else in the world. These basic conditions, reinforced by the U.S. sponsorship of Israel, precluded any serious or credible American effort to promote the unity and strength of the area as a whole. American policy still tended, moreover, to give tacit deference to the British lead, on the assumption that British interests and responsibilities were both primary, although this was qualified by Dulles's deep concern about the dangers of Soviet penetration and by his instinctive reluctance to support even residual forms of colonialism. As the tides of political conflict shifted with swift and treacherous unpredictability over these years, the central fact emerged that British and American interests and priorities were not at all the same. London wanted to maintain an effective political-military presence through which it could exercise a direct leverage in Middle East affairs; Washington was primarily concerned to see that the inevitable transition from colonialism to independence did not usher in Communist influence or control.

The Developing Miasma

The British-Egyptian agreement on the Suez base, concluded on July 27, 1954, seemed a responsible and salutary move toward orderly dis-

mantlement of the old colonial structure and the arrival at new arrangements consistent with the aspirations of Egypt's newly won independence.
Seen in isolation, it was. Yet it was also a catalyst, generating new
momentums and setting in motion new concerns. It provided for phased
British evacuation over twenty months and a seven-year right of reentry,
and it defined the defense area (within which an aggression from outside
would automatically permit British reactivation of the base) to include
Turkey, but to exclude Iran.[1] And it was embroidered with subtle
touches, being called an "agreement" rather than a "treaty" in deference
to Egyptian sensitivity to past humiliations, and providing that Britain
alone declared the 1936 treaty to be terminated, so that Nasser need not
risk admitting that the prior Egyptian abrogation had been in any way
invalid.[2]

Diehards in both countries promptly attacked the agreement, a group
of twenty-six Tories (who came to be known as the Suez Rebels) arguing
that British vital interests were being sacrificed to an unmanly policy of
"scuttle." Nasser's enemies in Cairo, on the other hand, saw in the document a reinforcement of covert British domination of Egypt. After a
noisy debate in Parliament, only the Suez Rebels voted against the agreement, giving Foreign Secretary Eden's moderate and transitional course
a solid 257 to 26 victory. But Nasser, who lacked the benefits of parliamentary procedure, had to consolidate popular support for his position by
braving an assassination attempt while he was speaking to a large crowd
in Alexandria's Liberation Square on October 6.[3]

Israel was disturbed at the prospective departure of British troops, for
the British military presence was regarded in Tel Aviv as a buffer in the
Arab-Israeli conflict and as a factor which lent credence to the Tripartite
Declaration of 1950 (by which Britain, France and the United States were
pledged to maintain a stable relationship between the disputants, and to
intervene militarily for this purpose if necessary). Tel Aviv was also
irritated by Dulles's continuing gestures toward a more evenhanded
Middle East policy, including a military aid agreement with Iraq, and
by American statements warning Israel to exercise restraint on immigration. Assistant Secretary of State Henry Byroade, while urging the Arabs
to accept the State of Israel as "an accomplished fact," had publicly
advised Tel Aviv to "drop the attitude of the conqueror" and "break
with the Zionist dogma of [unlimited] Jewish immigration." For so long,
said Byroade, as the potential magnitude of Israel was limited only by
"the total number of those of the Jewish faith in the entire world," the
Arabs would inevitably fear "a future attempt at territorial expansion
— and hence warfare of serious proportions."[4] Israel resented and resisted
such strictures, for the core of its leadership regarded national growth

as no more immoral than national birth. Thus, in Israel, the principal result of the British withdrawal agreement and American policy developments was to drive Israel toward military collaboration with the French.

The French, now facing armed rebellion in Algeria, were incensed that Nasser had offered a safe haven in Cairo for rebel leadership, as well as a few small arms shipments.[5] Given the political dynamics of Middle Eastern nationalism, it would have been difficult for him to have done less, but the French quickly developed the illusory obsession that Nasser was the root cause of their Algerian troubles, and that the troubles would cease if aid from Egypt were cut off. Official French opinion thus steadily persuaded itself of Nasser's total iniquity and of the need to see him destroyed. On the eve of the ill-fated Anglo-French military action against the Suez Canal in November 1956, Jacques Soustelle, a former governor-general of Algeria, declared that "in acting against Nasser, France is hitting the head of the octopus whose tentacles have for so many months been strangling French North Africa." [6]

French determination to destroy Nasser in order to save Algeria harmonized with Israel's determination to improve its security position by expanding its frontiers, especially to reopen the Strait of Tiran (at the mouth of the Gulf of Aqaba in southeastern Sinai) to Israeli shipping. The result was a secret collaboration between the two defense ministries without the knowledge of other elements of either government for many months. The prime mover in this enterprise was David Ben-Gurion, who had led Israel through the crucible years, who had built the Israeli army from the nuclei of the Haganah and Palmach, and whose temporary retirement into the Negev desert at the end of 1953 did not affect his de facto control of the Israeli defense ministry. The first fruit of this conspiracy, which began in July 1954 (the same month the British-Egyptian base agreement was signed) was a substantial package of French arms for Israel, an arrangement which involved a clear French violation of the Tripartite Declaration.[7]

The Baghdad Pact

When Iraq contracted for American arms in mid-1954, accepting all of the conditions required by United States foreign aid legislation, including the presence of an American military advisory and training group, Washington offered similar terms to Nasser. But he rejected the offer, on grounds that the conditions constituted unacceptable curtailments on Egyptian sovereignty; he also thought acceptance would bring trouble from his domestic opposition. At meetings in September with Nuri as Said, the tough, pro-British leader of Iraq, Nasser expressed the hope that the Arab states would sustain a "collective aloofness" from association with Western pacts. Nuri indicated his own deep commitment to a Western-oriented Iraqi policy, but nevertheless gave Nasser assurances that Iraq would not enter into a new, formal defense agreement with any Western power.[8] Turkey, with American encouragement, was then endeavoring to establish the nucleus of a "northern tier" alliance, and a Turkish-Pakistani pact was signed in late 1954, but there seemed to be no plan to extend this into the "southern tier" of Arab states.

Dulles, however, seemed determined not to leave any possible opportunity unexplored. No doubt he remained aware that the Arab states did not perceive a serious Communist threat and that Nasser was opposed to any Arab participation in a Western pact. But in mid-September 1954, he had just brought SEATO into being and was struggling with the confrontation at Quemoy. Regarding the Middle East as extremely vulnerable to Communism, he sent a new ambassador, Waldemar Gallman, to Iraq, instructing him "to see what could be done" to develop a regional defense arrangement that would include Iraq and possibly other Arab states.[9] But this was a tentative gesture compared to Eden's concurrent moves.

The British government was, in the fall of 1954, somewhat uncomfortable with the contingent nature of its access to the Suez base and was definitely looking for a secure alternative for the maintenance of a strong political-military presence in the Middle East. The natural alternative was Iraq, where British military bases were permitted under an existing twenty-five-year treaty that ran through October 1957. Strong national sentiment boiled just beneath the surface, but the monarchy still stood and control remained in the hands of Nuri as Said, who had shared combat with Lawrence of Arabia in the battles to overthrow the Turkish Empire during World War I, and whose position was dependent on British power and support. Eden thus conceived of the Baghdad Pact primarily as a means of reinforcing British influence in the area. By creating a strong and attractive focus in Iraq, he believed he could gradually isolate Nasser in the Arab world; and by including "northern tier" countries, who were being encouraged by Dulles to form an anti-Communist barrier, he expected to gain American adherence. The keys to the required north-south linkage were Nuri and the Turks.

By the end of 1954, the American embassies in Ankara and Baghdad were aware that the Turkish government desired to provide greater depth to its military position (against Russia) by an arrangement with Iraq to the south, that the British were urging this, and that Nuri "might" be interested. But it was believed that no definitive agreement was likely within eight or ten months.[10] Dulles was therefore genuinely surprised when the Turkish Prime Minister, Adnan Menderes, announced Iraq's adherence to the Turkish-Pakistani pact on January 12, 1955, immediately following a short visit to Baghdad. The treaty was signed on February 25, and British adherence in April became the vehicle for indefinitely extending British military rights in Iraq. Suddenly faced with the apparent fulfillment of his hopes to build another collective barrier to Communist advance across an area of strategic consequence, Dulles now surprisingly hesitated. Strong representations from the Near East Asian Affairs Bureau of the State Department apparently convinced him that overt American membership would antagonize not only Nasser, but other Arab leaders who shared his anti-British, anti-colonial sentiments. Zionist opinion did not appear to influence his thinking, and Congress showed no strong feeling one way or the other.[11] In response to British urging for full United States participation, Dulles finally agreed to designate Ambassador Gallman as an "observer" to the new pact organization in Baghdad, a compromise that Harold Macmillan thought "reflected the strange uncertainty of Dulles's own character." [12] But the uncertainty, if such it was, seemed grounded more in the circumstances than in Dulles's character: The sudden crystallization of the Baghdad Pact had revealed the discrepancies in British and American objectives; and indeed the Dulles compromise was no better than an awkward effort to meld two purposes which, despite a superficial parallelism, were rather different. Where Dulles aimed at blocking Communist penetration, and assumed this would require broad Arab sympathy and support, Eden aimed at maintaining British presence and power, and accepted the hostility of the Arab nationalists led by Nasser. The unhappy result was tacit American association with a British policy that seriously misjudged the surging tides of Arab nationalism, forgot the truth that Egypt is the inherent political focus of the Arab world, and underestimated the damage to Western interests that could be wrought by a resentful Nasser.

Nasser was, of course, astonished and outraged by the new pact and, after some delay, unleashed a violent propaganda campaign against Nuri over Radio Cairo, but neither this, nor an urgent meeting of other Arab premiers in Cairo, had any immediate effect on the matter. On February 26, 1955, Eden passed through Cairo on his way to a SEATO conference in Bangkok, and he and Nasser met for the first and only time. He greeted the Egyptian president in perfect Arabic and then went on to discuss the Koran and Arab poetry. As Nasser's biographer Mohamed Heikal later wrote: "It was a glamorous performance. He was the star of Western diplomacy who knew all the answers, talking to an unknown colonel with an uncertain future." [13] Eden was, however, receptive neither to Nasser's view that Arabs should avoid membership in Western defense pacts, nor to implied claims that Radio Cairo spoke for the Arab masses, but he did agree that Britain would refrain from attempts to bring other Arab states into the Baghdad Pact, in exchange for Nasser's promise to cease Egyptian attacks upon it.[14] It was an agreement that lasted for ten months, until December 1955, when a new and more militant Foreign Secretary, Harold Macmillan, tried to add Jordan.

The Soviet-Egyptian Arms Deal

Despite a spreading Arab hostility to the Baghdad Pact, there was in the winter of 1954–1955 a discernible "drift toward peace" in the Arab-Israeli conflict. The moderate Moshe Sharett still headed the government in Tel Aviv and, while border incidents between the two countries continued, they seemed stabilized at a low level of violence. Nasser, who was struggling for ascendancy against the right-wing Moslem Brotherhood and a host of intractable economic problems, told the British MP Richard Crossman that he intended to hold Egyptian arms purchases to a minimum consistent with the efficiency and contentment of the officer corps (recognizing that the junta he headed was the product of a military revolution). He showed no disposition for offensive war against Israel, and told Crossman he believed "the Israelis will destroy themselves if they go on spending 60 per cent of their budget on armaments." [15]

On the night of February 28, however, there occurred a savage, unprovoked Israeli raid on Gaza which transformed the hopeful possibilities for Egyptian-Israeli relations and sent a long shock wave down the corridor of time that came to its smashing climax twenty months later in the Anglo-French-Israeli attack on the Suez Canal. It was a signal to Nasser that Ben-Gurion (through his trusted agents in the defense ministry, Colonel Moshe Dayan and Shimon Peres) was reviving the policy of large-scale reprisals, combined with the threat of war and aimed at forcing a settlement; he concluded that it was now imperative that Egypt develop a reliable source of supply for modern arms. But the sources were very limited. The French were openly hostile. The British insisted, as a condition of delivery, that Egypt cease all opposition to the Baghdad Pact. On March 10, he submitted to Byroade (who was now U.S. ambassador in Cairo) a list which Washington regarded as both modest and reflecting a clear preoccupation with defense, as opposed to offensive war. Eisenhower characterized the request as "peanuts," yet no prompt action was taken.[16] One difficulty was that Nasser still resisted the legislative conditions of the foreign aid act, and there was a bureaucratic disinclination to find ways to relax these. There was also a reluctance to court British displeasure, to stir up Zionist sentiment in Congress, or to run against Dulles's known prejudice against rewarding neutralists. In any event, middle levels of the State and Defense Departments treated the Egyptian request as routine.

Nevertheless, by the time Nasser returned from Bandung in early May, Ambassador Byroade was able to inform him that Washington might provide the requested arms — but it would have to be on a strictly cash basis. It is plausible that this offer was a sincere effort to accommodate, by devising a deal that *could* circumvent the legislative conditions that Egypt opposed, even though Eisenhower later wrote in his memoirs that "our State Department, confident that he [Nasser] was short of money, informed him that payment would be expected in cash rather than barter." [17] But it does suggest that Washington's attitude was skeptical and not very forthcoming. Nasser told Byroade he could not accept the offer because the price ($27 million) would strain Egypt's reserves of foreign exchange. Thus apparently foiled in his efforts to obtain Western arms by French hostility, British calculation, and American rigidity, Nasser reluctantly turned to Russia.

According to one account, he drew the Soviet ambassador aside at a garden party at the Sudanese embassy in Cairo on May 18, and said to him, "We want to have arms from you; what will be your answer?" [18] According to another account, however, there was an agreement in principle to a Soviet arms deal as early as February. A rather mysterious Czech delegation appeared in Cairo during the second week of that month, from which there emerged vague talk of an agreement to trade Egyptian cotton for "heavy machinery." [19] A dispatch from Agence France Presse that same week, unnoticed at the time, stated that "Czechoslovakia is ready to exchange heavy arms for Egyptian cotton." [20] A pedestrian publication of the Soviet foreign ministry, appearing several years after the incident had ceased to be sensitive or newsworthy, stated that "Nasser's government concluded in February 1955 a commercial agreement with Czechoslovakia for the delivery of arms." [21]

February 1955 was also the month of a climactic power struggle in the Kremlin that deposed Malenkov and rather surprisingly elevated Bulganin instead of Molotov to the premiership. Molotov and Khrushchev had stood together in their opposition to Malenkov's policy of minimal nuclear deterrence and a major shift from capital goods to consumption, but their attitudes toward Soviet prospects in the Middle East were very different.[22] Khrushchev foresaw large new opportunities for influence in the Arab states. Molotov believed, on the contrary, that the whole of the Near East and South Asia was inhabited by unstable people who would prove to be unreliable allies, and that a Soviet attempt to arm them would only serve to pull the United States more strongly into the area.[23] He was fearful of overextending Soviet resources. The debate was more than academic; for Khrushchev, as secretary of the Communist party, was already making progressive encroachments upon Molotov's domain of foreign affairs.* On this analysis, Khrushchev had already made a secret offer of arms to Nasser by mid-February, and Molotov, just catching up with the information, expressed such vehement opposition that the majority in the Central Committee decided at the eleventh hour not to support him as Malenkov's successor. Bulganin became Khrushchev's figurehead candidate for the premiership, and received important support from Marshal Zhukov, who reflected the desire of the Red Army to rid itself of Bulganin (who was then defense minister) in order to make way for the appointment of a professional military officer to that post.[25]

Even after his defeat for the premiership, however, Molotov's continued resistance to an Egyptian arms deal was apparently strong enough to keep the matter in doubt through March and April, and thus to cause anxiety in Cairo. Sensing correctly that China had become, in certain respects, an arbiter of the internal Russian power struggles, Nasser enlisted Chou En-lai's assistance in Rangoon on April 19, on his way to Bandung. Chou, who was fast becoming the leading patron of the Third World, intervened on Nasser's behalf, and in the process strengthened Khrushchev and his activist supporters against Molotov.[26] Thus reassured, Nasser called in Ambassador Byroade on June 9 to inform him of what he called "tentative agreements" with the Soviets, but again expressed his preference for American arms.[27] Byroade, showing no emotion, said he would inform his government. There was no immediate response from Washington, but the following day the British ambassador (having been informed by Byroade) called on Nasser to issue a tough warning that, if Egypt took Soviet arms, the British would cut off the supply of ammunition and spare parts for British-made weapons in the Egyptian inventory. Nasser replied he could not accept ultimatums. On June 16, Nasser again told Byroade he still hoped to deal with the West and had, in consequence, postponed sending his military mission to Moscow. And once more he formally asked for American arms. On June 22, Byroade was able to tell him that Washington would entertain specific requests. On June 30, Nasser prepared a further pared-down list, which was valued by the State Department at less than $10 million. Remarkably, however, neither Washington nor London, although they read into Nasser's maneuver an attempt to blackmail them for better terms, appeared to regard the

* Treating the visit as an interparty matter, he had flown to Peking in September 1954 for direct talks with Mao, an act which acknowledged Chinese equality in the Communist movement. Molotov, the Foreign Minister, who opposed such a course, was conspicuously absent. Again, in May 1955, he made his famous pilgrimage to Tito, a reconciliation which Molotov also vigorously opposed.[24]

Soviet arms offer as anything more than a bluff. Even when intelligence reports began to document the outlines of a deal (which seemed to involve equipment in a wide value range, from $90 to $200 million), Dulles refused to accept the evidence; nor did any Western leader think the matter worth raising at the Geneva summit in July.

In mid-August, Kermit Roosevelt, the CIA Middle East expert, gave Dulles a short, sharp memorandum warning him that the Soviets were entirely serious about providing arms for Egypt. He carried the paper to Dulles's office and sat with him while he read it. Dulles, still not convinced, made the odd comment to Roosevelt that such a move "would be contrary to the Spirit of Geneva." [28] Three weeks later, however, Roosevelt was called from a vacation in Nantucket to attend another meeting with Dulles. Now gathered in the Secretary's office were his brother Allen Dulles; the Deputy Undersecretary, Robert Murphy; the Assistant Secretary for Near East Affairs, George Allen (who had succeeded Byroade); and the director of policy planning, Robert Bowie. At last the Secretary of State was convinced. What could be done? Roosevelt commented that the State Department had still given Nasser no definitive reply to his formal request of June 30. George Allen said this could not be so. Roosevelt insisted. Dulles then remarked that the Assistant Secretary had better find out. Allen immediately telephoned the Egyptian desk officer, who confirmed that Roosevelt was correct. Somewhat defensively, he then asserted that the lack of a definitive American answer made no real difference in any event, because Nasser's Soviet arms gambit was almost surely a bluff — the Soviets simply had no surplus to sell or give away. Three weeks earlier, such a comment would have been widely accepted; now it was received with skepticism. Secretary Dulles, who was troubled, asked Roosevelt to go to Cairo to persuade Nasser not to take Soviet arms. Both Roosevelt and Allen Dulles argued that it was already too late. Nevertheless, Roosevelt departed at once.[29]

A man who knew Nasser and got on well with him, Roosevelt soon confirmed that the die was cast. Before he could report this to Washington, however, he received a cable from Dulles indicating that the Secretary of State still clung to a fading hope that the worst had not happened. The British Foreign Secretary was with him, Dulles said, and *he* knew nothing of a Soviet arms deal with Nasser. Roosevelt cabled back, advising Dulles to read his newspaper the next morning.[30] Roosevelt was in Nasser's office on the evening of September 26 when the British ambassador, Sir Humphrey Trevelyan, telephoned for an urgent appointment. Nasser asked Roosevelt what he thought Trevelyan wanted. Roosevelt said he obviously wanted a verification of the arms deal. As the two men stood together watching Trevelyan's Rolls-Royce pull out of the British embassy compound across the Nile River, Nasser asked Roosevelt what he should tell him. Roosevelt suggested, half humorously, that "calling it a Czech deal might help to soften the impact; you might say you are dealing with Prague." Moments later Nasser, whose English was less than perfect, left Roosevelt and descended the steps of the Presidency to meet Trevelyan in the lower hall. In the ensuing brief exchange, he murmured something about "brog." [31] Trevelyan was not impressed, and London in a public statement that same night called it a Soviet-Egyptian arrangement.

One further effort was made to turn Nasser around — the dispatch of Assistant Secretary Allen to Cairo with a letter from Dulles that recognized Egypt's sovereign right to spend its own funds as it saw fit, but asked for a fuller explanation of Nasser's intentions.[32] It was an ill-conceived initiative, but official Washington was understandably preoccupied and jittery — President Eisenhower had suffered his heart attack just three days before and was still lying in an oxygen tent in Denver. Assistant Secretary Allen himself objected to the trip, feeling it could only make matters worse by appearing to the Arab world as a kind of American ultimatum, but Undersecretary Hoover insisted. Dulles, who was in New York at the United Nations, hastily signed the letter that Allen had drafted.[33]

As predicted, the visit was a reasonably cordial exercise in futility. Allen told Nasser, with something less than the whole truth, that the United States could understand a policy of neutrality, but that it was not neutral to accept arms from only one source. Nasser reiterated his exasperating difficulties in getting any clear or acceptable reply to numerous requests for American arms. He also dwelt at some length on his military assessment that Israel possessed superiority over all the Arab forces combined, and he characterized the Gaza raid of February 28 as the "turning point" which had required Egypt without more delay to redress the balance.[34] Allen expressed concern that the arms deal, by bringing a large number of Soviet technicians and advisers into Egypt, would prejudice Egyptian sovereignty. Nasser replied that he had not gotten rid of the British and refused an American military mission only to let the Russians overrun his country. That would be a dangerous and unpopular course, he said.[35]

Exactly when Nasser gave up on the possibility of obtaining Western arms is not precisely known, but the evidence suggests that he would have preferred a Western source of supply, if only for reasons of familiarity and convenience, if he had been able to obtain them under conditions that did not infringe his insistence on nonalignment (Mohamed Heikal later quoted from Chou En-lai's representations to the Kremlin that Nasser was a genuine and determined neutralist: "Nasser believes in the policy of non-alignment — as a long term strategy and not as a maneuver").[36] His overtures to Washington after Bandung, however, may have been designed primarily to make a record, showing that Egypt had earnestly sought a moderate scale of defensive arms from the West, but had been repeatedly rebuffed, thereby making an appeal to the Soviet Union unavoidable. A purpose for such a covering maneuver would have been to disarm the possibility of a violent American reaction to a deal that would open the Middle East to Soviet presence and presumably to increased influence. Both Nasser and Khrushchev were aware of United States actions in Guatemala in the spring of 1954 to unseat the Communist-oriented Arbenz regime and destroy several stockpiles of recently imported Soviet arms. Swift political action, military aid to selected rebels, and a range of covert guerilla operations had been employed. Neither Cairo nor Moscow wished to provoke a repetition of that response. If such was the purpose of Nasser's tactics, he succeeded, for Washington displayed little evidence of a Guatemala syndrome. As he departed Cairo, Assistant Secretary Allen told correspondents that, while the United States regretted the Soviet arms deal, it believed that Nasser's purpose was the defense of his country. In Washington, Dulles conceded that it was "difficult to be critical" of Egypt for seeking the arms which "they sincerely need for defense." [37] And perhaps not fully aware of the already burgeoning French arms flow to Israel, he added his hope that the United States could avoid participation in "what might become an arms race." [38]

Such was the chain of events that brought the Soviet Union into the Middle East — a move that demolished, at one stroke, the main objective of Dulles's Middle East policy and the principal reason he had labored to establish the "northern tier" barrier. The penetration, moreover, was clothed in irony, for it had been achieved not through dramatic aggression or subversion, but on the invitation of a local government and through a conventional instrumentality (a military assistance program) with respect to which the West had assumed it enjoyed a monopoly position.

21

The Fateful Aswan Renege

DISJOINTED WESTERN POLICIES that worked, wittingly and inadvertently, to isolate Nasser, thus opened a striking opportunity for Soviet policy to break the Western arms monopoly in the Middle East and establish Russia as a power factor on the scene. Yet this result did not produce a sobering and unifying effect in the Western Alliance. On the contrary, it served as a spur to counteractions that proved unfavorable for both stability and peace. It led the French to an immediate increase in arms shipments to Israel, which helped the bellicose faction in Tel Aviv to force out Moshe Sharett in November, restore Ben-Gurion to the premiership, and develop an urgent war plan for the invasion of the Sinai and the seizure of the strongpoint commanding the Strait of Tiran. It led the British to a misguided effort to bring Jordan into the Baghdad Pact, an effort whose failure brought to bear such intense political pressures on Eden that he lost his judgment, his honesty and his career. It led the United States, after tepid efforts to maintain American influence in Egypt, to Dulles's disastrous attempt to expose what he believed were empty Soviet promises by an abrupt withdrawal of the American offer to finance the Aswan High Dam. From the perspective of nearly twenty years, the unreason then prevailing in the policies of the leading Western nations is difficult either to believe or recapture.

Money for the Dam

The Aswan High Dam was a vast conception, technical and humane, designed to store and distribute the variable waters of the Nile and its tributaries so that productive, green and habitable land areas (a meager 15,000 of Egypt's total of 386,000 square miles) could be greatly enlarged. The Nile, wrote a British hydrologist long ago, "is the whole life of the country, and away from the river only a few nomads exist." [1] A more recent observer added that beyond the reach of the Nile waters, Egypt is all "shimmering sand and stone, part of the great desert that stretches from the Red Sea to the Atlantic." [2] In the Aswan High Dam, Egyptians saw the hope of their deliverance from grinding poverty. At Cairo's request, feasibility studies were undertaken by the World Bank in 1953, and by 1954 these had demonstrated to the bank's satisfaction that the dam project was both technically sound and within the capacity of Egypt's economy, assuming fair and reasonable outside financing arrangements. Eugene R. Black, president of the World Bank, an international civil servant, but also an American, reported to President Eisenhower at that time that construction of the dam was Egypt's highest economic and social priority. [3]

Immediately following the Soviet-Egyptian arms deal, the Soviets made an offer to finance the dam, but Nasser begged off, saying he was already talking to the World Bank. He then sent his ambassador in Washington to inform Dulles that Egypt would greatly prefer American to Russian assistance with the dam. It seemed further evidence of a serious commitment to nonalignment, and it offered the hope to the West that, by moving to underwrite this consequential and highly visible project, it could neutralize the effect of the Soviet arms deal. With President Eisenhower still in the early stages of recuperation from his heart attack, the U.S. government did not respond with alacrity, but on November 21, Eugene Black sat down in Washington with Undersecretary of State Herbert Hoover, Jr., the British ambassador, Sir Roger Makins, and the Egyptian finance minister, Abdel Kaissouny, to discuss Western financing for the dam. By December 16, they had reached agreement on a financing package for the first phase of construction whereunder the United States and Britain would provide cash grants of $70 million ($56 million from the United States and $14 million from Britain), and would also "be prepared to consider sympathetically" later grants up to an aggregate of $200 million as the work progressed. The World Bank would lend $200 million. contingent upon the Anglo-American grants. As the estimated total cost of the dam was $1.3 billion, the remaining burden on the Egyptian economy would be on the order of $900 million spread over fifteen to eighteen years. [4]

Nasser, who was unaccustomed to dealing with international banks, proved to be suspicious of conditions that seemed to him to infringe upon Egyptian sovereignty, and he declared categorically that he would never accept them. This problem sent Black to Cairo on January 24, 1956, with urgings from both Dulles and Eden that he be flexible, owing to the broad political importance of the project, and "not act like a banker." [5] After several notably inharmonious sessions, the astute, tough and charming Black won Nasser's confidence and his approval of the conditions set out in the bank loan. He could not, however, persuade him to accept also the conditions attaching to the American and British offers of grant money which, in the form of *aides-mémoires,* were sitting on Nasser's desk heavily marked with red pencil. Black explained that these offers contained standard loan conditions aimed at guarding against Egyptian inflation and at concentrating available Egyptian funds on the Aswan project, but Nasser was also worried by the absence of assured funding beyond the initial phase, and told Black "he was still going to see if he couldn't get some change in the terms . . ." [6] His refusal to close the deal quickly proved a fateful hinge, for a mere ten days later Dulles's enthusiasm for the project had markedly cooled, and later events in March and April reinforced the negative sentiments in both Washington and London.

Support for the Aswan High Dam presented definite political problems for the Eisenhower administration. Zionist opposition was predictable and reflexive; so too was the resistance of hard-liners in the Congress who scorned all neutralism and thought Nasser's purchase of Soviet arms was ideological treason. The most curious source of trouble, however, was a group of "cotton senators" from the South who asserted that the dam would, by increasing the acreage available for Egyptian cotton (fifteen to eighteen years thence) intensify a trade competition already tougher than their liking. Dulles could not ignore the aggregate of these pressures, but they do not appear to have been anything that could not have been overborne by a determined and popular President. A postmortem study by the Fulbright subcommittee (of the Senate Foreign Relations Committee) pointed out that the congressional opposition had been narrowly confined to the Senate Appropriations Committee, but that no serious effort was ever made to overcome it.[7] Dulles, who was cool to Nasser and convinced that neutralism or nonalignment was a political fiction, was unwilling to expend his own limited political capital with the Congress unless the political risks of the venture could be substantially reduced. And Eisenhower, recovering slowly from his heart attack, had neither the energy nor the political desire to make the fight.

Walking in the woods at Camp David on December 8, where Eisenhower was continuing his convalescence, Dulles explained the pros and cons to the President, and then recommended a special, very secret plan to improve the domestic risks: send a personal emissary to the Middle East in a renewed attempt to reach a basic Arab-Israeli settlement. Although no direct linkage between a settlement and the Aswan financing would be made, still Nasser would be given to understand that the West, by strengthening his domestic position via the Aswan financing, would be placing him in a safer position to negotiate a genuine peace with Israel.[8] Eisenhower approved the proposal and, after some discussion, made his choice of emissary: Robert B. Anderson, a Texas lawyer and businessman who had already served the administration as Secretary of the Navy and Deputy Secretary of Defense, and who would later return in 1957 as successor to Secretary Humphrey at the Treasury. On December 12, 1955, the *New York Times* reported that "the U.S. Government is tying its proposals for a ten-year aid program to build the High Aswan Dam in Egypt to a settlement of the Egyptian-Israeli disputes. The hope here is that the negotiations for economic aid to Egypt can lead to a general settlement of the disturbing Near East situation." Except for this one breach, however, the mission remained a secret for many years. One historian of the period learned of it from a reference in an early draft of Eisenhower's memoirs which did not appear in the published book.[9]

But the mission was destined to fail. Nasser was prepared to suggest a framework for peace talks and to develop formulae for possible settlements, but he could not speak for other Arab states, and could not accept politically intolerable terms — that is, terms which would so alienate Arab opinion as to bring about his own overthrow. Nor was Israel prepared for concessions. Ben-Gurion could not be persuaded that the Aswan High Dam, which would strengthen Nasser, was good for Israel.[10] Indeed, having returned to the cabinet as defense minister in November 1955, he was pressing the Israeli cabinet to approve a military seizure of the Sinai, and he launched a severe raid on Syria on December 12, which caused Egypt to respond with *fedayeen* terrorist attacks in order to prove the viability of the new Egyptian-Syrian alliance.[11] Anderson's effort had, moreover, to be carried on against the background of the December crisis in Jordan; all in all, it was not a propitious season for peacemaking. As Anderson shuttled quietly between Cairo and Tel Aviv, it became apparent that Dulles had failed to measure the full depth of the differences between the parties. Failure of the Anderson mission was undeniable by February, and it rapidly chilled the enthusiasm for the Aswan project which Dulles had conveyed to Black only ten days before. When, a few days later, Nasser submitted his request for substantial changes in the Anglo-American *aides-mémoires,* the temperature dropped to freezing in both Washington and London.

The Crisis in Jordan

In late 1955, for reasons that seemed grounded more in traditional, instinctive British concern to uphold the Hashemite family in Iraq and Jordan than in geopolitical considerations, Eden acceded to powerful urgings from fellow Arabists in the Foreign Office that Jordan be brought into the Baghdad Pact. The new Foreign Secretary, Harold Macmillan, a man of strong and unrepentant imperial tendencies, was in the vanguard of the effort, and Eden was persuaded — despite his private agreement with Nasser to freeze Arab membership in exchange for a suspension of overt Egyptian opposition to the pact (an agreement which Nasser had substantially honored).

As in the original approach to Iraq, the British put the Turks out in front, President Celal Bayar of Turkey traveling to Amman for a state visit in early November. Concurrently, Nuri in Iraq asked Washington to find some means of stopping American oil payments to Saudi Arabia for perhaps six months, in order to prevent Saudi financing of the anticipated street demonstrations against the pact in Jordan.[12] It was a bizarre request, and Eisenhower and Dulles promptly refused it. They also advised the British against an attempt to bring Jordan into the pact, but primarily on the grounds that no member should have a common border with Israel. But Macmillan had the bit in his teeth and Washington, like London, continued to underestimate the latent strength of Pan-Arabic feeling and the capacity of Radio Cairo to influence it. Against the background of hopeful British-American-Egyptian talks looking toward Western financing of the Aswan Dam, Nasser was slow to believe the violation of his agreement with Eden. But in early December, when the chief of the British imperial staff, General Sir Gerald Templer, arrived in Amman to consummate the military agreements, the scales fell from Egyptian eyes. As the Jordanian cabinet, which was riven by the issue of pact membership, began to break up between pro-Nasser nationalists and traditional supporters of the monarchy, Radio Cairo opened up on the Templer mission, calling it a Zionist-Imperialist plot to drag Jordan into a network of disastrous foreign alliances. Rioting broke out in several Jordanian cities with large-scale loss of life and on December 18 King Hussein found it prudent to drop the idea of joining the Baghdad Pact. Egypt, Syria, and Saudi Arabia at once sought to add insult to British injury by offering to substitute their own aid for the full amount of the long-standing British subsidy, which sustained the Jordanian army and thus the throne, but the king refused.[13]

The crisis was painful and costly for all concerned, and a harbinger of future troubles. Nasser concluded that Eden could not be trusted. Eden, who came under severe political attack at home for an ill-conceived and unsuccessful venture, concluded that Nasser was the supreme enemy of British influence in the Middle East. He also moved to assume personal control of foreign affairs by a cabinet shuffle that sent the fire-eating Macmillan to the Exchequer and named the more manageable Selwyn Lloyd to the Foreign Office. Dulles was made more keenly aware of crucial differences in American and British perceptions of interest in the Middle East, and of the many vicious crosscurrents beyond Washington's control.

Eden Loses His Touch

On March 1 there occurred another event in Jordan which, in retrospect, seems rather clearly to have marked the beginning of Eden's alarming and tragic deterioration. The acknowledged master of diplomacy, he began to appear, as Prime Minister, insufficiently rough and robust for the exercise of effective leadership in the contentious arenas of democracy. Possessing the technique of the specialist rather than the broad perspective of the statesman, he was soon being castigated by the London press for a "dithering" performance on both domestic and foreign issues. Said one newspaper, he was "a fidget, a fusspot . . . slow to make up his mind and quick to change it." An editorial in the *Daily Telegraph* of January 3, 1956, said that it was Eden's habit, when speaking, to make a point by placing a clenched fist in the palm of his other hand, "But the smack is seldom heard." Anthony Nutting, the young number three at the Foreign Office, later wrote that he came upon Eden the following day "positively writhing in the agony of this barbed shaft which . . . had struck him at his weakest point." [14] Eden was not, in fact, a tough planner with the tenacity to chart and hold steady to a long-term course. He was a negotiator, a tactician who planned his advance in limited moves; moreover, to the political pressures upon him were added the toxic effects of a damaged bile duct, operated on three times during 1953, yet still in imperfect repair, which was eating away at his whole system, edging his nerves and blurring his judgment.

On March 1, 1956, King Hussein abruptly dismissed Glubb Pasha, the British general who had built and who commanded the famous Arab Legion in Jordan. If Hussein's memoirs can be taken at face value, this action was "a strictly Jordanian affair. . . . My main motive in dismissing him was because we were in disagreement on two issues: the role of Arab officers in our Army, and defence strategy." [15] Nationalist sentiment was no doubt a factor, and it was being inflamed by daily personal attacks from Radio Cairo, depicting Glubb as the real ruler of Jordan. But whatever the mix of elements, King Hussein, who claimed to have ruminated on the matter for a year, brought the issue to a head on February 29 when a list of officers whom Glubb proposed for dismissal from the army was brought to him for signature. "Their only fault, as far as I could see," Hussein wrote, "was that they were nationalists and ambitious. . . . That night I decided Glubb . . . would have to go immediately." [16] Despite grave and angry warnings from the British ambassador of very serious consequences for "yourself, the monarchy, and the whole future of Jordan," [17] Glubb was gone by 7:00 A.M. on March 1. An era had ended.

Eden blamed Nasser totally for the Glubb dismissal. It put him in a passionate frenzy, and drove him to a declaration of personal war. As Anthony Nutting later wrote, on that "fatal day," Eden decided "the world was not big enough to hold both him and Nasser." [18] And from that point forward, Nutting believed, "Eden completely lost his touch." [19] After a desperate week of vainly trying to restore his domestic position by persuading Eisenhower to bring the United States fully into the Baghdad Pact, he was attacked in debate for a Middle East policy that was "ill-formed, ill-prepared . . . both weak and provocative at the same time," [20] and for the first time in his career, appearing ill and exhausted, he lost his temper in the House of Commons. Randolph Churchill, who bore him no love, wrote that this "marked the beginning of the disintegration of the personality and character that the public thought him to possess." [21] What seemed to goad him most was pressure from the right, from the small but vocal "Suez Rebel" group and the jingo press, both of whom reflected wounds to the national and imperial pride inflicted by the "Egyptian upstart." Julien Amery, one of the back-bench rebels, wrote a letter to the *Times* charging that Glubb's dismissal attested to "the bankruptcy of a policy of appeasement in the Middle East. . . . We are now very close to the final disaster." [22] Refusing to acknowledge that Britain now stood as a middle power in the shadow of thermonuclear giants, that it faced changes beyond its control in the Middle East, the Tory diehards and at least half of the British press insisted that "a lost grip . . . had to be recovered." It was enough to stampede Eden, who was relatively unaccustomed to harsh criticism, who had been perhaps too much "the 'Golden Boy' of the Conservative Party" basking "in the sunshine of Churchill's admiration." [23] In quick succession, he now associated himself with the French position on Algeria, reversed his position on the Aswan Dam, opened talks with his military chiefs that appeared predicated on the assumption of certain future conflict with Nasser, and began to treat every small incident in the Middle East as a major challenge to British authority (and to see Nasser's hand in every incident). This visible toughening of British policy, which ran hard against the grain of Eden's temperament and style, represented a victory for what another British minister called the "whiff-of-grapeshot school" led by "those overgrown Boy Scouts personified by Duncan Sandys." [24]

Nor was this the worst. Selwyn Lloyd brought back from an unhappy visit to Cairo the conclusion that Nasser was another Mussolini, and Eden was soon persuaded the analogy was apt, indeed was ready to believe that Nasser's willingness to negotiate the British withdrawal from Suez had been merely a means of clearing the way for the entry of Communism and a march against Israel. His insistence on the Mussolini analogy, which showed a total lapse of historical perspective, is difficult to explain in a man of such wide and deep experience. One concludes that the combined attacks on his political manhood and on his internal physical balance were bringing him to a state of controlled frenzy. In April, he received an able memorandum from the Foreign Office pleading for calm analysis and realism in dealing with Egypt. His response was to take Nutting away from a dinner at the Savoy Hotel where he was entertaining Harold Stassen, and to shout into the telephone: "What's all this nonsense about isolating Nasser or 'neutralising' him, as you call it? I want him destroyed, can't you understand? I want him removed, and if you and the Foreign Office don't agree, then you had better come to the Cabinet and explain why." [25]

An Anxious Spring

The Aswan matter thus drifted in a moribund state, while further developments — in London, Cairo, and Washington — conspired against its revival. Dulles's instinctive recoil from neutralism was not his only political allergy; he was also rendered nervous by any evidence of normal relations between the West and the Communist powers. Thus he viewed with wary distaste the visit to London of Khrushchev and Bulganin on April 18, a trip that had been arranged during that brief moment of East-West cordiality at the Geneva summit the preceding July. Although there were some hostile demonstrations, the British public and press treated "Khrush and Bulge," on the whole, with a warmhearted curiosity normally reserved for performing bears in a traveling circus, and the official talks were lively and unexpectedly friendly (Khrushchev later told the British ambassador in Moscow, "Bulganin can vote Labor if he likes, but I'm going to vote Conservative").[26] At a press conference on April 27, however, Khrushchev inadvertently triggered an Egyptian move toward Communist China which could only worsen the prospect for Aswan financing in Washington. Responding to a question about arms shipments to the Middle East, he denied that Soviet arms were going to Egypt (insisting with less than candor that they came from Czechoslovakia), but then went on to say that the USSR really preferred a general arms embargo in that area and would participate in this if it could be worked out by the United Nations.

It was a measure of the extreme anxiety in Cairo that Nasser read this remark as a serious threat to his continued flow of arms from Russia, and that he moved with unseemly haste (and no consultation) to recognize Red China. The move was a piece of sad and fateful foolishness, for, while the Red Chinese had little to offer in the way of modern arms, the act of inviting them into an already turbulent area could only set Washington's teeth on edge. As late as April 3, and in partial answer to Eden's emotional warnings that Nasser had become a clear enemy of the West, Dulles told a press conference he thought the Cairo regime was actuated by a desire for "genuine independence" and he saw no evidence of "vassalage to the Soviet Union." [27] But in Dulles's pantheon of devils, the Red Chinese represented perhaps the highest and purest evil, and this view was shared by a large majority of the Congress, the press, and the American people. That he was nettled and affronted by Nasser's action, and that it had some effect on the Aswan decision, seems clear from subsequent statements. A year later (April 2, 1957), in one of the varied defenses he employed to explain and defend his disastrous termination of the Western offer on Aswan, he told a press conference that Egypt's recognition of China "forced upon us an issue to which I think there was only one proper response: That issue was, do nations which play both sides get better treatment than nations which are stalwart and work with us?" [28] This variation on the theme of immoral neutralism was a particularly thin rationale for the Aswan renege, however, for the Soviet arms deal and the Western desire to neutralize its effect had, after all, been the primary motivating force behind the offer to finance Aswan. Nasser was already "playing both sides," and his recognition of China changed nothing of substance in that respect. As the Fulbright subcommittee pointed out in its later investigative report, Dulles really could not have it both ways: "To argue that the arms deal was both the reason for making the offer and also the reason for withdrawing the offer is wholly illogical." [29]

Eugene Black visited Nasser again on June 21 (in the course of a swing through several other Middle East countries), and found the Egyptian leader "rather surprised and hurt that he had gotten no answer to his suggested changes in the terms of the grants." [30] Nasser may have been hurt, but it is doubtful he was really surprised, for his own ambassador had hurried home from Washington on May 21 to tell him of the extra trouble stirred up by his recognition of China, and Eden's hostility was, of course, being spread daily upon the public record. Black again urged Nasser to retract his request for amendments, and accept the *aides-mémoires* as they were presented, but he left Cairo without knowing that Nasser would shortly decide to take this advice.

On his return to Washington, Black asked for an appointment with Dulles and, at a meeting which included Hoover and Murphy, reported the nature of his advice to Nasser and also the World Bank's unchanged view that the Egyptian economy could fully meet the burdens of the project. Dulles met the latter statement with heavy skepticism, remarking that he had "been thinking about this Aswan project, and I just wonder if this isn't too much for the Egyptian Government to undertake." [31] Black assured him there had been no change in the capacity of that economy since the deal was offered the preceding November; the general magnitude of Egypt's obligations under the Soviet arms deal had been known at the time and had not changed. Dulles, however, had turned off his mental hearing aid. He was now pacing slowly up and down the room, saying, "I just don't know whether we should go through with this or not." [32] Black, acknowledging that the project was large and difficult, said that, speaking purely as a banker, he would be saved a good deal of exertion if the deal were called off. But speaking as an American citizen, he was concerned. Recognizing that the Aswan Dam was the premium project for the Egyptian people, and that Nasser had staked his political fortune on public promises that it would be built, Black was afraid "Hell might break loose" if the American offer were terminated. At that point, Dulles gave him a cold sideways glance and walked out of the room, bringing the meeting to an abrupt close. [33]

The Miscalculation

Dulles had now rather evidently decided to let the Aswan offer lapse, although he appears to have withheld the fact of this decision from his State Department colleagues, his British and French allies, and possibly even from the President, who had by now suffered a new physical setback — a sharp attack of ileitis on June 8. Always sensitive to conservative opinion, Dulles accepted Treasury Secretary Humphrey's fear that the Egyptians would probably default along the way, leaving the United States to rescue the project with large infusions of capital or else to bear the stigma of its failure. This was a real and practical consideration, but Humphrey's opinion was largely intuitive, and quite superficial compared to the exhaustive studies made by the World Bank; it was, however, an opinion that came from a far more politically powerful quarter. In addition, Dulles distrusted Nasser and was rankled by the Egyptian temerity to try to bargain between the American and Russian offers. Himself the coldest of bargainers, never hesitant to exert tremendous pressure on an opponent, he was rather quick to characterize the same quality in others as "blackmail" — especially if he perceived that a moral issue was at stake along the spiked periphery where freedom confronted the Communist dictatorship. Finally, he was inwardly convinced that a system as evil as Soviet Communism could not really compete with the great citadel of American capitalism, that the Russian offer to build the Aswan Dam was an empty threat. The best way to prove this, and not only in the Middle East but across the whole span of the undeveloped world, was to let Russian backwardness join with Egyptian incompetence. The resulting humiliation would expose the emptiness of Soviet economic boasts and promises; at the same time, it would cause Nasser's fall from power, thus demonstrating the perils of neutralism.

If Mohamed Heikal's account is accepted, Nasser had also concluded by late June or early July that Dulles would terminate the Aswan offer. Talking to his agitated pro-American ambassador, Ahmed Hussein (who remained in Cairo for nearly two months before returning to see Dulles on July 19), Nasser said: "I have concrete evidence that even if you went back and accepted all their conditions, they will not give us the Aswan Dam." When the ambassador demurred, Nasser told him: "Well, all right. . . . Go and tell [Dulles] that we have accepted everything. But don't humiliate us. Because we are not going to get the High Dam." [34]

Word then reached Dulles in early July that Nasser now fully accepted the Anglo-American *aides-mémoires* and was sending his ambassador back to Washington to conclude the Aswan deal. It was an unwelcome surprise, for it created a deadline for decision and sharpened the context in which decision would have to be taken, making an angry reaction throughout the Arab world a virtual certainty. It would have been much easier if Cairo had simply chosen to accept Moscow's offer, permitting the Western offer to be superseded. But the new circumstances did not change the basic situation, as Dulles saw it, and they did offer a dramatic opportunity to demonstrate America's staunch resistance to "immoral blackmail." He carried the news to Eisenhower on July 13 at his Gettysburg farm, where the President was still recovering from his ileitis attack, and expressed the judgment that Cairo's shift of position probably meant that Nasser had failed to get a firm commitment from the Soviets.[35] Eisenhower expressed his annoyance at the complication, indicating that, in the circumstances and on the threshold of a presidential campaign, he should not be asked to take domestic political risks for Nasser. Still, the issue presented a quandary, and the President did not resolve it. While the discussion clearly moved in the direction of a negative decision, not only its manner and timing but even its substance were left largely to Dulles's discretion, pending consultation with the British and further reflection.

Dulles subsequently told the British ambassador that he was "dubious" about the loan, but would have to see the Egyptian ambassador on July 19. Makins's own advice, which was reinforced the next day by a further exchange of cables with Eden, was that Dulles should consider his decision with utmost care.[36] The British had no desire to make the loan; indeed, they were embarrassed that the offer still lay open for Nasser to pick up. At the same time, having negotiated long and painfully with Nasser, they feared a volatile reaction to a perceived slight. Uneasily, they decided to leave the matter to Dulles's judgment, but urged him "to play it long"; that is, to adopt the tactics of delay and avoid the dangers of a flat or abrupt rejection.[37]

In partial response to British advice, Dulles instructed Robert Bowie to draft a press statement that would minimize the sense of offense to the Cairo government. The product of Bowie's labor was conciliatory in tone, yet contained a comment on Egypt's credit standing and economic capacity that could only be read in Cairo as a gratuitous slur. It said that because of "developments" since December 1955, "the ability of Egypt to devote adequate resources to assure the project's success has become more uncertain than at the time the offer was made." Bowie has said subsequently that this language was designed primarily to assure congressional understanding and support for the decision, but was not intended to injure or provoke Nasser.[38] Since Dulles's aim was to hand the political-economic hot potato of the Aswan project to Cairo and Moscow in the belief that they could not make a success of it, there is no reason to doubt Bowie's recollection. Still, the statement reflects a remarkable insensitivity to the raw anxieties and pride of the Cairo regime, a deficiency that would almost surely have been corrected and softened if Dulles had shown it to Eugene Black, or the British ambassador. Moreover, the French ambassador in Washington, Couve de Murville, had told the State Department just a few days earlier that "to deny the loan . . . is a very dangerous action; it can affect the Suez Canal." [39] He had served in Cairo for several years. Dulles consulted with none of these men, and indeed brushed the final statement through the President in a meeting that lasted only twelve minutes.[40] In perhaps no other decision during his tenure at the State Department did he play so lone a hand.

The Renege

The fifty-minute meeting with Ambassador Hussein started at about 11:30 A.M. on July 19, with Dulles explaining in a kindly manner the difficulties he was encountering in the Congress. The ambassador sat nervously on the edge of the divan in the Secretary's office, while Dulles sat to one side in an armchair with his legs stretched out on the table. Undersecretary Hoover and Assistant Secretary Allen were also present on the American side, while one Egyptian diplomat accompanied his ambassador. An ebullient pro-American, Hussein said that he recognized the problems facing the United States, but that the Aswan High Dam was of absolutely transcendent importance to Egypt and the Middle East. He emphasized how much he personally wanted the West to support the project, and how concerned he was by the potential consequences of the Russian offer.⁴¹ Dulles nodded. Then speaking in his ponderous, pedantic style, slowly and powerfully, all in sad tones, he began to marshal the arguments in support of his conclusion that it was now impossible for the United States to participate in the Aswan project. About halfway through this exposition, Hussein caught the unmistakable drift, became agitated, and finally interrupted Dulles with an anguished plea. "Don't please say you are going to withdraw the offer," he said in effect, "because [and here he patted his pocket] we have the Russian offer to finance the dam right here." ⁴² This interjection apparently irritated Dulles, who resented any attempt to maneuver him, but it also gave him his cue. Although he must have known that Hussein's statement, far from being attempted blackmail, was the desperate plea of a pro-American Arab who feared that Soviet financing for the dam was inevitable if the United States withdrew its offer, Dulles retorted, in effect: "Well then, as you already have the money, you have no need of our support. The offer is withdrawn." ⁴³

It is plausible that Dulles was genuinely angry, that he brought the meeting to a more abrupt and heated conclusion than he had intended, and that it was Hussein's report of the discussion to Nasser, when coupled with the public statement, that produced the Egyptian leader's bitter reaction: "This is not a withdrawal," Nasser told Heikal and Foreign Minister Fawzi as he studied the radio messages on his aircraft, flying back to Cairo from a meeting in Brioni with Tito and Nehru. "It is an attack on the regime and an invitation to the people of Egypt to bring it down." ⁴⁴

Immediately after the meeting with the unhappy Hussein, Dulles joined Henry Luce and C. D. Jackson for lunch in his inner sanctum. The publisher and his senior editor (who had earlier served a stint as Eisenhower's assistant for "psychological strategy") found the Secretary exhilarated as he recounted his decision, especially his remark to Hussein that Nasser could "go to Moscow" for his money. But Jackson also gained the impression that Nasser was only an incidental factor, that Dulles had hurled his spear primarily at the Kremlin: he had decided to use the Aswan issue as a means of meeting Russia's "economic counteroffensive . . . there and then." [45] The Secretary emphasized his extreme allergy to "blackmail" and his refusal to temporize with any of its manifestations. He evidenced little or no concern with possible Egyptian retaliation. Yet by the end of the same working day, he had apparently suffered at least one or two pangs of doubt. About 7:30 P.M., his special assistant, William Macomber, was laboring in a small outer office, sorting out cables and memoranda to be sent on down the line for action, when he glanced up in surprise to find Secretary Dulles sitting directly before him, hat on and briefcase in hand. Macomber recalled his visual impression: "It looked like he had no neck. He had a perfectly normal neck. It was just a very big neck, and he was a very massive fellow." [46] After he had jumped to his feet and been waved back down again, the following colloquy occurred:

Dulles: Well, this has been quite a day.
Macomber: Yes, sir.
Dulles: Well, I certainly hope we did the right thing.
Macomber: Yes, sir, I hope so.
Dulles: I certainly hope we did the right thing.

Dulles then got up and walked out to the waiting elevator. He had never before stopped by Macomber's desk, and he never did again.[47]

Rationalization after the Fact

A week later, on July 26, when Nasser's amazing nationalization of the Suez Canal exposed the immensity of Dulles's miscalculation, a storm broke over him, raining down attacks on his competence and judgment like hailstones, and lasting for months and even years afterwards. Against these he developed a variegated and rather contradictory set of defenses, including (1) responsiveness to congressional feeling, (2) resistance to "blackmail," (3) weakness of the Egyptian economy, and (4) the claim that Nasser had deliberately provoked a negative action in order to justify his own prior decision to nationalize the canal. None of these proved particularly convincing to either critics or friends.

In reply to Senator Clifford Case during a hearing at which he was defending himself against the charge of having triggered the Canal seizure, he said: "There is one thing I want to make clear, Senator. I do not believe in the U.S. being blackmailed, and any time I sense a purpose on the part of any country to try to get money out of us by threatening that if we don't pay the money it will do something, at that point I say, 'Nothing doing.' " [48] But the blackmail charge stands on very slender evidence, residing chiefly in Ambassador Hussein's anguished interjection of July 19, and in an interview Nasser gave to the *New York Times* on April 2. On the earlier occasion, Nasser said he still held a Soviet offer to finance the dam and would "consider accepting" it if negotiations with Washington were to break down. But he added: "I do not mention the Soviet offer of aid as a threat or as bluff. The Soviet offer was very general and, really, we have not studied it." [49] He was still doing business with the World Bank and keeping the Russians at arm's length.

The assertion that the Egyptian economy was inadequate to the task of shouldering the Aswan burden was not much more impressive. Eugene Black, who was not consulted, continued to insist that the project was sound and the strength of the Egyptian economy adequate. And later events proved that that economy was able to carry about $900 million in capital burdens, in the context of an arrangement whereunder the Soviets supplied some $310 million (or nearly 20 percent less than the total amount of the Western offer). [50] Moreover, the economy concurrently assumed the added burden of a later Soviet arms deal that was arranged to replace Egyptian equipment losses suffered in the Suez War.

Even the President taxed his Secretary of State, raising questions he might better have asked before the renege. Dulles replied to one query by saying that, if he had not acted as he did, Congress would itself have imposed the termination "almost unanimously." [51] A year later, with a skeptical President still probing, Dulles introduced a wholly new line of defense. In a letter of October 30, 1957, he wrote: "President Nasser has since said that he planned for nearly two years to seize the Suez Canal Company, but was waiting for a good occasion. He knew that if he pressed for a decision from us when he did the result would be negative because the Congressional action had been announced.* Nevertheless he pressed for a definitive answer, and I suspect he did so in order to create the occasion for which he was looking." [52] Eugene Black called this theory "impossible — completely ridiculous," [53] and he was supported by the American, British, and French ambassadors in Cairo at the time. They all agreed that Nasser had contingency plans, but, in their considered judgment, he was not eager to cut short the Suez Canal Company's concession; if Dulles's negative had been couched in softer terms, they believed he would simply have picked up the Soviet offer. [54] On this analysis, Nasser reacted violently because he interpreted Dulles's statement and manner as designed to do him fatal political injury.

Yet it is necessary to ask, on Dulles's behalf, why the manner of the

* Presumably, this is a reference to the report of the Senate Appropriations Committee.

renege made such a difference, why the sensible course for Nasser, even after Dulles's abrupt "punch in the stomach," would not have been to embrace the Soviets? The answer may lie in veiled regions beyond reason, yet there are clues. There are the ingrained factors of Arab dignity and Arab revenge. There is also evidence of a distinct preference for relations with the West, notwithstanding the junta's bitter experience with colonial exploitation, and there is a discernible aversion to Communism (which time and attempted Russian-Egyptian collaboration have now confirmed). Aly Sabry, one of Nasser's closest aides, told an American shortly after the Canal seizure that "Nasser chose nationalization to keep free of Russia. Russian aid would have been the simple solution. . . . Nationalization was dangerous." [55]

From which emerges an irony. Dulles, bent upon pursuing his own highly abstract brand of global anti-Communism, was only incidentally interested in bringing Nasser down. His principal aim was to expose what he regarded as the pretensions of Soviet economic aid programs. Demonstration that these consisted of unfillable promises would break the momentum of the Soviet drive for "competitive coexistence"; that it might also humiliate regimes in small countries that had staked their own futures on those Soviet promises would be a salutary, but quite secondary, result. It was precisely Dulles's ignorance of Arabs, his tendency to treat Nasser as an undifferentiated pawn in a larger game, that produced the specifically Arablike and rashly human nationalization of the Suez Canal.

22

Cross-Purposes and Cardboard Proposals

Possessed of a trained lawyer's capacity to switch his attention quickly and almost totally from one problem to another, Dulles emplaned for Latin America on July 20 to join President Eisenhower at a meeting of the Organization of American States in Panama, apparently confident he had laid the Nasser problem to rest. Intent upon other matters, he took no notice of Nasser's first reaction, a speech delivered in a black rage on July 24, after five days of brooding on the American rebuff: "Our reply today is that we will not allow the domination of force and the dollar. I will tell you on Thursday, God willing, how Egypt has acted so that all its projects — such as this project — may be projects of sovereignty, dignity, and not those of humiliation, slavery, domination, rule, and exploitation. . . . When Washington sheds every decent principle on which foreign relations are based and broadcasts the lie, snare, and delusion that Egypt's economy is unsound, then I look them in the face and say: Drop dead of your fury for you will never be able to dictate to Egypt." [1]

Two days later, on July 26, having brought a daring plan of physical seizure to completion in record time, Nasser went to Alexandria by train to address a large expectant throng at sundown in Liberation Square. In a long, rhythmic, emotional speech, during which he descended often into the Arabic vernacular, he "played the throng like an immense organ" for two hours and forty-five minutes. "They are punishing Egypt," he declared of the Western powers, "because she refused to side with military blocs." [2] Russia had offered to finance the Aswan High Dam, but Nasser did not want Russian help; Egypt would build the dam with profits from the Canal. "This money is ours and this canal belongs to

Egypt because it is an Egyptian limited liability company. . . . We dug the Canal with our lives, our skulls, our bones, our blood." [3] By pre-arrangement, when he uttered the name of Ferdinand de Lesseps (the builder of the Suez Canal), as he was to do fourteen times in ten minutes, hand-picked civilian-military teams moved to take physical possession of the Suez Canal Company facilities at Port Said, Port Suez and Cairo. "Therefore, I have signed today and the government has approved . . . a resolution . . . for the nationalization of the Universal Company of the Suez Maritime Canal." [4] The deed was done.

When Dulles heard of the Canal nationalization and seizure, he was in Peru to attend inaugural ceremonies for the new President-elect, Manuel Prado Ugarteche. His first reaction was unvarnished shock and surprise; he was caught almost totally off guard. Still, it did not occur to him to rush home until he received a copy of Eden's July 27 cable to Eisenhower reflecting London's sense of anger, urgency, and immediate readiness to use force. Anxious to leave, but persuaded that he must stay at least until the ribbon of office had been bestowed on President Prado, he remained in Lima all during the twenty-eighth, perspiring uncomfortably in white tie and tails through a lengthy mass, several processions, a large ceremonial lunch, and finally the inaugural proceedings in the Peruvian senate. Preoccupied, his face set with worry, he glanced from time to time at the thin platinum pocket watch that had been a gift from his uncle Robert Lansing.

The Scene in London

Eden received news of the Canal seizure on the evening of July 26, while he was entertaining the young King of Iraq and his Prime Minister, Nuri as Said, at dinner at Ten Downing Street. The party immediately broke up and, as the Iraqis departed, Nuri expressed his anger not only at Nasser's act, but at his failure to consult with other Arab states before taking an action that would affect them all. He reportedly said to Eden: "Hit him, hit him hard, and hit him now." [5] Eden then went downstairs to the double-doored privacy of the cabinet room, accompanied by Selwyn Lloyd and the Marquess of Salisbury, who were among the dinner guests, and they were soon joined by the defense minister, the chiefs of staff, the French ambassador and the American chargé d'affaires (Ambassador Winthrop Aldrich being in the United States on leave). The dramatic meeting, late at night, to consider the course for embattled Britannia found most of the participants in full evening dress and decorations, "Anthony and Bobbety [Salisbury] with the sash and kneebreeches of the Garter." [6] Eden and the other ministers present were eager for immediate military action. But recognizing that Nasser's act of expropriation had certain precedent in law, they talked of issuing an order to withdraw all European canal pilots from Egypt, as this would, they judged, impair operation and maintenance of the Canal and thus constitute a technical violation of the 1888 Convention, justifying intervention. Long since determined upon a policy of force to bring Nasser down, Eden and his cabinet colleagues thus saw the new crisis as creating the pretext they had been seeking. What decided the issue in favor of delay that night was the adamant opposition of the military chiefs, who refused to risk an airdrop of troops on Suez unless land and naval forces could come to their support within twenty-four hours. But such was the state of British military unreadiness that this support would take six weeks to organize, equip and position. Pressure from the cabinet for an immediate airdrop was intense. It ended when the three military chiefs threatened to resign, but only the First Sea Lord, Admiral Louis Mountbatten, was opposed to a Suez War on the merits.[7]

From the beginning, Eden tried to keep the argument on political and emotional grounds, and away from the legalities of the question. In his definitive cable to Eisenhower of July 27, he called for a "firm stand" by Britain and the United States on pain of seeing the influence of both parties "irretrievably undermined" in the Middle East. In one sense this assessment was instinctively correct, for Nasser had rendered his nationalization speech with such emotion and ferocity, and with so undisguised an aim of striking a paralyzing blow at the whole Western position in the area, that its effect was to widen out the issues beyond a dispute over the Canal. Arab opinion was moved to transient ecstasy at the sight of Arab leadership facing down the financial exploiters of the West; at the same time Europe was astonished and then anxious at the realization that the "world's neck" had passed into unpredictable hands. Eden was quick to reinforce this feeling of anxiety: Nasser's "thumb on our windpipe," he asserted, was an intolerable state of affairs.

While Dulles was speeding home from Peru, Eisenhower was concluding that the first task was to cool off British and French emotion. He sent a cautionary reply to Eden and told him he was sending Robert Murphy to talk things over. From the outset, Eisenhower felt categorically that no justification for military action arose from the act of nationalization. He was also skeptical of the British view that Egypt lacked the technical competence to maintain Canal operations, for in his experience Suez was merely a ditch cut in the desert — a simple operation compared, for example, to the Panama Canal, where mechanical locks must be used to lift and lower the ships traversing a ruggedly uneven terrain. He felt the only way to determine whether or not Egypt was willing and able to meet its international obligations under the 1888 Convention was to wait and see.

Robert Murphy, in London, was given a small dinner on July 30 by his old Algiers colleague Harold Macmillan, who wrote in his memoirs: "Here was my opportunity and, with the Prime Minister's full acquiescence, I was determined to make full use of it." [8] On this occasion Murphy made clear he "was left in no doubt" that the British government regarded Suez as a test that "could be met only by the use of force," and he commented that this conclusion "seemed not unjustified." [9] Macmillan added that "we . . . did our best to frighten him, or at least to leave him in no doubt of our determination." [10] At lunch the following day, which included Eden, Lloyd and Salisbury as well as Macmillan, there was wider evidence of the jingo spirit and an unquestioning British assumption that the United States would give at least tacit support to an Anglo-French military operation. The British leaders assured Murphy there would be no need for direct U.S. help, except in the unlikely event of Russian intervention; in that case, as Murphy reported it, Eden said: "We do hope you will take care of the Bear." [11] Eisenhower's memoirs record the "depth of the regret I felt in the need to take a view so diametrically opposed to that held by the British." [12]

Enter the Secretary of State

After a taut talk with Eisenhower on July 31, Dulles, having just arrived from Peru, departed for London within two hours, carrying with him a letter for Eden from the President, a copy of the 1888 Convention, and a translation of Nasser's nationalization speech. Working with Herman Phleger on the plane, he set about to stress the legal issues which Eden was so ready to avoid, for Egypt's seizure of property on her own territory, when combined with both a readiness and an ability to compensate the former owners, was a right firmly established in international law. Moreover, as Nasser's expressed purpose was to use Canal profits to finance the Aswan Dam (as a means of avoiding further dependence on Russia), there seemed no reason to doubt that he had an incentive to maintain uninterrupted traffic through the waterway, and thus to charge fares that would promote traffic, as opposed to fares (and political obstructions) that would drive it around the Cape of Good Hope. It was also a fact that Egypt had physically controlled the Canal entrances since World War II (by reason of that fact it had effectively asserted the sovereign right to bar Israeli shipping since 1948).

But the Tory inner circle was impervious to such logic, and Dulles rather too quickly compromised a conclusive legal case.

Macmillan wrote: "I told Foster, as plainly as I could, that we just could not afford to lose this game. It was a question not of honour only but survival. . . . I think he was quite alarmed; for he had hoped to find me less extreme, I think." [13] If Nasser was allowed to "get away with it," the Tories argued, then Britain was finished as a world power. There was in this reaction — of the same men who had stood bravely against the perilous drift of 1938 — a tragic inability to transcend the Munich syndrome, a tragic tendency to equate Nasser with Mussolini (or Hitler), the Middle East with Europe, and 1956 with 1938. Yet however misguided the reaction, behind it lay a felt sense of impending doom. The anguished, terrible struggle for survival in World War II had brought the momentary exhilaration of richly deserved triumph, but there had followed a series of imperial erosions and defeats across the whole of that once-glorious span of authority on which the sun never set, forcing the sad awareness that Britain's strength was substantially spent. Now for reasons imbedded deep in the British psyche, Suez seemed the intolerable threat of coup de grace. In broad terms, the average Englishman shared this anxiety and foreboding. "If Eden's fevered policies had not struck a responsive chord in the hearts of half his countrymen," wrote one observer, "they would have been like a fuse without a bomb." [14]

In this atmosphere, Dulles labored to persuade the unpersuadable that an "international solution" could meet Britain's needs and win the overwhelming support of world opinion. Dominating the proceeding with his intellect and personal force, he made apparent headway by expressing sympathy for both the predicament and the impulse of his allies — a tactic that led to later difficulties, for while Murphy and others were inclined to discount several of the Secretary's offhand remarks (e.g., that Nasser must be made to "disgorge" the Canal), Dulles did not conceal the truth that he disliked Nasser and the Egyptians. And he refused to rest his case on the simple legal sufficiency of Nasser's expropriation. Had he done so, the outcome might have been quite different. But he insisted on sustaining a tortured ambiguity. He thought the seizure was legal, but he frowned upon it as bad international practice and so would not give it full countenance. [15] A vague insistence that "justice" must be done tended to mislead pent-up Tories into thinking that a difference over the means required to dispose of the problem was a relatively minor matter. Eden later wrote, accurately enough, that Dulles "agreed emphatically that the seizure of a great international waterway was intolerable." [16]

Out of this first meeting came an agreement to convene an international conference in London that would, Dulles hoped, bring world opinion to bear upon the equities in the case and thus cool the superheated Anglo-French determination to use force. The Western Big Three would submit to the conference a plan, designed by Dulles, creating an "international authority" to *operate* the waterway, ensure freedom of transit under the 1888 Convention, fix tolls, carry out improvements, and negotiate the compensation of the old Suez Canal Company. While all of this suggested that the United States had regained control of alliance diplomacy, the extent of Dulles's real persuasiveness is open to doubt. Britain and France had already accepted their inability to conduct military operations until at least the middle of September (a fact they carefully concealed from the Americans). So they had six weeks in which to rally domestic and world opinion to their support, and to lock the United States into a firm acceptance of their strategy. Equally to the point, the substance of Dulles's proposal must have invited skepticism, if its purpose was in fact to define a negotiable solution; for its implementation would effectively undo the Egyptian nationalization — indeed, it would involve a worse infringement on Egyptian sovereignty than the original concession of 1888. While this presented no problem for Eden and the French, it was a proposal that Nasser could not accept and survive — and must therefore reject — and it is probable that the Arabist Eden understood this more clearly than the Wall Street lawyer Dulles; the one knew the substantive texture of the people, the culture and the issues; the other was an ingenious deviser of ad hoc formulae based on rather abstract assessments of a required balance between equity and global order.

On the basic question of whether or not Dulles really believed in his proposal, and in others that he put forward during this bout of fevered diplomacy, there are differences of view. Robert Murphy had the impression that the Secretary was "merely throwing out ideas" [17] to gain time in the somewhat desperate hope that one of them would prove to be workable. But Herman Phleger, who accompanied him on the plane trip when the first proposal was developed, thought "the logic of it was wonderful" and never doubted Dulles's own conviction as to the efficacy of his handiwork.[18] Robert Bowie also thought Dulles believed his proposals provided a basis for serious negotiation and settlement.[19]

Aside from the question of whether or not the proposal would appeal to Nasser, the accompanying communiqué showed cavalier treatment of the legalities. Ignoring Egypt's insistence that only the Suez Canal Company was affected by nationalization, and that Egypt would fully meet its obligations to assure free passage through the waterway under the 1888 Convention, the London communiqué asserted that Nasser's action "threatens the freedom and security of the Canal." [20] And although the original de Lesseps concession of 1866 made clear that the company "being Egyptian, is governed by the laws and customs of the country," [21] the communiqué asserted that Nasser's action involved the seizure of "an international agency" and thus fell outside the boundary of the normal, justifiable nationalization of property. This was slippery and fallacious legalizing, and Dulles's full participation in it showed for the first time a view at some variance with Eisenhower's flat rejection of the moral and legal assertions of the Anglo-French. The difference remains, even when one acknowledges that Dulles faced the difficult problem of having to deal face-to-face with valued allies, to express sympathy, and to concede what he judged were secondary points, in the effort to bring them closer to the Eisenhower position of "no war." But during the critical three months following nationalization, Eisenhower and Dulles were not really on the same wavelength: Eisenhower was Olympian and categorical in his opposition to force; Dulles seemed more to share the Anglo-French anxiety that an unpredictable Nasser could not be trusted, and that force might thus be justified in the last resort. He conveyed this feeling to his allies with a prudent obliqueness, but he maddened them at critical junctures by suddenly shifting his stance to avoid the danger of a public difference with the President.

In the period between August 5 and the opening of the first London conference on August 16, Eden strove to persuade both Eisenhower and the British public that Nasser must be destroyed. Writing to Eisenhower, he assumed broad agreement "to undo what Nasser has done and to set up an International Regime for the Canal." [22] But he then pushed beyond the Canal issue to argue that, because Nasser's course "is unpleasantly familiar" and "the parallel with Mussolini is close," the "removal of Nasser, and the installation in Egypt of a regime less hostile to the West, must therefore rank high among our objectives." [23] On August 8, he attacked Nasser on British television, drawing an analogy with fascism and stating: "Why don't we trust him? The answer is simple. Look at his record. Our quarrel is not with Egypt, still less with the Arab world; it is with Colonel Nasser." [24] The Australian Prime Minister, Robert Menzies, was also brought in to assert the case for imperial destiny, and never mind the legalities. In a speech over the BBC facilities, arranged by Eden over the objections of its management that the BBC was not a propaganda arm of Her Majesty's Government, Menzies scorned the "disposition in some . . . quarters to find legal virtues in what Nasser has done. . . . If such nonsense is the law, why have any international agreements at all?" [25]

Eisenhower, who was growing annoyed at Eden's persistent efforts to push him beyond what he considered a clear and basic position — to

Arriving for the First London Conference
on the Suez Crisis (September 1956)

focus on the Canal problem and avoid any attempt to link it with the wider question of the Nasser regime — replied bluntly on September 2: "There must be no grounds for our several peoples to believe that anyone is using the Canal difficulty as an excuse to proceed forcibly against Nasser." [26]

The First London Conference

Dulles arrived back in London on August 15 in the wake of certain American press reports, traceable to an Eisenhower-Dulles meeting with congressional leaders on August 12, that the United States was softening its position on an international authority to *run* the Canal. According to a dispatch in the *Washington Post,* the United States would be content with an international body that was merely advisory to an operation run by Egypt. At lunch that day with Foreign Secretary Selwyn Lloyd and the French Foreign Minister, Christian Pineau, Dulles was confronted by adamant insistence that Britain and France would accept nothing less than an international authority with genuine operational control.[27] Whatever may have been in his mind by way of a compromise, he thus emerged with the realization that he would have to support the Anglo-French position, or cause an open split of the Western Big Three on the first day of the conference.

Unready to face a major breach, he went on to make an address the following afternoon, the centerpiece of which was a proposal that "the operation of the Suez Canal in accordance with the 1888 Treaty and the principles therein set forth" would be made the responsibility of an international operating board to be established by treaty and associated with the United Nations. The international confidence which previously rested upon the 1888 Convention and the Suez Canal Company had been "grievously assaulted," and the question was whether or not that confidence could "peacefully be repaired." If it could not, then "we face a future of the utmost gravity." He laid stress on the need to solve the "practical problem" of giving "effective practical expression to the principles of the 1888 Treaty." [28] As a whole, the speech was a superior example of lucid advocacy, demonstrating a mastery of the subject matter, a strong purpose and a moderate tone. Yet the fatal flaws remained: it argued from shaky legal premises for a proposal that was manifestly nonnegotiable.

The Indian counterproposal, introduced the following day, came much closer to being a practical and workable solution. The Indian spokesman, Krishna Menon, was a diplomat whose effectiveness suffered from the wide dislike of him in the West for both his neutralist views and his arrogance. But he asserted accurately that the effect of the Dulles proposal "is to repeal the act of nationalization; not to repeal it in the sense of replacing what was before, but to substitute an international body." This would not work, he said, because it did not reflect the realities of the situation: "The factual position is that the rulers of Egypt, whoever has sovereign power in Egypt, are really the people who can guarantee freedom of navigation." As Egypt had acted legally and properly in nationalizing the Canal, he found no merit in seeking to undo that act; there was, however, merit in creating an international *advisory* body to assure the right of free passage and fair tolls. Cutting the ground out from under Dulles's obscuring references to the evil of Egyptian political control, Menon argued that "our interest in this Canal is not a political one, it is a user interest, and that user interest can best be served by negotiation, by trying to make the interest a mutual one, by persuasion, by making Egypt a party to a solemn agreement which comes under the obligations of international law and of the Charter of the United Nations." He went on to recommend "a consultative body of user interests . . . with advisory, consultative and liaison functions . . . without prejudice to Egyptian ownership and operation." [29]

On August 19, Dulles received Eisenhower's cabled comments on his proposal of August 16. Although the President was unaware of the Indian proposal, his own thoughts coincided almost exactly: "Nasser may find it impossible to swallow the whole of this as now specified. . . . I see no objection to a board with supervisory rather than operating authority . . . with operating responsibility residing in someone appointed by Nasser, subject to board approval." [30] Dulles replied in considerable agitation on the twentieth that Anglo-French agreement to such modifications might well be impossible. Such a major concession, he thought, should be held in reserve "as a matter of last resort in order to obtain Egypt's concurrence." Eisenhower promptly cabled back, "I understand the box you are in," and left the matter to his Secretary of State, assuring him of his support and approval "in whatever action you finally decide you must take." [31]

A more detached, constructive, and imaginative reaction from Dulles could have made this a major turning point in the crisis. The American President was ready and willing to put his weight behind a proposal that Nasser would almost surely have accepted, that was supported by governments which, though small in number, represented a large percentage of the world's people — India, Russia, Indonesia and Ceylon. If vigorously led by the United States, this combination could almost certainly have isolated Britain and France at the conference and brought about a negotiation with Nasser which London and Paris could have threatened to disrupt by military action only at great peril to their reputations and their security. But Dulles could not transcend his abhorrence at the thought of even temporary alliance with Russia against America's traditional friends, or his dislike of neutralists. Moreover, his prestige and his intellectual vanity were now staked on his own proposal. He had the situation well in hand, he assured the President. And Eisenhower, husbanding his energies for the coming campaign for reelection, too readily receded from his instinctively sound feeling for the middle ground where serious negotiation was possible. By passively "leaving it to Foster," he lost the opportunity.

Dulles moved ahead with undiminished vigor to develop support for his own proposal. Applying considerable pressure on four countries who were heavily dependent on American economic and military aid — Turkey, Iran, Pakistan, and Ethiopia — he persuaded them to cosponsor a slightly amended resolution. In the end, eighteen nations lined up behind the United States position, while four nations — India, Russia, Indonesia and Ceylon — supported the Indian position. By prearrangement with Dulles, New Zealand's Foreign Minister, Thomas MacDonald, proposed that a committee of "assenting nations" call upon Nasser to present and discuss the eighteen-nation proposal, and the motion carried. Dulles wanted the committee to conduct genuine negotiations with Nasser, but Lloyd and Pineau adamantly insisted that the proposal must be presented on a take-it-or-leave-it basis. Soviet Foreign Minister Dmitri Shepilov protested, accurately, that this would be an "ultimatum" to Nasser.

Eden then made a major effort, directly and through Assistant Secretary Carl McCardle, to persuade Dulles that he was "the only one, the only man, who is capable of handling the matter in Cairo." [32] But Dulles, protesting he was too busy, insisted on returning to Washington. Here, again, an opportunity may have been lost. Eden's purpose in recruiting Dulles was no doubt to bind the United States more tightly to the enterprise wherever it led, yet if Dulles had gone to Cairo it is more than likely that a genuine negotiation would have ensued, moving the issues at least closer to settlement. But such a course would have meant placing the United States in the role of apparent spokesman for colonial-imperial interests, and it also carried with it a high risk of failure. Although he had invented, presented, argued for, and dragooned others into accepting what became the majority proposal, Dulles now wished to slip away from further responsibility. Caught between distasteful choices, his tactical sense prevailed. He cabled Eisenhower, saying, "I think it is preferable that we should become less conspicuous." [33] and returned home after agreeing that Menzies should lead the mission to Cairo.

The Menzies Mission

Sending Menzies was to guarantee failure, and failure was what Eden and Guy Mollet, the new French Premier, wanted. On a take-it-or-leave-it basis, the eighteen-nation proposal was doomed to rejection by Cairo irrespective of who made the presentation, for its unspoken premises were Egyptian technical incompetence and the unreliability of Nasser. Still, Menzies appears to have made the worst of a bad situation. Rugged, florid, with white hair and heavy jowls, the Australian Prime Minister was, at sixty-one, a man of blunt charm, ingrained prejudices, and hardly any feeling for the raw sensitivities of Asian and African nationalists. The Egyptian press thought him "blunt, hostile, and arrogant . . . a bull in a china shop." [34] After putting the proposal and engaging in several days of talk that showed no hope of agreement, he plainly warned Nasser of the seriousness of the Anglo-French military preparations. "Frankness as between two Heads of Government requires me to offer my personal opinion that you are facing not a bluff but a stark condition of fact which your country should not ignore." [35] As Heikal recalled the incident: "Menzies leaned forward over the desk, his thick eyebrows bristling, and growled: 'Mr. President, your refusal of an international administration will be the beginning of trouble.' " In response, Nasser closed the papers in front of him and said: " 'You are threatening me. Very well, I am finished. There will be no more discussions. It is all over.' " Menzies grew very red. Then the Ethiopian Foreign Minister and the American representative, Loy Henderson, intervened to smooth it out.[36]

At a press conference on August 31, President Eisenhower was asked if French military movements into Cyprus were consistent with the working out of a Suez settlement in a calm and deliberate atmosphere. His reply was that he was "not going to comment on the actions of any other government." But when pressed to say whether or not he had given any orders to American military forces as a result of the Canal nationalization, he replied he had done "nothing that isn't absolutely consistent" with his hopes for a peaceful settlement. Pausing, he then added: "We are committed to a peaceful settlement of this dispute, nothing else." [37] Menzies later claimed this statement had undermined his mission by so emphasizing United States commitment to a peaceful solution that Nasser felt safe in rejecting the eighteen-nation plan. But the Eisenhower remark, which Menzies appeared to confuse with a somewhat later one, provided no comfort to Egypt. On September 12, three days after Menzies had departed, Nasser told Ambassador Byroade he was sure that "the British and French are going to stay out there in the Mediterranean until they find a pretext to come in." [38] Anwar Sadat, a junta colleague who succeeded to the Egyptian presidency after Nasser's death, wrote a newspaper article on September 8 which said: "It has now become quite clear that Eden wants nothing but war. . . . He has no other course open to him than either to declare war or resign." [39]

Thrust and Parry

Anticipating failure of the Cairo talks, London and Paris pressed forward in early September with a three-part plan to bring matters to a head. One was to assure that their planned military assault on Alexandria (Operation Musketeer) would be ready to embark from Cyprus and Malta by September 15; a second was to order the European canal pilots off the job at about the same time, thereby disrupting ship traffic and creating the legal pretext for intervention; the third was to "go through the UN hoop." Both London and Paris understood that taking the issue to the United Nations was a gesture necessary to satisfy the amenities of international discourse before resorting to force. If the tactic was cynical, it was not insincere. They proposed to put forward a resolution embodying the eighteen-nation proposal that Menzies was at that moment presenting in Cairo. If, as seemed certain, the Soviets should veto it, or if, as seemed equally certain, attempts to amend it unfavorably should call forth their own veto, they would have exhausted the possibilities of international adjudication and freed themselves to act. The snarling of Canal traffic resulting from the departure of the European pilots would reinforce their case. They would knock out the Egyptian air force, land armed forces, and take possession of the Canal. Nasser would fall from power and the "international authority" scheme would be accepted by his successor.

Dulles, perceiving where this effort was leading, found himself in the curious position of opposing a move by his allies to obtain redress of their grievances through the United Nations — a position doubly awkward for a principal architect and champion not only of this permanent agency for international justice but also of the specific proposals on which the Anglo-French now chose to rest their case. Yet suddenly he was telling Eden and Mollet that the Security Council was like quicksand: "Once in it, we would not know how deep it would prove, or whether we would ever get out." [40] Eden sent him the draft resolution, which added nothing substantive or rhetorical to the Big Three communiqué of August 6 and the eighteen-nation proposal of August 23, but Dulles managed to find, as Macmillan complained, "every possible objection to almost every clause," [41] and refused to give assurance that the United States would reject any resolution falling short of the eighteen-nation formula, or would support allied "freedom of action" in the event the Anglo-French resolution was defeated.

While Eden and Mollet listened to these Dullesian reservations, they also moved their plans ahead, the British cabinet deciding to recall Parliament from summer recess for a meeting on September 12, at which time Eden could draw conclusions from the Cairo talks, announce his appeal to the United Nations, and make a veiled disclosure of contingent military plans. Eisenhower, poised for the electoral campaign which would officially get under way after Labor Day, was leaving the initiative and operational control in foreign policy almost entirely to Dulles. Thus left largely alone to face a concerted resurgence of Anglo-French determination to resolve the Suez crisis by force, the Secretary of State retreated to his cabin on Duck Island in Lake Ontario for the long Labor Day weekend, there to try to identify and develop a scheme that would both frustrate the Eden-Mollet intention to use the United Nations as a means of securing freedom of action for a military attack, and prevent their using a pilot shortage as a pretext. He set himself an immense task, but he tackled it with characteristic self-confidence and in characteristic solitude.

The SCUA Scheme

From his ruminations, as he chopped wood and washed dishes beside the lake in company with his wife, came forth what was to be known as the Suez Canal Users Association (SCUA), a scheme whereunder the users would band together, employ their own pilots, and transit the Canal according to their own needs; they would pay tolls to the SCUA and would pass on to Egypt what they considered a fair share. These "fresh thoughts," as Eden's memoirs characterized this new Dullesian ingenuity, were given to the British ambassador on September 4, who passed them to London. As well he might, Eden asked: "Is he serious?" Makins answered in the affirmative.[42] Opinions differ as to whether Dulles really believed this scheme could be made to work. But those who doubt it tend to miss the central fact that Dulles's modus operandi was essentially tactical. He was a man who went from the specific to the specific, without any enduring ideas to offer, and he was so susceptible to immersion in the twists and turns of his tactical ingenuity that he chronically lost his sense of proportion and not infrequently his sense of reality. The urgent tactical problem before him was to gain time.

At any rate, during the next six days he argued the case for SCUA, face-to-face and in the cable traffic, with remarkable zeal, ingeniously tailoring his approach to suit the prejudices and predilections of each individual who had to be persuaded. Thus, he presented SCUA to Eisenhower as a rather moderate measure, a device requiring Nasser to bargain because he could not oppose its operation unless he himself initiated force; and after all, SCUA would not take over the Canal, he told the President; its ships would merely pass through it.[43] To Eden he said the 1888 Convention gave Egypt no right to make a profit from the Canal; accordingly SCUA would legitimately deprive Nasser of Canal revenues without violating the treaty.[44] To the French ambassador he seemed to give assurances that the United States would do whatever was required to assert the full authority of the SCUA; at a minimum it would support economic sanctions if Nasser refused passage; and such economic deprivations were "certain to make Nasser a laughingstock throughout the world." [45]

In plain truth, as any casual observer could confirm, SCUA possessed a transparently grotesque, unreal quality. First, it repudiated the whole basis of the eighteen-nation proposal (which postulated the need for a new agreement with Nasser) by assuming that no new agreement was necessary. Second, it embodied the staggering presumption that somehow the problem could be handled on a purely technical level, bypassing the political questions of sovereignty and jurisdiction. As Dulles said a few days later at a press conference: "If we get operating problems out of the hands of diplomats, the statesmen, and get it down perhaps into a situation where practical ship operators are dealing with practical people on the part of Egypt, maybe some of these problems will be solvable." [46] Nasser quickly replied to this piece of nonsense by saying, "It is impossible to have two bodies to regulate navigation through the Canal"; and by way of example he suggested a "Port of London Users Association" which would operate at will in that harbor and pay the British what it thought was a fair share of the port charges.[47]

To Mollet and Pineau, the SCUA scheme was immediately seen as a device to postpone or prevent a showdown with Nasser. Selwyn Lloyd was also full of misgivings and Macmillan began to be "disillusioned as to Dulles's intellectual integrity over this whole affair." [48] Eden, however, was willing to listen. It seemed to him that so ardent an advocacy must mean Dulles and Eisenhower were seriously concerned and hence could not fail to support their own proposal. He was attracted by the element in the plan that called for paying Canal tolls to SCUA (and thus withholding them from Nasser). British and French pressure on various shippers had already cut Egypt's Canal tolls by more than 50 percent. If the United States fully cooperated, Nasser's revenues would

be reduced by another 35 percent! Moreover, Eden was certain that
SCUA would involve for Nasser a more serious affront to Egyptian
sovereignty and dignity than even the earlier proposal. As Nasser could
not acquiesce, SCUA was thus an opportunity to bind the United States
to a policy of severe economic pressure at the minimum, and possibly
to the acceptance of a military solution. Moreover, it was now becoming
apparent that ordering the European pilots off the job would not disrupt
Canal traffic, for the Egyptians were ready and able to run the show;
thus a different pretext was needed. After some further cable exchanges
on September 10 and 11 (in which Dulles adverted to the lawyer's dictum
that Egypt, having refused the eighteen-nation proposal, "could not
expect such good terms again"), Eden agreed to give SCUA a try, and
then insisted to the skeptical French that the scheme could be put to
Anglo-French purposes. Because a French military effort at Suez was
dependent upon British logistical support, they could only acquiesce.

The decision was to prove another humiliation for the tense and ail-
ing Prime Minister, not alone because he agreed to accept a tinsel-
thin plan, but because he agreed to sponsor it — which committed him,
but left Dulles in a more flexible position. Eden's press secretary loyally asserted to reporters that the plan was of British origin, but he
permitted himself the uneasy indiscretion that it had a "foster father." [49]
The thrust of the two-day debate in Parliament was accordingly altered: appeal to the UN would be deferred. Describing the SCUA plan
to the Commons on September 12, Eden acknowledged that "the attitude of the Egyptian Government will have an important bearing
on the capacity of the association to fulfill its functions." [50] From the
opposition benches rose up a roar of derisive, incredulous laughter, in
which even a number of Tories joined. But when the Prime Minister
went on to assert that, if Nasser should interfere with the operations
of the association, then Egypt would be in violation of the 1888 Convention, he was met with cries of "Deliberate provocation!" "What a
peacemaker!" "Resign!" Shouting above the tumult, Eden insisted that
what he was saying reflected "exchanges of views between three governments" and that, in the event of Egyptian interference, "Her Majesty's Government and others concerned will be free to take such further
steps as seem to be required." [51]

Eisenhower's concern at the increasingly emotional tone of Eden's
cables had led him to write the Prime Minister on September 2 saying,
"I must tell you frankly that American public opinion flatly rejects
the thought of using force," and urging British acceptance of SCUA.[52]
Now closely following the September 12 debate from Washington, Dulles quickly caught the drift of Eden's presentation and moved to make
certain his own position was publicly aligned with the President's.

He held an immediate press conference and coldly disassociated the United States from every implication of the SCUA plan that made it palatable to Eden. As Macmillan wrote bitterly, "Dulles, who had made the *statement* on SCUA quite correctly, and strictly in accordance with the agreed terms, fell down (as usual) on 'supplementary questions.' He said that, if opposed, American ships would *not* repeat *not* 'shoot' their way through the Canal. No. They would go round the Cape." [53] To Eden and the Tory inner circle, this refusal to leave even a shred of ambiguity regarding the use of force came as the harshest shock; it cut the last remaining strands of trust and engendered an enduring bitterness. And adding insult to injury, the timing of the Dulles press conference permitted Hugh Gaitskell, leader of the Labour opposition, to hurl the American Secretary of State's words across the well of the House of Commons as Eden prepared to wind up the debate. "Is he prepared to say on behalf of Her Majesty's Government," challenged Gaitskell, "that they will not shoot their way through the Canal?" [54] Amid rising tumult, Eden attempted a circuitous evasion, citing the unexceptionable dictum that no government could categorically deprive itself, in advance, of recourse to force. But, goaded, he added that "it would certainly be our intention . . . to refer a matter of that kind to the Security Council." [55]

The episode made for Dulles a prominent and permanent place in the British pantheon of devils. Eden, with elegant circumlocution, later called him a liar, writing in his memoirs that his difficulty in working with the Secretary of State "was to determine what he really meant and in consequence the significance to be attached to his words and actions." [56] Macmillan said: "It is only fair to the Ambassador, Winthrop Aldrich, to record that he was persistent in his warnings — he knew Dulles well." [57] Alastair Buchan, who acknowledged that Dulles's "skill with words enabled him to make rings around cleverer men than the British Foreign Secretary,* and gave him a complete dominance over his nominal master," considered Dulles "one of the most unattractive figures in modern history." [58] Even to more detached observers, the Dulles performance was dishonorable: he insisted on playing the leading role in formulating the "international authority" and SCUA plans, and he ardently advocated their adoption by his allies; the readiness of those allies to accept and pursue the proposals rested heavily on the supposition that the United States was a serious party at interest; moreover, by any objective reckoning, neither plan was realizable without concerted Western pressure and probably not without resort to force. Yet Dulles showed no hesitancy in backing away

* The reference here is to Eden rather than Macmillan or Lloyd.

from all such implications after his allies, at his urging, were publicly committed. He insisted, in short, on total control, but very limited responsibility. The result, as one careful British observer put it, was a performance marked by "a chilling dishonesty which has done permanent damage to his own reputation." [59]

At bottom the trouble seemed to lie in the Secretary of State's innate inability or refusal to build constructively upon Eisenhower's categorical opposition to the use of force. For the statesmanlike task of developing a genuine diplomatic solution (the elements of which became progressively clear), he assumed no responsibility. In part this was instinctive recoil from the knowledge that such a solution would have required collaboration with Russia and India against Britain and France, but it also reflected an enduring discrepancy in outlook between him and the President. He clung to the need for some abstract form of "justice" for Britain and France, and did not entirely rule out the legitimacy of force "in the last resort." As Allen Dulles, who was quite touchy and defensive about his brother's Suez performance, said much later to his CIA colleague, Richard Bissell: "Don't you realize that the individual who was really furious with the British and French and absolutely insistent on the action we took was Eisenhower not Foster?" Left alone, "Foster probably would have played this quite differently." [60] At the deepest level, however, there seemed a basic limitation of the man and his métier. For neither in this crisis (nor in others) did Dulles ever demonstrate the statesman's measure of disinterest, empathy and concern for the whole which are the supreme prerequisites of creative diplomacy. Only as these qualities are brought to bear can a higher harmony be fashioned from disparate and conflicting national interests. In the Suez crisis he never rose above the role of lawyer to the President engaged in an adversary proceeding with suspect allies; his tactical maneuvers were designed merely to keep them off balance, postpone a showdown, and thus buy time for Eisenhower's reelection.

The Second London Conference

Despite this massive display of ineptitude and disjunction, Dulles and Eden managed to reassemble the eighteen supporters of the earlier proposal for a second conference in London on September 19. But it was touch and go, for the other parties were bitterly affronted by the total absence of consultation on the SCUA proposals and by the implications of the proposals themselves. Without last-minute assurance from Dulles that SCUA was a purely voluntary undertaking imposing no obligations upon its members, there would have been no second conference. To most of these middle powers, SCUA appeared as either a plan for boycotting the Canal or as a pretext for a showdown leading to the use of force. And they disliked both, being opposed to the economic consequences of the one and the political-strategic consequences of the other. The estimated cost of a boycott was an extra $500 million a year for Western Europe, but Secretary Humphrey was opposed to any loans, except for oil imports from the United States. Moreover, Nasser had made clear on September 16 (three days in advance of the conference) his flat opposition to SCUA: "We shall not allow the Western-proposed Canal Users' Association to function through the Canal. We Egyptians shall run the Canal smoothly and efficiently"; if the Western powers attempted to force their way through, "then it would mean aggression and would be treated as such." [61] In answer to a question as to the role being played by Washington, he said, "Really, the United States is a puzzle to me. I am not able to follow it." [62]

The conference itself came close to being a personal disaster for Dulles, for the Anglo-French could see no merit in SCUA unless it led to force, while the other participants were now openly opposed both to force and to Dulles's apparently preferred course of economic boycott. Moreover, the conference debate cruelly exposed the hastily contrived and ramshackle illogic of the SCUA plan itself. There were three agenda items: (1) Menzies' report on his Cairo mission; (2) Nasser's proposal for a universal conference on Canal guarantees; and (3) the SCUA plan. The second item was contemptuously dismissed by the Western Big Three as "too imprecise to afford a useful basis for discussion," Dulles admitting as the conference closed that "we have not really ever discussed it." [63]

In a sharp speech, the Italian Foreign Minister, Gaetano Martino, challenged the right of SCUA to employ its own pilots, arguing that this would be a violation of the clear precedent in international law that the pilot is held responsible for the canal as well as the ship. From this it followed, he said, that ships seeking passage must accept pilots provided by the canal administration. He was supported in this contention by the Netherlands, Denmark, and Norway. Pakistan then urged that negotiations with Nasser be the sole purpose of SCUA, adding that, if SCUA were rejected by Nasser, the matter should be referred to the United Nations Security Council.[64] This latter was an unwelcome interjection to which Dulles responded the next day — a grim note of warning was sent to the Pakistani delegate stating that "it would be difficult for my Government to understand" Pakistan's rejection of SCUA, and asking if Pakistan (which was heavily dependent on American economic and military aid) ought not to weigh carefully the "pros and cons of precipitate negative action." [65] The Japanese delegate, who spoke next, raised a series of penetrating questions that rather pitilessly exposed the gossamer underpinnings of SCUA.

When Dulles rose to speak after the noon recess on September 21 (the last day of the conference), it was plain that the whole undertaking was in a state of intellectual shambles and on the verge of collapse. Control of events now visibly slipping from his hands, his own prestige at stake, he was faced with the necessity to restore some semblance of credibility to his brainchild, or else incur further damage to his reputation. His answers to the Japanese questions were not very effective. Would Egypt's cooperation be required for the operation of SCUA? Well, "de facto operating cooperation at the local level" would be required. So, contrary to what he had originally told Eden, some new agreement with Nasser was in fact needed. What if Egyptian law required that the Canal be operated exclusively with Egyptian pilots? Well, then, SCUA pilots would not have much to do "and that part of the plan would have collapsed." But the use of SCUA pilots was the very heart of the plan, for use of Egyptian pilots would mean Egyptian operation and control of the Canal. Would SCUA members be forbidden to use Egyptian pilots? Well, the United States "has no authority to enforce such a prohibition on its own shipowners, and no doubt other nations are in a similar position." The SCUA scheme, though it may have looked like a brilliant invention at Duck Island, was exposed as a strangely unreal and unworkable contrivance.[66]

His manner now reflecting resentment, worry, even a touch of panic, Dulles tried desperately to find and reflect a common denominator that would suffice to keep the eighteen nations from flying apart, that would hold them together in some semblance of concerted purpose — even in total inactivity if necessary. If there was a discernible majority view at the conference, it was that the Canal dispute should be taken to the United Nations without further delay. But by the richest irony, the Secretary of State who conceived peace and world order in Wilsonian terms was now opposed to such a course on tactical grounds: Security Council debate on a resolution unacceptable to Britain and France would lead to use of the veto power by those two nations. Such action would weaken the Charter which was passionately close to Dulles's heart. Worse still, it would fill American newspapers with accounts of the rift in the Western Alliance in the midst of a presidential campaign, one of whose prominent issues was the administration's handling of foreign policy. It would compel the United States to take a clear public position on the question of force; if that position was against force, but force was subsequently used, this fact could gravely embarrass Eisenhower's campaign, whatever the outcome of the conflict.

Casting about in this welter of contradictions for a common denominator that would pass muster at least temporarily, Dulles found and developed, in the course of his postluncheon remarks, the theme of moral immobilism. It was a formula that placed him morally behind the Anglo-French in their quest for "justice," yet sought simultaneously to prevent their taking any active steps to achieve it — whether by UN debate, economic sanction, or military force. On the one hand, he argued that a merely peaceful solution was not enough, that the nations present would be derelict in their moral duty to civilization and the United Nations Charter unless the solution were also just: "There has been exercised, and is being exercised, a great restraint in the face of a great peril. But you cannot expect that to go on indefinitely unless those of us who appreciate the problem, who are sympathetic with it, rally our forces to try to bring about a settlement which is not only a peaceful settlement but a settlement in conformity with the principles of justice and international law.' " To seek a solution merely devoid of war was to address "only half of the problem, and you cannot solve the problem just by half-way measures. . . . So I say, let's stick together in this proposition [SCUA] and continue to work not only for 'peace,' but for peace 'in conformity with the principles of justice and international law!' " [67]

But where did justice lie? Egypt was demonstrating its ability to run the Canal, and stood ready to convene a universal conference of users to work out guarantees of access, agreement on tolls, and related matters. Most of the nations at the conference were prepared to accept this situation and to work out a technical solution within the context of Egyptian control, believing that Nasser had a large political stake in making the Canal both an operational and a financial success. This was the essence of Eisenhower's repeatedly stated position; it had also seemed to be Dulles's position during his several rambling press conference appeals for practical, technical cooperation with the Egyptians at the working level. Yet Dulles had never in fact relinquished the contrary principle of user control — that is, political-operational control of the Canal by the user nations. It was imbedded in both the "international authority" and SCUA schemes, and it now remained integral to his conception of "justice." Thus did inner contradictions and irreconcilable purposes combine to paint him into a corner. A negotiable modus vivendi accepting Egyptian control was available, but he insisted that morally the situation demanded something more. This extra something was not negotiable; nevertheless, he insisted it could not be pursued either by economic sanction or by force. His position came to intellectual stultification. As he spoke, an intent hush descended upon his listeners, for the elderly Secretary was obviously struggling for coherence; he was close to tears, his glasses moist, his eyes blinking involuntarily, his voice choked with nervous tension.[68]

A less complex, less clever, more straightforward man would not have drifted into this untenable impasse. But Dulles had chosen to play a game that insisted at once on leading and frustrating the Anglo-French, while never deciding clearly what kind of solution, *within the realm of reality,* he wanted or was willing to put his country's weight behind. His "international authority" plan was a plausible basis for negotiation, but he proved unwilling (1) to pursue the Eisenhower-Indian proposal to transform it from an operating to an advisory authority, or (2) to accept any responsibility for talks with Nasser. The SCUA scheme was a logical monstrosity, but Dulles made it worse by refusing to support it even as an instrument of economic boycott. If his proposals were seriously advanced, that fact reflects badly on his judgment; if they were put forward primarily as a tactical means of holding off an explosion until Eisenhower was safely reelected, that fact indicates that his statecraft was capable of marked deception and cynicism. The chief mitigating factor in this harsh assessment — and it is a large one — is that the Anglo-French were never interested in a compromise settlement of the canal dispute, but were determined, for the sake of broader purposes, to bring Nasser down. Yet up to September 21, they had found no adequate pretext for war, and world opinion was gathering steadily behind the idea of a peaceful compromise. A strong American move for negotiations with Nasser might well have succeeded, but Dulles was not prepared to make it.

23

The Alliance in Peril

THE SCUA CONFERENCE COST Dulles his remaining credibility with the Anglo-French. They would be put off with empty gestures no longer. Although he had conversed at length with Eden in the late afternoon of September 21, just before emplaning for home, and had appealed to Eden (with what he took to be success) to keep the Suez matter out of the United Nations for the time being, Undersecretary Hoover met him at the Washington airport at 3:00 P.M. the following day with word that the Anglo-French were going at once to the United Nations. Dulles was visibly angered by this news. A few days later, Macmillan, who was in the United States on treasury business and saw Dulles alone, received a further outburst of the Secretary's indignation at the move to the UN: "He really felt that he had been badly treated. . . . We should get nothing but trouble in New York; we were courting disaster. (From the way Dulles spoke you would have thought he was warning us against entering a bawdy-house.)" [1] On Sunday, September 23, however, appearing on "Meet the Press," he maintained the curious double position that so tantalized his allies and confounded the middle powers, denying flatly that the United States had given tacit consent to the Anglo-French use of force if the United Nations failed to provide a solution, but repeating the line that peace and justice were two sides of the same coin. He wanted, he said, a solution that recognized "the real rights of the users." [2] But as fifteen nations gathered once more in London to go through the futile exercise of actually establishing the now thoroughly emasculated Suez Canal Users Association, he seemed to move closer to the President's unequivocal position. Answering a press conference question, he said: "There is talk about the 'teeth' being pulled out of it. There were never 'teeth' in it, if that means the use of force." [3]

UN Negotiations

By the time the Anglo-French resolution came up for UN debate in early October, Dulles had managed to delete its reference to a requirement for "international control," and had successfully insisted that the initial meetings should be private; he thought this would permit a freer exchange of views (it would also minimize publicity in the United States as the presidential campaign entered its climactic month).

Nasser continued to act with reason and restraint, instructing his Foreign Minister, Fawzi, to accept an international advisory board, even one organized by SCUA. During the private talks, Lloyd dictated "Six Principles" that should govern a Suez settlement, and Fawzi surprisingly expressed Egypt's agreement. When the UN Secretary-General, Dag Hammarskjöld, promptly made these public and secured their formal adoption by the Security Council on October 13, it seemed suddenly that the whole crisis had been brought to the edge of resolution. Fawzi reported to Cairo Hammarskjöld's judgment that "Selwyn Lloyd genuinely wanted an agreement but that Pineau did not"; [4] unfortunately, it also appeared to the Secretary-General that, while Lloyd was "nice, sentimental, easily agitated, and without influence," the "arrogant" Pineau was under orders not to reach an agreement. [5] Whatever the Anglo-French discrepancies in New York, Eden and Mollet were fully agreed that the situation had drifted uncomfortably close to a settlement, and one, moreover, that Nasser would survive! In an obvious attempt to present him with another unacceptable proposition, they thereupon introduced a rider to the principles requiring that Egypt "promptly" submit detailed implementing proposals, in advance of any further negotiations. But Russia and Yugoslavia vetoed this, and the "Six Principles" were left standing as the basis for negotiation.

This last development produced a brief period of euphoria in Washington that served both to delay the administration's realization that Anglo-French policy had gone underground, and to sharpen the shock of realization when it came. Dulles expressed to his staff the confident view that his delaying tactics had caused the Suez crisis to "wither on the vine," and Eisenhower confided his gratification to a television interviewer that "a very great crisis is behind us." [6] However, when Hammarskjöld urged further private negotiations to begin on October 29 in Geneva, Egypt agreed, but France and Britain backed sharply off.

War Preparations and Collusion

Meanwhile, the British and the French, jointly and separately, were advancing their plans for war, and the fateful collusion with Israel was also moving forward. Eden and Lloyd flew to Paris on September 26 for talks with Mollet and Pineau, whom they found in high spirits and "a very belligerent mood." [7] While the French leaders declined to disclose their developing arrangements with Israel, they were now so certain that Israel would provide a pretext for war against Nasser that they were willing to drop their objections to the United Nations debate. Unknown to the British, the French had decided to join Israel in attacking Nasser even without British participation. [8]

General Dayan, now the Israeli chief of staff, and an official party, including Golda Meir, were in Paris on September 29 with a final list of military equipment requirements — including 100 tanks, 300 half-track vehicles, 1,000 bazooka rocket launchers, and a squadron of transport planes. Back in Tel Aviv on October 2, Dayan issued the basic "early alert" order for the conquest of Sinai, setting October 20 as the tentative date for attack.

Although actual mobilization was postponed until the last possible moment, Israel began in early October to cultivate a crisis with Jordan as a cover for preparations against Nasser. As the British had as yet no clear view of French-Israeli plans, these actions very nearly led to a British-Israeli clash. Following a heavy Israeli raid on the Jordanian town of Qualqilya on October 10, King Hussein asked the British Middle East commander to honor the Anglo-Jordanian alliance, and squadrons of the RAF were very nearly sent into action against the Israeli air force. When London rescinded the order, a disillusioned Hussein sent his Foreign Minister to Cairo to ask for immediate assistance. Eden (who five days before had collapsed and lost consciousness in an elevator, with a fever fit so severe his aides thought he was going to die) was now stung by King Hussein's evident lack of confidence in the British government. He hastily cabled Nuri to send an Iraqi brigade. Israel then publicly warned that such an act would be "a direct threat to the security of Israel." Temporarily balked, Eden, who felt it was imperative to provide some measure of assistance for Hussein, now proposed that Nuri hold the troops in northeast Jordan far from the Israeli border, and that the force be reduced from a brigade to a regiment, but Israel refused to be mollified. Anthony Nutting advised Eden to stand firm behind Jordan even at the risk of war with Israel. [9]

With the fat nearly in the fire, Mollet hastily intervened with Eden to explain why an Anglo-Israeli clash would be fatal to the larger scheme, and the order to Iraq was rescinded. Dayan commented on this confusion of affairs in his diary entry of October 21: "I must confess to the feeling that, save for the Almighty, only the British are capable of complicating affairs to such a degree." [10]

At the eleventh hour, then, October 13, Mollet had sent emissaries to Eden to explain the urgent need to prevent the sending of Iraqi troops to Jordan, and to enlist the British in full-scale collusion against Nasser. Eden received them in his study at Chequers some thirty miles outside of London, accompanied only by Nutting and his private secretary. The French emissaries were Albert Gazier, minister of labor, and General Maurice Challe of the French air force. After dealing with the Iraqi matter, Challe outlined the basic plan. Israel would attack Egypt in the Sinai; Britain and France would then call upon both sides to withdraw from the Canal area, would land forces to "separate the combatants," and would occupy the Canal on the pretext of preventing damage to it. Challe did not say that Israel had definitely agreed to the plan, but made it clear that the plan proceeded from French-Israeli talks at the highest levels. Eden, who listened with mounting excitement, promised to send Nutting to Paris with a definitive British answer within two days.[11] He then telephoned Lloyd at the UN and instructed him to fly home immediately. But instead of sending the disillusioned Nutting, Eden went himself to Paris on October 16, accompanied by Selwyn Lloyd. There at a secret five-hour meeting with Mollet and Pineau, at which no notes were taken, the British leaders endorsed the French plan without reservation.[12] On October 18, Eden reported his discussions to the British cabinet, including, according to his less than candid memoirs, "the growing danger that Israel, under provocation from Egypt, would make some military move." [13] On October 19, the Anglo-French invasion commanders were told to prepare for action within ten days.

Eden's one-time protegé, Nutting, was appalled by the immorality of the war plan, by its violation of the United Nations Charter, and by the disastrous pitfalls in it for British interest in the Arab world. He foresaw accurately that it would not only provoke a widespread anti-Western reaction among the Arabs, ruinous to British interests and destructive of pro-Western Arab leaders like Nuri, but would also divide the Commonwealth, alienate the United States, and seriously disrupt European oil supplies. But Eden was beyond persuasion, and Nutting was pushed aside. Ben-Gurion and the Israeli military staff, however, saw these same British difficulties and therefore harbored dark suspicions that Eden would not, in the crunch, follow through on his promises. Ben-Gurion accordingly demanded the British commitment in writing.

Acting again as intermediary, the French arranged a deeply secret meeting in an undistinguished suburban villa at Sèvres (midway on the road from Paris to Versailles) to which Ben-Gurion, Dayan and Peres descended by plane through darkness and heavy fog on the night of October 22. When talks began the next morning, Ben-Gurion insisted to Selwyn Lloyd that British bombers must begin their attacks on the Egyptian air force *simultaneously* with the start of the Israeli ground attack; otherwise, he said, Israel's cities would be open to destruction from the air and the risk would be too high. But Anglo-French intervention was planned as a "police action," to "separate the combatants" in an ongoing battle; to maintain such a pretense required a certain interval of hostilities before the Anglo-French ultimatums could be issued, be rejected, and run their course. The British were angered at Ben-Gurion's persisting lack of faith, but after a further intercession by Pineau (who flew to London), Eden promised a written commitment to destroy the Egyptian air force if Israel would launch an attack in the direction of the Canal. As this did not fully meet Ben-Gurion's requirement for simultaneity, the French, who were far less concerned about secrecy than Eden, finally closed the gap by agreeing to deploy three French fighter squadrons to Israel, prior to hostilities. It is probable that Ben-Gurion exaggerated the air threat, for a basic element of the Israeli plan was a paratroop drop deep into the Sinai, only twenty miles from the Canal, and deliberately designed to confuse the Egyptians into thinking the operation was a reprisal raid, rather than part of a sustained invasion. Dayan doubted that Nasser's reaction would be a "rush to bomb civilian targets in Israel." [14]

The final accord at Sèvres was reached on October 24, a document in three copies. Israel would initiate action at dusk on October 29 with a para-drop at Mitla Pass to create the appearance of an immediate threat to the Canal. When the Anglo-French learned of this "threat," they would issue ultimatums on the afternoon of October 30 with a twelve-hour deadline. The ultimatums (predrafted at Sèvres) called for "temporary occupation" of the Canal Zone whether or not the combatants accepted a cease-fire. The Anglo-French force would accordingly attack Port Said at the mouth of the Canal and move down its length to cut off the Egyptian army's retreat from the Sinai. That army would then be trapped and destroyed between the Israeli and the Anglo-French forces. Israel agreed to stop ten miles east of the Canal, and Britain agreed to help Israel win an advantageous peace.[15] The British cabinet gave its final approval on October 25. Except for Sir Walter Monckton, who resigned as defense minister on October 11, deciding he could not accept responsibility for the coming war, but who agreed to remain in the cabinet as paymaster general for the sake of appearances, the cabinet stayed remarkably firm. Several other ministers suffered misgivings, but remembered the mood of imperial Götterdämmerung immediately after nationalization. Anthony Nutting, who was not a member of the cabinet, had told his superior, Selwyn Lloyd, that he would have to resign if "this sordid conspiracy" were carried through; [16] and he did so.

Eden, alone among the colluders, remained insistent on maintaining every aspect of the circumstantial pretexts for a "police action," and it was this rigidity that robbed the enterprise of whatever chances it may have had for political and military success. The central political requirement was for a swift military fait accompli. But Eden's determination to fight in the guise of a peacemaker meant he would not permit the ships at Malta to begin combat-loading until the *expiration* of the ultimatums. This, however, condemned the operation to an incredible ten-day lag (four days to load the ships and six days to sail the convoy to Egypt), an interval which was to be filled with air bombardment by the RAF. Only the French commander seems to have sensed the truth that world opinion would not tolerate ten days of bombing, but would act to halt the invasion. He was able to persuade his British military superior to grasp the nettle and begin loading the ships on October 27 (four days early) under the pretense of preparing for a previously scheduled training exercise. This reduced the lag to six days, but it was not enough.

The Hungarian Uprising

The official "clam-up" (as Ambassador Douglas Dillon in Paris dubbed it) of normal British and French communications with their American ally began about October 14, following Eden's meeting with General Challe. It covered all diplomatic and military levels, yet was not immediately noticed. Sir Roger Makins, the retiring British ambassador, had left Washington on October 11, and his successor, Sir Harold Caccia, did not arrive in Washington until November 8, having chosen to make the crossing by sea. The French ambassador, Hervé Alphand, was out of Washington; the Israeli ambassador, Abba Eban, was called to Tel Aviv.

The CIA began overflying the Middle East with U-2 aircraft at about the same time, and thus picked up a heavy increase in modern French fighter planes (Mystère IV) on Israeli airfields and also the beginnings of Israeli mobilization. But, as Israel had hoped, Eisenhower and Dulles drew the wrong conclusion. Surmising that Ben-Gurion's "obviously aggressive attitude" was aimed at Jordan and at action during the sensitive period of the American election, the President instructed Dulles to send the Israeli Prime Minister a blunt and personal warning that concern about the Jewish vote would not affect his stern determination to act against any disruption of peace in the Middle East: "Foster, you must not soften this thing and put it in diplomatic language. This has got to be absolutely my words." [17] Ben-Gurion continued, however, to hold the view that no American government would risk the Jewish vote to frustrate Israel in an election year.

By October 25, Dulles was uneasily aware of the deepening silence out of London, Paris, and Tel Aviv. Israel seemed to be mobilizing, and Anglo-French military preparations were evident at Cyprus and Malta. But by this time, his attention was focused on the dramatic unfolding of events in Eastern Europe. On October 19, the Polish government dismissed its Russian defense minister, Marshal Rokossovsky, and brought Wladyslaw Gomulka forward to be premier. Khrushchev flew to Warsaw with a threat to crush the dissidence with Russian military force, but the tough Poles defied him, declaring the whole nation would fight if necessary, and this led to negotiations and a dramatic agreement on a new basis. On October 22, in the wake of Gomulka's success, demonstrations broke out in the Hungarian capital of Budapest demanding the return of a Communist moderate, Imre Nagy. Here the Red Army did intervene with tanks and jet aircraft against rebel barricades, but the action served mainly to intensify the anti-Russian feeling of the populace. On October 24, Nagy was named premier and began to establish a reform government that could negotiate with the Soviets. Dulles followed these developments with fascination, telling his staff they represented a clear vindication of the liberation doctrine, and declaring to the Council on World Affairs in Dallas on October 26 that "the weakness of Soviet imperialism is being made manifest. Its weakness is not military weakness nor lack of material power. It is weak because it seeks to sustain an unnatural tyranny by suppressing human aspirations . . ." [18]

On October 30, the same day the Anglo-French ultimatums were issued, Khrushchev made the momentous offer to negotiate the full withdrawal of Red Army units from Hungary and establish a new basis of Soviet relationships throughout Eastern Europe — i.e., "noninterference in each other's internal affairs." He was working in very delicate circumstances to bring about a more rational, more "liberal" balance in an inherently unequal relationship, seeking to eliminate the most abrasive aspects of Russian domination without giving up what the Kremlin regarded as essential controls. For a breathless interlude, it appeared that a new modus vivendi between master and slave had been achieved. Allen Dulles

called it "a miracle." [19] He was somewhat premature. The more ardent
freedom fighters around Nagy broke (or could not exercise the necessary
discipline to maintain) the cease-fire; moreover, they pressed demands
(especially for Hungary's withdrawal from the Warsaw Pact) that even
Khrushchev was not prepared to accept. Negotiations broke down. The
Red Army reentered Budapest in force on November 4 and bloodily
crushed the rebellion. It was a decision made easier for the Kremlin by
the fact that the action of Israel, Britain and France undermined any
Western claim to higher morality.

The Suez War Begins

With Israeli mobilization now an evident fact, Dulles sent Ambassador
Aldrich to dine with Selwyn Lloyd on October 28, to ask its significance.
Lloyd said the British were in the dark, but had warned Israel not to
attack Jordan. Well, Aldrich asked, was Israel going to attack Egypt?
Lloyd said he had no information at all. Aldrich returned to the Foreign
Office thirty-six hours later at 10:00 A.M. on October 30, the morning
after the Israeli attack in the Sinai. In response to his urgent question as
to what the British now intended to do, Lloyd said that, in his own judgment, Britain would have to charge Israel as an aggressor against Egypt,
but that Mollet and Pineau were at that moment en route from Paris
and the matter had not been decided. He would arrange to see Aldrich
again after lunch. But in the afternoon, Lloyd having been called away
to the House of Commons, Aldrich was received at 4:45 by the permanent
undersecretary, Sir Ivone Kirkpatrick, who simply handed him the ultimatums, saying they were being made public at that moment. The failure
to inform the United States in advance was a calculated affront to Eisenhower and Dulles.[20]

Word of the Sinai invasion reached Eisenhower at about 6:00 P.M. on
October 29 (nearly six hours after it began) when he arrived in his aircraft, *Columbine,* for a campaign speech in Richmond, Virginia. Making
the speech, he hastened to Washington for a meeting at the White House
with Dulles, the intelligence men, and the military chiefs. That same
night he ordered Dulles to let Ben-Gurion have it with both barrels:
"All right, Foster, you tell 'em that, goddamn it, we're going to apply
sanctions, we're going to the United Nations, we're going to do everything that there is so we can stop this thing." [21] He also made an urgent
request for a UN Security Council meeting the following morning, and
issued a public reaffirmation of the Tripartite Declaration. Later that
evening, the U.S. ambassador to the United Nations, Cabot Lodge, was
offended when his British counterpart, Sir Pierson Dixon, told him

that London now regarded the Tripartite Declaration as "ancient history and without current validity," [22] and that Britain would take no action against Israel.

Eisenhower, astonished at Dixon's remark, cabled Eden asking for help "in clearing up my understanding as to exactly what is happening between us and our European allies." [23] Eden's reply was that Nasser's "equivocal attitude" toward the Tripartite Declaration had relieved the Western powers of their obligations thereunder, and that Egypt had brought the war on itself. Eisenhower at once cabled his stern disagreement, stating that the declaration "was a commitment among the three signatories and its validity in that respect was invulnerable to the reservations expressed on several occasions by both Israel and the Arabs." [24] This "transatlantic essay contest," as Eisenhower later described it,[25] was brought to a rude end the next day when news of the Anglo-French ultimatums reached the White House via the wire services, and before Ambassador Aldrich could report officially. Eisenhower was infuriated by both the substance and the insult, and not at all soothed by Eden's soon cabled explanation that he had decided not to "invite" United States association with the "declarations" because of his consideration for Eisenhower's "Constitutional and other difficulties" (i.e., the presidential election).[26]

On the morning of October 30, Lodge introduced an American resolution in the UN Security Council; it demanded that Israel withdraw behind the agreed armistice lines, and called upon other members to refrain from using force or the threat of force in the area, and also to refrain from aid to Israel. In response to this the British and French, who were determined to maintain their freedom to carry out their collusive war plan, vetoed the resolution, this being the first such British action in the history of the United Nations. A softer Russian resolution was then introduced, calling merely for a cease-fire and an immediate Israeli withdrawal; this too was vetoed by Britain and France. Temporarily, at least, the United Nations was paralyzed.

Eisenhower's genuine anger at news of the ultimatums, however, soon took a turn toward amazement and stupefaction as he contemplated the fact that his major allies would so rashly court the real risks of general war without even consulting the keystone member of the alliance. As Macmillan later noted, "the President is wounded and rather mystified." [27] Yet until the British bombing began, which dropped the final veil from Anglo-French intentions, he could not entirely repress an inherent optimism and an expression of faith in the British. Thus at 5:00 P.M. on October 30, he felt hopeful enough to tell Emmet Hughes that he thought the problem "will take care of itself if the Israelis stop fighting, and I'm pretty sure they will, with this ultimatum from the British."

And if not, asked Hughes, would the United States honor its obligation under the Tripartite Declaration by joining Nasser against the Western allies? "Hell, I don't know *where* we'll be at," the President replied.[28]

Nasser's first reaction to the Israeli attack was to believe it was a genuine invasion of the Sinai, but not to believe that Britain would jeopardize her remaining assets in the Arab world by conniving with Israel.[29] With the issuance of the ultimatums, however, he understood there was collusion among his enemies; then when the twelve-hour deadline passed without any overt act by the British or French (London inexplicably delayed the bombing until nightfall in Cairo on October 31, some twelve hours after the expiry of the ultimatums), he thought he was facing an Israeli attack plus an Anglo-French feint designed to prevent him from making a full defense in the Sinai. When bombing began at nightfall, however, Nasser realized an Anglo-French invasion was coming, making it imperative to extricate his army from the Sinai and draw it back into central Egypt.[30] Retreat began that night, and, although mercilessly pounded by Israeli and French air forces, the great bulk of the Egyptian army made good its escape to the Canal by the morning of November 2. Also, as soon as the British bombings began, the Egyptians sank a cement-loaded blockship athwart the Canal, as well as several other large vessels. Thus a total blockage of the waterway was the first result of Eden's action to "save the Canal." The Syrians blew up three pumping stations on the Iraq Petroleum Company line running across Syria to Tripoli, and Egypt began distributing arms and communication sets to the populace in anticipation of guerilla war.

Nothing had been said in the ultimatums about bombing, and it was impossible to square this action, which was directed solely against Egypt, with the declared aim of "separating the combatants." The other transparent discrepancy was the demand in the ultimatums that both combatants should halt 10 miles from the Canal (Israel to the east and Egypt to the west) — for at the moment they were issued, Egyptian forces were resisting the Israeli advance at least 100 miles east of the Canal. The ultimatums thus demanded that one party withdraw 110 miles, while inviting the other to advance 90 miles. The Labour opposition in the British House of Commons quickly smelled a rat, and the war minister's announcement of the bombing produced a pandemonium of such shouting, booing and disorder that debate had to be suspended for thirty minutes.[31]

The Eisenhower Speech

October 30 and 31 were days of tension and harried assessment at the White House. A campaign trip to Texas was cancelled, so that Eisenhower could remain at the center of events. He was distressed by the "complete mess and botch of things" created by Israel and his two major allies, but he did not seem to share his staff's thick and righteous wrath at the temerity of the London government so to complicate the position of the American President near the climax of his electoral campaign. Dulles shared the general anger on this point, but seemed more nettled by the way in which the Anglo-French depredations had prejudiced the West's moral posture with respect to events in Hungary: "It is nothing less than tragic that at this very time, when we are on the point of winning an immense and long-hoped-for victory over Soviet colonialism in Eastern Europe, we should be forced to choose between following in the footsteps of Anglo-French colonialism in Asia and Africa, or splitting our course away from their course." [32]

Sometime on October 30, Sherman Adams and others began to conclude that the President must make a "report to the nation" on the Suez crisis, although no one was clear as to what he should say. Undaunted by a lack of direction, however, a decision was made the following morning to request television time for 7:00 P.M. the same day (October 31), and Adams telephoned Dulles to ask for a speech draft which could be polished by Emmet Hughes and the President. Hughes had prepared a speech for delivery in Philadelphia on November 1 — a statement on the theme that the United States could not subscribe to one law for the weak and another for the strong, that there could be only one law or there would be no peace. It proved adaptable (with major and feverishly applied editorial work) to the new situation, and this was fortunate, for the Dulles text did not arrive at the White House until 3:15 and was then found to be useless. Hughes found Eisenhower "shaking his head sadly over it. . . . It recites and rambles with no force of argument." [33] So at 4:00 P.M. Hughes was forced to start fresh, dictating to two secretaries in relays, building on the Philadelphia speech with a desperate awareness of the seven o'clock deadline.

Dulles, who was called from the State Department to scan the pages as they emerged from the typewriter, seemed to Hughes almost totally exhausted, "ashen gray, heavy-lidded, strained," shaking his head in glazed disbelief at the news, just received, of British bombers over Cairo.[34] He suggested only the most trivial changes in the text while the President, to escape the tension, walked out on the White House lawn and began hitting golf balls from a point just beyond the windows of the cabinet room. At 6:45, dressed and fresh, Eisenhower sat down at his desk while Hughes, sitting opposite, finished underlining the large-type reading copy for "speech emphasis" with a grease pencil, handing it page by page to the waiting President. Receiving the final page at four minutes to seven, Eisenhower grinned and said to Hughes: "Boy, this is taking it right off the stove." [35] The speech, which the President read with calm and strong assurance, came out, Hughes thought, "surprisingly coherent." It was not a sharply anti-British or anti-French speech. Asserting that the United States had been neither consulted nor informed by its allies regarding "these actions . . . taken in error," Eisenhower said it was the nation's intention to maintain its allied partnership.[36] "At the same time it is — and it will remain — the dedicated purpose of your government to do all in its power to localize the fighting and to end the conflict." [37]

Emotional Climax and Physical Collapse

At Eisenhower's urgent request, Dulles went to the United Nations the following afternoon, where debate had now shifted to the General Assembly, to renew the pressure for immediate cessation of hostilities. Eisenhower insisted privately that the British were "still my right arm," but he and Dulles were agreed that there could be no special concessions for their wayward allies. The catalyst of the Anglo-French conspiratorial resort to force had had the effect of fusing (in an emotional sense perhaps even reversing) the positions of the two men. Before the event, the President had flatly and at times heatedly opposed the use of force as a means of settling the Canal dispute, while Dulles obliquely defended its legitimacy in the last resort. Now the President, while still firmly opposed, was more dispassionate, while Dulles took the Anglo-French action as a personal affront, a sinister breach of trust. He went to New York bearing an explosive resentment toward those who had cost him his hard-won control over the situation.

Macmillan, who acknowledged that the British cabinet had made a "profound miscalculation" of Washington's reaction, later wrote, not without prejudice or disproportion or a touch of malice, that "Dulles had all along regarded himself as the legal adviser in the Suez case. He had given much attention to the case and devised one contrivance after another. Now his clients had taken the matter out of his hands and acted on their own. This was an insult, almost a betrayal. Consequently, Dulles showed in the vital period a degree of hostility amounting almost to frenzy. . . . Perhaps the grim disease which was later to prove mortal had affected his psychological and intellectual equilibrium. . . . He clearly lost his temper; he may have also lost his nerve." [38]

To present the President's case against the use of force, it was necessary for Dulles to jettison whatever nuances he still clung to regarding the demands of "justice" for the Anglo-French over and above a merely peaceful solution. But this was easier now that there had been a flagrant transgression of a higher law, for nothing lay closer to Dulles's heart and mind than the sanctity of the United Nations. Thus, he found perfect harmony between his own theme and the President's in a defense of the resonant Wilsonian principle that international justice must be looked for within the structures and processes of the established world organization, that these were mankind's highest expression of decency, mutual accommodation, and law, that nothing justified breaching them for selfish ends. His speech was thus a sermon, an appeal to the ideals of Western Man and an implied demand that these ideals must be met at least by the leading nations of the Western world. No matter, for the moment, that the Soviet Union could not be brought to account for its savagery in Hungary or (on a far less glaring level of disparity) that India could not be forced to accept the United Nations resolution on Kashmir. In the Anglo-French-Israeli case, it was possible to appeal to reason, to exert moral pressure and, if necessary, economic and political sanctions!

Speaking slowly and powerfully from fragmentary notes, he called the military attacks "a grave error"; worse than that, they put in jeopardy the very existence of the United Nations. No doubt the world organization "may have been somewhat laggard, somewhat impotent in dealing with many injustices which are inherent in this Middle Eastern situation," and no doubt we ought to "give our most earnest thought to the problem of how we can do more to establish and implement principles of justice," but "the first thing is to stop the fighting as rapidly as possible lest it become a conflagration which would endanger us all. . . . What has been called a police action may develop into something which is far more grave." Accordingly, a failure to act strongly and promptly against the wrongdoing would condemn the United Nations to an "apparent impotence" that would lead other nations "to take into their own hands the remedying of what they believe to be their injustices." If that should happen, "the future is dark indeed." The United States was accordingly impelled to act against "three nations with whom it has ties, deep friendship, admiration and respect" because our "disagreement" with their actions "involves principles which far transcend the immediate issue." [39]

It was a speech of abstractions, but then much of the world lives by abstractions, and Dulles did so more than most. In retrospect, the Secretary thought it one of his best efforts. As he later told close associates, and especially churchmen, "If that had been my very last act on earth, it would have been exactly as I would have wished it. I would have liked it for my epitaph." [40] After a long and bitter debate, the U.S. resolution (essentially the same as the one vetoed in the Security Council) was adopted at 2:00 A.M. on November 2, by a vote of 65 to 5. Only Australia and New Zealand joined Britain, France and Israel in opposition; there

Recuperating at Key West after his first cancer attack, with Herbert
Hoover, Jr. (November 1956)

were six abstentions: Canada, Portugal, Belgium, the Netherlands, South
Africa, and Laos.

The terrible physical and mental strain of four months was now to
take its toll. It was perhaps 4:00 A.M. when Dulles went to bed in his
suite at the Waldorf, but he was back in Washington by noon and spent
the balance of the day at his desk. After a quiet dinner and some back-
gammon with his wife, he went to bed around ten o'clock. At midnight
on November 2, he was awakened by severe abdominal pains, which by
one o'clock had convinced him he must get to a hospital. In acute discomfort, he summoned his assistant, William Macomber, telling him first
to inform Hagerty, the White House press secretary, so that steps might
be taken to minimize the effect of his own physical setback on the
prominent campaign issue of the President's health. At the hospital, in
a performance which Macomber found an "enormously impressive" example of self-discipline and clinical detachment, he outlined three possibilities: a short illness lasting only a few days; a longer and more serious
disability extending over several weeks; or being "completely taken out."
Choosing to act on the most optimistic assumption, Dulles instructed
Macomber to have Hoover take charge of all policies in the Department,

except Suez. That situation he intended to manage even from the hospital; indeed, Macomber was to establish himself there the following Monday, so that messages and papers could be sent for Dulles's study and decision.[41] But the three-hour operation revealed cancer; it was serious; and Dulles did not return to the State Department until January. Control of Middle East policy passed, during a critical period, to other hands.

On November 17, after the Suez cease-fire was in effect, but during the period of American pressure for British, French and Israeli withdrawal, Selwyn Lloyd and the British ambassador came to pay a visit at Walter Reed Hospital. Dulles, in comfortable trousers, a sweater, and slippers, came slowly forward to meet them, shook hands, and immediately said: "Well, once you started, why didn't you go through with it and get Nasser down?" Lloyd was somewhat startled. Recovering, he said, "Foster, why didn't you give us a wink?" Dulles answered, "Oh! I couldn't do anything like *that!*" [42] Although some have cited this incident as evidence of a nasty sense of humor, there is more reason to regard it as a quite serious remark, revealing the enduring if subtle differences between Eisenhower and Dulles with regard to the ultimate legitimacy of force at Suez and, equally, the impossibility for Dulles to get more than an imperceptible half step out of cadence with the President.

24

Applying Principle

DESPITE DULLES'S RESOLVE to hold the reins on the fast horse of Suez, the cancer operation took him out of service for several weeks. From the morning of November 3, Eisenhower was in firm command of American policy in the Middle East, exerting a wide variety of pressures for a cease-fire and withdrawal, personally coordinating all major events, determined to act on pure principle as he understood it.

Eden Gives Way

Also on November 3, Egypt announced its full compliance with the UN demand for a cease-fire, and on the following day so did Israel — to the utter consternation of Britain and France! — for these acceptances meant that the basic condition of the ultimatums was met, and that all remaining pretext for the Anglo-French invasion was nullified. But the invasion force was now combat-loaded, moving across the Mediterranean and scheduled to land at Port Said in three days. When Ben-Gurion thus joined Nasser in accepting the cease-fire, Britain and France (as Dayan put it) "nearly jumped out of their skins." [1]

Ben-Gurion was moved by indications that Eden was faltering in the face of mounting pressures on every side. They came from the United States and the United Nations, and the Commonwealth was up in arms (Nehru called the collusive military action an extraordinary case of "naked aggression" in which "Israel is the invader and Egypt is made to suffer").[2] The situation in the House of Commons was an unmanageable tumult that seemed to threaten a breakdown of all political discourse: "A storm of booing would break out as soon as Anthony entered the Chamber, and would rise to a crescendo of hysteria when he actually rose to speak." [3] In the face of such pressures, and unable to provide persuasive answers to questions that punctured the moral pretension of the official posture, Eden gave the impression of a man looking for a way out. Now, however, he desperately urged Mollet to press Ben-Gurion to retract, and this Mollet did. Angry, but feeling he could not face the combination of American, Russian and United Nations pressures for withdrawal from the Sinai without strong Anglo-French support, Ben-Gurion reneged on the cease-fire on November 4 by insisting on a number of conditions plainly unacceptable to the UN.

Eden nevertheless continued to give way under severe pressure, which angered the impatient French, who had now ceased to be concerned with appearances. They devised an independent plan for a French paratroop attack on November 4, with open Israeli support and cover (the paratroops would drop inside Israeli lines near Kantara, then move out to seize the Canal), but Eden responded to this with outrage and indignation.[4] He now clutched at the straw of Anglo-French association with a larger UN peace-keeping force that seemed to be in the making, and persuaded Mollet that the British and French forces were the natural vanguard of a United Nations effort. In their joint reply to the United Nations, they accordingly promised to cease fire if the UN agreed "forthwith to limited detachments of Anglo-French troops to be stationed between the combatants." [5] The reply also included Eden's remarkably perfidious idea that the Anglo-French military presence was necessary "to secure the speedy withdrawal of Israeli forces"; [6] this was an argument that Mollet had reluctantly accepted as a means of getting Eden to speed up the landings, but it was too much for Ben-Gurion.

At 8:20 A.M. on November 5, British and French paratroops began stepping out of their transports six hundred feet above Port Said. Forty minutes later and several hundred miles to the south, the Israeli assault on the fortress at Sharm al-Sheikh, commanding the Strait of Tiran, gained for Israel the final and most important objective of the Sinai campaign — it opened the Gulf of Aqaba, permitting seaborne access via the Red Sea to the Israeli port of Elath. Within two hours, Ben-Gurion reinstated the Israeli agreement to the cease-fire, once more embarrassing the Anglo-French, who now had paratroop contingents on the ground, but amphibious forces still twenty-four hours from landing. Eden cabled Eisenhower insisting that the "police action" that had begun had to be carried through, if only to avoid a military vacuum while a United Nations force was being constituted. He added: "I have always felt . . .

that the Middle East was an issue over which, in the last resort, we would have to fight. . . . If we had allowed things to drift, . . . Nasser would have become a kind of Moslem Mussolini . . . taking the tricks all around the Middle East. . . . I am sure this is the moment to curb Nasser's ambitions. . . . By this means, we shall have taken the first step towards re-establishing authority in this area for our generation." [7]

Meanwhile, the Soviets, who had now crushed the Hungarian rebellion, proposed to Eisenhower the "joint and immediate use" of Soviet and American forces operating under a UN mandate to end the Suez war. Momentarily taken aback, Eisenhower soon pronounced the proposal "unthinkable" and an "obvious attempt" to divert world opinion from the bloody suppression of hope in Hungary.[8] He sharply warned Bulganin against Soviet intervention in the Middle East. There followed a series of ominously worded Soviet messages addressed to Britain, France and Israel that seemed to be thinly veiled threats of ballistic missile attacks. As a soldier, Eisenhower was not much impressed with these rumblings out of the Kremlin, but he was at the same time not averse to letting them add to the pressures on the three powers whom he was seeking to move toward cease-fire and withdrawal; indeed, there was indication during this period that the CIA manufactured several reports of Russian military activity which were without any basis in fact.[9]

Eden appears to have been equally unfrightened by the Soviet threats, feeling the primary Russian purpose was to prevent the United States from emerging from the crisis as the principal savior and protector of the Arabs. Nevertheless, he decided to quit shortly after receiving the Russian note, but his principal reason was the "threatened disaster to our whole economic position." [10] Britain's dollar reserves fell by $57 million in September and $84 million in October. But the November panic drained away $279 million, or 15 percent of London's total dollar reserves. Macmillan, perhaps the most avid supporter of the war against Nasser, was spun around by the financial crisis, telling Eden he could not any more be responsible for Her Majesty's Exchequer unless there was relief. But relief depended on stopping the war. The Secretary of the Treasury, George Humphrey, operating at Eisenhower's behest, firmly refused to approve a British request for a large withdrawal of dollars from the International Monetary Fund (with which London proposed to buy sterling and thus shore up its price). Humphrey told Macmillan that financial help would be forthcoming only if Britain promised an immediate cease-fire.

After a long and shattering day in Parliament, Eden telephoned Mollet at 1:30 A.M. on November 6 to express his view (which fell short of a final decision) that the game was up. Mollet, who opposed such a conclusion, but who seemed to misunderstand Eden's principal motivation, summoned Ambassador Dillon to the Matignon Palace within the hour to ask for U.S. assurances against a Russian attack on Anglo-French forces in the Middle East, explaining that such support was imperative if he were to hold the faltering British in line. While Dillon was still in Mollet's room, Eden telephoned again to say he had definitely decided to stop. Mollet then told Dillon that France had no choice but to comply, since French forces were dependent on British logistics. It is a measure of Eden's ambivalence or fatigue that these personal decisions at the highest level did not prevent the seaborne assault from going forward at dawn, and the cease-fire was not proclaimed until midnight of November 6 (some twenty-one hours after Eden's second phone call). Deciding that, with Israeli-Egyptian hostilities at an end, Britain had no choice but to abide by the language of its own ultimatum, the British cabinet acted at 10:00 A.M. In the French cabinet, however, the stubborn Pineau argued for going on without the British in full cooperation with Israel, but this ignored both the logistical factor and the evidence that even Israel was not prepared further to antagonize the United States. At 5:00 P.M. Mollet telephoned Eden with France's agreement to quit.

Eisenhower got the news at noon Washington time, on November 6, as he returned by helicopter from Gettysburg where he and Mrs. Eisenhower had cast their votes in the presidential election. He immediately telephoned Eden to offer congratulations, but also to caution him against setting any conditions on the cease-fire and to insist that none of the major powers should participate in the UN peace-keeping force. Thus was the fighting brought to an end.

Inexorable Logic

Eden, however, choosing to ignore Eisenhower's advice, sought with Mollet to include their troops in the UN emergency force and to delay any withdrawal until that force was fully established; they also wanted a major role in physically clearing the Canal. As Eden later wrote: "We were ashore with a sufficient force to hold Port Said. We held a gage. Nasser had received a humiliating defeat. . . . His position was badly shaken. Out of this situation intelligent statesmanship should, we thought, be able to shape a lasting settlement for the Arab-Israeli conflict and for the future of the canal." [11] Thus determined to maintain the Anglo-French military position as a strong bargaining counter, Eden sought simultaneously to effect a dramatic and visible repair of the broken bonds of alliance. On November 7 he telephoned Eisenhower to propose that he and Mollet should fly at once to Washington for a broad review of the whole situation. The President's steady inner self-confidence, forthrightness, dislike of pretense, and insistent refusal to personalize issues made him a bulwark of sanity and wise proportion in every crisis, but these same qualities led occasionally to a naïve disregard for appearances. On this occasion, his ingrained conviction that NATO was the indispensable cornerstone of Western security and his quiet sympathy for an old friend led him to give an affirmative off-the-cuff response to Eden's proposal. It was, after all, only a family quarrel; principle was one thing, but friendship and mutual interest were another.

The State Department, including Acting Secretary Hoover, was visibly dismayed by the impropriety of such a meeting. The United States had led the fight for the UN resolution against Britain and France, and the Anglo-French were still in defiance of the resolution. From his hospital bed, Dulles strongly concurred, fearing such a meeting would undermine the authority of the United Nations and suggest to the Arabs the existence of a permanent Anglo-American conspiracy. He intervened with blunt advice. The President accepted these representations "with reluctance and impatience," and telephoned the Prime Minister two hours later to rescind the invitation, telling Eden his advisers "think our timing is very, very bad. . . . We will have to postpone it a little bit. I am sorry." [12]

The next day, he paid a visit to Dulles at Walter Reed Hospital. Despite the myriad dangers and problems that swirled unresolved around his head, Eisenhower was a man of innate optimism and ebullience, and on this occasion he still carried the natural elation of both the fact and the margin of his reelection to the presidency just two days before.* The gaiety of his greeting to Dulles was, however, rather quickly absorbed in the Secretary's wholly somber response, and it became apparent to the President that he must explain himself and his humanitarian impulses to his principal adviser on foreign affairs. Sitting in a chair that required him to look up to the high hospital bed where Dulles sat like an old owl propped up by numerous pillows, the President seemed somewhat in the position of a schoolboy trying to explain away some misdeed to a skeptical and unyielding headmaster: "Foster, I understand why you thought it was a bad idea [to invite Eden] and why it should have been called off, and as you know we called it off. . . . But I want to explain to you what I had in my mind when I did it." [13] He went on at some length, but if he expected sympathy and understanding, he failed to get it. Nodding silently, the sixty-eight-year-old Dulles peered down at the man who had just been reelected to the highest office in the most powerful nation in the world. Only after Eisenhower had run out his string did he say anything, and then it

* In 1956, Eisenhower defeated Adlai Stevenson by 457 to 73 electoral votes. He carried 41 states to Stevenson's 7.

was a comment that crisply closed the subject: "Well, Mr. President, I think it was right that we called it off." [14]

For two weeks, Eden and Mollet clung fast to their defiant position on withdrawal, but when the UN emergency force arrived in Suez on November 21, Eisenhower moved with implacable determination to end the impasse. The desperate state of the pound sterling had forced Eden to a cease-fire. Now the urgent need for oil brought submission on the issue of withdrawal. The French, who had been less vulnerable on the monetary issue, were equally jeopardized by the prospect of a severe oil shortage; rationing had already begun in both countries and winter was coming on. Before Suez, 73 percent of Europe's oil came from the Middle East (one-half of that through the Canal), but with the Canal closed and the Syrian pipelines destroyed, Europe was drawing only 9 percent of its total requirements from that area. As 27 percent came from non–Middle East sources, this meant that total supply was down to 36 percent of normal. A supplement from the Western Hemisphere was urgently needed, but the United States insisted first on total withdrawal.

Although the Canadian Foreign Minister, Lester Pearson, had labored to create the UN emergency force in large part to provide a means of permitting the Anglo-French to give way with a semblance of dignity, there was never a serious chance that London and Paris could escape total withdrawal. The United Nations is a confederation of national sovereignties and its Charter provides no justifiable encroachment by one member on the territory of another; this strict and pristine rule is embedded in the very bone structure of the organization. Accordingly, the UN being seized of the Suez problem and the United States having committed itself to support of the UN, there could be no mitigation of the judgment. By an inexorable logic, Egypt had the sovereign right to refuse the presence of foreign forces on Egyptian soil. No matter what the extenuating circumstances, within the framework of a United Nations operation the Anglo-French withdrawal had to be total and unconditional. Such hard logic naturally generated resentment; indeed, anti-American feeling mounted throughout Europe. A resolution supported by 110 Tory members of the British Parliament congratulated Selwyn Lloyd for his efforts "to secure international control of the Suez Canal" and deplored "the attitude of America, which is gravely endangering the Atlantic Alliance." Harold Nicolson wrote in his diary that "for the moment, all Tory opinion, bemused though it be, is in favour of Eden. Simple minds work simply. The ladies of Bournemouth do not like the Russians, the Americans or Nasser: Eden has dealt a blow to these three enemies: therefore Eden must be right. It is as simple as that." [15] But Eden departed, sick and exhausted, for a rest in Jamaica on November 23, leaving R. A. Butler, the Lord Privy Seal, to bear the political onus of the inevitable capitulation. On November 30, President Eisenhower declared himself satisfied with Anglo-French assurances, and Selwyn Lloyd announced a phased troop withdrawal on December 3 which was duly completed on December 22.

Sanctimony at NATO

On November 18, Dulles flew off to Key West for further convalescence; on December 3 he was back in harness at the State Department, preparing for the December 11 meeting of the NATO Council which seemed certain, in the circumstances, to be a test of the alliance's capacity for survival. The bonds that held together the crucial American-British-French nucleus were torn or badly strained, and the prospects for quick repair clouded by embittered and distrustful personal relationships.

In a major address delivered on the second day of the conference, Dulles extended an olive branch to estranged allies and, displaying a hitherto unsuspected gift for understatement, admitted that "history may record that neither we nor our allies were without fault in our handling of the events which led to the crisis in which we now find ourselves." [16] Unfortunately, he did not stop there, but insisted on entering a claim to moral and tactical victory for the United States, and then, in his most egregious manner, went on to wrap himself in a mantle of such exclusive rectitude that he ended by exacerbating the already nettled state of his European colleagues. As the *London Times* of December 12 reported it, he did not hesitate to lecture his colleagues on morality, pointing out that even grave injustices were not grounds for resort to force, and that restraint in the face of provocation was proof of moral strength; indeed, that kind of strength "created a moral climate which stimulated and encouraged the forces which were destroying the Soviet system." [17] The Anglo-French action at Suez, he said, had violated not only the United Nations Charter, but also Article I of the North Atlantic Treaty (on the rather strained interpretation that that treaty requires all parties to renounce the use of force even with respect to problems outside the NATO area). Having thus laid down the dictum that force could not be justified by any nation under any circumstances, except self-defense, and that this stricture applied with particular point to members of NATO, he proceeded to make plain that the United States was exempt from such a rule because of its special position. As the nexus of numerous collective security arrangements, involving some forty other countries, the United States would insist on its right to act alone, indeed without any obligation to consult with its NATO allies, on matters beyond the NATO borders.

Without doubt, there was a case to be made for America's broad responsibilities and preeminent power position in the free world. But to link a naked claim to the unilateral use of force for oneself with a sanctimonious lecture on the immorality of force if contemplated by others was yet another example of that incredible Dullesian gratuitousness and insensitivity that left his admirers sadly shaking their heads and his critics gnashing their teeth. It also showed to perfection the now largely unconscious fusion of preacher, politican and lawyer. His instinct was to bind the other party (preferably to high moral principles), while preserving freedom of action for himself and his client. Obviously he had forgotten his private "why did you stop?" question to Selwyn Lloyd in the hospital. But if the moral discrepancy here involved entirely escaped him, it did not escape others. One London editorial, reflecting the mounting intensity of European reaction to the Dulles personality, began with the biblical quotation, "Thou hypocrite, first cast out the beam out of thine own eye."

At the same time he showed, in private meetings, a sharp resentment at suggestions, then circulating freely in the NATO Council and the European press, that he must bear a large measure of blame for having triggered the Canal nationalization, for having misled his allies, for having reduced NATO to its current state of malaise. In a talk on December 12, Macmillan found him "discursive and vague . . . in a querulous and unhappy mood." After complaining about the removal of Makins as British ambassador in Washington, "he went on to a long defence of himself and his policies . . . clearly hurt at the criticisms that had been made. He said that it was an error to believe that he and the President could be separated. He wrote most of the Presidential statements himself. When they had to be tough, they were made by the Secretary of State. . . . When they were idealistic, they were made by the President but written by the Secretary of State. He seemed very sensitive to any suggestion that there was a rift between them." [18]

Shoe-horning Israel

Immediately after accepting the cease-fire, Israel began its fight to retain the new lands won by military conquest. The basic theme of Ben-Gurion's speech to the Knesset on November 7 was that, as the Sinai was historically a part of Israel, there had been no invasion of Egypt. "Our operations were restricted to the area of the Sinai Peninsula alone." [19] The earlier armistice agreements and the boundaries they defined were accordingly "dead and buried and will never be resurrected." [20]

Eisenhower, who abhorred both Ben-Gurion's logic and his defiance of the UN, cabled him immediately that such intransigence could "impair the friendly cooperation between our two countries." [21] At the same time, Acting Secretary Hoover warned the Israeli Foreign Office of possible economic sanctions and of what he discerned as an incipient move by the neutral countries to expel Israel from the United Nations. Ben-Gurion took a prudent backward step on November 8, telling Eisenhower that "we have never planned to annex the Sinai," [22] but such was his tenacity that the last Israeli soldier was not pressured out of that peninsula until five months later, on March 16, 1957. But if Ben-Gurion now resigned himself to having eventually to yield up the Sinai, he remained adamant about Gaza and Sharm al-Sheikh, repeatedly defying UN resolutions over the next three months and lobbying tirelessly for sympathetic support in the American Jewish community. Eisenhower, however, who was consistently cavalier about the consequences of Zionist opposition at home, both before and after the election, gave him little room for encouragement: "I got calls from New York City and some of my friends [said]: 'Well, you've lost New York.' And I said I don't give a goddamn. . . . We thought the American Jew was . . . an American before he was a Jew so we'll just take the salt thataway." [23] He carried New York state by 1,600,000 votes.

On February 11, Dulles handed Ambassador Eban an *aide-mémoire* which expressed the considered American view that "Israeli withdrawal from Gaza should be prompt and unconditional." [24] With regard to Sharm al-Sheikh, however, he was more forthcoming, expressing the United States belief that the Gulf of Aqaba "comprehends international waters," thereby making it unlawful for any nation to "prevent free and innocent passage"; indeed, said Dulles, the United States was prepared, on behalf of American-registry vessels, to exercise the right of free and innocent passage "and to join with others to secure general recognition of this right." [25] This was a constructive American effort (which, however, fell short of a guarantee except as to ships of American registry) to provide free passage for Israeli shipping in the gulf and particularly through the Strait of Tiran, after the removal of Israeli armed forces from the commanding heights at the mouth of the gulf. Ben-Gurion, who held promises to be less valuable than physical control, did not budge.

By this time a large majority in the United Nations General Assembly was angry and restive at Israel's repeated defiance, and looking to the United States to apply the sanctions that would bring that Spartan country to heel. The latest Ben-Gurion intransigence convinced Dulles and Cabot Lodge that the United States must now take a public stand on severe sanctions against Israel, or else be confirmed at the United Nations as the creature of Jewish interests in America. On the Secretary of the Treasury's plantation in Thomasville, Georgia, where Eisenhower and Humphrey were shooting quail, they accordingly descended on February 16. Out of the meeting came a firm decision not only to suspend governmental assistance to Israel but also to eliminate the generous tax credits and to take other administrative action to restrict *private* assistance from American sources (the latter figure being roughly $100 million annually, comprising $40 million in cash gifts and $60 million in the purchase of Israel bonds; a record of the figures was available to the Treasury because of the tax deductions accorded both types of transaction). When the President returned to Washington, on February 20, to brief congressional leaders on this plan, the pervasiveness of Jewish influence in American politics quickly surfaced. Senator Lyndon Johnson was in the pro-Israeli vanguard for the Democrats, while the Senate Republican leader, William Knowland, threatened to resign from the U.S. delegation to the United Nations if any sanctions were applied against Israel. At a tense and strained meeting, Eisenhower refused to be deflected, but the congressional leaders pointedly declined to make his position their own.[26] In a television speech the following evening, he argued the literal letter of the law: "If the United Nations once admits that international disputes can be settled by using force, then we will have destroyed the very foundation of the organization. . . . The United Nations has no choice but to exert pressure upon Israel to comply with the withdrawal resolutions. . . ."[27] Six nations introduced a supporting UN resolution the next day. With a howl of rage, Ben-Gurion finally yielded on March 1.

Transition in London

As the bits and pieces of information about the Suez collusion began to find their way into the public domain, mainly from the insouciant French, they were met by categorical denials from the British defense and foreign ministries, and there was also a certain public disinclination in Britain to believe so unsavory a truth. Eden nevertheless returned from Jamaica on December 14 to a "malodorous" political atmosphere.[28] As he entered the House of Commons, he was met with "a stony silence from the Opposition and the feeblest of cheers from the Government benches. . . . It was a grim and revealing episode."[29] On December 20, he was cornered in a tight debate, and extricated himself only by making a directly false statement: "There was not," he said, "foreknowledge that Israel would attack Egypt." [30] Within a week his doctors advised him to resign, and he ended a long and largely illustrious career on January 9, 1957, leaving behind him a wounded but loyal Tory party and a deeply divided country. It was a towering personal and political tragedy. Eminently effective in the role of diplomatic specialist, which he performed with distinction for nine-tenths of his official life, he had failed as a political leader.

On his final day in office, just two hours before he bid farewell to the cabinet, he talked privately with Macmillan at Ten Downing Street in the one small drawing room with a "window to the west, looking over the garden," the only room on the north side that provided a "touch of warmth and glow" to the winter gloom of London.[31] Learning of Eden's decision, Macmillan found himself unprepared for the "sudden and tragic end to the adventure on which we had set out so gaily some twenty months before. . . . I can see him now on that sad winter afternoon, still looking so youthful, so gay, so debonair — the representative of all that was best of the youth that had served in the 1914–18 War." [32] He might have added that both he and Eden, and indeed many others in the Suez cabinet, were also among the best of those who in 1938 had "stood up to Hitler" and refused to "let Mussolini get away with it." That had been their triumph, and their supreme contribution to Britain and humanity. Their tragedy had been their strange collective lapse of historical perspective which led them to insist that Nasser was an incarnate Mussolini (and an incipient Hitler). More understandable, though no less tragic, had been their failure to perceive that ten years after the glorious copartnership of World War II, Britain was, in relation to the United States, only one among several middle powers in the constellation forming around the Washington superpower, that there was no longer an automatic identity of American and British interest, and that Washington was rather unlikely to support the last convulsive reflex of a spent imperial instinct.

After Eden had resigned, the Marquess of Salisbury and Lord Kilmuir were instructed to poll the cabinet to determine which one of the two obvious contenders for succession, R. A. Butler or Harold Macmillan, would be chosen. "Bobbety" Salisbury, who suffered a speech difficulty, asked each man, in the privacy of a small office off the cabinet room, "Well, which is it, Wab or Hawold?" [33] By this means it was decided that the name of Macmillan, the more traditional, the tougher, the more ruthless man, would be sent to the Queen.

The Suez debacle was a graveyard for careers and reputations on every side. Like Eden, Dulles was grievously wounded — in health and prestige — but unlike Eden (who lacked a politically invulnerable sponsor and protector), Dulles survived professionally. If there was in the whole inglorious spectacle any major figure who emerged with his reputation more or less intact, it was surely the President of the United States. Plunged into the fait accompli of Nasser's nationalization by Dulles's wholly private decision to use the Aswan issue as an anti-Soviet ploy in the global cold war, he immediately saw the Canal problem in true perspective and never changed his view. He can be faulted for not having insisted on a flatter, blunter presentation of his position, although his own statements were hardly subject to misinterpretation. But he was preoccupied with a campaign for reelection, he trusted Dulles, and his allies (who were bound by their own obsessions) were incapable of taking him at his word until it was too late. Yet even after the worst had happened, he retained a sense of proportion and an attitude of firm dispassion that were qualities displayed by no other participant.

25

On the Defensive

NINETEEN FIFTY-SEVEN was a year marked by steadily accelerating change in the world situation and by a deepening refusal of American policy to acknowledge or adjust to it. The "nuclear stalemate" was now nearly universally accepted as a political fact, and it strengthened the determination of the Third World countries to fashion a policy of "nonalignment" as between the two Superpowers, a fact which translated to relations with the West ranging from benign neutrality to outright hostility. Soviet offers of economic and military aid, and unqualified Soviet support for national independence in Asia and Africa, were meeting with a favorable response; "freedom from Communism" was not everywhere the instinctive, overriding consideration it had proved to be in the democratic West; there was rising resistance to the granting of air and naval bases, transit rights and other concessions which figured prominently in American calculations of feasible containment, military advantage, and prestige. Within the belt of Eastern Europe, the Soviets were faced with similar impulses to self-determination, flowing from the energies released by Khrushchev's de-Stalinization program and his endorsement of Tito's doctrine of "separate roads to Socialism." These currents had already produced the Polish and Hungarian challenges to Soviet authority and were generating a counterreformation movement in the Kremlin aimed at deposing the author of this dangerous liberal leniency. Accelerated change thus threatened the viability of old policies on both sides in the East-West struggle. Everywhere, arrangements and relationships which had long defined the postwar scene seemed to be shifting, breaking up, pulling loose from their moorings. Everywhere the yeast of change was at work, and more swiftly than most had imagined.

Arriving in Bonn (May 1957)

Mellow Immobility

In the face of universal gestation, the administration in Washington seemed to wrap itself in a deepening immobilism. Eisenhower was guarding his health and his peace of mind with longer and more frequent periods of rest and recreation, which led inevitably to a diminished sense of executive clarity and force throughout the administration. Dulles's views were by this time fully formed, and his natural tendencies to adhere to established positions and formulae were reinforced by both the President's waning energies and the increasing pressure of his own critics. Yet inside the thickening crust of official immobility, it seemed a time of personal mellowing. Entering upon his fifth year in office, Dulles was comfortably wedded to his job, widely admired for his technical mastery, "a genius for economizing the application of his brain . . . one of the great in-fighters of our time . . . a perfect advocate," [1] and made inwardly serene by the intellectual harmony and intimacy he had achieved with the President. This last was a deeply satisfying relationship, although it rarely extended into the social realm. Dulles did not golf, and Eisenhower turned to businessmen and old soldiers for diversion at stag dinners and at bridge.

As he approached his sixty-ninth birthday in February, the Secretary continued to work seven days a week at the same changeless pace, whether in Washington or traveling from important conference to trivial ceremony and back again, scribbling on his yellow pad, taking a cocktail with the staff, companioned by a devoted wife who carried his bed board. His work load was "prodigious," according to William Macomber but "he paced himself beautifully." He worked steadily; "I never saw him frantic . . . and he was never not working." [2] Saturdays and Sundays he rarely went to the office, but worked in his study at home, assisted by one of the three female secretaries who took turns on weekend duty and were treated as "part of the family," and it was on weekends that he turned to what he regarded as the more pleasurable, relaxing aspects of his job — like polishing a speech or drafting a letter to his friend Konrad Adenauer. [3] Though reserved and parental with his young special assistants ("We were not invited to do very much joking . . . you know, he was a very dignified man"), he was increasingly prone to wax philosophical at the end of the day: "The fact that you've got problems to deal with is natural and normal and not in itself a worrisome thing," he told Macomber; "you're never going to get to the point, where you've tidied up your problems. Problems come to you . . . the time to start worrying is if your problems don't change." [4] And listening to him,

Dictating to Phyliss Bernau at the State Department (1957)

An honorary locomotive engineer (1958)

Sailing on Lake Ontario (1958)

Macomber was certain that Dulles didn't mind the burden of problems, indeed relished them and the challenge they presented, that they were the meat and drink of his life: "That's part of the reason he didn't fret." [5]

With the three young female secretaries in his office he was often grandfatherly and jovial, feeding the fishes in their windowsill aquarium and exchanging kindly and hearty banter. For one of them, Phyliss Bernau (who later became Mrs. William Macomber), he showed a special affection, coming to regard and treat her, so it seemed to those who watched, as the daughter he would like to have had — pretty, cheerful, close at hand, attentive to his needs, appreciating his old-fashioned humor. He would joke with her about their respective waistlines, and hide her occasional box of candy, which was the signal for an elaborate charade to discover the culprit. He insisted that she accompany him on his flying trips to handle dictation, and he took vicarious pleasure in getting a firsthand account of her late evenings in London nightclubs or Paris restaurants in the company of young diplomats. If there occurred some mix-up in his schedule or some procedural gaffe in the outer office, it was Phyliss who was dispatched, wide-eyed and pretty, to the inner sanctum to break the unwelcome news: "Gosh, Mr. Dulles, what do you suppose just happened?" To her, he was the beloved "Boss," who sent her gifts and was "the greatest, the kindest, the wisest, and the most fun to be with." [6]

Returned from a trip to Iran in early February, the Secretary of State tried his hand at a piece of bureaucratic humor, based upon an enormous cake (decorated with the stars and stripes of the American flag) which he and Mrs. Dulles had found waiting for them one evening when they returned to their suite in Teheran. Acceptance of gifts from foreign powers being a matter hedged about with many restrictions for American officials, Dulles dictated a memorandum to the chief of protocol requesting "a ruling" on how he should dispose of the gift. Since it was reasonable to assume, he wrote, that the donor was a "king, prince or foreign state" and that he and Mrs. Dulles were the "joint donees," he had "decided to defer eating the cake until it could be returned to Washington and be personally inspected by the Chief of Protocol to determine whether or not the principle of 'de minimus' applied." There were, he acknowledged, complications in such a course. For one, Mrs. Dulles insisted on dividing the cake, on grounds that her half interest was not subject to government ruling, as she was not a "person holding any office of profit or trust . . . within the meaning of Section 9 of Article I of the Constitution"; this insistence distressed him, because it threatened to destroy "the cultural and artistic quality" of the cake's decoration, and because "partition is contrary to the basic foreign policy of the United States." A further complication was that, owing to inadequate "refrigerating facilities for conserving the cake" in his office, there was the "consequent danger" not only of deterioration, but equally of exposure to "the predatory instincts of various lady secretaries." Given "the complexity of the problem," he would appreciate a "prompt ruling" from the chief of protocol; he was also sending a copy of the memorandum to the legal adviser.[7]

Guarding the Flanks

Beyond the warmth of his inner circle, however, Dulles gave little evidence of a more flexible approach to the world, whether the near or distant parts of it. He continued, for example, to guard his bureaucratic flanks with undiminished vigor, viewing with dark suspicion any proposals from the White House staff that seemed aimed at placing one of their own — or indeed anyone who had some influence with the President — in a position to second-guess the Secretary of State, and quick to neutralize any developing signs of independence in what he considered his own domain.

A celebrated example of his technique (and one that tended to confirm

a rather widely held view that he regarded undersecretaries as super-
fluous) concerned Christian Herter, the governor of Massachusetts and
a serious student of foreign affairs, who, as a congressman in the late
1940s, had been instrumental in the passage of the Marshall Plan legislation. In mid-1956, Harold Stassen had shaken the proprieties of the
administration "family" by publicly recommending that the President
dump Nixon and choose Herter as his running mate in the 1956 election.
As there was indeed measurable unhappiness about Nixon in the liberal
wing of the party, the suggestion developed a genuine resonance and thus
presented a political problem. Herter may have been tempted to make a
public bid for the vice-presidency, but he had no wish to embarrass
Eisenhower, and it was soon arranged that if he would help to preserve a
solid front at the convention — by making the nominating speech for
Nixon — the President would be pleased to appoint him Undersecretary
of State.

Herter kept his part of the bargain and duly arrived at the State
Department in the spring of 1957 where Dulles, without much subtlety,
tried to break Eisenhower's commitment. Close friends of the Secretary
believe he may have sincerely decided he was acting in Herter's best
interests, but he told the governor, in effect: "You know, I think it
would be wiser for you if you started off as Assistant Secretary, so you'd
get into the family and you'd become known before you take this other
step." [8] Herter, a gentleman of austere spirit and forbearance, went away
from this meeting considerably disturbed, and took the problem to
William H. Jackson, the President's assistant for National Security Council affairs. As recounted by Arthur Krock (who knows how to embellish a
good story), the colloquy went something like this:

Jackson: Chris, aren't you Governor of Massachusetts?
Herter: Yes.
Jackson: Haven't you been Speaker of the House in Massachusetts?
Herter: Yes.
Jackson: Haven't you got a pretty nice house on the north shore?
Herter: Yes.
Jackson: Have you got all the money you need? Or your wife has?
Herter: Yes.
Jackson: Well, then, just tell [Dulles] you won't do it. That's all. That
   you insist upon [going in as Under Secretary]! [9]

Vice President Nixon was brought into the matter and was appalled:
"This cannot be. He must go in as Under Secretary." [10] So the President
was notified and he turned Dulles around, but Herter was not able to
function meaningfully until a year later when Dulles was overtaken by

terminal cancer. After three months, depressed by what he saw as the low morale of the Foreign Service and the "monarchic seclusion" in which Dulles worked, he confided to Emmet Hughes that it was "hard to know what use I am around here . . . no area of work is specifically my task. Everyone finds it difficult to know what Foster is either doing or thinking. So . . . I just keep trotting around after events, trying to piece together the true shape of them, so that I can at least be conversant with affairs when Foster is away from Washington. . . . I have left this office, many nights, thinking quite clearly that I should do only one thing. And that was — to go home and pack up my bags." [11]

A related incident involved Harold Stassen, the President's special assistant on disarmament, who was sometimes called "The Secretary for Peace" by the more romantic segments of the press, and who worked with enthusiasm and unquenchable ambition at carving out an independent sphere of authority and operations for himself. In the spring of 1957, the British had successfully tested their own H-Bomb at Christmas Island, and Macmillan was treading his careful but determined way toward an independent British stockpile, a task that involved evading the twin obstacles of bellicose Soviet demands for a cessation of all nuclear testing and mass protests from a British public that was deeply anxious for a halt to the arms race. Stassen, believing the Russians were sufficiently disturbed by the British progress in nuclear weaponry to make concessions for an agreement that would prevent the spread of a nuclear weapons capability to additional countries, prepared a proposal and secured Eisenhower's authority to use it as an informal "talking paper" in private discussions with the Russians and the British.[12] However, once engaged with the Russians, he handed them the paper (thirty pages of material) without any prior consultation with his allies. This action, inept or deliberate, angered and dismayed Macmillan, primarily because the paper contained a cutoff date for the manufacture of fissionable material for weapons purposes. After 1959 (when Stassen's plan assumed an effective inspection system could be installed), all new fissionable material would be allocated to nonweapons purposes. As this did not provide nearly enough time for Britain to build its weapons stockpile, Macmillan feared that American-Russian agreement would require "the abandonment of our nuclear ambitions." [13]

The Prime Minister expressed his dismay to Eisenhower in plain terms, saying that as "this is, after all, the greatest issue that faces the civilised world. . . . I would not be straight with you if I tried to disguise a certain feeling of distress that we were not told in advance that this document was to be given to the Russians." [14] Eisenhower's reply reflected his own distress that Stassen's handling of an "informal memorandum . . . without the knowledge or authorization of us here in

Washington" should have placed his ally in "an awkward position." [15] Dulles also telephoned Macmillan "to apologize at length," and the Prime Minister thought his apology was "all the more sincere because I knew he disliked Stassen and was jealous of his semi-independent position." [16] At the end of June, Dulles arrived in London to assume personal control of the disarmament negotiations, and Stassen was gradually but inexorably moved into limbo.

Accommodation to the Right

Similarly on policy matters, Dulles continued to follow the well-worn path of strident anti-Communism and opposition to negotiations with Russia or contacts with China until they evidenced a decisive "change of heart." Truman and Acheson had advocated and pursued a policy of creating "situations of strength" as a prerequisite to serious negotiations. However, what had been a condition precedent to constructive diplomacy gave the appearance, under Dulles, of having become the only goal. In word and deed Dulles seemed unable to articulate any purpose beyond preventing a further expansion of Communism. In part, his rigidly defensive posture seemed a response to the growing volume and vehemence of his critics: in 1957, the attacks that beat down upon him from Congress and the press were harsher and more relentless than ever before, and involved both his policies and his competence. He had emphasized American military and economic superiority as the basis for a strategy of instant nuclear retaliation, but the Soviets had now achieved nuclear stalemate; he had excoriated neutralism, but it seemed increasingly evident to thoughtful observers that a measured cultivation of neutralism was the only safe and rational way to deal with rising self-consciousness in the Third World; he had seemed to hold out the promise of "liberation," but the Soviets were stronger in their home bastion and more respectable outside it; he had preached America's need for friends and allies, but had himself become the principal object of allied distrust and even hatred. Moderates and liberals were demanding new approaches to China and the Third World, but the conservatives and members of the radical Right still pressed for clear-cut victory in the cold war, demanding a more aggressive policy. Such diverse figures as Senator Hubert Humphrey and the columnist Joseph Alsop regularly called for his resignation.

Caught in a nasty crossfire, he seemed very close in 1957 to the hapless state of official ineffectiveness to which Acheson had been reduced in 1950–1952, but which Dulles had promised himself would never happen to him. Deliberately or instinctively, he seemed to conclude that relative

safety was to be found with the conservatives and the right wing. Refusal
to accommodate the moderates and liberals could bring wounding slings
and arrows. But the power to do him in, so he reckoned, lay with the
virulent Communist-haters on the right — the archconservatives, the
residual McCarthyites, the China Lobby — and it was a power they would
use if he noticeably softened his position on the basic issues of the cold
war. Accommodation of the Right thus equated with personal survival,
and he continued to make it. It also seemed the best available antidote
to his second fear: namely, that any relaxation of international tension
would dangerously erode the already diminished sense of cohesion and
resolve among the non-Communist nations.

Throughout 1957, Dulles accordingly seemed almost willfully blind to
opportunities for useful accommodation with Russia and China, for a
more sympathetic approach to the Third World, indeed for a larger
understanding of what was happening in the vast land areas and populations beyond the United States. In the main, he seemed to occupy himself
with fighting rearguard actions in defense of policies and attitudes that
were increasingly out of touch, and to systematically chopping off the
intuitively wise, but vague and unsustained, initiatives of the President.
"I repeat it almost in my sleep," Eisenhower told a press conference on
June 26, that "there will be no . . . victorious side in any global
war. . . ." [17] But this invitation to a live-and-let-live understanding with
the Russians was followed a week later by Dulles's assertion that "American policy is conducted on the assumption, as a working hypothesis, that
free governments in the long run are going to prevail and despotic governments are going to go under." [18] Khrushchev replied that if the
Soviets "are confronted with conditions such as Dulles likes to put forward . . . it might take 200 years before we ever come together." [19]
From the sidelines Dean Acheson observed that "the idea that we are
engaged on a crusade or mission to vindicate vaguely and erroneously
conceived 'moral law' has led to actions which, I fear, are quite contrary
to our interests." [20] Again, on July 17, Eisenhower replied to a press conference question that he "couldn't see any harm" if the Soviet defense
minister, Marshal Zhukov, were to exchange visits with Secretary Wilson.
But when the Soviet embassy in Washington sought to pursue the matter,
Dulles quickly turned it off, saying the President's comment was "a
hypothetical answer to a hypothetical question." [21] Khrushchev later
complained that "we evaluated that press conference very carefully. . . .
We felt that this would contribute to an understanding. We wanted
Zhukov to go." But "we are a proud nation and we do not want to go
down on our knees to arrange these things." [22]

The Eisenhower Doctrine

The misconceived and mismanaged effort to bring Nasser down had left a residue of bitter anti-Americanism in Western Europe and of angry disillusion in America. Nasser, having precariously survived, was fast becoming the transcendent hero of fiercely xenophobic currents in Arab opinion that demanded unbridled national independence and sweeping social change. And with his army humiliated, the Sinai in Israel's hands, and the country enraged by the bombings and killings, he could no longer accept a Suez Canal arrangement based on Egyptian operation plus an international advisory board as envisaged by the "Six Principals" approved in October. Fawzi now informed Hammerskjöld that there could be no user participation in the management, even on an advisory basis.

In Britain, hostility to Nasser remained a central feature of Macmillan's new Tory government, but Eden's analogy with Mussolini and Fascism having proved generally unpersuasive, the new team developed a new line of argument. The Anglo-French action at Suez, explained one of the ministers, Peter Thorneycroft, had laid bare a plot by Russia to take over the whole Middle East, using Nasser as the Kremlin's instrument.[23] The French embellished this line by inviting Admiral Radford to their embassy in Washington to hear a report on vast Soviet arms caches discovered by the Israelis in the Sinai desert. But there seemed in fact no evidence that such stockpiles existed, and the Thorneycroft allegation may have been a deliberate distortion of rumors, for the real conflict between Communism and Nasserist Pan-Arabic nationalism was soon apparent. To a related Tory assertion that the Anglo-French intervention had actually saved the situation by bringing into being the UN emergency force, a leading Labour MP, Denis Healey, replied that this was "like Al Capone taking credit for improving the efficiency of the Chicago police."[24]

The charge of Egyptian-Russian conspiracy to communize the Middle East (though it ran counter to the Nasser regime's deep commitment to nonalignment and equally against Moslem society's ingrained antipathy to Communism) seemed a natural and convenient explanation of events to cold-war planners in Washington, both in the bureaucracy and at the cabinet level. Predictably, it triggered conditioned reflexes, and the result was to deepen the suspicion of Nasser, to confuse Arab nationalism with Communism, and to assume far greater Russian influence in the area than in fact existed. Nasser attempted to set the record straight, saying: "I vow I will not become the stooge or satellite or pawn or hireling of anybody. Just as Egypt is determined to have political independence, so also Egypt is determined to have and maintain [freedom] . . . from all foreign ideologies such as Marxism, racism, colonialism, imperialism, and atheism, all of which incidentally are European in origin." [25] But the West did not heed or believe him. Dulles and his colleagues discounted Egyptian determination to ̇be independent, in part because they did not believe Communist penetration could be effectively resisted by a posture of nonalignment, and in part because their resentment at Egypt's insistence on normal political intercourse with a Communist country clouded their assessment of the facts. Such misperceptions led predictably to actions which strengthened Soviet influence. Thus Undersecretary Hoover refused an Egyptian request for emergency food, fuel and medicine immediately after the fighting, and then compounded the resentment by refusing even to release enough of the Egyptian dollar reserves to permit Cairo's purchase of these necessities. No doubt, he thought by such refusals to weaken Communism, but Moscow promptly airlifted medical equipment and drugs, and shipped 60,000 tons of wheat.

Their minds focused on the large-scale ineptitude which had swept Britain and France from the scene and sharply increased Arab hostility to the West, Dulles and Eisenhower feared the Soviets would seize the opportunity to fill what they now perceived as a serious power vacuum, and without apparent hesitation they concluded that America must step into the breech. "The existing vacuum in the Middle East," the President told congressional leaders on New Year's Day, "must be filled by the United States before it is filled by Russia." [26] Dulles's operational response to this conclusion was entirely predictable: to put up another "stop sign"; to secure advance congressional approval for another contingent declaration of war in the pattern of SEATO and the Formosa Resolution. Thus, in early January 1957, the administration laid before Congress the Eisenhower Doctrine, a resolution "to deter Communist aggression in the Middle East area." It provided a special economic aid fund of $200 million, plus offers of military equipment and training. The heart of the proposal, however, was the declaration that "overt armed aggression from any nation controlled by international Communism" would be met by "the armed forces of the United States." [27] In another respect also, the dramatic move bore the familiar Dulles trademark — its development had been accomplished without any consultation with the United Nations, the European allies, or the members of the Baghdad Pact.

For the first time, this approach met with marked resistance in the Congress, mainly on the grounds that the threat of Soviet aggression to the Middle East seemed remote, but also because the Senate Foreign Relations Committee, in particular, had learned to be wary of Dulles crying wolf. Dangers to the area's stability were evident, but the senators found them related not to Soviet aggression or even infiltration, but to unbridled Arab nationalism that had been ignited by the Anglo-French and Israeli attacks on Egypt. Some members thought Dulles was deliberately raising the bogey of "International Communism" as a means of ensuring congressional support for the arms assistance and economic aid features of the resolution; certainly in his appearances before several congressional committees, he concentrated his sales effort on the most emotional and unlikely threat. The Suez Canal closure, the sabotage of oil pipelines, and Arab unrest, he argued, may have convinced the Kremlin rulers "that a great victory is almost within their grasp"; the greatest danger was thus "that ambitious despots may miscalculate." [28] Later in the month, trying to prod a determinedly deliberate Congress to swift action, he insisted that, if America should fail to act, the Middle East might soon be lost "in a great and maximum disaster" encompassing "the inevitability of a world war." [29]

The senators were frankly angered by this alarmist tone, and a new storm of criticism rose up against Dulles, which spread to his entire handling of Middle Eastern affairs, tracing back to his abrupt refusal of funds for the Aswan Dam. Senator Fulbright, noting that "a disastrous and remarkable collapse of our relations with our closest allies has taken place under the direction of the present Secretary of State," demanded a detailed accounting for the whole course of recent American policy in the Middle East.[30] Other legislators were irritated by yet another request for congressional "authorization" in a situation where the Constitution rather plainly gave the President inherent powers to act. Perhaps the widest resistance to the new gambit fed on the confusion surrounding the administration's intentions: the plan had been rushed to the Congress without the advice or knowledge of any interested or affected party; it envisaged U.S. military action independent of the United Nations (which Dulles had argued in November and December was a violation of the Charter); the resolution failed to define the area it covered (and the State Department conceded that no nation within the general area of the Middle East was now "controlled by international Communism"); an equal vagueness surrounded the possible forms of U.S. military action (no more than a battalion of marines was attached to the Sixth Fleet in the Mediterranean; otherwise it was a nuclear force). The proposed resolution possessed, in short, all the basic ingredients of the now standard Dullesian formula for brinkmanship: (1) an overstatement of the threat; (2) the development of an elaborate framework of specific "authority" within which the President could take or avoid action solely at his discretion; (3) ambiguous public warnings as to the likelihood of such action; and (4) extreme vagueness as to military means.

Britain and France were, of course, delighted with the new American move, not because of its stress on the Communist threat, but because it reinforced their view that a Western presence was required in the Middle East. Macmillan called the Eisenhower Doctrine "a recantation — an act of penitence — unparalleled in history." [31] Although this seemed hyperbolic, the "northern tier" countries of Turkey, Iran and Pakistan were equally enthusiastic. Much of the Arab world, however, took the new American initiative to mean another concerted effort to impose Western stability on the Middle East, to the advantage of American and European oil interests. The leaders of Egypt, Syria, Saudi Arabia, and Jordan, meeting in Cairo on January 19, categorically rejected the idea that a "power vacuum" existed in their area, and resolved "never to allow their countries to become a sphere of influence for any foreign power." [32] Iraq, Lebanon, and Saudi Arabia showed some interest in the idea of American protection, but the danger, as they saw it, was not "International Communism"; it was radical Nasserism. There is no doubt that the period following the Suez debacle presented a fluid situation in the Middle East, offering new opportunities, in certain countries, for the extension of Russian political and economic influence. There is equally no doubt that Khrushchev, sensing hesitation and disunity in the West, was in a mood to press for openings, and particularly to try to ride the strong anti-Western currents of Arab feeling. But the Eisenhower Doctrine was, in the circumstances, a rather blunt instrument, and particularly vulnerable to the charge that it was aimed primarily at preserving the status quo in a period of pervasive political, economic and social ferment. Khrushchev predicted that the Eisenhower Doctrine, because of its blatantly colonial overtones, would end up on "the garbage heap of history." [33]

After hearings extending over twelve weeks, and considerable amendment, Congress finally adopted the resolution and it was signed by the President on March 9. One result was to complete Dulles's efforts to encircle the Communist heartland with interconnected security pacts. As he said to the Senate Foreign Relations Committee: "Gradually, one part of the world after another is being brought into it, and perhaps we will end up with a, what you might call, universal doctrine reflected by multilateral treaties or multilateral world-wide authority from the Congress." [34] The latter phrase was an inaccuracy — probably inadvertent. The "multilateral world-wide authority" from Congress could be authority only for the unilateral use of American power.

Patching the Alliance

On February 26, Mollet and Pineau came to Washington in the first effort to repair the Western Alliance and, recognizing the inherent limitations, they seemed to make progress with Eisenhower and Dulles. Subdued but cordial talks were held on a wide range of subjects from Algeria and the Middle East to NATO, Euratom and the European Common Market. On March 20, the President and his Secretary of State journeyed to Bermuda for a similar two-day meeting with Macmillan and Selwyn Lloyd. The President, with his ingrained feeling for the importance of the Anglo-American tie, was clearly anxious to bind up the frayed strands, although he found it difficult at the outset to "talk constructively with our British colleagues . . . because of the blinding bitterness they felt toward Nasser"; indeed their obsession with "the possibilities of getting rid of Nasser" handicapped the common search for "a realistic method of operating the Canal." [35] But in an atmosphere marked by Eisenhower's cordiality and generosity of spirit, Macmillan managed rather brilliantly to submerge the Suez debacle without even repudiating the British policy. After the first day, the Prime Minister confided to his diary that "the atmosphere was very good . . . it is clear that we are not going to be the 'suppliants' or 'in the dock' at this conference. It is rather the other way round." Eisenhower told him privately that "he knew how unpopular Foster Dulles was with our people and with a lot of his people. But he must keep him. He could not do without him." [36]

Beyond a restoration of the amenities, the Bermuda meeting showed the two governments now substantially in accord that a serious power vacuum existed in the Middle East, and the President agreed the United States would now join the military planning committee of the Baghdad Pact, in addition to pressing on with the unilateral Eisenhower Doctrine. The "$64 question," [37] according to Macmillan, was whether or not the United States would wage political and economic warfare against Nasser (as Britain wanted to do) in the event Britain were forced to "eat dirt and accept a bad and unjust settlement" of the Suez Canal dispute.[38] Eisenhower's answer here did not reassure him, for he and Dulles proposed to unblock Egyptian currency and gradually resume surplus food shipments. Macmillan opposed the U.S. unfreezing of Egyptian funds because it would impose pressure on Britain to do the same, and he wished to avoid this while Nasser's claims against Britain for war damage were pending and unknown. Eisenhower also spoke at length of the "harm" done by the tendencies of both the British and American press to make the other country a scapegoat on Suez. He thought his own government had thus far made "very little effort to present the U.S. case as against that of UK or France," and he intended to continue such restraint, but he was disturbed at the steady abuse of American officials in the European press.[39] In a revealing aside, he told Macmillan that of course he himself "never read the newspapers or listened to the radio, but Mr. Hagerty told him about it," and he considered it "bad for good relations."[40] What mattered most to Eisenhower was a face-to-face understanding with Macmillan, and this was achieved.

On a more difficult matter, Eisenhower and Dulles reluctantly accepted the British decision to adopt its own "New Look" military strategy involving sharply reduced manpower and greater reliance on nuclear deterrence. Pressed by economic stringency, Macmillan had opted for the new British strategy in February, and only then had set out to persuade his WEU and NATO allies to accept it. They were all distressed, not only the Germans and the French, but even the Americans, for Washington did not equate its own reliance on mobile nuclear striking power with the situation of Britain. What aggrieved the European allies was the proposed cut in the British Army of the Rhine (from 80,000 to 50,000 men), for this both seemed a repudiation of Eden's commitment to WEU in 1954, and revived anxiety that West Germany would become the predominant military power on the Continent. Moreover, while there was no disagreement that in Europe ultimate reliance must be on nuclear retaliation, the new NATO commander, General Lauris Norstad, was pressing eloquently for "shield" forces of thirty divisions as the "irreducible minimum" to "force a pause" in a conventional Russian attack, thereby creating time for deliberation on a more consequential response by the highest NATO authorities.[41] His arguments were directed particularly against the budget-trimmers in Washington (of whom the President was one) who wanted to reduce American ground forces in Europe through the Radford Plan and similar devices. In the course of this debate, it became apparent that if *both* Britain and the United States withdrew troops from Europe, there would be no hope of building Norstad's shield force; indeed, it would be difficult to avoid troop cuts by every other NATO member.

As the exchanges continued through February and early March, Dulles found himself close to Norstad's view while Eisenhower tended to support Macmillan. Dulles's concern for nurturing the still-fragile political self-confidence in Europe was the basis of his opposition to American troop cuts. Norstad, on the other hand, made the purely military argument that a vital increment of security lay in a real "shield" as distinguished from a mere "trip-wire." Macmillan thought the practical distinction somewhat unreal, remarking that "all we could hope to do was to provide a period of delay with what some people call a shield and others a trip-wire," [42] and Eisenhower tended to agree.

The result was a compromise which sought to preserve both strategies. The United States agreed to strengthen the British deterrent by offering intermediate range ballistic missiles (IRBM) for emplacement in England under a joint operational arrangement that would leave custody of the nuclear warhead in American hands (as required by the Atomic Energy Act). Dulles and Norstad prevailed with respect to the retention of American forces in Germany; and at a special NATO meeting in April, the British agreed to postpone any troop withdrawals from the Continent until NATO could restudy the whole relationship between nuclear and conventional arms. Nothing effective could be done with the French, who had already withdrawn most of their combat contingents from NATO for service in Algeria.

The Doctrine Applied

The first challenge to the new status quo in the Middle East occurred in Jordan, in April, when the pro-Nasser government of Premier Nabulsi announced its intention to establish diplomatic relations with the Soviet Union. This offended King Hussein, who was quite alert to the difference between Nasserist and Russian influence, and who engineered a showdown on April 13 which succeeded in bringing the army over to his side, and forcing Nabulsi and several leading generals to flee. But the generals then established themselves in Syria, proclaiming Hussein's coup "an imperialist plot" and vowing his overthrow. This new situation presented the risk that King Hussein might fall and Jordan be thereafter carved up by Syria, Saudi Arabia, Iraq, and Israel.

The situation did not fit the formula of the Eisenhower Doctrine, nor was the survival of King Hussein a self-evident requirement of United States security; indeed, the American interest in Jordanian stability seemed a derivative of the British view that the Hashemite family (which was the base point of British power in Iraq) could not long survive there if its Jordanian wing were brought down. But the Eisenhower Doctrine, in its essence, transcended any tangible United States national interest. Reflecting the pure Dullesian approach, it was an abstract, inflatable, ideological device designed to control the pace, direction and nature of change throughout the Middle East by applying the unilateral police power of the United States, and it operated on the premise that all Russian, all local Communist, and most Nasserist influence was illegitimate. The factor of opposition to Nasser was probably subliminal, but showed itself in Dulles's persistent operational tendency to deny any distinction between radical Arabism and Communism. In some preliminary maneuvering, he sought to broaden the rationale for action in Jordan by asserting that U.S. policy was guided not alone by the Eisenhower Doctrine but also by the Tripartite Declaration of 1950. He then persuaded Eisenhower (who was golfing in Augusta) to authorize a statement saying that "both the Secretary of State and I regard the independence and integrity of Jordan as vital." [43] This was followed by a swift and well-publicized move of the Sixth Fleet (with its two aircraft carriers and 1,800 marines) to the Eastern Mediterranean, a move which effectively transformed a Jordanian matter into an international crisis. King Hussein did not formally request American assistance, since to do so would have played into the hands of his domestic opposition, but with this powerful backing he was able to deter the incipient rebels in Jordan and to reassert his own firm control.

In August there was more serious trouble in Syria. After the Syrian radio announced the expulsion of three U.S. embassy officials for subversive activities in an alleged plot to overthrow the regime of President Kuwatly, the army chief of staff resigned and was replaced by an officer known for his pro-Moscow sympathies. This new military commander then quickly signed an agreement with Russia for $500 million of economic and military aid. President Kuwatly, who was not the strong man in Damascus and who probably was not a party to the Soviet aid agreement, hurried off to confer with Nasser, while the fear quickly spread that Syria was about to be officially incorporated as a Soviet satellite. Intense diplomatic consultations followed in Ankara, involving the Turks, Iraqis and Jordanians, from which emerged an apparent conclusion that the new Syrian regime must be overthrown, and promptly — before a Soviet-Syrian mutual defense treaty could be signed and announced. Did this mean preemptive war? Eisenhower's memoirs tend to blur this reality, citing an agreement among the nations at Ankara that no military action would be taken "until Syria had actually committed aggression against her neighbors"; they anticipated, however, that "such provocation would be forthcoming in a short time." Beneath the euphemism, Eisenhower conceded that "we were being asked to give our tacit approval to an invasion of one sovereign nation by another." [44]

In any event, Washington showed no hesitation in making preliminary moves. Assurances were quietly given to Premier Menderes, King Faisal and King Hussein that the United States would expedite arms shipments, replace equipment losses, and take steps to prevent outside interference — from Russia or Israel. The Sixth Fleet once more steamed to the Eastern Mediterranean, and U.S. fighter aircraft were moved from Western Europe to the American base at Adana, Turkey. A senior diplomat, Loy

Henderson, was dispatched on a fact-finding trip which, surprisingly and to the great irritation of the Syrians, omitted a visit to Syria. From Turkey, however, he reported that Syria's pro-Soviet moves were "extremely serious," and his finding seemed to reinforce Washington's solid support for a bellicose decision. Eisenhower thought Iraq was the logical Arab power to take the initiative "in retaliation," [45] with the forces of Lebanon, Jordan, and Turkey massed on the other three Syrian frontiers to force a dispersal of Syrian troops. Prime Minister Macmillan, who thought the matter had gone rather too far, noted that paradoxically the British function had suddenly become "not to stimulate" but "to restrain the impetuousness of the State Department, which was interpreting the new 'Eisenhower Doctrine' with all the enthusiasm of recent converts." [46]

Even without British restraint, however, the war plan quickly came unstuck. Iraq could not attack Syria without courting the destruction of her oil pipelines which ran through the latter country and earned $200 million a year (or half the governmental revenue). Nor could attack be attempted without serious risk of nationalist efforts in Jordan and Saudi Arabia (aroused by Radio Cairo) to bring down the crowned heads of those two countries. When these truths sank in, King Hussein pointedly departed the Ankara meetings for a vacation in Italy, and King Saud intervened with a private warning that Washington was creating needless tumult and adding nothing to its own standing for wisdom among the Arabs. This latter move, which puzzled and irritated Dulles, underlined the fact that Radio Cairo had become, for certain purposes, a decisive political instrument. Reaching into every village square and coffee house throughout the Middle East, it was capable of arousing an intensely pro-Nasser, Pan-Arabic feeling among the common people of every Arab country. It thus served as a formidable deterrent to the attempt by any Arab government to align itself with the West against Nasser or Nasser's allies. This nationalism was not pro-Communist, but it was violently anti-Western, and the ruler of a fifteenth-century country whose people demanded more political change and economic improvement than he chose to give was not comfortable in the face of charges from the Egyptian Republic that he was a tool of United States policy.

Faced with this renewed evidence that Communism was not the decisive issue for Arabs, Washington found it prudent temporarily to restrain the Turks. Dulles told a press conference he thought things would work out peacefully. Syria took no provocative action; Moscow remained passive. At a September meeting of the heads of state of Saudi Arabia, Iraq, and Syria, King Saud declared publicly that he would "deplore" aggression against any Arab country, including Syria (a declaration which Allen Dulles thought was aimed at strengthening the internal position of President Kuwatly vis-à-vis his pro-Soviet colleagues).[47] Whatever the motivation, it signaled the end of any possibility that military action against Syria would be taken by another Arab state.

The Turks, however, increased their forces on the Syrian frontier from 32,000 to 50,000 and, with clandestine American encouragement, sought to maintain a state of tension, apparently persisting in the hope that a war of nerves could still unseat the new pro-Russian leadership in Damascus. The new Undersecretary of State, Christian Herter, thought such "clandestine American attempts to spur Turkish forces to do some vague kind of battle with Syria" were clumsy and ill-considered.[48] Syria soon filed a complaint with the United Nations; and on October 8, in an interview with James Reston, Khrushchev accused the United States of having urged Turkey (through Loy Henderson) to attack Syria. Applying his own happy brand of brinkmanship, he warned that "if the rifles fire, the rockets will start flying," in which case, Turkey would "not last one day."[49] Dulles felt called upon to respond in kind: "If there is an attack on Turkey by the Soviet Union, it would not mean a purely defensive operation by the United States, with the Soviet Union a privileged sanctuary from which to attack Turkey."[50] In the wake of these rhetorical pyrotechnics, the crisis was finally resolved on October 29 at a party in Moscow given by the Turkish ambassador; Khrushchev, arriving in jovial spirits, agreed there was no longer a threat to peace in the Middle East. The Turks reduced their forces on the border, and Syria withdrew its complaint to the United Nations.

26

A Time of Twilight

THERE WAS FURTHER EVIDENCE in the latter half of 1957 that the administration had settled into a rather fixed perception of the outer world and an established way of responding to the problems it presented. Definite and predictable patterns of behavior had developed, signaling the end of serious efforts to create new and innovative approaches. In a word, after five years in office, the Eisenhower team was showing signs of an intellectual and operational crystallization. More than ever it seemed in danger of being surprised or overwhelmed by dramatic events in a period characterized by accelerating change and by more aggressive initiatives out of both Russia and China.

The Rigid China Policy

Relative calm marked the situation in the Formosa Strait throughout 1956 and 1957. The cease-fire achieved after the Bandung conference held firm, and Peking turned its principal attention to extending normal diplomatic, trade and cultural relations both in Asia and beyond. Most of the major trading countries, including Japan, had by now eliminated the special restrictions on trade with China imposed at the time of the Korean War, and were moving to normalize economic relations. To this general trend, however, America's retention of "total embargo" was a conspicuous exception. Senators Fulbright and Humphrey, seeing "new forces astir," urged a reexamination of America's basic posture, but, even though the relaxation by other countries had reduced the Ameri-

"Don't You Ever Have Anything Fresh?"

From *Herblock's Special For Today*
SIMON & SCHUSTER, 1958

can policy to mere symbolic significance, Dulles clung stubbornly to the shopworn posture of total exclusion, throwing back the unpersuasive argument that "whatever others may do," the United States "ought not build up the military power of its potential enemy." [1]

This posture, of course, had its roots in domestic politics, but also in personal moral conviction; and by 1957 Eisenhower's sense of indignation at Peking seems to have exceeded Dulles's own. At the March meeting in Bermuda with the British, Dulles had expressed to Selwyn Lloyd the wish that London might adopt Washington's policy of non-recognition and opposition to UN membership for the Mao regime, as this would, he felt, make it easier for Washington to ease trade restrictions. Lloyd replied that he had come to believe the American policy was the more practical one, and he noted that recognition had been extended by a Labour government, but he saw no purpose in reversing the British position.[2] Eisenhower spoke at length on the "strong sentiment" in the United States against the Chinese Communists, and declared that if that regime ever got into the UN the United States might get out. Macmillan replied that this seemed to indicate a highly conditional American support for the UN, one confined to those situations where the UN agreed with the United States. Eisenhower then backed off somewhat, saying, well, he would fight to keep America in the UN if China were admitted, "but it would probably take a real effort on his part." [3]

A further consequence of this defensive mood was the administration's unwillingness to use the opportunity afforded by the lull to clarify the U.S. commitment in the Formosa Strait, or to take any other measures that might prevent or mitigate another predictable explosion over the offshore islands. In part this inattention was a consequence of Dulles's style — he was a crisis fire fighter, rushing from one quarter of the globe to another to quench the highest flames, and in 1956–1957 Taiwan and the offshore islands were only smoldering. But the immobilism here had deeper roots, reflecting the policy dilemma he had helped to create in 1954 by his espousal of Chiang's argument that Nationalist control of Taiwan depended on holding the offshore islands. By 1957, this view was a hardened conviction:

I realize full well that to many people, including some of the leaders of our Allies, it seems ridiculous to think of defending the off-shore islands . . . with the possibility of bringing on a major war with Communist China, perhaps also with the Soviet Union. But I strongly believe that to give them over to the Chinese Communists would not prevent war but promote it, because this would stimulate their desire and demands for more, namely, Formosa, and then the other free countries in the area. . . . Therefore, to me the defense of Quemoy is essential to the defense of Formosa.[4]

But could not the issues of Quemoy and Taiwan be disconnected by inducing Chiang to reduce the offshore island garrisons to token levels, as Eisenhower had urged in 1955? "I've talked on many occasions with the Generalissimo and I know that on this point Chiang would bow only to pressure so tremendous that it would in fact break him . . . the reaction in Formosa would defeat our own objectives." [5] The result was a policy of determined myopia, remarkable for the degree to which it abandoned Washington's power to control events, leaving the United States at the mercy of initiatives from either Chiang or the Chinese Communists that might carry it instantly to the brink of major war.

Despite Dulles's firm efforts to hold to the predetermined course, growing elements of American opinion showed themselves restive, and the hitherto closed subject of China was now being increasingly ventilated in congressional committees, public forums, classrooms, and the press. The application of logic to the problem revealed the possibilities of gradual change. Soon the Nationalist Chinese ambassador to Washington publicly complained of "an increasing trend among some American public opinion leaders to seek some kind of a compromise with Red China and appeasement of its aims," [6] and there followed in May a riot on Taiwan in which a mob sacked the American embassy and injured thirteen Americans while police stood quietly by. Ostensibly the violence was related to a dispute over criminal jurisdiction — popular resentment touched off by American insistence on maintaining jurisdiction in the criminal case of an American sergeant (a resident member of the military advisory group) charged with shooting a Chinese burglar. But foreign diplomats in Taipei, observing that spontaneous demonstrations did not occur on Taiwan, concluded that the riot was a calculated show of Chiang's displeasure with his Washington ally for permitting a dangerous drift in American opinion.

In apparent response, Dulles delivered in San Francisco, on June 28, a detailed restatement of U.S. policy toward China.[7] While he had little to say about Taiwan, he made clear that the inflexible line toward Peking was morally correct and would not be changed. Undercutting those who had professed to see a gradual mellowing of his attitude toward a settlement in Asia, Dulles asserted that "neither recognition, nor trade, nor cultural relations, nor all three would favorably influence the evolution of affairs in China." On the contrary, United States recognition of the Peking regime would simply "enhance their ability to hurt us and our friends"; admission of Communist China to the United Nations would implant in that organization "the seeds of its own destruction." In the same vein, he insisted that "nothing could be more dangerous than for the United States to operate on the theory that, if hostile and evil forces do not quickly or readily change, then it is we who must change to meet them. . . . If communism is stubborn for the wrong, let us be steadfast for the right." [8]

This restatement of Dulles's determination to keep China "in Coventry," condemned to eternal damnation for its Korean "aggression" and isolated from intercourse with respectable nations, rested heavily on the subjective factor of moral disapproval, which had been largely abandoned by modern diplomacy. Most nations, including the United States, now accord recognition if the government in question exercises de facto control of its national territory, but the act carries with it no implication of moral approval. Dulles understood this. In his first book, *War, Peace and Change* (1939), he had cogently argued the practical futility of refusing recognition to an existing national power, and in his second book, *War or Peace* (1950), he had recommended U.S. recognition of Communist China provided only that the Mao regime "proves its ability to govern China without serious domestic resistance." [9] Soon thereafter, however, he judged domestic political feelings to be too explosive for the application of logic. And now in 1957, he had need to bolster his own shaky position by reassuring the conservatives in Congress and by reasserting personal control of China policy as against the proponents of change in the press, the Congress, and even the State Department (Robert Bowie, who was leaving government that summer, had delivered himself of a long departing memorandum that urged a searching revision of the approach to Chiang and the problem of mainland China). Dulles thus declared in San Francisco that recognition was an instrument of national policy ("there is nothing automatic about it"), a means of exerting pressure which the United States must continue to use against the Peking regime, if only because disastrous consequences would flow from permitting that regime to gain "international standing and prestige." [10]

The substance of this speech was later incorporated, and elaborated, in a State Department memorandum sent to all American diplomatic posts in the Far East.[11] By its categorical judgments, it was intended to eliminate any reasonable basis for alternative policy positions. Seeming to reflect Dulles's personal hand, it was a crafty lawyer's brief, making much of its case with specious rationalizations that skillfully evaded the force of arguments on the other side. Judged in its entirety, it suggested why public opinion in many parts of the world found United States policy toward China to be not only unrealistic, but intellectually dishonest. The Chinese Communists failed to qualify for recognition, even by the usual objective tests, the memorandum argued, because they "have not completed their conquest of the country." But this was a reference to Taiwan, where Peking's failure to gain control was the direct consequence of total U.S. opposition, including military support

"However, We've Been Pretty Successful In Keeping American Newspapermen Out Of China"

From *Herblock's Special For Today*
SIMON & SCHUSTER, 1958

for the emigré faction. Conceding that the Peking regime was not "on the verge of collapse," the memorandum argued there was "equally no reason to accept its rule in mainland China as permanent." But no government anywhere is necessarily permanent, nor is recognition an irrevocable act. Again the memorandum asserted that the Peking regime represented only "a tiny minority" of the Chinese people and clearly did not represent "the will of the populace substantially declared." But general application of that principle would mean that only democratic regimes deserved and would receive American recognition. In fact, the United States was currently doing business not only with Soviet Russia, but with Spain, Portugal, Saudi Arabia, Pakistan, and Thailand, to name only some of the countries which were ruled by varying degrees of authoritarian or dictatorial governments, not one of which remotely approached the Jeffersonian ideal apparently required of Peking. Nor did the argument reflect the string of Latin American military juntas whose bloc-voting in the United Nations provided decisive support in the continued exclusion of Communist China from UN membership.

No Cultural Exchanges

In the June 28 speech, Dulles said: "We also doubt the value of cultural exchanges," and his actions in August suggested that the doubt extended as well to any form of communication. Peking had taken the initiative in 1956 to relax existing travel restrictions by inviting a number of American journalists to visit and report on China. The State Department's first reaction was to deny passports to the invited newsmen, using the boiler-plate argument that the United States could not validate a passport for travel to a country whose government the United States did not recognize. When the general manager of the Associated Press, reluctantly accepting this decision, wrote to the Secretary asking that he keep an open mind on the subject, particularly if the four remaining American civilians in Chinese prisons were released, Dulles made an oddly oblique response: "The United States Government is unwilling to change its policies toward Communist China," he replied, "when Chinese Communist authorities are using American citizens as political hostages for the very purpose of forcing us to modify these policies." [12] But this posture met with mounting criticism in the media, and Dulles was forced to address the question again a year later.

On August 22, 1957, the State Department announced a "compromise" whereunder a limited number of American news organizations would be permitted to accredit correspondents to Communist China for an experimental period of seven months; this seemed reasonable enough, until it became clear that the new policy would preclude the Chinese from selecting their own journalists for an exchange visit to the United States. The State Department based its case on the narrow grounds that American immigration law requires each visa application to be judged on its individual merit. According to Dulles's assistant John Hanes, the real sticking point for the Secretary of State was Peking's insistence on accepting only those newsmen to whom it had issued invitations. This was apparently agreeable to American news organizations, but not to Dulles. According to Hanes, the Chinese were privately informed that, as a practical matter, the Chinese newsmen selected by them would be admitted, but that they in turn would have to accept American journalists selected by American news organizations. According to Hanes, the Chinese refused reciprocity on that basis.[13] Some tincture of justification might be found for this narrow and technical legalism, but it offended the American press and showed the true measure of Dulles's enthusiasm for any contacts with China. Other edifying examples of American statesmanship vis-à-vis China in 1957 included the banning of a panda, sought by an American zoo, because it originated in China, and the indictment of an American stamp dealer because he imported Chinese government stamps.

The question has been asked by historians and journalists why Dulles did not hold more tenaciously to his sound Stimsonian doctrine (that diplomatic recognition acknowledges de facto control, but implies no moral approval), why he did not nurture it and harness it to Eisenhower's great political popularity and power in a major effort to recognize Communist China and establish direct and continuous relations with that government, as with the government of the Soviet Union. Had this been achieved, there is nothing to suggest that harmonious relations would have ensued, but the somber American tragedy in Vietnam during the 1960s would very probably have been mitigated, and perhaps even averted, by the fact that direct diplomatic association would have produced a better mutual understanding of Chinese and American purposes.

The answer to the question would seem to lie in an unsimple combination of perception, political will, emotional preference, self-protective prudence, and circumstance. With the Korean War still being fought and with the new internationalist administration in need of establishing some orthodox Republican credentials, the year 1953 would have been an impossible time for an approach to China, even for Eisenhower; nor is there any assurance that Peking would have responded favorably. In 1954, the prospect was virtually precluded by Dulles's obsessive belief that Peking's hand was behind the nationalist, anticolonialist rebellion in Indochina, and that Communist China posed a direct military threat to all of Asia. In late 1954 and early 1955, the situation at Quemoy would have made a conciliatory U.S. approach appear as a yielding to military pressure. But in the first year of the second term (during the long lull in the Formosa Strait and after the main force of the China Lobby was spent), if Eisenhower had advanced the argument that, out of his long military experience he had learned the vital importance of never losing contact with an enemy, and that diplomatic recognition was akin to establishing an outpost, it is probable he would have readily carried the day. He was uniquely trusted and liked by the American people. By 1957, however, Dulles was under such severe personal attack that the prospects of another major fight with fellow Republicans must have seemed wildly imprudent to him, perhaps even fatal to his retention of office. Moreover, such a move would have involved a wholesale repudiation of his assessment of events in Asia since 1951. For these reasons, the Secretary of State was not enthusiastic. In addition, by 1957, it was also evident that the President lacked the energy or desire to make such a fight — indeed that his emotional antipathy to Communist China had grown with the passage of time.

Thus hemmed in by domestic political attacks that reinforced his self-protective instincts, and dubious about the merits of the question, Dulles was also hobbled by an evident decline in presidential will. If he and Eisenhower had sat down sometime in late 1955 or early 1956 and planned a long-term approach to the problem of recognizing China, they might have been ready when circumstances were favorable. But under Eisenhower's conduct of the presidency, he did not initiate anything — problems came to him for judicial weighing and deciding. And Dulles's fast-paced, tactical style virtually precluded the possibility of a long-range plan on any subject.

Crisis in the Kremlin

Meanwhile, in the Soviet Union, Khrushchev was under pressure from elements in the Communist party who felt that his leniency with Tito and Gomulka and his domestic de-Stalinization program had led directly to the ill-fated Hungarian challenge. And indeed, having been led by Khrushchev down the path of "separate roads to Socialism," the Kremlin leaders now faced the doctrinal and practical problem of how to reconcile this new condition with an adequate degree of discipline and central direction, and how to make such a compromise stick with the increasingly disparate elements of the international movement. The contending forces were soon locked in a power struggle and Khrushchev's political life was at stake. Chou En-lai interrupted a missionary tour of Southeast Asia in January 1957 for emergency visits to Budapest, Warsaw and Moscow, his purpose being to mediate a dispute that threatened the Communist world with deepening factionalism and bloodshed. In Hungary, he endorsed the Soviet-imposed Kadar regime, and in Poland he persuaded Gomulka that "national communism" in that country must, as a practical matter, be tempered with acknowledgment that the Kremlin's interest could not be ignored. In Moscow, he joined in a public redefinition of the permissible limits of national independence "within the camp of Socialism." Taken altogether it was a brilliant and forceful performance, permitting Khrushchev to save his own position for the moment, and to stabilize the situation throughout Eastern Europe.

But the conflict was far from resolved, for the Khrushchev policy entailed, indeed encouraged, a general "loosening of fraternal bonds" in Eastern Europe, and this seemed to old-line Stalinists a course too dangerous to countenance. Their fear and anger were soon exacerbated by American credits to Poland in the spring and by further economic and military aid to Tito, including jet aircraft. Thus, when he returned from Finland in early June, Khrushchev found himself beset in the Presidium by enemies (Molotov, Malenkov, Kaganovitch, and Shepilov) demanding his immediate resignation. With great presence of mind, he managed to transfer the debate to the full Central Committee and thus gain time for rallying support in both the party and the military establishment. The defense minister, Marshal Zhukov, played a decisive role in the ensuing debate, which lasted from June 22 to June 29 and ended with the summary expulsion of his enemies (the "antiparty" plotters).

Significantly, none was killed or imprisoned, but all were farmed out to relatively inconsequential jobs — e.g., Molotov was sent as ambassador to the Mongolian People's Republic. The official account of the affair accused the "antiparty" group of being "shackled by old notions and methods" and thus out of touch with the new "advance towards Communism"; they "hampered in every way" the efforts of Chairman Khrushchev to carry out "the new pressing measures intended to ease international tension and promote universal peace." By July the remarkable Khrushchev had won another precarious victory over what Tito once called the "ingrown Stalinist tendencies" of the Soviet political system.

Flight of the Sputniks

What seemed, for a considerable time thereafter, the crowning consequence of the administration's inability or refusal to read the portents of a world gripped by accelerating change occurred in the early hours of Friday, October 4, 1957. Shortly after midnight, the Soviets announced that a man-made satellite called "sputnik" was orbiting the earth some 560 miles up at about 18,000 miles per hour. An almost visible tremor ran through the American body politic, knocking out the remaining footings on which Dulles had erected the policy to defeat Communism by bringing to bear Western superiority in economic strength, military power, and morality. Now a country supposedly hobbled by a technical backwardness inherent in the Communist system had hurled the first mechanism beyond the earth's atmosphere. The administration quickly sought to depreciate the achievement and its implications (various spokesmen calling it "a nice technical trick" and "an outer-space basketball game"), but this reaction wholly missed the unabashed wonder, combining excitement and fear, which the event had aroused throughout the world. And on November 2, the Soviets launched a second sputnik, this one a 1,100-pound vehicle with an air-conditioned compartment containing a dog.

These events did not change the power balance. Eisenhower said, accurately, in his State of the Union Message two months later that the Strategic Air Command and its naval air supplement remained "the most powerful deterrent to war in the world today." Moreover, the administration had a creditable record on ballistic missile development, in contrast with the slack attention given to that sector of science and armaments in the latter Truman years. Yet like lightning flashes that suddenly illuminate an entire landscape, the twin meteors made graphically clear that the basis of peace would henceforward be a balance of nuclear deterrence. They etched in the sky the end of pretensions to meaningful American nuclear superiority. They also sent a vivid political message to the Third World, which the *London Economist* translated thus: "We Russians, a backward people ourselves less than a lifetime ago, can now do even more spectacular things than the rich and pompous West, thanks to Communism." [14]

The administration now came under still further political attack for a serious failure to see and plan ahead, and for the first time sharp criticism extended to the President personally. Beyond the missile issue, his confused handling of the new budget * (where he had both countenanced and endorsed an attack by the Secretary of the Treasury upon his own presumably considered submissions) and his limp support for civil rights (followed by a sudden dispatch of federal troops to settle the Little Rock school crisis when confronted by a challenge to presidential power) raised new questions as to whether or not he was fully in touch with the affairs of his own administration. New doubts were

* FY1958 (beginning July 1, 1957).

cast on his physical vigor, and it was known that his staff went out of its way to "avoid upsetting the old man," his health rather than the coherence of the White House operation being their first concern. In the immediate aftermath of the sputniks, neither Eisenhower nor Dulles proved capable of a constructive initiative, and there was a noticeable drift in affairs. As the British ambassador, Sir Harold Caccia, informed Prime Minister Macmillan, the American reaction "has been something equivalent to Pearl Harbour [sic]; the . . . cocksureness is shaken." [15]

The British Initiative

It thus fell to the resilient Macmillan to seize the moment. His instinct was for a bilateral Anglo-American meeting both to strengthen the "English-speaking" entente (and the British role within it), and to make it the focus of a wider strategic reappraisal that would encompass the whole Western ability to meet the Russian challenge on every front and in every sphere of activity. Eisenhower quickly agreed to a meeting in Washington on October 23, and for the first time acknowledged to the British that "America cannot stand alone, still less 'go it alone.' " [16] It was a chastening moment.

Specifically, Macmillan sought repeal of the McMahon Act of 1946, which precluded the United States from sharing scientific data in the nuclear field with even its closest allies. The Bermuda agreement, in the spring, to emplace American-manned IRBM's in Britain had constituted a beginning, but Macmillan now wanted the means to achieve an independent British deterrent force with nuclear warheads of British design and manufacture. The administration agreed to see what could be worked out. The first day of talks, however, skated over and around the issues, with the President showing a tendency not to come to grips with what was to be done, or how, in a practical way. As Macmillan noted in his diary: "However, Foster was persistent, in his slow laborious way and at one time I thought we should get down to real business. But we didn't. Rather unfairly, I could not help thinking of the criticism of another statesman — 'his speech was slow, but it easily kept pace with his thought.' " [17] On the second day, Dulles proposed two Anglo-American committees — one on weapons collaboration, the other on scientific nuclear data — to work on the problem and render their reports before the day was out. He said that the administration would fight for an amendment to the McMahon Act which excluded Britain from its strictures, and which would thus permit technical assistance and an exchange of data. Macmillan had successfully, if partially and temporarily, revived the special Anglo-American relationship.

The question of how to come to practical grips with the need for a new approach had thus been answered initially by a bilateral solution. This done, the need to mitigate jealousies and misunderstandings became evident. By good fortune the NATO Secretary-General, Paul-Henri Spaak, was also in Washington, and he was quickly drawn into the discussions, from which emerged a plan to transform the regular NATO meeting in December into a gathering of the fourteen heads of government. The Washington communiqué said in part: because "self-sufficiency is now out of date," the two governments would urge NATO to adopt "an enlarged Atlantic effort in scientific research and development" in order to "permit close and fruitful collaboration of scientists and engineers." Seeking to offset the pervasive pessimism in the West, it added: "The free nations possess vast assets, both material and moral. These in the aggregate are far greater than those of the Communist world. We do not ignore the fact that the Soviet rulers can achieve formidable material accomplishments by concentrating upon selected development. . . . Despotisms have often been able to produce spectacular monuments. But the price has been heavy." [18]

The President under Stress

The political consequences of the sputniks continued to spread in the United States, revealing an acute national anxiety and self-doubt. Public concern about the adequacy of American deterrent power soon became a mushrooming concern that the entire American educational system was defective (especially in its failure to produce the requisite number and quality of scientists to assure the nation's technical superiority and thus its safety). A distinguished study panel (established the previous April by the office of defense mobilization) had rendered a report that now found its way into the public press. Known as the Gaither Report,* it found that the Soviet gross national product, although only one-third as large as the American economy, was growing perhaps twice as fast, and that Soviet expenditures for armed forces and heavy industry were equal to those of the United States. It also expressed the judgment that by 1959 the Soviets could possibly attack the United States with one hundred intercontinental ballistic missiles carrying megaton nuclear warheads, and that such an attack would find the bomber force of the Strategic Air Command on crowded airfields, vulnerable to destruction. Thus morbidly preoccupied with the "worst case" military contingency, no one in Wash-

---

* For its chairman, H. Rowan Gaither, President of the Ford Foundation. Members of the panel included Robert C. Sprague, William C. Foster, Robert Lovett, John J. McCloy, Frank Stanton, and Jerome B. Wiesner.

ington seemed to be listening when Khrushchev, who grasped the meaning of nuclear stalemate, came close to declaring a "no-first-use" policy on nuclear weapons. Addressing the Supreme Soviet on November 7, he said the USSR ruled out the achievement of its aims by "such monstrous means." The Soviet government "solemnly declare that our people have never thought, nor will they ever think, of using any means of destruction unless our country is attacked by imperialist countries." [19]

Eisenhower struggled to maintain the national sense of proportion against extremes of public anxiety, but he seemed defensive, besieged and a little bewildered. In a private talk with Emmet Hughes, he answered the latter's assertion that neither American foreign policy nor the Secretary of State commanded great confidence at home or abroad: "I know you're right to this extent — people just don't like that personality of Foster's, while they do like me. The fact remains that he just knows more about foreign affairs than anybody I know," except possibly himself. But "I can't take his job and move over there." [20] Were there alternatives? Possibly General Alfred Gruenther, who had succeeded him as NATO commander; "he's got what it takes. But a soldier in that job — with me here?" [21] In a rambling soliloquy, he also thought Gruenther could be the Republican presidential nominee in 1960, although his first choice was clearly his new Secretary of the Treasury, Robert Anderson, followed by William Rogers, Sherman Adams, and Richard Nixon in roughly that order. The problems of political succession and of finding qualified men for assignments of great consequence absorbed him, as they absorb all presidents, and especially at times when things are going badly. One thing he did not tell Hughes was that the previous winter, when Dulles was hospitalized with cancer, he had summoned Thomas E. Dewey from New York to discuss a cabinet post, but that Dewey had deflected the impending offer. As the New Yorker recalled it: "I got some whispers that he had something very serious on his mind. Foster was sick and Wilson was quitting — and I didn't know which it was, but we had quite a long talk and he was edging up to it." [22] At that point Dewey interrupted to remind the President that when he, Dewey, had set out in 1950 to sponsor Eisenhower for the presidency, he had categorically declared — in order to make certain his motives were not misunderstood — that he would never accept an appointment from President Eisenhower: "I just wanted him to understand that . . . I didn't ever want to embarrass him by turning anything down, but that I was not going to enter the government." [23]

Now in the waning days of the year as the shadows lengthened toward December, Eisenhower seemed to feel more than ever the stress and tension of the situation, and the burden and loneliness of his office. Writing to a friend on November 18, he said that ever since the fateful evening in mid-1956 when Nasser announced the nationalization of the Suez Canal, "I cannot remember a day that has not brought its major or minor crisis." [24] On November 25, while sitting at his White House desk after lunch, he experienced difficulty in picking up a paper that lay before him; as he glanced down on it, the printing seemed literally to run off the top of the page. He rang for his secretary, only to find when she came that he could not speak intelligibly. "Words — but not the ones I wanted — came to my tongue. It was impossible for me to express any coherent thought whatsoever." [25] The President had suffered the third breakdown of his health in twenty-six months, this time a "cerebral spasm," a mild stroke causing a temporary disconnection between his mental "dictionary" and the thought he wished to express. But unless recovery were reasonably swift, the result could be a progressive loss of memory and of the capacity for orderly analysis and decision. Burdened now with yet another setback, one both terrifying in its personal dimension and profoundly grave in its implications for Western leadership, and facing a time of unprecedented public anxiety, Eisenhower bravely determined to make a full recovery in time for the December NATO meeting, or, failing that, to resign. Once more his extraordinary physical resilience and strong will rescued him, yet the whole affair, which included an Atlantic crossing at low altitude to avoid strain on his heart, seemed to symbolize the sense of faltering infirmity that gripped the Western world.

Shadows on the Free World

With Dulles showing visible concern for the President's health and performance, Eisenhower read the opening passages of his speech without difficulty, then by prearrangement handed over the balance of the presentation to the Secretary of State. The words carried an undertone of uneasiness beneath the overt resolve, reflecting the air of undefinable disquiet that hung over the whole meeting: "We are here to re-dedicate ourselves to the task of dispelling the shadows that are being cast upon the free world. . . . This is a time for greatness. . . . We pray for greatness in the spirit of self-sacrifice, so that we may forsake lesser objectives and interests to devote ourselves wholly to the well-being of all of us. . . . All of us have a vital stake in this sense of increasing sacrifice. . . . The forces arrayed against us are formidable but not irresistible." [26]

The United States, Dulles announced, offered to provide intermediate range ballistic missiles to Europe under control of the NATO commander, and to establish a NATO stockpile of nuclear warheads under similar control; in addition it proposed a wider pooling of scientific and technical research and cooperation with a view to facilitating the production of modern weapons by the European countries. The reaction to these offers was decidedly mixed. France, in the throes of yet another governmental crisis in the approaching terminal illness of the Fourth Republic, and preoccupied by the savage Algerian struggle, was in a mood of ineffectual gloom and despondency. The West Germans were very reserved on the matter of receiving IRBM's, fearing both to provoke the Russians and complicate the question of unification. Adenauer told Macmillan privately he did not want the weapons on German soil, yet did not wish to take such a position openly.[27] The Scandinavians proved similarly aloof. What the European governments really wanted in the wake of the sputniks, and what their public opinion was beginning to demand, was a new effort to reach basic agreement with the Russians, an agreement that would place some reasonable controls on the terrible spiral of nuclear arms. More alert than Dulles to this political necessity, Macmillan took the lead in guiding the meeting to a position that balanced NATO acceptance of the American proposals with agreement to sponsor another conference with the Soviets, at the level of Foreign Ministers, and to accept any reasonable plan for arms reduction of which "reliable inspection" was an integral part. "The Americans did not much like this plan, but finally agreed," Macmillan wrote, when it became clear that this was the unavoidable price to be paid for NATO acceptance of nuclear weapons.[28] The meeting contributed its part to easing the fears aroused by the sputniks, but in the end only Britain, Italy and Turkey accepted the IRBM's.

Thus ended the cruelest year for the policy assumptions of which Dulles was the embodiment, and for the proclaimed policy itself of which he was the principal architect. Initiative had passed to the adversary. Washington was governed by old, tired, unimaginative men. It seemed a time of twilight.

27

Radical Nationalism in the Middle East

THE MIDDLE EAST SITUATION in 1958 was characterized by a gathering momentum of the forces of violent nationalism and Pan-Arabism and by a strong Western tendency to oppose these, albeit from several different vantage points and for ostensibly different reasons. London's assessment had the virtue of being most nearly accurate, seeing Nasserism as the principal threat to British interests in Jordan, Iraq, and the Persian Gulf. Washington, on the other hand, showed a persisting tendency to link radical Arab nationalism with "International Communism," with which in fact it had no internal connection, indeed to which it increasingly showed itself in open opposition, as the Soviet Union sought to scavenge the indigenous revolutionary impulses for its own purposes. Whether the American stance reflected Dulles's inability to perceive real distinctions, or was a deliberate ploy to strengthen domestic support for a policy of intervention by invoking the sacred theme of anti-Communism, was not wholly clear. Dulles's deep Wilsonian belief that the status quo, while not sacrosanct, must not be changed by force and violence, lived side by side with his equally deep suspicion of the Soviet-Egyptian relationship, and Nasser was without question a destabilizing force. Eisenhower on the other hand seemed merely confused: "If he [Nasser] was not a Communist, he certainly succeeded in making us very suspicious of him." [1] They were, however, in full agreement that the paramount need was order, and for its achievement they placed their faith mainly in military arrangements.

In Ankara on February 1 for a meeting of the Baghdad Pact, Dulles formalized the earlier American agreement to join the military planning committee, and indeed offered a three-star general to serve as full-time deputy director of the permanent staff, at the same time holding to the fiction that the United States was not really a full-fledged member of the alliance. A month later, he asserted that the Eisenhower Doctrine had in its first year of existence played a "decisive role . . . in strengthening the nations of the Middle East . . . to resist the insidious and ever-present threat of international communism." [2] In fact the results seemed rather more modest. It had provided some economic and military assist-ance to Iraq, Jordan, Lebanon and Saudi Arabia, but the very acceptance of these programs had aggravated tensions inside those nations and further separated their governments from public opinion. The doctrine had saved Jordan from diplomatic recognition of the Soviet Union, and perhaps from a civil war. American encouragement of Turkish pressure on Syria had not involved an invocation of the Eisenhower Doctrine, per se, but the pressure probably precipitated the dramatic act of union between Syria and Egypt which was proclaimed by Nasser and Kuwatly on February 1, 1958. Their urgent purpose in creating the United Arab Republic was to reestablish non-Communist control in Syria; the Syrian army was removed from politics, political parties were dissolved (with special measures taken to weaken the Communist party), and all key appointments were controlled from Cairo. It was in fact the Syrian army, fearful of growing Communist influence, that had been the prime mover in the effort to bring in the counterweight of Nasser's power and prestige. Thus strengthened, the Kuwatly government soon unmasked an intrigue against it that proved traceable directly to King Saud of Saudi Arabia, and the resulting revelations via Radio Cairo forced that king's virtual abdication in favor of a pro-Nasser brother.[3] The containment of Soviet influence in Syria was accordingly only rather indirectly attributable to the Eisenhower Doctrine.

The Trouble in Lebanon

In early May, when trouble broke out in small half-Christian, half-Moslem Lebanon, it was kindled by rebellious pro-Nasser nationalists protesting the conservative regime's association with the Eisenhower Doctrine and also the stated intention of President Camille Chamoun to remain in office beyond the legal expiration of his term in September. There was no evidence of Soviet involvement, but it was plain that the rebellion had Nasser's moral and material support, which now meant help from across the Syrian frontier. Except for the contagion of revo-lutionary Pan-Arabic feeling, the Lebanese army of 9,000 and a police force of 2,500 would have been sufficient to stifle the rebellion in the first forty-eight hours, but that feeling was, of course, the pervasive fact of life not only in Lebanon, but in every Arab nation. The Moslem group in the officer corps contained numerous influential Nasserists, while the Christian officers, trained by the French, were wholly professional and apolitical (as President Chamoun said of them: "They had no patriotic feeling whatever, and I think they were bored").[4] Of even greater importance, the army commander, General Fuad Shehab, was a moderate nationalist with presidential ambitions of his own, and showed himself unwilling to take decisive action against the rebels.

Despite the dearth of evidence that Lebanese independence was threatened by a Middle East country "under the control of International Communism," Dulles and the President quickly construed their authority under the Eisenhower Doctrine as broad enough to provide emergency assistance if Beirut should appeal for help. Dulles announced this finding on May 20, but preparatory actions had been taken three days before: accelerated deliveries of military equipment to Lebanon were ordered, the marine contingent with the Sixth Fleet was doubled, and a number of transport aircraft were dispatched from the United States to Germany, ostensibly to stand by for the evacuation of Americans from Beirut.

Congressional protests against this extremely broad interpretation of the doctrine were ignored. Meanwhile, the Lebanese Foreign Minister, Dr. Charles Malik, having held up a complaint to the United Nations for two weeks in deference to those Middle East leaders who hoped to settle the dispute "within the [Arab] family," formally charged the UAR on June 6 with "massive, illegal and unprovoked intervention." A former Iraqi premier weighed in against Nasser's aim "to turn the Arab States into satellites of Egypt by fomenting revolutions." [5] But except for accusing Nasser of "Communist methods," no suggestion was made that either the Soviet Union or "International Communism" was implicated.

The UN Security Council proposed to send an observation team and, with no objection from any major power, this was dispatched by June 14. Nor did Egypt raise any objection; indeed, Nasser called in the American ambassador and put forward suggested proposals for ending the trouble — Chamoun should finish out his term, but should then give way to General Shehab, as the strongest politician acceptable to both factors; in addition, the rebels should be granted full amnesty. In retrospect, Dulles's refusal to see these proposals as the ingredients of a reasonable settlement, and to use them as the point of departure for a serious negotiation between Chamoun and the rebels, perhaps with UN mediation, was rather clearly a missed opportunity. The final settlement consisted almost precisely of these terms, but there remained in Washington a basic antipathy to Nasser's Pan-Arabic aspirations, a state of mind which preferred military intervention to mediation. Dulles accordingly passed the proposals to Chamoun without endorsement, and Chamoun did not act on them. The observation team failed to stop the fighting, and indeed it greatly disheartened the Chamoun government by its report on July 4 that the "vast majority" of armed dissidents were Lebanese. This report may have been literally true, but it was misleading in the sense that it implied an absence of outside support from Egypt and Syria. Later evidence showed that the UN team had been able to work in the mountainous frontier area only during daylight hours and had thus missed a considerable flow of arms and saboteurs crossing into Lebanon after dark. Such a flow was proved when the U.S. Marine units later tapped the telephone lines between Damascus and the rebel center in Beirut.[6]

The Explosion in Iraq

With the scale and tempo of fighting on the rise in Lebanon, and with the Chamoun government moving toward an appeal to Washington for direct military intervention, the situation in Iraq suddenly blew up on the morning of July 14. On February 14, just two weeks following the proclamation establishing the political union of Egypt and Syria, King Faisal of Iraq and King Hussein of Jordan, who were blood relations, had moved to form a counterfederation, the Arab Union, as a means of strengthening their thrones and regimes against radical Pan-Arabism. Nasser was considerably annoyed, attacking this new combination at several mass rallies, and this no doubt sharpened the social and political tensions inside Iraq. On July 14, two brigades of the Iraqi army, whose loyalty to the king was known to be uncertain, were improvidently allowed not only to march through Baghdad on their way to another encampment, but contrary to the usual practice were issued live ammunition. Led by a brigadier named Kassim, who apparently decided to seize the opportunity presented, the troops attacked the Royal Palace and ran amok. King Faisal and the Crown Prince were brutally murdered. The Prime Minister, Nuri as Said, escaped in disguise, but was discovered the next day and not only killed but, as Macmillan wrote, "treated with utmost barbarity, his body being dragged naked through the streets for the delectation of the lowest section of the mob." [7] Kassim promptly declared that the uprising was a wholly independent act against Iraq's "corrupt ruling class," unrelated to any Nasserist plotting, and later evidence bore him out. So ended the Hashemite dynasty in Iraq. Inevitably, however, the event threw panic into the governments of Lebanon and Jordan, and President Chamoun promptly called in the American, British and French ambassadors to ask them all for immediate military help: "Well, you see what is happening . . . Lebanon is in real danger." [8]

Although there had been some prior Anglo-American discussions regarding joint military action in Lebanon, the American decision to intervene was taken unilaterally and without contemplation of British participation. Eisenhower and Dulles seem to have made a quick intuitive judgment that the risks of attempting to undo the new situation in Iraq were too great; nor was Jordan included in the focus of their attention. Dulles walked into a meeting of the National Security Council prepared to elaborate a recommendation for intervention in Lebanon, but the President waved him off: "Foster, I've already made up my mind. We're going in." [9] Congressional leaders, who were then called to the White House to be informed of the President's decision, presented, as expected, a mixture of reactions. Speaker Sam Rayburn feared the United States was involving itself in a civil war; Senator Fulbright seriously doubted that the crisis had any connection with Communism and accordingly felt the Eisenhower Doctrine did not apply. John Vorys of Ohio, a senior Republican member of the Foreign Affairs Committee, professed, however, to see the Soviet hand behind Nasser; and Carl Vinson, the leonine chairman of the House Armed Services Committee, supported the President and was ready to "go the distance." [10] Eisenhower, in later explaining his own thought process on this occasion, set out a balance sheet of pros and cons that, to say the least, did not seem self-evidently persuasive in favor of intervention. In Lebanon, he wrote, "the question was whether it would be better to incur the deep resentment of nearly all of the Arab world (and some of the rest of the Free World) and in doing so to risk general war with the Soviet Union or to do something worse — which was to do nothing." [11] Immediately after the decision was taken, on July 14, he telephoned to inform Macmillan, who said in jest, "You are doing a Suez on me." The President laughed.[12] The American ambassador in Beirut informed President Chamoun that "the American forces will be here tomorrow at two o'clock." [13]

Feeling that there had been inadequate consideration of the situation in Jordan, Macmillan called Eisenhower later that same night to propose that "it might well be better to act in both places rather than to let the situation drift." [14] Getting no definitive reply, but meanwhile receiving a "poignant" appeal for help from King Hussein, Macmillan assembled his military chiefs and was thereupon exposed to the equally poignant weakness of Britain's military position. It would be possible, said the military leaders, to airlift two battalions from Cyprus to Amman, but only if heavy weapons were left behind and only if Israel granted overflight rights. Feeling that after the Suez debacle London dare not act alone, Macmillan telephoned Dulles, who thought the operation "rash but praiseworthy" and promised moral and logistical support. The British cabinet thereupon decided to carry out "this rather 'quixotic' act," feeling that "we would not forgive ourselves if the King were murdered tomorrow, like the Royal Family of Iraq." [15]

Intervention

Poised off the Lebanese coast, the Sixth Fleet landed the first marine contingents on July 15, and they were quickly followed by airborne troops from Germany and additional marines, bringing total U.S. troop strength to 14,300. British paratroopers began landing in Jordan on July 17, and were quickly built up to a strength of 3,000. For the British this was perhaps the final rearguard action of empire in the Middle East and, though modest in scale, it was in continuous danger of losing its line of communication. The Israelis proved to be very sticky about overflight rights, some elements of the government at Tel Aviv preferring a Jordanian collapse that would provide a pretext for the Israeli seizure of the coveted West Bank territory. On August 3, when Israel demanded a total cessation of British overflights, the United States assumed responsibility for the British aerial supply line, flying materials from Cyprus to Amman in American military aircraft; Tel Aviv was not prepared to refuse Washington.

Although applauded by the "northern tier" countries, the intervention caused, as predicted, another violent outburst of anti-American and anti-British feeling in the Arab world, which Khrushchev naturally sought to exploit so that the Soviet Union might once more shine forth as the ardent defender of Arab rights. By numerous warnings, including a renewed threat to send "volunteers" to the Middle East, he succeeded in raising the public apprehension of war in much of the world, but in fact his policy was a model of operational caution. The intervention itself was also entirely peaceable, although the attitude of the Lebanese army was not precisely known in advance. General Shehab and the American ambassador, Robert McClintock, met the United States commander, Admiral Holloway, and the leading contingent of marines on the road from the airport and led them into the city of Beirut. There was some tension but no shots were fired in anger.*

Nasser, however, who was uncertain of both Soviet and American intentions, urgently boarded a plane for Moscow to deal with two somewhat contradictory problems: he wanted Russian assurances in the event

---

* The following day, additional combat marines came ashore across the bathing beaches in front of Beirut's expensive hotels. One private looked at the cluster of bikini-clad young women who were taking the sun, idly watching the operation or wholly indifferent. He put down his rifle, thoughtfully scanned the scene, and proclaimed in tones of wonder and appreciation: "So this is Eye-Rack."

the United States showed itself to be the spearhead of a new Western military campaign to bring him down; at the same time, he wanted to warn Khrushchev against any drastic or precipitous action until the situation was clearer. He had no desire for further Soviet intervention in the Middle East.

From all of this activity there ensued a flurry of confusing diplomatic exchanges. Khrushchev demanded a "Summit Conference" of the Big Four plus India, to be held within three days, in order to deal with "one of the gravest moments in history." Eisenhower replied that he was "not aware of any factual basis for your extravagantly expressed fear of the danger of general war." [16] But it proved impossible to ignore the acute anxiety of public opinion in Europe (including Britain) and throughout Asia, which carried with it the implicit demand that the Great Powers must come to an understanding that would spare mankind these frightful, unending alarms that turned every local problem into a global confrontation and brought the world to the apparent brink of catastrophe. While resisting any "Summit" on the 1955 Geneva model, Dulles accepted Macmillan's proposal that the heads of government should meet within the framework of the UN Security Council, as this seemed to provide a more mundane setting and thus to entail smaller risks in the likely event the conference failed. Here Khrushchev seemed tentatively willing, but General Charles de Gaulle, who was newly returned to power in France, not only expressed a strong preference for the original Russian proposal, but formally accepted the Russian invitation to parley at Geneva. With the West thus openly divided, Khrushchev added to the confusion, following a visit to Mao in early August. He now declared that a heads of government meeting within the framework of the UN Security Council was "inadmissible" because it would allow participation by Mao's nemesis, "the political corpse, Chiang Kai-Shek." The conference, he argued, must be a special meeting of the UN General Assembly.[17] The West accepted this modification.

Meanwhile, the Deputy Undersecretary of State, Robert Murphy, sat down in Beirut to mediate Lebanon's internal political disputes. He found Chamoun nervous, depressed, and near exhaustion after sixty-seven days as "a self-made prisoner" in the Presidential residence.[18] But thanks largely to Murphy's skillful efforts, an agreement was reached on July 31 providing for Chamoun's dignified departure and for a special election that would ensure success for General Shehab, the candidate of "national reconciliation." Murphy then flew to Baghdad for a quick visit to the new government of Iraq; Kassim received him cordially, and persuasively insisted that the condign actions taken against the monarchy had been of a purely internal character. He also expressed his suspicion of the purposes of American forces in Lebanon, and hoped they would soon be withdrawn. On the strength of Murphy's report, Washington extended diplomatic recognition on August 2 and even accompanied this with an "expression of its good wishes." [19]

Extrication

Thus, by the time the special General Assembly was convened on August 8, the danger of war in the Middle East had largely abated. The Soviet Union had made clear it would send no "volunteers," the political crisis in Lebanon was over, and the situation in Iraq was being understood and not exploited. The main problem now was how to extract the American and British troops. All through the latter part of July, the Security Council had sought a way to transfer to the UN the burden that the United States and Britain had unilaterally assumed, but, as in the Suez case, Nasser insisted on their unconditional withdrawal and was supported by repeated Soviet vetoes. Apparently undaunted, Dulles developed a six-point peace plan which Eisenhower personally presented to the General Assembly on August 13. Its basic premise, Wilsonian in its insistence on a comprehensive system of justice, was that the UN must develop alternatives to the American and British presence, in order to safeguard Lebanon and Jordan. As to the Middle East as a whole, it proposed "a standby United Nations Peace Force," measures to control inflammatory broadcasts across national boundaries, and a new effort at arms control, all of these being efforts to protect against "indirect aggression." [20]

The trouble, of course, was that not only Nasser but also most of the Arab states were opposed to measures that would inhibit a general development of the new nationalism under conditions and at a pace determined by Arabs; even the King of Jordan was unenthusiastic about a UN peace-keeping force on his territory, preferring arms and a direct promise of Anglo-American protection. Such vigorous opposition from the inhabitants of the region rendered the American proposals infeasible in the General Assembly. After nearly six weeks of impasse, during which General Shehab succeeded Chamoun in Lebanon and the Jordanian situation did not exceed the normal state of tension, a Sudanese resolution was unanimously accepted (on September 20) which vested wide discretion in Secretary-General Hammarskjöld to make "practical arrangements" to uphold "the purposes and principles of the Charter," and to "facilitate the early withdrawal" of American and British forces.[21] Its successful passage owed much to Nasser's willingness to drop, or at least to blur, his demand for unconditional withdrawal. Lebanon accepted the continued presence of the UN observer group, but declared itself no longer bound by the Chamoun government's endorsement of the Eisenhower Doctrine; there was to be no UN presence in Jordan; American and British forces were to leave by the end of October.

Once more Dulles had attempted to impose international authority, and safeguards for the status quo, through the agency of American power. He gained an initial success, but then foundered on the jagged realities of Arab nationalism. The net effect of the venture was a stable compromise in Lebanon, but at an enormous cost in general Arab distrust and ill will, a cost that illumined the continued failure of American policy to find a basis for constructive relations with the one man who was far and away the preeminent Arab leader and hero, and the embodiment of Arab aspirations. Nasser was not basically anti-Western, but he was determined to hold a middle position free of Western lead strings. Dulles's policies never sought to build upon these realities, but reflected always his preoccupation with the abstract macro-effort to control the pace and method of change and to arrest the spread of "International Communism." Fearing or misperceiving the Pan-Arabic movement, he seems to have acted out of unresolved contradictions within himself and within the fabric of American opinion: convinced that colonialism must come to an end, he was drawn in logic to an active sympathy for the rising forces of Arab nationalism, yet such a move was inhibited, not only by his Wilsonian insistence on a universal order, but more specifically in this case by the interests and judgments of his British ally. They were judgments that reinforced his own stubborn belief that Nasser was, wittingly or not, the principal agent of Soviet Communist expanion in the Middle East.

The substance of the agreement that Murphy negotiated in Beirut was a sensible compromise — it was, in fact, the only solution that could have prevented prolonged civil strife in which United States Marines would have faced the tragic task of defending an unpopular and unrepresentative government in Lebanon, and perhaps a spreading guerilla warfare throughout the area. Eisenhower later wrote that General Shehab was "almost ideal" because he was "acceptable to both the rebels and to the government." [22] Acceptance of the compromise showed Dulles's seasoned pragmatism and tactical skills, but it also raised the question of ends and means, of whether the crisis might not have been solved with less hoopla and fanfare and without military intervention if Dulles had been willing merely to urge Chamoun's serious consideration of proposals that embodied the elements of a rather evident practical settlement. Chamoun, who was treated to both the sweeping promises and the strict practical limits of the Eisenhower Doctrine, rather acutely perceived the contrast between the bold conception of Dullesian schemes at the outset and his readiness for retreat to rather riskless compromise at the end. As Chamoun saw it: "He didn't go to the end in any of his initiatives. . . . He used to start very great, very big, according to the mood of his heart, and then retreat when he was in touch with realities." [23] The settlement as finally negotiated by Murphy was almost precisely identical with the proposals put forward by Nasser in June.

The result of acting out of unresolved contradictions was that Dulles's Middle East policy was chronically fitful and episodic, reflecting short-term considerations and little or no long-range planning, powerfully reactive to "Communist-inspired" crises, yet slack and rather aimless in periods of relative calm. Many actions seemed irrelevant or had the effect of driving Nasser closer to the Russians. Thus, although as a barrier to Soviet influence to the south the Baghdad Pact had become a sieve, Dulles moved (on July 31) to reinforce it by entering upon separate bilateral security agreements with Turkey, Iran and Pakistan. In Baghdad itself, however (the ostensible seat of the alliance), tension mounted between local Communists and Nasserists. Kassim removed his pro-Nasser deputy, Colonel Arif, from political power by packing him off as ambassador to West Germany, and turned to greater reliance on local Communist groups who, following the demise of the monarchy, were among the few remaining organized political forces in Iraq. Matters came to a head on November 4 when the same Arif, who had secretly returned from Europe, was arrested in Baghdad. Severe repression followed against the Nasserists, including the meting out of several death sentences, which brought into the open the simmering antagonism between local Communists and Pan-Arabists. The Kassim government's pro-Russian sympathies continued to grow, and in the spring of 1959 Iraq formally withdrew from the Baghdad Pact and terminated all military agreements with the British. The last RAF units left the famous base at Habbaniyah on May 31. Without Iraq the pact reverted to a "northern tier" alliance, established its headquarters in Ankara, and changed its name to the Central Treaty Organization (CENTO). Soviet influence, whose southward movement it was intended to block, had long since leaped the barrier and established itself through economic and military assistance programs in Egypt, Syria and Iraq. Yet owing to the strong inertial tendency of institutions (including military alliances), CENTO has survived, albeit in a moribund state, to the present day.

Despite his fierce struggle against local Communists, however, Nasser's state relations with the Soviet Union appeared to be unaffected. On October 23, 1958, two years and three months after Dulles's fateful renege, Khrushchev announced Russia's readiness to provide technicians, machinery, tools, and money to help finance the Aswan High Dam. Nasser now accepted, and the ensuing agreement led to Russian collaboration on the project which was of surpassing interest and consequence for every Egyptian (as one historian wrote, it will be "seventeen times greater than the pyramid" and "will shelter, not a solitary dead soul, but endless millions of living souls until its story is as shrouded in legend as the pyramid's. It will be a legend of Nasser and the Russians in which any mention of the United States, which was otherwise the richest and most generous of nations, will be a footnote of irritability and meanness").[24] Questioned by a congressional committee regarding the implications of this new development, Dulles replied: "I don't think it is anything to get terribly excited about."

28

Reprise at Quemoy

Dulles's handling of the second Quemoy crisis in the early autumn of 1958 was probably, in purely technical terms, his most brilliant and successful piece of brinkmanship, yet (as discussed in chapter 26) the fact that such a performance was necessary said a good deal about his supreme unreadiness to lead public opinion toward acceptance of the need for any normalization of relations with Peking during the long lull between 1955 and 1958. It also reflected his ad hoc style, for, while Dulles was consumed by other crises, Chiang very substantially reinforced his offshore island garrisons (with the quiet encouragement of senior American military officers) and this, of course, enlarged the political consequences in the event they should be overrun. Neither Dulles nor Eisenhower seems to have been fully aware of this development until they were confronted with the new crisis.

The View from Peking

Communist China's decision to renew its military threat to Quemoy in August 1958 appeared to flow from a complex of domestic and foreign policy considerations. Confident about its stability and control at home, yet pessimistic about prospects for dramatic economic advance in the absence of drastic new programs, the regime had just launched the "Great Leap Forward" in industry and the agricultural communes. Although both were to prove devastating failures (and the communes to demonstrate the regime's utter readiness to pulverize human beings for the sake of the revolution), Mao and his colleagues appeared to be supremely confident at the outset.[1] In foreign affairs, there was a similar mix of dissatisfaction with the limited result of past efforts and of belief that events were now opening up new opportunities. The line of peaceful coexistence laid down at Bandung in the spring of 1955 had won for Peking a widening respect, but had done little to advance Mao's claim to China's seat in the United Nations and to diplomatic recognition by the United States. Restive, the regime was inclined to view the sputnik launchings not merely as having changed the psychology of the international scene, but as having produced an important shift in the actual balance of power.[2] In their own judgment on this point, the Russian leaders were more realistic, but the 1957–1958 period rather clearly marked the beginning of a more assertive Soviet conduct of foreign affairs, combining pungent Khrushchevian threats of nuclear destruction with efforts to begin a serious dialogue with the West at the heads of government level. It was also a brief period of relatively harmonious Moscow-Peking relations, and Khrushchev surely shared the assessment expressed in Mao's proclamation, made in the course of his November 1957 visit to Moscow, that "the East wind is now prevailing over the West wind."

The anti-American riot in Taipei, the extended American economic recession (1957–1958), and Washington's readiness to let the anti-Sukarno rebels in Indonesia go down to defeat (after giving them some aid) also contributed to Peking's conclusion that the United States might in 1958 be a less resolute opponent in the Formosa Strait, and that a further turning of the screws on Quemoy might now weaken Chiang's control of Taiwan.[3] Mao appeared to be impressed less by the American intervention in Lebanon than by the absence of an American effort to reverse the coup in Iraq.[4] But the Peking plan for renewing the threat to Quemoy was nevertheless a carefully calibrated combination of military and propaganda moves, and tightly controlled so that it could be pressed forward or quickly curtailed, depending on the nature and extent of the U.S. reaction. The military objective appeared to be a blockade of Quemoy, which, if effective, could cause the island to fall without a direct assault.

Although several air engagements and at least one naval encounter between Communist and Nationalist forces took place early in August, the artillery bombardment of Quemoy in the early evening of August 23 nevertheless achieved a stunning tactical surprise.[5] The Nationalist minister of defense, Yu Ta-wei, was that day on an inspection trip to Quemoy, and a banquet was planned in his honor. A large number of high-ranking officers, many from Taiwan, were gathering for dinner when the Chinese Communist artillery shells fell out of a calm blue sky like a sudden deadly hailstorm, many of them aimed at the banquet site.

Within a few seconds there were 200 casualties and, at the end of two hours, at least 500, of whom 200 were dead men. The Communist guns fired 40,000 rounds, and the disarray of the Nationalist garrison was so great that not an answering shot was fired during the first forty-five minutes. The defense minister escaped injury, but the casualties included a number of senior officers. The following day, the Communists fired 36,000 rounds against the island and bombed and strafed the western beaches with aircraft. The greatest military clash in the Formosa Strait since the attempted invasion of Quemoy in 1949 was under way.[6]

Initial Response

Confronted with this sudden new challenge, Dulles predictably sought to justify three years of mismanagement and errors of omission by appeal to moral principle. What was at stake, he declared, was "world order," and above all the principle that "armed force shall not be used to achieve territorial ambitions."[7] Such a dictum possessed legal and moral authority in the UN Charter as to relations between sovereign nations, but Dulles's use of it here conveniently ignored the truth that both international law and the overwhelming weight of world opinion were in no doubt that the offshore islands constituted an integral part of the territory of mainland China. He favored an immediate and unequivocal statement of American intentions to defend those islands, but the President preferred not to take such a flat position in advance, and instead instructed the Secretary of State to make public a letter of reply which Dulles had recently written to the chairman of the House Foreign Affairs Committee. Eisenhower seemed to fear that a categorical statement would intensify attacks by critics, both at home and abroad, and might provide Chiang with an additional handle for manipulating U.S. policy.[8] Since there were other offshore islands which the United States was clearly unwilling to defend, he may also have wanted to avoid defining any specific defense perimeter.

The text of the Dulles letter technically reserved the President's position, but it possessed an ambiguity only paper thin. Its key passage read: "It would be highly hazardous for anyone to assume that if the Chinese Communists were to attempt to change this situation by attacking and seeking to conquer these islands [Quemoy and Matsu] that this act could be considered or held to a 'limited operation.' It would, I fear, constitute a threat to the peace of the area."[9] A group of American military leaders arrived in Taiwan on August 26, and the following day Washington announced that the carrier *Essex* and four destroyers from the Sixth Fleet in the Mediterranean were en route to strengthen the

Seventh Fleet in the Formosa Strait. On August 31, Russia entered the picture by suggesting that the crisis might have global implications. *Pravda* declared ominously that "he who threatens today to attack the Chinese Peoples' Republic must not forget that he threatens the Soviet Union as well." Such actions, *Pravda* argued, could not be localized, but "will inevitably increase international tension and result in the spreading of the war to other areas." [10]

Meanwhile, the heavy artillery bombardment continued, reinforced by the employment of aircraft and PT boats against Nationalist ships bringing supplies from Taiwan, and accompanied by broadcasts calling on the Quemoy garrison to surrender: "Chinese Compatriots on Quemoy and Matsu: you have come to the critical moment of choice. . . . There is a road of life open for you — kill the US advisers and defect to our side. There is no other way out." [11] Your situation is as "hopeless as a pair of turtles entrapped in a flask." [12] Although the propaganda broadcasts had little effect, the military effort to blockade and isolate Quemoy appeared to be succeeding, for Nationalist efforts at resupply were disorganized and tentative.

During this initial period, Eisenhower received a "frantic" letter from Chiang that expressed in terms of anguish his fear that communications between Taiwan and Quemoy might be cut at any time, and that the Seventh Fleet might not be able to prevent a Communist assault on Taiwan itself; unless the Nationalists were allowed to take offensive air actions on a large scale, Quemoy might be doomed to starvation and surrender. What was needed, he argued, was a categorical statement of American intention to defend Quemoy and Matsu, and a broad delegation of authority to Admiral Smoot (the Taiwan defense commander) so that he could employ U.S. forces without reference to Washington. It was a blatant effort to force Eisenhower's hand. It was coolly rejected. The President thought Chiang's concern over Quemoy's vulnerability to blockade "totally inconsistent" with his obstinate "loading down the offshore islands with far more troops than were necessary for defensive purposes"; he disagreed with Chiang's lack of confidence in the Seventh Fleet, and he categorically refused to delegate authority for U.S. military action. Throughout the crisis, Eisenhower was "continually pressured" by both Chiang and American military leaders for a delegation of authority that would in effect place the question of war in the hands of a field commander. Knowing Chiang's basic desire to enmesh the United States in his struggle to regain the mainland, and understanding the latent itch of certain American commanders for a showdown with Communist China, he wisely refused. "I insisted that I would assess developments as they occurred. Therefore, I kept to myself the decision to employ U.S. forces." [13]

The Newport Memorandum

Eisenhower proved more susceptible to the Secretary of State's force-ful and rather crafty effort to nail him to a categorical commitment to defend Quemoy. With the supply situation visibly worsening, Dulles flew to Newport, Rhode Island, on September 4, where Eisenhower was vacationing, carrying with him a memorandum that reflected his own distillation of a broad assessment prepared by the Pentagon, the CIA, and the Far East bureau of the State Department. The document was a classic exposition of the "domino theory" carried to remarkable ex-tremes: in the absence of a manifest U.S. determination to protect Que-moy, it argued, the Communists would either overrun that island by amphibious assault, or bring about the collapse of its defenses by pro-tracted bombardment and blockade. This was a reasonably accurate statement. But the analysis then moved to two dubious conclusions: (1) that loss or surrender of Quemoy would expose Taiwan to action (subversive or military) which would "probably" lead to Chiang's over-throw and to the emergence of a government prepared to advocate union with Communist China; and (2) that, in such event, the whole United States "anti-Communist barrier" in the Western Pacific, including Ja-pan, Korea, Philippines, Thailand, Vietnam, Cambodia, Laos, Indonesia, Malaya, Burma, and even Okinawa "would probably come fully under Communist influence. . . . The consequences in the Far East would be even more far-reaching and catastrophic than those which followed when the United States allowed [*sic*] the Chinese mainland to be taken over by the Chinese Communists." Such an assessment led inexorably to one — and only one — course of action, an open and avowed readiness to de-fend Quemoy.[14] Nor was this the only requirement of the Dulles recom-mendation. If the Communists were to begin an assault, there "might" be a short period of time during which conventional weapons could per-suade them to reverse their effort, but in all proability nuclear weapons would have to be used. This would admittedly cause "a strong popular revulsion against the US in most of the world"; on the other hand, "if the matter were quickly closed, the revulsion might not be long-lived." In either case, the memorandum argued, it was necessary to accept the risks, for no alternative course was consistent with "the safety of the free world and our influence on it." [15]

With the passage of time and the exercise of power, Dulles seemed progressively to shed the philosophical inhibition regarding the actual use of force (as distinguished from the political threat to use it) with

Convoy

From *Herblock's Special For Today*
SIMON & SCHUSTER, 1958

which he had entered office. And by 1958, he seemed to have become convinced that tactical nuclear weapons could be used in local, limited situations without extreme consequences. At a conference to review military strategy (held at the marine base at Quantico, Virginia, on June 14, 1957), his remarks acknowledged that the growth of Soviet nuclear strength "tends . . . to diminish the efficacy of the threat of all-out use of US nuclear power as a deterrent to local attack." [16] Indeed, he admitted, it created a situation in which allies would be increasingly unwilling to permit their territory to be used for U.S. retaliatory bases, and would increasingly doubt the U.S. readiness to attack the Soviet Union. By mid-1957, then, Dulles understood the conditions of nuclear stalemate. He did not, however, accept them as controlling. There had to be a way out, and in his remarks at Quantico he stated conclusions as his own which were almost certainly derived from military technocrats of the Radford school. The "solution," he said, lies in the continued development and production of "small-yield nuclear weapons," for their use does not create the same "political difficulties" encountered in the contemplation of weapons of mass destruction. Knowledge that the United States possessed and would use small-yield nuclear weapons would thus "strengthen the cohesion of the collective security system" and "increase the Soviet risks of starting local actions." [17] This was a speech that might warm the hearts of modern major generals, but would appall serious statesmen. In 1958, however, Dulles appeared to be convinced that tactical nuclear weapons were politically efficacious in situations of limited war. He was not alone in this belief — it was indeed a current, fortunately short-lived, fashion among leading strategic thinkers.

At Newport, the President and the Secretary discussed the memorandum for a few minutes before Eisenhower agreed that, with minor editorial changes, it should form the basis of policy at Quemoy. He was in his golf clothes and anxious to be off to the links, and it is not clear whether or not he fully appreciated that he was approving the kind of categorical commitment he had hitherto striven to avoid. Still, the memorandum was an internal document, subject to amendment or cancellation. But Dulles then proposed, as Eisenhower was rising to leave, that it would be useful to communicate this stern expression of American resolve to the Chinese Communists and their allies, lest they miscalculate the risks. A direct presidential statement would be inappropriate, he thought, but perhaps something off the record would send the desired message to Peking. Once more Eisenhower quickly agreed, and then departed, leaving Dulles to conduct a press conference under the rule that his remarks would be attributable only to a "high official." In the course of that session, he declared that American determination to defend Quemoy was categorical and unequivocal. Within hours, the identity of the "high official" was disclosed by the press and, with the world aware that the statements made by the Secretary of State had immediately followed a meeting with the President, Eisenhower was painted into a corner. Dulles now possessed all the necessary ingredients for a rough confrontation at Quemoy — to threaten nuclear weapons in response to Chinese Communist attack, while seeking a basis for negotiations based on a "mutual and reciprocal renunciation of force, except in self-defense," which would leave Peking to pursue its territorial claims "by peaceful means." [18]

World Opinion

The tense confrontation at the very edge of the Chinese mainland was now, after ten days, raising temperatures all over the world and leading rapidly to the nearly total diplomatic isolation of the United States. Washington was castigated for grossly exaggerating the strategic importance of two flyspeck islands; for having permitted Chiang not only to remain in possession, but to enlarge and strengthen his garrisons there during the lull after 1955; and for now taking extreme and unjustified risks with the peace of the world. The *New Republic* for October 6, 1958, said editorially: "We consider the Administration's Quemoy policy indefensible morally, militarily and politically," and it laid stress on that principle of the UN Charter which prohibits intervention "in matters which are essentially within the domestic jurisdiction of any state." Dulles's effort to convert the United Nations into a vigilance committee (or to use the United States as a self-appointed committee of one) to enforce his own highly selective Charter principles was, the editorial said, profoundly disturbing, for it involved an evident distortion of international law.

The British Prime Minister perhaps epitomized the universal sense of unease and impotence in the face of another Dullesian exercise in brinkmanship: active support for Washington's policy was for Macmillan politically impossible — both official and unofficial British opinion held that Peking had "an unanswerable case to the possession of the islands"; at the same time, repudiation of Washington seemed equally impossible — it would "divide the free world" and definitely threaten the improved Anglo-American relations which Macmillan had done so much to rebuild after Suez. "So there we are." [19] On September 5, the British chargé in Washington was sent to see Dulles and obtain a fuller explanation of United States intentions in the Formosa Strait; the answers were not reassuring to London. Dulles told the British diplomat that, if the Communists attacked Quemoy with aircraft, an American reply against the mainland airfields would be necessary and could not hope to be effective without recourse to tactical nuclear weapons — "I hope no more than small air bursts without fallout. That is of course an unpleasant prospect, but one I think we must face up to." Reading the "simple and restrained" language in the reporting cable, Macmillan found himself "impressed," but also "somewhat depressed." [20]

Also on September 5, Dean Acheson spoke out for a growing segment of disturbed American opinion: "We seem to be drifting, either dazed or indifferent, toward war with China, a war without friends or allies, and over issues which the administration has not presented to the people, and which are not worth a single American life." [21] Dulles, his powerful sense of advocacy stimulated by this challenge, replied to Acheson and other critics by once more placing the broadest conceivable construction on the nature and meaning of the crisis, insisting at a press conference that "what is under threat, is the entire position of the United States and that of its free-world allies in the Western Pacific . . . what is at stake there are *the vital interests of the United States* [emphasis added] as well as the basic principle upon which world order is founded, which is that violence, force, shall not be used to acquire additional territory." [22] Such rash hyperbole was received in most countries as further evidence that American policy was wholly without a sense of proportion. Reinhold Niebuhr wrote: "Dulles forgets that what our allies like least of all is his tendency to equate our inflexibility with 'principle,' and their more flexible policy with 'expediency.' " [23] It seemed to many (in a period of revolutionary change which, since 1945, had not seen more than a few months go by without some manifestation of politically motivated violence) that Dulles was attempting both the morally arrogant and the physically impossible — to banish the legitimate use of force by every country in the world except his own.

Assertions from Washington combined with American air and naval activities in the Taiwan area nevertheless brought Peking to the realization that the risks of American military action in defense of Quemoy were serious. On September 6, Chou En-lai offered to resume ambassadorial talks in Warsaw, and announced a four-day cessation of Communist artillery fire. Breaking the tension with this show of flexibility, thereby reducing the risks of overt American military action, Peking gave away nothing of its substantive position and did not in fact start the talks (to which Dulles promptly agreed) until September 15. Meanwhile, the bombardment continued, although at a reduced rate of 12,000 rounds per day. At the talks, held in an old Polish castle, the United States ambassador to Poland, Jacob Beam, and his Chinese opposite

number, Wang Ping-nan, found themselves repeating positions set forth
in 1955. Beam demanded a cease-fire in the Formosa Strait as a prerequisite to discussion of other matters, but the Chinese replied that
the question of a cease-fire did not arise between China and the United
States because there was no fighting between those two countries; on the
other hand, the question of a cease-fire between the Mao regime and the
Nationalists was inadmissible because their relations were an internal
affair of China in which the United States had no voice. Wang then
said his government was prepared to allow the Nationalists to evacuate
Quemoy and Matsu unmolested, provided the United States agreed at
the same time to withdraw all of its forces from Taiwan and the Formosa
Strait.[24]

The diplomatic situation thus remained in impasse while artillery
bombardment and sporadic air battles continued, and the Seventh Fleet
escorted Nationalist supply vessels up to the three-mile limit. While the
Chinese Communists carefully refrained from interfering with the
United States Navy, they continued to plaster the unloading activities
on the beach, and the whole supply operation continued on a shaky
footing for several weeks, even with American support. Gradually, however, there was improvement in both technique and equipment. Regular airdrops were developed using C-46 transport planes, and extensive use was made of a tracked amphibious vehicle (the LVT), which
could swim out of a larger ship and run across the beach to a protected
unloading area. By the end of September, the Taiwan defense command
concluded that airdrops alone could sustain the garrison.[25]

Khrushchev reentered the picture on September 19 with a letter
that warned the United States against contemplating any kind of
nuclear attack against China, summoning Eisenhower to remember that
"the other side too has atomic and hydrogen weapons and the appropriate means to deliver them"; any such attack would "doom to certain
death sons of the American people" and "spark off the conflagration
of a world war."[26] The White House found this Orwellian effort so
intemperate in language and tone that it was curtly returned to the
Soviet embassy. Two days later Moscow assailed Eisenhower's rejection
of the note as evidence of an American unwillingness to listen to reason.[27]

Exchanges of this kind seemed to be moving world opinion to the
point of nervous breakdown and, even in the United States, domestic
support for a policy whose risks seemed wildly disproportionate to the
value of its objectives was visibly crumbling. The State Department
acknowledged receipt of five thousand letters on the Quemoy crisis, 80
percent of them critical or fearful.[28] Though Eisenhower insisted in a
major broadcast on September 27 that he was taking "the only position

. . . consistent with the vital interests of the United States and, indeed, with the peace of the world," [29] it did not prove a persuasive line of argument. The Democratic chairman of the Foreign Relations Committee, Senator Theodore Green, of Rhode Island, thought the offshore island crisis involved issues "not of vital concern to our own security," and told the President in a letter made public on September 29 that "it is my impression, confirmed by the press and my own mail, that United States military involvement in defense of Quemoy would not command that [congressional and public] support . . . essential to successful military action." [30] Eisenhower expressed shock at this public suggestion that America "could be defeated because of disunity at home," [31] but Green's letter and other manifestations of public opinion soon had their intended effect. Although the full record remains to be disclosed, it would be plausible to believe that Eisenhower himself (as he had done during the first Quemoy crisis in 1955) now began pressing against the vehement distortions of the Newport memorandum, striving to pull his tough Secretary of State back from the brink and restore a sense of proportion to the American position before wider interests at home and abroad were irreparably damaged. Some partial evidence exists. In a talk with the British Foreign Secretary, Selwyn Lloyd, on September 21 at Newport, the President said he was "against the use of even tactical atomic weapons in a limited operation." [32] In any event, Dulles soon performed a remarkable countermarch.

Washington Breaks the Tension

On September 30, Dulles told a press conference there was "no intention of modifying our policy," but then proceeded to a drastic shift of emphasis. Directly contrary to the thrust of his remarks at Newport and subsequently, he now wished to make clear that the United States had no legal commitment to defend Quemoy and Matsu. In addition, there was "no commitment of any kind" to assist Chiang's regime to return to the mainland, and he thought the prospect of a return under "their own steam" was "a highly hypothetical matter." He went on. The United States had reluctantly accepted, but never approved, Chiang's heavy concentration of forces on the offshore islands, and in fact regarded these troop dispositions as "rather foolish." Having in mind the morale on Taiwan, it was not wise to withdraw them "as a retreat under fire," but if a "reasonably dependable" cease-fire could be arranged, he thought "it would be foolish to keep these large forces on these islands." [33]

This definitive change in the tone and substance of the American posture was without question the product of intense heat in the domestic and international kitchens. It indicated (although, in the light of later American history, perhaps not conclusively) that in the nuclear age and the day of instantaneous communications not even the most powerful democratic government could long sustain a posture that most of its own electorate, and most of the world, considered to be both extremely dangerous and extremely unreasonable. But if this policy shift was received with general relief, the screams of anguish out of Taipei were audible in Washington almost before Dulles stopped speaking. Chiang, professing himself unable to believe that such scandalous words could have come from the mouth of the American Secretary of State, declared that if they really had been uttered, they were "incompatible with our stand." [34] Peking was quick to taunt him with this evidence that "the Americans will certainly abandon you." [35] But facing a steady buildup of American air and naval forces on Taiwan and in the straits area (as well as the growing effectiveness of the Nationalist air force, now equipped with the heat-seeking Sidewinder missile), and forced to concede that the Quemoy garrison could not, contrary to their earlier estimate, be effectively blockaded and starved out, Peking also perceived the Dulles gesture of September 30 as an opportunity to ease away from confrontation while it still seemed to be ahead. On October 6, the Chinese Communist minister of defense announced a one-week cease-fire in the straits area "out of humanitarian considerations," [36] provided only that the United States would cease its escort operations. When Washington complied with this condition, he announced a two-week extension, satisfying Peking's concern for appearances and "face" by emphasizing that this "unilateral and informal" gesture was not to be confused with the "two-Chinas" concept. How long the bombardment stopped was declared to be an internal Chinese matter. The claim to Taiwan remained.

Tough Talk in Taipei

After attending the funeral of Pope Pius XII on October 18, Dulles flew from Rome over the polar cap to Taiwan for three days of talks with Chiang Kai-shek. Whether moved by his own assessment or under orders from the President, he gave the ancient mandarin a stern lecture on the precarious nature of the Nationalists' position in the world community, and laid down several stringent conditions for continuing United States support. Speaking from a handwritten talking paper (set out on the pages of a lined yellow pad) which he had developed during the long flight from Rome, he made the following points to the Generalissimo (the italics are Dulles's own):

— The danger facing the GRC * is primarily political. It "stems from the world's longing for conditions of peace," but it includes a widespread feeling that the "relationship between GRC and CPR † not only endangers peace but that GRC *wants* it to endanger the peace and [to] involve the US, as the only means of returning to the mainland."
— The "civil" wars in Korea and Indochina have been "ended by armistice." Not so in the case of Taiwan. There is a "deep desire" in the free world to "see this 'trouble spot' liquidated in some way," and the free world looks to the GRC to make a contribution.
— The "international political situation today is serious as regards GRC. Except perhaps for the Republic of Korea and Vietnam, the *USA* is the *only* vigorous supporter of the GRC."
— "It has required the strongest representations from the US and its friends to prevent the community of free nations from according to the CPR the unlimited status of the only China, entitled without external interference to liquidate by force the remaining elements of the civil war and thus end the risk of general war."
— "It is doubtful whether even the US can long protect the GRC under present circumstances." There is need for a "fresh approach."

Turning from diagnosis to prescription, Dulles told Chiang:

— The GRC should make clear that "on a basis of *de facto* reciprocity" it will act "as though there were an armistice along the line of present division." This means an avoidance of commando raids, overflights, and "like provocations."
— As to the offshore islands, the GRC should "recognize the danger of opposing military forces being in close proximity" and "will accept any solution which seems dependably to assure that the islands will not be turned over to the Communists . . ."
— The "character and size of military forces of GRC on offshore islands and indeed generally will be reviewed from a military standpoint."
— More positively, the GRC should "dramatize the shift of effort to assure the survival of Chinese civilization. . . . It should seek solid yet dramatic ways to cast itself in the role of the custodian of China's

* Government of the Republic of China.
† Communist People's Republic.

Arriving in Rome for the funeral of Pope Pius XII,
with Clare Booth Luce and John McCone (October 1958)

real greatness" — i.e., education, art and other aspects of Chinese culture.[37]

The analysis reflected a lucid appreciation of the international political realities and of the need for Chiang to bend to them in order to maintain even a foothold in the community of nations. It contained a warning that Dulles and Eisenhower were fully aware that Chiang's strategy to regain the mainland was based in large part on exacerbating tensions in the straits area and thus involving the United States in military operations against the Chinese Communists. The essence of the proposed "fresh approach" was to demand from Chiang a de facto renunciation of force in the assertion of his claim to the mainland. Certain elements of this demand were quite specific — like the halting of all offensive military actions, including aerial reconnaissance of the mainland — but others were more tentative; thus, the size and character of the offshore garrisons was merely to be "reviewed" and, while acceptance of a "solution" to the offshore problem was required, it did not extend to abandoning the islands to Communist control. The idea of dramatizing the Nationalist regime as the inspired and devoted custodian of Chinese civilization was designed to provide sugar coating for the bitter pill of renunciation of force. With the Mao regime embarked on the staggeringly inhumane program of agricultural communes, this was an idea of at least transient attractiveness, although it had about it the air of a public relations "quick fix."

The official communiqué of the talks, issued October 23, just before Dulles departed for home, was heavily larded with the high-flown rhetoric of the cold war, proclaiming "solidarity" in relations between the two governments who, "united in their opposition to aggression," believe they "serve not only themselves but the cause of peace." Recent Communist aggression and propaganda in the Formosa Strait "have not divided them, as the Communists have hoped," but had in fact drawn them closer together. The "futile and dangerous policy" of the Mao regime which, with Soviet support, sought not only to conquer Taiwan, but also to force the United States to abandon its security commitments throughout Asia, "cannot possibly succeed." Buried in the penultimate paragraph was Chiang's important concession, wrapped in the conception of the Kuomintang as the keeper of Chinese civilization. The "sacred mission" of the Nationalist government was "the restoration of freedom to its people on the mainland." But since "the foundation of this mission" resided in "the minds and hearts" of the Chinese people, the "principal means" for achieving it must accordingly be in "the implementation of Dr. Sun Yat-Sen's three people's principles [nationalism, democracy, and social well-being] and not the use of force." [38]

The structural awkwardness of the last sentence, especially the fact that the reference to inhibition on force appears as an addendum, suggests there was much argument on whether or not to give the thought explicit expression. Dulles prevailed on this point, but was apparently not fully satisfied with the clarity and impact of the language, for he released his own much more specific statement in Washington the next day. This said in pertinent part: The Nationalist government "believes that its mission is to bring about the restoration of freedom to the people on the Mainland and to do so, not by the use of force, but by conduct and example which will sustain the minds and hearts of the mainland Chinese so that they are unconquerable." [39]

Quickly recognizing this further American effort to restrain Chiang, the Chinese Communists announced on October 25 that, following the expiration of their two-week cease-fire, they would bombard Quemoy only on alternate days of the month. Eisenhower "wondered if we were in a Gilbert and Sullivan war," [40] but the crisis was over.

Tactical Adjustment Only

As the crisis flickered out, insistent voices were raised both at home and abroad that the Nationalists should now be entirely withdrawn from the offshore islands. Such a move, it was agreed, would greatly strengthen international support for the position on Taiwan, as well as adding 100,000 troops for its military defense; and with the antagonists separated by 120 miles of open water, the prospect for stability in the straits area would be significantly improved. Yet Dulles revealed no plan to move beyond his verbal warning to Chiang against the use of force, not even to revive Eisenhower's 1955 proposal that the offshore garrisons be reduced to the status of outposts in order to remove them as "a thorn in the side of peace." Nor, as autumn passed into early winter, did either Eisenhower or Dulles show themselves any more inclined to lead a public opinion that was potentially more open-minded on the basic question of whether or not to grant Peking's claims to recognition and membership in the United Nations. On November 5, Eisenhower told a press conference he foresaw no change in the American position "as long as Red China continues to do some of the things which we cannot possibly stomach." [41] He had foremost in mind the holding of four American citizens in prison, but his moral repugnance extended to recent events in the Formosa Strait and to the total regimentation of life on the mainland.

On October 26, Peking announced the withdrawal of the last of its troops from North Korea, and called for a corresponding withdrawal of American and other United Nations forces from the south, as a prelude to organizing all-Korean elections under "neutral" supervision. Dulles promptly rejected this proposal, using the standard, but somewhat shopworn, argument that, whereas the Chinese would withdraw only fifty miles, the United States was being asked to withdraw ten thousand miles. His implicit assumption (which lay at the heart of U.S. Asian policy) was that Communist China remained eager to overrun South Korea, even though the latter country was now protected by a security treaty with the United States and by strong forces of its own, neither of which factors had been present in the 1950 situation.

On November 18, Dulles went to Cleveland to address the National Council of Churches, an occasion involving dinner with a number of old friends who had worked with him on the Commission on a Just and Durable Peace during World War II, including Roswell Barnes and Frederick Nolde. His speech that evening was a wide-ranging *tour d'horizon* which developed the theme of adapting to change (change from colonialism to independence, changes in physical power deriving from nuclear fission, changes in Communism induced by Western strength and the attraction of freedom). At the same time he stressed the reasons why he felt it would be a mistake to recognize Communist China or to allow that regime to enter the United Nations. His tone was morally righteous and he rehearsed all of the Western grievances against that regime beginning with its "aggression" in Korea. A majority of the churchmen present were evidently opposed to Dulles's position, and within a few hours of his talk they had voted a resolution that put the National Council of Churches on record as favoring steps that looked "toward the inclusion of the People's Republic of China in the United Nations and for its recognition by our Government." [42] As Ernest Gross recalled it, this "was strong and bitter medicine to Mr. Dulles," who felt the resolution was "a personal blow and a repudiation." [43] His sister, Eleanor Dulles, later wrote that he suffered "a deep sense of disappointment . . . a feeling of sadness that some of the churchmen had weakened in the face of pressures." [44] It was her contention that the basis of her brother's opposition to recognizing China was moral, that he could not reconcile it with the human rights of the people on Taiwan. The Cleveland resolution did not, however, propose mainland control over Taiwan; it implied a "two-Chinas" solution.

On December 4, in a major address at San Francisco, Dulles once more set himself categorically against recognition, asserting that affirmative action by the United States "would be a well-nigh mortal blow to the survival of the non-Communist governments in the Far East." [45] Why? Because the increase in Peking's prestige and influence would contribute an irresistible momentum to its subversive effort. Then, with a hyperbole that seemed an echo of General MacArthur and was to prove a harbinger of Lyndon Baines Johnson, he solemnly declared that recognition of Peking would "gravely jeopardize" the vital security interests of the United States: "The Pacific instead of being . . . a friendly body of water would in great part be dominated by hostile forces and our own defenses driven back to or about our continental frontiers." [46]

By the end of the year it was thus clear that the Secretary of State had once more demonstrated his unusual gift for tactical adjustment. The urgent problems had been to rescue the United States from acute diplomatic isolation and the administration from a progressive erosion of domestic support. These tasks were accomplished by a brilliant display of tactical skills, combining pressure, concession, and cunning. But beyond the placing of a poultice on the immediate crisis, there were no plans. Dulles displayed no instinct for using the flux of crisis as a point of departure for leading opinion in the construction of a new synthesis, or toward even the definition of a realistic Asian settlement. He chose once more to rehearse all the old arguments and parade all of the old fears, thus further to harden the official and public mindset. Beyond political prudence and moral scruple, his posture on China in the fall of 1958 was almost certainly influenced by the swift waning of his physical energy. Dulles was now seventy years old and dying of cancer. And from November 10 until he died the following May, his remaining energies were addressed primarily to the new and ominous crisis in Berlin.

29

Berlin—The Last Crisis

A T THE END of 1957, even in the depths of their anxiety about the
implications of the sputniks, the NATO allies had shown themselves willing to accept American intermediate range ballistic missiles
(IRBM) only on condition that a renewed effort would be made to reach
agreement with the Soviet Union on arms control and a reduction of
nuclear tensions. For their part, the Soviets were in a somewhat ambivalent position. They sensed an opportunity to push outward in the
Middle East and to support a new effort by Peking to resolve the
question of Taiwan. They also perceived a chance to solve the German
question, but here they acted as much from fear as from opportunity,
for their congenital anxiety about the rearmament of West Germany
was now aggravated by the specter that Bonn might receive nuclear
missiles. The Kremlin had consistently sought a disarmed and neutral
West Germany, and since 1955 had put forward or endorsed a number
of proposals for the disengagement of the major powers from both
Germanys, requiring Bonn to leave NATO and Pankow to leave the
Warsaw Pact. At the meeting of Foreign Ministers in October 1955,
following the Geneva summit, Molotov had indeed made clear the
Soviet aim of dismantling both "military groupings," but the West
understood that this would cause American and British troops to leave
the Continent and would break Western Europe into fragments, while
leaving Russian power fully intact in central Europe.

Crablike toward the Summit

On December 10, 1957, Bulganin advanced the Rapacki Plan * for a "nuclear-free zone" in an area embracing both Germanys, Poland and Czechoslovakia; at the same time he warned the West against the emplacement of IRBM's in West Germany: "One likewise cannot fail to take into account, for example, the fact that the placing of nuclear weapons at the disposal of the Federal Republic of Germany may set in motion such forces in Europe and entail such consequences as even the NATO members may not contemplate." [1] Moscow wanted to prevent Bonn from acquiring either direct or indirect access to nuclear weapons. On January 9, 1958, Bulganin sent a second letter calling for a summit conference to discuss the suspension of nuclear tests, the outlawing of nuclear weapons, and the acceptance of the Rapacki Plan. The British, who had long favored the idea of reducing tensions by means of a mutual thin-out or partial disengagement in central Europe (the Eden Plan of 1954 was a direct lineal forebear of the Rapacki Plan) were in the vanguard of an effort to organize a positive Western response and were prepared to go directly to the summit. But Eisenhower, who replied to Bulganin on January 12, was willing only to accept a summit conference as a possibility — after careful diplomatic preparation at staff levels, and also after a meeting of Foreign Ministers had made clear that tangible progress could be made on major issues if the heads of government were convened.[2] Dulles reaffirmed these caveats to Selwyn Lloyd at Ankara in February, but Khrushchev, who was rapidly consolidating his personal power in the Kremlin, was resolutely opposed to an intermediate meeting of Foreign Ministers. He wished to resolve the issues of Berlin and Germany, but he insisted that this be done in direct face-to-face meetings with the Western heads of government. The question of whether or not there would be East-West talks, and if so at what level, thus remained in an unresolved state through the winter. In Macmillan's view, the ultimate American position depended largely on Dulles: "On the Summit, . . . the President plays little or no part. . . . Foster Dulles will decide." [3] On March 29, an agreed Western note was finally developed and sent to Moscow, proposing that "diplomatic exchanges" should begin in Moscow the second half of April, looking to the prospect of a meeting of Foreign Ministers, but maintaining a highly contingent position on the matter of a summit conference. Khrushchev soon let it be known, however, that this timeworn approach was not

* Named for Adam Rapacki, the Polish Foreign Minister.

acceptable: "We have declared and declare now that we do not intend to meet to discuss the question of the people's democracies or the German question as raised by Mr. Eisenhower, Mr. Dulles, and Mr. Adenauer." [4]

On March 27, Bulganin resigned as premier in favor of Khrushchev, who also retained his post as chairman of the party, thus bringing both the government bureaucracy and the party apparatus under the control of one man for the first time since Stalin and apparently ending the period of collective leadership. Hammarskjöld told the British on April 1 that "Khrushchev is supreme, without challengers, and very confident of his own and Russia's strength. He will make no concessions. We must have Summit talks, but we shall achieve nothing serious, except perhaps on tests — that is, if we are ready to stop." [5] Washington and London were on record as being generally amenable to giving up nuclear tests if they could obtain a reliable inspection system, but this was a major sticking point, for the Soviets were adamantly opposed to allowing foreign inspectors inside their country, while the West insisted with equal vehemence that there could be no nuclear control agreement without on-site inspection. Khrushchev did agree, however, to a meeting of scientific experts in midsummer whose purpose was to devise technical safeguards against cheating, thus to narrow the area of suspicion between the parties and provide a more objective basis for mutual confidence in a test-ban agreement. These crablike movements toward some tentative stabilization of the nuclear arms race were interrupted by the Lebanon-Iraq crisis and the Kremlin's ensuing demands for several varieties of "emergency" summit meetings, but when these winds had blown themselves out, the prospect for deliberate East-West negotiations remained, although their content, method and timing were far from resolved.

Free Elections — the Untenable Formula

The issue of nuclear controls was intimately related to the issue of arrangements for European security and the issue of Germany and German unification. The Western position on unification continued to be that (1) it was desirable and (2) the only acceptable means for its achievement was free elections. This was a position based very largely on Adenauer's estimate of German psychology and his own domestic political situation, but by 1958 it was a position which only Dulles and the U.S. government continued to endorse with conviction. French and British support was tacit and reluctant, and there had also come into being a school of thought which favored German neutrality and another which believed that safety for the West required permanent de facto partition, with West Germany fully integrated in Western Europe.

The iron fact was that Germany would be unified on Soviet terms or it would not be unified, for Soviet control of the eastern segment gave it an absolute veto power in any merger negotiations. This fact had been apparent from the beginning, and had been underlined at the Geneva talks in 1955; moreover, by 1958 the general power balance in Europe had shifted to some extent in favor of the Soviets, owing to their growing strength in intermediate missiles. A number of observers accordingly began to point out that the Adenauer-Dulles formula was plainly unrealistic, had been outflanked and overtaken by events, and now threatened the West with new humiliations and dangers unless a more tenable alternative were quickly developed. George Kennan, who was perhaps the leading spokesman for the advocates of disengagement in Europe, delivered a celebrated lecture series over the BBC * in which he argued that central Europe presented "an extremely precarious situation" for two reasons: first, there was the particular danger that the East Germans might make another violent attempt to break away from Soviet control, and that the West Germans (now armed, as they had not been in 1953) would go to the rescue of their brothers and World War III would follow; second, a failure to reach an agreement providing for Soviet withdrawal from East Germany in the near future would doom all of Eastern Europe to permanent Soviet occupation and lead eventually to its full incorporation in the USSR. Kennan's proposed solution was a compromise on the question of free elections in order to achieve unification, neutralization and the withdrawal of all foreign forces from the center of Europe. He did not believe the Soviets would attack a Western Europe deprived of American and British forces, and he saw in a unified and neutral Germany the prospect of opening up hopeful vistas for Eastern Europe.[6]

A number of tough pro-NATO integrationists, personified perhaps by Dean Acheson, were scandalized by what they regarded as Kennan's amazing naïveté on the crucial issue of power and its relation to security for the West. A Germany unified yet severed from NATO would be, they feared, a huge menacing iceberg adrift in the center of Europe. Cut off from ties of military cooperation, the Germans would also become separated from the promising supranational experiments, and an isolated Germany would once again become an object of French suspicion and fear. Serious German-Polish frictions over disputed boundaries might well develop. Worst of all, there could be no assurance that German neutrality would endure; Germany was not Austria, and there was no precedent in history for the successful insulation of a large and vital country situated between two power systems and having ambitions of

* In the autumn of 1957.

its own. And if Germany did not remain neutral, it would surely not remained unarmed. In short, they argued, in the chill afterlight of German unification and neutrality, central Europe would present a situation ten times more precarious and less controllable than at present. If Western Europe was to live in reasonable safety and to continue exerting an attraction upon the satellite countries, the imperative condition was a West Germany integrated in Western Europe and in a NATO whose spinal column was the American connection. If this meant a Germany divided for the foreseeable future, so be it.

Adenauer, however, was unprepared to accept half a loaf. He wanted integration with the West, but he also insisted there could be no rational adjustment to the fact of an East German entity, even though it had been in existence for thirteen years. The near-absolute quality of his stubbornness on this issue was expressed in the sterile Hallstein Doctrine, under which Bonn warned all other countries against recognizing the East German regime and summarily cut its own diplomatic ties with any who ignored the warning. When Tito established diplomatic representation in Pankow, Bonn broke relations with Belgrade, thereby depriving itself of a promising avenue of advance to improved goodwill and understanding among those Eastern countries whose fear of German revanchism was still very much alive. Averell Harriman, who had a long experience with the Russians, believed they harbored a deep and genuine fear of an armed West Germany known to have influence over United States policy, but he doubted that Dulles granted any legitimacy to the Russian concern: "Foster gave in too much to Adenauer," who felt that "the way to get unification of Germany was to be stubborn about everything." [7] Harriman was certain that Adenauer had no aggressive aims, but this fact did not remove the reality of the Soviet apprehension. "Foster, I don't think, fully understood" this.[8]

On September 30, 1958, a Western note to Moscow once more stated that free elections offered the only acceptable method of achieving German unification. And on November 7, Dulles made a further statement. Referring to the agreement reached at the Geneva Summit Conference that the unification of Germany was a responsibility of the Four Powers, he said: "It was also agreed that Germany should be reunified in freedom by free elections. We hold to that." [9]

Berlin — the Deadline Crisis

It was against this background of dogmatic Western insistence on a German policy now beyond its power to fulfill that Khrushchev opened the "deadline crisis" of Berlin on November 10, 1958. Speaking to a

Soviet-Polish friendship meeting in Moscow, he charged that, contrary to the Potsdam Agreement, German "militarism, far from being eradicated, is rearing its head ever higher," [10] aided by the Western Powers who were thereby in violation of the Potsdam protocol.* The time had come, he said, for the signatories "to renounce the remnants of the occupation regime in Berlin," thereby making possible the development of a "normal situation" in the capital city of the German Democratic Republic. For their part, the Soviets would hand over their own remaining functions in Berlin to the East German authorities.[11] On November 27, the Soviets delivered a formal note to the other occupying powers which spelled out the terms and consequences of the Khrushchev proposal. It demanded a "solution" within six months, of which the central feature was "the conversion of West Berlin into an independent political unit — a free city, without any state, including both existing German states, interfering in its life." [12] It was to be neutral and disarmed. The deadline for Western acceptance of the proposal was underlined: There would be "no changes in the present procedure for military traffic . . . for half a year." [13] If there were no agreement by that time, Moscow would act unilaterally. Why had Khrushchev chosen this particular time to put forward so provocative a proposal? His answer, given at a special press conference, was that the West had persisted too long in its refusal to recognize the "reality" of two Germanys; it had proved unwilling to discuss a peace treaty on that basis, or even to accept a nuclear-free zone embracing the general area. "One must proceed from the real facts. . . . The war ended more than 13 years ago. . . . It is necessary, therefore, to find a solution that will end this abnormality." [14]

Dulles was quick to appreciate the bear trap in which Khrushchev had suddenly placed the West. The Western position in Berlin (surrounded on four sides by East German territory and having access only through narrow land and air corridors) was inherently tenuous, but Stalin's unsubtle efforts (in 1948–1949) to cut off Western access had been surmounted by the airlift, and Western superiority in overall power had served to hold off another crisis for ten years. But in 1958 Khrushchev did not mention access; he proposed rather to force the West to deal with the East German authorities, thereby creating a new set of relationships which, if accepted by the West, would seriously undermine their rights to Berlin deriving from the occupation statutes. Moreover, he was operating not only from a local power balance heavily in his favor, but

* The occupation rights of the Four Powers were in fact derived not from the Potsdam Agreement of 1945 (which concerned the regulation of German political and economic life), but from the Occupation Protocol of 1944. Khrushchev's error may have been deliberate.

from a recognized nuclear standoff, which he did not choose to leave implicit. The November 27 note said: "Methods of blackmail and reckless threats of force will be least of all appropriate in solving such a problem as the Berlin question. Such methods will not help solve a single question, but can only bring the situation to the danger point. But only madmen can go to the length of unleashing another world war over the preservation of privileges of occupiers in West Berlin. If such madmen should really appear, there is no doubt that strait jackets could be found for them . . ." [15] If the Western Powers should challenge or threaten to overpower the East German authorities after Moscow had turned over to them its own fuctions, the prospect was for a direct confrontation with the USSR under military conditions of extreme awkwardness and vulnerability for the West.

Asked at a press conference on November 26 (just one day before receipt of the formal Soviet note) if the West would deal with East German authorities if they manned the checkpoints along the access routes to Berlin, Dulles replied that, well, the West might deal with them as "agents" of the Soviet Union on a range of minor matters, so long as this did not involve a "substitution" of the German Democratic Republic for the Soviet Union. This remark caused an immediate shock in Germany, and Mayor Willy Brandt in Berlin was moved to charge Dulles with yielding to "salami tactics." Acording to Paul-Henri Spaak, however, Dulles did not intend by this remark to make a material concession, but only to clear away the underbrush of minor issues, so that the public could gain a clearer grasp of what was at stake. According to Spaak, he did not believe that the mere transfer of responsibility for stamping highway-access documents could ever find acceptance in Western opinion as justification for a hard policy of confrontation that might lead to war. [16] The Soviet provocation had to be greater. The following day Khrushchev moved to meet Dulles's need by making plain his intention to abolish the whole structure of the Berlin occupation regime and establish West Berlin as a "free city." This washed out the relevance of the "agent" theory. By the end of November, then, the West faced an exceedingly grim situation. Khrushchev could act unilaterally to substitute East German for Russian authority along the access routes. To accept this meant de facto recognition of East Germany and acknowledgment that the occupation rights could be modified without Western consent. To refuse would produce a new Berlin blockade and place the city in danger of slow strangulation. To challenge Khrushchev militarily could mean war. And a six-month deadline hovered over all.

The Soviet pressures, of course, met with different reactions in the several Western capitals. Eisenhower, who was vacationing in Augusta, told Dulles on the telephone that he would be willing to study the possibility of a free city if it included all of Berlin, but "if the proposal applied to West Berlin only, I would have nothing to do with it." [17] He was disturbed by a working paper from the British Foreign Office which Selwyn Lloyd had passed informally to Ambassador John Hay Whitney, for it suggested a British readiness to deal with East Germany on matters of Berlin access, and eventually to recognize that regime rather than expose Berlin to further blockade. Dulles assured him that Macmillan had personally repudiated the paper, but in fact it came close to representing the core British position. The Europeans as a whole were nervous, and inclined to focus on the vulnerabilities in the Western position.

To make a bad situation much worse, Dulles now suffered in early December a renewed and severe inflammation of his intestine, and was hospitalized at Walter Reed, making it very doubtful that he could fly to Paris for the annual mid-December meeting of the NATO Council. But NATO had now to deal urgently with the Soviet note on Berlin. Over the protest of his doctors, Dulles insisted on making the trip and left the hospital after five days. He was haggard and obviously ill, and it required a major exertion for him to see the conference through. During a pause at the delegates' buffet table, he glanced at the ample food and drink and remarked to a French diplomat: "I'll just have a cup of tea. It's about all I can take." [18] Spaak thought, however, that his very presence was reassuring to an anxious alliance and that his "granite-like" stand against Russian intimidation "meant a very great deal." [19] He charged Khrushchev with recklessness and urged that no negotiations be accepted under duress. He judged Moscow's tactics to be a severe war of nerves, requiring that the West be soberly prepared to go to nuclear warfare, if that proved necessary to protect West Berlin. If such resolve were shown, however, he was confident the crisis could be surmounted without war.[20] Because the issue of Berlin in isolation was so stark a contemplation, Dulles and the other NATO Foreign Ministers either consciously or unconsciously chose not to accept the narrow focus of the Russian note, but to interpret it as an attempt to reopen much broader questions. Walter Lippmann had earlier reflected this disposition of the State Department, writing on December 1 that the Soviets intended to employ Berlin "as an instrument for raising the whole question of Germany." [21] This American assessment was now incorporated in the NATO Council reply to Moscow of December 16 which, rejecting the demand for narrow negotiations about a "free city," declared that "the Council considers that the Berlin question can only be settled in the framework of an agreement with the USSR on Germany as a whole." [22] There was, however, much evidence in the note that Khrushchev was deliberately seeking to isolate the Berlin issue, and

Foreign Minister Andrei Gromyko confirmed this on December 25 in a protest that the NATO reply had not "correctly understood the intentions of the Soviet Union." [23]

After the NATO meeting Dulles flew directly to Jamaica for a rest, but returned in early January in time to meet with Anastas Mikoyan, who came to the United States ostensibly to stimulate East-West trade, but actually, as it appeared, to be on hand to explain the further Soviet initiative of January 10. On that day the Kremlin submitted to the Western powers a draft peace treaty for Germany, and called for a treaty conference and signing ceremony in Warsaw or Prague before the end of March. Both Germanys would be signatories, and the proposal was intimately linked to the "abnormal situation" in Berlin — with respect to the need for speedy conclusion of a German peace treaty, the USSR "would like to believe that the Government of the United States of America . . . will draw the necessary conclusions from the situation of the Berlin question . . ." [24] Khrushchev had dropped the other shoe. Within the tight deadline of May 27 (now only four months away), the West faced not only the "free city" proposal for Berlin, but a draft treaty for Germany as a whole. The "free city" proposal would make West Berlin a powerless hostage; the draft treaty would eclipse reunification by free elections. With respect to both proposals, Moscow threatened to act unilaterally, and appeared able to do so.

From reasonably cordial talks with Mikoyan, Dulles, however, gained the impression that the Soviets desired serious negotiations about Germany, and he thus opened up a new possibility at a press conference on January 13. Asked if his position was "no free elections, no unification," he replied, "Well, we have never said that. The formula of reunification by free elections was the agreed formula. It seems to us to be a natural method. But I wouldn't say that it is the only method by which reunification could be accomplished." [25] This remark threw Bonn once more into shock, and the German ambassador, Wilhelm Grewe, asked urgently for a clarification. Dulles retreated to the literal truth that he had merely given a technically precise answer to a question. Other means of reunification were "possible," he said, but the United States was still committed to a democratic electoral process.[26] It seemed apparent, however, that the Secretary of State was belatedly trying to gain some measure of freedom from Adenauer's tight and anxious embrace, and this was certainly the chancellor's assessment, for he promptly dispatched a special emissary, Herbert Dittman, for further consultation. In seeking to assure Adenauer, Dulles talked to Dittman in terms that suggested the extent to which he now saw himself, in these final months in office, as the personification of United States policy. Sitting on his comfortable leather couch with his feet up on the coffee table and doodling on the omnipresent yellow pad, he explained to Dittman that brinkmanship did in fact mean going to the abyss. This was the consequence, he said, of the fact that Soviet policy operates to expand every encounter to the edge of war. "I am forced to the abyss. I do not go there of my own volition. But when I am there, I am not willing to retreat. I have proved it at Quemoy." [27] But he further explained that a readiness to confront the abyss does not exclude flexibility where it is possible to be elastic without surrendering a fundamental position.[28] And soon he moved again toward greater elasticity, suggesting to a press conference on January 28 yet another alternative means of achieving German unity: "You can have a confederation which is, in fact, of very considerable progress toward reunification." [29] In his first direct confrontation with Russian, as distinguished from Chinese, power, Dulles seemed to be feeling for openings with great care.

The Military Constraints

The Western position in Berlin was marked by a conspicuous military weakness — local inferiority combined with the knowledge that this could be corrected only by invoking nuclear war. General Maxwell Taylor, the Army Chief of Staff, urged a conventional force strategy, involving the use of armed truck convoys, armed trains, infantry and tank escorts to "test Soviet intentions" in the Berlin corridors. Dean Acheson, a semiofficial spokesman for the Democratic party, acknowledging that nuclear weapons could not be used locally, agreed with Taylor that "the only visible alternative is to use western conventional power to remove obstacles to traffic to and from Berlin, both on land and in the air." [30] This line of reasoning was not, however, acceptable to Eisenhower, who felt it involved the danger of starting a land war which the West could not sustain, and of then being faced with the choice of accepting local defeat or *initiating* nuclear war. The division-size force which the Pentagon proposed for deployment in the Berlin corridors was, he felt, too strong for a probe and too weak to fight its way into Berlin; that much American force in the corridors would be played up in the press and would thus engage Soviet prestige, resulting in an even harder Soviet position. For his part, Dulles doubted that public opinion could be developed soon enough to support a major attempt to force the passage of Berlin before the May 27 deadline.[31] Both men seemed to be thinking in terms of avoiding a military showdown, considering that if worse came to worst they could revert to an airlift, as in 1948; but many in the Pentagon doubted that the airlift option remained open, for two reasons: the Berlin population was now larger and adapted to a higher standard of living than in 1948; and new Soviet radar jamming techniques might now seriously interrupt an all-weather, around-the-clock operation.

Such a narrowly circumscribed position drove the President back upon a deliberately ambiguous military posture. On the one hand, he was clear that "we are certainly not going to fight a ground war in Europe," nor was it likely that "we are going to shoot our way into Berlin." [32] Assuming he was not prepared to see the United States ejected and West Berlin slowly strangled, this left him with nuclear retaliation, but he publicly refused the logic of the equation.

Q. "Is the United States prepared to use nuclear weapons if necessary to defend free Berlin?

A. Well, I don't know how you could free anything with nuclear weapons. I can say this: the United States, and its allies, have announced their firm intention of preserving their rights and responsibilities with respect to Berlin." [33]

Privately, he did not seem entirely to rule out the possibility of opening the floodgates to Armageddon, saying to Vice-president Nixon and others assembled after an NSC meeting on December 11 that "in this gamble, we are not going to be betting white chips, building up the pot gradually and fearfully. Khrushchev should know that when we decide to act, our whole stack will be in the pot." [34] Yet the American contingency plan he approved that same day was a model of caution, containing built-in safeguards against rash action: (1) while the United States would refuse to allow East German authorities to stamp identification passes, there was no objection to *showing* such passes to such authorities for identification purposes; (2) if East German authorities were substituted for Soviet authorities, a small convoy with armed protection would attempt to go through; (3) if this were stopped, the attempt would be discontinued; (4) the convoy would fire only if fired on; (5) all Western traffic to Berlin would then be suspended, the West would publicize the fact of blockade and take the issue to the UN; (6) military preparations would then be intensified; (7) if moral and political pressures did not produce a solution, "use of additional force would be subject to governmental decision"; (8) in any event, the United States would "at once" make every effort to open talks with the Soviet Union at the level of Foreign Ministers. [35]

The Last Trip

With the clock ticking toward the May 27 deadline, the loose Western position, hastily pasted together at the NATO meeting in Paris, seemed grossly insufficient to form the basis for serious negotiations (it did not, of course, even take into account the Soviet note of January 10 and the accompanying draft of a German peace treaty). The Soviet initiatives had struck vital nerves in the West, but the responses were hardly uniform. The British, who believed Khrushchev was really seeking greater security for vulnerable Soviet positions in Eastern Europe, wanted early negotiations, were willing to deal with the East Germans, and strongly opposed the risk of armed probes on the access routes (on the ground that these would require the West to fire the first shots). They advocated a revival of the Eden and Rapacki plans (with some stronger provisions for inspection). The French, conversely, were opposed to early negotiations or any substantive concessions, including the acceptance of the East Germans as "agents"; they favored an airlift over a ground probe. The West Germans opposed any nuclear-free zone or other thin-out of forces, and found the "agent" theory anathema because it threatened eventual recognition of East Germany; they also preferred an airlift. If there was one point of unanimous agreement in Europe, it was opposition to "testing Soviet intentions" by risking a land war in the Berlin corridors. Otherwise the European responses reflected a picture of disarray. If something coherent was to be made of this mélange, it appeared that the United States would have to make it. And although he was a sick and dying man, Dulles thus embarked on yet another round of diplomatic consultations — with London, Paris, and Bonn — in an effort to construct a Western position that would hold together through a hard negotiation, or even through the grim contingency of Soviet interference with Western access to Berlin.

When Dulles arrived in London on February 4, Macmillan was "shocked at his appearance . . . it was clear to me now that he was a very sick man," [36] unable to hold on his stomach even the boiled egg and junket especially prepared for him. He wore a truss to support a hernia and was thin-lipped from his stern and dignified effort to suppress the pain. On points of substance, however, the prime minister was encouraged by his broad and tolerant reasonableness — in a private talk he gave the impression of having *"completely abandoned* the Pentagon plan" for a large-scale ground probe with tanks and artillery,[37] and Macmillan felt it was imperative that he repeat this view in the presence of his American colleagues, including Robert Murphy, who was a staunch advocate of the Pentagon view. This Dulles did. "I suspect," Macmillan wrote, "that it is the President who has overruled the soldiers. Indeed, when we were alone, Dulles as good as told me this." [38] Dulles also listened attentively to the British proposals for a nuclear-free zone in a defined forward sector of central Europe, but he remained solidly opposed to this or any other form of disengagement.

In mid-January 1959, the British Prime Minister, who was dealing with an anxious constituency and also faced with general elections in October, decided with characteristic political boldness to pick up "a sort of outstanding invitation to go to Moscow" which had been issued at the time of the Bulganin-Khrushchev visit to Britain in 1956.[39] He had in mind a solitary reconnaissance that might provide important mediation in the fateful Berlin impasse and that would (by both seeming and being a mission of peace) serve to steady British opinion and, not incidentally, to help the Tories at the polls. Two days before Dulles arrived in London, Macmillan had received Soviet acceptance of his proposed visit. Eisenhower and Dulles, who had, of course, been forewarned, were not overjoyed by the prospect, but, according to Macmillan, they were "not unsympathetic. . . . They say, in effect, that they have complete confidence in me and I must do whatever I think best." [40] Adenauer and De Gaulle had also conveyed their restrained approval, and Macmillan's carefully planned itinerary would carry him to Paris, Bonn, and Washington following his return from Moscow, so that his allies would be fully informed. When Dulles departed London, Macmillan felt "very sad. In spite of all the troubles and difficulties we had had with this strange man, I had grown to have an affection and respect for him." But "I felt that he was . . . doomed." [41]

In Paris, Dulles found De Gaulle shrouded in Olympian gloom, but determined to accept the risks inherent in defending Western rights in Berlin. He and Dulles agreed that, inasmuch as these rights had their juridical basis in the occupation statute, it would be unwise to allow the Berlin issue to go to the United Nations where there would be no assurance of a large or vigorous pro-Western majority. Although Dulles strove with singular willpower to suppress his pain, Couve de Murville said later: "It hurt us all to watch him. He was very tired. We knew then that he did not have very long to live." [42]

Between official engagements, however, Dulles found time for a talk with David Schoenbrun, the CBS Paris correspondent, who was just completing a biography of General de Gaulle.[43] Hunched in an armchair, looking very uncomfortable, and staring moodily into a long glass of whiskey and soda, he asked Schoenbrun to explain to him the motivations and idiosyncrasies of Le Grand Charlie. As they chatted, Dulles mentioned an incident of the previous July 6, when he had consulted De Gaulle on the prospective Lebanon intervention, and had recommended to the French president that France not participate in the military landings. To this De Gaulle had replied with imperial hauteur that "France will be present in the Lebanon," but in fact he did not follow through. He did, however, instruct Couve de Murville, the day following the landings, to issue a statement deploring the lack of

The last visit to see Adenauer in Bonn (February 1959)

allied unity and accusing the United States of not having consulted with France. Why had Dulles remained silent in the face of so blatant an untruth, Schoenbrun asked? "Well," Dulles replied, "there's no point — as President Eisenhower is fond of saying — of getting into a pissing contest with a skunk"; he was faced, he said, with the fact that he couldn't answer the attack "without contradicting the President of France," and he stirred up the ice in his drink with a thick forefinger and shook his head slowly.[44]

Also while in Paris, he dropped his guard to a concerned and admiring General Lauris Norstad, the NATO commander, briefly revealing something of the grim ordeal he was living through. Norstad, although privately shocked at Dulles's appearance, had said lightly that for a man who was still "running around" Europe after a stiff "bout with the doctors," he was delighted to say that the. Secretary looked "surprisingly well." [45] Dulles looked at him in pain and sadness, then slumped his head down on his chest and said: "Well, I'm tired. . . . You know, I can't rest in an airplane anymore." [46] That quiet haven between arduous engagements no longer existed. Norstad later reflected that this last round of diplomatic talks "must have been an almost unbearable ordeal for a proud man, because he wasn't the strong force that he'd been, and he knew that." [47]

In Bonn, Dulles and Adenauer achieved a general meeting of minds, encapsulated in Adenauer's phrase that there would be "no concessions without counter-concessions." [48] The old German remained exceedingly nervous about British proposals for a nuclear-free zone and profoundly suspicious of Macmillan's intentions in Moscow. But he was heartened by Dulles's report that De Gaulle stood ready to defend Western rights in Berlin, by war if necessary, and he accepted the American and British decision to seek negotiations before the May 27 deadline. Basically, he put his trust in Dulles and the United States to see the crisis through. It was indeed his only real choice, for the fate and future of the Federal Republic lay at that moment largely with the United States and the NATO alliance.

The meeting in Bonn was more notable for its human drama, the last poignant scene in the "love affair" between the two aging tartars who had stood together through many battles and must now part forever. As had become the chancellor's regular gesture of the unusual respect in which he held this man who was not a head of government, Adenauer met Dulles at the airport. A photograph was taken of the arriving Secretary of State standing in the doorway of his plane, waving to the chancellor who waited at the foot of the steps, his hand also outstretched. At their meeting in the Palais Schaumburg, Dulles leaned far back in his chair and rubbed his chest from time to time, his hands moving over his vest in a slow circular motion. He seemed tired and in pain, but his mind was clear. The anxious and troubled chancellor provided him with a special strained porridge during a break for refreshments, and Dulles, finding it unusually palatable, asked for the recipe. As they drove back to the airport, in the privacy of Adenauer's limousine, he told his host he had a hernia and would enter Walter Reed Hospital immediately on his return to Washington. He said that, except for President Eisenhower, no one else knew of this, but he wanted Adenauer to know so that he would not believe, upon learning of the hospitalization, that the problem was a recurrence of cancer. Adenauer was deeply convinced that Dulles was speaking the truth, as he then knew it.[49] It was a truth, no doubt, he desperately wanted to believe, but there had been a revealing episode in Mexico City three months before, in November. There to attend the inauguration ceremonies of the new president-elect, Dulles had suffered through a period of severe pain, lying on his bed at the American embassy with his hands pressed against his stomach. His friend the American ambassador, Robert C. Hill, wanted to summon doctors, but Dulles refused, saying he did not want to cause unfortunate diplomatic repercussions around the world, nor to take headlines away from the new Mexican president. In addition, he told Hill, "he suspected that for what was wrong with him the doctors could be of little assistance." [50]

Arriving back in Washington from Bonn, he asked the President for permission to turn over his duties temporarily to Undersecretary Herter, and immediately entered the hospital. A few days later, when the medical diagnosis showed a recurrence of the cancer, Dulles cabled Adenauer to express regret that "what I told you turned out to be wrong. But I am confident I can overcome this." [51] Soon, however, Adenauer also received two copies of the photograph taken at the Bonn airport. There was no inscription, but simply the words "John Foster Dulles" on both copies. In an accompanying note, the Secretary of State asked his friend to autograph one copy and send it to him at the hospital. Adenauer later said he knew then "that my friend Dulles was saying farewell to me forever." [52]

Macmillan in Moscow

Macmillan's trip to Moscow (between February 21 and March 3) proved a personal ordeal, yet one of immense practical value to the Western cause and to the ultimate easing of the grim Berlin crisis. He had to endure several blistering sessions at which Khrushchev criticized his allies — especially Eisenhower and Dulles — in harsh terms, as well as a surprising public speech in which the Russian leader both disparaged the West and offered Britain a "treaty of friendship and non-aggression" about which nothing had been said in the private discussions. Macmillan felt it necessary at their next meeting to point out to Khrushchev, with "much deliberation and seriousness," that Britain could not be separated from her allies either by stratagem or attacks upon their leaders.[53]

In a tough extemporaneous reply, in which he showed himself angry and disturbed, Khrushchev told Macmillan he really could not understand the West. "The Soviet Government had proposed a free city of West Berlin in which the population would be free of all danger and they were ready to surround this arrangement with all necessary guarantees. In their replies, the West talked about rights of access and occupation status which merely meant a continuation of the state of war. The West talked about defending three million people who did not need to be defended. But, when they talked about war, what was really involved were the deaths of hundreds of millions of people." [54] The Soviets, Khrushchev said, had advanced certain proposals regarding Germany, but the Western replies were not in any way responsive (as Macmillan translated this, "our last note of 16 February was not a reply to his note — it had no connection except a reference to the date").[55] Moreover, Western insistence on meetings at an intermediate level was merely, the Russian leader said, an attempt "to inveigle us in diplomatic talk, in the labyrinth of which the Soviet Union has had many years of experience — a bog without an exit." [56]

The status quo, Khrushchev insisted, must give way in Berlin, but Macmillan was confirmed in his earlier impression that the true Soviet motivation was defensive, that despite their new wealth and power the Russians were still obsessed by a sense of insecurity ("the old bogey of encirclement has not yet been laid"),[57] and that their primary aim was to stabilize the East German frontier with the West and the German-Polish borders. "By now," Khrushchev said, "enough time has passed and the situation has sufficiently changed for us to recognise that the difference between our systems must not create obstacles to the establishment of friendly relations between our peoples, between our countries. The social conditions in one country or another depend on the will of the people of a given country. We must recognise this fact, just as we recognise that the sun rises every morning, and must proceed from the fact that we live under different systems, but on one planet; that we breathe the same air, enjoy the blessings of nature and the warmth of the same sun." [58] Despite the conflict and tension of the meeting, Macmillan was encouraged by developments, and he found Khrushchev, "with all his faults and crudities" a charming contrast to the usual run of stony-faced and wooden Soviet bureaucrats. An "expansive, irrepres-

At Walter Reed Hospital with Foreign Minister Selwyn Lloyd,
President Eisenhower, and Prime Minister Macmillan (March 1959)

sible, eloquent . . . petulant, occasionally impossible, but not unlovable extrovert," Khrushchev seemed cast from an altogether different mold.[59]

In the final session, he made clear to Macmillan that his real desire was Western acceptance of East Germany and its existing frontiers. He was not interested in de jure recognition; de facto acceptance would be satisfactory. Moreover, he attached no particular significance to the deadline of May 27: "It could be 27 June or 27 August or any date we liked to name."[60] The main thing was progress toward serious agreement about Berlin. On March 2, the Soviet reply to the Western note of February 16 made a second notable shift. While asking for a summit conference to discuss European security, disarmament, a nuclear-free zone, and the mutual withdrawal of troops, it indicated that, if the Western powers were not yet ready for talks at the highest level, then there could be preliminary talks among the Foreign Ministers. With these two important "clarifications," which the Macmillan visit seemed to have been instrumental in bringing about, much of the intense anxiety was taken out of the "deadline crisis."

Macmillan arrived in Washington on March 20 to brief Eisenhower and Dulles on his trip to Russia, amid vocal American concern over the wide gap between the British and West German positions, and diplomatic rumors that Macmillan might be willing to enter into a treaty about East Germany. On the first day, the President, the Prime Minister and the Foreign Secretary journeyed to Ward 8 at Walter Reed Hospital for a visit with the Secretary of State. Sitting in a wheelchair in a silk dressing gown, looking very thin and "even emaciated," Dulles conducted "even more of a monologue than ordinarily" and seemed to Macmillan to be "*against* almost everything," especially a summit meeting.[61] Dulles made a forceful plea that nothing must be said or done to give people throughout the world the impression that the Soviets were now in the "driver's seat," insisting by implication that the Western threat of nuclear retaliation was still valid, had not been stalemated even in a situation like Berlin. Why, he asked, should the United States spend "$40 billion a year or more to create a deterrent and defensive power if, whenever the Soviets threatened us, our only answer would be to buy peace by compromise." [62] When Khrushchev made threatening speeches, Dulles said, the West should not become fearful "as though he were the Lord of Creation." [63] The conversation, as Eisenhower later remarked, turned out to be "anything but casual." [64] Macmillan found Dulles's spirited lecture "a splendid exhibition of courage and devotion," but "I felt that his illness had made his mind more rigid and reverting to very fixed concepts. I felt also sorry for the President." [65]

The most important difference between the U.S. and British approaches to the Berlin problem was the question of a summit. Despite the reasonably flexible Soviet note of March 2, Macmillan's central impression of his Russian visit was that effective negotiation was possible only with Khrushchev, and that an attempt to give the "usual quibbling answer" would merely irritate the Russian leader, thus intensifying all the uncertainties. On the other hand, a forthcoming acceptance of a summit conference would very probably have the effect of postponing a Berlin showdown at least until after such a meeting; and that would provide time for the West to concentrate on "the real problem — an acceptable compromise on Germany and Berlin." [66] Macmillan pressed Eisenhower hard and emotionally to accept this position: "I owe a duty to my people. This question of agreement now to a summit meeting is probably the most fateful decision I will ever have to make." Even recognizing the need to apply some discount to such a statement in a British election year, Eisenhower nevertheless felt there was "no question of his sincerity or the visible depth of his feelings." [67] After further consideration, he thus approved a British draft proposing a Foreign Ministers meeting on May 11 that would "prepare constructive proposals for consideration by a conference of Heads of Government later in the summer." It then added: "On this understanding and as soon as developments in the Foreign Minister's meeting justify holding a Summit Conference," the United States would be willing to participate.[68] This deft formula gave Macmillan reasonable assurance of a summit, yet permitted Eisenhower to hold the view that such a conference was not an automatic consequence of the lower-level preparation. On March 30, Khrushchev accepted this Western proposal.

30.

Death and Assessment

ULLES LEFT WALTER REED HOSPITAL on March 22 for his home in
Washington, and thence to Douglas Dillon's house in Hobe
Sound, his wife wanting him to be as comfortable as possible in a warm
climate. Through March and early April he continued to be surrounded
by the poignant conspiracy of hope; his doctors withheld a final opinion
and his friends and professional colleagues from the President on down
put a best face on the present and ignored the future. "We just didn't
talk about it," Allen Dulles said later, "because experience has shown
[that] sometimes the doctors are wrong. Rarely they're wrong in cancer,
but sometimes they're wrong." [1]

On February 17, the day after Dulles reentered the hospital, Lyndon
Johnson, the Democratic Majority Leader, had asked his Senate colleagues to resolve "that the Senate stand in silent prayer to the Almighty
for the early and complete recovery of the Secretary of State, the beloved John Foster Dulles"; and he had passed a copy of his accompanying remarks through William Macomber with the notation, "My
prayers and hopes are with you each hour. Lyndon." [2] From Joseph
Grew, former ambassador to Japan, now came a note: "Just a word
from an old friend to say that we are all pulling for you . . ." [3] Thruston
Morton, the junior senator from Kentucky and a former Assistant Secretary of State, sent him a gift: "My late father-in-law was one of your
most ardent and vocal admirers. He used to say that the only truly great
strengths left in the Free World were John Foster Dulles and good
bourbon whiskey. This whiskey will cure anything. I speak from years of
experience." [4]

As world opinion gradually became aware that the linchpin of American foreign policy had been perhaps permanently removed, there was belated realization of how extraordinarily strong Dulles had been and how much his certitude and omnipresence had become a part of the international structure that had been built to protect Western man from the twin fears of nuclear war and Communist inundation. His old friend Thomas E. Dewey seemed to speak for a great many: "They suddenly realized, most of them, [even those who] may have been hostile critics, [that] you, personally, are their sword and buckler. They discovered that they have been leaning on you for their own sense of personal security in a confusing and terrifying world; that you understood it and had the courage to stand up and protect them." [5] The *Reporter* said editorially: "There are so few men in our day and country with the capacity . . . to be themselves to the farthest reaches of loneliness and of risk. Mr. Dulles has proved to be one of the very, very few." [6] And his steadfast critic Richard Rovere wrote in the *New Yorker* that, as a consequence of his departure, there was now "a far wider appreciation of Mr. Dulles's services than there has been at any other time, and that this appreciation is in no sense the product of sympathy or pity or piety." [7] Harold Macmillan, speaking to the House of Commons, called him "a figure whose very bigness is hardly realised until we are threatened with its absence. He is one of those men whose devotion to duty and strength of purpose have made him a great, important and vital figure in the life of the world." [8] And even his major adversary in the Kremlin spoke with respect of his character and ability. "I feel very sorry for Dulles," Khrushchev told Dag Hammarskjöld. "I admire his intelligence, his wide knowledge, his integrity and his courage. Dulles invented brinkmanship, but he would never step over the brink." [9]

As Dulles sat in the Florida sun, trying to recover his strength from the debilitating effects of the radium treatments that were designed to retard the cancer, the situation drifted in anomaly. Although unable to make a further contribution to the Berlin crisis or to wider issues, he remained the Secretary of State; and it was clear that Eisenhower, trusting and revering him, would not ask for his resignation. The President waited, hoping against hope. Characteristically, it was Dulles himself who finally took the initiative. On April 11, Allen Dulles, who was vacationing at Palm Beach, received a call from Jerry Greene, the Secretary's special assistant, who said Foster wanted to see him as soon as possible. Allen motored over the short distance to Hobe Sound to find his brother lying in bed with a yellow legal pad on his legs; he had lost considerable weight and looked very weak. "I could see that my brother was in great pain." [10] The Secretary of State wanted Allen to go at once

Funeral services at Arlington Cemetery (May 27, 1959);
seated left to right: Mrs. Dulles, John Dulles,

Lillias Dulles Hinshaw, Avery Dulles, President and Mrs.
Eisenhower, Vice President and Mrs. Nixon

to Eisenhower, who was vacationing at Augusta, Georgia, and persuade the President to accept his resignation. While he did not give Allen the impression that he feared an imminent death, he was firm in his conviction that he could not recover "in time" to prepare for the Foreign Ministers talks now set for May 11, nor for the prospective summit conference thereafter. He had sketched out a letter of resignation on his yellow pad. It said:

Dear Mr. President:

It is apparent to me that I shall not be well enough, soon enough, to continue to serve as Secretary of State. Accordingly I tender my resignation to be effective at your convenience.

I am deeply grateful for the opportunities and responsibilities you have given me. I was brought up in the belief that this nation of ours was not merely a self-serving society, but was founded with a mission to help build a world where liberty and justice would prevail. Today that concept faces a formidable and ruthless challenge from international Communism. This has made it manifestly difficult to adhere steadfastly to our national idealism and national mission and at the same time avoid the awful catastrophe of war.

You, Mr. President, have given inspiring leadership in this essential task, and it has been a deep satisfaction to me to have been intimately associated with you in these matters. If I can, in a more limited capacity, continue to serve, I shall be happy to do so.

Gratefully yours,
JOHN FOSTER DULLES [11]

Allen chartered a plane and, accompanied by Jerry Greene, flew that same afternoon to see President Eisenhower in his spacious white brick cottage beside the Augusta golf course. They sat down together, with the press secretary, James Hagerty, also present. Eisenhower read the unsigned draft carefully and thoughtfully, then turned to Allen and said he did not want to cross this bridge until it was absolutely clear there was no alternative. Nor was he willing to do anything that might discourage the Secretary in his fight for recovery. "I remember very well the President's reaction," Allen recalled. "He was absolutely adamant about not accepting the resignation until he had had the final diagnosis of the doctors and their judgment that there was no hope of a recovery." [12] Allen argued for his brother, saying Foster felt that the coming Foreign Ministers meeting required a Secretary of State with full vigor, but Eisenhower was unmoved. So the matter was deferred, but not for long. The presidential aircraft, *Columbine*, was dispatched to return Dulles to Washington and the Walter Reed Hospital. Four days later the final medical judgment was rendered: the treatments had not arrested the cancer; it was spreading and there was no practical hope of recovery. Dulles telephoned Eisenhower on April 15, saying, "I can't continue and it isn't proper that I should." [13] A distressed and reluctant President at last accepted the inevitable, calling in Hagerty and directing him to make the announcement to the White House press corps. Then he stopped him and said, "No, Jim, I want to go down and do it myself." [14] It proved to be an emotional ordeal. On the following day he released the Secretary's letter together with his own reply:

Dear Foster:

I accept, with deepest personal regret and only because I have no alternative, your resignation as Secretary of State, effective upon the qualification of your successor.

In so doing, I can but repeat what the vast outpouring of affection and admiration from the entire free world has told you. You have, with the talents you so abundantly possess and with your exemplary integrity of character, employed your rich heritage as well as your unique experience in handling our relations with other countries. You have been a staunch bulwark of our nation against the machinations of Imperialistic Communism. You have won to the side of the free world countless peoples, and inspired in them renewed courage and determination to fight for freedom and principle. As a statesman of world stature you have set a record in the stewardship of our foreign relations that stands clear and strong for all to see.

By this letter I request you to serve in the future, to whatever extent your health will permit, as a consultant to me and the State Department in international affairs. I know that all Americans join me in the fervent hope that you will thus be able to continue the important contribution that only you can make toward a just peace in the world.

With affectionate regard,

As ever,

DWIGHT EISENHOWER [15]

Although Eisenhower had accepted Dulles's recommendation that Undersecretary Christian Herter should succeed him, there was an embarrassing hiatus of two days before the latter's appointment was announced, this being explained by Eisenhower's insistence that Herter, who suffered from serious arthritis, should first undergo a thorough physical examination. Yet even beyond this quite reasonable precaution there seemed in the President's approach a troubled hesitancy, a psychological unreadiness to take the inexorable next step. At Herter's swearing-in ceremony on April 18, he acted with unaccustomed brusqueness, giving the impression that the whole matter of bringing forth a successor to Dulles was deeply distasteful. The incident provided further embarrassment to the gentle and genteel man from Massachusetts, but Eisenhower's behavior reflected not a lack of confidence in Christian

Herter, but an emotional distress at the loss of Foster Dulles so deep that it temporarily affected his self-control.

On Sunday, May 24, 1959, Dulles died in his sleep. It had been a brave struggle and it was a brave death. Eisenhower called him "one of the truly great men of our time . . . a foe only to tyranny." [16] His body lay in state a day and a night in the Bethlehem Chapel of the vast Episcopal Cathedral that dominates the Washington skyline; then on May 27, at two o'clock in the afternoon, following a brief ceremony at the Cathedral, the solemn procession of a formal State Funeral began its slow march through the city and across the Potomac to Arlington Cemetery, the flag-draped caisson passing between row upon row of quiet, sympathetic onlookers along the way. The crowds were large. Eternally controversial in life, Dulles seemed in death to be recognized by admirers and critics alike as a man who had occupied so large a part of the diplomatic horizon for so long a time that his departure suddenly stirred anxiety because the void he left seemed of such immense proportions. There was, too, widespread respect for the brave stoicism of his final, painful months.

Adenauer came, unbidden, to say a final farewell to his old friend, and the other head of government in attendance was Menzies of Australia. Jean Monnet was there, as were Dag Hammarskjöld of the United Nations and Paul-Henri Spaak of NATO. The Foreign Ministers of the Soviet Union, West Germany, Britain, France and the United States (Gromyko, Von Brentano, Lloyd, Couve de Murville, and Herter) adjourned their fragile deliberations in Geneva to fly to Washington together in Herter's plane, thus passing May 27 (the original deadline on Berlin) not in confrontation but in peaceful tribute to the man who had long stood as chief defender of Adenauer's rigid policy of "no concessions" in central Europe. They were joined by Foreign Ministers or other ranking Cabinet officers of eleven other nations,* and by twenty-three honorary pallbearers selected by Mrs. Dulles.† As John Foster Dulles thus departed the scene, the American people and much of the world seemed to offer him belated appreciation, and to accept President Eisenhower's subsequent tribute: "His calm approach, his comprehension of the important factors in every problem, his firm conclusions, and his moral courage were majestic." [17]

* Belgium, Bolivia, Canada, Chile, Dominican Republic, Italy, Japan, Liberia, Netherlands, South Korea, Turkey.

† C. Stanton Babcock, Pemberton Berman, Arthur H. Dean, Thomas E. Dewey, C. Douglas Dillon, Harold Dodds, Charles C. Glover, Edward H. Greene, Morris Hadley, Robert F. Hart, Jr., Herbert C. Hoover, Jr., George M. Humphrey, C. D. Jackson, Joseph E. Johnson, Jean Monnet, George Murnane, Herman Phleger, Arthur W. Radford, John D. Rockefeller III, Dean Rusk, Eustace Seligman, Walter Bedell Smith, Henry Van Dusen.

Perspective

Twenty years after he entered office as Secretary of State and fourteen years after his death, John Foster Dulles looks like an impressive, head-strong man who was unquestionably the principal architect of foreign policy during the Eisenhower period, yet who left behind no very dis-tinguished or enduring monuments to his handiwork — with the notable exception of the Japanese peace treaty, and that, of course, was fashioned while he was a consultant to the previous administration. In fairness to Dulles, it must be said that the basic architecture of the postwar world — the containment strategy, the Truman Doctrine, the Marshall Plan, NATO, and the philosophy of foreign economic and military aid — was already in place when the Eisenhower administration came to office. And while there was no doubt room for new conceptions and new structures, the works of the Truman administration proved to have been soundly built, leaving Dulles little choice but to accept and utilize major elements of the legacy. While he tried hard to disguise that fact, employing both a dramatic rhetoric and a hyperthyroid activism to convey the impression of his own bold innovation, he succeeded chiefly in widening and institu-tionalizing the attitudes and structures of the cold war in American life.

Led by his self-righteous and apocalyptic style, the Eisenhower admin-istration moved to ring the Soviet Union and China with a comprehen-sive set of multilateral and bilateral anti-Communist alliances, whose development led in turn to a proliferation of American overseas military bases and to a dramatic rise in the flow of American military equipment for foreign armies. Bases must be manned and client armies trained and advised. By 1959, more than a million American officials, military and otherwise, including their dependents and servitors, were stationed in about forty-two countries. An anxious, often bemused, American people gave their active or their tacit consent. This vast formation represented unprecedented imperial power, yet that objective fact remained largely beyond recognition or acceptance by a public opinion that was now thor-oughly conditioned to the habit of their leaders to elevate every issue of foreign policy to the level of deadly clash between opposed moral absolutes. Dulles had led in the building of a powerful anti-Communist rationale which gave justification to dramatic and flar-flung American military deployments. As he quit the scene, there was as yet only the first glimmering awareness that this contribution also defined the philo-sophical limits of Dullesian diplomacy, that he possessed neither the per-ception of the opportunity, nor the will, to move beyond it.

Today this aspect of his legacy is more apparent. The slogans that have clung to his name -- "agonizing reappraisal," "liberation," "massive retaliation," "brinkmanship" — all share the same sad connotation of emptiness, indeed of semifraud. The collective security alliances he planned or put together — SEATO and CENTO — were in the 1950s not very different from the makeshift arrangements they appear today; at no time did they significantly strengthen the Western posture or enhance the diplomatic landscape, and their continued survival, in a moribund state, is attributable largely to the extraordinary norms of bureaucratic inertia. The Formosa Resolution and the Eisenhower Doctrine appear in retrospect as one-time devices formulated in haste to meet problems that were substantially misperceived, and to generate congressional support for potential American actions that seemed unclear even in the minds of Dulles and the President. There is a curiously ad hoc quality to the whole record.

Much of this is explainable by reference to the observable truth that Dulles was far more a tactician than a systematic strategist and planner, but also a tactician who operated on fixed moral or religious premises. Moved by strong but highly generalized articles of faith, and lacking the managerial instinct to develop an orderly and comprehensive plan of operations, he showed a marked tendency to move directly from the faith to the tactic, from an abstract premise to its direct application in a very specific situation. And as his premises seemed to him too basic for reexamination and his preference was for action, he was prone to expend almost all of his intellectual and physical energy on the short-term tactical requirements. Lawyerlike, he would apply his formidable powers of concentration to a suddenly urgent or dangerous development, but would rarely aim at more than temporary repair; and because he was insensitive to the interdependence of problems, he would frequently say or do things to help the immediate case, with only a dim awareness of the adverse effects he was producing on other and often more important cases.

One of his key premises was that the Communist system was not only inherently evil and immoral (which few doubted), but also inherently inferior to the West in material terms (which a good many doubted). Impelled by faith in this premise, he continued to pursue a policy of global pressure aimed at isolating, weakening, and eventually bringing down the major Communist adversaries in the world arena, trusting (as the West German ambassador, Albrecht von Kessel, said of him) "that Bolshevism was a product of the Devil and that God would wear out the Bolsheviks in the long run." [18] He resisted any earnest search for accommodation or even for serious negotiation, for his goal was not really coexistence based on a calculated balance of force; it was superiority and mastery based on a vague expectation that the West would maintain a

permanent power preponderance. There may have been a real opportunity to achieve a détente with the USSR in the fluid period immediately
following Stalin's death, and with the Chinese Communists in the long
lull between mid-1955 and mid-1958. But Dulles was geared, ideologically
and intellectually, for interminable struggle with the devil, and he clung
to his unexamined premise of inherent Western superiority long after
the Soviet Union had developed military and industrial strength, and
exportable economic surplus, of magnitudes that made a policy of concerted Western pressure manifestly unrealistic and unproductive. As a
consequence of his sluggish adjustment to these new realities (which also
included a rising determination of the Third World to achieve a position
of a genuine independence as between the two major power blocs), the
confident architect of pressure in the first Eisenhower term became the
exhausted firefighter in the second, dashing distractedly from one blaze
to another in a frenzied effort to stifle the flames of national rebellion
and revolution in the Third World.

The tragedy of this frustration, this stultification of Dulles's fine unfounded hopes, is that there might well have been a different outcome.
For the domestic political situation in the second term could very probably have sustained a different approach to the Third World, including
China. Through a demonstration of trustworthiness and practical wisdom, and through his instinctively prudent management of foreign policy
crises, Eisenhower had by the end of 1956 persuaded most of the congressional Republicans (who had oscillated wildly between isolationism
and imperialism) to support the foreign policies of an internationalist
Republican President, and indeed to assume a measure of personal
responsibility for them. Except for a few incorrigibles, the Republican
party was being brought out of isolation to the threshold of responsible
international behavior. The stage seemed set for constructive diplomacy.
But the popular President's energy was waning, while the unpopular
Secretary of State continued to pursue phantom goals and to judge that
his own survival still depended on accommodating the Republican right.
The result was that Dulles imposed a tenacious continuity on United
States policy at a time when conditions, at home and abroad, cried out
for searching reappraisal of basic premises, and when clear-headed, bold
political leadership might have produced changes in American relations
with Russia and China at least as significant as those finally achieved by
the Nixon-Kissinger initiatives of 1972. But the rigidity of Dullesian
priorities prevailed. Philosophically, for example, he was a strong anticolonialist, but as Soviet and Chinese offers of trade and aid gave Third
World countries a greater leverage vis-à-vis the West in their determined
efforts to achieve unfettered independence, he continued in sterile opposition to neutrality and nonalignment: it had adverse implications for

regional alliance arrangements and American military base rights, and these were the main ingredients of his policy of pressure and encirclement. Also, because he failed to see the practical limits for Russian and Chinese imperialism in their encounters with the resistant strength of nationalism in the newly independent countries (including Communist forms of nationalism), he continued to fear that *any* Communist presence among weak and backward peoples would lead to subversion and take-over that could only enhance the power and influence of Russia or China at the expense of the United States.

There was, however, no doubting his dominant influence. Conviction, intellect, knowledge, and power of advocacy gave him a preeminent place with the President, the cabinet, and in the wider public forums across the country and the world. His was the informing mind on American foreign policy; his speeches and policy statements — stamped with personal conviction, tight logic and moral fervor — provided a uniquely authoritative assessment of allies, adversaries, crises, and proposed courses of action. He was the dominant spokesman on foreign policy, and because he spoke so often, because the effect of his words was so often amplified by dramatic activity or dramatic inactivity, it is fair to say that what the average American citizen thought about the Communist system during the 1950s — the threats it posed, and how the United States should respond in a world of complexity and danger — was derived in no small part, directly or indirectly, from Dulles. For six years his simple sermons and bluntly righteous approach to the organization of defenses in Western Europe, the liberation of Eastern Europe, Russian influence in the Middle East, Peking's claim to Taiwan, and Communism's threat to Southeast Asia strongly shaped American attitudes and cast a long shadow upon the decade of the 1960s. To his credit (although greater credit was due President Eisenhower's firm restraint), Dulles avoided actual war, yet his strident approach to nearly every crisis weakened the trust and support of allies and led at times to the almost total diplomatic isolation of the United States.

The rigidity of his moral stance and the power of his advocacy also defined the limits of his constructive statesmanship. And in the longer perspective, as history is ultimately measured, it is these qualities that seem likely to deny him a place among the greatest American or foreign statesmen. For his real gift lay in adversary proceedings, in tactics, in handling (if not really solving) the urgent problem at hand, a problem not infrequently exacerbated by his own previous tactics. He lacked in large measure the statesman's dispassionate vision and the courage to peer across the perilous divide to the bristling trenches of alien ideology, to identify there, and then to build upon, the hidden elements of possible reconciliation. On the whole, he was too much the prudent political partisan, too much the advocate, too much the true believer to venture very far beyond the near-term interest of his client or to perceive the wisdom of yielding a few minor outposts for the sake of reconciling an enemy or of building greater stability into the larger situation. Where he thought morality or ideology were engaged, he was a compulsive and righteous combatant (though not always in the end an unyielding one), and he had also concluded that in such a public stance lay his surest hope of retaining office. The British Ambassador to the United States, Sir Oliver Franks, expressed an eloquent summary judgment:

Three or four centuries ago, when Reformation and Counter-Reformation divided Europe into armed camps, in an age of wars of religion, it was not so rare to encounter men of the type of Dulles. Like them . . . he came to unshakeable convictions of a religious and theological order. Like them, he saw the world as an arena in which the forces of good and evil were continuously at war.[19]

But one diplomat, who knew him better, perceived not only the moral believer, but also the wily and amoral tactician. As he put it, with less elegance but fuller truth, "Dulles was a curious cross between a Christer and a shrewd and quite ruthless lawyer."

Afterword

I N THE EARLY SUMMER of 1959, with Dulles less than two months in his grave, Eisenhower not only took personal command of American diplomacy, but gave its tone and style a turn so swift and sharp that the pattern of six years was utterly broken and the world was left in startled wonder. The President would repeatedly and vehemently deny that his new approach was in any way derived from the conclusion that Dulles's rigid negatives had progressively isolated the United States from the sympathies and the aspirations of most of mankind. Yet his thoughts and actions, reflecting as they did an instinctively different assessment of realities and potentialities in the outer world, seemed to speak the subconscious truth. Freed from the dominating influence of "the conscience and straitjacket of the free world" (as a European editorial had characterized the former Secretary of State), Eisenhower asked himself how "could I make the best use of this remaining time for the benefit of the United States?"[1] His answer was in essence — by reopening the lines of communication. The thrust of his new approach was to cut through the quibbling, tendentious underbrush of preconditions with which Dulles had hedged the American approach to coexistence, to break out of fixed and unyielding diplomatic postures, to open new dialogues, to build bridges.

The Dual Purpose Plan

It was an approach rooted in a Kansan's instinct for openness, and its beginnings were traceable backward in time to the end of 1958, when

Dulles was hospitalized with what few insiders doubted was terminal cancer. In December of that year, the President "began to re-examine the image of America across the world" and concluded he "did not like much of what he saw and heard." [2] A factor that disturbed but probably did not motivate him, yet was the uppermost concern of his cabinet and inner staff, was the parlous state of the Republican party facing a presidential race two years away without Eisenhower's surpassing popularity on the ticket. In the off-year congressional and gubernatorial elections just past, Republican candidates had suffered severe defeats from one end of the country to the other, largely, it seemed, because they were still addicted to running against "left-wing extremists" and the "retreat and appeasement" of the Truman-Acheson policy. To the President's global reflections the press secretary, James Hagerty (who seemed to have become the most influential White House adviser now that Foster Dulles was dead and Sherman Adams banished for petty corruption) added a sharp reminder of the domestic political dimension. He put forward a crisp memorandum which argued that the President could, by dramatizing his world role, simultaneously improve the American "image" abroad and assure the election of his chosen successor as President in 1960. The Hagerty plan called for extensive presidential goodwill tours, reaching to every quarter of the globe, combined with a readiness to participate in both a general summit conference of world leaders and bilateral talks with Premier Khrushchev. It involved also a general relaxation of protocol at all levels of American representation, looking to the development of a more informal, a more human "shirt-sleeves" diplomacy.

Once approved, the plan moved ahead initially with impressive sweep and dispatch. Vice-president Nixon went to Moscow in late July to open an American exhibition, and there engaged in his famous "Kitchen Debate" with Khrushchev. The President then set his own ambitious itinerary — four basic trips: (1) to Western Europe in the summer of 1959 to consult with his major allies; (2) to eleven nations on three continents in December 1959 — Italy, Turkey, Pakistan, Afghanistan, India, Iran, Greece, Tunisia, France, Spain, and Morocco; (3) to Latin America in the winter of 1960; and (4) to the Far East in the ensuing spring. Meanwhile, the Foreign Ministers meeting in Geneva was revealing a basic split in the Western position on Berlin — between the United States and Britain, who were prepared to consider a new contractual basis for their presence in that city, and France and West Germany, who felt that to concede "the right of belligerent occupation" would be tantamount to surrendering the Western position. The Soviet posture remained adamant for a "free city" of West Berlin and a German peace treaty. To relieve a situation that seemed to be approaching dangerous impasse, Herter and Eisenhower decided in late July to attempt bilateral diplomacy. And in early August, the President was able to announce the dramatic fact that Khrushchev had accepted an invitation to visit the United States the following month.

Things started well, as Eisenhower flew to Bonn in August to reassure the eighty-three-year-old Adenauer that the forthcoming Khrushchev visit to America contained no sinister portent for West Germany. Two hundred thousand friendly West Germans cheered the motorcade of gleaming Mercedes limousines, as the President stood with the chancellor in an open car acknowledging the welcome and the waving signs that said IKE, WE TRUST YOU, or simply WE LIKE IKE.[3] With official West German opinion driven to what seemed a political neurosis by the crisis in Berlin, Eisenhower told a press conference somewhat ambiguously that he would not, in talks with Khrushchev, be "conducting negotiations for anybody else"; he added more helpfully that his aim was simply to "explore" the Soviet Premier's mind, "to see whether there is any kind of proposal or suggestion that he can give that would make him a real leader in the search for peace."[4] In London, the President was warmly acclaimed not merely as the leader of a powerful ally, but as a remembered friend who had played a vital role in saving the life of Britain in a dark hour. To the British he gave equally warm and well-received assurances that America's purpose was "to be a loyal partner in our common enterprise" of advancing freedom and of furthering "a just and lasting peace."[5] Both parties seemed willing to forget the strained days of Suez. In Paris, the Garde Republicaine, resplendent in silver helmets, flashing lances and sabers, made up somewhat for the slightly smaller crowds. And in the hushed twilight of the Arc de Triomphe, with a reserved and soldierly De Gaulle beside him, the President rekindled the eternal flame at the base of the monument while a bugler sounded taps. Later at a ceremony where the enormous gold key to the city of Paris was bestowed, De Gaulle told the crowd of fifty thousand, with a majestic sweep of his arm toward his guest, that "all has gone well between us."[6]

Form versus Substance

All had gone well. Yet the uneasy feeling grew among the European press that they were witnesses to a pageant with a very thin or nonexistent script, that the unfolding events, warm with good feelings and rich in glamorous overtones though they might be, were essentially devoid of substance or serious diplomatic purpose. The *Manchester Guardian* said waspishly: "Mr. Eisenhower and Mr. Macmillan in the Chequers weekend have practiced golf shots, they have eaten grouse sent specially by the Queen from Balmoral, they have attended matins in the local church, they have paid a lightning visit to Oxford (while the rest of the company played croquet on the lawn), and they have talked over the future of mankind." [7] A special television program was arranged, which featured the President and the Prime Minister sitting comfortably in dinner jackets at Number Ten Downing Street. Macmillan opened brilliantly with, "Well, Mr. President, I want to start by saying how much we all welcome you here," and Eisenhower maintained the dazzling intellectual level of discourse by replying that "we are mighty glad to be back visiting again this lovely country." Macmillan then expressed his frank desire for a summit conference, to which Eisenhower, still fencing, replied that, if there was to be such a meeting, Khrushchev "had to understand beforehand that peace is an imperative." Macmillan hoped for American leniency on woolen exports, to which Eisenhower replied obliquely that the United States was fully in favor of a strong pound sterling.[8] Looking for meaning behind the façade, the *London Observer* put the finger on Hagerty who, "uneasy in foreign affairs, . . . devotes himself to selling the President's performance rather than to the issues and their implications. . . . He has brought the cultivation of the relationship between the President and the mass media to a fine Machiavellian art. Whether such an art is wholly desirable is quite another question." [9]

It was an incomplete, yet telling, appraisal of the trip. It was incomplete because it revealed only one (and in the President's mind surely the lesser) of the two main purposes of the odyssey now unfolding; for far above the effort to build images at home that could be translated into political support for the Republican party in 1960 stood Eisenhower's noble aim to communicate, to learn, to generate goodwill in the world. Yet the appraisal was also telling, in that the lack of substance in the performance applied almost as much to Eisenhower's higher purpose as to Hagerty's lower one. A limited goodwill tour could have served as the useful, perhaps indispensable preface to a serious and measurable shift of operational policy, but in this case the surface gesture was the dominant part of the reality. The Eisenhower administration in 1959 possessed neither the imagination, nor the intellectual coherence, nor the political will to effect a genuine change of course — in Germany, for example, or the Far East. Hemmed in by the thick webbing of intransigent treaty structures, entrenched programs and frozen attitudes that owed so much to Dulles, Eisenhower's global gregariousness did not generate enough thrust to achieve a breakout.

The ebullient Nikita Khrushchev arrived at Andrews Air Force Base outside Washington in early September, to the accompaniment of a twenty-one-gun salute, and for the next twelve days "entertained, jarred, angered and amused the American public with a transcontinental display of political showmanship." [10] Henry Cabot Lodge, assigned as his official escort, declaimed at public functions on the "economic humanism" of the American capitalist system, but after a few Khrushchevian rejoinders ("Only the grave can correct a hunchback!"), Emmet Hughes thought that Lodge's homilies, "intended to be assertive . . . succeeded only in sounding apologetic." [11] One Minnesota senator was reminded of a candidate in the late stages of a political campaign: "He has heard all the questions many times and his answers are sharp as hell." [12] The visit ended with private talks at Eisenhower's retreat, Camp David.

Khrushchev had written, on the eve of his visit, an article for *Foreign Affairs* that argued the necessity of a détente between the United States and Russia as a means of resolving the Berlin crisis and other outstanding problems. It was, in effect, a bid for a general two-power settlement, in which each would accept nuclear parity and noninterference in the affairs of the other. As to Germany, it would mean U.S. recognition of East Germany and acceptance of the Soviet position on West Berlin. The talks at Camp David were notable both for Khrushchev's explicit removal of a Berlin deadline (provided negotiations were not prolonged indefinitely) and for the absence of any agreement on the substance of a German-Berlin solution. But Eisenhower was sufficiently encouraged to accept the idea of a negotiated settlement on Berlin, and to seek agreement from his allies for a summit conference by the end of the year, to be followed in the spring or early summer by his own visit to Russia. In effect he and Khrushchev tacitly agreed to work toward general détente.[13]

A Triumphal Tour

Eisenhower's spectacular winter journey to eleven countries began on December 4 under hard, cold rain in Rome with "gutters gurgling with dirty water" and no crowds.[14] But in Ankara, a modest city of half a million, perhaps as many as four hundred thousand turned out to cheer and wave banners (TURKS ARE FRIENDS INDEED IKE) to the amazement of the Turkish officials. At a state dinner, the President told Turkish leaders their country was "a modern proving ground" for the achievement of democratic greatness.[15] The odyssey proceeded thence to Pakistan (in Ayub Khan's white Cadillac through large orderly crowds), to the mountain kingdom of Afghanistan (in an open Daimler through small but enthusiastic crowds, who rolled down the hillsides like tumble-weed to come nearer the honored visitor), and to a tumultuous welcome in India (where the President and Nehru were pelted with flowers along a twelve-mile stretch of the Kitchener Road leading into New Delhi while a large, excited crowd shouted, "Long live the king of America"). Addressing the Indian parliament, the President said, "Our hope is that we are moving into a better era." [16] Then on to Iran, Greece, Tunisia, and France.

The second visit to Paris was substantive, including not only private talks with De Gaulle (which produced no shift in the stubborn French refusal to make a serious military contribution to NATO), but also joint talks with Macmillan, Adenauer, and De Gaulle to settle the matter of a summit with Khrushchev. France was jealous, and West Germany suspicious, of the Camp David talks, and De Gaulle had asked in October for a postponement of the proposed December summit on the grounds that Camp David had not really produced "an effective reduction of tension." [17] His purpose, soon revealed, was to have his own bilateral summit with Khrushchev prior to a general conference. Adenauer had spent the autumn in furious activity, trying to coalesce opposition to any dramatic or substantive change in the status of Berlin, and Khrushchev noted in a Budapest speech that "Chancellor Adenauer is most active" in seeking "to prevent an improvement in the relations between states." [18] At Paris, Eisenhower gave his consent to the British concept of "a series of summits," and in deference to De Gaulle accepted a date in late spring for the first joint meeting with Khrushchev. There remained serious Western differences regarding the substance of a Berlin settlement, but there was agreement to propose an agenda strikingly similar to the one which had provided the basis of discussion for the Geneva summit of 1955: (1) Germany and Berlin, (2) disarmament, and (3) East-West relations. But now the communiqué contained no Dulles-ian caveats regarding preliminary meetings at lower levels.

Then for Eisenhower it was on to Spain and Morocco and further distribution of the thousands of medallions, gold in appearance and bearing the inscription PEACE AND FRIENDSHIP IN FREEDOM and, on the other side, IN APPRECIATION, D.D.E. On the night of December 23, 1959, safely returned and speaking from beneath the large and beautiful Christmas tree on the south lawn of the White House, the President addressed the American people in an exultant mood: "I wish every American — certainly every American recognized by his fellows as a leader . . . could see and hear what I have seen and what I have heard. The mutual understanding thereby created could in itself do much to dissolve the issues that plague the world. . . . I talked with kings and presidents, prime ministers and humble men and women in cottages and in mud huts. Their common denominator was their faith that America will help lead the way toward a just peace." [19]

It was almost inconceivable that such a voyage and such a speech could have been made while John Foster Dulles commanded at the State Department, and the two events seemed, at Christmastime in 1959, to promise — surely not the end of all hatred and conflict, but less tension and more understanding in the world, and perhaps future electoral success for the Republican party. The stuff of this last prospect showed in the latest Gallup poll, which found that, following the long December swing through middle Asia and northern Africa, Eisenhower was the world's "most admired man," [20] while the fragmented Democrats seemed wrapped in confusion and gloom. Whatever might be the substantive shortcomings of the administration's foreign policy, the earnest charm of Dwight Eisenhower and his ability to translate this into vast reservoirs of goodwill for America in distant lands seemed self-evidently a pearl of great price.

Sobering Realities

Yet the new tranquillity had an evanescent and gossamer quality that hovered on the surface of a hard substructure of entrenched attitudes, programs and procedures on both sides of the cold war, and of bitter, unresolved social-political conflict in many underdeveloped countries (some of it carrying strong anti-American overtones).

The ferment of anti-American feeling showed itself on the next segment of the Eisenhower odyssey, a long swing southward to Brazil, Argentina, Chile and Uruguay. Although the Brazilians were friendly, tragedy struck over Rio de Janeiro when two aircraft collided in heavy rain and fog, killing sixty people including nineteen members of the U.S. Navy Band who were arriving to play at Eisenhower's state dinner for President Kubitschek on the final night of the visit. In Buenos Aires, demonstrations by *Peronistas,* including some bomb-throwing, called forth very large and heavily armed units of the army, who lined the airport and the road leading to the city. Even with such massed protection, the President was helicoptered directly from his arriving aircraft to the American embassy. On the subsequent automobile ride to the congress, the horses of the Grenadier Guards kicked at the crowds while their riders layed about them with the flat of their sabers. The President was plainly disgusted by this display of excessive martial zeal, but *Peronistas* ganged up at several intersections, chanting "Pay-rone, Pay-rone" and trying to block the motorcade.[21] In Chile, after receiving a letter from leaders of the Chilean Students Union, which he found disturbingly cynical about the United States, Eisenhower tore up a prepared speech and rather naïvely lectured a student audience on their alleged misinformation. "We are not saints," he said, speaking of himself and his fellow countrymen. "We know we make mistakes, but our heart is in the right place." Moreover, United States aid was aimed at raising the living standards not only of the Latin American elites (as the students had charged), but of "every single individual in the nation." And "nothing could be more erroneous" than the charge that the United States neglects Latin America by making defense investments outside the hemisphere, for such investments protect Latin America.[22] In Uruguay the police used fire hoses and tear gas on rioting students.

The President returned home on March 7, evidently fatigued, but nevertheless confident that his new strategy for peace in the final year of his administration was working a discernible change in the world climate — toward relaxed tensions and flexibility and understanding, and away from war. Reporting to the nation the following day, he said, "There is a vast reservoir of respect, admiration and affection for the United States of America. . . . Two or three insignificant exceptions to this may have made a headline, but they were only minor incidents, lost in the massed welcome."[23]

The Fateful U-2 Incident

But now the built-in inertia of the vast, interlocking cold war mechanisms combined with a slack hand on the helm, bad luck, and a series of incredibly bad judgments to dash the hopes that Eisenhower held, and that thus far in his singular way he had so nobly advanced. On May 1, a mere two weeks before the scheduled summit meeting with Khrushchev in Paris, a black, high-level reconnaissance plane with unusually wide wings was sighted and shot down over Sverdlovsk, a large industrial complex in the Ural Mountains more than twelve hundred miles inside Russia. The aircraft, built by Lockheed Aircraft Company and equipped with high-altitude cameras, devices to measure the range of Soviet radar, and instruments for sampling the air to detect Soviet nuclear tests, was designated the U-2. It carried a single pilot and was headed from a base in Pakistan westward across the Soviet Union, at eighty thousand feet, to a landing field in Norway. It was operated by the CIA. Such planes had made similar journeys for nearly four years, and no Russian gun or interceptor aircraft had been able to reach the altitude of their flight, a fact that the Soviet government, aware of their presence, was not prepared to admit publicly. On this trip, however, the U-2 apparently lost some power and was forced to descend to a level within range. Suddenly it was hit, the pilot parachuting to safety complete with his Social Security card and an unused suicide needle.

In effect, a calculated risk had failed; the CIA had called the attention of the White House staff to the diplomatic risks of continuing the U-2 flights close to the coming Summit meeting. The matter was debated and weighed, in an effort to balance such risks against the felt need for intelligence information on the Russian missile program; it was agreed that the flights would continue through May 1. The U-2 that failed to reach Norway was the last scheduled flight until after the May 16 summit! [24] A fateful mishap had thus upset a close calculation. The President was informed at once that the plane had failed to reach its destination and that its limited fuel capacity precluded the possibility that it was still in the air.[25] Four days later (May 5), while Eisenhower was presiding over a meeting of the National Security Council, Moscow announced that an American reconnaissance aircraft had been shot down over Russian territory.[26]

The U-2 reconnaissance flights were operated under the "cover" of the space agency (NASA), for which the planes also flew unconcealed "weather research" missions. Earlier the same day (May 5), NASA had issued a statement reporting that one of its "Air Weather Service" planes was missing and presumed lost over southeastern Turkey, the pilot having radioed that he was "experiencing oxygen difficulties." The President expressed himself as content to stand on the NASA statement and await developments, but his NSC counsellors all urged a prompt and more plausible explanation, and Eisenhower yielded.[27] The State Department then issued an embellishment, conceding the possibility that the pilot of a "weather research" plane might have lost consciousness owing to the "reported difficulty with his oxygen equipment" and thus might have "accidentally violated Soviet airspace." [28]

But the next day (May 6) Khrushchev introduced the pilot to the world, complete with pictures of the special detection equipment and a detailed description of the intelligence mission. Caught in a lie, the State Department next (May 7) retreated to the murky line that, as a result of an investigation ordered by the President, it had been established that "insofar as the authorities are concerned, there was no authorization for any such flights as described by Mr. Khrushchev." [29] Allen Dulles offered to protect the President by accepting full responsibility and resigning.[30] It is possible that this new but more circuitous untruth, particularly if coupled with a resignation by the head of the CIA, might have met the diplomatic necessities of the situation, for Khrushchev was gambling heavily on achieving détente with the West as the necessary corollary to his internal policy of reduced arms spending and greater investment for the civilian economy. He had boasted of Soviet military strength in an effort to win U.S. acceptance of nuclear parity, but on January 14 he had announced a reduction of 1.2 million men in the armed forces by 1961. This move in conjunction with others seriously alienated the Soviet military leaders.[31] Khrushchev therefore needed more normal relations with the West, and was quite evidently seeking to exonerate Eisenhower. "I am quite willing to grant," he declared on May 7, "that the President knew nothing . . ."[32]

Unfortunately, the American statement (May 7) went on not only to acknowledge that U-2 flights had been "probably undertaken," but to justify them on the grounds of Soviet refusal to accept Eisenhower's "open skies" proposal of 1955. It was revealing of the depth of Khrushchev's domestic political difficulties that the USSR next (May 8) lodged a formal protest: "Does all this mean that, with the refusal of a number of states to accept this proposal for 'open skies,' the USA is attempting arbitrarily to take upon itself the right to 'open' a foreign sky?"[33] This skillful riposte in turn deepened the dilemma for the United States. Secretary Herter made one final effort to preserve the President and the summit, but the margin for maneuver was all but gone. Emerging from a meeting at the White House (May 9), he said, yes, the United States had been conducting U-2 flights for some years, but it had no choice in this matter since Russia's "secret preparation of armed might" was aimed at facing "the free world with the choice of abject surrender or nuclear destruction." However, "far from being damaging to the forthcoming meetings in Paris," the incident should "serve to underline" the need for a further effort to erect "effective safeguards against surprise attack and aggression."[34] With particular emphasis, he added that "specific missions of these unarmed civilian aircraft have not been subject to presidential authorization."

The confusions of the White House staff and the President's own imprecision of mind and tongue now worked, however, to remove even this last thin diplomatic poultice. Looking at the domestic implications of the Herter explanation, Hagerty and others were suddenly appalled by what they saw as Republican vulnerability to the Democratic charge that Eisenhower not only lacked control of the government, but was even unaware of espionage activities that could wreck his stated policy. The budding political prospects for the election, now only seven months away, were suddenly threatened by a killing frost. Caught between painful choices, they chose to throw away the remaining hope of a constructive dialogue with Khrushchev by arguing a line which, they thought, would prove invulnerable to domestic political attack. The President was now

spun around again. At a press conference (May 11), he assumed full responsibility for the flights. Such activity, Eisenhower now said, was "a
distasteful but vital necessity," given the Russian "fetish of secrecy and
concealment." [35] It had thus taken the administration only six days, as
Emmet Hughes commented acidly, "to transform an unthinkable falsehood into a sovereign right." [36]

The Soviet leader's reaction was a foregone conclusion, for the viability
of his policy inside the Kremlin depended heavily on his being able to
demonstrate Eisenhower's good faith to those colleagues on the Central
Committee who were wont to charge him with "appeasement" of capitalist America. The President's explicit and determined assumption of
personal responsibility for sending "spy planes" over the Soviet Union
made him a statesman with whom Khrushchev could no longer contemplate negotiation, whatever his personal preferences. That the Soviet
Union also conducted a wide range of espionage activities against the
United States was, of course, true, but it was not an argument Khrushchev
could use to maintain his position against his internal critics. Overt intrusions of Soviet airspace presented a special sensitivity. Quickly he declared, with rather evident regret: "You know my friendly attitude
toward the President. My hopes have not been justified. I am a human
being. . . . The Russian people would say I was mad to welcome a man
who sends spy planes over here." [37]

The final denouement was the summit meeting at Paris just three days
later, where Khrushchev coldly excoriated the United States ("a thief
caught red-handed in his theft"), demanded Eisenhower's apology for the
U-2 flights and punishment for those responsible, and withdrew the invitation for the President to visit Russia. It was a heated and dramatic
performance, yet one that bore the marks of elaborate preparation and
followed a prearranged line. He had good words for De Gaulle and
Macmillan, expressing regret that the summit had been "torpedoed by
the reactionary circles of the United States of America." [38] While the
Soviet premier spoke, the imposing and bemedaled defense minister,
Marshal Rodion Malinovsky, sat beside him as if to make certain that
the script was followed. Eisenhower accepted the verbal assault with
disciplined calm (although he blew up later at the American embassy),
and edged toward an apology by telling Khrushchev the flights had been
suspended and would not be resumed (which was, of course, a reversal
of his "vital necessity" statement of May 11). A deadlock being apparent,
Khrushchev collected his delegation and stalked out of the meeting never
to return. The new Eisenhower initiative, begun so bravely and hopefully
less than a year before, thus ended in a sad shambles of clumsy mismanagement, bad judgment, bad faith, and intellectual confusion.

Return to Cold War

A storm of public criticism was now building in Congress and the American press, and it was directed at Eisenhower personally for acts of omission and commission which seemed to have produced the debacle in Paris and thus to have shattered the hopes for détente. Pushed onto the defensive, the President responded, perhaps inevitably, by once more drawing taut the lines of the cold war, but this, of course, had the effect of further undercutting his basic aim and the theme of his long "journey for peace": "The plain truth is this: when a nation needs intelligence activity, there is no time when vigilance can be relaxed. . . . From Pearl Harbor we learned that even negotiation can be used to conceal preparations for surprise attack." [39] Stubbornly, he also announced his firm intention to go ahead with his Far East trip, and especially his planned visit to Japan, even though Tokyo had been convulsed for a month by anti-American demonstrations protesting the extension of the United States–Japan security treaty (passed on May 20 after 107 days of turbulent debate in the Diet), and there was no assurance that calm would descend simply because Eisenhower rode through the streets with the emperor. On the contrary. Both critics and concerned advisers counselled against the wisdom of a trip to the Far East so soon after the Paris experience, and especially against a visit to Japan; the risks of further humiliation, they thought, were too high.

But the President persisted, declaring that a decision to drop the three-day stopover in Tokyo would be up to the Japanese government. Thus, once more (on June 14) he was embarked, with the usual large retinue of official staff, Secret Service men, and journalists on a route that would take them first to Alaska and the Philippines and thence to Japan, Taiwan, Okinawa, and South Korea. Hagerty, who was sent ahead to scout the situation in Tokyo, soon found, however, that it was far worse than indicated by the brave reports emanating from the American embassy. His car was ganged at the airport by several thousand demonstrators, and he and Ambassador Douglas MacArthur II had to be extricated and flown to safety by helicopter. Advance Secret Service men, accompanying Hagerty, cabled the President's party in Manila that his life would be endangered unless the visit were radically changed. When the Japanese police began to express serious doubts of their ability to assure the President's safety, Prime Minister Nobusuke Kishi reluctantly cancelled the visit. Eisenhower had suffered another serious diplomatic defeat. The odyssey proceeded to its desultory conclusion.

Although it would have seemed in keeping with the President's natural candor and dignity to admit mistakes and acknowledge serious reversals, he chose instead, in a presidential election year, to stand and fight the critics. But he fought on slippery ground. No one disputed his insistence that, taken as a whole, the trips had provided a special "opportunity to emphasize and re-emphasize America's devotion to peace and justice" and to hold "valuable conversations between heads of state and governments." But denying both the complexity of a world in ferment and the glaring deficiencies of American judgment and management that had produced the overarching failure of the summit and the setback in Japan, he sought to blame the Communists for every manifestation of anti-Americanism encountered along the way; they had "sought every possible method" to disrupt his visits, because these were "of such positive value to the free world as to obstruct Communist imperialism." [40] "These disorders were not occasioned by America"; therefore, "We in the United States . . . [should not blame] ourselves for what the Communists do." [41] It was a line of defense received with skepticism by much of the American press. James Reston of the *New York Times* wrote that "President Eisenhower has devised a simple procedure for dealing with his critics and his defeats: He simply ignores the critics and claims victories. . . . The effect of this is serious in a democracy for it confuses the public, infuriates the political opposition and leaves mistakes unexplained and uncorrected." [42] The *St. Louis Post-Dispatch* doubted that the American President had been denied access to Japan merely by "a few nasty Communists." If Americans were to be faithful to truth, it said, "we must be prepared to admit" that the left-wing rioters could not have been effective "had not a large body of public opinion been hostile or apathetic to the new military treaty with the United States." [43] The *Washington Post* said: "It is tragic for the country" that Eisenhower's final months in office should be "marked by the collapse of the Summit Conference, the outburst of violence in Japan and a general resumption of the cold war." [44]

In the six months of its remaining life, the Eisenhower administration ran steadily down like a tired clock, its energies spent, its coherence blurred. But if these deficiencies, which were quite apparent at the time of Dulles's death, seem in retrospect to have foredoomed the President's final poignant effort to make a fresh start based on world realities too long ignored, it is also now apparent that Eisenhower was fatefully tripped by the elusive and capricious imponderables of history. Had the U-2 flights been suspended a month earlier, or had the pilot of the particular plane made it safely to Norway, or even had the administration handled the diplomatically explosive mishap with an astute, clearheaded determination to observe the accepted norms of international espionage, the Paris summit might well have proven the beginning of a hopeful dialogue, altered the character of the American debate on foreign policy (and perhaps the outcome in the 1960 election), and moved the world closer to sustainable détente. As things worked out, however, Eisenhower's humiliations and Khrushchev's harsh, self-protective exploitation of them had the effect of restoring to American politics an anti-Communist intensity that had slowly begun to fade. Suddenly, national pride, combined with renewed awareness of national peril, rose up to strengthen all the conformist tendencies and to weaken the impulse for rational inquiry into political alternatives to cold war. The subliminal influence of a hundred simplistic, repetitive Dullesian sermons now showed itself in two hundred newspaper editorials and a thousand political speeches. Indeed, although their accents and rhythms were different, the fervent anti-Communist absolutes of John Foster Dulles were embedded in the very bone structure of John Fitzgerald Kennedy's inaugural address.

Notes

CHAPTER ONE
In the Beginning

1. State Department Press Release #40, January 22, 1953.
2. *Department of State Bulletin*, XXVIII, February 9, 1953, p. 216.
3. Author interview with Lincoln Gordon, August 4, 1972.
4. Elliott Bell, Oral History interview, p. 27.
5. *Department of State Bulletin*, XXVIII, February 9, 1953, p. 240.
6. Ibid.
7. Ibid., p. 239.
8. "Father" to "Foster," April 29, 1924, Dulles Papers.
9. Louis L. Gerson, *John Foster Dulles*, pp. 6–7.
10. Margaret Edwards, Oral History interview.
11. Diary of Mrs. Allen Macy Dulles, February 25, 1893, Dulles Papers.
12. Gerson, *Dulles*, p. 4; also Eleanor Lansing Dulles, *The Last Year*, p. 129.
13. Eleanor Lansing Dulles, *Last Year*, p. 161.
14. Ibid., p. 160.
15. Allen Dulles, Oral History interview, p. 10.
16. Author interview with Eleanor Lansing Dulles, October 15, 1971.
17. Allen Dulles, Oral History interview, p. 8.
18. Ibid., p. 13.
19. Ibid., p. 10.
20. Ibid., p. 11.
21. Bristol to JFD, June 1, 1955, Dulles Papers.
22. JFD to Bristol, June 13, 1955, Dulles Papers.
23. Margaret Edwards, Oral History interview.
24. James Reston, Oral History interview, p. 23.

CHAPTER TWO
Princeton, the Hague, and Paris

1. Allen Dulles, Oral History interview, p. 3.
2. Eleanor Lansing Dulles, *The Last Year*, p. 125.

3. Arthur Krock, Oral History interview, p. 7.
4. Ibid., p. 1.
5. John Robinson Beal, *John Foster Dulles*, p. 32.
6. Ibid.
7. Louis L. Gerson, *John Foster Dulles*, p. 7.
8. Essay written at Princeton on "Pragmatism," Dulles Papers.
9. Senior thesis at Princeton, "The Theory of Judgment," Dulles Papers.
10. Beal, *Dulles*, p. 44.
11. Ibid., p. 48.
12. Author interview with Henry P. de Vries, September 21, 1971.
13. C. L. Sulzberger, *A Long Row of Candles*, p. 748.
14. Eleanor Lansing Dulles, *Last Year*, p. 127.
15. Ibid.
16. Allen Dulles, Oral History interview, p. 3.
17. Charles Lucet, Oral History interview.
18. Beal, *Dulles*, p. 53.
19. Ibid., p. 52.
20. Ibid., pp. 54–55.
21. Ibid., p. 55.
22. Ibid., p. 58.
23. Arthur Krock, Oral History interview, pp. 8–9.
24. Ibid., p. 2.
25. Robert Lansing, *The Peace Negotiations: A Personal Narrative* (Boston: Houghton Mifflin, 1921), p. 199.
26. Arthur Krock, Oral History interview, p. 12.
27. Private memorandum, December 19, 1922, Dulles Papers.
28. Beal, *Dulles*, p. 65.
29. Ibid., p. 67.
30. Ibid., p. 64.
31. Michael A. Guhin, *John Foster Dulles*, p. 30.
32. Ibid., p. 31.
33. Allen Dulles, Oral History interview, p. 26.
34. Ibid., p. 29.
35. Wilson to JFD, June 27, 1919, Dulles Papers.

CHAPTER THREE
Struggle and Success in Wall Street

1. John Robinson Beal, *John Foster Dulles*, p. 71.
2. Michael A. Guhin, *John Foster Dulles*, p. 37.
3. Eustace Seligman, Oral History interview.
4. Thomas E. Dewey, Oral History interview, p. 10.
5. John Coleman Bennett, Oral History interview, p. 23.
6. Elliott Bell, Oral History interview, p. 2.
7. Eustace Seligman, Oral History interview, p. 3.
8. Author interview with Henry P. de Vries, September 21, 1971.
9. Reinhold Niebuhr, "The Moral World of John Foster Dulles," *New Republic*, December 1, 1958, p. 8.
10. Sir Oliver Franks, Oral History interview, pp. 6–8.
11. Ibid., pp. 6–7.
12. Avery Dulles, Oral History interview, p. 2.
13. David Bruce, Oral History interview, p. 19.
14. Avery Dulles, Oral History interview, p. 5.
15. David Bruce, Oral History interview, p. 17.

16. Roderic O'Connor, Oral History interview, pp. 155–156.
17. Author interview with Eleanor Lansing Dulles, October 15, 1971.
18. Roderic O'Connor, Oral History interview, p. 85.
19. David Schoenbrun, Oral History interview, p. 71.
20. Roderic O'Connor, Oral History interview, pp. 147–148.
21. Avery Dulles, Oral History interview, p. 10.
22. Ibid., p. 9.
23. Ibid., p. 12.
24. Allen Dulles, Oral History interview, p. 34.
25. Author interview with Henry Brandon, December 7, 1971.
26. Roscoe Drummond and Gaston Coblentz, *Duel at the Brink*, pp. 229–230.

CHAPTER FOUR
Response to World Crisis

1. John Foster Dulles, *War, Peace and Change*, p. ix.
2. John Foster Dulles, "The Road to Peace," *Atlantic Monthly*, October 1935, p. 496.
3. "Peaceful Change within the Society of Nations," speech at Princeton, March 19, 1936, Dulles Papers.
4. Ibid.
5. Ibid.
6. Thomas E. Dewey, Oral History interview, p. 6.
7. John J. McCloy, Oral History interview, p. 5.
8. Louis L. Gerson, *John Foster Dulles*, p. 18.
9. John Foster Dulles, *War, Peace and Change*, p. 58.
10. Author interview with Robert Amory, October 6, 1971.
11. John Foster Dulles, *War, Peace and Change*, p. ix.
12. Ibid., p. 8.
13. Ibid., pp. 57–58.
14. Ibid., p. 82.
15. Ibid., pp. 48–49.
16. Ibid., p. 81.
17. Ibid., p. 150.
18. Ibid., p. 168.
19. Federal Council of Churches publicity release, 1944, Dulles Papers.
20. Ibid.
21. Marquis Childs, Oral History interview, p. 2.
22. Samuel Cavert, Oral History interview, pp. 12, 8.
23. Richard M. Fagley, Oral History interview, p. 29.
24. John Robinson Beal, *John Foster Dulles*, p. 86.
25. Speech at Princeton Theological Seminary, May 16, 1945, Dulles Papers.
26. "America's Role in World Affairs," address to Detroit YMCA, October 28, 1939, Dulles Papers.
27. JFD to Lindbergh, November 1939, Dulles Papers.
28. Speech to Foreign Policy Association, March 18, 1939, Dulles Papers.
29. Draft of Dulles letter, April 1940, Dulles Papers.
30. Address to Detroit YMCA, October 28, 1939, Dulles Papers.
31. "The Christian Forces and a Stable Peace," address to YMCA National Board, New York City, January 25, 1941, Dulles Papers.
32. "Toward World Order," address at Ohio Wesleyan University, March 5, 1942, Dulles Papers.
33. Report to Federal Council of Churches on trip to England, August 1942, Dulles Papers.
34. Ibid.

35. Notes of trip to England, July 1942, Dulles Papers.
36. *The Diaries of Sir Alexander Cadogan, O.M., 1938–1945,* edited by David Dilks, p. 462.
37. Thomas E. Dewey, Oral History interview, pp. 2–3.
38. Ibid., pp. 3–4.
39. Ibid., p. 11.
40. Richard Rovere, Oral History interview, p. 2.
41. Henry P. Van Dusen, ed., *The Spiritual Legacy of John Foster Dulles* (Philadelphia: Westminster Press, 1960), p. 21.
42. Ibid., p. 93.
43. Ibid., pp. 93–94.
44. John Coleman Bennett, Oral History interview, p. 6.
45. Ibid., p. 4.
46. Henry Van Dusen, Oral History interview, pp. 37–38, 53.
47. Beal, *Dulles,* pp. 90–91.
48. Van Dusen, ed., *Spiritual Legacy,* p. 110.
49. Gerson, *Dulles,* p. 25.
50. Cordell Hull, *Memoirs,* II (New York: Macmillan, 1948), p. 1686.
51. Arthur H. Vandenberg, Jr., and Joe Alex Morris, eds., *The Private Papers of Senator Vandenberg* (Boston: Houghton Mifflin, 1952), p. 88.
52. Hull, *Memoirs,* II, p. 1693.
53. Thomas E. Dewey, Oral History interview, p. 14.
54. Beal, *Dulles,* p. 98.
55. Address to National Study Conference on the Churches and a Just and Durable Peace, Detroit, January 16, 1945, Dulles Papers.
56. Ibid.
57. Ibid.
58. Address to Economic Club of Detroit, February 1945, Dulles Papers.
59. "From Yalta to San Francisco," address to Foreign Policy Association, March 17, 1945, Dulles Papers.
60. Gerson, *Dulles,* p. 40.
61. Thomas E. Dewey, Oral History interview, p. 48.

CHAPTER FIVE
Discovering the Russians

1. John Foster Dulles, *War or Peace,* p. 29.
2. Louis L. Gerson, *John Foster Dulles,* p. 44.
3. John Foster Dulles, *War or Peace,* p. 12.
4. Ibid., p. 9.
5. Ibid., p. 12.
6. Ibid., p. 9.
7. Ibid., p. 10.
8. Ibid., p. 7.
9. Gerson, *Dulles,* p. 45.
10. John Foster Dulles, "Thoughts on Soviet Foreign Policy," *Life,* May 3, 1946, pp. 113–118.
11. Ibid., p. 123.
12. Ibid., p. 124.
13. Ibid., May 10, 1946, p. 120.
14. Luce to JFD, June 16, 1946, Dulles Papers.
15. Muste to JFD, June 11, 1946, Dulles Papers.
16. Vandenberg to JFD, May 13, 1946, Dulles Papers.
17. Kohlberg to JFD, May 1946, Dulles Papers.

18. Symington to JFD, September 17, 1946, Dulles Papers.
19. Copies in Dulles Papers.
20. Speech to Daily Press Association, Chicago, February 10, 1947, Dulles Papers.
21. Speech, July 15, 1946, Dulles Papers.
22. Private memorandum, 1944, Dulles Papers.
23. JFD to Vandenberg, March 29, 1947, Dulles Papers.
24. Ibid.
25. Transcript of radio broadcast, April 29, 1947, Dulles Papers.
26. Swope to JFD, June 28, 1948, Dulles Papers.
27. Tabouis to JFD, July 29, 1948, Dulles Papers.
28. JFD to Tabouis, August 2, 1948, Dulles Papers.
29. James B. Reston, "John Foster Dulles and His Foreign Policy," *Life*, October 4, 1948, p. 132.
30. Ibid., p. 141.
31. Memorandum for the record, July 19, 1948, Dulles Papers.
32. JFD to Vandenberg, September 28, 1948, Dulles Papers.
33. JFD cable to Dewey, October 10, 1948, Dulles Papers.
34. Memorandum from Marshall to JFD, October 25, 1948, Dulles Papers.
35. Memorandum from JFD to Marshall, October 27, 1948, Dulles Papers.
36. JFD cable to Dewey, October 28, 1948, Dulles Papers.
37. JFD cable to Dewey, October 30, 1948, Dulles Papers.
38. David Schoenbrun, Oral History interview, p. 101.
39. JFD cable to Dewey, November 3, 1948, Dulles Papers.

CHAPTER SIX
Pleasures and Perils of Partisanship

1. John Robinson Beal, *John Foster Dulles,* p. 106.
2. Thomas E. Dewey, Oral History interview, p. 36.
3. Ibid., p. 35.
4. Acheson to JFD, May 9, 1949, Dulles Papers.
5. Beal, *Dulles,* p. 108.
6. Speech in Cleveland, January 17, 1945, Dulles Papers.
7. George V. Allen, Oral History interview.
8. *Congressional Record,* September 21, 1949, p. 13086.
9. Ernest Gross, Oral History interview, p. 44.
10. Beal, *Dulles,* p. 111.
11. Thomas E. Dewey, Oral History interview, p. 11.
12. Roderic O'Connor, Oral History interview, p. 6.
13. Thomas E. Dewey, Oral History interview, pp. 37–38.
14. Beal, *Dulles,* p. 113.
15. Ibid., p. 114.
16. Ibid.
17. Roderic O'Connor, Oral History interview, p. 13.
18. Ibid., p. 14.
19. Avery Dulles, Oral History interview, pp. 29–30.
20. Robert Murphy, Oral History interview.
21. John Foster Dulles, *War or Peace,* p. 8.
22. Ibid., p. 165.
23. Ibid., p. 205.
24. Ibid., p. 206.
25. Ibid., p. 252.
26. Ibid., p. 247.
27. Ibid., pp. 175–176.

28. Ibid., p. 247.
29. Author interview with Lucius Battle, October 4, 1971.
30. Ibid.
31. Ibid.
32. Memorandum of conversation with Vandenberg, March 30, 1950, Dulles Papers.
33. Ibid.
34. Ibid.
35. Memorandum of conversations with Rusk and Acheson, March 30, 1950, Dulles Papers.
36. Ibid.
37. Ibid.
38. Louis L. Gerson, *John Foster Dulles,* p. 57.
39. Ibid., pp. 58–59.
40. Ibid., pp. 60–61.

CHAPTER SEVEN
Japanese Peace — Korean War

1. Frederick S. Dunn, *Peacemaking and the Settlement with Japan,* p. 54.
2. Ibid., p. 55.
3. Ibid., pp. 60–61.
4. Dean Acheson, *Present at the Creation,* p. 428.
5. John Robinson Beal, *John Foster Dulles,* p. 116.
6. Acheson, *Creation,* p. 428.
7. Dunn, *Peacemaking,* p. 77.
8. Ibid., p. 86.
9. Transcript of press conference, July 11, 1951, Dulles Papers.
10. Louis L. Gerson, *John Foster Dulles,* p. 62.
11. Elliott Bell, Oral History interview, p. 8.
12. Dunn, *Peacemaking,* pp. 100–101.
13. *New York Times,* May 19, 1949.
14. Ibid., January 6, 1950.
15. Acheson, *Creation,* p. 357.
16. *New York Times,* May 11, 1950.
17. *Department of State Bulletin,* XXIII, July 3, 1950, pp. 12–13.
18. Ibid., p. 13.
19. John M. Allison, Oral History interview, p. 7.
20. I. F. Stone, *The Hidden History of the Korean War,* p. 27.
21. Ibid., p. 21.
22. John M. Allison, Oral History interview, pp. 10–11.
23. John M. Allison, *Ambassador from the Prairie, or Allison Wonderland* (Boston: Houghton Mifflin, 1973), p. 129.
24. Ibid., p. 131.
25. Ibid., p. 132.
26. Ibid., p. 135.
27. Ibid., p. 135.
28. John M. Allison, Oral History interview, p. 12.
29. Ibid., p. 13.
30. John M. Allison, *Ambassador from the Prairie,* p. 137.
31. Ibid., p. 138.
32. Ibid.
33. Ibid., p. 139.
34. Ibid.
35. Stone, *Korean War,* pp. 72–74.

36. *Khrushchev Remembers*, p. 368.
37. Speech at Vanderbilt University, June 4, 1950, Dulles Papers.
38. Draft of letter from JFD to Muste, March 24, 1951, Dulles Papers.
39. JFD to Muste, March 26, 1951, Dulles Papers.
40. Richard H. Rovere and Arthur M. Schlesinger, Jr., *The General and the President*, p. 92.
41. Ibid., p. 97.
42. *New York Times*, June 28, 1950.
43. Ibid.
44. Acheson, *Creation*, p. 428.
45. John Allison, Oral History interview, p. 18.
46. Ibid., pp. 20–21.
47. JFD to Truman, January 10, 1951, Dulles Papers.
48. John Allison, Oral History interview, p. 27.
49. Ibid.
50. Ibid., pp. 25–26.
51. David Bruce, Oral History interview.
52. Memorandum entitled "Japan and China," presented to Ambassador Franks, January 9, 1954, Dulles Papers.
53. Ibid.
54. Acheson, *Creation*, p. 541.
55. Ibid., p. 539.
56. *Newsweek*, September 10, 1951, p. 30.
57. Acheson, *Creation*, p. 546.
58. Ibid., pp. 548–549.
59. Memorandum of conversation with Truman, October 3, 1951, Dulles Papers.
60. Memorandum to Acheson, October 22, 1951, Dulles Papers.
61. Memorandum presented to Franks, January 9, 1954, Dulles Papers.
62. Informal memorandum, March 6, 1952, Dulles Papers.
63. Ibid.
64. Acheson, *Creation*, p. 759.
65. Ibid.
66. Ibid.
67. Ibid., p. 605.
68. Ibid., p. 604.
69. John Allison, Oral History interview, p. 23.

CHAPTER EIGHT
"Victory" and the American Temperament

1. Statement to the press, June 30, 1950, Dulles Papers.
2. Author interview with Lucius Battle, October 4, 1971.
3. Ibid.
4. Memorandum entitled "Estimate of the Situation," November 30, 1950, Dulles Papers.
5. Ibid.
6. [George Kennan], "The Sources of Soviet Conduct," *Foreign Affairs*, July 1947, p. 576.
7. Ibid.
8. James Burnham, *The Coming Defeat of Communism*, p. 138.
9. Dean Acheson, *Present at the Creation*, p. 451.
10. Ibid.
11. Richard H. Rovere and Arthur M. Schlesinger, Jr., *The General and the President*, p. 134.

12. Acheson, *Creation,* p. 454.
13. Rovere and Schlesinger, *General and President,* p. 140.
14. Ibid., p. 170.
15. Ibid., p. 8.
16. Ibid., p. 226.
17. Ibid., pp. 234–235.

CHAPTER NINE
The Partisan's Return

1. Speech to National Farm Institute, Des Moines, Iowa, February 16, 1952, Dulles Papers.
2. Louis L. Gerson, *John Foster Dulles,* p. 69.
3. Ibid., pp. 69–70.
4. Ibid., pp. 74–75.
5. Author interview with William B. Macomber, January 7, 1972.
6. John Foster Dulles, "A Policy of Boldness," *Life,* May 19, 1952, p. 146.
7. Ibid.
8. Ibid., p. 151.
9. Ibid., p. 148.
10. Ibid., p. 151.
11. Ibid., p. 154.
12. Ibid., p. 157.
13. Author interview with Emmet J. Hughes, December 5, 1972.
14. Eisenhower to JFD, April 15, 1952, Dulles Papers.
15. Gerson, *Dulles,* pp. 74–75.
16. Ibid., pp. 75–76.
17. Joseph C. Harsch, Oral History interview, p. 10.
18. Gerson, *Dulles,* p. 82.
19. Richard H. Rovere, *The Eisenhower Years,* p. 56.
20. Author interview with Emmet J. Hughes, December 5, 1972.
21. Rovere, *Eisenhower Years,* p. 61.
22. Speech to Pittsburgh Foreign Policy Association, May 15, 1952, Dulles Papers.
23. Speech in Bloomfield, New Jersey, October 10, 1952, Dulles Papers.
24. Transcript of television program "Pick the Winner," August 21, 1952, Dulles Papers.
25. Gerson, *Dulles,* p. 90.
26. Joseph Alsop, *Washington Post,* October 2, 1952.
27. Dwight D. Eisenhower, *Mandate for Change,* p. 142.
28. *New York Times,* August 17, 1952.
29. Senate Committee on Foreign Relations, *Hearing on Confirmation of John Foster Dulles as Secretary of State,* January 15, 1953, pp. 15, 26.
30. Campaign speech, November 3, 1952, Dulles Papers.

CHAPTER TEN
The New Dispensation

1. Emmet John Hughes, *The Ordeal of Power,* pp. 19–20.
2. Ibid., p. 37.
3. Author interview with Emmet J. Hughes, November 2, 1971.
4. Letter to author from John J. McCloy, August–October 1972.
5. Letter to author from Milton S. Eisenhower, December 20, 1972.
6. Eustace Seligman, Oral History interview, p. 21.

7. Letter to author from Milton S. Eisenhower, December 20, 1972.
8. Author interview with Emmet J. Hughes, November 2, 1971.
9. Hughes, *Ordeal of Power*, p. 50.
10. Ibid., pp. 51–52.
11. Roderic O'Connor, Oral History interview, p. 25.
12. Sherman Adams, Oral History interview, pp. 13, 9.
13. Ibid., pp. 2–3.
14. Ibid., p. 5.
15. Ibid.
16. Ibid., p. 8.
17. Ibid., pp. 13–14.
18. Thomas E. Dewey, Oral History interview, pp. 33–34.
19. John Hanes, Oral History interview, pp. 8–9.
20. Thomas E. Dewey, Oral History interview, p. 34.
21. Charles E. Bohlen, Oral History interview, p. 22.
22. Roderic O'Connor, Oral History interview, p. 125.
23. Ibid., pp. 125–126.
24. John Service, Oral History interview.
25. Roderic O'Connor, Oral History interview, p. 129.
26. Ibid., pp. 134–135.
27. Author interview with Eleanor Thomas Elliott, May 9, 1972.
28. Ibid.
29. Author interview with Roderic O'Connor, June 24, 1971.
30. Thomas S. Gates, Oral History interview, pp. 10–11.
31. Dwight D. Eisenhower, *Mandate for Change*, p. 367.
32. Letter to author from Stuart Hedden, October 5, 1972.
33. Ibid.
34. Douglas MacArthur II, Oral History interview, pp. 40–41.
35. Author interview with Robert Amory, October 6, 1971.
36. Roderic O'Connor, Oral History interview, p. 44.
37. Author interview with William B. Macomber, January 7, 1972.
38. Thomas E. Dewey, Oral History interview, pp. 31–32.
39. Ibid., p. 33.
40. John W. Wheeler-Bennett and Anthony Nichols, *The Semblance of Peace*, p. 597.
41. Joseph C. Harsch, Oral History interview, p. 15.
42. James B. Reston, Oral History interview, pp. 22–23.
43. Richard Rovere, Oral History interview, p. 15.
44. John Hanes, Oral History interview, p. 123.
45. James B. Reston, Oral History interview, pp. 22, 25.
46. Ibid., pp. 8, 6.
47. Author interview with Henry Brandon, December 7, 1971.
48. David Schoenbrun, Oral History interview, p. 71.
49. Roderic O'Connor, Oral History interview, p. 32.
50. *Congressional Record*, May 8, 1951, p. 5045.
51. Robert Griffith, *The Politics of Fear*, p. 199.
52. William Harlan Hale, " 'Big Brother' in Foggy Bottom," *Reporter*, August 17, 1954, p. 15.
53. Ibid., pp. 15–17.
54. John Hanes, Oral History interview, p. 81.
55. Dean Acheson, *Present at the Creation*, p. 712.
56. Joseph C. Harsch, "John Foster Dulles: A Very Complicated Man," *Harper's*, September 1956, p. 30.
57. John Hanes, Oral History interview, p. 72.
58. George F. Kennan, Oral History interview, p. 10.
59. Ibid., p. 12.
60. Hughes, *Ordeal of Power*, p. 120.
61. John Hanes, Oral History interview, p. 15.

62. Hale, " 'Big Brother,' " p. 13.
63. Ibid.
64. John Hanes, Oral History interview, p. 91.
65. Ibid., p. 77.
66. Ibid., p. 81.
67. Charles E. Bohlen, Oral History interview, p. 13.
68. Ibid., pp. 13–14.
69. Ibid., p. 13.
70. John Hanes, Oral History interview, p. 81.
71. Robert J. Donovan, *Eisenhower,* p. 87.
72. John Hanes, Oral History interview, p. 116.
73. Donovan, *Eisenhower,* p. 89.
74. John Robinson Beal, *John Foster Dulles,* p. 143.
75. Charles E. Bohlen, Oral History interview, p. 16.
76. Author interview with Charles E. Bohlen, August 17, 1972.
77. Charles E. Bohlen, Oral History interview, p. 30.

CHAPTER ELEVEN
Policy Beginnings (Part One)

1. *Department of State Bulletin,* XXVIII, February 9, 1953, p. 212.
2. Ibid.
3. Roscoe Drummond and Gaston Coblentz, *Duel at the Brink,* p. 83.
4. *Department of State Bulletin,* XXVIII, February 9, 1953, p. 214.
5. Author interview with Lincoln Gordon, August 4, 1972.
6. Drummond and Coblentz, *Duel at the Brink,* p. 85.
7. Richard Goold-Adams, *John Foster Dulles,* p. 69.
8. *New York Times,* February 3, 1953.
9. Richard P. Stebbins, *The United States in World Affairs 1953* (New York: Harper & Brothers for the Council on Foreign Relations, 1954), p. 26.
10. *Department of State Bulletin,* XXVIII, February 9, 1953, p. 212.
11. Goold-Adams, *Dulles,* p. 71.
12. Roderic O'Connor, Oral History interview, p. 86.
13. Ibid.
14. Ibid., p. 79.
15. Author interview with Henry Brandon, December 7, 1971.
16. Dwight D. Eisenhower, *Mandate for Change,* p. 148.
17. Statement to the press, March 20, 1953, Dulles Papers.
18. Emmet John Hughes, *The Ordeal of Power,* p. 109.
19. Speech to White House Conference for the Advertising Council, March 24, 1953, Dulles Papers.
20. Hughes, *Ordeal of Power,* p. 103.
21. Ibid.
22. Ibid., p. 113.
23. Ibid., p. 109.
24. Ibid., p. 110.
25. Ibid., p. 119.
26. Ibid., p. 113.
27. Ibid.
28. *New Yorker,* May 2, 1953, p. 108.
29. Speech to American Society of Newspaper Editors, April 18, 1953, Dulles Papers.
30. Private memorandum, late April 1953, Dulles Papers.
31. Stebbins, *U.S. in World Affairs 1953,* p. 133.
32. Louis L. Gerson, *John Foster Dulles,* p. 134.

33. Ibid., p. 136.
34. Goold-Adams, *Dulles*, p. 101; also Gerson, *Dulles*, p. 136.
35. Goold-Adams, *Dulles*, p. 101.
36. *New York Times*, September 4, 1953.
37. Hughes, *Ordeal of Power*, p. 86.
38. Ibid., pp. 86–87.
39. Gerson, *Dulles*, pp. 119–120.
40. Hughes, *Ordeal of Power*, p. 144.
41. Ibid.
42. Ibid., p. 145.

CHAPTER TWELVE
Policy Beginnings (Part Two)

1. Richard Goold-Adams, *John Foster Dulles*, p. 93.
2. Richard P. Stebbins, *The United States in World Affairs 1953* (New York: Harper & Brothers for the Council on Foreign Relations, 1954), p. 187.
3. Emmet John Hughes, *The Ordeal of Power*, p. 137.
4. Ibid., p. 148.
5. Charles E. Bohlen, Oral History interview, p. 24.
6. Ibid.
7. Dean Acheson, *Present at the Creation*, p. 564.
8. Kennett Love, *Suez*, p. 196.
9. Private memorandum, June 1, 1953, Dulles Papers.
10. Author interview with Roderic O'Connor, June 24, 1971.
11. Roderic O'Connor, Oral History interview, p. 76.
12. Love, *Suez*, p. 235.
13. *Department of State Bulletin*, XXVIII, June 15, 1953, p. 835.
14. Ibid.
15. Love, *Suez*, p. 272.
16. Ibid.
17. Ibid., p. 273.
18. Author interview with Herman Eiltz, August 18, 1972.
19. Roderic O'Connor, Oral History interview, p. 75.
20. *Department of State Bulletin*, XXVIII, June 15, 1953, p. 834.
21. Abba Eban, Oral History interview, p. 15.
22. Ibid., pp. 16–17.
23. Ibid., p. 17.
24. Robert J. Donovan, *Eisenhower*, p. 120.
25. Ibid., p. 126.
26. Louis L. Gerson, *John Foster Dulles*, p. 139.
27. Richard H. Rovere, *The Eisenhower Years*, p. 159.
28. Dwight D. Eisenhower, *Mandate for Change*, pp. 244–245.
29. Ibid., p. 246.
30. Ibid., pp. 248–249.
31. Gerson, *Dulles*, p. 141.
32. Roscoe Drummond and Gaston Coblentz, *Duel at the Brink*, p. 86.
33. Ibid.
34. Gerson, *Dulles*, p. 141.

CHAPTER THIRTEEN
Massive Retaliation and the New Look

1. John Foster Dulles, "A Policy of Boldness," *Life,* May 19, 1952, p. 146.
2. Ibid., p. 151.
3. John Foster Dulles, *War or Peace,* p. 233.
4. Ibid., pp. 238–239.
5. Ibid., p. 239.
6. Ibid., p. 235.
7. *New York Times,* May 1, 1953.
8. Ibid.
9. Omar Bradley, "This Way Lies Peace," *Saturday Evening Post,* October 15, 1949, p. 33.
10. Warner R. Schilling, Paul Hammond and Glen H. Snyder, *Strategy, Politics and Defense Budgets,* p. 412.
11. Ibid., p. 413.
12. Ibid., pp. 407–409.
13. Ibid., p. 426.
14. Ibid., p. 427
15. *Boston Herald,* October 19, 1953.
16. *New York Times,* October 21, 1953.
17. Author interview with Robert Bowie, February 29, 1972.
18. "Evolution of Foreign Policy," speech to Council on Foreign Relations, January 12, 1954 (Department of State Press Release #8).
19. Ibid.
20. Ibid.
21. Walter Lippmann, *New York Herald Tribune,* March 18, 1954.
22. Eustace Seligman, Oral History interview, pp. 22–23.
23. John Foster Dulles, "Policy for Security and Peace," *Foreign Affairs,* April 1954, p. 356.
24. Ibid., p. 359.
25. Ibid., pp. 357–358.
26. Ibid., p. 358.
27. Walter Lippmann, *New York Herald Tribune,* March 18, 1954.

CHAPTER FOURTEEN
"United Action" in Indochina

1. Robert F. Randle, *Geneva 1954,* p. 322.
2. Dean Acheson, *Present at the Creation,* p. 303.
3. Norman A. Graebner, *The New Isolationism: A Study in Politics and Foreign Policy Since 1950* (New York: Ronald Press, 1956), p. 45.
4. Ibid., p. 28.
5. *New York Times,* September 25, 1953.
6. Victor Bator, *Vietnam,* p. 228.
7. *New York Times,* April 30, 1954.
8. *Department of State Bulletin,* XXIX, September 14, 1953, p. 342.
9. *Foreign Ministers' Meeting, Berlin Discussions, January 25–February 18, 1954,* Department of State Publication #5399, p. 41.
10. Ibid., p. 47.
11. *Documents on American Foreign Relations 1954* edited by Peter V. Curl (New York: Harper & Brothers for the Council on Foreign Relations, 1955), p. 219.

12. *New York Times,* February 25, 1954.
13. Ibid., February 23, 1954.
14. Ibid., February 25, 1954.
15. Ibid.
16. Bator, *Vietnam,* p. 30.
17. Ibid., p. 35.
18. Ibid., p. 34.
19. Ibid., pp. 34–35.
20. *New York Times,* March 24, 1954.
21. Arthur W. Radford, Oral History interview, p. 46.
22. Ibid., p. 55.
23. Ibid., pp. 46–47.
24. James Shepley, "How Dulles Averted War," *Life,* January 16, 1956, p. 72.
25. Dwight D. Eisenhower, *Mandate for Change,* p. 345.
26. Transcript of press conference, London, April 13, 1954, Dulles Papers.
27. Department of State, *American Foreign Policy 1950–55, Basic Documents,* II, pp. 2374–2376.
28. *New York Times,* March 30, 1954.
29. Chalmers M. Roberts, "The Day We Didn't Go to War," *Reporter,* September 14, 1954, pp. 31–32.
30. Eisenhower, *Mandate,* p. 347.
31. Randle, *Geneva,* p. 64.
32. Richard H. Rovere, *The Eisenhower Years,* p. 193.
33. Ibid.
34. Ibid., p. 191.
35. Eisenhower, *Mandate,* p. 346.
36. Ibid., p. 347.
37. Ibid., p. 348.
38. Bator, *Vietnam,* p. 54.
39. Randle, *Geneva,* p. 79.
40. Department of State Press Release #192, April 13, 1954.
41. Randle, *Geneva,* p. 80.
42. Bator, *Vietnam,* p. 62.
43. Anthony Eden, *Full Circle,* p. 110.
44. Eleanor Lansing Dulles, "Time and Decisions," *Forensic Quarterly,* August 1969, p. 277.
45. *New York Times,* May 4, 1954.
46. Fletcher Knebel, "We Nearly Went to War Three Times," *Look,* February 8, 1955, p. 26.
47. Eisenhower, *Mandate,* p. 350.
48. Ibid.
49. Eden, *Full Circle,* p. 113.
50. Ibid., pp. 114–115.
51. Ibid., p. 114.
52. Eisenhower, *Mandate,* p. 351.
53. Ibid., p. 350.
54. Ibid.
55. Eden, *Full Circle,* p. 116.
56. Ibid.
57. Ibid.
58. Ibid., p. 117.
59. Ibid., p. 118.
60. Bator, *Vietnam,* p. 71.
61. Ibid.
62. Randle, *Geneva,* p. 102.
63. Eden, *Full Circle,* p. 119.

64. Randle, *Geneva*, p. 103.
65. Eisenhower, *Mandate*, p. 352.
66. Randle, *Geneva*, p. 104.
67. Eisenhower, *Mandate*, p. 352.
68. Kay Halle, *Irrepressible Churchill: A Treasury of Winston Churchill's Wit* (New York: World, 1966), p. 325.

CHAPTER FIFTEEN
The Geneva Negotiations — 1954

1. *New York Times*, April 27, 1954.
2. Anthony Eden, *Full Circle*, p. 125.
3. Ibid., p. 127.
4. Ibid., p. 123.
5. *Department of State Bulletin*, XXX, May 17, 1954, p. 740.
6. *London Times*, May 6, 1954.
7. James Shepley, "How Dulles Averted War," *Life*, January 16, 1956, p. 72.
8. *London Times*, August 11, 1954.
9. Ibid., May 22, 1954.
10. Author interview with Robert Bowie, February 29, 1972.
11. *New York Times*, April 27, 1954.
12. Donald Lancaster, *The Emancipation of French Indochina* (Oxford: the University Press, 1961), p. 316.
13. Robert F. Randle, *Geneva 1954*, pp. 163–164.
14. Ibid., pp. 206–207.
15. Ibid., p. 210.
16. *London Times*, May 7, 1954.
17. Victor Bator, *Vietnam*, p. 99.
18. Walter Lippmann, *New York Herald Tribune*, May 6, 1954.
19. *New York Times*, May 7, 1954.
20. Ibid., May 8, 1954.
21. Randle, *Geneva*, p. 177.
22. Ibid., p. 219.
23. Ibid., pp. 220–221.
24. Dwight D. Eisenhower, *Mandate for Change*, pp. 358–359.
25. Author interview with Robert Bowie, February 29, 1972.
26. Mike Gravel, ed., *The Pentagon Papers*, I, p. 125.
27. Ibid.
28. Ibid., p. 129.
29. "Security in the Pacific," address to Los Angeles World Affairs Council, June 11, 1954 (Department of State Press Release #318).
30. Gravel, ed., *Pentagon Papers*, I, p. 128.
31. Eden, *Full Circle*, p. 133.
32. Bator, *Vietnam*, p. 101.
33. Randle, *Geneva*, p. 226.
34. Ibid., p. 231.
35. Ibid., p. 234.
36. Gravel, ed., *Pentagon Papers*, I, p. 138.
37. Ibid.; also Eisenhower, *Mandate*, p. 365.
38. *Le Monde*, February 12, 1954.
39. *New York Times*, June 16, 1954.
40. Randle, *Geneva*, pp. 281–282.
41. *London Times*, June 26, 1954.
42. Eden, *Full Circle*, p. 147.

43. Randle, *Geneva*, p. 292.
44. Eden, *Full Circle*, p. 150.
45. Ibid., p. 149.
46. Randle, *Geneva*, pp. 304–305.
47. Gravel, ed., *Pentagon Papers*, I, p. 145.
48. *Department of State Bulletin*, XXXI, July 26, 1954, p. 121.
49. Eisenhower, *Mandate*, p. 369.
50. Randle, *Geneva*, p. 316.
51. Roscoe Drummond and Gaston Coblentz, *Duel at the Brink*, p. 123.
52. Eden, *Full Circle*, p. 156.
53. Ibid.
54. Gravel, ed., *Pentagon Papers*, I, p. 152.
55. Ibid., p. 155.
56. *Le Monde*, July 17, 1954.
57. Randle, *Geneva*, p. 339.
58. Ibid., pp. 339–340.
59. Gravel, ed., *Pentagon Papers*, I, p. 154.
60. Ibid., p. 160.
61. Randle, *Geneva*, pp. 340–341.
62. Gravel, ed., *Pentagon Papers*, I, pp. 571–572.
63. Ibid., p. 568.
64. Ibid., p. 569.
65. Ibid., p. 571.
66. Ibid., p. 162.

CHAPTER SIXTEEN
Vietnam — Aftermath and Prologue

1. Robert F. Randle, *Geneva 1954*, p. 356.
2. *New York Times*, July 22, 1954.
3. Ibid., July 25, 1954.
4. Randle, *Geneva*, p. 359.
5. *New York Times*, July 22, 1954.
6. John Foster Dulles, *War or Peace*, p. 205.
7. Ibid.
8. Mike Gravel, ed., *The Pentagon Papers*, I, p. 212.
9. Anthony Eden, *Full Circle*, pp. 158–159.
10. Richard P. Stebbins, *The United States in World Affairs 1954* (New York: Harper & Brothers for the Council on Foreign Relations, 1955), p. 258.
11. Gravel, ed., *Pentagon Papers*, I, p. 212.
12. Richard Bissell, Oral History interview, p. 8.
13. Victor Bator, *Vietnam*, p. 163.
14. *Department of State Bulletin*, XXXI, September 27, 1954, p. 432.
15. Ibid.
16. *New York Times*, May 30, 1962.
17. Bator, *Vietnam*, p. 168.
18. Daniel Lerner and Raymond Aron, eds., *France Defeats EDC* (New York: Praeger, 1957), p. 10.
19. Randle, *Geneva*, p. 373; also *New York Times*, August 23, 1954.
20. *New York Times*, August 22 and August 25, 1954.
21. Richard Goold-Adams, *John Foster Dulles*, p. 145.
22. Ibid., p. 147.
23. Ibid., p. 151.
24. Ibid., p. 152.

25. Ibid., p. 148.
26. JFD statement to NATO Council, September 29, 1954, Dulles Papers.
27. Ibid.
28. Ibid.
29. Eden statement to NATO Council, September 29, 1954, Dulles Papers.
30. Ibid.
31. Ibid.
32. Goold-Adams, *Dulles*, p. 157.
33. Statement to NATO Council, October 3, 1954, Dulles Papers.
34. Eden to JFD, October 4, 1954, Dulles Papers.
35. Gravel, ed., *Pentagon Papers*, I, p. 210.
36. Ibid., p. 204.
37. Author interview with Robert Amory, April 11, 1972.
38. Gravel, ed., *Pentagon Papers*, I, pp. 213–214.
39. Ibid., p. 214.
40. *Department of State Bulletin*, XXXI, October 11, 1954, p. 534.
41. Ibid.
42. Gravel, ed., *Pentagon Papers*, I, p. 221.
43. *Department of State Bulletin*, XXXI, November 15, 1954, p. 735.
44. Gravel, ed., *Pentagon Papers*, I, p. 223.
45. Ibid.
46. Ibid., p. 222.
47. Ibid.
48. Ibid., p. 215.
49. Ibid., p. 216.
50. Ibid.
51. Ibid., p. 217.
52. Ibid.
53. Ibid.
54. Ibid., p. 218.
55. Ibid., p. 224.
56. Ibid.
57. Ibid.
58. Ibid., p. 225.
59. Ibid., p. 228.
60. Ibid.
61. Ibid., p. 229.
62. Ibid., p. 228.
63. Ibid., p. 227.
64. Ibid., p. 232.
65. Ibid.
66. Ibid., p. 233.
67. Ibid.
68. Ibid., p. 234.
69. Ibid., p. 235.
70. Ibid., p. 234.
71. Ibid., p. 236.
72. Ibid.
73. Ibid., p. 237.
74. Ibid.
75. Ibid.
76. Ibid., pp. 237–238.
77. Ibid., p. 238.
78. Ibid.
79. Ibid., pp. 238–239.
80. Ibid., p. 241.

CHAPTER SEVENTEEN
Ambiguity at Quemoy

1. John Foster Dulles, *War or Peace*, p. 190.
2. Karl Lott Rankin, *China Assignment*, p. 113.
3. Ibid., p. 194.
4. *New York Times*, June 30, 1954.
5. Morton H. Halperin, *Communist China and the Offshore Islands 1949–1965* (unpublished manuscript), ch. 4, p. 14.
6. Ibid., p. 17.
7. Dwight D. Eisenhower, *Mandate for Change*, p. 462.
8. Ibid.
9. Rankin, *China Assignment*, p. 204.
10. Chalmers M. Roberts, "Battle on the 'Rim of Hell': President vs. War Hawks," *Reporter*, December 16, 1954, p. 12.
11. Ibid.
12. Rankin, *China Assignment*, p. 206.
13. Ibid., p. 207.
14. Eisenhower, *Mandate*, p. 464.
15. Roberts, "Battle on the 'Rim of Hell,' " p. 12.
16. Ibid.
17. Eisenhower, *Mandate*, p. 464.
18. Roberts, "Battle on the 'Rim of Hell,' " p. 12.
19. Rankin, *China Assignment*, p. 207.
20. Eisenhower, *Mandate*, p. 463.
21. Morton H. Halperin and Tang Tsou, "United States Policy Toward the Offshore Islands," *Public Policy*, XV (Cambridge: Harvard University Press, 1966), pp. 120–121.
22. Stewart Alsop, "The Story Behind Quemoy: How We Drifted Close to War," *Saturday Evening Post*, December 13, 1958, p. 86.
23. Halperin and Tsou, "U.S. Policy Toward the Offshore Islands," *Public Policy*, XV, pp. 121–122.
24. Rankin, *China Assignment*, p. 168.
25. Roberts, "Battle on the 'Rim of Hell,' " p. 13.
26. Eisenhower, *Mandate*, p. 465.
27. Roberts, "Battle on the 'Rim of Hell,' " p. 11.
28. Ibid.
29. Eisenhower, *Mandate*, p. 464.
30. Ibid.
31. Ibid., p. 465.
32. Ibid., p. 466.
33. Ibid.
34. Ibid., p. 483.
35. Alsop, "The Story Behind Quemoy," p. 87.
36. Eisenhower, *Mandate*, p. 467.
37. Transcript of press conference, January 24, 1955, Dulles Papers.
38. Eisenhower, *Mandate*, p. 470.
39. Ibid., p. 472.
40. Ibid., p. 475.
41. Ibid., p. 469.
42. *Department of State Bulletin*, XXXII, February 28, 1955, p. 330.
43. Notes for speech to SEATO Council, February 21, 1955, Dulles Papers.
44. Eisenhower, *Mandate*, p. 475.
45. *Christian Science Monitor*, March 3, 1955.
46. Richard H. Rovere, *The Eisenhower Years*, p. 263.

47. Rankin, *China Assignment*, p. 225.
48. Eisenhower, *Mandate*, p. 476.
49. Ibid.
50. Ibid.
51. Ibid., p. 477.
52. Ibid.
53. Rovere, *Eisenhower Years*, p. 356.
54. *New York Times*, March 13, 1954.
55. Ibid., March 18, 1954.
56. Author interview with Robert Bowie, February 29, 1972.
57. Transcript of Eisenhower press conference, March 16, 1955, Dulles Papers.
58. Halperin, *Communist China and the Offshore Islands*, ch. 5, p. 9.
59. Rovere, *Eisenhower Years*, p. 248.
60. Ibid., p. 263.
61. Ibid., p. 248.
62. Eisenhower, *Mandate*, pp. 479–480.
63. Ibid., p. 481.
64. *New York Times*, March 26, 1955.
65. *U.S. News and World Report*, March 25, 1955, pp. 30–32.
66. Eisenhower, *Mandate*, pp. 478–479.
67. *New York Times*, March 29, 1955.
68. Eisenhower, *Mandate*, p. 611.
69. Ibid., p. 481.
70. Halperin, *Communist China and the Offshore Islands*, ch. 5, p. 16.
71. *New York Herald Tribune*, April 22, 1955.
72. George McTurnan Kahin, *The Asian-African Conference*, p. 62.
73. Halperin, *Communist China and the Offshore Islands*, ch. 5, p. 17.
74. Ibid.
75. Eisenhower, *Mandate*, p. 483.

CHAPTER EIGHTEEN
To the Summit

1. *New York Times*, October 28, 1954.
2. Richard H. Rovere, *The Eisenhower Years*, p. 235.
3. Department of State Bulletin, XXXI, November 1, 1954, p. 636.
4. Speech notes for NATO Council meeting, December 15, 1955, Dulles Papers.
5. Roscoe Drummond and Gaston Coblentz, *Duel at the Brink*, p. 133.
6. Ibid., p. 134.
7. Ibid., p. 141.
8. Harold MacMillan, *Tides of Fortune*, pp. 587–588.
9. Ibid., p. 591.
10. Drummond and Coblentz, *Duel at the Brink*, p. 137.
11. Macmillan, *Tides*, p. 599.
12. Drummond and Coblentz, *Duel at the Brink*, pp. 137–138.
13. Transcript of press conference, Vienna, May 15, 1955, Dulles Papers.
14. Macmillan, *Tides*, p. 608.
15. Rovere, *Eisenhower Years*, p. 271.
16. Ibid., p. 272.
17. Briefing memorandum for Eisenhower, June 18, 1955, Dulles Papers.
18. Ibid.
19. *New York Times*, July 16, 1955.
20. Ibid.
21. Macmillan, *Tides*, pp. 616–617.
22. Rovere, *Eisenhower Years*, p. 280.

23. Ibid., pp. 281–282.
24. Roderic O'Connor, Oral History interview, p. 79.
25. Ibid., p. 81.
26. Richard P. Stebbins, *The United States in World Affairs 1955* (New York: Harper & Brothers for the Council on Foreign Relations, 1956), p. 64.
27. Rovere, *Eisenhower Years*, p. 290.
28. Transcript of press conference, Geneva, July 23, 1955, Dulles Papers.
29. Macmillan, *Tides*, p. 619.
30. Ibid.
31. Ibid., p. 616.
32. Ibid., p. 621.
33. Ibid.
34. *New York Times*, July 19, 1955.
35. Macmillan, *Tides*, p. 620.
36. Stebbins, *U.S. in World Affairs 1955*, p. 66.
37. Roscoe Drummond, *New York Herald Tribune*, August 1, 1955.
38. Transcript of press conference, Geneva, July 23, 1955, Dulles Papers.
39. Macmillan, *Tides*, pp. 622–624.
40. Rovere, *Eisenhower Years*, p. 283.
41. *New York Times*, December 14, 1955.
42. JFD cable to United States Mission Chiefs, August 15, 1955, Dulles Papers.
43. Ibid.
44. Ibid.
45. Ibid.

CHAPTER NINETEEN
A Gathering Immobility

1. Richard H. Rovere, *The Eisenhower Years*, p. 354.
2. Ibid., pp. 310–311.
3. *New Yorker*, October 8, 1955, p. 182.
4. Rovere, *Eisenhower Years*, p. 336.
5. Eisenhower to JFD, October 1955, Dulles Papers.
6. *New York Times*, March 1, 1956.
7. Roscoe Drummond and Gaston Coblentz, *Duel at the Brink*, p. 36.
8. Ibid., pp. 35–36.
9. *New York Times*, February 15, 1956.
10. James Shepley, "How Dulles Averted War," *Life*, January 16, 1956, p. 77.
11. Ibid., p. 78.
12. Ibid., p. 77.
13. Ibid., p. 72.
14. Ibid., p. 70.
15. *New York Times*, January 20, 1956.
16. *Life*, January 30, 1956, p. 20.
17. *New York Times*, January 15, 1956.
18. Ibid., January 6, 1956.
19. Ibid.
20. Richard P. Stebbins, *The United States in World Affairs 1956* (New York: Harper & Brothers for the Council on Foreign Relations, 1957), p. 16.
21. *New York Times*, February 26, 1956.
22. Stebbins, *U.S. in World Affairs 1956*, p. 18.
23. Robert J. Donovan, *Eisenhower*, p. 389.
24. Richard P. Stebbins, *The United States in World Affairs 1955* (New York: Harper & Brothers for the Council on Foreign Relations, 1956), p. 121.
25. Ibid., p. 122.

26. *New York Times,* November 16, 1955.
27. George McTurnan Kahin, *The Asian-African Conference,* p. 81.
28. *New York Times,* June 7, 1956.
29. *Department of State Bulletin,* XXXIV, June 18, 1956, pp. 999–1000.

CHAPTER TWENTY
The Middle East — Prelude to Crisis

1. Kennett Love, *Suez,* p. 186.
2. Ibid., p. 188.
3. Ibid., p. 189.
4. Ibid., pp. 71–72.
5. Ibid., pp. 133–135.
6. Ibid., p. 129.
7. Ibid., p. 75.
8. Ibid., p. 196.
9. Author interview with Herman Eiltz, August 18, 1972.
10. Ibid.
11. Ibid.
12. Harold Macmillan, *Riding the Storm,* p. 94.
13. Mohamed Hassanein Heikal, *The Cairo Documents* (Garden City: Doubleday, 1973), p. 74.
14. Love, *Suez,* p. 201.
15. Ibid., p. 14.
16. Ibid., p. 88
17. Dwight D. Eisenhower, *Waging Peace,* p. 24.
18. Love, *Suez,* p. 90.
19. Uri Ra'anan, *The USSR Arms the Third World,* p. 78.
20. Ibid., p. 79.
21. Ibid., p. 76.
22. Ibid., pp. 86–87.
23. Ibid., pp. 86–90.
24. Ibid., pp. 89–90.
25. Ibid., pp. 97–98.
26. Ibid., pp. 140–142.
27. Author interview with Kermit Roosevelt, August 5, 1971.
28. Ibid.
29. Ibid.
30. Ibid.
31. Ibid.
32. Love, *Suez,* p. 284.
33. Ibid.
34. Ibid., p. 287.
35. Ibid.
36. Ra'anan, *The USSR Arms the Third World,* p. 142.
37. Love, *Suez,* p. 289.
38. Ibid.

CHAPTER TWENTY-ONE
The Fateful Aswan Renege

1. Kennett Love, *Suez,* p. 298.
2. Ibid.

3. Eugene R. Black, Oral History interview, p. 16.
4. Ibid., p. 6.
5. Ibid., p. 8.
6. Ibid., p. 10.
7. Love, *Suez,* p. 324.
8. Ibid., p. 308.
9. Ibid., p. 713.
10. Ibid., p. 309.
11. Ibid., p. 308.
12. Ibid., p. 203.
13. Ibid., p. 204.
14. Anthony Nutting, *No End of a Lesson,* p. 25.
15. Love, *Suez,* p. 208.
16. Ibid., p. 209.
17. Ibid., p. 210.
18. Nutting, *Lesson,* p. 18.
19. Ibid., p. 32.
20. Love, *Suez,* p. 214.
21. Randolph S. Churchill, *The Rise and Fall of Sir Anthony Eden* (New York: Putnam's, 1959), p. 228.
22. *London Times,* March 6, 1956.
23. Nutting, *Lesson,* p. 26.
24. Ibid., p. 36.
25. Ibid., pp. 34–35.
26. Love, *Suez,* p. 259.
27. *New York Times,* April 4, 1956.
28. Ibid., April 3, 1957.
29. Love, *Suez,* p. 317.
30. Eugene R. Black, Oral History interview, p. 13.
31. Ibid., p. 14.
32. Ibid.
33. Ibid.
34. Mohamed Hassanein Heikal, *The Cairo Documents* (Garden City: Doubleday, 1973), p. 65.
35. Love, *Suez,* p. 322.
36. Herman Finer, *Dulles over Suez,* p. 46.
37. Ibid.
38. Author interview with Robert Bowie, February 29, 1972.
39. Finer, *Dulles over Suez,* p. 47.
40. Love, *Suez,* p. 325.
41. George V. Allen, Oral History interview.
42. Finer, *Dulles over Suez,* p. 48; also George V. Allen, Oral History interview.
43. Ibid.
44. Heikal, *Documents,* p. 68.
45. Finer, *Dulles over Suez,* p. 52.
46. William B. Macomber, Oral History interview, p. 55.
47. Ibid.
48. Finer, *Dulles over Suez,* p. 53.
49. *New York Times,* April 2, 1956.
50. Love, *Suez,* p. 317.
51. Dwight D. Eisenhower, *Waging Peace,* p. 33.
52. JFD to Eisenhower, October 30, 1957, Dulles Papers.
53. Love, *Suez,* p. 320.
54. Ibid., p. 322.
55. Ibid., p. 323.

CHAPTER TWENTY-TWO
Cross-Purposes and Cardboard Proposals

1. Kennett Love, *Suez*, p. 338.
2. Ibid., p. 347.
3. Ibid., p. 349.
4. Ibid., p. 350.
5. Ibid., p. 354.
6. Ibid.
7. Ibid., p. 370.
8. Harold Macmillan, *Riding the Storm*, p. 104.
9. Robert Murphy, *Diplomat Among Warriors*, p. 380.
10. Macmillan, *Storm*, p. 105.
11. Murphy, *Diplomat*, p. 381.
12. Dwight D. Eisenhower, *Waging Peace*, p. 41.
13. Macmillan, *Storm*, p. 106.
14. Love, *Suez*, p. 419.
15. William B. Macomber, Oral History interview, p. 57.
16. Anthony Eden, *Full Circle*, p. 487.
17. Robert Murphy, Oral History interview, p. 57.
18. Herman Phleger, Oral History interview, p. 49.
19. Author interview with Robert Bowie, February 29, 1972.
20. Love, *Suez*, p. 386.
21. Ibid., p. 385.
22. Ibid., p. 394.
23. Ibid.
24. Ibid., p. 395.
25. Ibid., p. 402.
26. Ibid., p. 395.
27. Herman Finer, *Dulles over Suez*, p. 143.
28. Ibid., pp. 152–154.
29. Ibid., pp. 157–159; also Love, *Suez*, p. 405.
30. Love, *Suez*, p. 405.
31. Ibid.
32. Finer, *Dulles over Suez*, p. 173.
33. Love, *Suez*, p. 412.
34. Ibid., p. 417.
35. Ibid., p. 416.
36. Mohamed Hassanein Heikal, *The Cairo Documents* (Garden City: Doubleday, 1973), p. 102.
37. *New York Times*, September 1, 1956.
38. Love, *Suez*, p. 418.
39. Ibid., p. 417.
40. Macmillan, *Storm*, p. 118.
41. Ibid., p. 119.
42. Finer, *Dulles over Suez*, p. 218.
43. Ibid., p. 215.
44. Love, *Suez*, p. 425.
45. Finer, *Dulles over Suez*, p. 218.
46. Ibid., p. 234.
47. Love, *Suez*, p. 429.
48. Macmillan, *Storm*, p. 121.
49. Love, *Suez*, p. 427.
50. Ibid., p. 426.
51. Ibid., pp. 426–427.

52. Eisenhower, *Peace,* p. 667.
53. Macmillan, *Storm,* p. 125.
54. Love, *Suez,* p. 428.
55. Ibid.
56. Eden, *Full Circle,* p. 71.
57. Macmillan, *Storm,* p. 123.
58. Alastair Buchan, "Le chevalier mal fet," *Twentieth Century,* March 1960, p. 237.
59. Richard Goold-Adams, *John Foster Dulles,* p. 224.
60. Richard Bissell, Oral History interview, p. 27.
61. Finer, *Dulles over Suez,* p. 248.
62. Ibid.
63. Love, *Suez,* p. 437.
64. Ibid.
65. Finer, *Dulles over Suez,* p. 256; also Love, *Suez,* p. 438.
66. Love, *Suez,* p. 437.
67. Ibid.
68. Finer, *Dulles over Suez,* pp. 258–259.

CHAPTER TWENTY-THREE
The Alliance in Peril

1. Harold Macmillan, *Riding the Storm,* pp. 135–136.
2. Transcript of "Meet the Press," September 23, 1956, Dulles Papers.
3. *New York Times,* October 3, 1956.
4. Mohamed Hassanein Heikal, *The Cairo Documents* (Garden City: Doubleday, 1973), p. 168.
5. Ibid.
6. Robert Murphy, *Diplomat Among Warriors,* p. 388.
7. Kennett Love, *Suez,* p. 441.
8. Ibid.
9. Anthony Nutting, *No End of a Lesson,* p. 89.
10. Love, *Suez,* p. 449.
11. Ibid., pp. 450–452.
12. Ibid., p. 452.
13. Anthony Eden, *Full Circle,* p. 574.
14. Love, *Suez,* p. 465.
15. Ibid., pp. 465–466.
16. Ibid., p. 453.
17. Ibid., p. 454.
18. Herman Finer, *Dulles over Suez,* p. 351.
19. Love, *Suez,* p. 561.
20. Ibid., p. 504.
21. Ibid., p. 503.
22. Dwight D. Eisenhower, *Waging Peace,* p. 679.
23. Ibid., p. 678.
24. Love, *Suez,* p. 505.
25. Eisenhower, *Peace,* p. 77.
26. Love, *Suez,* p. 506.
27. Macmillan, *Storm,* p. 179.
28. Emmet John Hughes, *The Ordeal of Power,* p. 216.
29. Love, *Suez,* p. 482.
30. Ibid.
31. Nutting, *Lesson,* p. 128.
32. Love, *Suez,* p. 561.
33. Hughes, *Ordeal of Power,* pp. 219–220.

34. Ibid., p. 220.
35. Ibid., p. 221.
36. Ibid.
37. Love, *Suez*, p. 519.
38. Macmillan, *Storm*, pp. 157–158.
39. Finer, *Dulles over Suez*, pp. 394–396; also Love, *Suez*, pp. 562–563.
40. William B. Macomber, Oral History interview, p. 59.
41. Ibid., pp. 63–66.
42. Finer, *Dulles over Suez*, pp. 446–447.

CHAPTER TWENTY-FOUR
Applying Principle

1. Kennett Love, *Suez*, p. 573.
2. Ibid., p. 562.
3. Ibid., p. 560.
4. Anthony Nutting, *No End of a Lesson*, p. 135.
5. Love, *Suez*, p. 571.
6. Ibid., p. 574.
7. Ibid., p. 578.
8. Ibid., p. 614.
9. Ibid., p. 615.
10. Anthony Eden, *Full Circle*, p. 622.
11. Ibid., pp. 624–625.
12. Love, *Suez*, p. 643.
13. William B. Macomber, Oral History interview, p. 117.
14. Ibid., p. 118.
15. Love, *Suez*, p. 654.
16. *London Times*, December 12, 1956.
17. Ibid.
18. Harold Macmillan, *Riding the Storm*, p. 178.
19. Love, *Suez*, p. 637.
20. Ibid., p. 638.
21. Ibid., p. 639.
22. Ibid., p. 640.
23. Ibid., p. 641.
24. Ibid., p. 664.
25. Ibid.
26. Ibid., p. 666.
27. Ibid.
28. Nutting, *Lesson,* p. 163.
29. Love, *Suez*, p. 657.
30. Nutting, *Lesson,* p. 164.
31. Macmillan, *Storm*, p. 180.
32. Ibid., pp. 180–181.
33. Ibid., p. 182.

CHAPTER TWENTY-FIVE
On the Defensive

1. Karl G. Harr, Jr., Oral History interview, pp. 30–31.
2. William B. Macomber, Oral History interview, pp. 12–13.
3. Ibid., p. 13.

4. Ibid., pp. 13–14, 88.
5. Ibid., p. 88.
6. Bernau to JFD, January 12, 1959, Dulles Papers.
7. Memorandum to Chief of Protocol, February 1958, Dulles Papers.
8. Arthur Krock, Oral History interview, p. 32.
9. Ibid., p. 33.
10. Ibid.
11. Emmet John Hughes, *The Ordeal of Power*, p. 254.
12. Dwight D. Eisenhower, *Waging Peace*, p. 472.
13. Harold Macmillan, *Riding the Storm*, p. 300.
14. Ibid., p. 301.
15. Ibid., pp. 303–304.
16. Ibid., p. 304.
17. *New York Times*, June 27, 1957.
18. Ibid., July 3, 1957.
19. Richard P. Stebbins, *The United States in World Affairs 1957* (New York: Harper & Brothers for the Council on Foreign Relations, 1958), p. 127.
20. Dean Acheson, "Foreign Policy and Presidential Moralism," *Reporter*, May 2, 1957, p. 14.
21. *New York Times*, October 9, 1957.
22. Ibid.
23. Anthony Nutting, *No End of a Lesson*, p. 147.
24. Ibid.
25. Kennett Love, *Suez*, p. 645.
26. Eisenhower, *Peace*, p. 178.
27. *New York Times*, January 6, 1957.
28. Senate Committee on Foreign Relations, *Hearings on the President's Proposal on the Middle East*, January 14, 1957, p. 5.
29. Ibid., January 24, 1957, p. 208.
30. Richard Goold-Adams, *John Foster Dulles*, p. 240.
31. Macmillan, *Storm*, p. 511.
32. Stebbins, *U.S. in World Affairs 1957*, p. 176.
33. Ibid., p. 177.
34. Notes for testimony before the Senate Foreign Relations Committee, February 1957, Dulles Papers.
35. Love, *Suez*, pp. 657–658.
36. Macmillan, *Storm*, pp. 250–251.
37. Personal notes on the Bermuda conference, March 21–24, 1957, Dulles Papers.
38. Macmillan, *Storm*, p. 253.
39. Personal notes on the Bermuda conference, March 21–24, 1957, Dulles Papers.
40. Macmillan, *Storm*, p. 255.
41. *Department of State Bulletin*, XXXVI, February 18, 1957, pp. 251–255.
42. Macmillan, *Storm*, p. 292.
43. Eisenhower, *Peace*, p. 195.
44. Ibid., p. 198.
45. Ibid.
46. Macmillan, *Storm*, pp. 277–278.
47. Eisenhower, *Peace*, p. 202.
48. Hughes, *Ordeal of Power*, pp. 253–254.
49. Eisenhower, *Peace*, p. 204; also Goold-Adams, *Dulles*, p. 253.
50. Eisenhower, *Peace*, pp. 203–204.

CHAPTER TWENTY-SIX
A Time of Twilight

1. A. Doak Barnett, *Communist China and Asia*, p. 453.
2. Notes on Bermuda conference, March 21–24, 1957, Dulles Papers.
3. Ibid.
4. Andrew H. Berding, *Dulles on Diplomacy*, pp. 59–60.
5. Ibid., p. 60.
6. Richard P. Stebbins, *The United States in World Affairs 1957* (New York: Harper & Brothers for the Council on Foreign Relations, 1958), p. 224.
7. *Department of State Bulletin*, XXXVII, July 15, 1957, pp. 91–95.
8. Ibid., pp. 93–95.
9. John Foster Dulles, *War or Peace*, p. 190.
10. *Department of State Bulletin*, XXXVII, July 15, 1957, p. 94.
11. State Department Press Release #459, August 11, 1958.
12. JFD to general manager, Associated Press, September 6, 1956, Dulles Papers.
13. Author interview with John Hanes, November 10, 1972.
14. *London Economist*, October 12, 1957.
15. Harold Macmillan, *Riding the Storm*, p. 320.
16. Ibid.
17. Ibid., p. 321.
18. U.S.-British communiqué, Washington, October 25, 1957, Dulles Papers.
19. Richard P. Stebbins, *The United States in World Affairs 1958* (New York: Harper & Brothers for the Council on Foreign Relations, 1959), p. 11.
20. Emmet John Hughes, *The Ordeal of Power*, p. 251.
21. Ibid.
22. Thomas E. Dewey, Oral History interview, p. 22.
23. Ibid.
24. Dwight D. Eisenhower, *Waging Peace*, p. 226.
25. Ibid., p. 227.
26. Eisenhower statement to NATO meeting, December 16, 1957, Dulles Papers.
27. Macmillan, *Storm*, p. 335.
28. Ibid., p. 337.

CHAPTER TWENTY-SEVEN
Radical Nationalism in the Middle East

1. Dwight D. Eisenhower, *Waging Peace*, p. 265.
2. Richard P. Stebbins, *The United States in World Affairs 1958* (New York: Harper & Brothers for the Council on Foreign Relations, 1959), p. 186.
3. Eisenhower, *Peace*, pp. 262–264.
4. Camille Chamoun, Oral History interview, p. 32.
5. Richard P. Stebbins, *U.S. in World Affairs 1958*, p. 197.
6. Robert Murphy, *Diplomat Among Warriors*, p. 402.
7. Harold Macmillan, *Riding the Storm*, p. 510.
8. Camille Chamoun, Oral History interview, p. 13.
9. Karl G. Harr, Jr., Oral History interview, p. 53.
10. Eisenhower, *Peace*, p. 272.
11. Ibid., p. 274.
12. Macmillan, *Storm*, p. 512.
13. Camille Chamoun, Oral History interview, p. 14.

14. Macmillan, *Storm*, p. 513.
15. Ibid., pp. 517–518.
16. *Department of State Bulletin*, XXXIX, August 11, 1958, pp. 229–233.
17. Stebbins, *U.S. in World Affairs 1958*, p. 313.
18. Murphy, *Diplomat*, p. 400.
19. Stebbins, *U.S. in World Affairs 1958*, p. 209.
20. Ibid., pp. 212–213.
21. Ibid., p. 215.
22. Eisenhower, *Peace*, p. 286.
23. Camille Chamoun, Oral History interview, pp. 5 and 8.
24. Kennett Love, *Suez*, p. 297.

CHAPTER TWENTY-EIGHT
Reprise at Quemoy

1. Dwight H. Perkins, *Market Control and Planning in Communist China* (Cambridge: Harvard University Press, 1966), pp. 82–89.
2. Morton H. Halperin, *Communist China and the Offshore Islands, 1949–1965* (unpublished manuscript), ch. 6, p. 4.
3. Ibid., p. 5.
4. Ibid.
5. *New York Times*, August 8 and August 13, 1958.
6. Halperin, *Communist China and the Offshore Islands*, ch. 7. pp. 2–3.
7. JFD to Chairman, House of Foreign Affairs Committee, August 23, 1958, Dulles Papers.
8. Dwight D. Eisenhower, *Waging Peace*, p. 296.
9. Ibid.
10. Richard P. Stebbins, *The United States in World Affairs 1958* (New York: Harper & Brothers for the Council on Foreign Relations, 1959), p. 319.
11. Halperin, *Communist China and the Offshore Islands*, ch. 7, p. 12.
12. Ibid., p. 11.
13. Eisenhower, *Peace*, pp. 298–299.
14. Ibid., pp. 691–692.
15. Ibid., p. 693.
16. Remarks to military strategy conference, Quantico, Virginia, June 14, 1957, Dulles Papers.
17. Ibid.
18. Eisenhower, *Peace*, p. 300.
19. Harold Macmillan, *Riding the Storm*, p. 544.
20. Ibid., pp. 546–548.
21. Stebbins, *U.S. in World Affairs 1958*, p. 320.
22. *New York Times*, September 10, 1958.
23. Reinhold Niebuhr, "The Moral World of John Foster Dulles," *New Republic*, December 1, 1958, p. 8.
24. Halperin, *Communist China and the Offshore Islands*, ch. 8, p. 17.
25. Eisenhower, *Peace*, p. 303.
26. *New York Times*, September 20, 1958.
27. Ibid., September 22, 1958.
28. Stebbins, *U.S. in World Affairs 1958*, p. 121.
29. *Department of State Bulletin*, XXXIX, September 29, 1958, p. 483.
30. *New York Times*, October 5, 1958.
31. Ibid.
32. Macmillan, *Storm*, p. 555.
33. *New York Times*, October 1, 1958.

34. Ibid., October 2, 1958.
35. Stebbins, *U.S. in World Affairs 1958*, p. 328.
36. Ibid.
37. Talking paper for meeting with Chiang Kai-shek, Taipei, October 21, 1958, Dulles Papers.
38. *Department of State Bulletin*, XXXIX, November 10, 1958, pp. 721–722.
39. Statement to the press, October 24, 1958, Dulles Papers.
40. Eisenhower, *Peace*, p. 304.
41. Stebbins, *U.S. in World Affairs 1958*, p. 339.
42. *New York Times*, November 22, 1958.
43. Ernest Gross, Oral History interview, p. 56.
44. Eleanor Lansing Dulles, *The Last Year*, pp. 198–199.
45. *Department of State Bulletin*, XXXIX, December 22, 1958, p. 992.
46. Ibid.

CHAPTER TWENTY-NINE
Berlin — The Last Crisis

1. Jack M. Schick, *The Berlin Crisis*, p. 8.
2. Harold Macmillan, *Riding the Storm*, p. 470.
3. Ibid., p. 477.
4. *New York Times*, April 4, 1958.
5. Macmillan, *Storm*, p. 483.
6. George F. Kennan, *Russia, the Atom and the West* (New York: Harper & Brothers, 1958), pp. 34–38.
7. W. Averell Harriman, Oral History interview, pp. 27–28.
8. Ibid., p. 31.
9. Schick, *Berlin Crisis*, p. 31.
10. Ibid., p. 11.
11. Ibid.
12. Ibid., p. 13.
13. Ibid., p. 14.
14. Ibid., p. 16.
15. Ibid., p. 15.
16. Roscoe Drummond and Gaston Coblentz, *Duel at the Brink*, pp. 202–203.
17. Dwight D. Eisenhower, *Waging Peace*, pp. 333–334.
18. Drummond and Coblentz, *Duel at the Brink*, p. 208.
19. Ibid.
20. Ibid., p. 209.
21. *New York Herald Tribune*, December 1, 1958.
22. Schick, *Berlin Crisis*, p. 20.
23. Ibid.
24. Ibid., p. 21.
25. Ibid., p. 37.
26. Drummond and Coblentz, *Duel at the Brink*, p. 209.
27. Ibid., p. 210.
28. Ibid.
29. Schick, *Berlin Crisis*, p. 38.
30. Dean Acheson, "Wishing Won't Hold Berlin," *Saturday Evening Post*, March 7, 1959, p. 86.
31. Eisenhower, *Peace*, pp. 340–341.
32. *New York Times*, February 19, 1959.
33. Schick, *Berlin Crisis*, p. 52.
34. Eisenhower, *Peace*, pp. 338–339.

35. Ibid., p. 341.
36. Macmillan, *Storm,* p. 587.
37. Ibid.
38. Ibid., p. 588.
39. Ibid., p. 582.
40. Ibid., p. 583.
41. Ibid., p. 589.
42. Drummond and Coblentz, *Duel at the Brink,* p. 213.
43. David Schoenbrun, Oral History interview, p. 3.
44. Ibid., pp. 5–8.
45. Lauris Norstad, Oral History interview, pp. 30–31.
46. Ibid., p. 31.
47. Ibid., p. 39.
48. Drummond and Coblentz, *Duel at the Brink,* p. 222.
49. Ibid., pp. 220–221.
50. Ibid., p. 225.
51. Andrew H. Berding, *Dulles on Diplomacy,* p. 43.
52. Drummond and Coblentz, *Duel at the Brink,* p. 223.
53. Macmillan, *Storm,* p. 610.
54. Ibid., p. 614.
55. Ibid., p. 611.
56. Ibid., p. 605.
57. Ibid., p. 601.
58. Ibid., p. 604.
59. Ibid., p. 608.
60. Ibid., p. 625.
61. Ibid., p. 644.
62. Eisenhower, *Peace,* p. 353.
63. Ibid.
64. Ibid., p. 352.
65. Macmillan, *Storm,* p. 644.
66. Ibid., p. 636.
67. Eisenhower, *Peace,* p. 355.
68. Ibid., p. 697.

CHAPTER THIRTY
Death and Assessment

1. Allen Dulles, Oral History interview, p. 79.
2. Johnson to JFD, February 17, 1959, Dulles Papers.
3. Grew to JFD, February 15, 1959, Dulles Papers.
4. Morton to JFD, early February 1959, Dulles Papers.
5. Dewey to JFD, February 17, 1959, Dulles Papers.
6. *Reporter,* April 30, 1959, p. 1.
7. *New Yorker,* April 25, 1959, p. 93.
8. Louis L. Gerson, *John Foster Dulles,* pp. 321–322.
9. Ibid., p. 322.
10. Allen Dulles, Oral History interview, p. 80.
11. Ibid., p. 83.
12. Ibid., p. 84.
13. Roscoe Drummond and Gaston Coblentz, *Duel at the Brink,* p. 227.
14. Ibid.
15. Dwight D. Eisenhower, *Waging Peace,* p. 358.
16. Ibid.

17. Richard Challener, "John Foster Dulles: An Electronic Portrait," lecture at Princeton University, December 9, 1970.
18. Ibid.
19. Ibid.

AFTERWORD

1. Dwight D. Eisenhower, *Waging Peace*, p. 485.
2. Merriman Smith, *A President's Odyssey* (New York: Harper & Brothers, 1961), p. 250.
3. Ibid., pp. 43–44.
4. Ibid., p. 45.
5. Ibid., p. 49.
6. Ibid., p. 65.
7. Ibid., p. 58.
8. Ibid., pp. 59–60.
9. Ibid., pp. 40–41.
10. Emmet John Hughes, *The Ordeal of Power*, pp. 290–291.
11. Ibid., p. 291.
12. Ibid.
13. Jack M. Schick, *The Berlin Crisis*, pp. 98–102.
14. Smith, *Odyssey*, p. 75.
15. Ibid., p. 83.
16. Ibid., p. 109.
17. Schick, *Berlin Crisis*, pp. 105–106.
18. Ibid., p. 106.
19. *New York Times*, December 24, 1959.
20. Smith, *Odyssey*, p. 142.
21. Ibid., p. 164.
22. Ibid., p. 173.
23. *New York Times*, March 9, 1960.
24. Author interview with Robert Amory, October 6, 1971.
25. Eisenhower, *Peace*, p. 543.
26. Ibid., p. 548.
27. Ibid.
28. Ibid., p. 549.
29. *New York Times*, May 8, 1960.
30. David Wise and Thomas B. Ross, *The U-2 Affair*, p. 101.
31. Schick, *Berlin Crisis*, p. 108.
32. *New York Times*, May 8, 1960.
33. Schick, *Berlin Crisis*, p. 114.
34. Smith, *Odyssey*, pp. 191–192.
35. *New York Times*, May 12, 1960.
36. Hughes, *Ordeal of Power*, p. 301.
37. *New York Times*, May 12, 1960.
38. Schick, *Berlin Crisis*, p. 119.
39. Smith, *Odyssey*, p. 207.
40. Ibid., p. 240.
41. *New York Times*, June 28, 1960.
42. Smith, *Odyssey*, p. 241.
43. Ibid., p. 239.
44. Ibid., p. 241.

Bibliography

BOOKS

Acheson, Dean. *Present at the Creation: My Years in the State Department.* New York: W. W. Norton, 1969.

Adams, Michael. *Suez and After.* Boston: Beacon Press, 1968.

Adams, Sherman. *Firsthand Report: The Story of the Eisenhower Administration.* New York: Harper & Brothers, 1961.

Barnett, A. Doak. *Communist China and Asia: A Challenge to American Policy.* New York: Random House, 1960.

Bator, Victor. *Vietnam, A Diplomatic Tragedy: Origins of the United States Involvement.* Dobbs Ferry: Oceana, 1965.

Beal, John Robinson. *John Foster Dulles: 1888–1959.* New York: Harper & Brothers, 1959.

Berding, Andrew H. *Dulles on Diplomacy.* Princeton: Van Nostrand, 1965.

Brown, John Mason. *Through These Men: Some Aspects of Our Passing History.* New York: Harper & Brothers, 1952.

Burnham, James. *The Coming Defeat of Communism.* London: Jonathan Cape, 1950.

Cadogan, Sir Alexander. *The Diaries of Sir Alexander Cadogan, O.M., 1938–1945,* Edited by David Dilks. New York: Putnam's, 1972.

Cameron, Allan W. *Vietnam Crisis: A Documentary History,* vol. I, 1940–1956. Ithaca: Cornell University Press, 1971.

Churchill, Randolph S. *The Rise and Fall of Sir Anthony Eden.* New York: Putnam's, 1959.

Donovan, Robert J. *Eisenhower: The Inside Story.* New York: Harper & Brothers, 1956.

Drummond, Roscoe, and Coblentz, Gaston. *Duel at the Brink: John Foster Dulles' Command of American Power.* Garden City: Doubleday, 1960.

Dulles, Eleanor Lansing. *John Foster Dulles: The Last Year.* New York: Harcourt, Brace & World, 1963.

Dulles, John Foster. *War or Peace.* New York: Macmillan, 1950.

———. *War, Peace and Change.* New York: Harper & Brothers, 1939.

Dunn, Frederick S. *Peacemaking and the Settlement with Japan.* Princeton: Princeton University Press, 1963.

Eden, Anthony. *Full Circle.* Boston: Houghton Mifflin, 1960.

Eisenhower, Dwight D. *Mandate for Change: 1953–1956.* Garden City: Doubleday, 1963.

———. *Waging Peace: 1956–1961.* Garden City: Doubleday, 1965.

Finer, Herman. *Dulles over Suez: The Theory and Practice of His Diplomacy*. New York: Quadrangle Books, 1964.

Gerson, Louis L. *John Foster Dulles. The American Secretaries of State and Their Diplomacy*, vol. 17. New York: Cooper Square Publishers, 1967.

Goold-Adams, Richard. *John Foster Dulles: A Reappraisal*. New York: Appleton-Century-Crofts, 1962.

Graebner, Norman, ed. *An Uncertain Tradition: American Secretaries of State in the Twentieth Century*. New York: McGraw-Hill, 1961.

Gravel, Mike, ed. *The Senator Gravel Edition: The Pentagon Papers*. Boston: Beacon, 1971.

Griffith, Robert. *The Politics of Fear: Joseph R. McCarthy and the Senate*. Lexington: University of Kentucky Press, 1970.

Guhin, Michael A. *John Foster Dulles: A Statesman and His Times*. New York: Columbia University Press, 1972.

Hughes, Emmet J. *America the Vincible*. Garden City: Doubleday, 1959.

———. *The Ordeal of Power: A Political Memoir of the Eisenhower Years*. New York: Atheneum, 1963.

[Khrushchev, Nikita.] *Khrushchev Remembers*. Translated and edited by Strobe Talbott. Boston: Little, Brown, 1970.

Kissinger, Henry A. *The Necessity for Choice: Prospects of American Foreign Policy*. New York: Harper & Brothers, 1960.

Love, Kennett. *Suez: The Twice Fought War*. New York: McGraw-Hill, 1960.

Macmillan, Harold R. *Tides of Fortune: 1945–1955*. New York: Harper & Row, 1969.

———. *Riding the Storm: 1956–1959*. New York: Harper & Row, 1971.

Menzies, Sir Robert. *Afternoon Light: Some Memoirs of Men and Events*. New York: Coward-McCann and Geoghegan, 1967.

Murphy, Robert. *Diplomat Among Warriors*. Garden City: Doubleday, 1964.

Neustadt, Richard. *Alliance Politics*. New York: Columbia University Press, 1970.

Nutting, Anthony. *No End of a Lesson: The Story of Suez*. New York: Clarkson N. Potter, 1967.

Ra'anan, Uri. *The USSR Arms the Third World: Case Studies in Soviet Foreign Policy*. Cambridge: MIT Press, 1969.

Randle, Robert F. *Geneva 1954: The Settlement of the Indochinese War*. Princeton: Princeton University Press, 1969.

Rankin, Karl Lott. *China Assignment*. Seattle: University of Washington Press, 1964.

Reischauer, Edwin O. *The United States and Japan*. Cambridge: Harvard University Press, 1950.

Robertson, Terrence. *Crisis: The Inside Story of the Suez Conspiracy*. London: Hutchinson of London, 1964.

Rovere, Richard H. *The Eisenhower Years*. New York: Farrar, Strauss & Cudahy, 1956.

Rovere, Richard H., and Schlesinger, Arthur M., Jr. *The General and the President: The Future of American Foreign Policy*. New York: Farrar, Strauss & Young, 1951.

Schick, Jack M. *The Berlin Crisis: 1958 to 1962*. Philadelphia: University of Pennsylvania Press, 1971.

Schilling, Warner; Hammond, Paul; and Snyder, Glen H. *Strategy, Politics and Defense Budgets*. New York: Columbia University Press, 1962.

Sheehan, Neil; Smith, Hendrick; Kenworthy, E. W.; and Butterfield, Fox, eds. *The Pentagon Papers* (New York Times Edition). New York: Bantam Books, 1971.

Stalin, Joseph. *Problems of Leninism*. Moscow: Foreign Language Publishing House, 1945.

Stone, I. F. *The Hidden History of the Korean War*. New York: Monthly Review Press, 1952.

Sulzberger, C. L. *A Long Row of Candles*. New York: Macmillan, 1969.

Wynn, Wilton. *Nasser of Egypt: The Search for Dignity*. Cambridge: Arlington Books, 1959.

MAGAZINE ARTICLES

Acheson, Dean G. "Foreign Policy and Presidential Moralism." *The Reporter*, May 2, 1957, pp. 10–14.
———. "Wishing Won't Hold Berlin." *Saturday Evening Post*, March 7, 1959, p. 32.
Alsop, Stewart. "The Story Behind Quemoy: How We Drifted Close to War." *Saturday Evening Post*, December 13, 1958, p. 26.
Bradley, Omar. "This Way Lies Peace." *Saturday Evening Post*, October 15, 1949, p. 33.
Buchan, Alastair. "Le chevalier mal fet." *Twentieth Century* (London), March 1960, pp. 235–240.
Dulles, Eleanor Lansing. "Time and Decisions." *The Forensic Quarterly*, August 1969, pp. 277–285.
Dulles, John Foster. "The Dawes Report and the Peace of Europe." *The Independent*, April 26, 1924, p. 218.
———. "The Road to Peace." *Atlantic Monthly*, October 1935, pp. 492–499.
———. "Thoughts on Soviet Foreign Policy and What To Do About It." *Life*, May 3, 1946, pp. 112–126.
———. "Thoughts on Soviet Foreign Policy and What To Do About It." *Life*, May 10, 1946, pp. 118–130.
———. "To Save Humanity from the Deep Abyss." *The New York Times Magazine*, July 30, 1950, p. 5.
———. "A Policy of Boldness." *Life*, May 19, 1952, pp. 146–160.
———. "Policy for Security and Peace." *Foreign Affairs*, March 16, 1954, pp. 353–364.
Hale, William Harlan. "'Big Brother' in Foggy Bottom." *The Reporter*, August 17, 1954, pp. 10–17.
Harsch, Joseph C. "John Foster Dulles: A Very Complicated Man." *Harper's Magazine*, September 1956, pp. 27–34.
[Kennan, George F.] "The Sources of Soviet Conduct." *Foreign Affairs*, July 1947, pp. 566–582.
Knebel, Fletcher. "We Nearly Went to War Three Times." *Look*, February 8, 1955, pp. 26–27.
Niebuhr, Reinhold. "The Moral World of Foster Dulles." *The New Republic*, December 1, 1958, p. 8.
Roberts, Chalmers M. "Battle on the 'Rim of Hell': President vs. Warhawks." *The Reporter*, December 16, 1954, pp. 11–14.
Shepley, James. "How Dulles Averted War." *Life*, January 16, 1956, pp. 70–80.

DULLES PAPERS

The John Foster Dulles Papers are deposited at Princeton University. The collection includes speeches, statements, press releases, press conferences and interviews, articles and reports, notes, memoranda, and correspondence.

The Dulles Oral History Collection comprises about three hundred tape-recorded interviews with men and women who knew and worked with Dulles at various times in his life. All of the interviews have been reduced to manuscript and, with a few exceptions, all are available to scholars on the same basis as the Dulles Papers. They are located with the papers at the Princeton University Library. Research for this book included study of the Oral History interviews given by each of the following:

Sherman Adams	Roswell Barnes
George V. Allen	Loftus E. Becker
Joseph Alsop	Elliott V. Bell
Stewart Alsop	John Coleman Bennett

Andrew H. Berding
Richard M. Bissell
Eugene R. Black
Charles E. Bohlen
Robert R. Bowie
Willy Brandt
Herbert Brownell
David K. E. Bruce
Arleigh Burke
James F. Byrnes
Charles P. Cabell
Camille Chamoun
Lucius D. Clay
J. Lawton Collins
James B. Conant
John Sherman Cooper
Thomas E. Dewey
C. Douglas Dillon
Allen W. Dulles
Avery Dulles
Abba Eban
Dwight D. Eisenhower
Eleanor Thomas Elliott
Richard M. Fagley
Thomas K. Finletter
Sir Oliver Franks
Thomas S. Gates
Andrew Goodpaster
Gordon Gray
John W. Hanes
Bryce N. Harlow
Karl Harr, Jr.
Averell Harriman

Joseph C. Harsch
John M. Hightower
Julius Holmes
Emmet J. Hughes
Jacob K. Javits
George F. Kennan
Arthur Krock
Curtis E. LeMay
Henry Luce
Charles Lucet
Douglas MacArthur II
Carl McCardle
John J. McCloy
Phylis Bernau Macomber
William Butts Macomber
Thruston Morton
Robert Murphy
Lauris Norstad
Roderic L. O'Connor
Herman Phleger
Arthur W. Radford
James B. Reston
Matthew B. Ridgway
Richard H. Rovere
David Schoenbrun
William Scranton
Eustace Seligman
John Stewart Service
Gerard C. Smith
Paul-Henri Spaak
Harold Stassen
Nathan Twining

Index